SSC Cumulative Title Index, Vols. 1-65

"A & P" (Updike) 13:372, 398-99; 27:320-30
"A la Víbora de la mar" (Fuentes) 24:29, 32, 57-8, 71-2
A. Lincoln, Simulacrum (Dick) 57:82
"A un dîner d' athées" (Barbey d'Aurevilly) 17:6-8, 11-12, 17, 19-20, 33-4, 37, 43-4
"A une heure du matin" (Baudelaire) 18:19, 41-2, 45-7, 49
"Aaron Trow" (Trollope) 28:317, 319, 323-24, 330-33, 349, 357
"The Abandoned House" (Michaels) 16:316
"L'abandonné" (Maupassant) 1:259
"Abashiri made" (Shiga) 23:352
"The Abbé Aubain" (Mérimée) 7:290, 292, 295, 300
"The Abbess of Castro" (Stendhal)
    See "L'Abbesse de Castro"
"L'Abbesse de Castro" (Stendhal) 27:230-31, 247, 249-50, 262-63
"The Abbey Grange" (Doyle) 12:60, 62
"The Abbot's Ghost; or, Maurice Treherne's Temptation" (Alcott) 27:4, 57
ABC Book (Tolstoy) 9:386-87
"Abdias" (Stifter) 28:272-74, 276-81, 283, 290-91, 295-99
"The Abduction from the Seraglio" (Barthelme) 2:46, 51-2; 55; 92
"Abdul Azziz Has His: An Adventure in the Yildiz Kiosk" (Leacock) 39:267
"El abejorro" (Unamuno) 11:312
Abel Sánchez (Unamuno)
    See Abel Sánchez: Una historia de pasión
Abel Sánchez: Una historia de pasión (Unamuno) 11:314, 317, 325, 337-39, 345, 347, 349, 351
"Abel Staple Disapproves" (Coppard) 21:27
"Abencaján el Bojarí, muerto en su laberinto" (Borges) 4:30, 35; 41:72, 81-82, 125
"Abenjacán el-Bokhari, Dead in his Labryrinth" (Borges)
    See "Abencaján el Bojarí, muerto en su la-berinto"
"Abenjacán the Bojarí, Dead in His Labyrinth" (Borges)
    See "Abencaján el Bojarí, muerto en su la-berinto"
"Abenjacán the Buckharian, Dead in His Labyrinth" (Borges)
    See "Abencaján el Bojarí, muerto en su la-berinto"
Die Abenteuer in der Sylvesternacht (Hoffmann) 13:188-89, 210
"Abie's Irish Rose" (Lardner) 32:134
"The Abortion" (Gilchrist) 63:36
"The Abortion" (Walker) 5:412, 414
"About How Ivan Ivanovič Quarreled with Ivan Nikiforovič" (Gogol)
    See "The Tale of How Ivan Ivanovich Quar-relled with Ivan Nikiforovich"
"About Love" (Chekhov)
    See "O ljubvi"
"About Sevka" (Pilnyak) 48:283

"About the Devil" (Gorky)
    See "O cherte"
"About the Old and Young Pamukovices" (Andrić)
    See "O starim i mladim Pamukovicima"
"About the Siskin Who Lied and the Woodpecker Who Loved the Truth" (Gorky)
    See "O chizhe, kotoryi lgal, i o diatle liu-bitele istiny"
"Above the River" (Williams) 31:334
"El abrazo de Vergara" (Alarcon) 64:2-3, 6, 28-30, 39
"Abril es el mes más cruel" (Cabrera Infante) 39:18, 22
"Abroad" (Gordimer) 17:157, 160
"Abrogast von Andelon und Elisa von Portugal, Albrecht von Werdenberg und Amisa von" (Arnim) 29:10
"Absalom, My Son" (Warner) 23:370-71
"An Absence" (Ginzburg)
    See "Un assenza"
"The Absence of Mr. Glass" (Chesterton) 1:131; 46:110, 133
"Absent without Leave" (Boell) 23:2-3
"Absent-Mindedness in a Parish Choir" (Hardy) 2:206, 215, 217
Absolute Love (Jarry)
    See L'amour absolu
"The Absolute Proof" (Čapek)
    See "Naprostý dukaz"
"Absolution" (Fitzgerald) 6:46, 77, 81, 83-4, 86, 100, 102-03
"Absorbed in Letters" (Akutagawa Ryūnosuke) 44:44, 47, 54;
"Abyss" (Ford) 56:184, 197
"Accents of Death" (Farrell) 28:92
"An Acceptable Level of Pain" (Lenz) 33:338
"Acceptance of Their Ways" (Gallant) 5:139-40
"Access" (Abish) 44:15, 20, 26
"Access to the Children" (Trevor) 21:231, 233, 260; 58:200, 204-6, 252
"Accident" (Farrell) 28:94
"An Accident" (Narayan) 25:132, 154
"The Accident" (Williams) 31:319, 329-30, 343, 345, 364
"Accident Zone" (Campbell) 19:75
"Accidente" (Pardo Bazán) 30:262
"The Accompanist" (Pritchett) 14:263, 273
"Accompanists" (Davie) 52:11
"According to His Lights" (Galsworthy) 22:91
"According to the Pattern" (Evans) 43:19, 28
"An Account of Some Strange Disturbances in an Old House on Aungier Street" (Le Fanu)
    See "Some Strange Disturbances in an Old House on Augier Street"
"Account of Spring Breezes and Autumn Rain" (Tanizaki)
    See "Shumpū shūu roku"
"An Accursed Race" (Gaskell) 25:55, 60, 66
"The Accuser and the Accused" (Singer) 53:274
"Ace in the Hole" (Updike) 13:351-52; 27:329

"Aceite guapo" (Castellanos) 39:46, 57
"El acercamiento a Almotásim" (Borges) 4:4, 16; 41:53-55, 97, 163
"The Achievement of the Cat" (Saki) 12:314, 327
"Achilles' Heel" (O'Connor) 5:370, 372
Acia (Turgenev)
    See Asya
"Acme" (Galsworthy) 22:79, 101
El acoso (Carpentier) 35:91-2, 106, 114-15, 128
Acres and Pains (Perelman) 32:211, 219, 224-25, 230
"Acrobats in the Park" (Welty) 51:319
"Across Paris" (Aymé) 41:4
Across Paris (Aymé)
    See Across Paris and Other Stories
Across Paris and Other Stories (Aymé) 41:3-4
"Across the Airshaft" (Fisher) 25:17, 19
"Across the Bay" (Bates) 10:118, 134
"Across the Bridge" (Boell)
    See "An der Brücke"
"Across the Bridge" (Greene) 29:212
"Across the Gulf" (Davis) 38:110
"Across the Plains" (Moorhouse) 40:309
Across the River and into the Trees (Hemingway) 25:79
"Across the Straits" (Lawson) 18:220
"Across the Wide Missouri" (Wideman) 62:264-67, 283, 315, 317, 320
"An Act of Reparation" (Warner) 23:373
"Acting Captain" (Lewis) 40:271, 276
"Action Will Be Taken" (Boell) 23:8, 10
Actions and Reactions (Kipling) 5:272, 283-85
"The Actor and the Alibi" (Chesterton) 1:138; 46:113, 135
"Acts of God" (Boyle) 16:157
"Acuérdate" (Rulfo) 25:245, 249, 265, 268
"Ad Astra" (Faulkner) 1:147
Ad olam (Agnon) 30:38, 40, 43, 46-7, 57-62, 71
"Ad porcos" (Bioy Casares) 17:56
"Adam and Eve" (Kazakov)
    See "Adam i Eva"
"Adam and Eve" (Machado de Assis)
    See "Adão e Eva"
"Adam and Eve and Pinch Me" (Coppard) 21:17
Adam and Eve and Pinch Me (Coppard) 21:2, 4, 7, 15, 18, 20
"Adam i Eva" (Kazakov) 43:56, 58-62, 65-9
"Adam, One Afternoon" (Calvino)
    See "Un pomeriggio Adamo"
Adam, One Afternoon, and Other Stories (Calvino)
    See L'entrada en guerra
Adam, Where Art Thou? (Boell)
    See Wo warst du, Adam?
"Adam's Bride" (Jolley) 19:221, 233
"Adam's Death" (Boyle) 5:57
"Adão e Eva" (Machado de Assis) 24:127, 129, 153
Adenei hanahar (Appelfeld) 42:4, 11-13

"Adieu" (Balzac) 5:17-18, 22, 24, 31, 33; 59:16-17, 19-20
"Adieu" (Endō) 48:212
"Adieu, New-York!" (Morand) 22:174
Los adioses (Onetti) 23:247, 253, 257-58, 260, 274, 276-79
"The Adjuster" (Fitzgerald) 6:46
"An Adjustment of Nature" (Henry) 49:197, 200
"Adjustment Team" (Dick) 57:106
"Admirals" (Chabon) 59:79
"Admiral's Night" (Machado de Assis) 24:140, 152
Admiralteiskaia igla (Nabokov) 11:124-25
"The Admiralty Spire" (Nabokov)
    See *Admiralteiskaia igla*
"The Admirer" (Singer) 3:378, 384
"Admiring the Scenery" (O'Faolain) 13:284-86, 288, 297, 300, 302-05, 307, 309
"Admonition" (Dazai Osamu) 41:232
"Adobe House in a Provincial Garden" (Platonov)
    See "Glinyanyy dom v uyezdnom sadu"
"Adolescence" (Wescott) 35:363-64, 368, 370, 372
Adolescent (Dostoevsky)
    See *Podrostok*
"Adoration" (Gilchrist) 14:157; 63:15
"Adrift Just Off the Islets of Langerhans: Latitude 38 54'N, Longitude 00'13'" (Ellison) 14:109-11, 115, 118-21
Adult Entertainment (Metcalf) 43:152-56, 165-67
"The Adult Holiday" (Spencer) 57:213
"The Adulterous Woman" (Camus)
    See "La femme adultère"
"Adultery" (Dubus) 15:74, 76, 87, 89-90, 92-4, 98, 100
Adultery, and Other Choices (Dubus) 15:72-3, 75-6, 80-1, 92
"Advancing Luna—and Ida B. Wells" (Walker) 5:412-13
"El Advenimiento del Aguila" (Castellanos) 39:49, 73
"Adventure" (Anderson) 1:18, 58
"The Adventure" (Boell) 23:10
"The Adventure" (Lagerkvist)
    See "Äventyret"
"An Adventure" (Platonov) 42:248
"An Adventure from a Work in Progress" (Thomas) 3:402, 407; 44:357, 359
"The Adventure of a Bather" (Calvino) 48:147
"The Adventure of a Clerk" (Calvino) 3:116
"The Adventure of a Near-sighted Man" (Calvino) 48:147
"Adventure of a Photographer" (Calvino) 3:111
"The Adventure of a Poet" (Calvino)
    See "L'avventura di un poeta"
"The Adventure of a Reader" (Calvino) 3:112
"The Adventure of a Soldier" (Calvino) 48:146-47
"Adventure of a Traveller" (Calvino) 3:111; 48:147
"The Adventure of Charles Augustus Milverton" (Doyle) 12:61
"The Adventure of Gloria Scott" (Doyle) 12:57
"The Adventure of Lieutenant Jergounoff" (Turgenev)
    See "Istoriya leytenanta Ergunova"
"The Adventure of Peter Black" (Doyle) 12:50
"The Adventure of Shoscombe Old Place" (Doyle) 12:51-2, 63
"The Adventure of Six Napoleons" (Doyle) 12:55
"The Adventure of the Black Fisherman" (Irving) 2:241, 247
"The Adventure of the Blanched Soldier" (Doyle) 12:51-2
"The Adventure of the Blue Carbuncle" (Doyle) 12:55, 66, 68, 73-4
"The Adventure of the Cardboard Box" (Doyle) 12:62-4

"The Adventure of the Copper Beeches" (Doyle) 12:51, 55, 58-9, 68, 71-3
"The Adventure of the Creeping Man" (Doyle) 12:52, 63-4
"The Adventure of the Dancing Men" (Doyle) 12:49, 51
"Adventure of the Deserted Residence" (Machen) 20:206
"The Adventure of the Empty House" (Doyle) 12:61
"The Adventure of the Engineer's Thumb" (Doyle) 12:51, 58, 66, 68, 72-4
"The Adventure of the Englishman" (Irving) 2:262
"The Adventure of the German Student" (Irving) 2:241, 256-57, 261
"The Adventure of the Golden Pince-Nez" (Doyle) 12:62
"The Adventure of the Greek Interpreter" (Doyle) 12:51, 55
"The Adventure of the Illustrious Client" (Doyle) 12:54, 64
"The Adventure of the Mason" (Irving) 2:266
"The Adventure of the Missing Three-Quarter" (Doyle) 12:50-2
"Adventure of the Mysterious Picture" (Irving) 2:261, 265
"The Adventure of the Mysterious Stranger" (Irving) 2:261
"The Adventure of the Naval Treaty" (Doyle) 12:50-1, 58-60
"The Adventure of the Noble Bachelor" (Doyle) 12:53, 66, 71, 75
"The Adventure of the Norwood Builder" (Doyle) 12:51-2
"The Adventure of the Red-Headed League" (Doyle) 12:50, 54-5, 66, 70-1, 73
"The Adventure of the Reigate Puzzle" (Doyle) 12:58-9
"The Adventure of the Retired Colourman" (Doyle) 12:50
"The Adventure of the Second Stain" (Doyle) 12:51, 53, 62
"The Adventure of the Silver Blaze" (Doyle) 12:51
"The Adventure of the Speckled Band" (Doyle) 12:58-9, 66, 68, 71, 73-4
"The Adventure of the Stockbroker's Clerk" (Doyle) 12:50-1, 55
"The Adventure of the Sussex Vampire" (Doyle) 12:52, 63
"The Adventure of the Three Gables" (Doyle) 12:52, 64
"The Adventure of the Veiled Lodger" (Doyle) 12:52, 63
"The Adventure of the Yellow Face" (Doyle) 12:50-2, 58
"The Adventure of Wisteria Lodge" (Doyle) 12:62-3
"Adventure Story" (Atwood) 46:75
Adventures du Baron de Gangan (Voltaire) 12:340
Adventures in the Skin Trade, and Other Stories (Thomas) 3:396, 403-04; 44:323-24, 334, 341-42, 344, 354, 360-61
"The Adventures of a Breach-of-Promise Swindler" (Čapek)
    See "Příběhy sňatkového podvodníka"
"Adventures of a Dead Man" (Bulgakov) 18:90
"The Adventures of a Melody" (Peretz) 26:206
"Adventures of a Monkey" (Zoshchenko) 15:391-93, 399
"The Adventures of Chichikov" (Bulgakov) 18:73-4, 91, 98-9
"The Adventures of Françoise and Suzanne" (Cable) 4:49
"The Adventures of Frederick Pickering" (Trollope) 28:320, 323, 332-34, 348
Adventures of Gerard (Doyle) 12:81-2
"The Adventures of John Longbowe" (Harte) 59:311

Adventures of Martin Hewitt (Morrison) 40:332, 349
The Adventures of Menakhem-Mendl (Aleichem) 33:45, 47, 57
The Adventures of Sherlock Holmes (Doyle) 12:68, 72-4
"The Adventures of Simon and Susanna" (Harris) 19:196
"The Adventures of the Bruce-Partington Plans" (Doyle) 12:51-2, 55-6
"Advice to Young Men" (Chesnutt) 7:14
"Aepyornis Island" (Wells) 6:388, 399
"Aerial Ways" (Pasternak)
    See "Vozdushnye puti"
"The Aeroplanes at Brescia" (Davenport) 16:161, 165, 167, 170, 176, 197
"Los afanes" (Bioy Casares) 17:87, 95
"Afar a Bird" (Beckett) 16:123, 125-26
"The Affair at 7, Rue de M—" (Steinbeck)
    See "L'affaire du l'avenue de M—"
"The Affair at Coulter's Notch" (Bierce) 9:49
"The Affair at Grover Station" (Cather) 2:102; 50:77, 91, 99, 187, 231
"An Affair of Honor" (Nabokov) 11:117
"An Affair of Outposts" (Bierce) 9:60, 96
"The Affair of the Clasps" (Gorky) 28:145, 149, 158
"The Affair with the Clasps" (Gorky)
    See "The Affair of the Clasps"
"L'affaire du l'avenue de M—" (Steinbeck) 11:255-56, 258
"Affection" (Barthelme) 55:94, 109-11
"L'affichage céleste" (Villiers de l'Isle Adam) 14:377, 381-83, 390, 396
"The Aficionados" (Carver) 8:50
"Afloat" (Beattie) 11:10-11, 13, 29
Afloat (Maupassant)
    See *Sur l'eau*
"Afonka Bida" (Babel) 16:52, 58
"Afra" (Pardo Bazán) 30:266, 280-81, 283-84
"El afrancesado" (Alarcon) 64:2-3, 30, 38
"Africa Emergent" (Gordimer) 17:57, 160, 174
"The African Magician" (Gordimer) 17:156, 162, 173-74
"African Morning" (Hughes) 6:116-17, 122
African Stories (Lessing) 6:189-91, 196, 212, 214-15, 217-18; 61:99-100, 102-4
"Africans" (Pilnyak) 48:286
"After Dark in the Playing Fields" (James) 16:251
"After Dinner" (Cortázar) 7:70
"After Fourteen Years" (O'Connor) 5:381, 387, 392
"After Holbein" (Wharton) 6:422-23
After Lazarus: A Filmscript (Coover) 15:58-9, 61
"After Lunch" (Cortázar) 7:70
"After Rain" (Trevor) 58:254, 260, 262-63, 275-76, 287
After Rain (Trevor) 58:252-54, 258, 262-63, 272, 274-77, 286, 298
"After Strange Gods" (Norris) 28:205, 207
After Such Pleasures (Parker) 2:273-74
"After the Ball" (Collier) 19:109, 112
"After the Ball" (Tolstoy) 9:367, 379, 388, 394-95
"After the Battle" (Babel) 16:12, 26-28, 30, 52, 54, 57-8
"After the Buffalo" (Algren) 33:114
"After the Denim" (Carver) 8:14; 51:5-6, 14-15
"After the Fair" (Thomas) 3:399; 44:325, 332, 354
"After the Fireworks" (Huxley) 39:159, 173
"After the Funeral: In Memory of Anne Jones" (Thomas) 44:338
"After the Game" (Dubus) 15:86, 100
"After the Race" (Joyce) 3:205, 208-09, 226, 231, 234, 247-48; 26:46-7; 44:263, 288; 64:252-57
"After the Race" (Somerville & Ross) 56:317
"After the Show" (Wilson) 21:320, 324, 337-39
"After the Sirens" (Hood) 42:138-39, 231, 235

"After the Storm" (Hemingway) **1**:216, 234
"After the Sun Has Risen" (Farrell) **28**:94
"After The Theatre" (Chekhov) **51**:37
"After the Wedding" (Appelfeld)
     See "Ahar hahatunah"
"After the Winter" (Chopin) **8**:93
"After Twenty Years" (Henry) **49**:197
"After You, My Dear Alphonse" (Jackson)
     39:210, 211, 219, 220, 224, 225, 229
"After You've Gone" (Adams) **24**:18
After You've Gone (Adams) **24**:16-19
After-Hours (Cortázar)
     See *Deshoras*
"After-Image" (Caldwell) **19**:5
"Afternoon" (Ellison) **26**:8, 21, 28
"Afternoon" (Sansom) **21**:86-7
"Afternoon Dancing" (Trevor) **58**:231
"Afternoon in Linen" (Jackson) **39**:211, 220, 222, 224
"An Afternoon Miracle" (Henry) **5**:162, 181
"Afternoon of a Playwright" (Thurber) **1**:424
"Afternoon of an Author" (Fitzgerald) **6**:60
"Afternoon Waltz" (O'Hara) **15**:277, 284
"An Afternoon with the Old Man" (Dubus) **15**:74
"Afterthoughts by the Author" (Dick) **57**:78
"Afterward" (Wharton) **6**:433
"Afterword" (Kelly) **50**:288
"Agafia" (Chekhov) **2**:155; 8; **51**:82, 106-7
"Again" (Campbell) **19**:71, 75
"Again the Antilles" (Rhys) **21**:49, 61
"Against the Odds" (Trevor) **58**:299
"Agatha" (O'Hara) **15**:282-83
"Agathon, or Concerning Wisdom" (Čapek) **36**:95
Age (Calisher) **15**:12-14
L'âge de discrétion (Beauvoir) **35**:46, 48-53, 72-3, 79, 81-3, 85
"The Age of a Wart" (White) **39**:347-49
The Age of Amazement (Appelfeld)
     See *Tor Hapela'ot*
"The Age of Desire" (Barker) **53**:140, 142-43, 153, 157-58, 162, 168-70, 175
The Age of Discretion (Beauvoir)
     See *L'âge de discrétion*
"The Age of Genius" (Schulz) **13**:336, 344
"The Age of Lead" (Atwood) **46**:79-81, 98
The Age of Miracles (Gilchrist) **63**:5-7, 16, 18, 20-21, 28, 33-34
The Age of Wonders (Appelfeld)
     See *Tor Hapela'ot*
"The Aged Susano-ono-mikoto" (Akutagawa Ryūnosuke) **44**:62
"Agnes" (Gordon) **59**:230, 260, 265, 267-68, 278, 280
"Agony" (Lish) **18**:283
Agostino (Moravia) **26**:131-33, 136, 140-41, 143, 146, 156, 180, 182-83
"The Agreement" (Barthelme) **55**:9-10, 87
"Agunot: A Tale" (Agnon) **30**:6-8, 10, 66, 69
"Aguri" (Tanizaki) **21**:181
Ah King (Maugham) **8**:374, 378
"Ah Life, Ah Death, Ah Music, Ah France" (Saroyan) **21**:149
"Ah Q cheng-chuan" (Lu Hsun)
     See "Ah Q zheng zhuan"
"Ah Q zheng zhuan" (Lu Hsun) **20**:126, 129-30, 145, 150-51
"Ah Q—The Real Story" (Lu Hsun)
     See "Ah Q zheng zhuan"
"Ah, the University!" (Collier) **19**:101, 109
"Ah, Well" (Lawson) **18**:243
"Ah, Woe Is Me" (Gordimer) **17**:152, 160, 167
"Ahar hahatunah" (Appelfeld) **42**:13, 45-46
Ahasverus död (Lagerkvist) **12**:184, 186-90, 192, 198
"Ahead" (Aldiss)
     See "The Failed Men"
"Ah-Ha" (Saroyan) **21**:165-66
"Ah-ha Ah-ha" (Saroyan) **21**:166
"Ahí, pero dónde, cómo" (Cortázar) **7**:61-2
Ahí y ahora (Cortázar) **7**:91

Die Ahnenprobe (Tieck) **31**:286
"El ahogado más hermoso del mundo" (García Márquez) **8**:160, 167-70, 183, 186
"Ahoy, Sailor Boy" (Coppard) **21**:27
Aika (Endō) **48**:191, 198-99, 203
"The Air Disaster" (Ballard) **53**:21
The Airs of Earth (Aldiss) **36**:18
"Airwaves" (Mason) **4**:1
"Akai mayu" (Abe) **61**:5, 22, 25, 27
"Akanishi Kakita" (Shiga) **23**:345
Akëdysséril (Villiers de l'Isle Adam) **14**:378-79, 383-84, 386, 388-90
"Akhnilo" (Salter) **58**:190, 193
"An Akoulina of the Irish Midlands" (Lavin) **4**:182-83
"Akuma" (Tanizaki) **21**:195, 208
"Al yad hahof" (Appelfeld) **42**:5-6
"Alas, Poor Bollington" (Coppard) **21**:11, 28
"Alas, Poor Maling" (Greene) **29**:183-84
"Alaska" (Adams) **24**:13
"Albatross" (Thomas) **20**:317
"Albergo Empedocle" (Forster) **27**:74, 83, 99, 102-03, 108, 119
"Albert" (Tolstoy) **9**:376, 389-90, 393; **30**:332
"Albert Nobbs" (Moore) **19**:298, 303, 310-11
"Albert Savarus" (Balzac) **5**:27
"Albert und Concordia" (Arnim) **29**:29-30
"Albertine" (Dreiser) **30**:142
Albertus, ou l'âme et le péché: légende théologique (Gautier) **20**:10, 24
"Album de familia" (Castellanos) **39**:30, 75, 76
Album de familia (Castellanos) **39**:30, 44, 46, 47, 51, 55, 60, 61, 72, 75, 80
"The Alchemist" (Lovecraft) **52**:262, 264, 287, 290, 334
Ale verk (Peretz) **26**:222
"Alec" (O'Connor) **5**:371, 390
"Alec's Cabin" (Stuart) **31**:227, 236
"Aleksandrit" (Leskov) **34**:110, 119
"The Aleph" (Borges)
     See "El aleph"
"El aleph" (Borges) **4**:25, 28, 31-2, 34; **41**:65-66, 134, 160-61, 164
El aleph (Borges) **4**:15, 18-20, 34, 36, 39-41; **41**:53, 60, 65, 115-17, 134, 157, 161-62
The Aleph, and Other Stories, 1933-1969 (Borges)
     See *El aleph*
"Alexander" (Bates) **10**:111-12, 124, 132
"Alexander the Great" (Čapek) **36**:95, 130
"Alexandra" (Cather) **50**:232
"Alexandrian Tale" (Machado de Assis)
     See "Conto alexandrino"
"The Alexandrite" (Leskov)
     See "Aleksandrit"
"L'alfabeto" (Moravia) **26**:148
"Alguien desordena estas rosas" (García Márquez) **8**:154, 158
"Alguien que anda por ahí" (Cortázar) **7**:83-7, 90-1
The Alhambra (Irving) **2**:242-46, 251, 254, 265, 268
"The Alibi" (du Maurier) **18**:127, 132
"Alibi Ike" (Lardner) **32**:114, 125, 145, 148, 155, 168
"Alice" (Barthelme) **55**:12
"Alice Doane's Appeal" (Hawthorne) **39**:121
"Alice Dugdale" (Trollope) **28**:311, 318, 322-23, 335, 356
"Alice, Falling" (Millhauser) **57**:155, 157, 162, 181, 183, 185
"Alice Long's Dachsunds" (Spark) **10**:360, 362, 367, 371
"Alice Who Sees Mice" (Cisneros) **32**:8, 41
"Alicia and I Talking on Edna's Steps" (Cisneros) **32**:29
"Alicia's Diary" (Hardy) **2**:211, 214
"The Alien Corn" (Maugham) **8**:356-57, 366, 369, 378-79
"An Alien Flower" (Gallant) **5**:124, 132-33
"An Alien in the Pines" (Garland) **18**:154, 160

"The Alien Skull" (O'Flaherty) **6**:262, 280; **60**:183
"Alien Territory" (Atwood) **46**:74, 83
"The Aliens" (McCullers) **9**:342-43, 347, 354, 356
"Los alimentos terrestres" (Arreola) **38**:7-8, 10, 22-23
"Alipaša" (Andrić) **36**:65, 67, 78
"Alix de Morainville" (Cable) **4**:60
"Alix's Refusal" (Colette) **10**:292
"Alkmene" (Dinesen) **7**:165
"All, All Wasted" (Aiken) **9**:12, 14
"All at One Point" (Calvino) **3**:103, 108; **48**:65-6, 104, 155, 157
"All Avoidable Talk" (Narayan) **25**:133, 156
"All Fires the Fire" (Cortázar)
     See "Todos los fuegos el fuego"
All Fires the Fire, and Other Stories (Cortázar)
     See *Todos los fuegos el fuego*
All Gone (Dixon) **16**:218
"All Hallows" (de la Mare) **14**:70, 71, 83, 92
"All Lovers Love the Spring" (Gordon) **15**:104-05
All on the Irish Shore (Somerville & Ross) **56**:294, 308, 314, 317
"All Saints" (Bowen) **3**:40, 42
"All Shook Up" (Boyle) **16**:144-45
"All Sorts of Impossible Things" (McGahern) **17**:299, 304, 309
"All Souls'" (Wharton) **6**:423, 426-27
"All Stories Are True" (Wideman) **62**:286-88, 290
All Stories are True (Wideman) **62**:273-75, 277, 286, 288, 296
"All Strange Away" (Beckett) **16**:117
"All Summer in a Day" (Bradbury) **29**:80-1
"All That GlistersIsn't Gold" (Betts) **45**:28-9
"All That Glitters" (Clarke) **3**:134
"All That Messuage" (Morrison) **40**:337, 355, 367
All That Rises Must Converge (O'Connor)
     See *Everything That Rises Must Converge*
"All the Assholes of the World and Mine" (Bukowski) **45**:64
"All the Birds Come Home to Roost" (Ellison) **14**:124
"All the Dead Pilots" (Faulkner) **1**:147
"All the Girls He Wanted" (O'Hara) **15**:248, 255, 264, 266
"All the Good People I've Left Behind" (Oates) **6**:250, 252-53
All the Good People I've Left Behind (Oates) **6**:247-48, 250, 252-54
"All the King's Horses" (Vonnegut) **8**:434
"All the Other Stories" (Calvino) **3**:101
"All the Pussy We Want" (Bukowski) **45**:56
All the Sad Young Men (Fitzgerald) **6**:46, 94
"All the Sounds of Fear" (Ellison) **14**:105
"All the Time in the World" (Clarke) **3**:135
"All Things Are Nothing to Me" (Farrell) **28**:118, 120-21
"All Through the Night" (Algren) **33**:107
"All uscita" (Pirandello) **22**:234
"All You Zombies" (Heinlein) **55**:190
"Allal" (Bowles) **3**:69
"Allan and Adelaide: An Arabesque" (Ligotti) **16**:286
"Allegiance" (Taylor) **10**:375-79
"An Allegory of Man's Fate" (Hood) **42**:188-89, 205
"Allende la verdad" (Pardo Bazán) **30**:262
"Aller et retour" (Barnes) **3**:7-8, 10, 14-17, 24
"The Alligators" (Updike) **13**:356
"All-seeing" (Moravia) **26**:160-61
"The All-Seeing" (Nin) **10**:303-04
"Un alma pura" (Fuentes) **24**:29, 32, 57-8, 62, 70, 73
"Alma Redeemed" (Malamud) **15**:235
"Al-Mamon" (Gogol) **4**:83; **52**:104
"An Almanac of Pain" (Dazai Osamu) **41**:247-48, 250
"The Almighty Test" (Sansom) **21**:127

"The Almond Tree" (Grimm and Grimm) **36**:203

"The Almond Tree" (de la Mare) **14**:80

"Almost a Gentleman" (Lewis) **40**:271, 276

"Alms Giving" (Moore)
See "An Déirc"

"The Aloe" (Mansfield) **9**:279, 282, 284, 301-03, 309; **23**:158; **38**:230

"Aloha Oe" (London) **4**:269

"Alone" (O'Hara) **15**:248, 265, 267, 274-76

"Alone" (Pilnyak) **48**:285

"Alone" (Singer) **3**:360-61, 364; **53**:294

Alone Against Tomorrow: Stories of Alienation in Speculative Fiction (Ellison) **14**:143-47

Alone with the Horrors (Campbell) **19**:86-8

"Along Memory Lane" (Svevo)
See "L'avvenire dei ricordi"

"Along the Edges" (McGahern) **17**:319

"Along the Road" (Kazakov) **43**:58

"Along the Road" (Pilnyak) **48**:287

"Along the Shore" (Appelfeld)
See "Al yad hahof"

"The Alphabet" (Walser) **20**:355-56

"An Alpimalyan Dialogue" (Turgenev) **7**:335

"An Alpine Idyll" (Hemingway) **1**:210, 217; **36**:291; **63**:56-57

"Als der Krieg ausbrach" (Boell) **23**:2-4, 43-4, 46

"Altar Boy" (Fante) **65**:95, 97, 102

"The Altar of the Dead" (James) **8**:269, 302, 304, 307-09

"The Altar of the Family" (Wilding) **50**:347-48

"Altdeutsche Landsleute" (Arnim) **29**:29-30

Das alte Buch und die Reise ins Blaue hinein (Tieck) **31**:284, 286

Der Alte vom Berge (Tieck) **31**:275

Alternating Currents (Pohl) **25**:227, 229-30, 232, 234

"Alternatives" (Adams) **24**:5, 13

Altogether: The Collected Stories of W. Somerset Maugham (Maugham)
See *East and West: The Collected Short Stories of W. Somerset Maugham*

"Aluteh" (Far) **62**:32, 40

"Always Something to Do in Salinas" (Steinbeck) **11**:253

"Alyosha the Pot" (Tolstoy) **9**:379, 389

"Am I Not Your Rosalind?" (Thurber) **1**:420, 425; **47**:377

"Am I Spoiling You" (Bambara)
See "The Apprentice"

"Am I Your World?" (Saroyan) **21**:162

"Am Strande von Tanger" (Salter) **58**:173, 186, 189-90

"Amalia" (Ferré) **36**:159

"Amanda and Love" (Freeman) **47**:102

L'amant (Duras) **40**:64-65, 72-74, 76-78, 96, 99-105, 107-23, 127-32, 134, 144-51

"L'amante di Gramigna" (Verga) **21**:283, 292, 298-99, 304, 308, 313

L'amante infelice (Moravia) **26**:138, 143, 162

"El amante liberal" (Cervantes) **12**:3, 5, 7-8, 14-16, 18, 34, 44

"Les amants de Tolède" (Villiers de l'Isle Adam) **14**:390, 394, 397

"Amargura para tres sonámbulos" (García Márquez) **8**:154-55, 157-58, 182

Amateurs (Barthelme) **2**:47; **55**:99, 14, 44, 86-6, 105-6, 118-21

"The Amazon" (Leskov)
See "Voitel' nica"

"The Ambassador from Wall Street" (Auchincloss) **22**:4

"The Ambassadress" (Auchincloss) **22**:3, 38

"The Ambitious Guest" (Hawthorne) **3**:182, 186-87

"The Ambitious Sophomore" (Vonnegut) **8**:431

"Ambrose His Mark" (Barth) **10**:41, 45-6, 53-4, 56, 60-1, 63, 89, 95, 97-8, 100

"Ambuscade" (Faulkner) **1**:170, 177

"An Ambuscade" (Harris) **19**:183

"L'ame de la maison ou la vie et la mort d'un grillon" (Gautier) **20**:15

"America First" (Auchincloss) **22**:43

"The American Bakery" (Apple) **50**:23, 34, 38

An American Dream Girl (Farrell) **28**:98

"An American Dutchman" (Clarke) **45**:95

American Earth (Caldwell) **19**:3-6, 9-13, 23, 25, 29-30, 34, 57

"American Express" (Salter) **58**:172, 174-76, 186, 193-94, 196

"American Honeymoon" (Benét) **10**:149

"The American Paul Johnson" (Moorhouse) **40**:301

"The American Poet's Visit" (Moorhouse) **40**:285, 290, 293, 302, 310

"The American Wife" (O'Connor) **5**:373

"The Americanizing of Pau Tau" (Far) **62**:13, 19, 50-51, 58, 60, 75, 99

The Americans, Baby (Moorhouse) **40**:285-89, 291-92, 294, 297, 300-304, 308-11, 322-24

"The American's Tale" (Doyle) **12**:81, 84-5

"Les ames du purgatoire" (Mérimée) **7**:283-4, 289-90, 292

"Les amies de pension" (Villiers de l'Isle Adam) **14**:378, 396

"El amigo de la Muerte" (Alarcon) **64**:2-3, 8, 15-19, 28-29

"Los amigos" (Cortázar) **7**:70, 88-9

"Las amistades efímeras" (Castellanos) **39**:35, 73, 75

"Amnesty" (Gordimer) **17**:182, 184, 187-88, 191

"Amo, amas, amat, amamus, amatis, Enough" (Perelman) **32**:222, 234

"Among School Children" (Welty) **51**:295

Among the Camps (Page) **23**:285

"Among the Corn Rows" (Garland) **18**:142, 144, 154, 159, 168-69, 172, 176, 180

"Among the Dahlias" (Sansom) **21**:90, 92, 95, 112-13

Among the Dahlias (Sansom) **21**:84, 112-14, 116, 126-27

Among the Lost People (Aiken) **9**:6, 28

"Among the Massagetae" (Hesse) **9**:244

"Among the Mourners" (Gilchrist) **63**:6-7

"Among the Paths to Eden" (Capote) **2**:74-5; **47**:38, 42-5, 48-9

"Among the Pictures Are These" (Campbell) **19**:73

"Among the Roses" (Lessing) **61**:113, 115, 120, 125-26

"Among Those Present" (Benét) **10**:154

"Amor" (Lispector) **34**:185, 188, 191, 193, 195-200, 202, 205, 214, 217-19, 221

"El amor asesinado" (Pardo Bazán) **30**:264

"El amor que asalta" (Unamuno) **11**:312-13

L'amore coniugale, e altri racconti (Moravia) **26**:134-35, 138, 140, 150-51, 162

Amores y amoríos, historietas en prosa y verso (Alarcon) **64**:2

"Gli amori difficili" (Calvino) **48**:34, 80, 150

Gli amori difficili (Calvino) **3**:111-13, 116-18; **48**:34, 80, 150

Amori senza amore (Pirandello) **22**:275

La amortajada (Bombal) **37**:2-3, 9, 18-21, 23-24, 27, 29-30, 32, 36-39, 41, 47

"Amour" (Maupassant) **1**:278, 280

L'amour absolu (Jarry) **20**:50, 53, 61-2, 66

"L'amour du naturel" (Villiers de l'Isle Adam) **14**:396

"Amour dure" (Lee) **33**:302, 304-05, 309

L'amour en visites (Jarry) **20**:50

"L'amour suprême" (Villiers de l'Isle Adam) **14**:379, 384-85, 387, 390, 396

L'amour suprême (Villiers de l'Isle Adam) **14**:378, 396-97

The Amulet (Meyer)
See *Das Amulett*

Das Amulett (Meyer) **30**:187, 209-12, 214-18

"Der Amüsierdoktor" (Lenz) **33**:327, 331-32

"An Amusing Adventure" (Zoshchenko) **15**:399

"Amy Foster" (Conrad) **9**:143

"An der Brücke" (Boell) **23**:5, 11, 34

"Ana María" (Donoso) **34**:4, 21, 25, 30, 32, 49

"Anabella's Hat" (Michaels) **16**:309

"Anacleto morones" (Rulfo) **25**:251, 262, 265, 270-71

"Anagram" (Thomas) **44**:336

Analytical Studies (Balzac)
See *Etudes analytiques*

"Ananias" (Harris) **19**:149, 158, 180

"An Anarchist" (Conrad) **9**:157, 179, 181-83, 185

"Ancestors" (Woolf) **7**:381, 389

"Ancient Gentility" (Williams) **31**:333

"The Ancient Seal" (Stifter) **28**:281, 283

"& Answers" (Oates) **6**:232

"And Baby Makes Three" (Selby) **20**:278

"And Even Beyond" (Peretz) **26**:194

"And He Built a Crooked House" (Heinlein) **55**:162, 185, 214

"And Man" (Saroyan) **21**:143, 151

"And of Clay Are We Created" (Allende) **65**:7, 33-34, 47-50

And Other Stories (O'Hara) **15**:286

"And Some More" (Cisneros) **32**:5

"And the Crooked Shall Become Straight" (Agnon)
See "Vehaya he'akov lemishor"

"And the Moon Be Still as Bright" (Bradbury) **29**:50; **53**:195-96, 201-5, 209, 246, 251, 253, 257-59, 262

"And Then" (Barthelme) **2**:47; **55**:44, 88

And Tomorrow, Monday (Pirandello)
See *E domani lunedi*

And Where Were You, Adam? (Boell)
See *Wo warst du, Adam?*

And You, Too (Endō)
See *Nanji mo mata*

"Andare verso il popolo" (Moravia) **26**:163, 180

"¡Buena pesca!" (Alarcon) **64**:2, 5, 9, 28-29; 31

André Walter (Gide) **13**:59

"Andrea" (O'Hara) **15**:285

"Andreas Thameyer's Last Letter" (Schnitzler)
See "Andreas Thameyers letzter brief"

"Andreas Thameyers letzter brief" (Schnitzler) **15**:377

"Andrei Kolosov" (Turgenev) **7**:313, 320, 323-24, 335, 339-40, 359; **57**:288-90, 292

"Andrej Kolosov" (Turgenev)
See "Andrei Kolosov"

"Andrey Kolosov" (Turgenev)
See "Andrei Kolosov"

"Andrey Satchel and the Parson and Clerk" (Hardy) **2**:215

"Androcles and the Army" (O'Connor) **5**:369, 374

"Andromache" (Dubus) **15**:73-4, 81

"Androygenus" (Singer) **53**:305, 313

"The Andventure of the Devil's Foot" (Doyle) **12**:63

"L'ane" (Maupassant) **1**:259

L'Ane d'or (Nerval) **18**:371

"L'Ane et le cheval" (Aymé) **41**:10, 15, 18

Anecdotes of Destiny (Dinesen) **7**:175

"Anedota pecuniária" (Machado de Assis) **24**:128

"Der Anfang von etwas" (Lenz) **33**:318-20, 327

L'angeau (Mauriac) **24**:164, 166-7, 174, 181-2

"The Angel" (Andersen) **6**:15

"The Angel and the Sweep" (Coppard) **21**:12

"The Angel at the Grave" (Wharton) **6**:414

"El ángel de la Guarda" (Alarcon) **64**:2-3, 28, 30, 38

"Angel in the Pasture" (Stuart) **31**:241-42

"Angel Levine" (Malamud) **15**:168, 170-71, 173, 203-04, 207-09, 214, 220

"The Angel of Mons" (Machen)
See "The Bowmen"

"The Angel of the Bridge" (Cheever) **1**:96, 100, 110

"The Angel of the Lord" (Howells) **36**:387-90, 397

"The Angel of the Odd" (Poe) **1**:407-08

"An Angel on the Porch" (Wolfe) **33**:376, 383-84, 386, 399, 401

"Angel Pond Lure of the North" (Leacock) **39**:265

"The Angel Was a Yankee" (Benét) **10**:154, 160

"Angela" (Farrell) **28**:89, 92

"Angela" (Mukherjee) **38**:238-39, 252, 254, 265, 278

Angela Borgia (Meyer) **30**:187, 190, 195, 241, 244-45

"Angelic Butterfly" (Levi)
   See "Angelica Farfalla"

"Angelica Farfalla" (Levi) **12**:278

Angelika, die Geueserin and Cosmusm, der Seilspringer (Arnim) **29**:5

Angélique (Nerval) **18**:362-65

"Angels at the Ritz" (Trevor) **21**:233, 262; **58**:200, 207-8, 212, 230

Angels at the Ritz, and Other Stories (Trevor) **21**:233, 237, 260, 262; **58**:200, 206-8

"Angels Unawares" (Henderson) **29**:327

"Anglicization" (Zangwill) **44**:378, 390

"The Anglo-Saxons of Auxierville" (Stuart) **31**:244

"L'angoscia" (Moravia) **26**:182

Angry Candy (Ellison) **14**:141-42

"Angst" (Oates) **6**:241

"Anguish" (Chekhov) **51**:58-60, 78

"Anika's Times" (Andrić)
   See "Anikina vremena"

"Anikina vremena" (Andrić) **36**:33, 38, 43, 46, 48, 52, 66

"The Animal Game" (Machado de Assis) **24**:139, 155

"The Animal in the Synagogue" (Kafka) **60**:243-44

"Animal Sketches" (Shiga) **23**:346

"Animal Woods" (Calvino) **48**:146

"Animals or Human Beings" (Wilson) **21**:358, 362

"Anita G." (Kluge) **61**:74

"Ann Lee's" (Bowen) **3**:54

Ann Lee's (Bowen) **3**:37, 39-40, 55

Ann Lee's and Other Stories (Bowen) **28**:4

"Ann Lisbeth" (Andersen) **6**:14-15; **56**:37

"Anna" (Dubus) **15**:96

"Anna, Lady Baxby" (Hardy) **60**:179

"Anna Lisa's Nose" (Berriault) **30**:96-7

"Anna na shee" (Chekhov) **51**:29, 58, 61, 64, 69, 194

"Anna on the Neck" (Chekhov) **2**:131, 157;

"Anna, Part I" (Gilchrist) **14**:157-60

"Anna Trivia Pluralized" (Perelman) **32**:229

"Annamalai" (Narayan) **25**:139, 145, 154-55, 164-65, 176

"Anne" (Beauvoir) **35**:60, 62-4, 66-71

"Anne" (Davis) **38**:122-23

"Anner Lizer's Stumblin' Block" (Dunbar) **8**:120-21, 129, 136

"Annette Delarbre" (Irving) **2**:241, 251, 259

"Anneve" (Caldwell) **19**:56

"Gli anni-lucci" (Calvino) **3**:92; **48**:70-1

"Anniversary" (Aiken) **9**:13, 31

"An Anniversary" (de la Mare) **14**:79, 84, 89

"Anniversary" (Lardner) **32**:133-34, 138, 140-41, 145, 149, 160, 162

"The Anniversary" (Price) **22**:367

"L'annonciateur" (Villiers de l'Isle Adam) **14**:381-87, 389-90, 395-96

The Annotated H.P. Lovecraft (Lovecraft) **52**:354

Annouchka (Turgenev)
   See *Asya*

"Announcement" (Arreola)
   See "Anuncio"

"The Annual Conference of 1930 and South Coast Dada" (Moorhouse) **40**:291

"The Annuity" (Pirandello) **22**:227-28

"El año en Spitzberg" (Alarcon) **64**:8, 31

"An Anonym" (Čapek) **36**:130

"Anonymiad" (Barth) **10**:40, 43-4, 46-8, 52, 54-6, 64, 74, 78-80, 83, 86-8, 90-1, 98-9 100-02

"An Anonymous Story" (Chekhov) **2**:130-31, 157-58

"Another American Tragedy" (Collier) **19**:107-10, 112

"Another April" (Stuart) **31**:232-33, 266

"Another Christmas" (Trevor) **21**:262; **58**:225, 288

"Another Community" (Narayan) **25**:134, 139, 141, 157

"Another Country" (Hemingway)
   See "Let It Go"

"Another Day Another Dollar" (Selby) **20**:254-55, 258-59, 263, 267-69, 271-72

"Another face" (Agnon)
   See "Panim aherot"

"Another Hanging" (Stuart) **31**:234, 236, 267

"Another Man's Wife" (Anderson) **1**:39

"Another Pair of Hands" (Spark) **10**:370

"Another Part of the Sky" (Gordimer) **17**:151

"Another Story" (Cheever) **1**:112

"Another Time" (O'Brien) **10**:346-47

"Another Wife" (Anderson) **1**:31, 50-1

"Another World" (Campbell) **19**:77

"Ansell" (Forster) **27**:99, 103-04, 119

"The Answer" (Pirandello) **22**:254-55

"The Answer Depends" (O'Hara) **15**:262

"Answer to Prayer" (Wells) **6**:392

"Answers to a Questionnaire" (Ballard) **53**:67

"The Antagonists" (Chekhov) **51**:90

"The Antchar" (Turgenev) **7**:318-19

"Antes da ponte Rio-Niterói" (Lispector) **34**:209, 211

The Antheap (Lessing) **6**:189-91, 193-94, 196; **61**:100, 131

"Anthony: Who Sought Things That Were Lost" (Waugh) **41**:325

"Anti-bureaucratisation and the Apparatchiki" (Moorhouse) **40**:322

"Antico furore" (Moravia) **26**:164

"The Antidote" (Narayan) **25**:140, 155

"Antigona" (Bunin) **5**:113

"Antigone" (Bunin)
   See "Antigona"

"The Antique Ring" (Hawthorne) **3**:189, 191

"The Antiquities of Elis" (Davenport) **16**:170, 176, 178, 195-96

"Antlers" (Bass) **69**:16, 20

"Antlers" (Kazakov) **43**:61

"Antonie" (Villiers de l'Isle Adam) **14**:382

"Antónov Apples" (Bunin) **5**:81, 100

"Antonovskie jabloki" (Bunin) **5**:98-9

"Ants and the Fire" (Solzhenitsyn)
   See "Koster i murav'i"

"The Ant's Wedding" (Levi) **12**:275, 277

"Anuncio" (Arreola) **38**:12

"Anxiety" (Paley) **8**:411-12

"Any Purple Subjunctives Today?" (Perelman) **32**:213

"Any Reasonable Offer" (Vonnegut) **8**:433

Anya Kōro (Shiga) **23**:363

The Anything Box (Henderson) **29**:316

"Anyuta" (Chekhov) **51**:33, 54, 57

"Anywhere Out of the World" (Baudelaire)
   See "N'importe où hors du monde"

"Apacalipsis de Solentiname" (Cortázar) **7**:83, 86, 88, 90-1

"Apada" (Tagore) **48**:310-11

"A-pao" (P'u Sung-ling) **31**:196-97

"Apartment" (Cowan) **28**:83

"The Ape" (Pritchett) **14**:271

"The Ape Lady in Retirement" (Boyle) **16**:148, 154

"Apellesova cherta" (Pasternak)
   See "Il tratto di Apelle"

"The Aperture Moment" (Aldiss) **36**:11-12, 25

"Aphrodite" (Platonov) **42**:254

"A-Playin' of Old Sledge at the Settlemint" (Murfree) **22**:188, 207-8

"Apocalypse at Solentiname" (Cortázar)
   See "Apacalipsis de Solentiname"

"An Apocryph" (Čapek)
   See "Crucifixion"

Apocrypha (Čapek) **36**:112, 129

Apocryphal Stories (Čapek)
   See *Kniha apokryfů*

"Um apólogo" (Machado de Assis) **24**:128, 130

"An Apologue" (Hawthorne) **39**:126

"The Apology" (Barthelme) **55**:106

"The Apostate" (London) **4**:263, 291-92

"An Apostle of the Tulles" (Harte) **8**:247-49; **59**:310

"The Apparatus for the Chemical Analysis of the Last Breath" (Villiers de l'Isle Adam)
   See "L'appareil pur l'analyse chimique du dernier soupir"

"L'appareil pur l'analyse chimique du dernier soupir" (Villiers de l'Isle Adam) **14**:379, 396

"Apparition" (Maupassant) **1**:265, 281

"An Apparition in the Engineers' Castle" (Leskov) **34**:127

"Appeal to the Authorities" (Dazai Osamu) **41**:238-39, 244-45

"Appearance and Reality" (Maugham) **8**:380

"An Appearance of Life" (Aldiss) **36**:11

"Appearances" (O'Hara) **15**:290

"The Apple" (Wells) **6**:359, 383

"Apple Girl" (Calvino)
   See "La ragazza mela"

"The Apple Tree" (Bowen) **3**:33, 41

"The Apple Tree" (du Maurier) **18**:137-38

"The Apple Tree" (Freeman) **47**:163

"The Apple Tree" (Galsworthy) **22**:61, 75-6, 80, 84, 86-8, 90, 94-7, 99-102

"The Apple Tree" (Mansfield) **9**:282, 284; **38**:204

The Apple Tree: A Short Novel and Some Stories (du Maurier) **18**:126, 130, 137

"Apples" (Campbell) **19**:71, 75

"Apples and Pears" (Davenport) **16**:185-89

Apples and Pears, and Other Stories (Davenport) **16**:183-89, 199-200

"The Apple-Tree Table" (Melville) **1**:294-95, 298

"An Application for a Film Grant" (Moorhouse) **40**:323

"An Appointment with the General" (Greene) **29**:216, 223, 226-27

"The Apprentice" (Bambara) **35**:15, 26, 28-9, 38-41

"The Apprentice" (Dybek) **55**:124-25, 127, 134, 136, 130, 141

"Apprentice" (Warner) **23**:368

"The Approach to al Mu'tasim" (Borges)
   See "El acercamiento a Almotásim"

"The Approach to Almotasim" (Borges)
   See "El acercamiento a Almotásim"

"April 2000: The Third Expedition" (Bradbury) **29**:50, 68-75; **53**:187-88, 190, 195, 197, 201-4, 207, 211, 222, 248-49, 252-54

"April 2026: The Long Years" (Bradbury) **29**:69

"April and May Mornings" (Alarcon)
   See "Mañanas de abril y mayo"

"April Fish" (Gallant) **5**:151

"April in Paris" (Le Guin) **12**:232

"April is the Cruelest Month" (Cabrera Infante)
   See "Abril es el mes más cruel"

"April, Late April" (Wolfe) **33**:401

"The April Witch" (Bradbury) **29**:47; **53**:215

"Àpropos of the Kreutzer Sonata" (Leskov) **34**:119

"Apropos of the Wet Snow" (Dostoevsky) **2**:169, 187

Apt Pupil (King) **17**:262-66, 271, 273; **55**:243-46

"Apuntes de un rencoroso" (Arreola) **38**:5

Aqua quemada (Fuentes) **24**:43-4, 61-2, 75

"Aquarius" (Thomas) **20**:287, 317-19

"The Aquatic Uncle" (Calvino)
See "Lo zio acquativo"
Aquis Submersus (Storm) **27**:281, 284, 286-87,
289, 291-96, 302-03, 308-14
"Arabesque: The Mouse" (Coppard) **21**:15, 17,
26
Arabesques (Gogol) **4**:104; **29**:142
"Araby" (Joyce) **3**:202-03, 205, 208, 217-18,
225, 231, 234, 237, 242, 245-46, 249;
26:46-7, 50, 73, 79, 83; **44**:235-319; **64**:196,
256
"Araki Thomas" (Endō) **48**:208
"Arap Petra Velikogo" (Pushkin) **55**:288-89
Arap Petra Velikogo (Pushkin) **27**:129, 148,
162-63, 165, 178, 182, 186, 188
"Ararat" (Henderson) **29**:316, 326
"The Arbiter" (Auchincloss) **22**:35, 39, 45
"El árbol" (Bombal) **37**:9, 23, 26-27, 30, 33,
36-39, 44
Arcadian Adventures with the Idle Rich
(Leacock) **39**:257, 262, 263, 265, 271, 273
"Arcadian London" (Dickens) **17**:123
"Archangel" (Updike) **13**:390, 397
"The Archduchess" (du Maurier) **18**:127
Arctic Summer, and Other Fiction (Forster)
27:115
"Arcturus, the Hound" (Kazakov)
See "Arktur—gončij pes"
"Ardagh" (Le Fanu)
See "The Fortunes of Sir Robert Ardagh"
"Ardessa" (Cather) **2**:99, 110-11; **50**:78
"Ardid de guerra" (Pardo Bazán) **30**:272
"Ardor/Awe/Atrocity" (Abish) **44**:7-9, 12, 15,
19
"Are These Actual Miles?" (Carver) **8**:47
"Are You a Doctor?" (Carver) **8**:9-10, 18, 32,
34, 47
"Arena" (Pardo Bazán) **30**:261
"Arethusa" (Freeman) **47**:103, 118-20, 163
"Argamak" (Babel) **16**:27-8, 52, 56
"The Argentine Ant" (Calvino)
See *La formica Argentina*
"Argo and his Master" (Svevo)
See "Argo e il suo padrone"
"Argo e il suo padrone" (Svevo) **25**:329, 331-
32, 336
"Argon" (Levi) **12**:255-57, 259, 264
"The Argonauts" (Pavese) **19**:369
"The Argonauts of North Liberty" (Harte)
8:214, 216-17, 223
"The Argonauts of the Air" (Wells) **6**:359, 367,
374, 380, 383, 388, 403
"The Argument" (Dixon) **16**:211
"Aria" (Barthelme) **55**:109
"L'aria buona" (Calvino) **48**:82-3
"Aria Marcella, Souvenir de Pompei" (Gautier)
20:3, 5-8, 16-20, 35
"Ariadna" (Chekhov)
See "Ariadne"
"Ariadne" (Chekhov) **2**:131-32, 157; **28**:60;
51:26, 32-3, 75-6, 128, 171, 174, 191-92,
194-96, 207, 209
"Ariel. A Legend of the Lighthouse" (Alcott)
27:58
"Arina" (Pilnyak) **48**:284
"The Aristocrat" (Pritchett) **14**:270, 293, 296
"Arktur, gonchii pes" (Kazakov)
See "Arktur—gončij pes"
"Arktur—gončij pes" (Kazakov) **43**:47, 49, 51,
54, 62-3, 66-7, 69
"Arktur—Hunting Dog" (Kazakov)
See "Arktur—gončij pes"
*Armance; ou, Quelques scènes d'un salon de
Paris en 1827* (Stendhal) **27**:232, 252-55,
258, 264-71
"Armande" (Colette) **10**:274-75, 293
"Las armas secretas" (Cortázar) **7**:50, 53-8,
70-1
Die arme Baronin (Keller) **26**:92-3, 102-04,
110
Der Arme Spielmann (Grillparzer) **37**:84-191
"Der Arme Wohltäter" (Stifter) **28**:284, 288

"The Armenian & the Armenian" (Saroyan)
21:133
"Army of Occupation" (Boyle) **5**:64, 74-5
"Around the Bend in Eighty Days" (Perelman)
32:229
Around the Day in Eighty Worlds (Cortázar)
See *La vuelta al día en ochenta mundos*
"Around the Dear Ruin" (Berriault) **30**:96-7
*Around the Mountain: Scenes from Montreal
Life* (Hood) **42**:143, 150-54, 158, 162,
182-83, 196-97, 199, 203-04, 213-22,
239-43
"Around the World Fliers" (Williams) **31**:334
"Around Theatres" (Hood) **42**:217, 220
"Arrangement in Black and White" (Parker)
2:274-75, 278, 280, 283, 286
"Arrangements" (Dixon) **16**:216
"The Arrest of Lieutenant Golightly" (Kipling)
5:288, 290
"The Arrow of Heaven" (Chesterton) **1**:128;
46:111, 113, 134, 141
Arrowroot (Tanizaki)
See *Yoshinokuzu*
"Arrowroot Leaves in Yoshino" (Tanizaki)
21:192
"Arsène Guillot" (Mérimée) **7**:279, 290-2, 300
"Art and Mr. Mahoney" (McCullers) **9**:332,
343, 345-46, 354, 359
"Eine Art Erzahlung" (Walser) **20**:345
"The Art of Book-Making" (Irving) **2**:254
"The Art of Courtly Love" (Garrett) **30**:164
"The Art of Living" (Gardner) **7**:224-28, 235,
240
The Art of Living, and Other Stories (Gardner)
7:223-28, 235
"Artemis, the Honest Well-Digger" (Cheever)
1:107-08; **38**:46
"Arthur Gordon Pym" (Poe)
See *The Narrative of Arthur Gordon Pym,
of Nantucket*
"Arthur Jermyn" (Lovecraft)
See "Facts concerning the Late Arthur Jer-
myn and His Family"
"Arthur Smith salva sin alma" (Castellanos)
39:49, 57
"Arthur Smith Saves His Soul" (Castellanos)
See "Arthur Smith salva sin alma"
"Arthur Snatchfold" (Forster) **27**:90, 94, 96,
102-07, 123
"Artificial Flowers" (Čapek)
See "Falešné květiny"
"The Artificial Nigger" (O'Connor) **1**:343, 345,
347, 353; **23**:185, 206, 236-37; **61**:189, 191
An Artificial Nigger (O'Connor)
See "The Artificial Nigger"
"Artificial Roses" (García Márquez) **8**:185
"The Artist" (Galsworthy) **22**:99
"The Artist at Work" (Camus)
See "Jonas ou l'artiste au travail"
"The Artist of the Beautiful" (Hawthorne)
3:169-71, 174, 183-84; **39**:121
"Un Artista" (Svevo) **25**:353
"The Artistic Career of Corky" (Wodehouse)
2:342
"The Artistic Personality" (Auchincloss)
22:40-1
"The Artist's Child" (Gissing) **37**:72, 75
"An Artist's Story" (Chekhov) **2**:131, 139, 157;
28:62-3; **51**:33
"The Artist's Turn" (Narayan) **25**:140
"The Artless Age" (Glasgow) **34**:65-6, 71, 76,
78, 81, 102-03
"The Artus Exchange" (Hoffmann)
See "Der Artushof"
"Der Artushof" (Hoffmann) **13**:183, 223
"Aru ahō no isshō" (Akutagawa Ryūnosuke)
44:44, 69, 83-4, 89
"Arvie Aspinall's Alarm Clock" (Lawson)
18:201, 238, 241
"Arxierej" (Chekhov) **2**:131, 148-49, 157-58;
51:84, 93, 124, 143, 148-50, 198

"As academias de Sião" (Machado de Assis)
24:128-30
"As águas do mundo" (Lispector) **34**:231,
233-34
"As Boys to Wanton Flies" (Wilding) **50**:347
"As Breathing and Consciousness Return"
(Solzhenitsyn)
See "Dykhanie"
"As Far as Abashiri" (Shiga)
See "Abashiri made"
"As in the Good Old Days" (Čapek) **36**:115
As Sad as She Is (Onetti)
See *Tan triste como ella*
"As Strong as a Man" (Suckow)
See "A Great Mollie"
"Ascension" (Thomas) **20**:324-25, 327-28
"El asesino" (Arreola) **38**:9, 21
"Ash" (Campbell) **19**:74
'Ashan (Appelfeld) **42**:3-5, 43
"Ash-Cake Hannah and Her Ben" (Dunbar)
8:122
"The Ashen Moon" (Shiga)
See "Hai-iro no tsuki"
Ashenden; or, The British Agent (Maugham)
8:365, 367, 376-78, 380, 383
"Ashes of Descending Incense, First Brazier"
(Chang) **28**:29; 32; 35-36
"Ashes of Descending Incense, Second
Brazier" (Chang) **28**:32; 35
"Ashikari" (Tanizaki) **21**:182-83, 185, 188-89,
191, 195
"The Ash-Tree" (James) **16**:225, 229-30, 232,
234-36, 240-41, 251, 253, 256
Así en la paz como en la guerra (Cabrera
Infante) **39**:7, 9, 10, 12, 17-19, 21-24
"Así y todo" (Pardo Bazán) **30**:264, 266
Asia (Turgenev)
See *Asya*
"Asigh" (Lavin) **4**:167-68, 181-83
"El asistente" (Alarcon) **64**:2-3
Asja (Turgenev)
See *Asya*
"Aska and the Wolf" (Andrić)
See "Aska i vuk"
"Aska i vuk" (Andrić) **36**:35, 38, 43, 73
"Aspects of the Dying Process" (Wilding)
50:347
Aspects of the Dying Process (Wilding) **50**:344,
346, 349, 352
"The Aspern Papers" (Bellow) **14**:25
"The Aspern Papers" (Ozick) **60**:335
The Aspern Papers (James) **8**:275, 300, 321-22,
324, 332, 335; **47**:202, 204, 267
"Asphodel" (Welty) **1**:467-69, 472; **51**:265, 318
An Aspidistra in Babylon: Four Novellas
(Bates) **10**:122
"Aspirin Is a Member of the NRA" (Saroyan)
21:132, 136, 142, 166
"The Assassination of John Fitzgerald Kennedy
Considered as a Downhill Motor Race"
(Ballard) **1**:70-1, 75
"The Assassination Weapon" (Ballard) **53**:17
L'assassinio di via Belpoggio (Svevo) **25**:357,
362
"Assault" (Oates) **6**:243
"The Assembly" (Borges)
See *El congreso*
"The Assembly" (Gallant) **5**:147
Assembly (O'Hara) **15**:251, 252, 261, 279, 280-
81, 287
"Un assenza" (Ginzburg) **65**:115, 130, 132
"The Assessor of Success" (Henry) **5**:187
Assez (Beckett) **16**:71, 76-8, 83, 87, 95-9, 122,
135
"The Assignation" (Poe) **1**:394; **22**:304-07;
54:209, 211-16
"The Assistant" (O'Hara) **15**:279, 285
"The Assistant Producer" (Nabokov) **11**:113,
128
"The Associated Un-Charities" (Norris) **28**:214
"Assommons les pauvres" (Baudelaire) **18**:34,
47, 49-53

"Assumption" (Beckett) **16**:72

"The Assyrian" (Saroyan) **21**:155, 157

The Assyrian, and Other Stories (Saroyan) **21**:155

"Astley's" (Dickens) **17**:134

"An Astrologer's Day" (Narayan) **25**:132, 138, 140, 152-53, 155, 160-61, 169

An Astrologer's Day and Other Stories (Narayan) **25**:132-33, 135, 137, 139, 152, 154-55

"The Astronomer" (Betts) **45**:7, 19, 28-30, 36, 38

"The Astronomer" (Updike) **13**:389

The Astronomer and Other Stories (Betts) **45**:3-4, 7-8, 10, 28-30

Asya (Turgenev) **7**:320, 323-24, 326-27, 334, 337, 339, 347-52, 360; **57**:302-3, 385

"At a Dinner of Atheists" (Barbey d'Aurevilly) See "A un dîner d' athées"

"At Age Forty-Seven" (Zoshchenko) **15**:407

"At Chênière Caminada" (Chopin) **8**:95, 99, 110

"At Christmas-Time" (Chekhov) **2**:130-31; **51**:48

"At Dawn" (Rulfo) See "En la madrugada"

"At Daybreak" (Calvino) **3**:109; **48**:65, 132, 154, 160

"At Daybreak" (Rulfo) See "En la madrugada"

"At Evening, a Geranium" (Pirandello) See "Di sera, un geranio"

"At First Sight" (Adams) **24**:10

"At First Sight" (Campbell) **19**:62, 73

"At First Sight" (de la Mare) **14**:71, 74, 89

"At Geisenheimer's" (Wodehouse) **2**:355

"At Hemdat's" (Agnon) **30**:68

"At Home" (Chekhov) See "V rodnom uglu"

"At Home in Auschwitz" (Borowski) See "Auschwitz, Our Home"

"At Kinosaki" (Shiga) See "Kinosaki nite"

"At Laban's Well" (Coppard) **21**:19

"At Last" (Stoker) **62**:252

"At Lehmann's" (Mansfield) **23**:137

"At One O'Clock in the Morning" (Baudelaire) See "A une heure du matin"

"At Paso Rojo" (Bowles) **3**:59, 61-2, 66, 79

"At Sallygap" (Lavin) **4**:169, 171-72, 175, 178-79, 182

"At Shaft 11" (Dunbar) **8**:120-21, 127, 129, 131, 136, 139-40, 143

"At Sundown" (Saroyan) **21**:161

"At Teague Poteet's: A Sketch of the Hog Mountain Range" (Harris) **19**:131, 174-75, 179, 181

"At the Barber's" (Zoshchenko) **15**:407-08

"At the Bay" (Mansfield) **9**:278, 280, 282-83, 286, 288-92, 300, 302, 305-07, 309; **23**:139-41, 143, 153-54, 158-59; **38**:204, 229

"At the Beach" (Adams) **24**:11

"At the Bedside of a Dying Man" (Peretz) See "By a Dying Man's Pillow"

"At the 'Cadian Ball" (Chopin) **8**:72, 91, 95, 99, 106-07

"At the Castle" (Čapek) **36**:82, 93, 124-25

"At the Doctors" (Andrić) See "Kod lekara"

"At the Drug Store" (Taylor) **10**:398-400, 418

"At the Edge of the World" (Leskov) See "Na kraju sveta"

"At the End of the Mechanical Age" (Barthelme) **2**:47; **55**:44, 87

"At the End of the Passage" (Kipling) **5**:264, 271-72, 274, 278, 280-81, 290-91

"At the Front" (Williams) **31**:305

"At the Gate" (Pirandello) See "All uscita"

"At the Kirks" (Gordon) **59**:261, 265

"At the Krungthep Plaza" (Bowles) **3**:80

"At the Landing" (Welty) **1**:468; **51**:259, 269, 281, 319

"At the Mountains of Madness" (Lovecraft) **52**:269, 354-56

At the Mountains of Madness, and Other Tales of Terror (Lovecraft) **52**:252, 270, 272-77, 280, 286-90, 313, 320, 337-38, 341, 343, 351

"At the Mouse Circus" (Ellison) **14**:115

"At the Outset of the Day" (Agnon) **30**:4

"At the Portal" (Narayan) **25**:134-35, 154

"At the Prophet's" (Mann) **5**:323

"At the Rainbow's End" (London) **4**:286

"At the Rendezvous of Victory" (Gordimer) **17**:171

"At the Salt Marsh" (Gorky) **28**:158

"At the Seminary" (Oates) **6**:255-56

"At the Sign of the Savage" (Howells) **36**:397

"At the Start of the Day" (Solzhenitsyn) **32**:395

"At the Station" (Kazakov) See "Na polustanke"

"At the Tolstoy Museum" (Barthelme) **2**:31, 35, 40, 48, 56; **55**:3-6, 60-5, 84

"At the Turn of the Road: An Irish Girl's Love Story" (Moore) **19**:345

At the University (Storm) See *Auf der Universität*

"At Third Hand: a Psychological Inquiry" (Howells) **36**:387

"Athénaïse" (Chopin) **8**:66, 72-3, 78, 86, 96, 99, 113-14

"Athene, Goddess of the Brave" (Auchincloss) **22**:52

"Atomo verde número cinco" (Donoso) **34**:8-11, 17, 33

The Atonement (Tagore) See "Prayaschitta"

"The Atrocity Exhibition" (Ballard) **1**:75

The Atrocity Exhibition (Ballard) **1**:70-1, 76-8, 80-3; **53**:6, 8, 11-12, 14-17, 19, 25-7, 33, 40, 52-4, 67-8, 91-2, 94-7, 99-113, 120, 122, 124-5

"Atrophy" (Wharton) **6**:424

"Attack" (O'Connor) **5**:371, 391

"An Attack of Nerves" (Chekhov) **2**:153, 155-56; **41**:199; **51**:25, 82, 84

"An Attack on Lenin" (Zoshchenko) **15**:407

"Attalie Brouillard" (Cable) **4**:59

Attendance List for a Funeral (Kluge) See *Lebensläufe*

"The Attila" (Narayan) **25**:140-41, 154

"Attitude" (Lewis) **40**:281

"Attracta" (Trevor) **21**:235, 247, 262; **58**:226, 237, 242, 275, 278

"Attractive Modern Homes" (Bowen) **3**:54

"Au clair de la lune" (Aymé) **41**:10

"Au large" (Cable) **4**:58-9

"Au Seabhac" (O'Flaherty) **6**:286-89

"Au tombeau de Charles Fourier" (Davenport) **16**:168-69, 175, 177, 191, 193

"L'auberge" (Maupassant) **1**:265; **64**:317, 320

L'Auberge rouge (Balzac) **5**:18, 31, 33; **59**:11-14

"An Auction" (Crane) **7**:108, 110

Auf dem Staatshof (Storm) **27**:282, 286

"Auf der Galerie" (Kafka) **29**:343

Auf der Universität (Storm) **27**:282, 286

Der Aufruhr in den Cevennen (Tieck) **31**:273, 275-76, 283, 287-88

"Auguiano Religious Articles Rosaries Statues" (Cisneros) **32**:38

"August" (Schulz) **13**:330-31, 339

"August Afternoon" (Caldwell) **19**:25-7, 32, 39, 46

"August Eschenburg" (Millhauser) **57**:158-59, 167, 172, 175

August Holiday (Pavese) See *Feria d'agosto*

"August Holiday Fun" (Moravia) See "Scherzi di Ferragosto"

"Augustus" (Hesse) **9**:234

"Aunt Cora" (Wilson) **21**:358, 363

"Aunt Fountain's Prisoner" (Harris) **19**:124, 173, 178

"Aunt Gertrude" (Pritchett) **14**:263, 271

Aunt Jo's Scrap-Bag (Alcott) **27**:7-12, 22, 42-3, 50, 57

Aunt Jo's Scrap-Bag: My Boys (Alcott) **27**:42

"Aunt Juley's Courtship" (Galsworthy) **22**:70

"Aunt Lucy's Search" (Chesnutt) **7**:13

"Aunt Lympy's Interference" (Chopin) **8**:84

"Aunt Mandy's Investment" (Dunbar) **8**:121, 127, 137, 143, 147

"Aunt Mathilde's Drawings" (Wilson) **21**:358-59

"Aunt Mimy's Son" (Chesnutt) **7**:28

"Aunt Tempy's Revenge" (Dunbar) **8**:122

"Aunt Tempy's Triumph" (Dunbar) **8**:122

"Auntie Bissel" (Suckow) **18**:413, 422, 424

"Auntie Toothache" (Andersen) **56**:34-5, 37

"The Aunt's Story" (White) **39**:288-89

"Auprès d'un mort" (Maupassant) **1**:281

Aura (Fuentes) **24**:29, 33-8, 43-51, 58-62

Aurélia (Nerval) **18**:334-37, 355, 361-62, 366-68, 373-81, 383-84

"The Aurelian" (Nabokov) **11**:130

"Aurora" (Morand) **22**:156-57, 165

Aus dem Leben eines bekannten Mannes (Hoffmann) **13**:187, 189

"Auschwitz, Our Home" (Borowski) **48**:5, 6, 15

"The Aussolas Martin Cat" (Somerville & Ross) **56**:301, 333-4, 340

"The Author of Beltraffio" (James) **8**:300, 304-05, 345, 350

"The Author of the Acacia Seeds and Other Extracts from the 'Journal of the Association of Therolinguistics'" (Le Guin) **12**:230, 235

"The Author's Chamber" (Irving) **2**:265

"An Author's Confession" (Gogol) **4**:83

"Author's Outline of 'The Mute'" (McCullers) **9**:343

"Autobiografija" (Andrić) **36**:50, 69-73

"The Autobiography" (Andrić) See "Autobiografija"

"Autobiography" (Atwood) **2**:15

"An Autobiography" (Gallant) **5**:133

"Autobiography: A Self-Recorded Fiction" (Barth) **10**:41-2, 46, 53-4, 60, 64, 72, 76-9, 80, 84, 91 97-8

"Autobiography of an Omnibus" (Alcott) **27**:43

"Ha' Autobus ha'Aharon" (Agnon) **30**:22, 37, 54

"Autofac" (Dick) **57**:41, 44, 52-53, 108

"L'automa" (Moravia) **26**:142, 146-47, 152, 155, 164-65, 182

L'automa (Moravia) **26**:141-42, 146, 148-49, 152-53, 155, 161-62, 164, 180, 182

"Die Automate" (Hoffmann) **13**:209, 213-14, 219

"The Automaton" (Moravia) See "L'automa"

"The Automobile That Wouldn't Run" (Caldwell) **19**:25, 39, 42, 47

"La autopista del sur" (Cortázar) **7**:54-5, 61

"Autre étude de femme" (Balzac) **5**:32-3, 35-6, 39

"Autres temps" (Wharton) **6**:424-26, 436

"Autrui" (Arreola) **38**:3, 7, 23, 25-28

"Autumn I" (Mansfield) **9**:284

"Autumn II" (Mansfield) See "The Wind Blows"

"Autumn Afternoon" (Bradbury) **53**:267

"Autumn in the Oak Forest" (Kazakov) See "Osen v dubovykhlesakh"

"Autumn in the Woods" (Kazakov) See "Osen v dubovykhlesakh"

"Autumn Loneliness" (Boell) **23**:38

"The Autumn Mountain" (Akutagawa Ryūnosuke) See "Shūzan zu"

"Autumn Sunshine" (Trevor) **21**:247, 262

"Gli avangnardisti a Mentone" (Calvino) **3**:97; **48**:36

"Gli avanguardisti a Mentone" (Calvino) **48**:36

"L'avaro" (Moravia) **26**:163

"Avec la bebe-sitter" (Updike) **13**:385

"L'aventure de Walter Schnafs" (Maupassant) **1**:263

"Äventyret" (Lagerkvist) **12**:181, 191

"Avenue Junot" (Aymé) **41**:17

"The Average Man" (Chekhov)
   See "Obyvateli"

"Averroes's Search" (Borges)
   See "La busca de Averroes"

"L'aveu" (Maupassant) **1**:263, 274; **64**:334, 336

"Avey" (Toomer) **1**:441, 443-45, 451, 453, 458-59; **45**:191, 204-06, 226-29, 232, 236-40, 260, 262, 265, 268, 286, 288, 319, 325, 349-51, 362, 367, 380-81

"The Aviator" (Walser) **20**:364

"Aviv kar" (Appelfeld) **42**:4-6

"Avremi Bass" (Peretz) **26**:202

"L'avvenire dei ricordi" (Svevo) **25**:360

"L'avventura di un impiegato" (Calvino) **48**:43

"L'avventura di un poeta" (Calvino) **3**:111, 116; **48**:80, 146-41

"L'avventura di uno sciatore" (Calvino) **48**:43

"An Awakening" (Anderson) **1**:34, 44-5

"Awakening" (Babel) **16**:36, 41-2, 59

"The Awakening" (Clarke) **3**:143, 148

"Awakening" (Pavese) **19**:375

"The Awakening of Rollo Podmarsh" (Wodehouse) **2**:344

"The Awful Fate of Mr. Wolf" (Harris) **19**:172

"The Awful Gladness of the Mate" (Wodehouse) **2**:356

"Awful When You Think of it" (Greene) **29**:201

"The Awful Woman with the Spectacles" (Leacock) **39**:266

"The Axe" (Narayan) **25**:154

"Axolotl" (Cortázar) **7**:58, 63-4, 66-7, 70-5, 81

"Azalia" (Harris) **19**:124, 131, 149, 179

"Azathoth" (Lovecraft) **3**:273

"Azélie" (Chopin) **8**:110

"Azraël" (Villiers de l'Isle Adam)
   See "L'annonciateur"

"Baa, Baa, Black Sheep" (Kipling) **5**:277-78, 283, 293; **54**:86-8, 90-3, 107-8

"Las babas del diablo" (Cortázar) **7**:54, 65-6, 68-9, 86

"Bab'e carstuo" (Chekhov) **2**:156-57; **51**:79, 84, 144, 176-78, 191, 193-94, 196-97

"Babel's Children" (Barker) **53**:140, 154, 156, 158-59

"Baberu no tô no tanuki" (Abe) **61**:13, 22-23, 27

The Babe's Bed (Wescott) **35**:372-76

"Babes in the Woods" (Henry) **5**:193; **49**:206

"The Babes in the Woods" (O'Connor) **5**:380

"Babette's Feast" (Dinesen) **7**:166, 195

"The Babies in the Bush" (Lawson) **18**:220

"The Babus of Nayanjore" (Tagore) **48**:301

"Baby" (Barthelme) **55**:76

"Baby" (Campbell) **19**:87

"Baby" (Chekhov) **2**:155; **51**:111-12, 180, 182, 205

"The Baby" (Moravia) **26**:139, 150

"Baby" (Saroyan) **21**:159-60

"Baby H. P." (Arreola) **38**:5, 8, 12, 22, 30

"A Baby in the Siege" (Harris) **19**:182

Baby, It's Cold Inside (Perelman) **32**:212, 226-27, 229, 236, 245

"Baby Mike" (Farrell) **28**:96

"The Baby Party" (Fitzgerald) **6**:46, 94-5

"A Baby Tramp" (Bierce) **9**:87

"The Babylon Lottery" (Borges)
   See "La lotería en Babilonia"

"The Babylon Night" (Morand)
   See "La nuit de Babylone"

"Babylon Revisited" (Fitzgerald) **6**:47, 51, 53, 60, 63-4, 72, 74, 76, 81, 85-6, 99-100, 104; **31**:1-38

"Baby's Breath" (Bambara) **35**:42

"The Baby's Christmas" (Harris) **19**:182

"The Baby's Fortune" (Harris) **19**:182

"The Babysitter" (Coover) **15**:30, 38, 40, 48, 50-1

"The Bachelor" (Stifter)
   See "Der Hagestolz"

"The Bachelor's Supper" (Aiken) **9**:6, 13

"Bachmann" (Nabokov) **11**:124

"Back before Day" (Price) **22**:379-81

"The Back Drawing-Room" (Bowen) **3**:40, 54

"Back for Christmas" (Collier) **19**:108-10, 112

"Back from Java" (Aldiss) **36**:14

Back in the World (Wolff) **63**:261-62, 264, 300-321, 325

"The Back of Beyond" (Maugham) **8**:375

"Back to the Bush" (Leacock) **39**:364

"Back to the Sea" (Moravia)
   See "Ritorno al mare"

"The Background" (Saki) **12**:311

"Backseat" (Wideman) **62**:273, 277, 281, 283-86, 289-90

"The Backslider" (Fisher) **25**:17-20, 22, 25, 27

"Backwards" (Aymé) **41**:5

"Backwater" (Aldiss) **36**:26-7

"The Backwater" (Turgenev) **7**:320, 335; **57**:296-97, 303

"Bad Characters" (Stafford) **26**:279, 281, 286, 310

Bad Characters (Stafford) **26**:279-80

"Bad Company" (de la Mare) **14**:80, 88, 90

"A Bad Day" (Nabokov) **11**:132-33

"Bad Dreams" (Taylor) **10**:379-80, 384, 389, 393

"The Bad Glazier" (Baudelaire)
   See "Le mauvais vitrier"

"Bad News" (Atwood) **46**:74-5

Bad Saint Vitalis (Keller)
   See *Der Schlimm-heilige Vitalis*

"The Bad Woman" (Fante) **65**:92

Badenheim 1939 (Appelfeld) **42**:3, 15-19, 21-26, 31

"The Badger from the Tower of Babel" (Abe)
   See "Baberu no tô no tanuki"

"The Bag" (Saki) **12**:315

"The Bag of Gold" (Howells) **36**:399

Bagai' haporeh (Appelfeld) **42**:3, 5, 8, 43

"Bagombo Snuff Box" (Vonnegut) **8**:433, 437

"Bagovah hakar" (Appelfeld) **42**:5, 8, 45, 47-48

"The Bagpipes of Spring" (Benét) **10**:150

"Der Bahnhof von Zimpren" (Boell) **23**:6

Bahnwärter Thiel (Hauptmann) **37**:196-201, 207-8, 213-18, 220-24, 226-29, 231, 241-44, 252-53, 257-62

"Bai guang" (Lu Hsun) **20**:136

"The Bailbondsman" (Elkin) **12**:93, 95, 106-07, 110, 112, 114, 116

Le baiser au lépreux (Mauriac) **24**:159-60, 162, 179-80, 182, 206

"Bait" (Campbell) **19**:75

"Bajron u Sintri" (Andrić) **36**:50

Bakante bilder (Peretz) **26**:218, 223

"The Baker's Dozen" (Saki) **12**:328

"The Baker's Story" (Naipaul) **38**:300, 323, 328, 346-47

"Le bal de sceaux" (Balzac) **5**:4, 29

"Balaam" (Harris) **19**:131

Balaam and His Ass (Harris) **19**:49

"Balaam and His Master" (Harris) **19**:149, 182

Balaam and His Master, and Other Sketches and Stories (Harris) **19**:146-47, 149, 180-82

"Balada o Juraji Čupovi" (Čapek) **36**:99, 128

"The Balance" (Waugh) **41**:322, 326-28, 338-39, 352, 360

"Balance His, Swing Yours" (Stegner) **27**:197, 202

"The Balcony" (Irving) **2**:266

"The Balek Scales" (Boell)
   See "Die Waage der Baleks"

"De balística" (Arreola) **38**:4, 8, 10, 12, 21, 23

"The Ball" (Akutagawa Ryūnosuke)
   See "Butōkai"

"Ball der Wohltäter" (Lenz) **33**:317, 321-24, 326-27

"Ball of Fat" (Pardo Bazán) **30**:291

"A Ball of Malt and Madame Butterfly" (Kiely) **58**:145-46, 158, 167-68

"Ballad" (Arreola) **38**:13

"A Ballad" (Bunin)
   See "Ballada"

"A Ballad" (McGahern) **17**:315, 317

"The Ballad of Juraj Čup" (Čapek)
   See "Balada o Juraji Čupovi"

The Ballad of the Sad Cafe: The Novels and Stories of Carson McCullers (McCullers) **9**:322-26, 329, 331-32, 334-35, 338, 341-42, 344-46, 350, 353, 355, 358; **24**:231-86

"Ballada" (Bunin) **5**:115

"Ballet for Opening Day" (Algren) **33**:96

"The Ballet Girl" (Coppard) **21**:11, 29

"The Ballet of Central Park" (Boyle) **5**:66

"The Ballet of the Nations" (Lee) **33**:307

"The Balloon" (Barthelme) **2**:31, 33, 36, 42; **55**:4, 23, 28, 32, 35, 44, 51-4, 62, 64, 85, 88, 91, 94, 108

"The Balloon Hoax" (Poe) **1**:406

"The Ballroom" (Sansom) **21**:87, 126

"The Ballroom of Romance" (Trevor) **21**:253, 260, 265, 270-71, 273; **58**:218, 223, 231, 252, 271, 280

The Ballroom of Romance, and Other Stories (Trevor) **21**:232, 235-37, 261; **58**:200, 204, 264

"The Balsam Fir" (Freeman) **47**:105

"Baltasar Gérard (1555-1582)" (Arreola) **38**:9, 13

"Balthazar's Marvelous Afternoon" (García Márquez)
   See "La prodigiosa tarde de Baltazar"

"The Baluchiterium" (Updike) **13**:348, 360

"Bananafish" (Salinger)
   See "A Perfect Day for Bananafish"

"The Bandits" (Akutagawa Ryūnosuke)
   See "Chūtō"

"Bandits" (Aleichem) **33**:51-2

"Bandy Callaghan's Girl" (Norris) **28**:201, 207

"Bang-Bang You're Dead" (Spark) **10**:353, 356-60, 364-65, 367, 370

"The Banishment of Ming and Mai" (Far) **62**:50, 54-55

"Bank Holiday" (McGahern) **17**:306, 311, 317-18, 321

"Bankruptcy" (Dazai Osamu) **41**:229, 233

"The Banks of the Jordan" (Trollope)
   See "A Ride across Palestine"

Bannen (Dazai Osamu) **41**:241, 246, 271

The Banner of the Upright Seven (Keller)
   See *The Flag of the Seven Upright Ones*

"Banquet in Honor" (Hughes) **6**:122

"The Banquet of Crow" (Parker) **2**:280, 285

"Banya" (Zoshchenko)
   See "The Bath"

"Un baptême" (Maupassant) **1**:256, 259, 284

"Baptizing" (Munro) **3**:331, 339-40

"The Bar Light-house" (Freeman) **47**:147

"Bar Titanic" (Andrić)
   See "Bife titanik"

"Bara no Yūrei" (Kawabata) **17**:242

Barabbas (Lagerkvist) **12**:178-8, 183, 185, 187, 189, 193-4, 197-203

"Barbados" (Marshall) **3**:299-300, 302-04, 306-08, 316-17

"Barbara of the House of Grebe" (Hardy) **2**:204, 209, 214-15, 221; **60**:179, 205-7, 212-14, 217, 219-20

"The Barbarian Woman" (Walser) **20**:348

"The Barbecue" (Dixon) **16**:206, 211

"The Barber" (Bates) **10**:112

"The Barber Whose Uncle Had His Head Bitten Off by a Circus Tiger" (Saroyan) **21**:133

"Barbie-Q" (Cisneros) **32**:8

"A Barefaced Lie" (West) **16**:402-03

"The Barefoot Saint" (Benét) **10**:145, 153

"Barker's Luck" (Harte) **8**:222, 244
"Barn Burning" (Faulkner) **1**:163, 165
"Barnby Robinson" (Warner) **23**:372
"Barneti Graven" (Andersen) **56**:37
"Barney Take Me Home Again" (Lawson) **18**:211
"Barnja" (Chekhov) **51**:102-3, 107-8
"Barnum Museum" (Millhauser) **57**:156-57, 166-67, 172, 181-82, 185
The Barnum Museum (Millhauser) **57**:155-57, 161, 164, 168, 172-73, 178, 180, 182-85, 187
"Baron Dorn" (Andrić) **36**:65
The Baron in the Trees (Calvino)
   See *Il barone rampante*
"Baron von Leisenborg's Destiny" (Schnitzler) **61**:306, 308
Il barone rampante (Calvino) **3**:89-91, 93-5, 99, 117-18; **48**:44-5, 52, 84, 90-1, 150-51, 153, 164
"Barrack Room Fiddle Tune" (Ross) **24**:307, 311, 323-24
The Barracks Thief and Other Stories (Wolff) **63**:263, 300, 316, 321
"The Barrel" (Maupassant) **1**:269
"The Barricade" (Hemingway) **1**:208
"The Barrow" (Le Guin) **12**:210, 213, 216, 218, 247-48
"Bartleby, the Scrivener: A Story of Wall-Street" (Melville) **1**:293, 295, 297-98, 303-04, 311, 317, 322-23, 325, 328, 331; **17**:326-92; **46**:335
"Baryshnia-krest'ianka" (Pushkin) **27**:129, 141-43, 166, 168, 171, 186; **55**:308
"Bás na Bó" (O'Flaherty) **6**:287-88
"Basement" (Bambara) **35**:22-3, 34
"The Basement" (Lagerkvist) **12**:179, 182, 196-7
"The Basement Room" (Greene) **29**:182, 185-86, 192-93, 199, 213-14, 216-17, 220
The Basement Room and Other Stories (Greene) **29**:213
"Basil and Cleopatra" (Fitzgerald) **6**:50
"Basil from Her Garden" (Barthelme) **55**:117
"Basilisk" (Ellison) **14**:102-05
"Básník" (Čapek) **36**:98, 102, 121, 127
"The Basque and Bijou" (Nin) **10**:326
"Bastille Day" (Berriault) **30**:98
"The Bat Who Got The Hell Out" (Thurber) **47**:363
"Batard" (London) **4**:288-89
"The Bath" (Carver) **8**:15, 19-24, 26-7, 30, 39, 56-60; **51**:14
"The Bath" (Zoshchenko) **15**:388, 409-10
"The Bathroom Dance" (Jolley) **19**:234
The Battle (Kluge)
   See *Schlachtbeschreibung*
"The Battle Ax" (Leskov)
   See "Voitel' nica"
"Battle Keaton Dies" (Stuart) **31**:225, 230-31, 234, 251
"The Battle of Grünwald" (Borowski) **48**:7
The Battle of Life (Dickens) **49**:66, 158
"The Battle of Sempach" (Walser) **20**:356-59
"The Battle of the Frogs and Mice" (Lovecraft) **52**:287
"Battle with the Bees" (Stuart) **31**:265
"Battleground" (King) **17**:261
"The Battler" (Hemingway) **1**:242, 244-45, 247; **40**:166, 209, 221, 249, 251; **63**:40, 79, 83
"Der bau" (Kafka) **5**:206, 209, 241; **60**:235, 240
"Baum Gabriel, 1935 - ( )" (Gallant) **5**:137-38
"Bavarian Gentians" (Lawrence) **4**:233
"Baxter's Procrustes" (Chesnutt) **7**:15; **54**:27-8, 52-4
"Bay City Blues" (Chandler) **23**:59, 65, 67-8, 72, 82-3, 88, 109
"HaBayit" (Agnon) **30**:22-3, 26, 34
Bayou Folk (Chopin) **8**:65-8, 72, 77, 84, 88-9, 93, 97, 103-08, 110-11, 114

"Be This Her Memorial" (Evans) **43**:16-17, 27-8, 36-7
"The Beach" (Cowan) **28**:76; 80
"The Beach Murders" (Ballard) **1**:72-4; **53**:20, 55
"The Beach of Falesá" (Stevenson) **11**:269, 279, 283-84, 286-87, 296, 299; 237-58, 249
"The Beach Party" (Grau) **15**:148, 160
"Beachworld" (King) **55**:250
"The Beam" (Grimm and Grimm) **36**:200
"The Bear" (Faulkner) **1**:148, 152-58, 167, 172-74, 182; **35**:135-214; **42**:107
"A Bear Hunt" (Faulkner) **1**:177
"The Beard" (Singer) **3**:375
"The Bearer of Burdens" (Zangwill) **44**:378, 389
"The Bear-Hunt" (Tolstoy) **9**:387
"Bearskin" (Grimm and Grimm) **36**:228
The Beast in Me, and Other Animals: A New Collection of Pieces and Drawings about Human Beings and Less Alarming Creatures (Thurber) **1**:425
"The Beast in the Cave" (Lovecraft) **52**:262-64, 267, 287, 290-91
"The Beast in the Jungle" (James) **8**:302, 307-09, 320, 326, 338-40, 342, 347
"The Beast That Etcetera" (Ellison)
   See "The Beast That Shouted Love at the Heart of the World"
"The Beast That Shouted Love at the Heart of the World" (Ellison) **14**:106-07, 115, 117
"Beasts" (Betts)
   See "Beasts of the Southern Wild"
Beasts and Super-Beasts (Saki) **12**:288, 291, 294-96, 307-09, 313-14, 323, 329, 332
"Beasts of the Southern Wild" (Betts) **45**:3, 6, 31, 39-43
Beasts of the Southern Wild and Other Stories (Betts) **45**:3, 5, 21, 25-6, 30-2
"Beat Me" (Perelman) **32**:202
Beatrice (Schnitzler)
   See *Frau Beate und ihr Sohn*
"Beatrice Trueblood's Story" (Stafford) **26**:284, 299
"Beau Séjour" (Lewis) **34**:159, 167, 177
"The Beauties" (Chekhov) **2**:156; **51**:117-19, 121, 126
"Beautiful and Cruel" (Cisneros) **32**:6, 32
"A Beautiful Child" (Capote) **2**:81
"Beautiful Girl" (Adams) **24**:3-4, 6, 13
Beautiful Girl (Adams) **24**:2-3, 13, 15
"A Beautiful nature" (Frame) **29**:110
"The Beautiful Stranger" (Jackson) **9**:272
"The Beautiful Suit" (Wells) **6**:361-62, 376, 391
"Beauty" (Greene) **29**:200-01, 230
"Beauty" (O'Flaherty) **6**:262, 285
"Beauty and Beast" (Sansom) **21**:86, 88
"Beauty Spots" (Kipling) **5**:280
"Beca" (Andrić) **36**:32
"La beca" (Unamuno) **11**:312
"Because of the Dollars" (Conrad) **9**:152
Bech: A Book (Updike) **13**:356, 366-68, 379-82
"Bech Enters Heaven" (Updike) **13**:380, 383
"Bech in Rumania" (Updike) **13**:380
"Bech Panics" (Updike) **13**:380-81
"Bech Swings?" (Updike) **13**:380
"Bech Takes Pot Luck" (Updike) **13**:380
"Becker and the Boys from the Band" (Moorhouse) **40**:301
"Becker on the Moon" (Moorhouse) **40**:290, 301
"The Becker Wives" (Lavin) **4**:166-67, 184-90, 192
"The Beckoning Fair One" (Campbell) **19**:83
"Becky" (Toomer) **1**:445, 456-58; **45**:170, 186, 198, 203, 215, 253, 260, 264-65, 268, 275, 285, 290-91, 349-50, 355, 357-58, 374
"The Bedfordshire Clanger" (Bates) **10**:117
"The Bedjacket" (Frame) **29**:108
Bednye lyudi (Dostoevsky) **44**:95, 111, 116, 122-24, 147, 157, 160, 162, 165, 167-69

"The Bedroom Eyes of Mrs. Vansittart" (Trevor) **58**:278
Bedtime Stories (Dazai Osamu)
   See *Otogi zōshi*
"Bedtime Story" (Campbell) **19**:76, 78
Beer and Cold Cuts (Williams) **31**:333
"Beer at the Corner Bar" (Bukowski) **45**:51, 63
"The Bees" (Zoshchenko) **15**:407-08
Beffe della morte e della vita (Pirandello) **22**:275
"Before Breakfast" (Cather) **2**:93-4; **50**:54-5, 87-8, 156, 158, 213-16, 233-34, 236, 253-54
"Before Eden" (Clarke) **3**:127
"Before the Deluge" (Rhys) **21**:56
"Before the Grand Jury" (Stuart) **31**:226
"Before the Law" (Kafka)
   See "Vor dem gesetz"
"Before the Low Green Door" (Garland) **18**:148, 154, 160, 182-83, 185
"Before the Party" (Maugham) **8**:359, 362, 366-67, 372
"Before the Storm" (Campbell) **19**:72, 90
"Before the War" (Atwood) **2**:16
"Beg Karčić's Dream" (Andrić)
   See "San bega Karčića"
"The Begetting of the Two Swineherds" (Stephens) **50**:321
"The Beggar" (Chekhov) **51**:77
"The Beggar and the Diamond" (King) **17**:295
The Beggar Maid: Stories of Flo and Rose (Munro)
   See *Who Do You Think You Are?*
"Beggars" (Clarke) **45**:113
"The Beggars" (O'Flaherty) **6**:276-78
"The Beggars" (Pavese) **19**:386
"Beggar-Student" (Dazai Osamu) **41**:232
"Begger Woman of Locarno" (Kleist)
   See "Das Bettelweib von Locarno"
"The Beginning" (Grau) **15**:162
A Beginning, and Other Stories (de la Mare) **14**:79, 85, 89, 92
"The Beginning of an Idea" (McGahern) **17**:307, 323
"The Beginning of Homewood" (Wideman) **62**:264, 266-67
"The Beginning of Something" (Dixon) **16**:207, 214
"Beginnings" (Coover) **15**:45-6
"Behind a Mask: Or, A Woman's Power" (Alcott) **27**:4-5, 12-7, 28, 31, 50, 57, 61-2
Behind a Mask: The Unknown Thrillers of Louisa May Alcott (Alcott) **27**:35, 61
Behind the Beyond (Leacock) **39**:262, 266
"Behind the Blue Curtain" (Millhauser) **57**:180, 183, 186
"Behind the Scenes at a Whist Game" (Barbey d'Aurevilly)
   See "Le dessous de cartes d'une partie de whist"
"Behind the Shade" (Morrison) **40**:328, 337, 367
"Behind the Singer Tower" (Cather) **2**:99, 103-04, 111; **50**:69, 71, 77, 159-63
"Behind the Times" (Doyle) **12**:89
"Behold the Incredible Revenge of the Shifted P.O.V." (Lish) **18**:280
"Behold the Key" (Malamud) **15**:169, 181, 222
"The Beige Dolorosa" (Harrison) **19**:216-17
Beim Bau der Chinesischen Mauer (Kafka) **5**:206
Beim Vetter Christian (Storm) **27**:280, 282
"Being an Angel" (Campbell) **19**:77-8
"Being Kind to Titina" (White) **39**:280-281, 284, 286, 289, 291-93, 295, 317, 325, 344
"Being Moral" (Michaels) **16**:311
"Being Stolen From" (Trevor) **58**:281-82
Ein Bekenntnis (Storm) **27**:279, 282, 307
Bekomat hakarka (Appelfeld) **42**:3, 8-9
"Bel Colore" (Galsworthy) **22**:58
"Un bel gioco dura poco" (Calvino) **3**:97; **48**:37
A bela e a fera (Lispector) **34**:229, 233, 235
"Belaja lošad'" (Bunin) **5**:98

"Belated Flowers" (Chekhov) **51**:209

"The Belated Travellers" (Irving) **2**:262

A Beleaguered City: Tale of the Seen and Unseen (Oliphant) **25**:179-82, 186, 193, 197, 199, 201-5, 207-08

"Belize" (Gilchrist) **14**:157-58

Belkin Tales (Pushkin)
See *Povesti Belkina*

"The Bell" (Andersen) **6**:6-8, 15, 30, 33; **56**:8-11

"The Bell" (de la Mare)
See "Out of the Deep"

"The Bell Remembered" (Wolfe) **33**:399

"La bella durmiente" (Ferré) **36**:135-37, 150, 156, 161-62, 169-70, 173

"Bella Fleace" (Waugh)
See "Bella Fleace Gave a Party"

"Bella Fleace Gave a Party" (Waugh) **41**:311, 323, 325, 328, 330, 340

"The Bella Lingua" (Cheever) **1**:93, 106, 112; **38**:53

"Bella vista" (Colette) **10**:274

La bella vita (Moravia) **26**:162

The Bellarosa Connection (Bellow) **14**:50, 56, 58-61

"La Belle Bayadère" (Alcott) **27**:44

"La belle Dorothée" (Baudelaire) **18**:3-7

"A Belle of St. Valerien" (Harris) **19**:183

"La Belle Zoraïde" (Chopin) **8**:71, 87, 90-1, 106

"Bellerophoniad" (Barth) **10**:44, 49-52, 54, 56, 61, 64-9, 91-3, 101-02

"Belles Demoiselles Plantation" (Cable) **4**:48, 53, 62-4, 66-7, 73-4

"La belleza ideal" (Alarcon) **64**:3, 5-6, 28-30

"The Bellin' of the Bride" (Stuart) **31**:231

"The Bell-Ringer of Angels" (Harte) **8**:214, 248-49; **59**:307

"The Bell-Tower" (Melville) **1**:298, 303

"The Belobrysov Story" (Bulgakov) **18**:91

"Below the Mill Dam" (Kipling) **5**:268, 283

"The Belt" (Moravia) **26**:172

"La belva" (Pavese) **19**:366, 388

"Ben sete 'arim" (Agnon) **30**:53-5, 66

"The Bench" (Dixon) **16**:207-08, 212-13

"The Bench" (Jolley) **19**:221

"The Bench of Desolation" (James) **8**:277, 304

"Beneath the Cards of a Game of Whist" (Barbey d'Aurevilly)
See "Le dessous de cartes d'une partie de whist"

"Beneath the Willow-Tree" (Andersen) **6**:30

"Benediction" (Fitzgerald) **6**:45, 57-8

"Bénéficies de Guerre" (Morand) **22**:159

"The Benefit of the Doubt" (London) **4**:291

"Benefit Performance for Lord Cuzon" (Bulgakov)
See "Lord Curzon's Benefit Day"

"The Benefits of American Life" (Farrell) **28**:100

"Benighted" (de la Mare) **14**:90

"Benito Cereno" (Melville) **1**:293, 295-300, 303-04, 310-12, 320-23, 328, 330; **17**:328, 338, 361; **46**:335

"The Bênitou's Slave" (Chopin) **8**:89

"Benjamin Button" (Fitzgerald)
See "The Curious Case of Benjamin Button"

Benya Krik the Gangster, and Other Stories (Babel) **16**:14

"An Beo" (O'Flaherty) **6**:286-88

"Ber-Bulu" (Hammett) **17**:222

Berecche and the War (Pirandello)
See *Berecche e la guerra*

Berecche e la guerra (Pirandello) **22**:231, 275

"Berenice" (Poe) **1**:396, 398; **22**:291, 329, 334; **54**:161, 185, 209, 229, 231

"Berestechko" (Babel) **16**:9, 27-8, 31, 52, 55-7

Bergkristall (Stifter) **28**:298

Bergkristall (Stifter) **28**:272

"Die Bergwerke zu Falun" (Hoffmann) **13**:205, 209-11, 218, 220, 252, 255, 257

"Bericht für eine Akademie" (Kafka) **60**:253

"Ein Beriht für eine Akademie" (Kafka) **5**:215-16, 220, 231; **29**:332, 345, 369-70; **35**:264

"Berkeley House" (Adams) **24**:15

"A Berlin Diary" (Isherwood) **56**:200, 211

"A Berlin Diary (Autumn 1930)" (Isherwood) **56**:203, 222, 225-26

"A Berlin Diary (Winter 1932-33)" (Isherwood) **56**:203, 209-10, 224

The Berlin of Sally Bowles (Isherwood) **56**:218

The Berlin Stories (Isherwood) **56**:211

Die Berlocken (Keller) **26**:103-04, 110

"Bernadette" (Gallant) **5**:122, 125, 139

"Bernice Bobs Her Hair" (Fitzgerald) **6**:58, 96

"Berry" (Hughes) **6**:121, 142

"The Berry Patch" (Stegner) **27**:197, 227

"Bertha" (Appelfeld) **42**:44-45

"Bertie Changes His Mind" (Wodehouse) **2**:356

"Bertram and Bini" (Kipling) **5**:274

"Beryl" (Metcalf) **43**:73

"The Beryl Coronet" (Doyle) **12**:52, 58, 66, 71-3

"Der beschriebene Tännling" (Stifter) **28**:299

"Beside the Brandy Still" (Andrić)
See "Kod kazana"

"Beside the River" (Boell) **23**:38

"Bess" (Phillips) **16**:336, 338-39

"Bess Waters" (Price) **22**:385

"Bessmertie" (Platonov) **42**:250

"Bessy's Troubles at Home" (Gaskell) **25**:58

"The Best and Worst People and Things of 1938" (Saroyan) **21**:163

"The Best China Saucer" (Jewett) **6**:166

Best Ghost Stories of J. S. Le Fanu (Le Fanu) **14**:237

Best of Aldiss (Aldiss) **36**:18

The Best of Arthur C. Clarke: 1937-1971 (Clarke) **3**:149

The Best of H. E. Bates (Bates)
See *Seven by Five: Stories 1926-61*

The Best of John Collier (Collier) **19**:109

The Best of Philip K. Dick (Dick) **57**:78, 102, 138

The Best of S. J. Perelman (Perelman) **32**:220

The Best of Saki (Saki) **12**:320

The Best of Simple (Hughes) **6**:137

The Best of the Lot (Suckow) **18**:400-01, 403

Best Science Fiction Stories of Brian W. Aldiss (Aldiss)
See *But Who Can Replace a Man?*

The Best Short Stories of J. G. Ballard (Ballard) **1**:74

Best Supernatural Stories (Lovecraft) **52**:254

"The Best Years" (Cather) **2**:93-4, 105; **50**:59, 65-7, 85, 107, 105, 156-58, 213-15, 254

Bestiario (Arreola) **38**:36

Bestiario (Cortázar) **7**:50-1, 53-4, 69-70

"The Bestiary" (Arreola) **38**:12-13

Bestiary (Arreola)
See *Bestiario*

Bestiary (Cortázar)
See *Bestiario*

"Bestre" (Lewis) **34**:160, 167, 176, 178

"Best-Seller" (Henry) **5**:159

"The Bet" (Chekhov) **2**:130

"La bête à Maître Belhomme" (Maupassant) **1**:259, 273, 281

"Bethulah" (Zangwill) **44**:375, 388

"The Betrayer of Israel" (Singer) **3**:383

Die Betrogene (Mann) **5**:313-16, 324-26, 340-42

"The Betrotal" (Aymé) **41**:26

"The Betrothed" (Chekhov)
See "Nevesta"

Betrothed (Agnon) **30**:5, 12-13, 15, 34, 37, 75-7, 79-80

"Das Bettelweib von Locarno" (Kleist) **22**:115, 117, 137, 142, 146

"Better Morphosis" (Aldiss) **36**:28

"Better Than to Burn" (Lispector)
See "Melhor do que order"

"Better Think Twice about It, and Twelve Other Stories" (Pirandello) **22**:226, 228-29, 272

"Betty" (Atwood) **2**:14, 22; **46**:45, 76, 78, 81, 94

"Between Men" (Lessing) **6**:197, 200, 207

"Between Rounds" (Henry) **49**:197

Between the Dark and the Daylight (Howells) **36**:357, 360-61, 365, 382, 400

"Between the Devil and the Deep Sea" (Kipling) **5**:268

"Between Two Cities" (Agnon)
See "Ben sete 'arim"

"Between Two Cliffs" (Peretz)
See "Tzvishen Zwee Berg"

"Between Two Kisses" (Čapek) **36**:87

"Between Two Mountains" (Peretz)
See "Tzvishen Zwee Berg"

"Between Two Shores" (Glasgow) **34**:59, 64, 77, 80, 99

"Between Zero and One" (Gallant) **5**:134, 144

"Beverly Home" (Johnson) **56**:237, 242, 245, 264, 267

"Bewitched" (Wharton) **6**:422, 427

"A Bewitched Place" (Bulgakov) **18**:89

"A Bewitched Place" (Gogol)
See "Zakoldovannoe mesto"

"The Bewitched Spot" (Gogol)
See "Zakoldovannoe mesto"

"The Bewitched Tailor" (Aleichem)
See "Der farkishefter shnayder"

"Beyond" (Faulkner) **1**:162

"Beyond Doubt" (Heinlein) **55**:216

"Beyond Lies the Wub" (Dick) **57**:69-70, 119, 122-24, 137-39, 151

"Beyond the Bayou" (Chopin) **8**:89, 104

"Beyond the Curve" (Abe) **61**:9

Beyond the Curve (Abe) **61**:8-11

"Beyond the End" (Barnes)
See "Spillway"

"Beyond the Glass Mountain" (Stegner) **27**:195, 197

"Beyond the Pale" (Kipling) **5**:261-62, 273; **54**:79

"Beyond the Pale" (Trevor) **21**:247-48, 262, 269; **58**:226, 233, 242, 249-50, 275

Beyond the Pale, and Other Stories (Trevor) **21**:262; **58**:200, 212-13, 289, 291, 299

"Beyond the Wall of Sleep" (Lovecraft) **3**:258, 268; **52**:264-65, 270

Beyond the Wall of Sleep (Lovecraft) **52**:291

"Beyond Words" (Campbell) **19**:77, 87

"Bezhin Lea" (Turgenev) **7**:316, 345; **57**:266, 281

"Bežin Meadow" (Turgenev)
See "Bezhin Lea"

"Bezlyub'e" (Pasternak) **31**:117

Bianche e nere (Pirandello) **22**:231, 275

"La biblioteca de Babel" (Borges) **4**:6-7, 18, 29; **41**:61, 64, 69, 76-79, 137, 152, 158, 166

"La Bicha" (Pardo Bazán) **30**:266

"Bicultural Angela" (Hood) **42**:217, 221

"A Bicycle Gymkhana" (Norris) **28**:214

"Bicycles, Muscles, Cigarettes" (Carver) **8**:10, 20, 42

"Bidan" (Galsworthy) **22**:101

"Bien Pretty" (Cisneros) **32**:10, 16, 34, 38-9

"Los bienes ajenos" (Arreola) **38**:11

"Les bienfaits de la lune" (Baudelaire) **18**:4

"The Bienfilâtre Sisters" (Villiers de l'Isle Adam)
See "Les demoiselles de Bienfilâtre"

"Bienvenido, Bob" (Onetti) **23**:246, 249-50, 252

"Bife titanik" (Andrić) **36**:37, 46, 74, 77

"Big Bertha Stories" (Mason) **4**:2

"The Big Black and White Game" (Bradbury) **29**:42

"Big Black Good Man" (Wright) **2**:364

"Big Blonde" (Parker) **2**:273-74, 276, 278-81, 284

"Big Boy Leaves Home" (Wright) **2**:360-61, 363, 365, 367-69, 371-76, 379-81, 386-90
"The Big Broadcast of 1938" (Barthelme) **2**:26; **55**:10, 19
"Big Buck" (Caldwell) **19**:17
"Big Business Bolshevik" (Kluge) **61**:74
"Big Claus and Little Claus" (Andersen)
　　See "Lille Claus og Store Claus"
"Big Fiddle" (Boyle) **5**:66-8
"Big Game" (Boyle) **16**:156-57
"The Big Game" (Coppard) **21**:11
"Big Game Hunt" (Clarke) **3**:133-34
"The Big Garage" (Boyle) **16**:140-42
The Big Hunger: Stories 1932-1959 (Fante) **65**:92, 94, 112
"Big Kids and Little Kids" (Suckow) **18**:393
"The Big Knockover" (Hammett) **17**:200-1, 215, 219, 224, 230
The Big Knockover: Selected Stories and Short Novels (Hammett) **17**:201-4, 212
"Big Leaguer" (Fante) **65**:78
"Big Mama's Funeral" (García Márquez)
　　See "Los funerales de la Mamá Grande"
Big Mama's Funeral (García Márquez)
　　See *Los funerales de la Mamá Grande*
"Big Meeting" (Hughes) **6**:119, 122, 132-33
"The Big Outside World" (Beattie) **11**:25
"The Big Stick" (Sansom) **21**:84
"Big Swallow and Little Swallow" (Pirandello)
　　See "Rondone e rondinella"
"The Big Town" (Lardner) **32**:118, 131
The Big Town: How I and the Mrs. Go to New York to See Life and Get Katie a Husband (Lardner) **32**:127, 141, 148-49, 152-56
"Big Two-Hearted River" (Hemingway) **1**:208, 214, 220, 231, 234, 240, 243-48; **40**:155, 168, 209, 214, 250; **63**:39-40, 42-45, 79, 81-83, 86-91, 98-101, 125
"Big Volodya and Little Volodya" (Chekhov)
　　See "Volodja boloj i Volodja malen'kij"
"Big Wheels: A Tale of the Laundry Game" (King) **17**:275
"The Bigot" (Page) **23**:307
"Bijou" (Dybek) **55**:134
"Les bijoux" (Maupassant) **1**:273, 286, 288; **64**:352
"The Bill" (Malamud) **15**:169, 175, 202, 222-23
"The Bill" (Moravia) **26**:141
"Bill" (Powers) **4**:375, 381-82
"Bill Sprockett's Land" (Jolley) **19**:233
"Bill the Ventriloquial Rooster" (Lawson) **18**:206, 218, 263
"Billenium" (Ballard) **1**:68-9, 75; **53**:8-9, 29, 49
"Billy" (Gordon) **59**:237, 260, 263, 265
"Billy and the Gargoyles" (Auchincloss) **22**:3, 33, 48, 53
Billy Budd, Sailor: An Inside Narrative (Melville) **1**:294-303, 305-16, 318, 321, 329; **46**:155-382
Bing (Beckett) **16**:76-85, 122
"Biografía de Tadeo Isidoro Cruz (1829-1874)" (Borges) **4**:9; **41**:59
"Biography of Tadeo Isidoro Cruz" (Borges)
　　See "Biografía de Tadeo Isidoro Cruz (1829-1874)"
"Bird" (Hesse) **9**:244
A Bird in the House (Laurence) **7**:246-49, 251, 253-60, 262-64, 266-72
"A Bird of Bagdad" (Henry) **5**:196
"The Bird of Love" (Far)
　　See "Children of Peace"
"Bird of Prey" (Collier) **19**:109, 111
"The Bird of Travel" (de la Mare) **14**:66, 67, 80, 85, 90
"The Birds" (du Maurier) **18**:125-26, 130, 137-38
"Birds" (Schulz)
　　See "Ptaki"
"The Birds and the Foxes" (Thurber) **1**:426, 431

"The birds began to sing" (Frame) **29**:110
"Birds on the Western Front" (Saki) **12**:314
"Birjuk" (Turgenev) **57**:266
"Birth" (Nin) **10**:299-305
"Birth" (O'Flaherty) **6**:262
"The Birth, Life and Death of an Underground Newspaper" (Bukowski) **45**:64
"The Birth of a Man" (Gorky) **28**:137, 139, 147
"A Birthday" (Mansfield) **9**:281, 284, 302-03; **23**:139
"The Birthday Gift" (Narayan) **25**:142
"The Birthday of the Infanta" (Wilde) **11**:364-65, 372, 374, 376, 382-83, 394-97, 399, 407-09
"The Birthmark" (Agnon) **30**:3
"The Birthmark" (Ellison) **26**:8, 21, 26-7, 29
"The Birthmark" (Hawthorne) **3**:159, 168-70, 178, 183-84, 189, 191-94; **39**:91
"The Bisara of Pooree" (Kipling) **5**:262, 265
"Biscuits" (Metcalf) **43**:78
"Bisei no shin" (Akutagawa Ryūnosuke) **44**:90
"Bishop" (Barthelme) **55**:100-9
"The Bishop" (Chekhov)
　　See "Arxierej"
"The Bishop of Borglum" (Andersen) **6**:18
"The Bishop's Beggar" (Benét) **10**:156
"The Bishop's Feast" (Rhys) **21**:55
"The Bishop's Fool" (Lewis) **34**:157
"The Bishop's Robe" (Singer) **3**:374
"A Bit of Advice" (Aleichem)
　　See "An eytse"
"A Bit of Business" (Trevor) **58**:254, 261-62, 275-76
"A Bit of Shore Life" (Jewett) **6**:166
"A Bit of Young Life" (Gordimer) **17**:153, 168
"A Bit off the Map" (Wilson) **21**:321, 323, 339, 365
A Bit off the Map (Wilson) **21**:320, 328, 336-38, 357, 362
"The Biter Bit" (Sansom) **21**:116-17
"Bitter Honeymoon" (Moravia) **26**:138-39, 142
Bitter Honeymoon, and Other Stories (Moravia)
　　See *I racconti*
"Bitter Sorrow for Three Sleepwalkers" (García Márquez)
　　See "Amargura para tres sonámbulos"
"Bitterness for Three Sleepwalkers" (García Márquez)
　　See "Amargura para tres sonámbulos"
"Blacamán el bueno vendedor de milagros" (García Márquez) **8**:167-69, 186
"Blacamán the Good, Vendor of Miracles" (García Márquez)
　　See "Blacamán el bueno vendedor de milagros"
"The Black Bird's Mate" (O'Flaherty) **6**:280
"Black Boy" (Boyle) **5**:56
"Black Bread" (Verga) **21**:298
"The Black Cat" (Poe) **1**:389-90, 406, 408; **34**:241-42, 244, 274; **35**:298, 307-11, 313-15, 320, 343, 345-46; **54**:198, 218
"Black Death" (Hurston) **4**:142
"The Black Dog" (Coppard) **21**:3
The Black Dog (Coppard) **21**:3, 8, 15, 19
"Black Ephram" (Garland) **18**:154
"The Black Eyes" (Alarcon)
　　See "Los ojos negros"
"The Black Ferris" (Bradbury) **29**:63
"The Black Godmother" (Galsworthy) **22**:75
"Black Horses" (Pirandello) **22**:229
"Black Is My Favorite Color" (Malamud) **15**:173-74, 207-09
"A Black Jack Bargainer" (Henry) **5**:162, 170
"Black Joe" (Lawson) **18**:202
"The Black Lights" (Jones) **56**:273
"The Black Madonna" (Lessing) **61**:99-100
"The Black Madonna" (Spark) **10**:350-52, 355, 359, 361, 366, 368
Black Magic (Morand)
　　See *Magie noire*

"The Black Magic of Barney Haller" (Thurber) **1**:415; **47**:376-77
The Black Man and Other Tales (Stevenson) **51**:240
"Black Man and White Woman in Dark Green Rowboat" (Banks) **42**:60
"The Black Mare" (O'Flaherty) **6**:264, 281
"The Black Mate" (Conrad) **9**:179
"The Black Monk" (Chekhov)
　　See "ёrnyji monax"
"Black Pits of Luna" (Heinlein) **55**:165, 230
"The Black Prince" (Grau) **15**:147, 150, 156, 151, 164
The Black Prince, and Other Stories (Grau) **15**:148-52, 154, 156, 160, 164
"The Black Rabbit" (O'Flaherty) **6**:274, 281
"The Black Sheep" (Boell)
　　See "Die schwarzen schafe"
"Black Sheep No. Five: Clarence" (Dreiser) **30**:151
"Black Sheep No. Four: Ethelda" (Dreiser) **30**:151
"Black Sheep No. One: Johnny" (Dreiser) **30**:151
"Black Sheep No. Six: Harrison Barr" (Dreiser) **30**:151
"Black Sheep No. Three: Bill" (Dreiser) **30**:151
"Black Sheep No. Two: Otie" (Dreiser) **30**:151
"Black Shylock" (Auchincloss) **22**:13-14
"The Black Swan" (Mann)
　　See *Die Betrogene*
"Black Tickets" (Phillips) **16**:325, 327-28
Black Tickets (Phillips) **16**:325, 327-31, 333-34, 336-37, 339
"The Black Tsar" (Morand)
　　See "Le tsar noir"
"The Black Veil" (Dickens) **17**:117, 121, 125-26
"Black Venus" (Carter) **13**:17-20, 32-35
Black Venus (Carter) **13**:13-15, 17-18
"The Black Wedding" (Singer) **3**:359, 375-76
Black Wine (Campbell) **19**:83, 87
The Blackamoor of Peter the Great (Pushkin)
　　See *Povesti Belkina*
"Blackberry Winter" (Warren) **4**:387-94, 396-99, 401-04; **58**:301-56
"The Blackbird" (O'Flaherty) **6**:268, 280
"Blackbird in a Bramble Bough" (Kiely) **58**:147, 153-55
"Blackbird Pie" (Carver) **8**:51
"Blacked Out" (Campbell) **19**:73
"Blackmail" (Galsworthy) **22**:79, 101
"Blackmailers Don't Shoot" (Chandler) **23**:56-8, 66, 68, 78, 80, 84-6, 91, 96, 102, 106
"Blades of Steel" (Fisher) **25**:5-6, 14-20, 22-3, 25-6
Blandings Castle (Wodehouse) **2**:346-47, 353
"The Blank Page" (Dinesen) **7**:200
"The Blast of God" (Evans) **43**:12-13, 23
"The Blast of the Book" (Chesterton) **1**:131; **46**:110, 136
"The Blazing Fire" (Čapek)
　　See "Živý plamen"
Le blé en herbe (Colette) **10**:262
"The Bleeding Heart" (Stafford) **26**:274, 276-77, 281, 283, 312
"Bless Me, Father" (Dubus) **15**:83
"Bless Me, Father, For I Have Sinned" (Bradbury) **29**:87
"Blessed Assurance" (Hughes) **6**:123-24
"A Blessed Deceit" (Dunbar) **8**:122
"The Blessed Man of Boston, My Grandmother's Thimble, and Fanning Island" (Updike) **13**:400
"The Blessing" (Powers) **4**:368-70, 373
"Blessings" (Dubus) **15**:85
"Blessings of Railway" (Narayan) **25**:137-38, 140
"Blight" (Dybek) **55**:130-34, 136-38, 142-43, 155-54
"The Blind" (Pavese) **19**:365
"Blind Dog" (Narayan) **25**:138, 140, 154, 169

"Blind Frank" (Steinbeck) **11**:203
"Blind Geronimo and His Brother" (Schnitzler)
    See "Der blinde Geronimo und sein Bruder"
"Blind Girls" (Phillips) **16**:328
"Blind Lightning" (Ellison) **14**:113-15, 117
"Blind Love" (Pritchett) **14**:259, 261, 266, 268, 280-81, 285-86, 289
Blind Love, and Other Stories (Pritchett) **14**:255, 267
"The Blind Man" (Chopin) **8**:100
"The Blind Man" (Lawrence) **4**:231, 233-36, 242-46
"The Blind Man" (Stephens) **50**:315, 316
"A Blind Man's Tale" (Tanizaki)
    See "Mōmoku monogatari"
"Blind Tom" (Davis) **38**:117-19, 133-34, 137-39
"Der blinde Geronimo und sein Bruder" (Schnitzler) **15**:343, 345, 377; **61**:308
"Blinder" (Gordimer) **17**:171, 194
"Blindfold" (Oates) **6**:231
"The Blinding of One-Eyed Bogan" (Lawson) **18**:242
"Bliss" (Mansfield) **9**:276, 279-80, 295, 297, 299, 301, 305-07, 309-11, 314; **23**:164
Bliss, and Other Stories (Mansfield) **9**:279, 281; **23**:139; **38**:203
"The Blizzard" (Banks) **42**:68-9
"The Blizzard" (Pushkin)
    See "Metel"
"The Blizzard" (Singer) **3**:374
"The Blockade" (Chang) **28**:25; 28; 34
"The Blond Beast" (Wharton) **6**:435
Der blonde Eckbert (Tieck) **31**:271, 276-79, 281, 292-93, 296
"Blood" (Singer) **3**:356, 358, 364, 375; **53**:293, 305
"Blood Lust" (O'Flaherty) **6**:261, 269, 277, 283
"The Blood of the Martyrs" (Benét) **10**:142, 152, 154, 156
"Blood of the Walsungs" (Mann)
    See *Wälsungenblut*
"Blood Relatives" (Apple) **50**:23, 45
"Blood, Sea" (Calvino)
    See "Il sangue, il mare"
"Blood Soup" (Dybek) **55**:130
"Blood-Burning Moon" (Toomer) **1**:443, 445, 450, 452-53, 458; **45**:184, 186, 188-89, 202-05, 223, 231-32, 236-37, 240, 253, 260, 265, 267-68, 275-77, 279, 290-92, 297, 320, 325-26, 331, 333-37, 340, 356, 359, 368, 374, 377, 383, 386
"Bloodfall" (Boyle) **16**:141-42, 144, 151
"The Blood-Feud of Toad-Water" (Saki) **12**:328
"Bloodshed" (Ozick) **15**:302, 304, 306, 317; **60**:315-16, 333
Bloodshed and Three Novellas (Ozick) **15**:302, 304-06, 308-10, 315, 317-18, 323, 326, 333
"Bloodstain" (Stegner) **27**:214
"Blood-Swollen Landscape" (Oates) **6**:250
"The Bloody Chamber" (Carter) **13**:5-9, 11-12, 17, 23, 26-28, 30
The Bloody Chamber, and Other Stories (Carter) **13**:5-8, 17, 23, 27-8, 30
"The Bloomsbury Christening" (Dickens) **17**:110-11, 116, 120, 136
"The Blow" (O'Flaherty) **6**:260, 282, 287
"Blow-Up" (Cortázar)
    See "Las babas del diablo"
"Blowups Happen" (Heinlein) **55**:163, 218-19, 234
"Blue and Green" (Kazakov) **43**:57-8
"Blue and Green" (Woolf) **7**:374-75, 398
"The Blue Background" (Aldiss) **36**:20, 22
"Blue Boy" (Caldwell) **19**:9, 38
"The Blue Cart" (Naipaul) **38**:318
"The Blue Chrysanthemum" (Čapek)
    See "Modrá chryzantéma"
"The Blue Cross" (Chesterton) **1**:119, 123, 133, 135, 138; **46**:113, 117, 125-28, 132, 139, 142-43, 145, 147-49, 153
"Blue Dave" (Harris) **19**:131, 146-47, 151, 176
"The Blue Dress" (Trevor) **58**:213, 256

"The Blue Hotel" (Crane) **7**:104-06, 108-16, 127, 129, 142-43, 145, 151-52, 154-55; **56**:72-81, 85-6, 105
"Blue Island" (Powers) **4**:368, 372
"The Blue Lenses" (du Maurier) **18**:127-28
"Blue Life" (Gorky)
    See "The Sky-blue Life"
"The Blue Light" (Grimm and Grimm) **36**:228-29
"The Blue Mesa" (Cather) **50**:232
"The Blue Moccasins" (Lawrence) **4**:220
"Blue Moon" (Phillips) **16**:335-36, 338
"The Blue Room" (Mérimée)
    See "La chambre bleue"
"Blue Spanish Eyes" (Thomas) **20**:323, 325, 328
"The Blue Woman" (Donoso) **34**:21
"Bluebeard's Egg" (Atwood) **2**:17, 21; **46**:38, 43, 50-3, 55-6, 96
Bluebeard's Egg (Atwood) **2**:17-18, 20-2; **46**:38, 43-6, 49, 51-3, 65, 69, 74, 76, 78-9, 81, 91-2, 95
"Bluebell Meadow" (Kiely) **58**:157, 159, 163
"Blue-Dog Eyes" (García Márquez)
    See "Ojos de perro azul"
"The Blue-Eyed Buddhist" (Gilchrist) **14**:158
"Bluegill" (Phillips) **16**:335-38
"Bluejay Yarn" (Twain) **6**:310; **34**:308
"The Blues I'm Playing" (Hughes) **6**:121-22, 129, 134-36
"The Blue-Winged Teal" (Stegner) **27**:195, 198, 201-04
"Blumenthal on the Air" (Chabon) **59**:71, 73, 75-77
"Blumfeld, an Elderly Bachelor" (Kafka) **5**:243-44
"Bluzdajuscije ogon'ki" (Leskov) **34**:108
Bo ni natta otako (Abe) **61**:13
"La boa" (Arreola) **38**:11
"Le Boa" (Duras) **40**:3, 6-7, 9, 65, 133-35
"The Boa" (Duras)
    See "Le Boa"
"The Boarding House" (Dickens) **17**:110, 113, 117, 120
"The Boarding House" (Joyce) **3**:201, 205-07, 234, 237, 247-48; **26**:46-7, 50; **44**:269, 284; **64**:222, 241, 244, 259
"The Boar-Pig" (Saki) **12**:295, 307, 320, 325
"Boat Animals" (Aldiss) **36**:14, 20
"Boat Trip" (Walser) **20**:354, 363-66
"Boaz the Teacher" (Aleichem) **33**:19
"Bobbio's Ave Maria" (Pirandello) **22**:255
Bödeln (Lagerkvist) **12**:177, 180, 182, 185, 193, 197
"Bodies in the Moonlight" (Hughes) **6**:117-18, 127
"Bodily Secrets" (Trevor) **21**:246-47; **58**:280
"The body" (Lispector)
    See "O corpo"
The Body (King) **17**:263-64, 267, 272, 276-78, 280, 284-85; **55**:243-44, 246-49, 253, 259
"The Body Beautiful" (Perelman) **32**:204
"The Body Politic" (Barker) **53**:140, 142-43, 157-58, 162-63, 168-69, 176
"The Body-Snatcher" (Stevenson) **11**:269-70, 282, 296, 306; **51**:237, 240-43, 248
The Bodysnatcher (Onetti)
    See "Just a Little One"
"Le Boeufs" (Aymé) **41**:6
"The Bog King's Daughter" (Andersen)
    See "Dynd-Kongens Datter"
"The Bog Man" (Atwood) **46**:79-81, 98
"The Bogey Man" (Coppard) **21**:7, 9
"Bogg of Geebung" (Lawson) **18**:248, 250
"The Bogus Policeman" (Aymé) **41**:5
Boh (Moravia) **26**:180
"The Bohemian Girl" (Cather) **2**:96-7, 101, 103-05, 108; **50**:59, 63, 72, 84, 97, 200-01, 205, 207-08, 240, 245-47
"Boiled Alive" (Campbell) **19**:70-1
"The Boiler Room" (Sansom) **21**:82, 86, 99
"Boitelle" (Maupassant) **1**:263

"Les Boîtes de peinture" (Aymé) **41**:8, 14-15
"Le Bol de punch" (Gautier) **20**:5, 10-11, 22
"A Bold Deserter" (Harris) **19**:182
"The Bold Dragoon" (Irving) **2**:256
"Boles" (Gorky) **28**:160, 190
"Bol'shoe serdtse" (Pilnyak) **48**:268-69
"The Bomb Shop" (O'Faolain) **13**:314
"Bombard" (Maupassant) **1**:263; **64**:288-91
"Bombolo" (Pirandello) **22**:241
"Bon Voyage" (Benét) **10**:149
"Bona and Paul" (Toomer) **1**:444, 446, 450, 452-54, 458-62; **45**:173, 209-11, 231-32, 237, 240, 242, 244, 246, 260, 265-66, 269-70, 277, 287, 303, 318-19, 326, 359, 362, 367, 370, 380-81, 383
"Bonanza 1972 in Toronto" (Clarke) **45**:72
"Bonaventure" (Gallant) **5**:144
Bonaventure: A Prose Pastoral of Acadian Louisiana (Cable) **4**:48, 50-1, 53, 58-60, 62, 73, 75
"Bon-Bon" (Poe) **54**:166-67
"The Bond" (Singer) **3**:385, 387; **53**:327, 330
"Bone Bubbles" (Barthelme) **2**:31; **55**:4, 67, 74, 108-9, 111, 117
"The Bone Setter" (Le Fanu)
    See "The Ghost and the Bone Setter"
"The Bonefires" (Pavese) **19**:369
"Bones and Bouquets" (Davie) **52**:6, 8, 11
"Bones of Contention" (O'Connor) **5**:371, 377
Bones of Contention, and Other Stories (O'Connor) **5**:364, 371, 377, 380, 382
"The Bonfire" (O'Hara) **15**:283
"The Bonfire" (Sansom) **21**:118-20
"Le bonheur dans le crime" (Barbey d'Aurevilly) **17**:6-8, 11, 13-16, 19-20, 26, 44
"Bonn Diary" (Boell)
    See "Hauptstädtisches Journal"
"La Bonne Peinture" (Aymé) **41**:5, 17-18, 32
"Les bons chiens" (Baudelaire) **18**:39
"Bontche Schweig" (Peretz)
    See "Bontsye Shvayg"
"Bontsie Silent" (Peretz)
    See "Bontsye Shvayg"
"Bontsye Shvayg" (Peretz) **26**:194, 197, 201-2, 207, 209, 220
"Bonvalpaša" (Andrić) **36**:65, 67
"The Bonzo's Secret" (Machado de Assis)
    See "O segrêdo do bonzo"
"The Boogeyman" (King) **55**:260-61
"The Book" (Schulz)
    See "Księga"
A Book (Barnes) **3**:3-4, 14, 22, 26
"The Book and Its Contents" (Kelly) **50**:289
The Book Class (Auchincloss) **22**:29-30, 33, 47, 50-1
"The Book of Blood" (Barker) **53**:136, 156-57, 162-63
The Book of Brian Aldiss (Aldiss)
    See *The Comic Inferno*
The Book of Deeds (Agnon)
    See *Sefer ha-Maasim*
Book of Fables (Agnon)
    See *Sefer ha-Maasim*
"Book of Harlem" (Hurston) **4**:155
The Book of Sand (Borges) **41**:131, 133-34, 157, 160, 162, 167
The Book of the American Indian (Garland) **18**:146, 177-79, 186-88
"The Book of the Dead" (Kawabata)
    See "Shisha no Sho"
"The Book of the Grotesque" (Anderson) **1**:57
The Book of the State (Agnon) **30**:68
Book That Doesn't Bite (Valenzuela)
    See *Libro que no muerde*
"The Book-Bag" (Maugham) **8**:357, 360-61, 375, 378
"The Bookkeeper's Wife" (Cather) **2**:99, 110; **50**:78, 232
Books of Blood (Barker) **53**:150, 153-54, 156, 161, 163, 165-68, 171, 174, 176-77, 179
"The Bookshop" (Huxley) **39**:153-54, 161

"Boom" (Norris) **28**:213

Boom Town (Wolfe) **33**:347, 375

"Boors Carousing" (Warner) **23**:370

"Boots" (Hood) **42**:187

"The Boots of Buffalo Leather" (Grimm and Grimm) **36**:228-29

"Bop Bop against That Curtain" (Bukowski) **45**:55

"A Border Incident" (Cheever) **38**:43

"The Border Line" (Lawrence) **4**:219, 238

"A Border-Line Case" (du Maurier) **18**:129, 135

"Borealis" (Morand) **22**:181

"Boredom" (Gorky) **28**:145-46, 160

"Borges" (Borges)
   See "Borges y yo"

"Borges and I" (Borges)
   See "Borges y yo"

"Borges and Myself" (Borges)
   See "Borges y yo"

"Borges y yo" (Borges) **41**:46, 148-49, 151, 157, 164, 167

Borghesia (Ginzburg) **65**:128, 134

"A Boring Story" (Chekhov)
   See "A Dreary Story"

"Born Bad" (Cisneros) **32**:6, 43

"A Born Farmer" (Jewett) **6**:156, 158

"A Born Genius" (O'Faolain) **13**:283-84, 309, 312, 314

"The Boscombe Valley Mystery" (Doyle) **12**:66, 68-71, 73-4

"The Bosom of the McRorys" (Somerville & Ross) **56**:301, 320, 333-4, 339

"The Boss" (Gorky)
   See "Khoziain"

"The Boss" (Stephens) **50**:312, 316

"A Botanist's Romance" (Davie) **52**:4, 6

"Both Parties Concerned" (Salinger) **65**:312-13

Bötjer Basch (Storm) **27**:286

"Die Botschaft" (Boell) **23**:5

"Le Bottes de sept Lieues" (Aymé) **41**:10

"The Bottle" (Zoshchenko) **15**:404

"The Bottle Imp" (Stevenson) **11**:268-69, 283, 296, 298; **51**:219, 240, 247-49

"A Bottle of Brown Sherry" (Kiely) **58**:149

"A Bottle of Milk for Mother" (Algren) **33**:87, 90-3, 100, 104-05, 109

"A Bottle of Perrier" (Wharton) **6**:423-24

"Bottle Party" (Collier) **19**:98, 103-04, 112

"Bottomless Hell" (Dazai Osamu) **41**:257

"The Bottomless Well" (Chesterton) **1**:122

Bought and Sold (Moravia)
   See *Il paradiso*

"Boule de suif" (Maupassant) **1**:255-57, 259, 263, 266, 269, 271-76, 281-83, 286-88, 290

"Boulôt and Boulotte" (Chopin) **8**:88, 102-03

"Bouncing Bet" (Freeman) **47**:105, 162

"The Bouquet" (Chesnutt) **7**:3, 16, 22-3, 29-30, 33, 36; **54**:9

"La bourse" (Balzac) **5**:29

"Bow Down, Isaac" (Aiken) **9**:7, 13, 42

"The Bowl" (de la Mare) **14**:87

"The Bowmen" (Machen) **20**:155, 157, 163, 166, 200

The Bowmen and Other Legends of the War (Machen) **20**:196

"The Bowmen of Shu" (Davenport) **16**:184-85, 187-88

"The Box" (Endō) **48**:209-10, 212

"A Box of Ginger" (Calisher) **15**:5, 15, 17

"Box Seat" (Toomer) **1**:440, 443, 445-48, 450-53, 458; **45**:190-92, 194-95, 200, 207-09, 211, 229-30, 232-33, 237-40, 244, 250-52, 260, 266, 268, 277, 287, 326, 336, 347-48, 351, 362, 367, 370, 380-83, 386

"A Box to Hide In" (Thurber) **1**:414, 417

"Los Boxers" (Cisneros) **32**:35

"Boxes" (Carver) **8**:43

A Boy and His Dog (Ellison) **14**:99-100, 115, 117, 124, 128-29, 138, 140-41

"The Boy and the Bayonet" (Dunbar) **8**:122, 147

"A Boy Asks a Question of a Lady" (Barnes) **3**:10-11

"Boy in Rome" (Cheever) **1**:100; **38**:53, 62; **57**:10

"The Boy Knows the Truth" (Singer) **3**:380

"The Boy Prodigy" (Tanizaki)
   See "Shindō"

A Boy Suffers (Meyer)
   See *Das Leiden eines Knaben*

"The Boy Who Hated Girls" (Vonnegut) **8**:431

"Boy with a Bible" (Borowski) **48**:4-5

"Boyhood" (Farrell) **28**:120

Boyhood (Tolstoy)
   See *Otrochestvo*

"Boys and Girls" (Farrell) **28**:110

"Boys and Girls" (Munro) **3**:321, 343-44

"Boys! Raise Giant Mushrooms in Your Cellar!" (Bradbury) **29**:58, 62

"A Boy's Town" (Howells) **36**:398

"A Boy's Will" (Frame) **29**:97-8

Boži muka (Čapek) **36**:81, 88-9, 91-2, 96-7, 109-10, 121-26, 130

Bracebridge Hall (Irving) **2**:240, 244-46, 251, 254-55, 258-59, 265

"Braids" (Aquina) **37**:44

"Brain Damage" (Barthelme) **2**:32-3, 39-40, 42, 47, 55; **55**:4-6, 13-14, 67, 72, 111

"Brainsy" (O'Faolain) **13**:291, 312

"Brakes and White Vi'lets" (Freeman) **47**:84, 101

The Bram Stoker Bedside Companion (Stoker) **62**:237, 252-53

"A Branch of the Service" (Greene) **29**:223, 230

"A Branch Road" (Garland) **18**:143, 150, 154-56, 159, 168-70, 172, 175-76, 192-93

"A Brand-New Approach" (Bioy Casares) **17**:75

"The Brandon House and the Lighthouse" (Jewett) **6**:154, 167

"Braska Comes Through" (Stuart) **31**:248

"Die Brautwahl" (Hoffmann) **13**:186

"The Brave Little Tailor" (Grimm and Grimm) **36**:229-30

"The Bravest Boat" (Lowry) **31**:43-4, 46, 48, 51-4, 59, 61-2, 71-5, 81, 84, 86-7

"Brazil" (Marshall) **3**:299, 300, 302-04, 306, 317

"A Breach of Promise" (Narayan) **25**:133, 135, 160, 162

"Bread" (Atwood) **2**:19-20

"Bread Alone" (O'Hara) **15**:248-49

"Bread from Stones" (Garrett) **30**:166, 180

"Bread in Uzok" (Caldwell) **19**:41

"The Bread of Charity" (Turgenev) **7**:318

The Bread of Those Early Years (Boell)
   See *Das Brot der frühen Jahre*

"Bread, Sugar, and Milk" (Moorhouse) **40**:289, 292

The Break of Day (Colette)
   See *La naissance du jour*

"Break On Through" (Jones) **56**:273, 275, 277

"Breakfast" (Bowen) **3**:54; **28**:4

"Breakfast" (Cortázar)
   See "Desayuno"

"Breakfast" (Farrell) **28**:125

"Breakfast" (Steinbeck) **11**:225-26, 233-34, 238-39, 241

Breakfast at Tiffany's (Capote) **2**:67-76, 78-9, 81; **47**:16-17, 21-2, 28-9, 34, 37-8, 45-6, 55, 58, 63, 70

"Breakfast at Twilight" (Dick) **57**:105, 109

"The Break-In" (Adams) **24**:11

"Breaking Off" (Hood) **42**:176, 191

The Breaking Point (du Maurier) **18**:127-28, 130, 132

"Breaking Strain" (Clarke) **3**:144, 150

"Breaking the Ice" (Thomas) **20**:320, 322, 325

"Breaking the News" (Boell)
   See "Die Botschaft"

"Breaking the News" (Nabokov) **11**:117

"The Breaking Up of the Winships" (Thurber) **1**:419, 435

"The Breakthrough" (du Maurier) **18**:129

"A Breath" (Pirandello)
   See "Soffio"

"Breath" (Price) **22**:386

"Breath from the Sky" (McCullers) **9**:342, 345, 354-55

"The Breath of Humanity" (Pilnyak)
   See "Chelovecheskiy veter"

"A Breath of Lucifer" (Narayan) **25**:139

"Breathing" (Solzhenitsyn)
   See "Dykhanie"

The Breathing Method (King) **17**:265-67, 272-73, 280; **55**:243-44

"Bred in the Bone" (Page) **23**:307

"The Breech" (Hammett) **17**:217

"Breeders" (Thomas) **20**:324, 327

"The Bremen Town Musicians" (Grimm and Grimm) **36**:208

"Brethren" (Bunin) **5**:80-2, 87-8, 93-7, 106, 115

"A Breton Inkeeper" (Lewis) **34**:164, 166, 177

"A Breton Journal" (Lewis) **34**:176-77

A Brian Aldiss Omnibus (Aldiss) **36**:18

"The Bridal Night" (O'Connor) **5**:363-64, 371, 377, 380, 383, 390, 395, 398

"The Bridal of Death" (Stoker) **62**:250

"The Bridal Party" (Fitzgerald) **6**:48, 61

"Bridal Sheets" (Lavin) **4**:165, 167, 180-81

"Bride and Bridegroom" (Tagore)
   See "Patra o Patri"

"The Bride Comes to Yellow Sky" (Crane) **7**:104-05, 108-09, 116-17, 126-27, 149, 151; **56**:97, 69-71, 75, 105

"The Bride of Christ" (Farrell) **28**:94, 118

"The Bride of Christ" (Gordimer) **17**:157

"The Bride of Innisfallen" (Welty) **51**:260, 262, 272

The Bride of Innisfallen (Welty) **1**:476, 479, 484, 495; **51**:263, 281, 318-19

"The Bridegroom" (Gordimer) **17**:154

"The Bridegroom Cometh" (Pilnyak)
   See "Zhenikh vo polunochi"

"The Bridegroom's Body" (Boyle) **5**:58-63, 66, 68

"The Bridge" (Dixon) **16**:216

"The Bridge of Dreams" (Tanizaki)
   See "Yume no ukihashi"

"The Bridge on the Žepa" (Andrić)
   See "Most na Žepi"

"The Bridge-Builders" (Kipling) **5**:267, 283, 294; **54**:70, 72, 79

"Bridges" (Andrić)
   See "Mostovi"

"Bridging" (Apple) **50**:32, 36, 45

Brief Candles (Huxley) **39**:171-74, 176

"The Brief Cure of Aunt Fanny" (Dunbar) **8**:122, 149

"The Brief Début of Tildy" (Henry) **5**:171; **49**:197

"The Brigade Commander" (Babel) **16**:26, 29, 50

"The Brigadier" (Turgenev)
   See "Brigadir"

"The Brigadier and the Golf Widow" (Cheever) **38**:50, 61, 68; **57**:9

"The Brigadier and the Golf Widow" (Wolff) **63**:268

The Brigadier and the Golf Widow (Cheever) **1**:94-5, 100; **38**:44, 63, 66; **57**:2

"Brigadir" (Turgenev) **7**:316, 320-21, 324, 337, 358

"The Brigands" (Villiers de l'Isle Adam)
   See "Les brigands"

"Les brigands" (Villiers de l'Isle Adam) **14**:381, 395-96

"Briggita" (Stifter) **28**:276, 290, 298-99, 301-03

"Bright and Morning Star" (Wright) **2**:363, 368, 373, 375, 377, 379-83, 387-88, 391-92

"The Bright Boy" (Machen) **20**:163, 198

"The Bright Day" (Grau) **15**:159

"The Bright Side" (Galsworthy) **22**:63, 78, 101

"The Bright Sun Will Bring It to Light" (Grimm and Grimm) **36**:229-30

"A Bright Sunday in Madison" (Narayan) **25**:135

"Brighten's Sister-in-Law" (Lawson) **18**:202-03, 229-30, 232, 241, 262

"Brigid" (Lavin) **4**:167

"The Brilliant Leaves" (Gordon) **15**:104, 108-09, 116, 139, 142

"Brillo" (Ellison) **14**:123

"Bring, Bring" (Aiken) **9**:12-13, 40

Bring! Bring! (Aiken) **9**:3, 5, 6, 28

"British Guiana" (Marshall) **3**:299-300, 302, 305, 317

"A briv tsu a gutn fraynd" (Aleichem) **33**:43

"Broadcast" (Campbell) **19**:87

"A Broadsheet Ballad" (Coppard) **21**:29

Brodie (Borges)
See *El informe de Brodie*

Brodie's Report (Borges)
See *El informe de Brodie*

"The Broken Boot" (Galsworthy) **22**:74, 78, 101

"Broken Field Running" (Bambara) **35**:15, 26, 28-30, 39-41

"The Broken Giraffe" (O'Hara) **15**:286

"The Broken Heart" (Irving) **2**:243, 245

"Broken Homes" (Trevor) **21**:234, 262; **58**:209, 213

"Broken Merchandise" (Bukowski) **45**:52

"The Broken Nest" (Tagore)
See "Nashtanir"

"The Broken Pot" (Narayan) **25**:137-38, 141

"Broken Stairways, Walls of Time" (Ballard) **53**:131

"Broken Sword" (Chesterton)
See "The Sign of the Broken Sword"

"Broken Ties" (Tagore)
See "Chaturanga"

Broken Ties and Other Stories (Tagore) **48**:321-22

"The Broken Wheel" (Saroyan) **21**:133-34

"Broken Wings" (James) **8**:304, 306

"A Broken World" (O'Faolain) **13**:283-84, 287, 293, 298, 300, 302, 306, 309, 316-17

"Brokers' and Marine-Store Shops" (Dickens) **17**:133

"Bronda" (Appelfeld) **42**:11

"The Bronze Door" (Chandler) **23**:64, 110-11

"Bronze Leaves and Red" (Davenport) **16**:198

"The Brooch" (Faulkner) **1**:165

"The Brood" (Campbell) **19**:71, 75

"Brooklyn" (Marshall) **3**:300, 302, 304-05, 307-08, 314-17

"Brooksmith" (James) **8**:304, 306

"Broomsticks" (de la Mare) **14**:68, 69, 87

Broomsticks, and Other Tales (de la Mare) **14**:82, 86

Das Brot der frühen Jahre (Boell) **23**:12

"Brotcotnaz" (Lewis) **34**:161-62

"The Brother" (Coover) **15**:33, 35, 48, 59

"Brother" (Greene) **29**:183, 212

"Brother" (Kipling) **54**:121

"Brother" (O'Brien) **10**:345

"Brother and Sister" (Grimm and Grimm)
See "Brüderchen und Schwesterchen"

"Brother André, Père Lamarche and My Grandmother Eugenie Blagdon" (Hood) **42**:184

"Brother Bear Learns to Comb His Head" (Harris) **19**:194

"Brother Boniface" (Lavin) **4**:183

"Brother Death" (Anderson) **1**:32, 37, 39, 50-1, 56-7

"Brother Earl" (Anderson) **1**:52

"Brother Francis" (Čapek) **36**:129

"Brother Lustig" (Grimm and Grimm) **36**:196-99, 228

"Brother Rabbit and the Chickens" (Harris) **19**:197

Brother Rabbit and the Mosquitoes (Harris) **19**:189, 195

"Brother Rabbit Ties Mr. Lion" (Harris) **19**:197

"Brother Rabbit's Courtship" (Harris) **19**:195

"Brother Rabbit's Love-Charm" (Harris) **19**:196

"Brother Tiger and Daddy Sheep" (Harris) **19**:194

"A Brother to Diogenes" (Page) **23**:288, 307, 312

"Brother Wolf Says Grace" (Harris) **19**:150

"The Brotherhood Movement" (Bioy Casares) **17**:75

"Brothers" (Anderson) **1**:52

"Brothers" (Bunin)
See "Brethren"

"Brothers" (Lu Hsun)
See "Dixiong"

"Brothers and Sisters" (Le Guin) **12**:210-11, 213-16, 249-50

"The Brother's House" (Algren) **33**:88, 106

Brothers of the Head (Aldiss) **36**:10, 15-18

"Brothpot" (Verga) **21**:284

"Brown Dog" (Harrison) **19**:211-15

"The Brown Grass" (Cowan) **28**:78-80

"The Brown Hand" (Doyle) **12**:62, 64

"The Brown House" (Yamamoto) **34**:348-49, 352, 358, 364

"Brown of Calaveras" (Harte) **8**:214, 236, 244, 246-48; **59**:338

"Brownie" (Gissing) **37**:73, 79

Brownie (Gissing) **37**:67, 79

"Brüderchen und Schwesterchen" (Grimm and Grimm) **36**:225-26

"Brugglesmith" (Kipling) **5**:266

"Brummy Usen" (Lawson) **18**:239

"Bruno" (Warner) **23**:376

"The Brushwood Boy" (Kipling) **5**:266-67, 273-74, 283; **54**:79, 98

"The Brute" (Čapek) **36**:93, 124

"The Brute" (Conrad) **9**:152, 176, 183

"La bûche" (Maupassant) **1**:274

"Buchilo" (Platonov) **42**:266-67

"The Bucket of Blood" (O'Hara) **15**:281

"Buckeye Hollow Inheritance" (Harte) **8**:218

"The Buckles of Superior Dosset" (Galsworthy) **22**:71

"The Buckley Lady" (Freeman) **47**:84-85, 106

"Buckthorne and His Friends" (Irving) **2**:241, 251, 261-62

"The Buckwheat" (Andersen) **6**:7, 12, 18, 34

"The Buddies" (Farrell) **28**:91

"Buddy" (Dixon) **16**:217

"La buenaventura" (Alarcon) **64**:2-4, 9

"Buenaventura Durruti's Funeral" (Moorhouse) **40**:324

"Los buenos tiempos" (Pardo Bazán) **30**:264

"O búfalo" (Lispector) **34**:185, 189-90, 195-97, 201-02

"The Buffalos" (Williams) **31**:303, 354, 359, 361

"Bugle Song" (Stegner) **27**:195-97, 215, 222-23

"Building Alive" (Sansom) **21**:81, 83, 90, 92, 124

"The Building Site" (Duras) **40**:65

"Building Speculation" (Calvino)
See "La speculazione edilizia"

"Build-Up" (Ballard) **1**:68, 76-7; **53**:8-9, 29, 42, 45, 49-50, 91

"An Buille" (O'Flaherty) **6**:286-89

"Buiyon no tsuma" (Dazai Osamu) **41**:238-42, 244-45, 251, 253-54, 263

"Bukoemov" (Gorky) **28**:146

"Bulbs" (Davie) **52**:4-5

Bulemanns Haus (Storm) **27**:278

"Bulfinch" (Cheever) **38**:44; **57**:3

"The Bulgarian Poetess" (Updike) **13**:367, 374-75, 378, 380-81

"The Bull" (Pavese) **19**:369

"The Bull That Thought" (Kipling) **5**:279, 286

"Bullring of the Summer Night" (Algren) **33**:95

"The Bull-Run Style" (Lawson) **18**:233

"The Bully" (Dubus) **15**:74

"Bums at Sunset" (Wolfe) **33**:369

"Bums in the Attic" (Cisneros) **32**:31

"Bunches" (Andrić)
See "Snopići"

"A Bundle of Letters" (James) **8**:299

"Bunner Sisters" (Wharton) **6**:418, 422, 433

Bunte Steine (Stifter) **28**:272, 279, 283, 286, 288-89, 292, 300, 302-03

"La buonissima madre" (Svevo) **25**:336, 360

"The Burden of Loveliness" (Williams) **31**:327, 334

"The Bureau of Frauds" (P'u Sung-ling)
See "K'ao-pi ssu"

"The Burglar's Christmas" (Cather) **2**:100; **50**:72-3, 93-4

"The Burial of the Guns" (Page) **23**:295-96, 298, 307

The Burial of the Guns (Page) **23**:283, 285, 291, 326, 328

"The Burial of the Rats" (Stoker) **62**:233, 243, 253-54

"Buried Lives" (Mukherjee) **38**:245, 254, 267-68, 282-83

"Una burla riuscita" (Svevo) **25**:328-32, 335-37, 340-50, 352-53, 357-58, 363-65

"The Burning" (Welty) **1**:476, 479, 484; **27**:332, 338; **51**:305

"The Burning Baby" (Thomas) **3**:399, 407; **44**:323, 328, 336-38, 342, 344, 346, 354, 357-59

"Burning Chrome" (Gibson) **52**:16-18, 22, 32

Burning Chrome (Gibson) **52**:15-18, 21-2, 26-7, 30, 32, 34-6, 41-3, 47, 54

"The Burning Eyes" (Gordon) **15**:128-29, 142

The Burning Flames, and Other Stories (Rulfo)
See *El llano en llamas, y otros cuentos*

"The Burning House" (Beattie) **11**:10, 13, 22, 29

The Burning House (Beattie) **11**:7, 9, 10-12, 19, 22-4, 26-7, 29, 32

"The Burning Plain" (Rulfo) **25**:265, 268, 270

The Burning Plain, and Other Stories (Rulfo)
See *El llano en llamas, y otros cuentos*

"The Burning Shame" (Twain) **34**:295

"Burning the Bed" (Betts) **45**:3

"The Burnt Ones" (White) **39**:330

The Burnt Ones (White) **39**:278-80, 282-83, 288, 292-94, 300, 303, 205-06, 309, 312, 316, 318, 320, 324, 335, 337, 343, 345

Burnt Water (Fuentes)
See *Aqua quemada*

"The Burrow" (Kafka)
See "Der bau"

"Burutu Moon" (Hughes) **6**:118

"The Bus" (Singer) **3**:381-82

"Bus Ride" (Fante) **65**:92

"The Bus to St. James's" (Cheever) **1**:100, 106; **38**:55

"La busca de Averroes" (Borges) **4**:26, 37, 41

"La Buse et le cochon" (Aymé) **41**:8, 15

"The Bush Undertaker" (Lawson) **18**:201, 206-07, 218, 221, 237-39, 241, 245, 259

"The Busher Comes Back" (Lardner) **32**:143

"A Busher's Letters Home" (Lardner) **32**:141-43, 150, 152, 159

Bushūkō hiwa (Tanizaki) **21**:182-86, 189-91, 195, 198, 219, 224, 226

The Bushwackers and Other Stories (Murfree) **22**:187

"The Bushwhackers" (Murfree) **22**:187

"Business Is Business" (Boell)
See "Geschäft ist Geschäft"

"The Business Man" (Poe) **1**:407; **54**:181

"Business Talk" (Apple) **50**:23, 33-4, 45

"The Business Venture" (Spencer) **57**:220-21, 224, 229-31, 242, 244

"Busride" (Cortázar)
See "Omnibus"

"A Busy Day in a Lawyer's Office" (Chesnutt) **7**:14

"A Busy Man" (Nabokov) **11**:133

"But at the Stroke of Midnight" (Warner) **23**:376

"But It's Going to Rain" (Lispector)
　See "Mas vai chover"
"But We Are Not Strangers" (Kazakov) 43:67
But Who Can Replace a Man? (Aldiss) 36:18
"Butcher Bird" (Stegner) 27:196-97
"Butcher Rogaum's Door" (Dreiser) 30:1237, 127, 129-30, 132
"Butōkai" (Akutagawa Ryūnosuke) 44:64, 78
"Butter Butter for a Boat" (Jolley) 19:245
"Butterball's Night" (Cortázar)
　See "La noche de Mantequilla"
"Buttercup Night" (Galsworthy) 22:63, 101
"Butterflies" (Trevor) 58:200
"The Butterfly" (Andersen)
　See "Sommerfuglen"
"The Butterfly" (Chekhov)
　See "Poprygin'ia"
"The Butterfly" (O'Hara) 15:282
"The Butterfly and the Traffic Light" (Ozick) 15:298, 313
"Buying a Horse" (Howells) 36:399
"By a Dying Man's Pillow" (Peretz) 26:204-05, 217
"By Courier" (Henry) 49:197, 200
"By Himself" (Pirandello)
　See "Da sé"
"By Moonlight" (Mansfield) 9:286; 23:146, 153-54
"By My Troth, Nerissa" (Aiken) 9:13
"By Oneself" (Pirandello)
　See "Da sé"
By Shore and Sedge (Harte) 59:310
"By Special Request" (Waugh) 41:330
"By the Brandy Still" (Andrić)
　See "Kod kazana"
"By the Gods' Mouth" (Fuentes)
　See "Por boca de los dioses"
"By the Mouth of the Gods" (Fuentes)
　See "Por boca de los dioses"
"By the People" (Faulkner) 1:178
"By the Road" (Bunin) 5:106
"By the Sea" (Adams) 24:9
"By the Shore" (Appelfeld)
　See "Ahar hahatunah"
"By the Water" (Bowles) 3:71-2
"By the Waters of Babylon" (Benét) 10:154, 157
"By Word of Mouth" (Kipling) 54:72-4
"Byezhin Prairie" (Turgenev)
　See "Bezhin Lea"
Byl'yo (Pilnyak) 48:248, 252, 265
"Byron in Sintra" (Andrić)
　See "Bajron u Sintri"
"The Bystander" (Berriault) 30:96-7
"Byvshii lyudi" (Gorky) 28:136-37, 146, 151, 157, 183, 185, 189, 191
Byways (Hesse) 9:230
"The Byzantine Omelet" (Saki) 12:295
"C. Musonius Rufus" (Davenport) 16:169, 171, 175, 177, 191
Cabal (Barker)
　See *Nightbreed*
The Cabal and Other Stories (Gilchrist) 63:9, 26
"The Cabalist of East Broadway" (Singer) 3:374, 383-84
"The Caballero's Way" (Henry) 5:167
"El caballo blanco" (Pardo Bazán) 30:290
Cabbages and Kings (Henry) 5:155, 160, 162-63, 167-69, 172; 49:205
"Cabecita blanca" (Castellanos) 39:75, 76
"The Cabin" (Carver) 8:50
"The Cabinet of Edgar Allan Poe" (Carter) 13:16-18, 20
"The Cabulliwallah" (Tagore) 48:301
"La cachet d'onyx" (Barbey d'Aurevilly) 17:9-13, 17-18
"Cäcilie" (Kleist)
　See *Die heilige Cäcilie; oder, die Gewalt der Musik*
"Cadbury, the Beaver Who Lacked" (Dick) 57:68

"A Caddy's Diary" (Lardner) 32:117, 123, 146, 149, 154-55
"Cadence" (Dubus) 15:73-4, 100
"The Cadjer" (Galsworthy) 22:58
"Cafard" (Galsworthy) 22:62-3, 101
"Café des exilés" (Cable) 4:58, 62, 68
"La Cafetière" (Gautier) 20:4, 9-10, 13, 16-17
"Caffs, Pools and Bikes" (Sansom) 21:106, 108, 126
"The Cage Birds" (Pritchett) 14:284, 298
"The Cage of Sand" (Ballard) 53:8
"The Caged Lion" (Norris) 28:205, 207
"Cahoots" (Dunbar) 8:122, 132, 145
"Cain and Artyom" (Gorky)
　See "Kain i Artem"
"Cain Rose Up" (King) 17:274; 55:243-44, 246-49, 253, 259; 55:250
"A Cake of Soap" (Lu Hsun)
　See "Feizao"
Cakes and Ale and Twelve Stories (Maugham) 8:384
"El calamar opta por su tinta" (Bioy Casares) 17:95
"Calf of Gold" (Kelly) 50:286-87, 303
"Calico Shoes" (Farrell) 28:87, 112
Calico Shoes and Other Stories (Farrell) 28:86, 100, 118-22
"The Californian's Tale" (Twain) 26:331
"Caline" (Chopin) 8:94
"The Caliph and the Cad" (Henry) 5:158
"The Caliph, Cupid, and the Clock" (Henry) 5:158; 49:197
"The Call" (Cowan) 28:82
"Call and I Follow, I Follow!" (Perelman) 32:243
"Call at Corazón" (Bowles) 3:59, 61-2, 66, 69, 77, 79
"Call Me, Call Me" (O'Hara) 15:252
"Call Me Knacknissel" (Aleichem) 33:74
"The Call of Blood" (Cervantes)
　See "La fuerza de la sangre"
"The Call of Cthulhu" (Lovecraft) 3:258, 261, 263-64, 269-70, 274, 278, 280, 283, 290; 52:253, 255-56, 261, 268-70, 280, 308-9, 320, 330, 333, 336-37, 347-49, 352-54
"The Call of the Tame" (Henry) 5:191, 194
"A Call on Mrs. Forrester" (Thurber) 1:431
Call to Arms (Lu Hsun)
　See *Nahan*
"The Call to Duty" (Pirandello) 22:226, 229
"Calla-Lillies and Hannah" (Freeman) 47:103
"Calling" (Ford) 56:184, 196
"Calling All Moths: Candle Dead Ahead" (Perelman) 32:229
"Calling Card" (Campbell)
　See "First Foot"
"Calling Cards" (Bunin)
　See "Vizitnye kartochki"
"Calling Jesus" (Toomer) 1:445, 447, 450; 45:208, 225, 238-40, 253, 260-62, 264-65, 268, 277, 355, 381-82
"The Calm" (Carver) 8:14, 42; 51:5, 15
"Le Calmant" (Beckett) 16:73-5, 87, 89-91
"The Calmative" (Beckett)
　See "Le Calmant"
Calvaries (Čapek)
　See *Boží muka*
"Calvary" (Evans) 43:29
"La camara in attesa" (Pirandello) 22:232-33, 285-86
"The Camberwell Beauty" (Pritchett) 14:262-63, 266, 272
The Camberwell Beauty, and Other Stories (Pritchett) 14:267, 301, 305
"Cambio de armas" (Valenzuela) 14:353, 355-6, 358
Cambio de armas (Valenzuela) 14:352, 355, 359, 366-67, 372
"The Camel's Back" (Fitzgerald) 6:45, 59, 96-7
"La camera e la strada" (Moravia) 26:148
"El Camino de Santiago" (Carpentier) 35:91, 97, 99, 101-03, 105

"Il campo di granturco" (Pavese) 19:385
"Can All This Grandeur Perish?" (Farrell) 28:92, 130
Can All This Grandeur Perish? and Other Stories (Farrell) 28:99, 122
"Can I Stay Here?" (O'Hara) 15:262, 283
Can Such Things Be? (Bierce) 9:59
"Can You Carry Me?" (O'Hara) 15:270
"La cana" (Pardo Bazán) 30:278-80
"Canadian Experience" (Clarke) 45:76, 78-9, 84, 91-2, 103-04, 106, 111, 113
"The Canals of Mars" (Boyle) 5:55
"The Canary" (Mansfield) 9:282, 306, 310, 313; 38:230
"A Canary for One" (Hemingway) 1:209, 217, 232, 237; 63:52, 56, 58
Canary in a Cat House (Vonnegut) 8:428
"Cancel All I Said" (Collier) 19:103, 110
"La canciónde Peronelle" (Arreola) 38:6
Candide; or, Optimism (Voltaire)
　See *Candide; ou, L'optimisme*
Candide; ou, L'optimisme (Voltaire) 12:338-44, 347-55, 357-62, 364-65, 368-69, 372-74, 376-78, 383-90, 393-6, 400
"The Candles" (Agnon)
　See "HaNerot"
"Candles" (Singer)
　See "Nerot"
"Candles for the Madonna" (Boell) 23:11
"Candleshine" (Benét) 10:149
"The Candy Country" (Alcott) 27:44
"The Candy That Is Not Sweet" (Far) 62:50, 53
"Candy-Man Beechum" (Caldwell) 19:9, 16-17, 21-3, 28-9, 36-9
Cane (Toomer) 1:439-55, 458-60, 462; 45:167-393
"The Cane in the Corridor" (Thurber) 1:420, 422; 47:303
"Canon Alberic's Scrap-Book" (James) 16:232, 234-36, 238, 242, 248, 250-52, 255-57
The Canopy of Time (Aldiss) 36:18
"Canta l'epistola" (Pirandello) 22:229, 233, 248-50, 266-67
Cantar de ciegos (Fuentes) 24:29, 31, 33, 37, 51-2, 55-8, 62, 71-2, 75
"Cantelman's Spring-Mate" (Lewis) 34:254-56, 165, 172, 175
"The Canterbury Pilgrims" (Hawthorne) 3:185-86
"The Canterville Ghost: A Hylo-Idealistic Romance" (Wilde) 11:372, 376, 399-401, 407
"Cantiga de esponsais" (Machado de Assis) 24:129
"Um cão de lata ão rabo" (Machado de Assis) 24:130
The Cape Cod Lighter (O'Hara) 15:281-82
"Cape Race" (de la Mare) 14:82, 86, 89
Capel Sion (Evans) 43:3, 6, 13, 15, 18, 26-7, 36, 39
"The Capital in My Notebook" (Bulgakov) 18:90
"The Capital of the World" (Hemingway) 1:217, 232, 234, 245; 25:113; 40:209, 211
"A Capitalist" (Gissing) 37:52
"La capitana" (Pardo Bazán) 30:272
"The Capitulation of Jean Jacques" (Galsworthy) 22:90
"Cap'n Jollyfax's Gun" (Morrison) 40:329
A Capote Reader (Capote) 47:63
"Caprice" (Verga)
　See "Fantasticheria"
"The Captain" (Dubus) 15:93
"The Captain" (Michaels) 16:305, 307-10
"Captain Blood" (Barthelme) 55:93, 111, 115
"Captain Boldheart" (Dickens) 17:124
"Captain Candelario's Heroic Last Stand" (Ferré)
　See "La extraña muerte del capitancito Candelario"
"Captain d'Arce's Memoirs" (Verga)
　See "I Ricordi del Capitano d'Arce"

"The Captain Has Bad Dreams" (Algren) **33**:88, 105, 110

"The Captain Is Impaled" (Algren) **33**:105

"The Captain of 'The Camel'" (Bierce) **9**:80

"Captain Sands" (Jewett) **6**:167

Captain Shigemoto's Mother (Tanizaki)
See *Shōshō Shigemoto no haha*

"The Captains" (Jewett) **6**:154, 167

The Captain's Daughter; or, the Generosity of the Russian Usurper Pugatscheff (Pushkin)
See *Kapitanskaya-dochka*

"The Captain's Doll" (Lawrence) **4**:197, 204, 210-12, 223-26, 234-36, 239-40

"The Captain's Doll" (Wilson) **21**:364

"The Captain's Gift" (Stafford) **26**:278-79, 283, 285, 301, 307

"The Captain's Son" (Taylor) **10**:396-97, 399, 402

"The Captive" (Gordon) **15**:105-06, 110, 117, 128, 133

"The Captive" (Kipling) **5**:283

"The Captive" (Pirandello) **22**:226, 229, 265

"The Captive" (Singer) **3**:374, 384; **53**:330

"The Captives" (Benét) **10**:154

"Captivity" (Henderson) **29**:328

"The Captured Shadow" (Fitzgerald) **6**:49

"The Captured Woman" (Barthelme) **2**:46; **55**:86

Captures (Galsworthy) **22**:65-6, 77, 97, 99, 101-02

"Car Crash While Hitchhiking" (Johnson) **56**:236, 239, 247, 254, 258, 264, 266-68

"The Car We Had to Push" (Thurber) **1**:431

La cara de la desgracia (Onetti) **23**:247, 250, 252, 260-61, 279-80

"The Carafe" (Zoshchenko) **15**:407-08

"Carancro" (Cable) **4**:58

"Las caras de la verdad" (Bioy Casares) **17**:59

Caravan: The Assembled Tales of John Galsworthy (Galsworthy) **22**:67-9, 73-9

"Carbo-Loading" (Apple) **50**:23, 32, 34

"Carbon" (Levi) **12**:257, 259, 262, 265, 268, 280

"El carbonero alcalde" (Alarcon) **64**:3

"Carcassonne" (Faulkner) **1**:181

"The Cardinal's First Tale" (Dinesen) **7**:162-63, 172, 186, 194, 198

"The Cardinal's Third Tale" (Dinesen) **7**:168, 200

The Cardinals, with Meditations and Short Stories (Head) **52**:219-20, 230-31, 235, 240-43

"Cards" (Beattie) **11**:26, 29

"A Career" (Narayan) **25**:141, 155

"The Career of Nightmares" (Ligotti) **16**:293

"Careful" (Carver) **8**:26, 31, 35, 51

"The Careful Man" (Galsworthy) **22**:98

"Careful, Sharp Eggs Underfoot" (Betts) **45**:4, 28-9

"Careless Talk" (Bowen) **3**:31; **28**:7

"Careless Talk" (Gallant) **5**:151

"A Careless Widow" (Pritchett) **14**:300

A Careless Widow, and Other Stories (Pritchett) **14**:300

"The Caress" (O'Flaherty) **6**:267

"The Caretaker" (Moravia) **26**:139

"Caricature" (Singer) **3**:359, 375

"La caricia más profunda" (Cortázar) **7**:58, 61, 63

"Carma" (Toomer) **1**:456-57; **45**:199, 237, 260, 264-65, 267, 285, 331, 335, 374

"Carmen" (Lardner) **32**:145

Carmen (Mérimée) **7**:276, 280-2, 285-6, 290, 294-6, 305-06, 308

"Carmilla" (Le Fanu) **14**:221, 223, 225, 233-38, 243-45, 251

Il carnevale de Morti (Pirandello) **22**:231, 275

"Carnival" (Caldwell) **19**:41

"Carnival" (Dinesen) **7**:190-91

"Carnival of Madness" (Bradbury)
See "Usher II"

The Carnival of the Dead (Pirandello)
See *Il carnevale de Morti*

"The Carnival of the Stone Children" (Gilchrist) **63**:8

"A Carolina" (Machado de Assis) **24**:155

"Carpe Noctem, If You Can" (Thurber) **1**:424

"Carpenters" (Salinger)
See "Raise High the Roofbeam, Carpenters"

"The Carriage Lamps" (Crane) **7**:104; **56**:111

"La carriola" (Pirandello) **22**:270

Carry On, Jeeves (Wodehouse) **2**:337, 346

Carry-Over (Suckow) **18**:404

"Carta a un senorita en París" (Cortázar) **7**:56-7, 61, 70-1

"Carta a un srta. en París" (Cortázar)
See "Carta a un senorita en París"

"Carta a un Zapatero" (Arreola) **38**:10

"La Carte" (Aymé) **41**:16-17, 19-21, 26-28

"A Cartomante" (Machado de Assis) **24**:128, 134

"Cartoon" (Coover) **15**:60

"The Cartouche" (de la Mare) **14**:79

"The Caryatids" (Dinesen) **7**:167, 191-92, 203-04

"Čas" (Čapek) **36**:110

"Un cas de divorce" (Maupassant) **1**:286

"Le cas de Madame Luneau" (Maupassant) **1**:259, 286

"Cas voli Bozijej" (Leskov) **34**:108

"Caša" (Andrić) **36**:33

"Casa al mare" (Ginzburg) **65**:115, 130

"Casa Anna" (Taylor) **10**:379

"La casa de Asterión" (Borges) **4**:7, 10, 25; **41**:72

"La casa del Granella" (Pirandello) **22**:256, 259

"La casa en la arena" (Onetti) **23**:246, 251-52, 279

"Casa tomada" (Cortázar) **7**:53, 81

"Casa velhas" (Machado de Assis) **24**:155

"Casada e viúva" (Machado de Assis) **24**:131

"El casamiento engañoso" (Cervantes) **12**:21, 24, 33-4, 37-8, 40

Casanovas Heimfahrt (Schnitzler) **15**:352, 371, 376

Casanova's Homecoming (Schnitzler)
See *Casanovas Heimfahrt*

The Case Against Tomorrow (Pohl) **25**:212

"A Case for Kop" (Boell) **23**:8, 36

"A Case for Lombroso" (Norris) **28**:197, 206-07, 214

"A Case for Prosecution" (Čapek) **36**:130

"A Case for the Oracle" (Lawson) **18**:250

"Case Histories" (Kluge) **61**:74

Case Histories (Kluge)
See *Lebensläufe*

"A Case History" (O'Hara) **15**:252, 280

"A Case in a Thousand" (Beckett) **16**:72

"The Case of 'Ca'line': A Kitchen Monologue" (Dunbar) **8**:122, 127, 147

"The Case of Dimity Ann" (Thurber) **47**:383

"A Case of Identity" (Doyle) **12**:49, 51, 59, 66-8, 70-1, 73

"The Case of Lady Sannox" (Doyle) **12**:64

"The Case of Lieutenant Yelaghin" (Bunin)
See "The Elaghin Affair"

"The Case of Lord Cornphillip" (Waugh) **41**:331

"A Case of Metaphantasmia" (Howells) **36**:360-61, 363-64, 397

"The Case of Smith vs. Jones" (Twain) **26**:326

"The Case of The Lost Parent" (Kelly) **50**:288

"The Case of the Lost Relation" (Kelly) **50**:207

"A Case That Was Dropped" (Leskov)
See "Pogassee delo"

"The Case with the Child" (Čapek)
See "Případ s dítětem"

The Case-Book of Sherlock Holmes (Doyle) **12**:62

"The Cask of Amontillado" (Poe) **1**:378, 394, 407-08; **22**:293; **34**:264-65; **35**:297-354; **54**:180, 185, 188-89, 209

"Cassandra" (Mansfield) **9**:282

"Cassation" (Barnes) **3**:6, 10, 16, 24-5

"The Cassowary" (Bowen) **3**:33

Cast a Cold Eye (McCarthy) **24**:215-18

"Casting the Runes" (James) **16**:227, 230, 233, 236, 245, 248, 252-53, 255

"The Casting Vote" (Murfree) **22**:211

"The Castle of Crossed Destinies" (Calvino) **3**:101-02

The Castle of Crossed Destinies (Calvino)
See *Il castello dei destini incrociati*

"The Castle of the King" (Stoker) **62**:251

"Castles in the Air" (Greene) **29**:219

"Castor and Pollux" (Warner) **23**:384

"A Casual Incident" (Farrell) **28**:111

"The Casualty" (Boell) **23**:38

"Casualty" (Wolff) **63**:275, 277

The Casualty (Boell) **23**:36

The Casuarina Tree (Maugham) **8**:366-67, 371, 374

"Časy" (Turgenev) **7**:324-25, 327, 358

"The Cat" (Cheever) **38**:43

"The Cat" (Freeman) **47**:164

"The Cat" (Saroyan) **21**:135

The Cat (Colette)
See *La chatte*

A Cat, a Man, and Two Women (Tanizaki)
See *The Cat, Shōzō, and Two Women*

"The Cat in the Hat for President" (Coover) **15**:45-6

"Cat in the Rain" (Hemingway) **1**:244-45; **63**:55, 81, 124

"The Cat Jumps" (Bowen) **3**:41, 53; **28**:9, 12

The Cat Jumps and Other Stories (Bowen) **3**:33, 41; **28**:4

"A Cat Named Dempsey" (Benét) **10**:154

"Cat Scratch Fever" (Kelly) **50**:291

Cat Scratch Fever (Kelly) **50**:290-92

The Cat, Shōzō, and Two Women (Tanizaki) **21**:186, 192, 218

"The Cat That Walked by Himself" (Kipling) **5**:284

"Cat up a Tree" (Sansom) **21**:83, 92

"Cat Within" (Narayan) **25**:157

"The Cat Woman" (Dybek) **55**:125, 127, 136-37, 140, 142

"The Catalan Night" (Morand)
See "La nuit Catalane"

"Catalina" (Villiers de l'Isle Adam) **14**:397

Catalogue of the Exhibition: The Art of Edmund Moorash 1810-1846 (Millhauser) **57**:158, 173, 176

"The Catalonian Night" (Morand)
See "La nuit Catalane"

"A Catastrophe" (Wells) **6**:389

"The Catbird Seat" (Thurber) **1**:422, 425, 431-32, 435; **47**:365, 374-75, 382, 389-90

"The Catch" (Gordimer) **17**:151-52, 166

The Catch (Oe)
See *Shiiku*

"The Catechist" (Barthelme) **2**:37, 39, 55; **55**:10, 29, 821

"Caterina" (Moravia) **26**:144, 165

"Cathay" (Millhauser) **57**:155-56, 167, 172

"Cathedral" (Carver) **8**:26, 30, 34-5, 40-1, 43-4, 48-9, 51

Cathedral (Carver) **8**:17, 20, 23, 26-8, 30-2, 34, 39-40, 46, 49, 55-61

"The Cathedral Builder" (Auchincloss) **22**:34, 50

"Catherine Carmichael" (Trollope) **28**:317, 322, 327, 349, 356

"Catman" (Ellison) **14**:109-10

"Cats" (Shiga) **23**:346, 349

"Cats and Students, Bubbles and Abysses" (Bass) **60**:5, 8

The Cat's Cradle Book (Warner) **23**:367, 380

"The Cats of Ulthar" (Lovecraft) **3**:262; **52**:285, 297, 359

"The Cat's Point of View" (Čapek) **36**:84

"The Cattle Dealers" (Chekhov) **2**:128

"The Cattle Pen" (Leskov) **34**:127

"A causa secreta" (Machado de Assis) **24**:128, 133

"Cause of Death: Hooked Nose" (Boell) **23**:36

"The Cause of the Difficulty" (Harris) **19**:183

"Caution" (Naipaul) **38**:306, 327

"Caution—Soft Prose Ahead" (Perelman) **32**:202, 211

Il cavaliere inesistente (Calvino) **3**:90-1, 99, 106-07, 117; **48**:34-5, 44-6, 49, 90, 92, 150, 155, 165-66

"Cavalleria Rusticana" (Verga) **21**:283-84, 286, 295, 298-301, 305

Cavalleria Rusticana, and Other Tales of Sicilian Peasant Life (Verga)
   See *Vita dei campi*

"Un cavallo nella luna" (Pirandello) **22**:275

"Un cavallo sulla luna" (Pirandello) **22**:279

"Cavanelle" (Chopin) **8**:94, 108, 111

"Cavar un foso" (Bioy Casares) **17**:95

"The Cave" (Bass) **60**:42

"The Cave Man as He Is" (Leacock) **39**:265

"Caveat Emptor" (Stafford) **26**:279, 282

"La caverna" (Arreola) **38**:4

"Caviar" (Boyle) **16**:144

"C'è qualcuno che ride" (Pirandello) **22**:261, 269

"Cecino e il bue" (Calvino) **48**:99

"Cefalea" (Cortázar) **7**:58

"Čekárna" (Čapek) **36**:92, 110, 122-23

"The Celebrated Jumping Frog of Calaveras County" (Twain) **6**:300, 309-12, 316-21; **26**:357; **34**:288-346

The Celebrated Jumping Frog of Calaveras County, and Other Sketches (Twain) **34**:322, 336

"A Celebrity" (Machado de Assis) **24**:153

"Celephaïs" (Lovecraft) **52**:281, 285-86, 298-300, 335, 342, 359, 361-62

"La céleste aventure" (Villiers de l'Isle Adam) **14**:390

"The Celestial Omnibus" (Forster) **27**:74-77, 81, 83, 85-6, 99, 102, 111, 114-15, 123

The Celestial Omnibus (Forster) **27**:68-70, 74, 76, 89-90, 97, 108, 112, 124

"The Celestial Plot" (Bioy Casares) **17**:85

The Celestial Plot (Bioy Casares)
   See *La trama celeste*

"Celestial Publicity" (Villiers de l'Isle Adam)
   See "L'affichage céleste"

"The Celestial Railroad" (Hawthorne) **3**:178, 181, 183

Les célibataires (Balzac)
   See *Le curé de Tours*

Celibate Lives (Moore) **19**:297-300, 302-04, 308, 310-11, 318

Celibates (Moore) **19**:310, 341-43, 346

The Celibates' Club (Zangwill) **44**:365, 375, 378, 381-82

"The Cellars" (Campbell) **19**:62, 74, 81, 86, 88, 90

"Celle-ci et Celle-là ou la Jeune-France passionnée" (Gautier) **20**:10, 12, 14, 24

"El celoso extremeño" (Cervantes) **12**:3-4, 8, 14, 16-17, 21, 23, 33-4, 37, 39

"Čelovek v futljare" (Chekhov) **2**:139, 141, 143, 155, 157; **28**:54-6, 63, 65-72; **51**:85-6, 92, 128, 138, 147, 209

"The Cemetery at Kozin" (Babel) **16**:27-8, 31, 55

"The Cemetery in the Demesne" (Lavin) **4**:166, 176

"The Cenci" (Stendhal)
   See "Les Cenci"

"Les Cenci" (Stendhal) **27**:231-39, 241-42, 244-47, 249, 261

"The Census Takers" (Pohl) **25**:224

"Centaur in Brass" (Faulkner) **1**:177

"Central Time Control" (Ballard) **53**:42

"Ceremonias de rechazo" (Valenzuela) **14**:355, 358-59

"The Ceremony" (Machen) **20**:200

"Le Cerf et le chien" (Aymé) **41**:6

"Cerium" (Levi) **12**:256, 258, 265, 280

"ёrnyji monax" (Chekhov) **2**:126, 131-32, 143, 147-48; **28**:60; **41**:199-200; **51**:114-16, 129-30, 143-44, 191, 196-97

"Certain Considerations" (Pirandello)
   See "Certi obblighi"

A Certain Lucas (Cortázar)
   See *Un tal Lucas*

Certain Women (Caldwell) **19**:21-2, 42, 55-6

"Certi obblighi" (Pirandello) **22**:253

"The Certificate" (Agnon)
   See "HaTe'udah"

"Čertogon" (Leskov) **34**:114

"Červená povídka" (Čapek) **36**:96, 110

"Chablis" (Barthelme) **55**:76

"Chac Mool" (Fuentes) **24**:30, 38-41, 43-5, 52-5, 59, 62, 64-8, 82

"Chacun sa chimère" (Baudelaire) **18**:4-5, 17-18, 35

"Chad Gadya" (Zangwill) **44**:373

"Chagrin d'Amour" (Hesse) **9**:231, 235

"Chagrin in Three Parts" (Greene) **29**:202

"The Chain" (Wolff) **63**:274, 276, 335-36

"A Chain of Love" (Price) **22**:360, 363, 374, 384

"The Chain Smoker" (Pritchett) **14**:286

"La chaîne d'or" (Gautier) **20**:2, 15

"Chains" (Dreiser) **30**:110, 122, 145

Chains (Dreiser) **30**:110, 122, 152-53, 159

"Chai-p'ing kung-tzu" (P'u Sung-ling) **31**:199

"The Chair" (Davenport) **16**:185, 187

"Châli" (Maupassant) **1**:259

"The Challenge" (O'Flaherty) **6**:277-78

"The Challenge From Beyond" (Lovecraft) **52**:277

"Chambers" (Dickens) **17**:123

"La chambre" (Sartre) **32**:255-9, 261, 263-4, 267-70

"La chambre 11" (Maupassant) **1**:288; **64**:283, 285-91

"La chambre bleue" (Mérimée) **7**:277, 296-7.

Chambre d'hotel (Colette) **10**:269-70

"La chambre double" (Baudelaire) **18**:5, 8, 18

"The Champ" (Boyle) **16**:140-41, 151-52

Le Champ d'Oliviers (Maupassant) **1**:273, 283

"Champion" (Lardner) **32**:117, 127, 129, 131-32, 136, 138, 143, 146, 148-49, 152, 154-55, 160-61, 163, 168-69

"The Champion" (Stuart) **31**:234, 264-65

"The Champion of the Weather" (Henry) **5**:159

"Chance" (Dazai Osamu) **41**:251

Chance Aquaintances (Colette)
   See *Chambre d'hotel*

"A Chance for Mr. Lever" (Greene) **29**:183, 186, 212, 217

"The Chance of Araminta" (Freeman) **47**:102

"Chanclas" (Cisneros) **32**:31

"A Change" (Narayan) **25**:137, 141

"Ch'ang-ê" (P'u Sung-ling) **31**:207, 209

"A Change of Circumstances" (Morrison) **40**:366

"A Change of Cover" (Kluge) **61**:50

"A Change of Heart" (Jewett) **6**:156, 158

A Change of Light, and Other Stories (Cortázar) **7**:62-3

"A Change of Office" (Sansom) **21**:105, 110, 126

"A Changed Man" (Hardy) **60**:182

A Changed Man (Hardy) **60**:177

A Changed Man, The Waiting Supper, and Other Tales, concluding with the Romantic Adventures of a Milkmaid (Hardy) **2**:210-11, 214-15, 220-21; **60**:182

"The Changeling" (Hood) **42**:238

"Chang-shih fu" (P'u Sung-ling) **31**:200

"Chanson d'été" (Bulgakov) **18**:90

"La chanson vitrier" (Baudelaire) **18**:63

"Le chant du coq" (Villiers de l'Isle Adam) **14**:396

"Chantal" (Beauvoir) **35**:60, 62, 64-6, 68-70

"Les Chantiers" (Duras) **40**:3, 9

Les chants de Maldoror: Chant premier (Lautréamont) **14**:167-212

"Chants the Epistle" (Pirandello)
   See "Canta l'epistola"

"Le chapeau chinois" (Villiers de l'Isle Adam)
   See "Le secret de l'ancienne musique"

"The Chaplet" (Saki) **12**:288

"A Chapter in the History of a Tyrone Family" (Le Fanu) **14**:220, 237, 239, 247

"Charade" (Auchincloss) **22**:51

"Charity" (Dybek) **55**:127-28

"Charity" (Ford) **56**:184, 196

"Charity" (O'Flaherty) **6**:264

"Charles" (Jackson) **9**:249; **39**:211, 219, 220, 222, 225

"Charles O'Malley" (Somerville & Ross) **56**:294

"Charles Ryder's Schooldays" (Waugh) **41**:331, 346-49

Charles Ryder's Schooldays (Waugh)
   See *Charles Ryder's Schooldays and Other Stories*

Charles Ryder's Schooldays and Other Stories (Waugh) **41**:329-31, 333-37

"El charlestón" (Donoso) **34**:30, 32, 49

"Charleston" (Donoso)
   See "El charlestón"

El charlestón (Donoso) **34**:24-5, 49-50

Charleston and Other Stories (Donoso)
   See *El charlestón*

"Charlie" (Chopin) **8**:84, 86

Charlie in the House of Rue (Coover) **15**:47, 59-60

"Charlie's Greek" (O'Faolain) **13**:320

"Charlotte Esmond" (Bates) **10**:112

"The Charlottenburg Night" (Morand)
   See "La nuit de Charlottenburg"

"A Charm" (Kipling) **5**:283

"The Charmed Spot" (Gogol)
   See "Zakoldovannoe mesto"

"A Charming Family" (Gissing) **37**:56

"Charnel House of the Moon" (Ligotti) **16**:277

"An Charraig Dhubh" (O'Flaherty) **6**:287

"The Chase" (Calvino) **48**:86, 88, 155

"The Chase" (Moravia) **26**:159, 161

"The Chaser" (Collier) **19**:98, 102, 105, 109, 111-12

"The Château of Prince Polignac" (Trollope) **28**:317-18, 328, 330, 343, 347

"The Chatelaine of Burnt Ridge" (Harte) **59**:308

"Le chat-qui-pelote" (Balzac)
   See "La maison du chat-qui-pelote"

"Chattanooga-Choo-Choo" (Donoso) **34**:8-9, 13, 17, 32-3

La chatte (Colette) **10**:225-56, 262, 265, 269-71, 276-77

"Chattery Teeth" (King) **17**:295

"Chaturanga" (Tagore) **48**:316

"Chava" (Aleichem) **33**:29

"Chawdron" (Huxley) **39**:162, 173, 176-77

Chayka (Chekhov) **51**:26

"Che ti dice la patria?" (Hemingway) **1**:232

"Che yü" (P'u Sung-ling) **31**:190

"Cheap in August" (Greene) **29**:200-02, 217

"The Cheapjack" (O'Connor) **5**:371, 389

"An Chearc Uisce" (O'Flaherty) **6**:287

"Che-Che-O" (Platonov) **42**:248

Cheering from the Sidelines (Lu Hsun)
   See *Nahan*

"The Cheery Soul" (Bowen) **3**:32, 54; **28**:3

"A Cheery Soul" (White) **39**:280, 282-83, 287, 291-94, 299-300, 316-17, 325, 327, 329, 344

"Cheese" (Coppard) **21**:16

"The Cheese Stands Alone" (Ellison) **14**:127

"Le Chef d'oeuvre inconnu" (Balzac) **5**:12, 16, 23, 48-9; **59**:21, 33-39, 55, 58-59, 61-62, 64

"Chefs Chafe as Steak Smugglers Flood Turkish Baths" (Perelman) **32**:240

"Chelkash" (Gorky) **28**:134, 136-37, 148, 154-56, 159, 178, 188-89

"Chelovecheskiy veter" (Pilnyak) **48**:265

"Chelovék na chasákh" (Leskov) **34**:117
"The Chemist's Wife" (Chekhov) **51**:89
"Ch'eng hsien" (P'u Sung-ling) **31**:190, 192
"Ch'eng the Immortal" (P'u Sung-ling)
   See "Ch'eng hsien"
Chéri (Colette) **10**:253-55, 257-58, 262, 267,
   270, 277-78, 282, 285-86, 288
"Cherries" (Dazai Osamu)
   See "Ōtō"
The Cherry Garden (Chekhov)
   See *Visňevyi sad*
The Cherry Orchard (Chekhov)
   See *Visňevyi sad*
"The Cherry Tree" (Coppard) **21**:16, 28
"Cherti" (Chekhov) **51**:180
"Chertopolokh" (Pilnyak) **48**:264-65
"The Cheshire Cheese" (Pilnyak)
   See "Ye Olde Cheshire Cheese"
"Chesniki" (Babel) **16**:26, 50, 58
"The Chess Match" (Hood) **42**:141
"The Chest and the Ghost" (Stendhal)
   See "Le coffre et le revenant"
"The Chestnut Tree" (Pritchett) **14**:271
"Chestnuts" (Lewis) **40**:281
"A cheval" (Maupassant) **1**:278, 280
"Un cheval de race" (Baudelaire) **18**:6, 20
"Le Chevalier double" (Gautier) **20**:8, 15, 31
"The Chevalier of the Place Blanche" (Rhys)
   21:56
"La chevelure" (Baudelaire) **18**:8
"La Chevelure" (Maupassant) **64**:316, 322-27
"Chi shêng" (P'u Sung-ling) **31**:204-05
"Chia êrh" (P'u Sung-ling) **31**:204
"Chia Feng-chih" (P'u Sung-ling) **31**:199
"Chiao Mi" (P'u Sung-ling) **31**:204
"Chiao-na" (P'u Sung-ling) **31**:205-6, 209
"Ch'iao-niang" (P'u Sung-ling) **31**:207, 209
"Chiao-nu" (P'u Sung-ling) **31**:196
"Chichi" (Dazai Osamu) **41**:249, 251
"Chichi Haha" (Kawabata) **17**:245-46
"Chichi yo, anata wa doko e ikuno ka?" (Oe)
   20:223-28
"Chickamauga" (Bierce) **9**:53-7, 64, 68, 70, 75,
   77, 87
"Chickamauga" (Wolfe) **33**:354, 372-75
Chicken Inspector No. 23 (Perelman) **32**:225,
   228, 242
"Chicken Pie" (Wilding) **50**:359
"Chicken-Grethe" (Andersen) **6**:7
"Chief Justice Harbottle" (Le Fanu)
   See "Mr. Justice Hartbottle"
"The Chief Mourner of Marne" (Chesterton)
   1:128, 138; **46**:111, 114, 135, 141
"Le Chien" (Aymé) **41**:6
"Le chien" (Maupassant) **1**:259
"Le chien et le flacon" (Baudelaire) **18**:17, 33
"Chiisai arubamu" (Dazai Osamu) **41**:256
"Chijin no ai" (Tanizaki) **21**:183-84, 192-93,
   195
"The Child" (Bates) **10**:112
"Child" (Frame) **29**:106
"Child" (Galsworthy) **22**:98
"The Child Born Out of the Fog" (Nin) **10**:301,
   303
"Child by Tiger" (Wolfe) **33**:364, 377, 386-87,
   389-91
The Child in Chains (Mauriac)
   See *L'enfant chargé de chaînes*
"A Child in the Dark, and a Foreign Father"
   (Lawson) **18**:258, 263
"The Child in the Grave" (Andersen) **6**:15, 26
"A Child of Christmas: A Christmas Tale of
   North and South" (Harris) **19**:183
"The Child of God" (O'Flaherty) **6**:262, 269-
   70, 281
"Child So Fair" (Betts) **45**:2
"The Child That Went with the Fairies" (Le
   Fanu) **14**:223
"The Child Who Favored Daughter" (Walker)
   5:403, 409-11
"The-Child-Who-Was-Tired" (Mansfield) **9**:286,
   310, 316; **23**:130

"Childhood" (Hesse)
   See "Kinderseele"
Childhood (Pilnyak)
   See *Detstvo*
Childhood (Tolstoy)
   See *Detstvo*
Childhood and Adolescence (Tolstoy)
   See *Detstvo*
Childhood and Other Neighborhoods (Dybek)
   55:125-30, 134-35, 137-40, 142, 150-51,
   156
"Childhood: At Grandmother's" (Babel) **16**:36
"A Childhood Incident" (Hood) **42**:191
"Childhood is Not Forever" (Farrell) **28**:122
Childhood Is Not Forever (Farrell) **28**:112, 116,
   121
"The Childhood of a Leader" (Sartre)
   See "L'Enfance d'un chef"
"The Childhood of Luvers" (Pasternak)
   See "Detstvo Luvers"
"The Childhood of Zhenya Luvers" (Pasternak)
   See "Detstvo Luvers"
"The Childish Fear" (Campbell) **19**:81
"The Children" (Algren) **33**:87-8, 106
"Children" (Ford) **56**:144-45, 151-52, 155-56,
   160, 171-73, 175, 177, 193-95
"The Children" (Oates) **6**:225
"Children" (Tanizaki)
   See "Shōnen"
Children and Older People (Suckow) **18**:391,
   394, 405
"Children Are Bored on Sunday" (Stafford)
   26:276-77
Children Are Bored on Sunday (Stafford)
   26:274, 281, 285, 307
"Children Are Civilians Too" (Boell) **23**:11
Children Are Civilians, Too (Boell) **23**:11
"The Children Green and Golden" (Metcalf)
   43:106
"Children of Captivity" (Somerville & Ross)
   56:294
"Children of Peace" (Far) **62**:50, 74
Children of the Bush (Lawson) **18**:241, 257
Children of the Frost (London) **4**:258, 282,
   285-88
"Children of the Great" (Lewis) **34**:163, 165
"The Children of the Night" (Pohl) **25**:224, 230
"The Children of the Pool" (Machen) **20**:177,
   198
The Children of the Pool (Machen) **20**:166,
   177-78, 194, 197
"The Children of the Zodiac" (Kipling) **5**:283,
   286
"Children on Their Birthdays" (Capote) **2**:61,
   63-6, 70, 72-3, 75-8; **47**:4, 10-13, 17, 31,
   37, 45, 54-5, 58
"The Children's Campaign" (Lagerkvist)
   See "Det lilla fälttåget"
"The Children's Game" (Stafford) **26**:300-07
"The Children's Grandmother" (Warner) **23**:370
"Children's Story" (Banks) **42**:60
"A Child's Christmas in Wales" (Thomas)
   44:341
"A Child's Dream of a Star" (Dickens) **17**:124,
   131
"The Child's Evening Prayer" (Andersen) **6**:15
A Child's Garden of Curses (Perelman) **32**:245
"A Child's Heart" (Hesse) **9**:227
"Child's Play" (Adams) **24**:17-18
"Child's Play" (Trevor) **58**:253, 258-59, 276,
   286-87
"Childybawn" (O'Faolain) **13**:288, 297, 301
"A Chilhowee Lily" (Murfree) **22**:212
"The Chimera" (Cheever) **1**:97, 105
"The Chimera" (Pavese) **19**:388
Chimera (Barth) **10**:44, 48-53, 55-7, 60-1, 64-5,
   68-9, 70-2, 74, 81, 83-4, 91, 93-5 100-04
The Chimes (Dickens) **17**:99, 101, 103-09, 115,
   127, 129-30, 132; **49**:7, 41, 66, 77-8, 101,
   155, 158, 174
"The Chimney" (Campbell) **19**:71
"Ch'in Kuei" (P'u Sung-ling) **31**:201

"Chin Music" (Stoker) **62**:252
"Ch'in shêng" (P'u Sung-ling) **31**:205, 207
"China" (Donoso) **34**:13-14, 30, 32, 49
"The Chinago" (London) **4**:263
"The Chinaman" (Wideman) **62**:262-65, 267,
   290
"The Chinaman's Ghost" (Lawson) **18**:245
"A chinela turca" (Machado de Assis) **24**:129
"A Chinese Boy-Girl" (Far) **62**:32, 35-38, 41,
   50, 77
"A Chinese Feud" (Far) **62**:31
"A Chinese Ishmael" (Far) **62**:11, 35, 37, 39-40
"The Chinese Lily" (Far) **62**:50, 55, 95
"A Chinese Perspective" (Aldiss) **36**:11
"Chinese Story" (Pilnyak) **48**:295-97
Chinese Story and Other Tales (Pilnyak)
   48:295-97
"A Chinese Tale" (Bulgakov) **18**:72-4, 99
"A Chinese Tom-Boy" (Far) **62**:77
"Ch'ing-mei" (P'u Sung-ling) **31**:207, 209-10
"The Chink" (Stegner) **27**:198-200, 202, 204-
   05, 224
"The Chink in Armor" (O'Hara) **15**:254-55
"Chin-ling Yi" (P'u Sung-ling) **31**:205
"Chintamans and Birds" (Čapek)
   See "Čintamani a ptáci"
"Il chiodo" (Pirandello) **22**:269
"A Chip of Glass Ruby" (Gordimer) **17**:155,
   161, 173, 181
"Chip Off the Old Block" (Stegner) **27**:227
"Chippy" (Narayan) **25**:134, 138, 140, 155-56
"Chistyi ponedel'nik" (Bunin) **5**:114
"Chitatel" (Gorky) **28**:187
"Chiu yu" (P'u Sung-ling) **31**:205-06
"Chiu-shan wang" (P'u Sung-ling) **31**:208
"The Choice" (Galsworthy) **22**:74, 79
"The Choice" (Wharton) **6**:418
"Choice Grain" (Leskov)
   See "Otbornoje zerno"
"A Choice of Butchers" (Trevor) **58**:230, 274
"A Choice of Profession" (Malamud) **15**:170,
   173, 175, 220-21
"Chopin in Winter" (Dybek) **55**:130, 132, 137,
   139-41, 153-54
"Chor' i Kalinyč" (Turgenev) **7**:313, 342, 362;
   57:264, 266-67, 283
"The Chords of Youth" (Bates) **10**:139
"The Chorus Girl" (Chekhov) **2**:130, 137, 139;
   51:49-50, 52, 88
"The Chosen" (Carpentier) **35**:106
"Choteau" (Bass) **60**:4-5, 30, 32
"Ch'ou hu" (P'u Sung-ling) **31**:204, 206, 208
"Chou San" (P'u Sung-ling) **31**:204-05
"Chrisp Street, Poplar" (Morrison) **40**:354
"The Christening" (Lawrence) **4**:197, 202, 234
"A Christian Education" (Spencer) **57**:198, 254
"A Christian Education" (Warren) **4**:390, 394,
   396; **58**:336, 354
"Christine's Letter" (Coppard) **21**:27
"Christmas" (McGahern) **17**:298, 302
"Christmas" (Nabokov) **11**:132-33
"The Christmas Banquet" (Hawthorne) **3**:181,
   183
Christmas Books (Dickens) **49**:38, 42, 49, 51,
   97-8, 101, 103, 105, 107, 162, 182
"Christmas by Injunction" (Henry) **5**:162
A Christmas Carol (Dickens)
   See *A Christmas Carol. In Prose. Being a*
   Ghost Story of Christmas
"A Christmas Carol for Harold Ross" (Boyle)
   5:64
A Christmas Carol. In Prose. Being a Ghost
   Story of Christmas (Dickens) **17**:99, 101,
   103-04, 108, 113-20, 124, 127, 129-30, 132,
   139, 143, 145-48; **49**:3-188
Christmas Chimes (Dickens)
   See *The Chimes*
"Christmas Day at Kirby Cottage" (Trollope)
   28:317, 332, 341, 348, 355
"Christmas Day at Thompson Hall" (Trollope)
   28:322-23, 332, 335, 346, 348, 355

"Christmas Day in the Workhouse" (Wilson) **21**:321-22, 330, 332, 339, 355, 360

"A Christmas Dinner" (Dickens) **17**:110, 116; **49**:164-65

"A Christmas Dream, and How It Came True" (Alcott) **27**:44

"Christmas Eve" (Gogol)
See "Noč pered roždestvom"

"Christmas Eve at Johnson's Drugs N Goods" (Bambara) **35**:27, 29

"Christmas Eve in the Streets" (Morrison) **40**:365

"Christmas Every Day" (Boell)
See "Nicht nur zur Weihnachtzeit"

Christmas Every Day and Other Stories Told for Children (Howells) **36**:400

"The Christmas Eves of Aunt Elise: A Tale of Possession in Old Grosse Pointe" (Ligotti) **16**:271, 278, 283

"Christmas Gift" (Warren) **4**:388-90, 394; **58**:310, 317, 354

"A Christmas in Wyoming" (Gilchrist) **63**:36

"Christmas is a Sad Season for the Poor" (Cheever) **1**:107

"Christmas Jenny" (Freeman) **1**:191; **47**:93, 104, 147, 168, 190

"A Christmas Memory" (Capote) **2**:67, 72-3, 75-6; **47**:19, 38, 40-2, 55-6, 63

"Christmas Morning" (O'Connor) **5**:378

"A Christmas Party and a Wedding" (Dostoevsky)
See "A Christmas Tree and a Wedding"

"A Christmas Recollection" (Page)
See "Polly: A Christmas Recollection"

"A Christmas Song" (Bates) **10**:117

"Christmas Story" (Mauriac)
See "Conte de Noël"

"A Christmas Story" (Naipaul) **38**:321, 328, 346

"A Christmas Tale" (Oliphant) **25**:194-95, 204

"A Christmas Tree and a Wedding" (Dostoevsky) **2**:171, 190, 193-95, 197

"Christmas with Two Children's Stories" (Hesse) **9**:241, 244

"Christopherson" (Gissing) **37**:52-3, 64, 81

"Christos v gost'ax u muzika" (Leskov) **34**:108

"Chromium" (Levi) **12**:256, 268

"The Chronic Argonauts" (Wells) **6**:388

Chronicle of a Death Foretold (García Márquez)
See *Crónica de una muerte anunciada*

The Chronicles of Aunt Minervy Ann (Harris) **19**:147, 150-51, 155

Chronicles of Bustos Domecq (Bioy Casares)
See *Crónicas de Bustos Domecq*

The Chronicles of Clovis (Saki) **12**:287-88, 293, 323, 330-35

Chronicles of Golden Friars (Le Fanu) **14**:220, 245

Chronicles of Martin Hewitt (Morrison) **40**:332, 349

Chronicles of the Canongate (Scott) **32**:285-86, 292, 298-302, 304-05, 317-19

Chroniques (Maupassant) **64**:310

Chroniques du XXme siècle (Morand) **22**:172

Chroniques italiennes (Stendhal) **27**:230-32, 247-50, 260-63

"Chronopolis" (Ballard) **1**:69, 84; **53**:9-10, 29, 42, 49

Chronopolis, and Other Stories (Ballard) **1**:71

"Chrysalis" (Bradbury) **29**:82

"The Chrysanthemums" (Steinbeck) **11**:207, 210, 214, 221, 223-37, 240-41, 244; **37**:321-62

"Chu Chu, The Devotion of Enriquez" (Harte) **8**:228

Chuanqi (Chang) **28**:20; 26; 31; 38; 40

"An Chulaith Nua" (O'Flaherty) **6**:287

"Chul'dik i Epishka" (Platonov) **42**:266

"Chums" (Gorky) **28**:137

"Chun Ah Chun" (London) **4**:269

"The Church at Novograd" (Babel) **16**:25, 28, 52, 56

"The Church in High Street" (Campbell) **19**:61, 66, 72, 90

"A Church Mouse" (Freeman) **47**:85, 105, 145, 147, 149, 151, 168, 191

"The Church That Was at Antioch" (Kipling) **5**:272

"The Church with an Overshot Wheel" (Henry) **5**:163, 180-81

"Chūtō" (Akutagawa Ryūnosuke) **44**:74-5

"The Chymist" (Ligotti) **16**:266, 269, 271, 280-81, 283

"Ciaula Discovers the Moon" (Pirandello) **22**:250

"Cicadas" (Bunin) **5**:82

"Cicely's Dream" (Chesnutt) **7**:22-3, 33-4, 37; **54**:9, 11, 13, 49, 58-61, 64

"The Cicerone" (McCarthy) **24**:215-16, 224, 226-27

"Ciclismo en Gringnan" (Cortázar) **7**:95

"The Cigarstore Robbery" (Hemingway) **1**:208

"Ćilim" (Andrić) **36**:43

"Cimutti" (Svevo) **25**:329

"Cinci" (Pirandello) **22**:240, 244

"Cinderella" (Grimm and Grimm) **36**:190, 196, 208

"The Cinderella Waltz" (Beattie) **11**:8

"The Cinema" (Salter) **58**:173-74, 176, 190-91, 196

"Cinnamon Roses" (Freeman) **47**:105

Cinnamon Shops (Schulz) **13**:326-27, 332, 343-44

Cinque romanzi brevi (Ginzburg) **65**:115, 119, 126, 130-32, 140, 145

"Čintamani a ptáci" (Čapek) **36**:97, 99, 127

"La ciociara" (Moravia) **26**:151

"Circe" (Welty) **51**:263, 305

"A Circle in the Fire" (O'Connor) **1**:343-44, 347, 356; **23**:185, 235; **61**:227-28, 234, 237

"A Circle in the Water" (Howells) **36**:397-98

"Circle of Prayer" (Munro) **3**:348

"The Circular Ruins" (Borges)
See "Las ruinas circulares"

"The Circular Valley" (Bowles) **3**:66, 69-71, 79

"Circumstantial Evidence" (Bradbury)
See "April 2000: The Third Expedition"

"Circus" (Andrić)
See "Cirkus"

"The Circus" (Porter) **4**:331-34, 340, 353; **31**:175; **43**:182, 258-9, 201, 305-6

"The Circus" (Saroyan) **21**:172

"Circus at Dawn" (Wolfe) **33**:369, 401

"The Circus at Denby" (Jewett) **6**:150, 155, 167

"The Circus at Luxor" (Naipaul) **38**:346

"The Circus Horse" (Colette) **10**:292

"The Circus in the Attic" (Warren) **4**:387-89, 391, 395-98, 404; **58**:310, 317, 336, 354-55

The Circus in the Attic, and Other Stories (Warren) **4**:387-90, 393, 396-97; **58**:308-9, 316-17, 336, 339, 344-47, 354

"Circus in Town" (Ross) **24**:305, 310-11, 315, 319, 323

"Cirkus" (Andrić) **36**:66-7

"The Cistern" (Bradbury) **29**:66

"Cities" (Kelly) **50**:286-88

Cities (Kelly) **50**:289, 295

"Citizen" (Pritchett) **14**:297

"Citizens of the Third Grade" (Saroyan) **21**:163

"La citta" (Pavese) **19**:378, 385

"The City" (Bradbury) **29**:81

"The City" (Hesse) **9**:230, 235

"The City" (Pavese)
See "La citta"

"The City" (Updike) **13**:403, 409

"City Boy" (Michaels) **16**:301, 303, 312, 321

"The City Coat of Arms" (Kafka) **29**:371

"City Life" (Barthelme) **2**:40; **55**:13-14, 74, 76, 84, 119

"City Life" (Gordon) **59**:261

City Life (Barthelme) **2**:30-5, 37-9; **55**:3-7, 9, 11, 13-15, 27-9, 31, 34-6, 39, 51, 53, 56-7, 66-7, 74-6, 82, 88, 111

"A City of Churches" (Barthelme) **2**:37, 39, 41, 54; **55**:41,73

"The City of Dreadful Night" (Henry) **5**:188, 197

"City of Golddiggers" (Kluge) **61**:56

"City of London Churches" (Dickens) **17**:123

"The City of Refuge" (Fisher) **25**:4-5, 7-9, 13, 17-27

"A City of the Dead, a City of the Living" (Gordimer) **17**:171, 174, 191

"The City of the Living" (Stegner) **27**:195, 198, 219-20, 223-26

The City of the Living, and Other Stories (Stegner) **27**:193, 196-99, 207, 219

The City of the Yellow Devil (Gorky) **28**:135

"The City on the Neva" (Solzhenitsyn)
See "Gorod na Neve"

Ciudad Real (Castellanos) **39**:29, 47, 49, 50, 55, 56, 73

"Civil War" (O'Flaherty) **6**:262, 274

Claire Lenoir (Villiers de l'Isle Adam) **14**:376

"The Clairvoyant" (Čapek)
See "Jasnovidec"

The Clairvoyant (Gass) **12**:148

"The Clam" (P'u Sung-ling)
See "Ge"

"Clancy in the Tower of Babel" (Cheever) **1**:107; **38**:52

"Clara" (Meyer) **30**:249

"Clara" (O'Brien) **10**:333

"Clara Milich" (Turgenev)
See "Klara Milich"

"Clarence" (Dreiser)
See "Black Sheep No. Five: Clarence"

"Clarence" (Harte) **8**:222, 251-52

"Clarisa" (Allende) **65**:10, 26, 51

"Clarissa" (Morand) **22**:156-57, 165, 168

"Clarissa and the Depths" (Betts) **45**:4, 28-9

"Class" (Bukowski) **45**:53-4

"The Classical Annex" (Forster) **27**:93, 96, 107

Claudine à l'école (Colette) **10**:269

Claudine at School (Colette)
See *Claudine à l'école*

"Claudius' Diary" (Shiga)
See "Kurōdiasu no nikki"

"Claudius' Journal" (Shiga)
See "Kurōdiasu no nikki"

"Clave para un amor" (Bioy Casares) **17**:58

"El clavo" (Alarcon) **64**:2-3, 5-6, 9, 19, 28-31, 36, 38-39

"The Claxtons" (Huxley) **39**:158-59, 173, 177

"Clay" (Joyce) **3**:205, 209, 211, 221-22, 226, 233-34, 237, 247; **26**:46-7, 50, 61, 79; **44**:264, 284; **64**:242, 244, 259

"Clay" (White) **39**:280, 283, 286, 289-90, 292-93, 297, 312, 316-17, 323, 325, 328-29, 336, 344

"La Clé sous le paillasson" (Aymé) **41**:23

"Clean Minded People" (Bradbury) **53**:208

"A Clean, Well-Lighted Place" (Hemingway) **1**:216, 230, 232, 237-38; **36**:294, 298-99; **40**:154-269

"The Cleaner's Story" (Sansom) **21**:83

"The Clear Track" (O'Hara) **15**:289

"A Cleared Path" (Gilman) **13**:141-42

"A Clearing in the Sky" (Stuart) **31**:235, 264

Clearing in the Sky and Other Stories (Stuart) **31**:234-35, 243, 261, 264

"The Clemency of the Court" (Cather) **2**:96, 100, 103, 105; **50**:59-60, 68-9, 71, 73, 89-91, 104, 106

"Clement Moore's Vocation" (Davis) **38**:120-21

"Clementina" (Cheever) **1**:100, 107; **38**:53

"Clementine" (Caldwell) **19**:56

"Clerkenwell" (Morrison) **40**:353

"The Clerk's Quest" (Moore)
See "Tóir Mhic Uí Dhíomasuigh"

"The Clerk's Tale" (Pritchett) **14**:271

"Clever Elsie" (Grimm and Grimm) **36**:188

"The Clever Little Tailor" (Grimm and Grimm) **36**:229-30
"The Clever Little Trick" (Zoshchenko) **15**:404
"A Clever-Kids Story" (Beattie) **11**:6, 15-16
The Clicking of Cuthbert (Wodehouse) **2**:344, 354
"The Climber" (Mason) **4**:3
"The Climbers" (Andrić) **36**:78-9
Clive Barker's Books of Blood, Vols. I-III (Barker) **53**:136-42, 145
Clive Barker's Books of Blood, Vols. IV-VI (Barker) **53**:136-42, 145
Clive Barker's Books of Blood, Volume 1 (Barker) **53**:140, 168
Clive Barker's Books of Blood, Volume 2 (Barker) **53**:143, 173, 178
Clive Barker's Books of Blood, Volume 3 (Barker) **53**:143, 175
Clive Barker's Books of Blood, Volume 4 (Barker)
    See *The Inhuman Condition: Tales of Terror*
"The Cloak" (Gogol)
    See "Shinel"
"The Clock" (Baudelaire)
    See "L'horloge"
"A Clod of Earth" (Akutagawa Ryūnosuke)
    See "Ikkai no tsuchi"
"A Clod of Soil" (Akutagawa Ryūnosuke)
    See "Ikkai no tsuchi"
"Clone" (Cortázar) **7**:69-71
"Clorinda Walks in Heaven" (Coppard) **21**:27
Clorinda Walks in Heaven (Coppard) **21**:7-8, 15
"A Close Shave" (Stuart) **31**:251
Closed All Night (Morand)
    See *Fermé la nuit*
"The Closed Door" (Andrić)
    See "Zatvorena vrata"
"The Closed Door" (Donoso)
    See "La puerta cerrada"
"Closed Space" (Beckett) **16**:123, 126
"Closer to You" (Bradfield) **65**:68
"Clothe the Naked" (Parker) **2**:275, 280-81, 286
"The Cloud" (Fowles) **33**:233, 235-36, 240, 242-44, 246-49, 258, 260-61, 263-64, 266, 274-76, 278-80, 289-90
"Cloud and Sun" (Tagore)
    See "Megh o Roudra"
"Cloud, Castle, Lake" (Nabokov)
    See "Oblako, ozero, bashnia"
"The Cloud Sculptors of Coral D" (Ballard) **53**:72, 74, 77
"Cloud Sculptures" (Ballard) **53**:79
The Cloven Viscount (Calvino)
    See *Il visconte dimezzato*
"Clowns in Clover" (Gordimer) **17**:153
"The Club Bedroom" (Auchincloss) **22**:10
"Le club des hachichins" (Gautier) **20**:16, 23-5, 31
"Club of Misunderstood Men" (Chesterton) **46**:117
"The Club of Queer Trades" (Chesterton) **46**:115
The Club of Queer Trades (Chesterton) **1**:120, 122, 139; **46**:119, 121
"Clyde" (Farrell) **28**:100
"Clytie" (Welty) **1**:466, 468, 471, 481, 495; **51**:282, 305-6, 318-19, 338, 340
"Cmyk . . . Cmyk . . . Cmyk!" (Turgenev)
    See "Stuk...stuk...stuk"
"The Coach House" (Chekhov) **2**:128
"The Coachman" (Gorky)
    See "Izvozchik"
The Coast of Chicago (Dybek) **55**:130-34, 137-43, 145, 150-52, 154, 156
"The Coat of Many Colors" (Far) **62**:32, 35, 37-38
"Cobardía" (Pardo Bazán) **30**:294
"Coburg House" (Hardy) **60**:188
"The Cobweb" (Saki) **12**:296
"The Coca-Cola Kid" (Moorhouse) **40**:289

"Cock Crow" (Gordon) **15**:123-24, 126
"Cock-a-Doodle-Doo!" (Melville) **1**:295, 298, 303, 305, 322; **17**:363
"Cockadoodledoo" (Singer) **3**:358
"The Cockatoos" (White) **39**:302, 309-11, 319-20, 324-27, 329-31, 346
The Cockatoos (White) **39**:301, 303-04, 306, 308-10, 319-20, 337, 343, 345-46, 350, 352
"Cockney Corners" (Morrison) **40**:353
"Cockroaches" (Schulz) **13**:333-34
"Cocktail Party" (Arreola) **38**:21
"Cocky Olly" (Pritchett) **14**:300
"Coco" (Maupassant) **1**:275
"The Cocoons" (Ligotti) **16**:282-84
"Cocotte" (White) **39**:293
"Le Cocu nombreux" (Aymé) **41**:22-24
"Coda" (Selby) **20**:253, 255-57
"The Code of the Herdsman" (Lewis) **34**:165, 173, 177
"Un coeur simple" (Maupassant) **1**:286
Un coeur simple (Flaubert) **11**:37, 45-6, 54-6, 58-66, 70-1, 80-1, 84, 87, 91, 94, 96-9, 101, 103; **60**:110-16, 118-19, 123, 126, 128, 130-33, 135-39, 154, 159-60, 162-64, 166, 168-72
"The Coffer and the Ghost" (Stendhal)
    See "Le coffre et le revenant"
The Coffin-Maker (Pushkin)
    See "Grobovshchik"
"Le coffre et le revenant" (Stendhal) **27**:247-49, 259
"Coggin's Property" (Stoker) **62**:252
"Cogwheel" (Akutagawa Ryūnosuke)
    See "Haguruma"
"The Coice of a Bride" (Hoffmann)
    See "Die Brautwahl"
"A Coincidence" (Farrell) **28**:100
"Coitus 80" (Ballard) **53**:19
"The Cold" (Warner) **23**:370
"Cold Autumn" (Bunin) **5**:115-16
"A Cold, Calculating Thing" (O'Hara) **15**:252
"A Cold Day" (Saroyan) **21**:143
"Cold Ground Was My Bed Last Night" (Garrett) **30**:166
Cold Ground Was My Bed Last Night (Garrett) **30**:173-74
"The Cold Heights" (Appelfeld)
    See "Bagovah hakar"
"The Cold House" (O'Hara) **15**:258, 265
"Cold Print" (Campbell) **19**:61-2, 64, 66, 71-3, 81, 88, 90-1
Cold Print (Campbell) **19**:66, 70-2, 80, 87, 90
Cold Snap (Jones) **56**:276-77, 279-80, 284-85
"Cold Spell" (Lewis) **40**:282
"Cold Spring" (Appelfeld)
    See "Aviv kar"
"Cold-Blooded" (Atwood) **46**:74-5, 99
"Colic" (O'Flaherty) **6**:271
"Coll. SS. Trins. Ap. Toron.—A Fable" (Clarke) **45**:79-80, 91, 103
"Collaboration" (Collier) **19**:98, 114
Collages (Nin) **10**:305-06, 308
Collected Fictions (Borges) **41**:157, 159, 162-63, 166
Collected Ghost Stories (James) **16**:227, 230-32, 239, 241, 246, 249, 251, 255
Collected Short Fiction (Cather)
    See *Willa Cather's Collected Short Fiction, 1892-1912*
Collected Short Stories (Forster) **27**:97-8, 103
Collected Short Stories (Huxley) **39**:161-62
The Collected Short Stories of Conrad Aiken (Aiken) **9**:9, 12, 28, 41
The Collected Stories (Babel) **16**:6, 8, 11, 14, 17, 19, 21, 25, 35, 41, 59
The Collected Stories (Boyle) **16**:155
Collected Stories (García Márquez) **8**:182-84
Collected Stories (Gilchrist) **63**:27-29, 35-36
Collected Stories (Greene) **29**:208, 213, 216-17
Collected Stories (Lavin) **4**:174
Collected Stories (Lessing) **6**:196, 218-19; **61**:94, 96-97

Collected Stories (Malamud)
    See *The Stories of Bernard Malamud*
Collected Stories (Mansfield) **9**:281
The Collected Stories (McGahern) **17**:318, 322
Collected Stories (O'Connor) **5**:398
The Collected Stories (Price) **22**:384-85, 388
Collected Stories (Pritchett) **14**:301
The Collected Stories (Thomas) **44**:340-41
The Collected Stories (Trevor) **21**:260-61, 264; **58**:222, 228-30, 241, 263, 277, 283, 288-90, 295-97
Collected Stories I (Spark) **10**:359-60, 368
Collected Stories: 1939-1976 (Bowles) **3**:65, 68-9
The Collected Stories of Caroline Gordon (Gordon) **15**:137-38, 141
Collected Stories of Charles Chesnutt (Chesnutt) **54**:50-54
The Collected Stories of Colette (Colette) **10**:280, 291
Collected Stories of Eileen Chang (Chang) **28**:30; 37
The Collected Stories of Ellen Glasgow (Glasgow) **34**:68
The Collected Stories of Eudora Welty (Welty) **51**:297-98, 300-08, 310-11, 314-18
The Collected Stories of Hortense Calisher (Calisher) **15**:7-8, 15, 19, 21
The Collected Stories of Isaac Bashevis Singer (Singer) **3**:383-84; **53**:274, 327
The Collected Stories of Jean Stafford (Stafford) **26**:281, 285-86, 289-91, 312
The Collected Stories of Katherine Anne Porter (Porter) **4**:347, 351, 358, 361; **31**:167; **43**:236, 240, 245, 290, 303-14
The Collected Stories of Louis Auchincloss (Auchincloss) **22**:52-3
The Collected Stories of Peter Taylor (Taylor) **10**:389
The Collected Stories of Philip K. Dick (Dick) **57**:68, 78, 114, 127, 151
The Collected Stories Of Seán O'Faoláin (O'Faolain) **13**:313
Collected Stories of Wallace Stegner (Stegner) **27**:220, 222-23, 226-27
Collected Stories of William Faulkner (Faulkner) **1**:151, 161-62, 177, 181; **42**:116-18
Collected Stories to Collected Short Stories (Huxley)
    See *Collected Short Stories*
The Collected Tales of A. E. Coppard (Coppard) **21**:18
The Collected Tales of E. M. Forster (Forster) **27**:74
Collected Work (Andrić) **36**:50-1
Collected Works (Bunin) **5**:99
Collected Works (Harte) **59**:332
Collected Works (Walser) **20**:339
The Collected Works of Edgar Allan Poe (Poe) **54**:154, 156-60, 223, 237
Collected Works of Henry Lawson (Lawson) **18**:210
Collected Writings (Bierce) **9**:75
"The Collection" (Pritchett) **14**:296, 298
"A Collection of Bones" (Davie) **52**:8
Collection of Fairy Tales (Dazai Osamu)
    See *Otogi zōshi*
"The Collector" (Auchincloss) **22**:13
"The Collector" (Clarke) **45**:75-6, 88-9, 96
"Collector" (Cowan) **28**:81
"Collector of Innocents" (Auchincloss) **22**:49
"The Collector of Treasures" (Head) **52**:194, 202-4, 206-7, 216, 218, 228, 237-38, 247
The Collector of Treasures and Other Botswana Village Tales (Head) **52**:187-88, 190, 192-93, 205, 208-12, 214, 236
"Collectors" (Carver) **8**:11, 19; **51**:12
"Le collier" (Maupassant) **1**:259
"Colloquy" (Jackson) **9**:252; **39**:211, 223, 224, 225, 228

"The Colloquy of Monos and Una" (Poe) 1:401-02; 34:250, 258; 35:310
Colomba (Mérimée) 7:276-7, 280-3, 290, 294-5, 300-05, 308
Le Colonel Chabert (Balzac) 5:8, 18, 24-7; 59:16-19, 21
The Colonel Has No One to Write Him (García Márquez)
See *El colonel no tiene quien le escribe*
"Colonel Julian" (Bates) 10:117
Colonel Julian, and Other Stories (Bates) 10:115-17
El colonel no tiene quien le escribe (García Márquez) 8:162, 185, 192-97
"Colonel Starbottle for the Plaintiff" (Harte) 8:229
"Colonel Starbottle's Client" (Harte) 8:216, 245
"The Colonel's Awakening" (Dunbar) 8:121, 127, 131, 148
"The Colonel's Foundation" (Auchincloss) 22:53
"The Colonel's Lady" (Maugham) 8:366, 380
"The Colonel's 'Nigger Dog'" (Harris) 19:182
"El coloquio de los perros" (Cervantes) 12:4, 8, 14-16, 21, 24, 26-8, 33-4, 37-8,
"Colorado" (Beattie) 11:4-5, 7, 17
"The Colored Girls of Passenack—Old and New" (Williams) 31:302, 332, 357, 359
Colored Stones (Stifter)
See *Bunte Steine*
"Colour and Line" (Babel) 16:22, 27, 59
"The Colour Out of Space" (Lovecraft) 3:261, 263, 267-69, 274, 281, 290-91; 52:252, 270, 305, 319-20, 337, 348-49, 351, 354, 362
"The Colt" (Stegner) 27:194, 196-97, 199
"Come Again Tomorrow" (Gordimer) 17:165
"Come Along, Marjorie" (Spark) 10:355-57, 359, 365, 370
Come Along with Me (Jackson) 9:254; 39:210
Come Back, Dr. Caligari (Barthelme) 2:26-9, 31, 37-9, 46, 49, 51; 55:10-11, 14-15, 70, 28, 30, 66-7, 74, 106
"Come Dance with Me in Ireland" (Jackson) 39:210, 211, 224, 225
"Come in if You Love Money" (Algren) 33:96-7
"Come on a Coming" (Dixon) 16:208
"Come On Back" (Gardner) 7:224-25, 227-28, 235, 240-41
"Come On, Wagon" (Henderson) 29:317
"Come Out the Wilderness" (Baldwin) 10:2-3, 5, 7-9
"Começos de Uma Fortuna" (Lispector) 34:194
"The Comedian" (Narayan) 25:140-41
La Comédie humaine (Balzac) 5:6-13, 16-17, 19-20, 26-33, 43, 48; 59:6, 11, 32, 41
"Les comédiens sans le savoir" (Balzac) 5:31
"Comedy Cop" (Farrell) 28:90
"Comedy Entombed: 1930" (Williams) 31:327, 333, 345, 348-49
"Comedy Evening" (Walser) 20:353
"A Comedy in Rubber" (Henry) 5:158
"Comedy Is Where You Die and They Don't Bury You Because You Can Still Walk" (Saroyan) 21:144
"The Comedy of War" (Harris) 19:183
"La Comendadora" (Alarcon) 64:3, 5-6, 9, 26, 28, 39, 44
"Comet" (Salter) 58:195-96
"The Comet" (Schulz)
See "Kometa"
"The Comforts of Home" (O'Connor) 1:343-44, 351, 353, 365; 61:201, 203
The Comic Inferno (Aldiss) 36:18
"Comic Strip" (Garrett) 30:165
"Coming Apart" (Walker) 5:412-14
"Coming, Aphrodite!" (Cather) 2:91-2, 95, 104, 111-14, **50**:53, 57, 76, 95, 141, 214, 232, 241, 243-44, 248
"Coming Attractions" (Wolff) 63:261, 301-3, 306, 310, 318-21, 338
"Coming Down the Mountain" (Stuart) 31:265

"Coming, Eden Bower!" (Cather)
See "Coming, Aphrodite!"
"Coming Home" (Bowen) 3:40
"Coming into His Kingdom" (McGahern) 17:302, 322
"The Coming of Abel Behenna" (Stoker) 62:238, 253-54
"The Coming Out of Maggie" (Henry) 5:171, 197; 49:197
"Coming to Grief" (Barker) 53:150-53, 157-59, 162, 172-73
Command, and I Will Obey You (Moravia)
See *Una cosa è una cosa*
A Commentary (Galsworthy) 22:59-60, 97, 99
"Commerce and Sentiment" (Harris) 19:183
"A Committee-Man of 'The Terror'" (Hardy) 2:220
The Common Chord (O'Connor) 5:364-65, 371, 378, 380, 383-84
"A Common Confusion" (Kafka) 5:207
"The Common Day" (Cheever) 38:54
"Common Meter" (Fisher) 25:14, 16-20, 22-3, 25
"The Common Round" (Mansfield) 9:304
Common Sense (Heinlein) 55:171-73, 214, 232, 234
"Common Sense Should Tell You" (O'Hara) 15:250
"A Commonplace Story" (Gordimer) 17:167
"Communion" (Coppard) 21:11, 15
"Communist" (Ford) 56:137-38, 140-41, 144, 146, 152, 172-73, 177, 194
"The Commuter" (Dick) 57:106
"Cómo perdí la vista" (Bioy Casares) 17:83
"The Companion" (Campbell) 19:65, 75
"The Companion" (Machado de Assis) 24:153
Company (Beckett) 16:100-02, 110-12, 115, 129, 134, 137
"Company for Gertrude" (Wodehouse) 2:346
"The Company Is Not Responsible" (McCarthy) 24:221-22
"Company Manners" (Gaskell) 25:65-6
"A Company of Laughing Faces" (Gordimer) 17:155-56, 161
"The Company of the Dead" (Price) 22:384, 386
"The Company of Wolves" (Carter) 13:5, 7, 9, 13-14, 27, 28
The Company She Keeps (McCarthy) 24:212-13, 215-19, 221, 228
"The Compartment" (Carver) 8:26, 32, 35
The Compass Rose (Le Guin) 12:235
"A Compatriot" (Bunin) 5:81
"Compatriots from an Earlier Age" (Arnim)
See "Altdeutsche Landsleute"
"Compensation" (Galsworthy) 22:74, 79
"Competition at Slush Creek" (Stuart) 31:252
"The Competitor" (Galsworthy) 22:99
"The Complaint Ledger" (Chekhov) 2:130
Complete Collected Stories (Pritchett) 14:302-03, 305
Complete Collected Works and Letters (Chekhov) 51:135, 170, 175, 187, 209, 211
Complete Father Brown (Chesterton) 46:142-43
The Complete Fiction of Bruno Schulz (Schulz) 13:342
"A Complete Life" (Pilnyak) 48:284-85, 292
"The Complete Life of John Hopkins" (Henry) 5:159, 188
The Complete Short Stories (Trollope) 28:332-33, 343, 349-51
The Complete Short Stories of Ernest Hemingway (Hemingway) 40:191-92; 63:118-19, 121
The Complete Short Stories of Thomas Wolfe (Wolfe) 33:396-99
The Complete Stories of Erskine Caldwell (Caldwell) 19:19-20, 25
The Complete Stories of Flannery O'Connor (O'Connor) 61:147, 187-93, 197, 218, 229-35, 237

Complete Tales of Uncle Remus (Harris) 19:193-97
Complete Works (Borges)
See *Obras completas*
Complete Works (Peretz)
See *Ale verk*
The Complete Works of Edgar Allen Poe (Poe) 54:154, 156-60, 237
The Complete Works of Nathanael West (West) 16:367
The Completion of Love (Musil)
See "Vollendung der Liebe"
"A Complicated Nature" (Trevor) 21:262; 58:208, 231
"Compression" (Thomas) 20:323-26, 328
"Compulsory Figures" (Thomas) 20:320, 322
"Comrade Stanley" (Farrell) 28:98, 122, 125
"Comrades" (Gordimer) 17:186, 188
"Comrades in Arms" (Gissing) 37:64-5
"The Comte de Pralines" (Somerville & Ross) 56:320
Le Comte de Saint-Germain (Nerval) 18:371
"Comte Hippolit" (Hoffmann)
See "Der Vampyrismus"
"Con legítimo orgullo" (Cortázar) 7:94
"Con todo el respeto debido" (Allende) 65:39
"The Concentration City" (Ballard)
See "Build-Up"
"Concerning the Bodyguard" (Barthelme) 2:44; 55:57, 59-60
"Concerning Wet Snow" (Dostoevsky)
See "Apropos of the Wet Snow"
"Concert" (Wideman) 62:269, 281
"Le conchiglie e il tempo" (Calvino) 48:155
Concierto barroco (Carpentier) 35:130-34
"Conclusion" (Gorky) 28:146
"The Concrete Mixer" (Bradbury) 29:42, 62
"Concussion" (Campbell) 19:63, 74, 78, 86, 92
"Condemned Door" (Cortázar) 7:69
"El condenado" (Arreola) 38:7, 9
Condensed Novels, and Other Papers (Harte) 8:225, 230, 249
"The Condominium" (Elkin) 12:93-5, 106-07, 110
"Conducta en los velorios" (Cortázar) 7:92
"The Conductor and a Member of the Imperial Family" (Bulgakov) 18:90
"The Conductor Kalina's Story" (Čapek)
See "Historie dirigenta Kaliny"
"The Cone" (Wells) 6:361, 383
"Coney Island" (Beattie) 11:25-6, 29
Confabulario (Arreola) 38:3-13, 18, 20-21, 23-26, 28-29
Confabulario Total, 1941-61 (Arreola) 38:12-13
Confabulario y Varia invencion (Arreola) 38:8
"The Conference" (Singer) 3:385, 388
"A Conference of the Powers" (Kipling) 5:259
Conference-ville (Moorhouse) 40:294-97, 304-305, 307, 309, 323-24
"Confession" (Andrić) 36:45, 70
"Confession" (Gorky)
See "Ispoved"
"The Confession of Brother Grimes" (Warren) 4:390, 394, 396; 58:336, 354
"The Confessional" (O'Faolain) 13:293
"Le confessioni del vegliardo" (Svevo) 25:334, 340, 350, 352-53, 360-61
"Confessions of a Baby Chick" (Perelman) 32:240
"Confessions of a Man Insane Enough to Live with Beasts" (Bukowski) 45:64
"Confessions of a Pornographer's Shroud" (Barker) 53:137, 154, 157, 162-63, 168
"Confidencia" (Pardo Bazán) 30:295
"Confidencias de un lobo" (Bioy Casares) 17:53, 56
"Confissões de uma viúva moça" (Machado de Assis) 24:131
"Le confitéor de l'artiste" (Baudelaire) 18:4-5, 8, 18
"A Conflict Ended" (Freeman) 1:196-97, 199; 47:118-19, 148-49, 151, 162, 182, 186

"Confused" (Singer) 3:384
"Confused Head" (Shiga) 23:333
"The Conger Eel" (O'Flaherty) 6:269, 274
El congreso (Borges) 4:27-8
The Congress (Borges)
　　See *El congreso*
Conjugal Love (Moravia)
　　See *L'amore coniugale, e altri racconti*
The Conjure Woman (Chesnutt) 7:2-5, 7-12, 14,
　　26, 30, 33, 38-40, 43; 54:8-9, 14, 20-5, 27-
　　48, 63-4
"The Conjurer's Revenge" (Chesnutt) 7:6-7,
　　10, 18, 42; 54:35, 49-40, 42, 44-5
"The Conjuring Contest" (Dunbar) 8:122, 149
"Connections" (Davie) 52:6
"The Connoisseur" (de la Mare) 14:70, 82
The Connoisseur, and Other Stories (de la
　　Mare) 14:70
"The Connoisseurs" (Stafford) 26:298
"The Connor Girls" (O'Brien) 10:334, 341
"A Conquest of Humility" (Freeman) 1:198
"Conscience" (Galsworthy) 22:74, 101
"The Conscript" (Balzac) 5:12-13
"A Conscript's Christmas" (Harris) 19:181-82
"Consequences" (Cather) 2:110-11, 115; 50:77
"Conservatory" (Barthelme) 2:51
"Consolation" (Pardo Bazán) 30:290
"Consolation" (Verga) 21:298
"Consolations of Age" (Aldiss) 36:20
"The Consolations of Horror" (Ligotti) 16:261,
　　271, 277-78, 283, 285, 288, 294
"A Consolatory Tale" (Dinesen) 7:164, 186,
　　193, 200
"A Conspiracy of Silence" (Somerville &
　　Ross) 56:301, 316, 333, 338
"The Constant Tin Solider" (Andersen)
　　See "Den standhaftige Tinsoldat"
"A Constellation of Events" (Updike) 13:402
"The Consummation" (Galsworthy) 22:98
"Conte de fin d'été" (Villiers de l'Isle Adam)
　　14:390
"Conte de Noël" (Aymé) 41:13
"Conte de Noël" (Mauriac) 24:185, 198-99, 208
"Conte du milieu" (Aymé) 41:10
Contes cruels (Villiers de l'Isle Adam) 14:377-
　　78, 380-81, 391, 395-96, 403, 411
Contes cruels: Nouveaux contes cruels (Villiers
　　de l'Isle Adam) 14:404, 412
Contes de la bécasse (Maupassant) 1:257
Contes drolatiques (Balzac) 5:19-21
Les Contes du chat perché (Aymé) 41:4-5, 7,
　　10, 13-16, 18-19
Contes philosophiques (Balzac)
　　See *Romans et contes philosophiques*
"The Contessina" (Bowen) 3:40
"The Contest" (Paley) 8:388, 394, 398
"A Contest" (Svevo)
　　See "Una lotta"
"The Contest for Aaron Gold" (Roth) 26:251-53
"A Contest of Ladies" (Sansom) 21:84, 94, 111,
　　126
A Contest of Ladies (Sansom) 21:84, 90-1, 112,
　　126
"The Contest of the Minstrels" (Hoffmann)
　　See "Der Kampf der Sänger"
Continent (Crace) 61:30-33, 35, 38-40, 42-44
The Continental Op (Hammett) 17:212-13, 217,
　　227
"Continuation of the Yellow Millet" (P'u
　　Sung-ling)
　　See "Hsü huang-liang"
"Continuity of Parks" (Cortázar) 7:54, 70, 83
"Conto alexandrino" (Machado de Assis)
　　24:128-30, 133, 152-53
Contos flumineneses (Machado de Assis)
　　24:131-32, 151
"The Contract" (Anderson) 1:52
"Contract" (Lardner) 32:128, 133, 135-36, 138,
　　140, 145
"A Contract" (Svevo)
　　See "Un contratto"
"Contratreta" (Pardo Bazán) 30:272

"Un contratto" (Svevo) 25:334, 360
"Contrition" (Dubus) 15:74, 83
"The Convalescence of Jack Hamlin" (Harte)
　　8:247, 249
"Convention" (Dreiser) 30:112, 114, 122, 156
"The Conventional Wisdom" (Elkin) 12:99
"A Conversation" (Aiken) 9:14
"A Conversation" (Turgenev) 7:335
"Conversation at Night" (Bunin)
　　See "A Night Conversation"
"Conversation in the Atomic Age" (O'Hara)
　　15:250, 258
"The Conversation of Eiros and Charmion"
　　(Poe) 1:402
"A Conversation on Feet" (Davie) 52:7
"Conversation Piece, 1945" (Nabokov) 11:109-
　　10, 112-13, 127
"Conversation with Goya" (Andrić)
　　See "Razgovori sa Gojom"
"A Conversation with My Father" (Paley)
　　8:390, 392, 395, 399-402, 405, 407, 415-16,
　　418
"Conversations at Night" (Le Guin) 12:211,
　　213, 216
"Conversations in a Dead Language" (Ligotti)
　　16:271, 275, 292, 294, 297
"Conversations with Goethe" (Barthelme) 2:51;
　　55:111, 115
Conversations with Leukothea (Pavese)
　　See *Dialoghi con Leucò*
"Converse at Night" (Dinesen) 7:168, 171, 186
"The Conversion" (Banks) 42:52-3
"A Conversion" (Morrison) 40:328, 330, 354,
　　366, 368
"The Conversion of Aurelian McGoggin"
　　(Kipling) 5:261, 274
"The Conversion of Sum Loo" (Cather) 2:102;
　　50:91, 100, 107
"The Conversion of the Jews" (Roth) 26:229,
　　234, 248, 257-60, 265-66
"The Conversion of William Kirkwood"
　　(McGahern) 17:305, 323
"El converso" (Arreola) 38:8
"The Convert" (Lavin) 4:165-68
"A Convert of the Mission" (Harte) 8:216, 254
"The Converts" (Zangwill) 44:378
Los convidados de agosto (Castellanos) 39:29,
　　33, 34, 37, 38, 42, 43, 55, 59, 73
"Le convive des dernières fêtes" (Villiers de
　　l'Isle Adam) 14:378, 381-82, 384, 388-90,
　　393-94
"Le convive inconnu" (Villiers de l'Isle Adam)
　　See "Le convive des dernières fêtes"
"Cookie" (Taylor) 10:382, 390
"The Cookie Lady" (Dick) 57:107
"The Cooking Lesson" (Castellanos)
　　See "Lección de cocina"
"Cool Air" (Lovecraft) 3:258, 262, 274; 52:254,
　　269, 291, 320, 346-47
*A Cool Million: The Dismantling of Lemuel
　　Pitkin* (West) 16:343-48, 354-56, 362,
　　366, 379-85, 387-94, 399-400, 402-03, 405-
　　08, 411, 415, 418
"Coordination" (Forster) 27:86, 103, 114
"The Cop and the Anthem" (Henry) 5:173, 187;
　　49:197, 201-02
"Copenhagen Season" (Dinesen) 7:166, 169-71,
　　186, 190-91
"The Copper Charm" (Morrison) 40:329
"Cops and Robbers" (Stafford) 26:278, 283,
　　285, 308
The Copy-Cat, and Other Stories (Freeman)
　　47:86, 133
"Un coq chanta" (Maupassant) 1:272
"Cora Unashamed" (Hughes) 6:109-10, 118-19,
　　121-23, 129
"El corazón perdido" (Pardo Bazán) 30:264
"La corde" (Baudelaire) 18:35, 39
"The Corduroy Pants" (Caldwell) 19:36
"The Coreopsis Kid" (Calisher) 15:5, 15-17
Corilla (Nerval) 18:362, 367, 369

"Ćorkan and the German Woman" (Andrić)
　　See "Ćorkan i švabica"
"Ćorkan i švabica" (Andrić) 36:37-8, 42, 54,
　　66
"Corkscrew" (Hammett) 17:216, 222, 230
"The Corn Planting" (Anderson) 1:37
"The Cornac and His Wife" (Lewis) 34:147,
　　161, 169
"The Corner" (Cowan) 28:76; 81
"A Corner in Dwarfs" (Stoker) 62:252
Corner of the Woods (Storm)
　　See *Waldwinkel*
"The Cornet" (Alarcon)
　　See "La corneta de llaves"
"Cornet at Night" (Ross) 24:290-92, 294-98,
　　306, 310-11, 314-15, 319, 323-24
"The Cornet Yelagin Affair" (Bunin)
　　See "The Elaghin Affair"
"La corneta de llaves" (Alarcon) 64:2, 4, 38
"El coro de ángeles" (Alarcon) 64:28-29
"The Coronation of Thomas Shap" (Lovecraft)
　　52:361
"The Coroner" (Chekhov) 51:99-100
"La corpana" (Pardo Bazán) 30:272
"O corpo" (Lispector) 34:185, 189, 191, 195,
　　197, 201-02
"Corporal of Artillery" (Dubus) 15:73
"Correspondence" (McCullers) 9:332-34, 343,
　　345, 358
"A Correspondence" (Turgenev)
　　See "Peripiska"
A Correspondence (Turgenev) 7:317-18, 320,
　　324-26, 328, 361
"A Correspondence Course" (Gordimer) 17:171,
　　173, 193
"Corrido" (Arreola) 38:7, 10
"The Corsican Inn" (Pritchett) 14:268, 298
"Cortés and Montezuma" (Barthelme) 55:26,
　　91
"The Cortez Gang" (Algren) 33:96
"Cortigiana stanca" (Moravia) 26:138, 163,
　　179, 182
"Cortísimo metraje" (Cortázar) 7:95
"Corto Viaggio sentimentale" (Svevo) 25:331-
　　33, 336-38, 351-52, 354-57, 360, 363
*Corto viaggio sentimentale e altri racconti
　　inediti* (Svevo) 25:329-30, 332-33, 338
Una cosa è una cosa (Moravia) 26:159-62, 165,
　　173, 180
"Cosè il re" (Verga) 21:292
"Cosmic Casanova" (Clarke) 3:133
Le cosmicomiche (Calvino) 3:92-6, 98-100,
　　103-04, 106-07, 110, 112, 116-17; 48:33-4,
　　48, 57, 59, 61, 63, 65, 67, 69, 73-5, 77, 80,
　　83, 103-5, 114, 127, 131, 136, 150, 153,
　　159, 166-67
Cosmicomiche vecchie e nuove (Calvino)
　　48:149-50, 152, 158, 166
Cosmicomics (Calvino)
　　See *Le cosmicomiche*
Cosmicomics Old and New (Calvino)
　　See *Cosmicomiche vecchie e nuove*
"A Cosmopolitan" (Galsworthy) 22:93
Cosmopolitans (Maugham) 8:366, 380
"A Cosmopolite in a Café" (Henry) 49:197
"The Cossack" (Chekhov) 51:83
The Cossacks (Tolstoy) 30:317, 331
"The Cost of Living" (Fuentes)
　　See "El costo de la vida"
"The Cost of Living" (Gallant) 5:130, 140-41,
　　149
"The Cost of Living" (Malamud) 15:173-75
"El costo de la vida" (Fuentes) 24:45, 56-8, 62,
　　74
Costumes by Eros (Aiken) 9:4, 28
"The Cosy Room" (Machen) 20:163, 197
The Cosy Room (Machen) 20:166, 177-78, 186,
　　194, 197
"La Côte Basque, 1965" (Capote) 47:65-7
"The Cottagette" (Gilman) 13:126, 145
"The Cottonwood Part One: Story of Sun
　　House" (Silko) 37:303

"Cottonwood Part Two: Buffalo Story" (Silko) 37:303

"Cottonwood Parts One and Two" (Silko) 37:308

"A Council of State" (Dunbar) 8:122, 124-25, 128, 136, 141, 144, 150

"A Council of War" (Gilman) 13:143

"Councillor Krespel" (Hoffmann)
See "Rat Krespel"

"Counsel for Oedipus" (O'Connor) 5:370

"Count Magnus" (James) 16:228-30, 232, 237-38, 243, 245, 250-52, 256

"The Count of Crow's Nest" (Cather) 2:100, 102; 50:68, 76, 93, 152, 184-86

"The Count of Monte Cristo" (Calvino) 3:93, 95-6; 48:115, 134, 138-39, 160

"Counter Movement" (Davie) 52:8

"The Counterfeit Coin" (Baudelaire)
See "La fausse monnaie"

"Counterparts" (Joyce) 3:200-01, 205, 209, 226, 231, 234, 246, 249; 26:46-7; 44:263, 284; 64:208-12, 218-19, 233, 258-59, 261-62, 264

"Countess" (Le Fanu)
See "A Passage in the Secret History of an Irish Countess"

"Countess Varazoff" (Alcott) 27:57

Counting (Phillips) 16:332

"Counting the Waves" (Farrell) 28:94

"The Counting-House" (Turgenev) 7:313

"Country" (Phillips) 16:327

"The Country Church" (Irving) 2:244

"The Country Doctor" (Kafka)
See "Ein landarzt"

"The Country Doctor" (Turgenev) 57:266

"The Country Doctor" (Williams) 31:354

A Country Doctor's Notebook (Bulgakov)
See *Zapiski iunogo vracha*

"Country Full of Swedes" (Caldwell) 19:4, 6, 9, 12-13, 17, 19, 22-4, 27, 34, 39, 42, 47

"The Country Funeral" (McGahern) 17:319-22, 324

"The Country Husband" (Cheever) 1:90, 100-02; 38:50, 55-6, 61, 68, 71, 78, 80-4, 88-90; 57:9

"The Country Inn" (Turgenev)
See "The Inn"

"A Country Love Story" (Stafford) 26:274, 277, 283, 285, 307, 312

"The Country of the Blind" (Wells) 6:361-62, 368-73, 376-79, 383-84, 391-92, 399-400, 405

The Country of the Blind, and Other Stories (Wells) 6:359-61, 366, 380, 391-92

"Country Rain" (Williams) 31:314, 327, 354

"Country Roads" (Pilnyak) 48:290-91

"Country Society" (Bates) 10:118

"A Country Tale" (Dinesen) 7:168-69

"A Country Walk" (Sansom) 21:84, 91-2, 126

"The Count's Courtship" (de la Mare) 14:66, 81, 86

"The Coup de Grâce" (Bierce) 9:55-6, 75-7

"Le coup de pistolet" (Mérimée) 7:277

"A Coupla Scalped Indians" (Ellison) 26:11

"Le Couple" (Aymé) 41:19

"A Couple of Fools" (Bates) 10:131

"A Couple of Hamburgers" (Thurber) 1:418-19

"A Couple of Winos" (Bukowski) 45:58-9

"Coupon" (Čapek)
See "Kupón"

"Coups de couteaux" (Mauriac) 24:183, 185, 196, 198-201, 204-07

"Courage" (Galsworthy) 22:58, 74, 79

"The Courageous Tailor" (Grimm and Grimm) 36:191

"Court in the West Eighties" (McCullers) 9:342, 345, 356

"The Courtesy Call" (Dazai Osamu)
See "A Visitor"

"The Courting of Dinah Shadd" (Kipling) 5:260, 263-64, 274

"The Courting of Sister Wisby" (Jewett) 6:152, 160, 162, 178

"Courtly Vision" (Mukherjee) 38:264, 274, 277

The Courts of Love (Gilchrist) 63:7-8, 28

"A Courtship" (Faulkner) 1:151, 178

"Courtship" (O'Brien) 10:334, 341

"The Courtship of Mr. Lyon" (Carter) 13:6, 9, 25, 30-31

"The Courtship of Susan Bell" (Trollope) 28:318, 327-28, 333, 348

"Cousin Larry" (Parker) 2:280, 283

Cousin Phillis (Gaskell)
See *Cousin Phyllis*

Cousin Phyllis (Gaskell) 25:32, 38, 40, 45-6, 49-50, 54, 57-8, 61, 63-4, 74-7

"Cousin Poor Lesley and the Lousy People" (Elkin) 12:117

"Cousin Teresa" (Saki) 12:295, 302, 312

"Cousins" (Bellow) 14:43, 46, 58

The Cousins (Spencer) 57:219-21, 223-24, 226, 229, 231, 244

"The Covenant" (Auchincloss) 22:44

A Covenanting Story-Book (Stevenson) 51:242

Coventry (Heinlein) 55:169-71, 199, 202, 211, 231

"The Coverfield Sweepstakes" (Norris) 28:203

Covering End (James) 8:296

"The Covering of Blood" (Agnon) 30:71-4

"Cow and Gate Baby Contest" (Naipaul) 38:331

"A Cow in the House" (Kiely) 58:149-50

"The Coward" (Barnes) 3:18-22

"A Coward" (Wharton) 6:414

"Cowboys" (Salter)
See "Dirt"

"The Cow's Death" (O'Flaherty) 6:274

"The Cowslip Field" (Bates) 10:120, 131-32, 139

Cow-Wheat (Pilnyak) 48:264-65

"The Coxon Fund" (James) 8:317, 348

Crab Apple Jelly (O'Connor) 5:362, 364, 371, 377-78, 380, 383

"Crabforth" (Sansom) 21:124

"The Cracked Looking-Glass" (Porter) 4:327, 329-30, 339-40, 342, 360; 43:170, 173, 177, 181, 185, 223, 235, 247, 292

"Cracker Prayer" (Hughes) 6:138

"Crackling Mountain" (Dazai Osamu)
See "The Crackling Mountain"

"The Crackling Mountain" (Dazai Osamu) 41:234, 236, 264, 276

Crackling Mountain (Dazai Osamu)
See *Crackling Mountain and Other Stories*

Crackling Mountain and Other Stories (Dazai Osamu) 41:263, 276

The Crapshooter (Steinbeck) 11:248

"Craven Arms" (Coppard) 21:8, 15

"Crawford's Consistency" (James) 32:108

"The Crazy Batlen" (Peretz) 26:201

"The Crazy Beggar-Student" (Peretz)
See "The Crazy Batlen"

"Crazy, Crazy, Now Showing Everywhere" (Gilchrist) 14:154

"Crazy Crowd" (Wilson) 21:319, 322, 325, 327, 330, 336, 338, 342-44, 349, 352, 365

"The Crazy Hunter" (Boyle) 5:58-9, 61-3, 65-6, 68-9

The Crazy Hunter: Three Short Novels (Boyle) 5:66

Crazy Like a Fox (Perelman) 32:205, 213, 220, 229, 237-39

"Crazy Sunday" (Fitzgerald) 6:47, 52, 60-1, 77-9

"The Creamery Man" (Garland) 18:160

"The Creamery Manager" (McGahern) 17:320, 322

"Created He Them" (London) 4:253

"Creation" (Tanizaki) 21:190

"The Creation of Beauty: A Study in Sublimation" (Greene) 29:219

"Creative Frenzy" (Akutagawa Ryūnosuke) 44:64

"The Creative Impulse" (Maugham) 8:369, 378-79

"The Creative Instinct" (Maugham) 8:358

"The Creature" (O'Brien) 10:332-33

"The Creatures" (de la Mare) 14:65, 80, 83, 85

"Creatures of Apogee" (Aldiss) 36:19, 24, 27

Creatures of Circumstance (Maugham) 8:380

"Creatures That Once Were Men" (Gorky)
See "Byvshii lyudi"

"Crèche" (Ford) 56:184, 197

"A Credibility Gap" (Gordimer) 17:157

Credos and Curios (Thurber) 1:424; 47:379

"The Creeping Siamese" (Hammett) 17:224

"Cremona Violin" (Hoffmann) 13:225

"A Crepe for Her Brother" (Betts)
See "The Sympathetic Visitor"

"Le crépuscule du soir" (Baudelaire) 18:5, 8, 17, 33

"Cressy" (Harte) 8:221

"Crevasse" (Faulkner) 1:147

"Crewe" (de la Mare) 14:73, 80, 84, 88-9, 90-1

"The Cricket" (P'u Sung-ling)
See "Ts'u-chih"

"The Cricket on the Hearth" (Dickens) 17:103, 116, 127-28; 49:66, 158

"Criers and Kibitzers, Kibitzers and Criers" (Elkin) 12:94-5, 116-18

"Crime and Punishment" (Narayan) 25:133, 139, 156

"The Crime at Pickett's Mill" (Bierce) 9:98

"Crime at the Tennis Club" (Moravia)
See "Delitto al circolo di tennis"

"Le crime au père Boniface" (Maupassant) 1:274

"Crime in the Cottage" (Čapek)
See "Zločin v chalupě"

"Crime in the Post-Office" (Čapek)
See "Zločin na poště"

"The Crime of Gabriel Gale" (Chesterton) 1:124

"The Crime of Professor Sandwich" (Benét) 10:149

"The Crime of S. Karma" (Abe)
See "S. Karuma-shi no hanzai"

"The Crime of the Communist" (Chesterton) 46:136

"The Crime Wave at Blandings" (Wodehouse) 2:344, 346, 349

"Crimen libre" (Pardo Bazán) 30:279

"Crimes of Conscience" (Gordimer) 17:171, 174, 193

"The Criminal" (Dazai Osamu) 41:240, 245

"The Criminal" (Tanizaki) 21:194

"Criminal Courts" (Dickens) 17:115

"A Criminal Star" (Stoker) 62:250, 252

"The Crimson Curtain" (Barbey d'Aurevilly)
See "Le rideau cramoisi"

"The Crimson Island" (Bulgakov) 18:74, 91, 110

"The Cripple" (Andersen)
See "Krøblingen"

"The Crisis" (Barthelme) 55:106, 108

"The Crisis" (Zoshchenko) 15:400

"The Critic" (Galsworthy) 22:99

"Critical Mass" (Clarke) 3:134

"Critique de la vie quotidienne" (Barthelme) 2:39-40, 42, 55

"La Critique de la Vie Quotidienne" (Barthelme) 55:31, 82, 109

"Croatoan" (Ellison) 14:115-17, 128

"The Crocodile Pagoda" (Far) 62:50

Crónica de una muerte anunciada (García Márquez) 8:167, 173-82, 186, 190, 200-04

Crónicas de Bustos Domecq (Bioy Casares) 17:48, 52, 74-5, 84, 86; 19:48; 48:36-7, 42

Cronopios and Famas (Cortázar)
See *Historia de cronopios y de famas*

"The Crooked Branch" (Gaskell) 25:37-8, 46-7, 50-1, 60, 73

"The Crooked Made Straight" (Agnon)
See "Vehaya he'akov lemishor"

"Crooken Sands" (Stoker) 62:234, 242, 253-54

"The Crop" (O'Connor) 61:225

The Croquet Player (Wells) 6:400-02
"Crosby" (Hood) 42:175, 191
"Cross Country" (Crace) 61:31
"Crossbones" (Michaels) 16:302
"Cross-Country Snow" (Hemingway) 1:217, 244; 40:209, 211; 63:72, 75, 81, 90
"Crossing Friends" (Abish) 44:2
"Crossing into Poland" (Babel) 16:25, 28-9, 31, 33
"Crossing the Border" (Oates) 6:248-49
Crossing the Border: Fifteen Tales (Oates) 6:226-29, 231, 247-48, 250, 253-54
"Crossing the Great Void" (Abish) 44:10, 16, 19-20
"Crossing the Line" (McGahern) 17:315, 323
"Crossing the Rubicon" (Thomas) 20:289, 296-98, 308, 317, 319
"Crossing the Zbruck" (Babel) 16:51-4, 56, 58
"Crouch End" (King) 17:295
"The Crow Catcher" (Arreola) 38:12-13
"The Crow Comes Last" (Calvino) 48:150
"The Crow in the Woods" (Updike) 13:400
"The Crowd" (Bradbury) 29:65, 75, 88
"The Crowd Master" (Lewis) 34:163-64
"Crowds" (Baudelaire)
See "Les foules"
"Crown Fire" (Caldwell) 19:5, 8
"A Crown of Feathers" (Singer) 3:374
A Crown of Feathers, and Other Stories (Singer) 3:374-76, 380, 382, 384; 53:325
"The Crowning Offer" (Auchincloss) 22:33
"The Croxley Master" (Doyle) 12:89
"Cruce de caminos" (Unamuno) 11:312-13
Crucial Instances (Wharton) 6:413
"Crucifixion" (Čapek) 36:114, 117
"Cruel and Barbarous Treatment" (McCarthy) 24:213
"The Cruel Master" (Oates) 6:237
"Cruel Star" (Borowski) 48:17
"Cruise (Letters from a Young Lady of Leisure)" (Waugh) 41:311, 323, 330-31, 340
The Cruise of "The Breadwinner" (Bates) 10:129-30
"The Cruise of the 'Idlewild'" (Dreiser) 30:107, 126
The Crusade of the Excelsior (Harte) 8:245; 59:294, 306-7, 309
"La cruz de palo: Novela romántica" (Alarcon) 64:25-26, 30-31
"La cruz de palos" (Alarcon) 64:2, 7, 25
"Cry Hope, Cry Fury!" (Ballard) 53:72-3, 77, 79, 128, 131
"Cry of Peacock" (Galsworthy) 22:70
"The Crying Organ" (Moorhouse) 40:298
"Crystal Ball" (Grimm and Grimm) 36:192
"The Crystal Egg" (Wells) 6:383, 389-91, 393-94, 404-05
"The Crystal Fantasy" (Kawabata)
See "Suishō Gensō"
"The Crystal Garden" (Ballard) 53:131
"The Crystal Ship" (Vinge) 24:328, 330, 332, 334-35, 339-40
"Crystals" (Calvino)
See "I cristalli"
"Cuando las mujeres quieren a los hombres" (Ferré) 36:144, 146-47, 149, 157-59, 171
"Cuando se estudia gramática" (Cabrera Infante) 39:22
"Cuarta versión" (Valenzuela) 14:355, 367
"Cuarta vigilia" (Castellanos) 39:49
"Cuatro socialistas" (Pardo Bazán) 30:271
"The Cuckoo Clock" (Pritchett) 14:269, 298
"The Cuckoo-Spit" (Lavin) 4:172, 176, 183, 185
"Čudo u Olovu" (Andrić) 36:38, 52, 55
"Cuello de gatito negro" (Cortázar) 7:61, 69
"Cuento primitivo" (Pardo Bazán) 30:296
"Cuento soñado" (Pardo Bazán) 30:265
Cuentos (Donoso) 34:14-15, 20-3, 49-50

Cuentos amartorios (Alarcon)
See *Novelas cortas: Cuentos amartorios*
Cuentos, articulos y novelas (Alarcon) 64:7
Cuentos completos (Onetti) 23:258
Cuentos de amor (Pardo Bazán) 30:264-65, 267, 269-70
Cuentos de Eva Luna (Allende) 65:2-3, 6-7, 9-12, 26, 32-34, 36-37, 39, 46-54
Los cuentos de Juan Bobo (Ferré) 36:146
Cuentos de la tierra (Pardo Bazán) 30:263
Cuentos de Marineda (Pardo Bazán) 30:270, 293-94
Cuentos nuevos (Pardo Bazán) 30:262-63, 270-71
Cuentos sacroprofanos (Pardo Bazán) 30:276
Cuentos trágicos (Pardo Bazán) 30:278
"El cuervero" (Arreola) 38:10
"La cuesta de las comadres" (Rulfo) 25:245, 247, 249-50, 255, 258, 262, 264-65, 273, 280
"The Cuff Link" (Pardo Bazán) 30:290
"La culpable" (Pardo Bazán) 30:266-67
"Cunner-Fishing" (Jewett) 6:155, 167
"The Cunning Snake" (Harris) 19:162-63
"The Cup of Coffee" (Auchincloss) 22:51
"A Cup of Cold Water" (Wharton) 6:424
"Cup of Life" (Bulgakov) 18:91
"The Cup of Life" (Bunin) 5:90, 92, 109
The Cup of Life (Bunin) 5:90
"A Cup of Tea" (Mansfield) 9:310
"The Cupboard of the Yesterdays" (Saki) 12:310, 328
"Cupid and Chow-Chow" (Alcott) 27:17-22
Cupid and Chow-Chow (Alcott) 27:43
"Cupid's Arrows" (Kipling) 5:261
"La cura delle vespe" (Calvino) 48:82
"Cura pastoralis" (Hood) 42:140, 184, 187, 204
"Curado" (Pardo Bazán) 30:272
"The Curate's Friend" (Forster) 27:72-4, 86, 112-14, 119
Curator Carsten (Storm)
See *Carsten Curator*
"The Curb in the Sky" (Thurber) 1:418, 425; 47:389-90
"The Cure" (Cheever) 1:89; 38:55
"The Cure" (Colette) 10:280
Le curé de Tours (Balzac) 5:5, 7-8, 18, 25-6
The Curé of Tours (Balzac)
See *Le curé de Tours*
"The Curfew Tolls" (Benét) 10:154
"El curioso impertinente" (Cervantes) 12:3-4, 9-15
"A Curious Call" (Alcott) 27:43
"The Curious Case of Benjamin Button" (Fitzgerald) 6:59, 79-80, 92
"Curious if True" (Gaskell) 25:37, 47, 55, 61-3, 73
"The Curse" (Clarke) 3:124, 143-44
"The Cursed Play" (Tanizaki) 21:194
"The Curtain" (Chandler) 23:59, 65-7, 72-3, 80-3, 87, 92, 97-8, 106-07
"The Curtain Blown by the Breeze" (Spark) 10:356, 359, 361, 370-71
"The Curtain Falls" (Harris) 19:183
"A Curtain of Green" (Welty) 1:465-67, 469, 471, 476, 481-82, 484, 487, 496; 51:254, 257, 306, 314-17
A Curtain of Green and Other Stories (Welty) 51:254, 281-83, 306-7, 314, 318-21, 338
"A Curved Line" (Saroyan) 21:132
"The Custard Heart" (Parker) 2:275, 280-81, 286
"The Custody of the Pumpkin" (Wodehouse) 2:346-47
"Custom House" (Hawthorne) 39:129
"The Custom of the Country" (O'Connor) 5:370-71, 384, 387, 389
"Custom-Made Bride" (Vonnegut) 8:432, 436
"Customs" (Oates) 6:227, 248-50
"Cut" (Dixon) 16:204, 210
"Cut Glass Bowl" (Fitzgerald) 6:57
"Cutta Cord-la" (Harris) 19:162

"Cvety zapozdalye" (Chekhov) 51:103, 106
"Cy" (Dixon) 16:207, 211
"Cycling in Gringnan" (Cortázar)
See "Ciclismo en Gringnan"
"The Cyclone" (Hesse) 9:230-32, 235
Cyclone and Other Stories (Narayan) 25:137-38, 152, 155
"C.Y.E." (McCarthy) 24:215-16
"Les Cygnes" (Aymé) 41:8
"Le Cygnes" (Aymé) 41:15
"Cynthia" (Huxley) 39:153-54, 167
"Cyprian's Narrative" (Hoffmann)
See "Der Vampyrismus"
"Da sé" (Pirandello) 22:255, 279
Da Vinci's Bicycle (Davenport) 16:173-74, 176-77, 179-80, 182-83, 185, 187, 190, 193-98
"Dada" (Boyle) 16:141, 143
"Daddy Deering" (Garland) 18:160, 176, 194
"Daddy Garbage" (Wideman) 62:261, 263
"Daddy Jake the Runaway" (Harris) 19:147, 151, 187
Daddy Jake the Runaway, and Short Stories Told after Dark by Uncle Remus (Harris) 19:130, 147-48, 195-96
"Daddy's Girl" (Jones) 56:285
"The Daemon Lover" (Jackson) 9:267, 272; 39:209, 210, 211, 212, 213, 214, 216, 217, 218, 220, 223, 224, 225, 227, 228, 229
The Daffodil Sky (Bates) 10:118-19
"The Dagger with Wings" (Chesterton) 1:130-31; 46:109-110, 125
Dago Red (Fante) 65:73-76, 84, 86, 93-95, 97, 99-102
"Dagon" (Lovecraft) 3:258, 262, 268, 272-73, 282, 285, 289; 52:263, 267, 287, 294, 334, 337, 343, 345, 356
Dagon and Other Macabre Tales (Lovecraft) 52:262-64, 285, 292, 335, 341-43, 345-46
"Daidoji Shinsuke no Hansei" (Akutagawa Ryūnosuke) 44:82
"The Daisy" (Andersen) 6:3, 7
Daisy Miller: A Study (James) 8:264, 274, 291, 298-99, 309-14, 334, 336-38; 32:54-110; 47:200, 238, 332, 337-38
"Daisy Overend" (Spark) 10:359-60
"Dalyrimple Goes Wrong" (Fitzgerald) 6:45, 57
"Dama de pensamientos" (Arreola) 38:11
"La dama joven" (Pardo Bazán) 30:272-73
"Dama s sobačkoj" (Chekhov) 3:127-28, 131-33, 135, 150, 155, 157; 28:60, 62-3, 41:194, 203; 51:26, 58, 60, 62, 70-1, 78-9, 84, 93, 117, 119, 122, 124, 135, 148, 157, 198, 208-10, 212-14
"Damballah" (Wideman) 62:261, 273-75, 289, 322-24, 328-29
Damballah (Wideman) 62:260-68, 271, 273-79, 284-85, 288, 293, 295, 307, 314, 322
The Damned Yard (Andrić)
See *Prokleta avlija*
"Dan u Rimu" (Andrić) 36:46
"Danae" (Galsworthy) 22:72-3
"The Dance" (Andrić)
See "Igra"
"The Dance" (Thomas) 20:321
"The Dance at Chevalier's" (Cather) 2:101, 105, 107; 50:59, 62, 78, 99
"The Dance of Death, or the Lovely and Pleasant" (Agnon) 30:66, 81-6
"The Dance of the Chain" (Moorhouse) 40:310
"Dance of the Happy Shades" (Munro) 3:321, 328-30, 335, 346
Dance of the Happy Shades (Munro) 3:320, 322, 328-29, 331, 335, 343-44, 347
"The Dancin' Party at Harrison's Cove" (Murfree) 22:184, 186, 188, 196, 198, 203-04, 206-08, 217
"Dancing Girls" (Atwood) 2:6-8, 10, 12; 46:26-8, 33, 35, 43, 58, 92
Dancing Girls, and Other Stories (Atwood) 2:3-7, 10, 13-16, 20-2; 46:25-9, 32, 36-40, 43, 46, 51, 57-8, 60, 62-3, 76-8, 80, 84, 91-2, 94-5

"The Dancing Mistress" (Bowen) **3**:30, 43, 54
"The Dancing Party" (Gordon) **59**:262
"Dancing with Both Feet on the Ground"
    (White) **39**:347, 349
Dandelion Wine (Bradbury) **29**:43, 45, 52, 86;
    53:184-86, 188, 234-35, 264-66
"Dandelions" (Metcalf) **43**:109
"The Dandy Frightening the Squatter" (Twain)
    6:300; **59**:210; **34**:294, 297-98, 301
"Dandy Jim's Conjure Scare" (Dunbar) **8**:122,
    149
"The Dane's Breechin'" (Somerville & Ross)
    56:301, 308
"The Dane's Place" (Donoso)
    See "Dinamarquero"
"Danger!" (Doyle) **12**:80
"The Danger in the House" (Thurber) **1**:429
"The Danger of Shadows" (Benét) **10**:160
"Danger Wears Three Faces" (Bradbury)
    See "The Great Hallucination"
"The Dangerous Age" (Sansom) **21**:114
A Dangerous Perfume (Nin) **10**:306
"A Dangerous Woman" (Farrell) **28**:111
A Dangerous Woman and Other Stories
    (Farrell) **28**:110-11
"Les dangers de l'inconduite" (Balzac) **5**:4
"Daniel Jovard ou la Conversion d'un
    classique" (Gautier) **20**:5, 10, 12
"Daniel Webster and the Ides of March"
    (Benét) **10**:153, 158
"Daniel Webster and the Sea Serpent" (Benét)
    10:144, 153, 158
"Danny" (Jewett) **6**:150, 167
"Danny Sahib" (Mukherjee) **38**:240
"Danny's Girls" (Mukherjee) **38**:238, 254, 266,
    273
"Danse Pseudomacabre" (Williams) **31**:305,
    319-20, 325, 329, 364
"Dante and the Lobster" (Beckett) **16**:64, 69,
    92-3
"Dante Street" (Babel) **16**:59
"Daoine Bochta" (O'Flaherty) **6**:287, 289
"Daphne's Lover" (Taylor) **10**:400, 416-17
"Daphnis and Chloe" (Moore) **19**:293
"Darby Dallow Tells His Tale" (Coppard) **21**:8
"Darcy in the Land of Youth" (O'Connor) **5**:371
"Dare's Gift" (Glasgow) **34**:57-8, 61-3, 66-7,
    70, 73, 79-80, 82, 84-5, 87-8, 90, 92, 94-7,
    100
"The Daring Young Man on the Flying
    Trapeze" (Saroyan) **21**:131-32, 135-36,
    140, 142, 152, 157, 174-75
*The Daring Young Man on the Flying Trapeze,
    and Other Stories* (Saroyan) **21**:130-33,
    136, 139, 141, 143, 145-46, 152, 154, 158-
    59, 165-67, 174
"Darius & the Clouds" (Cisneros) **32**:5
"The Dark" (Updike) **13**:348
Dark Alleys (Bunin)
    See *Dark Avenues*
"Dark Avenues" (Bunin) **5**:115
Dark Avenues (Bunin) **5**:82, 90, 113-16
"A Dark Brown Dog" (Crane) **7**:130
"Dark Came Early in That Country" (Algren)
    33:95, 98
Dark Carnival (Bradbury) **29**:39, 43, 59, 75,
    86, 88-9
"The Dark Chamber" (Ligotti) **16**:296
"The Dark City" (Aiken) **9**:13-14, 31
Dark Companions (Campbell) **19**:65, 75-6, 78,
    84, 87
Dark Feasts: The World of Ramsey Campbell
    (Campbell) **19**:70-1, 78, 86, 93
"Dark Glasses" (Hood) **42**:141, 168-69 171,
    188-89, 205
"The Dark Glasses" (Spark) **10**:356
Dark Glasses (Hood) **42**:141, 150, 162, 167-71,
    187-90, 204-05, 213, 215, 219-20, 222
"Dark in the Forest, Strange as Time" (Wolfe)
    33:369-70, 382
"The Dark Men" (Dubus) **15**:77-9

A Dark Night's Passing (Shiga)
    See *Anya Kōro*
"A Dark Night's Work" (Gaskell) **25**:46, 50-2,
    58-60, 67
"The Dark Show" (Campbell) **19**:74
"Dark They Were, and Golden-Eyed"
    (Bradbury) **29**:61, 82; **53**:196-97, 207,
    247-50, 253
"The Dark Walk" (Taylor) **10**:392, 411
"The Darkening Moon" (Stafford) **26**:281, 289
The Dark-Eyed Lady (Coppard) **21**:19
Darkness (Mukherjee) **38**:238, 240, 247, 250,
    254, 257, 263-65, 269-73, 277-79, 281, 291,
    294
"Darkness Box" (Le Guin) **12**:232
"The Darling" (Bradfield) **65**:59-63, 65-68
"The Darling" (Chekhov) **2**:131-32, 135
"Darling" (Dixon) **16**:207, 211
"Darling" (Stephens) **50**:315
"The Darling River" (Lawson) **18**:206
"The Darning Needle" (Andersen) **6**:20
"A Dashing Fellow" (Nabokov) **11**:117
"Dasi the Bridegroom" (Narayan) **25**:141,
    154-55
"Dates and Times" (Pilnyak) **48**:287
"Datos para entender a los perqueos"
    (Cortázar) **7**:95
"Datura Fastuosa" (Hoffmann) **13**:221-23,
    225-26
"Daughter" (Caldwell) **19**:9, 27-8, 33, 38
"The Daughter" (Suckow) **18**:389, 401, 409
"Daughter of Albion" (Chekhov) **2**:126
"A Daughter of the Aurora" (London) **4**:286
"A Daughter of the Lodge" (Gissing) **37**:56, 64,
    81
"The Daughter of the Regiment" (Kipling)
    5:260
*The Daughter of the Storage and Other Things
    in Prose and Verse* (Howells) **36**:400
"The Daughter of the Yen Family" (P'u
    Sung-ling)
    See "Yen Shih"
"Daughters" (Anderson) **1**:52
Daughters of Fire (Nerval)
    See *Les filles du feu*
"The Daughters of the Late Colonel"
    (Mansfield) **9**:280-81, 300, 303-06, 310;
    23:154; **38**:229
"The Daughters of the Vicar" (Lawrence) **4**:197-
    98, 202, 204, 212, 233
Däumchen (Tieck) **31**:275
"Daumier" (Barthelme) **2**:39, 42, 49, 55;
    55:31-3, 67-8, 76, 85, 94
"De Daumier-Smith's Blue Period" (Salinger)
    2:293, 301, 315; **28**:262; **65**:304-5, 309-10,
    321
"The Daunt Diana" (Wharton) **6**:421, 428
"Dave's Neckliss" (Chesnutt) **7**:18; **54**:42-6, 48
"David Gaunt" (Davis) **38**:96, 114
"David Swan" (Hawthorne) **3**:160
"Dawn" (Powers) **4**:370
Dawn Ginsbergh's Revenge (Perelman) **32**:201,
    214, 218-20, 226, 238
"The Dawn in Erewhon" (Davenport) **16**:162-
    67, 169-70, 176, 183, 185-86, 197
"The Dawn of Another Day" (Williams) **31**:306,
    323-24
"Dawn of Remembered Spring" (Stuart) **31**:234
"A Day" (Pirandello)
    See "Una giornata"
"A Day" (Trevor) **58**:253, 261, 287
"The Day after Christmas" (Andrić)
    See "Na drugi dan Božića"
"Day after Day" (Lispector)
    See "Dia após dia"
"A Day after Saturday" (García Márquez) **8**:185
"The Day Before" (Endō)
    See "Sono zenjitsu"
"The Day Before" (Spencer) **57**:198, 214-15,
    239, 241
"The Day before the Revolution" (Le Guin)
    12:231, 234, 241

"The Day He Himself Shall Wipe My Tears
    Away" (Oe)
    See "Mizu kara waga namida o nuguitamo
    hi"
"A Day in Coney Island" (Singer) **3**:374
"A Day in Harmenze" (Borowski) **48**:5-7, 16
"A Day in Rome" (Andrić)
    See "Dan u Rimu"
"A Day in the Country" (Millhauser) **57**:154
"A Day in the Jungle" (Jackson) **9**:258
"A Day in the Life of a Galactic Empire"
    (Aldiss) **36**:28
"A Day in the Life of Able Charlie" (Pohl)
    25:236
"Day Million" (Pohl) **25**:214, 221, 225, 234-35
Day Million (Pohl) **25**:229, 232
"The Day Mr. Computer Fell Out of the Tree"
    (Dick) **57**:68
"The Day My Days as a Child Ended"
    (Cabrera Infante)
    See "El día que terminó mi niñez"
"The Day of Forever" (Ballard) **53**:9-11, 60
"A Day of Grace" (Garland) **18**:154, 160, 181,
    183
"The Day of Judgment" (Evans) **43**:18
"A Day of Our Life" (Bulgakov) **18**:90
*A Day of Pleasure: Stories of a Boy Growing
    Up in Warsaw* (Singer) **53**:325
"The Day of Silence" (Gissing) **37**:55, 80-1
The Day of Silence and Other Stories (Gissing)
    37:80
"The Day of the Boomer Dukes" (Pohl) **25**:232
"Day of the Butterfly" (Munro) **3**:329-30, 337
"The Day of the Dying Rabbit" (Updike)
    13:359-61
"The Day of the Landslide" (Rulfo)
    See "El dia del derrumbe"
The Day of the Locust (West) **16**:345-49, 355-
    57, 359-62, 364, 366-67, 369-74, 379, 381,
    383-85, 387-89, 394, 396, 399-402, 406-08,
    411, 414-15, 418
"The Day of the Sheep" (Frame) **29**:109, 118
"A Day on a Selection" (Lawson) **18**:200, 237-
    38, 240-41
"A Day Out" (Sansom) **21**:118
"The Day Resurgent" (Henry) **5**:188
"A Day Saved" (Greene) **29**:184
"The Day the Dam Broke" (Thurber) **1**:426,
    428, 432
"The Day the Icicle Works Closed" (Pohl)
    25:220, 230, 232
"The Day the Lift . . ." (Sansom) **21**:118, 127
"The Day the Martians Came" (Pohl) **25**:220
"The Day the Pig Fell into the Well"
    (Cheever) **1**:100; **38**:52, 55
"The Day They Burned the Books" (Rhys)
    21:49, 65, 69
"The Day We Got Drunk on Cake" (Trevor)
    58:200, 203, 207, 212
*The Day We Got Drunk on Cake, and Other
    Stories* (Trevor) **21**:230, 232, 236, 254,
    261; **58**:199-200, 202, 204
"The Day We Talked about James Thurber"
    (Bukowski) **45**:57, 61
"A Day with Conrad Green" (Lardner) **32**:136,
    138, 140, 146, 149, 152, 154-55, 163, 169
"A Day with Pegasus" (Ross) **24**:291, 296, 306-
    07, 310-12, 315-16, 323
Daybreak (Schnitzler)
    See *Spiel im Morgengrauen*
"Daydream of a Drunken Housewife"
    (Lispector)
    See "Devaneio e Embriaguez duma Ra-
    pariga"
"Daydreams" (Chekhov)
    See "Mety"
"The Daydreams of a Drunken Woman"
    (Lispector)
    See "Devaneio e Embriaguez duma Ra-
    pariga"
Daylight and Nightmare (Chesterton) **1**:140
"Days" (O'Hara) **15**:253

Days and Nights: Journal of a Deserter (Jarry)
See *Les jours et les nuits: Roman d'un dé-
serter*
Day's End and Other Stories (Bates) **10**:111
"A Day's Lodging" (London) **4**:253
"Days of Heaven" (Bass) **60**:16, 19-20
"Days of Sunshine" (Benét) **10**:149
"A Day's Pleasure" (Garland) **18**:154, 160
"A Day's Pleasure" (Howells) **36**:399
A Day's Pleasure and Other Sketches
(Howells) **36**:399-400
"A Day's Work" (Capote) **2**:81
"A Day's Work" (Porter) **4**:339-40, 342, 360;
43:177, 186, 235, 248, 292
The Day's Work (Kipling) **5**:266-68, 273-74,
283, 294-95; **54**:69
"Dayspring Mishandled" (Kipling) **5**:270, 278,
282-83, 299-303
"Dazzle" (Bradfield) **65**:58, 60, 62-63, 66, 68
"Dazzle" (Capote) **47**:63-4
"The Dazzling Light" (Machen) **20**:200
"De Mortuis" (Collier) **19**:102, 109-10, 112
"The De Wets Come to Kloof Grange"
(Lessing) **6**:186, 189; **61**:100, 119, 123,
125-26
"The Deacon" (Updike) **13**:361
"Dead" (Barker) **53**:139
"The Dead" (Joyce) **3**:202-06, 208, 210-11,
214-15, 217, 223-26, 228, 232-40, 242-45,
247, 249; **26**:32-86; **44**:236, 244, 263-65,
268-70, 279, 284, 288; **64**:196-200, 202,
222-28, 231, 244, 247, 259, 266-70, 272,
274, 276, 278
"The Dead" (Oates) **6**:225, 234, 254
"The Dead Are Silent" (Schnitzler)
See "Der toten schweigern"
"The Dead Astronaut" (Ballard) **53**:8, 55,
117-18
"The Dead Child" (Andersen)
See "The Child in the Grave"
"The Dead Fiddler" (Singer) **3**:369, 384;
53:339-40
"The Dead Girl" (Agnon) **30**:66
"The Dead in Korea" (Dybek) **55**:141
Dead Leaves (García Márquez)
See *La hojarasca*
"The Dead Leman" (Gautier) **20**:3
"Dead Mabelle" (Bowen) **3**:30, 44, 54
"The Dead Man" (Borges)
See "El muerto"
"The Dead Man's Revenge" (Lovecraft) **52**:262
"Dead Mule" (Betts) **45**:21
"The Dead Queen" (Coover) **15**:43-6
"Dead Roses" (White) **39**:279-82, 284, 290,
292-94, 297, 309, 312, 316-17, 336-37, 339,
344
"The Dead Season" (Schulz)
See "Martwy sezon"
"The Dead Sexton" (Le Fanu) **14**:238
"The Dead Time" (Ballard) **53**:21, 122-23
"The Dead Walk" (Bulgakov) **18**:90
"Dead Yellow Women" (Hammett) **17**:201, 222-
24, 226, 230
"The Deadly Mission of P Snodgrass" (Pohl)
25:234
"The Deal" (Michaels) **16**:301-03
"The Deal" (Tagore) **48**:325, 328
"A Deal in Wheat" (Norris) **28**:198
*A Deal in Wheat and Other Stories of the New
and Old West* (Norris) **28**:198-200
"Dean of Men" (Taylor) **10**:390, 399, 415, 418
"Deanna and the Ayatollah" (Hood) **42**:235
Dear Baby (Saroyan) **21**:154-55
"Dear Greta Garbo" (Saroyan) **21**:132
"Dear John" (Updike) **13**:367
"Death" (Anderson) **1**:30, 42
"Death" (Calvino) **3**:110; **48**:106, 138, 142-43,
157, 160
"Death" (Svevo)
See "La morte"
"Death" (Turgenev) **57**:266, 287
"Death and Decision" (Stuart) **31**:227, 236, 252

"Death and the Cherry Tree" (Bates) **10**:121
"Death and the Child" (Crane) **7**:100-01, 104-
08; **56**:88, 106-10
"Death and the Compass" (Borges)
See "La muerte y la brújula"
"Death and the Senator" (Clarke) **3**:147
"Death Beckons" (Pilnyak) **48**:286
"Death by Landscape" (Atwood) **46**:80, 98
"Death Comes to a Hero" (Gilchrist) **63**:7
"Death Constant beyond Love" (García
Márquez)
See "Muerte constante más allá der amor"
Death Dance: Twenty-Five Stories (Wilson)
21:339
"The Death Disease" (Bradbury) **53**:246
"The Death Disk" (Twain) **26**:331
"Death Has Two Good Eyes" (Stuart) **31**:266-67
"Death in Jerusalem" (Trevor) **21**:247, 262, 265
"Death in Midsummer" (Mishima) **4**:313-14,
318, 321-22
Death in Midsummer, and Other Stories
(Mishima) **4**:313-18, 321-23
"Death in Sinan Monastery" (Andrić)
See "Smrt u sinanovoj tekiji"
"Death in Sinan's Tekke" (Andrić)
See "Smrt u sinanovoj tekiji"
"A Death in the Country" (Benét) **10**:142, 149,
156-57
"A Death in the Desert" (Cather) **2**:90-1, 98,
103, 105, 113; **50**:57-9, 80, 82, 107, 110-11,
122, 135-36, 139, 187, 195-97, 239, 241,
247, 264-65
"A Death in the Forest" (Anderson) **46**:18, 20
"Death in the Sunday City" (Sansom) **21**:126
"Death in the Wings" (Stoker) **62**:247
"Death in the Woods" (Anderson) **1**:31, 37-8,
40, 50-2, 56, 58-62; **46**:2-22
Death in the Woods (Anderson) **1**:31, 37, 50-1,
56; **46**:17
Death in Venice (Mann)
See *Der Tod in Venedig*
"The Death of a Bachelor" (Schnitzler) **15**:343;
61:306
"The Death of a Civil Servant" (Chekhov) **51**:92
"Death of a Doctor" (Davie) **52**:8
"Death of a Doctor and Other Stories" (Davie)
52:6, 8, 10-11
"Death of a Freedom Fighter" (Borowski) **48**:4,
6-7
Death of a Huntsman (Bates) **10**:119-20, 128-29
"The Death of a Kinsman" (Taylor) **10**:415
"Death of a Lesser Man" (Berriault) **30**:96-8
"Death of a Martyr" (Akutagawa Ryūnosuke)
See "Hōkyōnin no shi"
"The Death of a Political Boy" (Oe)
See "Seiji shonen shisu"
"Death of a Professor" (Trevor) **58**:299, 301
"The Death of a Traveling Salesman" (Welty)
1:466, 472, 481, 493, 497; **51**:258, 263-64,
200, 282-83, 318-19, 321
The Death of Ahasuerus (Lagerkvist)
See *Ahasverus död*
"The Death of Ankou" (Lewis) **34**:153, 161-62
169
"The Death of Archimedes" (Čapek) **36**:117,
129
"The Death of Baldy" (Sansom) **21**:88
"The Death of Baron Gandara" (Čapek)
See "Smrt barona Gandary"
"The Death of Children" (Saroyan) **21**:133
"Death of Distant Friends" (Updike) **13**:404
"The Death of Dolgushov" (Babel) **16**:12, 24,
28-30, 41, 53, 58
"The Death of Edward Lear" (Barthelme) **2**:49,
52; **55**:91
"The Death of Halpin Frayser" (Bierce) **9**:70,
85-6
The Death of Ivan Ilych (Tolstoy)
See *Smert Ivana Ilyicha*
"The Death of Justina" (Cheever) **1**:100; **38**:50,
54, 61, 84, 88; **57**:9
"The Death of Ligoun" (London) **4**:287

"The Death of Lully" (Huxley) **39**:154
"The Death of Me" (Lish) **18**:275, 281, 283
"The Death of Me" (Malamud) **15**:174, 216,
227
The Death of Methusaleh, and Other Stories
(Singer) **3**:389; **53**:271-74, 303, 327
"The Death of Methuselah" (Singer) **3**:389
"The Death of Monga" (Lewis) **40**:280
"The Death of Mrs. Sheer" (Oates) **6**:224
"The death of my mother and my new mother"
(Shiga)
See "Haha no shi to atarishi haha"
"The Death of Old Arkhipov" (Pilnyak)
See "Smert starika Arkhipova"
"The Death of Peggy Meehan" (Trevor) **21**:263;
58:230, 241
"The Death of Stevie Long" (O'Faolain) **13**:315
"The Death of the Father" (Bukowski) **45**:51
"The Death of the Father II" (Bukowski)
45:62-3, 65
"The Death of the Laird's Jock" (Scott) **32**:319
"The Death of the Lion" (James) **8**:281, 306,
317
"The Death of the Martians" (Bradbury) **53**:248
The Death of the Poet (Tieck)
See *Der Tod des Dichters*
"The Death of the Prophet" (Baldwin) **10**:17
"The Death of the Right Fielder" (Dybek)
55:130, 145, 148-49, 155
"The Death of The Tiger" (Castellanos)
See "La muerte del tigre"
"Death Register" (Akutagawa Ryūnosuke)
See "Tenkibo"
"Death Rides the Rails to Poston" (Yamamoto)
34:357
"Death Scenes" (Atwood) **46**:75, 83
Death, the Proud Brother (Wolfe) **33**:346-47,
349, 367, 371-72, 375, 380
"The Deathbird" (Ellison) **14**:115, 118, 138,
140-41, 143, 145-46
*Deathbird Stories: A Pantheon of Modern
Gods* (Ellison) **14**:118, 121
"Deaths" (Pilnyak)
See "Smerti"
"Deaths at Sea" (Dubus) **15**:90
"Death's Friend" (Alarcon)
See "El amigo de la Muerte"
Debits and Credits (Kipling) **5**:275, 279, 283,
296; **54**:73, 94
"Debris" (Coover) **15**:47
"The Debt" (Wharton) **6**:421, 429
"A Debt of Honour" (Pritchett) **14**:255, 298
"Debts" (Paley) **8**:399, 403, 407
"Un début dans la vie" (Balzac) **5**:8-9
The Decameron (Boccaccio) **10**:163-247
"The Deceitful Marriage" (Cervantes)
See "El casamiento engañoso"
"The Deceived" (Mann)
See *Die Betrogene*
"The Deceptive Mat" (Far) **62**:50, 53
"The Decision" (O'Hara) **15**:250, 252, 254-55,
258
"Decline and Fall" (Bukowski) **45**:60-2, 68
Decline and Fall (Waugh) **41**:311, 318-22, 326,
328, 330, 336, 342-43, 345, 350-53, 355-66
"Decline & Fall of Dingdong-Daddyland"
(Algren) **33**:107
The Declining Years (Dazai Osamu)
See *Bannen*
"Décoré" (Maupassant) **1**:256, 263; **64**:287-88,
291
"Découverte" (Maupassant) **1**:259
"A Decrepit Clan" (Leskov) **34**:129
"Le Décret" (Aymé) **41**:11, 16, 18-19, 21-24,
26-28
"DeDe's Talking, It's Her Turn" (Gilchrist)
14:154
"Dedication" (King) **17**:295
"Deductible Yacht" (Auchincloss) **22**:5
"A Deed of Vengeance?" (Stoker) **62**:248
"Deeds of Light" (Price) **22**:388
"Deep End" (Ballard) **1**:69; **53**:8, 50

"The Deep River: A Story oF Ancient Tribal Migration" (Head) **52**:188, 190, 193, 195, 201-2, 206, 210-11, 214, 223, 227, 236, 247

Deep Sightings and Rescue Missions (Bambara) **35**:42

Deephaven (Jewett) **6**:150, 154-57, 165-69

"Deephaven Cronies" (Jewett) **6**:150, 167

"Deephaven Excursions" (Jewett) **6**:150, 168

"Deephaven Society" (Jewett) **6**:154, 167

"Deer Dance/For Your Return" (Silko) **37**:309

"Deer in the Works" (Vonnegut) **8**:438

"Deer Season" (Beattie) **11**:6

"Deer Song" (Silko) **37**:309

"Defeat" (Boyle) **5**:66

"Defeat" (Galsworthy) **22**:63, 95, 101-02

"The Defeat of the City" (Henry) **5**:184

"The Defeated" (Gordimer) **17**:151

"The Defection of Mary Ann Gibbs" (Dunbar) **8**:122

"The Defence of Semidvorie" (Platonov) **42**:254

"A Defender of the Faith" (Dunbar) **8**:122, 132

"Defender of the Faith" (Roth) **26**:228, 231-32, 235-36, 239-42, 245, 249-50, 252, 257, 265-66, 268-70

"The Defenders" (Dick) **57**:41, 52-53, 91, 103, 107

"The Defenestration of Ermintrude Inch" (Clarke) **3**:134

"The Defenseman" (Banks) **42**:70

"A Defensive Diamond" (Saki) **12**:296, 327

"An Déirc" (Moore) **19**:319, 322, 324, 326, 328, 332, 334-35, 337

Deirdre (Stephens) **50**:306, 317-26, 330, 332-33, 308-09

"Delia" (Gordon) **59**:230, 260, 265, 267-68, 278-80

"The Deliberation of Mr. Dunkin" (Dunbar) **8**:119, 121, 131, 136, 143

The Delicate Nature (Bates) **10**:118

"The Delicate Prey" (Bowles) **3**:59-63, 66, 72, 77

A Delicate Prey and Other Stories (Bowles) **3**:58-65, 67, 70-2, 76-7, 79-80

"Delilah and the Space-Rigger" (Heinlein) **55**:186, 201

"Delincuente honrado" (Pardo Bazán) **30**:264-65

"Delitto al circolo di tennis" (Moravia) **26**:163

"Delivering" (Dubus) **15**:75, 81, 89, 96

"Dell Goes Into Politics" (Moorhouse) **40**:286, 311

"Delphine" (Morand) **22**:156-57, 165

"The Delta at Sunset" (Ballard) **1**:69; **53**:11, 46-7, 50

"Delta Autumn" (Faulkner) **1**:166; **35**:140-41, 143, 145-48, 153-54, 157, 164-65, 167, 169, 173-74, 176, 178, 181, 190, 193-94, 198, 201-03

Delta of Venus (Nin) **10**:305, 307, 324-25, 327

Delta Wedding (Welty) **51**:260-61, 272, 274, 285, 318

"The Deluge at Norderney" (Dinesen) **7**:163, 170, 174, 176, 179-80, 182-83, 186, 190, 195-98, 200, 204

"Delusion for a Dragon Slayer" (Ellison) **14**:108, 118, 120

"The Demi-Gods" (Galsworthy) **22**:91

The Demi-Gods (Stephens) **50**:326

"Demise of an Attitude" (Kluge) **61**:75

"Les demoiselles de Bienfilâtre" (Villiers de l'Isle Adam) **14**:377-81, 383, 385-86, 393, 396, 411

"A Demon" (O'Brien) **10**:347

"Le Démon de la connaissance" (Mauriac) **24**:184, 197-98, 200, 203, 205-06

"The Demon Lover" (Bowen) **3**:31-2, 41, 50-2, 54; **28**:1-17

The Demon Lover and Other Stories (Bowen) **3**:30-3, 41, 44, 48, 50-2; **28**:2-7, 9-10, 14-17

"The Demon of Perversity" (Poe) See "The Imp of the Perverse"

Demons and Darkness (Collier) **19**:105

Demons by Daylight (Campbell) **19**:60-3, 70, 73, 75, 78, 81-93

"The Demonstrators" (Welty) **1**:488; **27**:353; **51**:285-86, 318-19

"Demos" (Galsworthy) **22**:98

"Dendorokakariya" (Abe) **61**:9-10, 17, 21

"Dendrocacalia" (Abe) See "Dendorokakariya"

"The Dentist and the Gas" (Leacock) **39**:262

"Dentistry and Doubt" (Updike) **13**:351, 354, 395

"An Deóraidhe" (Moore) **19**:319-21, 323, 330, 334-35

"Departure" (Anderson) **1**:31, 42, 45-6

"The Departure of Emma Inch" (Thurber) **47**:367, 379-80

"Departures" (Barthelme) **55**:116, 120

"Depend on Aunt Elly" (Algren) **33**:88, 107, 110-11, 113

"The Dependents" (Chekhov) **51**:89

Le dépeupleur (Beckett) **16**:71-2, 76-7, 88, 94, 98, 102, 105-07, 115, 123

"The Depths" (Campbell) **19**:87

"A Deputy Waiter" (Stoker) **62**:252

"El derecho de asilo" (Carpentier) **35**:116-19

"Derletzebrief eines literaten" (Schnitzler) **15**:355, 361-64

"Dermuche" (Aymé) **41**:13, 17

Derriere chez Martin (Aymé) **41**:20, 23

"Derring-Do" (Capote) **2**:81

"Derzelez at the Inn" (Andrić) **36**:54

"Des Journées entières dans les arbres" (Duras) **40**:3-6, 77

Des journées entières dans les arbres (Duras) **40**:3, 9-10, 13-14, 65, 133-35

"Desayuno" (Cortázar) **7**:95

"The Desborough Connections" (Harte) **8**:220

"A Descendant of Kings" (Williams) **31**:302, 324, 331, 359, 361

"A Descendant of the Cid" (Pardo Bazán) See "El nieto del Cid"

"A Descent into the Maelström" (Poe) **1**:385, 400, 402; **22**:300; **34**:249-50; **35**:310, 321-22

"Descent of Man" (Boyle) **16**:142, 148-49, 153

"The Descent of Man" (Wharton) **6**:428-29

The Descent of Man (Wharton) **6**:420-21

Descent of Man, and Other Stories (Boyle) **16**:140-41, 143-44, 149-50, 154

Description of a Battle (Kluge) **61**:75

"Description of a Fight" (Kafka) **29**:349; **35**:240

"Descriptions of a Battle" (Kafka) See "Description of a Fight"

"A desejada das gentes" (Machado de Assis) **24**:129

"Desert Breakdown, 1968" (Wolff) **63**:263, 301, 312, 315-16, 318, 320, 322, 338

"The Deserter" (Babel) **16**:35

"A Desertion" (Crane) **7**:106

"Le désespoir de la vieille" (Baudelaire) **18**:17, 32, 59, 64-5

Deshoras (Cortázar) **7**:79

"Design for Departure" (Algren) **33**:87-89, 102-03, 110

"Le désir de peindre" (Baudelaire) **18**:6-7, 18

"Le désir d'être un homme" (Villiers de l'Isle Adam) **14**:381, 384, 387, 389-90, 396

"Desire" (Beattie) **11**:11, 20

"Desire" (Stephens) **50**:306, 314-15, 331

Desire (O'Flaherty) See *Dúil*

"Desire in November" (Calvino) **3**:112

"The Desire to Be a Man" (Villiers de l'Isle Adam) See "Le désir d'être un homme"

"The Desired Payment" (Bulgakov) **18**:89

"Désirée's Baby" (Chopin) **8**:66, 68, 74-6, 81-4, 91-2, 99, 103, 105-06

"Las desnudas" (Pardo Bazán) **30**:272

"The Desperado" (Turgenev) See "Otchayanny"

"A Desperate Character" (Turgenev) See "Otchayanny"

"Desquite" (Pardo Bazán) **30**:268-69

"Le dessous de cartes d'une partie de whist" (Barbey d'Aurevilly) **17**:7, 10-12, 15, 17-21, 27-8, 30-4, 38-9, 43-4

Destinies (Mauriac) See *Destins*

"El destino" (Pardo Bazán) **30**:272

Destins (Mauriac) **24**:160, 165, 174, 201

El destripador (Pardo Bazán) See *Un destripador de antaño*

"Un destripador de antaño" (Pardo Bazán) **30**:262, 269, 272

Un destripador de antaño (Pardo Bazán) **30**:270

"The Destruction of Kreshev" (Singer) **3**:358-59, 368, 375, 383-84; **53**:338

"The Destruction of the Goetheanum" (Salter) **58**:173, 190-91

"Destruction of the Man" (Pirandello) See "La distruzione dell'uomo"

"Destructions" (Andrić) See "Razaranja"

"The Destructors" (Greene) **29**:204-09, 212-15, 217, 222

"Details of a Sunset" (Nabokov) See "Katastrofa"

"Detroit Skyline, 1949" (Mason) **4**:4,

Detstvo (Pilnyak) **48**:254

Detstvo (Tolstoy) **9**:374-76, 380, 383, 399, 401-03; **30**:331; **45**:155

"Detstvo Luvers" (Pasternak) **31**:95-6, 98, 102, 107-08, 111-20

"Deutsches Requiem" (Borges) **4**:9, 18, 24-6, 30, 37, 40-2

"Deux acteurs pour un rôle" (Gautier) **20**:31

"Deux amis" (Maupassant) **1**:275

"Deux augures" (Villiers de l'Isle Adam) **14**:381, 395-96

"Les deux pigeons" (Laforgue) **20**:101-2, 105

"Les deux rêves" (Balzac) **5**:31; **59**:11

"Devaneio e Embriaguez duma Rapariga" (Lispector) **34**:187, 194-95, 197-98, 202, 217, 221

"The Devil" (Tanizaki) See "Akuma"

"The Devil" (Tolstoy) **9**:377-78; **30**:312, 317, 319, 328, 339-40, 342-43

"The Devil: A Sequel" (Tanizaki) See "Zoku Akuma"

The Devil and All (Collier) **19**:105

"The Devil and Daniel Webster" (Benét) **10**:143-44, 152-54, 156-58

"The Devil and his Grandmother" (Grimm and Grimm) **36**:228-29

"The Devil and Irv Cherniske" (Boyle) **16**:151, 153

"The Devil and Television" (Stuart) **31**:227, 236, 250

"The Devil and Tobacco" (Akutagawa Ryūnosuke) See *Tobaku tu akuma*

The Devil and Tobacco (Akutagawa Ryūnosuke) See *Tobaku tu akuma*

"The Devil and Tom Walker" (Irving) **2**:241, 247-48, 250-51, 254, 262; **37**:267

"The Devil at Noon" (Tanizaki) See "Hakūchyukigo"

"The Devil, George and Rosie" (Collier) **19**:104-05

"The Devil Has Many Faces" (Stuart) **31**:250

"The Devil in the Belfry" (Poe) **1**:407; **54**:191

"The Devil Makes the Law" (Heinlein) See *Magic, Inc.*

"The Devil with the Three Golden Hairs" (Grimm and Grimm) **36**:223

"The Devil-Drive" (Leskov) See "Čertogon"

"The Devil's Church" (Machado de Assis) See "A igreja do diabo"

"Devil's Ford" (Harte) **59**:306

The Devil's Larder (Crace) **61**:33-43, 46-47
"The Devil's Race-Track": Mark Twain's Great Dark Writings (Twain) **6**:336
"The Devil's Sooty Brother" (Grimm and Grimm) **36**:199, 228-29
"The Devil's Spittle" (Cortázar)
　　See "Las babas del diablo"
The Devil's Yard (Andrić)
　　See *Prokleta avlija*
"The Devoted Friend" (Wilde) **11**:375-76, 380, 386, 395, 398, 407, 409
"The Devotée" (Tagore)
　　See "Tapashwini"
"Devotion without End" (Peretz) **26**:211, 215
"Di grasso" (Babel) **16**:10-11, 16, 36, 41, 59
"Di sera, un geranio" (Pirandello) **22**:260
"Di shtot fun di kleyne mentshelek" (Aleichem) **33**:45
"Dia após dia" (Lispector) **34**:211
"El Dia de Muerte" (Bradbury) **29**:47; **53**:215
"El dia del derrumbe" (Rulfo) **25**:255, 265, 271-74
"El día des las madres" (Fuentes)
　　See "Mother's Day"
"El día que terminó mi niñez" (Cabrera Infante) **39**:23
"Le diable" (Maupassant) **1**:270, 284
"Diable—A Dog" (London)
　　See "Batard"
"Diaboliad" (Bulgakov) **18**:72, 74, 93-5, 97, 99, 104, 113
Diaboliad, and Other Stories (Bulgakov)
　　See *D'iavoliada*
Les diaboliques (Barbey d'Aurevilly) **17**:2-4, 7-8, 10-13, 15, 17-21, 24-5, 30, 33-4, 39-41, 43-4
"Diagnosis" (Wharton) **6**:424
"Dial F for Frankenstein" (Clarke) **3**:145
"The Dialectic" (Farrell) **28**:122, 125
Dialoghi con Leucò (Pavese) **19**:364-65, 371-72, 386, 388-89
"Diálogo del espejo" (García Márquez) **8**:154-56, 182
"Dialogue" (Lessing) **6**:200-04
"Dialogue in a Mirror" (García Márquez)
　　See "Diálogo del espejo"
"The Dialogue of the Dogs" (Cervantes)
　　See "El coloquio de los perros"
Dialogues de bêtes (Colette) **10**:261, 272
Dialogues with Leucò (Pavese)
　　See *Dialoghi con Leucò*
"El diamante" (Arreola) **38**:22
"El diamante de Villasola" (Unamuno) **11**:312
"The Diamond as Big as the Ritz" (Fitzgerald) **6**:46-7, 58-60, 88, 92, 100-02
"A Diamond Guitar" (Capote) **2**:67; **47**:38, 50, 55-6, 58
"The Diamond Maker" (Wells) **6**:383, 388, 408
"The Diamond Mine" (Cather) **2**:91-2; **50**:69, 95, 241
"The Diamond Necklace" (Maupassant)
　　See "La parure"
"The Diamond of Kali" (Henry) **5**:184
"Diane de Foret" (Bradbury) **53**:267
"Diary, 1900" (Hesse) **9**:230
"Diary of a Forgotten Transcendentalist" (Bradfield) **65**:67-68
"The Diary of a Knight of King Arthur" (Lewis) **40**:280
"Diary of a Madman" (Gogol) **4**:82-3, 88, 91, 98, 100-01, 105-07, 122, 124, 126, 128-29; **29**:127-28, 132, 135, 143, 148, 152, 163; **52**:83, 92-3, 103, 105-8, 122-23, 129, 132
"Diary of a Madman" (Lu Hsun)
　　See *Kuangren riji*
"The Diary of a Madman" (Tolstoy)
　　See *Zapiski sumasshedshego*
"The Diary of a Meshumad" (Zangwill) **44**:377-67, 370, 372, 375, 387
"Diary of a Sixteen-Year-Old" (Kawabata)
　　See "Jūrokusai no Nikki"

"The Diary of a Superfluous Man" (Turgenev)
　　See "Dnevnik lišnego čeloveka"
"The Diary of an African Nun" (Walker) **5**:402, 404
"Diary of Hamlet" (Shiga) **23**:363
"The Diary of K. W." (Berriault) **30**:95-8, 104
"The Diary of Mr. Poynter" (James) **16**:223-24, 229-30, 232-33, 235, 249, 255
"A Diary of Old New York" (Auchincloss) **22**:43
"A Diary of Sudden Death; By a Public-Spirited Observer on the Inside" (Bierce) **9**:83
"The Diary of the Rose" (Le Guin) **12**:230, 237-38
Los días enmascarados (Fuentes) **24**:30, 32, 37-8, 40-1, 43-4, 46, 52-6, 58, 62
D'iavoliada (Bulgakov) **18**:72-3, 91-2, 97-100
"Dichter und Komponist" (Hoffmann) **13**:191
Dichterleben (Tieck) **31**:271-73, 276, 282-83, 287, 289-90
"Dick Boyle's Business Card" (Harte) **8**:216, 252
"Dick Denver's Idea" (Galsworthy) **22**:91
"Dickon the Devil" (Le Fanu) **14**:223
"Did Henry Miller Walk in Our Tropical Garden" (Wilding) **50**:347
"Did I Invite You?" (Pritchett)
　　See "Did You Invite Me?"
"Did You Ever Dream Lucky?" (Ellison) **26**:11
"Did You Invite Me?" (Pritchett) **14**:285, 298
"Diddling Considered as One of the Exact Sciences" (Poe) **1**:407
"An die Musik" (Le Guin) **12**:211-12, 214, 219-20, 222-23, 245, 250
"The Die-Hard" (Benét) **10**:154
Dietegen (Keller) **26**:91, 95, 107
"Dieu d'amour" (Wharton) **6**:428
"The Difference" (Glasgow) **34**:58, 64-7, 71, 75, 78, 80-1, 94-5, 100-02
"The Difference" (Tagore) **48**:333-34
"Different Clowns for Different Towns" (Algren) **33**:96
"Different Faces" (Agnon)
　　See "Panim aherot"
Different Seasons (King) **17**:262-67, 271-73, 275, 282, 284; **55**; 243, 246
"A Difficult Case" (Howells) **36**:390-93, 396-98
Difficult Loves (Calvino)
　　See *Gli amori difficili*
"Difficult People" (Chekhov) **2**:155
"Digging Our Own Graves" (Farrell) **28**:99, 125
"Digroyse behole fun di kleyne mentshelekh" (Aleichem) **33**:7
"Díles que no me maten!" (Rulfo) **25**:246, 249, 253-54, 261, 265, 272-73, 275, 278, 280
"The Dilettante" (Mann) **5**:320, 323, 330, 335-37
"The Dilettante" (Wharton) **6**:424
"A Dill Pickle" (Mansfield) **9**:309-10
"Dinamarquero" (Donoso) **34**:30, 49
"The Diner Out" (Auchincloss) **22**:38
"Ding Dong" (Beckett) **16**:93
Ding Dong Bell (de la Mare) **14**:90, 92
"Dingle the Fool" (Jolley) **19**:223
"Dinner" (Lardner) **32**:133, 135, 138, 140-41, 167-68
"A Dinner at Poplar Walk" (Dickens) **17**:120; **49**:164
"Dinol and Crede" (Moore) **19**:299, 311
"The Dinosaurs" (Calvino)
　　See "I dinosauri"
"Díoltas" (O'Flaherty) **6**:287-88
"Dionea" (Lee) **33**:302, 309
"El dios de los toros" (Bioy Casares) **17**:68, 70
"The Diploma" (Pirandello)
　　See "La patente"
"The Diplomat" (Auchincloss) **22**:44
"The Diplomat" (Machado de Assis) **24**:153
"Direction of the Road" (Le Guin) **12**:234
"Dirt" (Salter) **58**:172, 190, 192, 196

"The Dirty Girl" (Wilding) **50**:346
"Dirty Wedding" (Johnson) **56**:234, 261, 266
"The Disappearance of Actor Benda" (Čapek) **36**:105
"The Disappearance of an Actor" (Čapek) **36**:127-28
"Disappearing Creatures of All Kinds" (Hood) **42**:236
"The Disappearing Duke" (Chandler) **23**:110
"The Dis-Associated Charities" (Norris)
　　See "The Associated Un-Charities"
The Disaster Area (Ballard) **53**:114
"The Discarded" (Ellison) **14**:103, 113-15, 117
"The Discarders" (Jolley) **19**:233
"The Discharged" (Čapek) **36**:106
"The Disciple" (Aiken) **9**:4, 12-13
"The Discipline" (Clarke) **45**:73, 78, 83-4, 88, 97
"El discípulo" (Arreola) **38**:6-7, 21
"El disco" (Borges) **41**:167
"Discord" (O'Faolain) **13**:284-286, 288, 293, 309, 315
"The Discounters of Money" (Henry) **5**:159
"Discourse of a Lady Standing a Dinner to a Down-and-out Friend" (Rhys) **21**:62
"Discourse on the Tachanka" (Babel) **16**:27, 55
"A Discovery in the Woods" (Greene) **29**:187, 189
"A Discreet Miracle" (Allende) **65**:10
"Discussion with the Fest Coordinators" (Kluge) **61**:74
"The Disease" (Bradbury) **53**:249, 253
"El disfraz" (Pardo Bazán) **30**:272
"A Disgrace to the Family" (Boyle) **5**:64
"Disguise" (Singer) **53**:273, 305
"Disillusioned" (de la Mare) **14**:83, 86
"Disillusionment" (Mann) **5**:321, 330
"The Disinherited" (Bowen) **3**:33, 41, 45, 48-9, 51; **28**:9
"The Disintegration Machine" (Doyle) **12**:79
"The Disk" (Borges)
　　See "El disco"
"The Dismissal" (Bowles) **3**:75, 80
"Disneyad" (Apple) **50**:8, 17, 32, 45
"Disobedience" (Moravia) **26**:132-33, 136
Disobedience (Moravia)
　　See *La disubbidienza*
Disorder and Early Sorrow (Mann) **5**:310-12, 323, 350
"The Displaced Person" (O'Connor) **1**:335-36, 338, 343-45, 347, 359; **23**:205, 235; **61**:159-64, 166-67, 240
"Displaced Persons" (Sansom) **21**:90, 94
"The Distance" (Bass) **60**:42
"Distance" (Carver) **8**:4-5, 29, 42, 59; **20**-1
"Distance" (Oates) **6**:236-37
"Distance" (Paley) **8**:416-17
"The Distance of the Moon" (Calvino)
　　See "La distanza della luna"
"The Distances" (Cortázar)
　　See "Lejana"
"A Distant Episode" (Bowles) **3**:59, 61-2, 66-9, 72, 78
"Distant Music" (Beattie) **11**:4, 6-7, 17
"The Distant Past" (Trevor) **21**:248, 260-62; **58**:225, 233, 237, 271, 275, 287
The Distant Past, and Other Stories (Trevor) **21**:253
"La distanza della luna" (Calvino) **3**:92, 103, 107, 109; **48**:46, 64, 66-7, 69, 72-3, 77, 104, 132-33, 154, 156, 158
Distortions (Beattie) **11**:2-5, 11-12, 15-16, 18-23, 26-8, 30-2,
"The Distracted Preacher" (Hardy) **2**:203, 205, 208, 213-15, 219-21; **60**:178
"Distraction" (Pirandello) **22**:249
"The District Doctor" (Turgenev) **57**:281
"La distruzione dell'uomo" (Pirandello) **22**:280
"The Disturber" (Villiers de l'Isle Adam)
　　See "L'inquiéteur"
"The Disturber of Traffic" (Kipling) **5**:283

La disubbidienza (Moravia) **26**:133, 140, 143, 146, 156, 158, 165-66, 169-71, 182, 185-86
"The Ditch" (O'Flaherty) **6**:265
"The Diver" (Dinesen) **7**:163, 167-68, 171
"The Diver" (Pritchett) **14**:260-61, 288-89, 299
Divers Vanities (Morrison) **40**:329, 333, 349
A Diversity of Creatures (Kipling) **5**:275, 282-84
"Dividends" (O'Faolain) **13**:300
"The Division" (Turgenev) **7**:318
"A Division in the Coolly" (Garland) **18**:148, 160, 184
"The Divorce" (Gilchrist) **63**:6
"Divorcing: A Fragment" (Updike) **13**:387
"Dixiong" (Lu Hsun) **20**:149
"Dizzy-Headed Dick" (Dunbar) **8**:122
"D'javoliada" (Bulgakov)
　See "Diaboliad"
"Djinn, No Chaser" (Ellison) **14**:127
"Djoûmane" (Mérimée) **7**:285, 296-8
"Djuna" (Nin) **10**:300-01, 317
Dlia pol'zy dela (Solzhenitsyn) **32**:330, 333, 335-37, 340, 364, 390, 395, 397
"Dnevnik lišnego čeloveka" (Turgenev) **7**:314, 318-20, 339; **57**:293,297
"Do the Dead Sing?" (King)
　See "The Reach"
"Do You Know This Man?" (Auchincloss) **22**:51
"Do You Like It Here?" (O'Hara) **15**:266
"Do You Want to Make Something Out of It?" (Thurber) **1**:428
"Do Your Christmas Necking Now" (Perelman) **32**:240
"Doc Marlowe" (Thurber) **1**:414; **47**:303
"Doc Mellhorn and the Pearly Gates" (Benét) **10**:143, 154, 159-60
"Doc Rivers" (Williams)
　See "Old Doc Rivers"
"Las doce figuras del mundo" (Bioy Casares) **17**:70
"The Dock-Witch" (Ozick) **15**:297, 300, 312-13, 326
"Doc's Story" (Wideman) **62**:268, 273, 279
"The Doctor" (Dubus) **15**:70, 77-9
"The Doctor" (Gallant) **5**:135, 139
"The Doctor" (Williams) **31**:329
"The Doctor and His Divorced Wife" (Agnon)
　See "The Doctor's Divorce"
"The Doctor and His Divorcée" (Agnon)
　See "The Doctor's Divorce"
"The Doctor and the Doctor's Wife" (Hemingway) **1**:208, 217, 234, 241, 245; **63**:42, 65-70, 103, 106
Doctor Brodie's Report (Borges)
　See *El informe de Brodie*
"Dr. Bullivant" (Hawthorne) **3**:164
"Doctor Chevalier's Lie" (Chopin) **8**:73
"Doctor Crombie" (Greene) **29**:200-01
"Doctor Havel after Ten Years" (Kundera) **24**:88-9, 91-2, 103
"Doctor Havel after Twenty Years" (Kundera) **24**:100, 104, 107-08, 118
"Doctor Havel Ten Years Later" (Kundera)
　See "Doctor Havel after Ten Years"
"Dr. Heidegger's Experiment" (Hawthorne) **3**:154, 178, 186-87
Doctor Jekyll and Mr. Hyde (Stevenson)
　See *The Strange Case of Dr. Jekyll and Mr. Hyde*
Doctor Martino, and Other Stories (Faulkner) **1**:180
"The Doctor of Hoyland" (Doyle) **12**:88
"A Doctor of Medicine" (Kipling) **5**:285
"The Doctor of Silence" (Kelly) **50**:295
Doctor of Silence (Kelly) **50**:289-90, 292, 299-301
"Doctor or Patient?" (Peretz)
　See "Rofe' o chole?"
"Doctor Tarr and Professor Fether" (Poe)
　See "The System of Doctor Tarr and Professor Fether"

"Doctor Tristan's Treatment" (Villiers de l'Isle Adam)
　See "Le traitement du docteur Tristan"
"The Doctors" (Barnes) **3**:9-10
"The Doctor's Case" (King) **17**:295
"The Doctor's Divorce" (Agnon) **30**:3, 48, 54,63-6
"The Doctor's Horse" (Freeman) **47**:164
"The Doctor's Son" (O'Hara) **15**:247, 252, 256-57, 265-66, 286
The Doctor's Son, and Other Stories (O'Hara) **15**:249, 263, 264-67, 273-74
"A Doctor's Visit" (Chekhov)
　See "Sluaj iz praktiki"
"The Doctor's Wife" (Ozick) **15**:297, 300, 313-14; **60**:312
"The Doctor's Word" (Narayan) **25**:138, 140, 153, 155-56
"Dodu" (Narayan) **25**:135, 137, 156, 160
Dodu and Other Stories (Narayan) **25**:137, 152
"Doe" (Coppard) **21**:29
"A Doer of the World" (Dreiser) **30**:112
"Dog" (Kelly) **50**:290
"The Dog" (Shiga) **23**:346
"The Dog" (Turgenev)
　See "Sobaka"
"Dog Days" (Dixon) **16**:217
"The Dog Explosion" (Hood) **42**:187
"The Dog Hervey" (Kipling) **5**:275, 284-85
"The Dog It Was That Died" (Galsworthy) **22**:63, 79, 101-02
"A Dog Named Trilby" (Hughes) **6**:122
"Dog of Timothy's" (Galsworthy) **22**:71
"Dog Scent" (Zoshchenko) **15**:406
"The Dog Shiro" (Akutagawa Ryūnosuke) **44**:53
"The Dog that Bit People" (Thurber) **47**:370
"Doge und Dogressa" (Hoffmann) **13**:183-84
"A Dog's a Dog" (Collier) **19**:111
The Dogs' Colloquy (Cervantes)
　See "El coloquio de los perros"
"A Dog's Death" (Price) **22**:376
"The Dogs in the Great Glen" (Kiely) **58**:148, 157
"Doing Right" (Clarke) **45**:73, 75, 78, 88, 103
"Doing Time with Public Enemy No. 1" (Bukowski) **45**:56
Doktor Murkes gesammeltes Schweigen, und andere Satiren (Boell) **23**:8, 36
"Dokutan" (Tanizaki) **21**:209-10
"Dolan's Cadillac" (King) **17**:294
"The Doldrums" (Galsworthy) **22**:72-3, 91
"The Doll" (Chesnutt) **7**:17; **54**:50-1, 53
"The Doll" (Fuentes)
　See "El Muñeco"
"The Doll Queen" (Fuentes)
　See "La muñeca reina"
Dollari e vecchie mondane (Calvino) **3**:91; **48**:80, 147
Dollars and the Demi-Mondaine (Calvino)
　See *Dollari e vecchie mondane*
"Dolls" (Campbell) **19**:76, 85
"The Doll's House" (Mansfield) **9**:280, 282, 286, 301-05, 308, 311, 313; **23**:153, 164, 169
"The Dolls' Journey" (Alcott) **27**:43
"Dolph Heyliger" (Irving) **2**:241, 247-48, 251, 254, 256, 259-60
"The Dolt" (Barthelme) **2**:38, 52; **55**:32, 40, 44, 74, 88
"Dom pod kruchei" (Kazakov) **43**:53
"Dom s mezoninom" (Chekhov) **51**:26, 58, 60, 70-1, 79, 128, 136, 146, 172-73, 189, 194, 199, 207, 214
"The Domain of Arnheim" (Poe) **22**:303, 305
"Le domande" (Moravia) **26**:148
"A Domestic Dilemma" (McCullers) **9**:323, 331-32, 343, 353-54, 356, 359-60
Domestic Happiness (Tolstoy)
　See *Semeinoe schaste*
"Domestic Life in America" (Updike) **13**:385-86, 388-89

Domestic Relations: Short Stories (O'Connor) **5**:371, 375
"Domingo" (Castellanos) **39**:45, 75, 76
"El dominó verde" (Pardo Bazán) **30**:264-65
"Don" (Dixon) **16**:207, 212
Don Candelbro e Campagnin (Verga)
　See *Don Candelro*
Don Candelro (Verga) **21**:294-95
"Don Carmelo's Salvation" (Pardo Bazán)
　See "La salvación de don Carmelo"
Don Correa (Keller) **26**:103-04, 110
"Don Joaquin" (Cable) **4**:58
"Don Juan (Retired)" (O'Connor) **5**:369, 371
"Don Juan's Temptation" (O'Connor) **5**:366, 371, 389
"El don rechazado" (Castellanos) **39**:39, 49
"El don supremo" (Bioy Casares) **17**:53
"Dona Benedita" (Machado de Assis) **24**:128
"Doña Faustina" (Bowles) **3**:64, 66, 80, 83
"Dona Paula" (Machado de Assis) **24**:153
Donde viven las águilas (Valenzuela) **14**:366
"Donnerhugel's Narrative" (Scott) **32**:288-89, 291, 300
"Le donneur d'eau bénite" (Maupassant) **1**:281
"Les dons des fées" (Baudelaire) **18**:17, 19, 43
"Don't Bother Coming" (Hood) **42**:236
"Don't Die" (Lish) **18**:283
"Don't Let Them" (Cortázar)
　See "No te dejes"
"Don't Let's Be Dramatic" (Moravia) **26**:160
"Don't Look Now" (du Maurier) **18**:129-30, 133, 137
Don't Look Now (du Maurier)
　See *Not after Midnight*
"Don't Smoke on the Apron" (Sansom) **21**:127
"Don't Take No for an Answer" (Garrett) **30**:163, 172, 180
"Don't You Hear the Dogs Barking?" (Rulfo)
　See "No oyes ladrar los perros"
"The Doom of the Darnaways" (Chesterton) **1**:131, 138; **46**:110, 113, 134
"The Doom of the Griffiths" (Gaskell) **25**:54-5
A Doom on the Sun (Thomas) **44**:333
"The Doom That Came to Sarnath" (Lovecraft) **52**:285-86, 309, 357-58
"The Door: A Prologue of Sorts" (Coover) **15**:33, 35, 51
"The Door in the Wall" (Wells) **6**:361-62, 368-70, 376, 381, 383-84, 391-92, 404, 406
"The Door of Opportunity" (Maugham) **8**:357, 374
"The Door of the Trap" (Anderson) **1**:27, 39, 52
"The Doorbell" (Nabokov) **11**:133
"The Doorkeeper" (Stifter)
　See "Tourmaline"
"The Doorkeeper at the Mansion" (Stifter)
　See "Tourmaline"
"Doorstep Acquaintance" (Howells) **36**:399
"Doorways" (McGahern) **17**:299, 308-09, 318-19, 321
"Doppelgänger" (Lewis) **34**:163, 165, 179-80
Ein Doppelgänger (Storm) **27**:306, 311
"Die Doppeltgänger" (Hoffmann) **13**:206
"El Dorado: A Kansas Recessional" (Cather) **2**:101, 105; **50**:59, 77, 104-05, 187
"Dorfgeschichte" (Walser) **20**:333
"Doroga" (Babel) **16**:36, 59
Dorotheas Blumenkörbchen (Keller) **26**:100, 108
"Dorothée" (Baudelaire)
　See "La belle Dorothée"
"Dorothy" (Caldwell) **19**:34, 37, 41-2
"Dorothy and My Grandmother and the Sailors" (Jackson) **39**:210, 211, 222
The Dorrington Deed-box (Morrison) **40**:332, 349
"Dos ángeles caídos" (Alarcon) **64**:2, 7, 25-26, 30-31
Dos ángeles caidos y otros escritos olvidados (Alarcon) **64**:2, 7
"Dos cartas" (Donoso) **34**:30, 49

"Las dos doncellas" (Cervantes) **12**:4-5, 14, 17-18, 21, 26, 34, 37, 44

"Las dos Elenas" (Fuentes) **24**:29, 32, 51, 55-6, 58, 61-2, 70, 72

"Dos fantasías memorables" (Borges) **4**:16

"Las dos glorias" (Alarcon) **64**:28

Dos madres (Unamuno) **11**:313, 323-25, 327, 347, 356

"Dos meserl" (Aleichem) **33**:66, 71

"Dos palabras" (Allende) **65**:3, 26, 46-47, 53-54

"Los dos retratos" (Alarcon) **64**:28

"Dos retratos" (Alarcon) **64**:2, 30

"Los dos reyes y los dos laberintos" (Borges) **4**:28, 30-1, 35

"Dos Shtraiml" (Peretz) **26**:201-02, 220, 222-23

"Dos tepl" (Aleichem) **33**:19, 26-7, 35-9

"Dos teppel" (Aleichem)
    See "Dos tepl"

Las dos Venecias (Ferré) **36**:146, 155

"'Dossing Out' and 'Camping'" (Lawson) **18**:215

"Dossy" (Frame) **29**:101, 105

The Double (Dostoevsky)
    See *Dvoynik*

"Double Birthday" (Cather) **2**:99, 113-15; **50**:105, 208

"A Double Buggy at Lahey's Creek" (Lawson) **18**:201-06, 229, 262

"The Double Chamber" (Baudelaire)
    See "La chambre double"

"The Double Corner" (Stegner) **27**:197, 218

"Une double famille" (Balzac) **5**:22, 29-31

"Double Feature" (Selby) **20**:258

"The Double Gap" (Auchincloss) **22**:14, 21-2, 41-2

"The Double Happiness Bun" (Gilchrist) **14**:154

La double méprise (Mérimée) **7**:276, 281, 283, 286, 290-2, 304

"The Double Mistake" (Mérimée)
    See *La double méprise*

"Double Talk" (Nabokov)
    See "Conversation Piece, 1945"

"A Double Tragedy" (Alcott) **27**:34, 58

A Double-Barrelled Detective Story (Twain) **6**:295

"A Double-Dyed Deceiver" (Henry) **5**:182; **49**:205

".007" (Kipling) **5**:266, 268, 279

"Doubles" (Hood) **42**:175, 177, 192, 205

"Doubting Makar" (Platonov)
    See "Usomnivshiisia Makar"

"Doubts" (Akutagawa Ryūnosuke) **44**:45

"The Dove Came Down" (Wescott) **35**:357, 363, 369-72, 374-75

"The Dove of Chapacalco" (Porter) **31**:162-63; **43**:229-30

"The Dover Road" (Machen) **20**:197

"The Doves Nest" (Mansfield) **9**:280;

The Doves' Nest, and Other Stories (Mansfield) **9**:281; **23**:137

"Dowa" (Akutagawa Ryūnosuke) **44**:69

"Down at the Dinghy" (Salinger) **2**:290-91, 295-96, 298-300, 314; **65**:294, 296, 304-5, 308-9, 318, 321

"Down at the Dump" (White)
    See "Down in the Dump"

"Down at the Hydro" (Sansom) **21**:117, 127

"Down by the Riverside" (Wright) **2**:360-61, 363, 365-69, 371, 374-75, 379-81, 387, 390-91

"Down in the Dump" (White) **39**:280-82, 287, 289, 291-94, 296, 299, 307, 312, 315-16, 318-19, 325, 327, 329, 336, 339-42, 344

"Down Pens" (Saki) **12**:306

"Down, Satan!" (Barker) **53**:142, 156, 162-63

"Down Then by Derry" (Kiely) **58**:155-56, 163

"Down There" (Campbell) **19**:88

"Down with All Hands" (Algren) **33**:108

"Downers" (Michaels) **16**:308

"Downhill" (Beattie) **11**:17, 28

"The Downward Path to Wisdom" (Porter) **4**:339-40, 342, 359; **43**:177, 182, 190-92, 292

"Downwind from Gettysbury" (Bradbury) **29**:56

"The Dowry of Angyar" (Le Guin) **12**:219, 224

Dr. Brodie's Report (Borges)
    See *El informe de Brodie*

"Dr. Faustus" (Benét) **10**:145

"Dr. Locrian's Asylum" (Ligotti) **16**:269, 278-80, 283, 296

"Dr. Mejzlík's Case" (Čapek)
    See "Případ dra Mejzlíka"

Dr. Murke's Collected Silences (Boell)
    See *Doktor Murkes gesammeltes Schweigen, und andere Satiren*

"Dr. Perelman, I Presume; or, Small Bore in Africa" (Perelman) **32**:213

"Dr. Tarr and Prof. Fether" (Poe) **34**:281

"Dr. Voke and Mr. Veech" (Ligotti) **16**:261, 265, 276, 284

"Dr. Woolacott" (Forster) **27**:90, 96, 102-07

"Dracula's Guest" (Stoker) **62**:244, 253-54

Dracula's Guest, and Other Weird Stories (Stoker) **62**:253-54

"Draft" (Beckett) **16**:108

"The Dragon" (Akutagawa Ryūnosuke) **44**:57-8;

"The Dragon" (Bradbury) **53**:191

"The Dragon" (Spark) **10**:367, 370

"The Dragon at Hide and Seek" (Chesterton) **1**:140

"Dragonflies" (Shiga) **23**:346

La dragonne (Jarry) **20**:50

"The Dragon's Teeth" (Gordon)
    See "One against Thebes"

"The Drama" (Chekhov) **51**:77

"Dramas" (O'Brien) **10**:346

"Un drame au bord de la mer" (Balzac) **5**:11-13, 16, 26, 31

"The Draped Mirrors" (Borges) **41**:102

"Drawing In" (Campbell) **19**:75

"Drawing Names" (Mason) **4**:5

"Drawing Room B" (O'Hara) **15**:250

"The Drawing-Room" (Trevor) **58**:211

"Dread" (Barker) **53**:137-38, 140, 143, 157-58, 162-63

"Dreaded Hell" (Onetti)
    See "El infierno tan temido"

"A Dream" (Howells) **36**:352-56, 396-97

"A Dream" (Peretz)
    See "A Kholem"

"A Dream" (Turgenev)
    See "Son"

"The Dream" (Turgenev)
    See "Son"

"Dream Cargoes" (Ballard) **53**:67

"A Dream Come True" (Onetti)
    See "Un sueño realizado"

The Dream Department (Perelman) **32**:201, 205

A Dream Fulfilled, and Other Stories (Onetti)
    See *Un sueño realizado y otros cuentos*

"The Dream in the Dead House" (Stoker) **62**:246

"Dream Journeys" (Hesse) **9**:230-32, 236

Dream Journeys (Hesse) **9**:230

The Dream Life of Balso Snell (West) **16**:345-47, 349-51, 354, 361-67, 369, 377, 379, 383-87, 389-90, 393-94, 396-98, 402-03, 406-11, 415, 417

"Dream of a Mannikin; or, The Third Person" (Ligotti) **16**:261, 263, 265, 271, 273, 275-78, 283, 288

"The Dream of a Queer Fellow" (Dostoevsky)
    See "The Dream of a Ridiculous Man"

"The Dream of a Ridiculous Man" (Dostoevsky) **2**:166, 183, 185

"The Dream of an Hour" (Chopin)
    See "The Story of an Hour"

"A Dream of Armageddon" (Wells) **6**:360, 383-84, 391, 404

"The Dream of Beg Karčic" (Andrić)
    See "San bega Karčića"

"A Dream of Butterflies" (Trevor) **21**:262; **58**:256

"The Dream of Duncan Parrenness" (Kipling) **54**:79

"The Dream of lusheng" (Akutagawa Ryūnosuke) **44**:57-8

"A Dream of Oblómov's Grandson" (Bunin) **5**:81, 90

"A Dream of Red Hands" (Stoker) **62**:253-54

"The Dream of the Consortium" (Millhauser) **57**:182-83, 189

"The Dream of the Gods" (Hesse) **9**:243

"Dream of the Wolf" (Bradfield) **65**:60-61, 66, 68, 70

Dream of the Wolf (Bradfield) **65**:61-64, 67

"A Dream of Wolves" (P'u Sung-ling) **31**:198

"Dream Sequence" (Hesse) **9**:234-35

"The Dream Soldier" (Abe) **61**:11

"The Dreamer" (Fante) **65**:75

"Dreamer in a Dead Language" (Paley) **8**:410

"The Dreamers" (Dinesen)
    See "Drømmerne"

"Dreamers of the Ghetto" (Zangwill) **44**:364

Dreamers of the Ghetto (Zangwill) **44**:366, 370, 373, 388

"The Dreaming Child" (Dinesen) **7**:165, 171

"The Dreaming in Nortown" (Ligotti) **16**:284

"The Dream-Quest of Unknown Kadath" (Lovecraft) **52**:324

"Dreams" (Akutagawa Ryūnosuke) **44**:51

"Dreams" (Chekhov) **2**:156; **51**:69, 82, 156

"The Dreams in the Witch-House" (Lovecraft) **3**:258, 260, 263, 268, 272, 274-76, 282; **52**:274, 284, 290, 333, 338, 351

"The Dreams of Chang" (Bunin) **5**:80-1, 83-4, 93

"The Dreams That Failed" (Far) **62**:50, 53

Dreamtigers (Borges)
    See *El hacedor*

"A Dreary Story" (Chekhov) **2**:126, 131, 143, 150, 156; **41**:199-201; **51**:28, 81, 83-4

"Die drei Erznarren" (Arnim) **29**:5, 29

Drei Frauen (Musil) **18**:292-93, 297, 322-23, 325

Die drei gerechten Kammacher (Keller) **26**:91, 107, 116, 125-26

Die drei liebreichen Schwestern und der gluckliche Farber (Arnim) **29**:5-8

"Drei Matones" (Peretz) **26**:196, 202, 215

"Drei Schmiede ihres Schicksals" (Stifter) **28**:291

"Drenched in Light" (Hurston) **4**:136-38, 149-50

"A Dresden Lady in Dixie" (Chopin) **8**:94

"The Dress" (Thomas) **3**:399, 408; **44**:322, 333-34, 337-38, 344, 354

"Dressed Like Summer Leaves" (Dubus) **15**:87

"A Dressmaker" (Warner) **23**:373

"The Dreydl" (Aleichem) **33**:17-18

"Dreyfus in Kasrilevke" (Aleichem) **33**:47

"Dried Fruit" (Moore) **19**:340-41

"Drift" (Cowan) **28**:80

Drift (Cowan) **28**:76-80

"Drifted Back" (Lawson) **18**:248, 250

"Drifting Apart" (Lawson) **18**:229

"Drifting Crane" (Garland) **18**:147, 176, 187-88

"Drifting Down Lost Creek" (Murfree) **22**:188, 190, 196, 203, 206, 208, 215, 218

"Drink to Me Only with Labyrinthine Eyes" (Ligotti) **16**:265, 269, 271, 274, 276, 278, 294

"The Drive Home" (Banks) **42**:69

"A Drive in the Country" (Greene) **29**:183, 186, 193, 212-13

Driving Blind (Bradbury) **29**:66; **53**:267

"Le droit du passe" (Villiers de l'Isle Adam) **14**:396

"Le drôle" (Mauriac) **24**:189-99, 206

Droll Stories (Balzac)
    See *Contes drolatiques*

"Drømmerne" (Dinesen) **7**:167, 170, 174, 191, 195, 197-98, 200, 209

The Drop of Blood (Pardo Bazán)
   See *La gota de sangre*
"A Drop of Water" (Andersen)
   See "Vanddraaben"
"Dropped Dead: A Ghost Story" (Howells)
   36:398
"The Drover's Wife" (Lawson) **18**:201-02, 206,
   216-17, 219-23, 225-27, 248-51, 259, 263
"The Drowned Giant" (Ballard) **1**:68, 74; **53**:9,
   48
"The Drowned Girl" (Gogol)
   See "Majskaja noč, ili Vtoplennica"
"Drowne's Wooden Image" (Hawthorne) **3**:185
"Drowning" (Boyle) **16**:142, 151, 156
"Drüben auf den Inseln" (Lenz) **33**:317, 319
"The Drum" (Coppard) **21**:16
"The Drummer of All the World" (Laurence)
   7:245, 248-50, 256, 260-61, 272
The Drummer of the Eleventh North
   Devonshire Fusiliers (Davenport) **16**:199-
   200
"The Drums of the Fore and Aft" (Kipling)
   5:264-65, 269, 273
"Drunk with Love" (Gilchrist) **14**:157
Drunk with Love (Gilchrist) **14**:156-59; **63**:7,
   15, 21, 28
"The Drunkard" (O'Connor) **5**:369, 371, 378
"Drunkard's Death" (Dickens) **17**:116, 125
"The Drunkard's Dream" (Le Fanu) **14**:220,
   222-23
"A Drunken Steam-Engine" (Bulgakov) **18**:90
The Dry Heart (Ginzburg)
   See *E stato così*
"Dry September" (Faulkner) **1**:148, 180-81
Dry Valley (Bunin)
   See *Sukhodol*
"The Dryad" (Andersen) **6**:7
"The Dualists; or, the Death Doom of the
   Double Born" (Stoker) **62**:247
Dubliners (Joyce) **3**:201-03, 205-07, 210, 213-
   14, 216-18, 224-26, 228-30, 233-35, 237-
   39, 244-45, 247-49; **26**:32, 36, 39-40, 46-
   53, 67-70, 72, 76-7, 82, 84; **44**:235-36, 238,
   243, 254, 262-65, 268, 275, 277, 279, 282,
   284, 288, 291-97, 299-303, 305-09, 313,
   315, 317; **64**:196, 202-6, 208, 210, 220-24,
   226-28, 230-31, 233-35, 240-43, 245-46,
   250, 252-64, 273
Dubrovsky (Pushkin) **27**:164, 175-76, 185
"The Duc De L'Omellette" (Poe) **22**:305;
   35:336
"The Duchess" (Cheever) **1**:106
"The Duchess and the Bugs" (Thurber) **1**:430
"The Duchess and the Jeweller" (Woolf) **7**:377,
   388
"The Duchess at Prayer" (Wharton) **6**:413, 415,
   428
"The Duchess of Hamptonshire" (Hardy) **2**:204;
   180, 205, 208
"The Duchess of Palliano" (Stendhal)
   See "La Duchesse de Palliano"
La Duchesse de Langeais (Balzac) **5**:43-5, 47
"La Duchesse de Palliano" (Stendhal) **27**:249-
   50, 261
"The Duckling" (Andersen)
   See "Den grimme [dJ]lling"
"The Duckling" (Solzhenitsyn)
   See "Utenok"
"The Ducks" (Carver) **8**:10
"Dudley for the Dartmouth Cup" (Taylor)
   10:379
Due cortigiane e Serata di don Giovanni
   (Moravia) **26**:185
"Le due maschere" (Pirandello) **22**:275
"The Duel" (Borges)
   See "El duelo"
"The Duel" (Chekhov)
   See "Duèl"
"Duèl" (Chekhov) **2**:131, 143, 145, 150-51,
   155, 157; **41**:189-224; **51**:79, 83, 85, 90-1,
   114, 128, 135, 157, 166, 173-74, 176-78,
   180-86, 188, 193, 195, 202

"The Duel" (Conrad) **9**:163, 183
"The Duel" (Henry) **5**:191
"The Duel" (Kleist)
   See *Der Zweikampf*
"The Duel of Dr. Hirsch" (Chesterton) **1**:138;
   46:113, 133
"A Duel without Seconds" (Barnes) **3**:13
"El duelo" (Borges) **4**:20, 27
"Dúil" (O'Flaherty) **6**:286, 288-89
Dúil (O'Flaherty) **6**:285-89
"Duke of Portland" (Villiers de l'Isle Adam)
   14:381, 384, 388, 390-91, 393-96
"The Duke's Reappearance" (Hardy) **2**:210
Dulcima (Bates) **10**:117-18
"The Dulham Ladies" (Jewett) **6**:160
"A Dull Story" (Chekhov)
   See "A Dreary Story"
"Dullborough Town" (Dickens) **17**:123
"Dulse" (Munro) **3**:346
"The Dumb Girl" (Peretz) **26**:205
"Dumb Show" (Aldiss) **36**:5
"The Dumb Witness" (Chesnutt) **54**:42, 53
"Dumbledon Donkey" (Coppard) **21**:12
"Dumbrovic" (Farrell) **28**:126
"Dummy" (Carver) **8**:5, 29, 34
"The Dummy" (Jackson) **39**:211, 224, 227
"Dundun" (Johnson) **56**:234, 237, 240, 260,
   264, 266-67
"The Dunwich Horror" (Lovecraft) **3**:258-59,
   263, 269-70, 274-76, 290-92, 294; **52**:271,
   274, 279, 282-83, 289, 311, 315, 322, 337,
   349-50, 354, 362
The Dunwich Horror, and Others: The Best
   Supernatural Stories of H.P. Lovecraft
   (Lovecraft) **52**:265, 268, 270-72, 283, 288,
   291, 318, 336, 338-39, 343-44, 346-50, 352
"Dunyazadiad" (Barth) **10**:48-9, 51, 54, 56, 61,
   66, 68-9, 71, 91, 93-7, 101-05
Duo (Colette) **10**:262-65, 269
"The Duplicity of Hargraves" (Henry) **5**:159,
   171; **49**:203
"Duracok" (Leskov) **34**:111-12
"Durasa" (Tagore) **48**:338
"Durbuddhi" (Tagore) **48**:304, 307-8
"During a Winter Night" (Warner) **23**:380
"During the Encampment" (Andrić)
   See "Za logorovanja"
"During the Jurassic" (Updike) **13**:360, 387
"Dushenka" (Chekhov) **51**:34-5, 54-6, 78, 135,
   144, 207
"Dusie" (Barnes) **3**:10, 16
"Dusk" (Saki) **12**:296, 305, 315
"Dusk" (Salter) **58**:195-96
Dusk and Other Stories (Salter) **58**:172-76, 185,
   190-96
"Dusk before Fireworks" (Parker) **2**:273-74,
   281, 284-85
"Dusky Ruth" (Coppard) **21**:2, 15-16, 18, 20,
   25, 29
"Dust" (Fisher) **25**:6, 17, 20, 25-6
"The Dust Garden" (Ferré) **36**:157
"Dutch Courage" (Kipling) **5**:264
"The Dutch Letters" (Moorhouse) **40**:299, 307,
   324
"Dux gospozi Zanlis" (Leskov) **34**:113
"Dvadtsat' shest' i odna" (Gorky) **28**:134, 136-
   37, 146, 160, 163-64, 167-68, 171, 176-77,
   179, 189, 191
"Dvoe v dekabre" (Kazakov) **43**:68-9
Dvoinik (Dostoevsky)
   See *Dvoynik*
Dvoynik (Dostoevsky) **44**:93-177
"The Dwarf" (Bradbury) **29**:67, 87, 89
"Dwarf House" (Beattie) **11**:15-16
"Dwellers in the Valley" (Lewis) **40**:280
"Dying" (Schnitzler)
   See "Sterben"
"Dying Fires" (Norris) **28**:210-11
"Dykhanie" (Solzhenitsyn) **32**:351
"Dynamite Hands" (Jones) **56**:276
"The Dynamiter" (Stevenson)
   See *The New Arabian Nights*

"Dynd-Kongens Datter" (Andersen) **6**:13-15,
   35-7; **56**:31
"Džan" (Platonov) **42**:2546, 259-61, 264
E domani lunedì (Pirandello) **22**:232, 234, 275
"E due" (Pirandello) **22**:234
E stato così (Ginzburg) **65**:116, 125, 131-32,
   136
"Each Other" (Lessing) **6**:197, 200, 214, 218
"The Eagle Trees" (Jewett) **44**:179-81
"The Ear of Grain" (Grimm and Grimm) **36**:199
"Early Afternoon" (O'Hara) **15**:248, 274
"An Early Christmas" (Price) **22**:384, 388
"Early Coaches" (Dickens) **17**:133
"An Early Evening Conversation" (Andrić)
   See "Razgovor predveče"
"The early Life of Daidoj Shinsuke"
   (Akutagawa Ryūnosuke)
   See "Daidoji Shinsuke no Hansei"
"Early Morning Rabbits" (Metcalf) **43**:79, 100,
   104-5, 107, 158-59, 163
Early Prose Writings (Thomas) **44**:340-41
"Early Sorrow" (Mann)
   See *Disorder and Early Sorrow*
Early Stories (Bowen) **3**:40; **28**:4
"The Ears of Johnny Bear" (Steinbeck) **11**:207-
   08, 225, 229-30, 233-34, 242-44; **37**:357
"Earth 18" (Pohl) **25**:225
"The Earth Gives All and Takes All" (Evans)
   43:22-3, 25, 27
The Earth Gives All and Takes All (Evans)
   43:15, 22-3, 38
"The Earth is a Syllable" (Lewis) **40**:278
"The Earth Men" (Bradbury) **53**:202-5, 207,
   210, 222, 246, 249-50, 252-53
"Earth, Moon" (Boyle) **16**:142
"Earthbound" (Oliphant) **25**:180, 184, 196-200,
   203, 208-09
"Earthbred" (Evans) **43**:28
"Earthquake Almanac" (Twain) **34**:326
"The Earthquake in Chile" (Kleist)
   See "Das Erdbeben in Chili"
"Earth's Holocaust" (Hawthorne) **3**:162, 181-
   82, 189
East and West: The Collected Short Stories of
   W. Somerset Maugham (Maugham) **8**:356,
   358, 360, 370, 380, 382
East India and Company (Morand) **22**:167, 182
"An Easter Carol" (Clarke) **45**:72, 81, 93-4,
   112-13
"The Easter Egg" (Saki) **12**:298, 306, 329
"The Easter Egg Party" (Bowen) **3**:43, 47
"Easter Eve" (Chekhov) **2**:130; **41**:190; **51**:34,
   36, 44, 46, 70, 150, 159-60, 163-64, 199
"The Easter of the Soul" (Henry) **5**:188
"The Easter Procession" (Solzhenitsyn) **32**:365,
   393, 395
"The Easter Wedding" (Dunbar) **8**:122, 136
"Easter Weekend 1971" (Kluge) **61**:56
"An Eastern Tale" (Chekhov) **51**:78
"The Eastmill Reception Centre" (Metcalf)
   43:101, 155-56, 166
Eastward Ha! (Perelman) **32**:230, 233-34
"An Easy Life" (Kazakov) **43**:49, 67
"Eating" (Bass) **60**:41
"Eating Out" (Michaels) **16**:308
"Eating the Placenta" (Dixon) **16**:208
The Ebony Tower (Fowles) **33**:233-69, 275-76,
   283, 287-88, 291-95
"The Eccentric Seclusion of the Old Lady"
   (Chesterton) **1**:120
"Echo" (Barth) **10**:42, 47, 52-4, 59-61, 75-6,
   80-1, 85, 89, 95, 99, 102
"The Echo" (Bowles) **3**:59, 61-2, 66, 72, 77, 79
"The Echo and the Nemesis" (Stafford) **26**:274,
   277, 283-84, 312
"Echoes" (Dinesen) **7**:173-74
Echoes from the Macabre (du Maurier) **18**:130
"Echo's Bones" (Beckett) **16**:106-08
"The Eclipse" (Spencer) **57**:198, 213
Eclogues (Davenport) **16**:183, 187-89
L'école des femmes (Gide) **13**:72, 95, 100-02,
   104, 105

"Economic Conference, 1934" (Lowry) **31**:42

"The Ecstasy and Suffering of Toma Galus" (Andrić)
  See "Zanos i stradanja Tome Galusa"

"The Ed Sullivan Show" (Barthelme) **55**:73

"Eddie" (Schulz) **13**:334

"Eddie Mac" (McGahern) **17**:305

"The Edge" (Narayan) **25**:159, 175

"The Edge of the Evening" (Kipling) **5**:269

"The Edge of the World" (Cheever) **1**:88; **38**:43

"Editha" (Howells) **36**:349, 351-52, 357, 371-74, 377, 379, 382-83, 385, 394, 397, 399

"The Editor" (Tagore)
  See "Shampadak"

"The Editor Regrets..." (Pritchett) **14**:297

An Editor's Tales (Trollope) **28**:311, 313, 316, 320, 322-24, 332-33, 336, 339, 341-42, 353-54

"Edmund" (Hesse) **9**:230-31, 236

"Edna's Husband" (Farrell) **28**:122

"Edna's Ruthie" (Cisneros) **32**:32

Edo and Enam (Agnon) **30**:5, 15, 24, 26-8, 30, 32-4, 71, 75

"An Education" (Ozick) **15**:302, 305, 316-17

"Education of a Stuffed Shirt" (Machado de Assis) **24**:136, 138, 152

"The Education of Audrey" (Mansfield) **9**:301

"The Educational Experience" (Barthelme) **2**:53

"Edward" (Waugh)
  See "Edward of Unique Achievement"

"Edward and God" (Kundera) **24**:87-95, 102-03, 107, 111, 118-21, 124-25

"Edward and Pia" (Barthelme) **2**:30; **55**:108

"Edward of Unique Achievement" (Waugh) **41**:328

"Edward Randolph's Portrait" (Hawthorne) **3**:179, 182

Eekenhof (Storm) **27**:281, 286

"The Effective Remedy" (Bulgakov) **18**:89

"Effigy of War" (Boyle) **5**:63-4

Les égarements de Minne (Colette) **10**:257

"Eger" (Chekhov) **2**:155; **51**:58, 102, 105-6, 151-53

"The Egg and the Hen" (Lispector)
  See "O ovo e a galinha"

"The Egg Race" (Updike) **13**:386

"El egía" (Arreola) **38**:6

"L'église" (Balzac) **5**:14, 23, 31

"The Egoist" (Collier) **19**:103

"Egotism; or, The Bosom Serpent" (Hawthorne) **3**:159, 178, 183, 189; **39**:91

"Egotists" (O'Faolain) **13**:309

"An Egyptian Cigarette" (Chopin) **8**:99

"Egyptian Darkness" (Bulgakov) **18**:86, 88

"Egyptian Nights" (Pushkin)
  See "Yegipetskiye nochi"

Die Ehenschmiede (Arnim) **29**:5

"Eidolons" (Ellison) **14**:142

Eigensinn und Laune (Tieck) **31**:275

Eight Men (Wright) **2**:364, 366, 370, 386, 388

"Eight O'Clock One Morning" (Grau) **15**:149, 160

"Eighteen Springs" (Chang) **28**:26

18 Stories (Boell) **23**:6, 8-9

"1830" (Davenport) **16**:161, 165-66, 170, 183

"The Eighth Day" (Apple) **50**:23, 32-4

"The Eighth Voyage of Sinbad" (Millhauser) **57**:155, 158, 160, 165-66, 181, 183-85

"Eileen" (Gordon) **59**:230, 260, 265, 267-68, 278-80

"Die Einfahrt" (Walser) **20**:341

Einsichten und Ausblicke (Hauptmann) **37**:246

"Einstein Crosses the Elbe Near Hamburg" (Lenz)
  See "Einstein überquert die Elbe bei Hamburg—Geschichte in drei Sätzen"

"Einstein überquert die Elbe bei Hamburg—Geschichte in drei Sätzen" (Lenz) **33**:330, 337

Einzug in ein neues Haus (Hesse) **49**:211

"Eiros and Charmion" (Poe)
  See "The Conversation of Eiros and Charmion"

"Eisenheim the Illusionist" (Millhauser) **57**:155, 158, 168-69, 172, 177, 183, 186

"Either of One or of No One" (Pirandello)
  See "O di uno o di nessuno"

"Ekatri" (Tagore) **48**:316

"Ekskurzija" (Andrić) **36**:43

"The Elaghin Affair" (Bunin) **5**:82-3, 85, 87, 103, 108-09, 115, 119

The Elaghin Affair, and Other Stories (Bunin) **5**:82

"The Elaghin Case" (Bunin)
  See "The Elaghin Affair"

"The Elder Lady" (Borges) **4**:19

"The Elder Mother" (Andersen)
  See "The Elder-Tree Mother"

"Elder Pill, Preacher" (Garland) **18**:154, 160, 163, 176

"The Elder Sister" (Tagore) **48**:326, 328

"The Elder-Tree Mother" (Andersen) **6**:3-4, 14, 24

"Eldorado" (Lessing) **61**:100

Eldorado (Lessing) **6**:191, 194-95

"Eleanor's House" (Cather) **2**:99, 103; **50**:77, 85, 153-54, 200-01, 204

"Electioneerin' on Big Injun Mounting" (Murfree) **22**:188, 207-09, 218

"The Electric Ant" (Dick) **57**:49, 61, 84

The Electrical Experience (Moorhouse) **40**:288, 290-92, 294-98, 303-305, 308-09, 321-22

"Electricity" (Crace) **61**:30-32

"El Elefante X" (Arreola) **38**:36-39

"Elegies" (Price) **22**:370

"Elegy" (Čapek) **36**:89, 107, 121-23

"Elegy for a Freelance" (Carter) **13**:4

"An Elegy for Alma's Aunt Amy" (Suckow) **18**:393, 395, 413, 422, 424

"The Element Follows You Around, Sir!" (Lowry) **31**:42-3

"Elementals" (Benét) **10**:145

"Der Elementargeist" (Hoffmann) **13**:215

"Elements of True Manhood" (Jewett) **6**:167

"Eleonora" (Poe) **22**:291

"Elephant" (Carver) **8**:43

"Elephant and Colosseum" (Lowry) **31**:40, 43-8, 51, 59-61, 63-4, 66, 71-5, 79, 82, 84-5

"An Elephant Never Forgets" (Wilson) **21**:358-59

"Les Eléphants" (Aymé) **41**:8

"Elephants to Ride Upon" (Thomas) **20**:317-18

"Elethia" (Walker) **5**:413

"The Elevator" (Coover) **15**:30-1, 38-40, 48, 50

"Eleven" (Cisneros) **32**:8, 52

"Eleven O'Clock" (Pritchett) **14**:270

Eleven Stained-Glass Segments (Endō) **48**:191

"The Eleventh-Hour Guest" (Villiers de l'Isle Adam)
  See "Le convive des dernières fêtes"

"The Elfin Mound" (Andersen) **6**:7

"Eli the Fanatic" (Roth) **26**:229, 232, 234-35, 245-46, 249, 252, 257, 259, 265, 268

"Elias" (Tolstoy) **9**:388

"Elias Wildmanstadius ou l'Homme moyenage" (Gautier) **20**:10-11

Eligible Men (Elkin)
  See *Searches and Seizures*

"Elijah's Goblet" (Zangwill) **44**:378

"Die Elixiere des Teufels" (Hoffmann) **13**:188

"Elixirs of the Devil" (Hoffmann)
  See "Die Elixiere des Teufels"

"Elizabeth" (Adams) **24**:13

"Elizabeth" (Dreiser) **30**:148

"Elizabeth" (Jackson) **9**:252, 266, 270-71; **39**:211, 212, 223, 224

"Elizabeth Stock's One Story" (Chopin) **8**:100

"Elk" (Bass) **60**:37

"Ella and the Chinese" (O'Hara) **15**:263

"Ellen Adams Wrynn" (Dreiser) **30**:140-141

"The Elm Log" (Solzhenitsyn) **32**:395

"The Elm Tree" (Freeman) **47**:105

"Elmer and Edna" (Suckow) **18**:390

"The Elm-Tree Mother" (Andersen)
  See "The Elder-Tree Mother"

"Elogio da vaidade" (Machado de Assis) **24**:128-29

Elogio de la sombra (Borges) **41**:157, 166

"The Elopement of Allen Poole" (Cather) **50**:73, 91-2

"An Eloquence of Grief" (Crane) **7**:130

"Elphenor and Weasel" (Warner) **23**:384

"Elsewhen" (Heinlein) **55**:218

"Elsie in New York" (Henry) **5**:194

"Elsket" (Page) **23**:285, 297

Elsket, and Other Stories (Page) **23**:285

"Eltha" (Suckow) **18**:393, 414, 417-18, 422, 424-25

"L'elu des rêves" (Villiers de l'Isle Adam) **14**:390, 393

"Em" (Dixon) **16**:210

"The Emancipator" (Gilchrist) **14**:157-59

"Emanuela" (Dreiser) **30**:141-42

"The Embarkment for Cythera" (Cheever) **1**:93

"An Embarrassing Situation" (Chopin) **8**:72

Embarrassments (James) **47**:338

"The Embrace at Vergara" (Alarcon)
  See "El abrazo de Vergara"

"Emden" (Narayan) **25**:169

"Emelyan and the Empty Drum" (Tolstoy)
  See "The Empty Drum"

"Emelyan Pilyai" (Gorky) **28**:139, 145

"The Emerald" (Barthelme) **55**:108, 114

"Emergency" (Johnson) **56**:234, 237, 240, 264, 266-67

"Emergency Exit" (Coppard) **21**:22

"Emeryt" (Schulz) **13**:328

Emilie (Nerval) **18**:362, 364

"Eminence" (Suckow) **18**:391-92, 411

"The Emissary" (Bradbury) **29**:86-7

"Emma Bovary" (Moore) **19**:344-45

"Emma Zunz" (Borges) **4**:16, 18-19, 23, 37, 39, 40; **41**:117, 124, 162, 164, 168-79

"Emmanuele! Emmanuele!" (Gordon) **15**:107-08, 121, 138, 142

"Emotional Bankruptcy" (Fitzgerald) **6**:50

"The Emperor's New Clothes" (Andersen)
  See "Keiserens nye Kl[dj]der"

"Empire" (Ford) **56**:138-39, 141, 145, 149, 152, 159-60, 174, 187, 194-95

"The Empire of the Ants" (Wells) **6**:361, 365, 382, 391-92, 403

"The Empty Amulet" (Bowles) **3**:76

"The Empty Drum" (Tolstoy) **9**:377, 380, 388

"An Empty Purse" (Jewett) **6**:156

"The Empty Room" (Caldwell) **19**:5-6

"The Empty Street" (Cowan) **28**:75, 77

The Empty Street (Cowan) **28**:74-6

"En defensa de la Trigolibia" (Fuentes) **24**:38, 53-5

"En el gran ecbó" (Cabrera Infante) **39**:18, 23

"En el presidio" (Pardo Bazán) **30**:279

"En famille" (Maupassant) **1**:259-60, 263, 272, 274, 278

"En la madrugada" (Rulfo) **25**:245, 249-50, 255, 257-58, 262-63, 265-66, 273-75

"En la Noche" (Bradbury) **29**:42

En tranvía (Pardo Bazán) **30**:270, 272

"En verdad os digo" (Arreola) **38**:4, 7-8, 22-23

"En voyage" (Maupassant) **1**:280; **64**:283, 291

"En wagon" (Maupassant) **1**:263

"The Enamored Youth" (Hesse) **9**:243

"El encaje roto" (Pardo Bazán) **30**:264

"The Encantadas; or, The Enchanted Isles" (Melville) **1**:293, 297-99, 303-04, 308, 310-11, 321-22, 329

"The Enchanted Bluff" (Cather) **2**:97, 102, 104-05, 108; **50**:63, 75, 124, 229, 233, 236, 249, 253

"The Enchanted Fruit" (Campbell) **19**:74, 84

"An Enchanted Garden" (Calvino)
  See "Un giardino incantato"

The Enchanted House (Musil)
  See *Die Versuchung der Stillen Veronika*

"The Enchanted Kiss" (Henry) **5**:159, 163
Enchanted Night (Millhauser) **57**:189-90
"Enchanted Palace" (Kiely) **58**:146
"The Enchanted Pilgrim" (Leskov)
    See "Očarovannyj strannik"
"The Enchanted Sea-Wilderness" (Twain) **6**:337
"The Enchanted Spot" (Gogol)
    See "Zakoldovannoe mesto"
"The Enchanted Wanderer" (Leskov)
    See "Očarovannyj strannik"
"The Enchantress" (Bates) **10**:123
"The Enchantress" (Stevenson) **51**:248-49
The Enchantress, and Other Stories (Bates)
    10:123
"Encher Tempo" (Machado de Assis) **24**:145
"The Encounter" (Ballard) **53**:5, 8, 48
"The Encounter" (Borges)
    See "El encuentro"
"An Encounter" (Coover) **15**:46
"An Encounter" (Joyce) **3**:201, 205, 208, 217-
    18, 225-26, 230, 232, 234, 237, 247;
    26:46-7, 50; **44**:262-63, 265, 288, 290-92,
    294-95, 297, 299, 311; **64**:222
"Encounter at Dawn" (Clarke) **3**:127, 135, 143
"Encounter with Evil" (Cortázar)
    See "Encuentro con el mal"
Encounters (Bowen) **3**:29, 40
"Encrucijada" (Bioy Casares) **17**:53, 56
"El encuentro" (Arreola) **38**:11
"El encuentro" (Borges) **41**:176
"Encuentro con el mal" (Cortázar) **7**:94
"The End" (Beckett)
    See "La Fin"
"The End" (Borges)
    See "El fin"
"End Game" (Ballard) **53**:11, 44
"The End of a Career" (Stafford) **26**:279, 283-
    84, 301, 316
"The End of a Good Man" (O'Faolain) **13**:288,
    293
End of a Mission (Boell)
    See *Ende einer Dienstfahrt*
"End of a Summer's Day" (Campbell) **19**:63-4,
    71, 73, 88, 92
"The End of a War" (Lenz) **33**:337-38
"End of August" (Pavese)
    See "Fine d'agosto"
"The End of Christy Tucker" (Caldwell) **19**:18,
    38
"The End of Ice" (Moorhouse) **40**:290
"The End of It" (Hood) **42**:138, 146, 189, 205,
    226, 234-35
"The End of Oplatka" (Čapek)
    See "Oplatkuv konec"
"The End of Something" (Hemingway) **1**:208,
    234, 244-45; **40**:209; **63**:72, 81, 83, 91
"The End of the Beginning" (Bradbury) **29**:78
"The End of the Beginning" (Norris) **28**:201
"The End of the Duel" (Borges) **4**:20, 33-4
End of the Game (Cortázar)
    See *Final del juego*
"End of the Line" (Campbell) **19**:88
The End of the Night (Mauriac)
    See *La fin de la nuit*
"The End of the Old Folks' Home" (Babel)
    16:24
"The End of the Party" (Greene) **29**:184-85,
    190, 193
"The End of the Passage" (Kipling)
    See "At the End of the Passage"
"The End of the Story" (London) **4**:256
"The End of the Tether" (Conrad) **9**:140-41,
    143, 145
"The End of the Vendetta" (Davis) **38**:110
"The End of the World" (Adams) **24**:16-17
"The End of the World" (Turgenev) **7**:335
The End of the World, and Other Stories
    (Gallant) **5**:130
"An End of Troubles" (Narayan) **25**:138, 141
"The End of Wisdom" (Chesterton) **1**:140
"Das Ende der Welt" (Walser) **20**:334-35

Ende einer Dienstfahrt (Boell) **23**:9, 11, 19,
    22-3, 33
"Endicott of the Red Cross" (Hawthorne)
    3:175-76
"Ending" (Grau) **15**:163
Endless Mountains (Price) **22**:384, 387
"L'endormeuse" (Maupassant) **1**:284
"The Enduring Chill" (O'Connor) **61**:201,
    203-4, 206, 208, 225
"An Enduring Friendship" (O'Faolain) **13**:297
"Enemies" (Chekhov) **2**:158; **51**:30, 124, 159-
    60, 164, 166-68
"Enemies" (Gordimer) **17**:153, 187
"The Enemies" (Gordon) **15**:119
"The Enemies" (Thomas) **3**:407-09; **44**:322,
    328, 332-33, 338, 346, 357-58
*Enemies of the System: A Tale of Homo
    Uniformis* (Aldiss) **36**:10-12, 15, 17
"The Enemies to Each Other" (Kipling) **5**:283;
    54:94
"The Enemies United" (Thomas) **44**:333
"The Enemy" (Naipaul) **38**:300, 320, 322, 327,
    345
The Enemy (Mauriac)
    See *Le mal*
"Energetic" (Walser) **20**:355
"L'Enfance d'un chef" (Sartre) **32**:254-55, 258-
    61, 270, 272
"L'enfant aux souliers de pain" (Gautier) **20**:16
L'enfant chargé de chaînes (Mauriac)
    24:172,176-79
"L'enfant malade" (Colette) **10**:274-76
"Engine Driver's Wife" (Platonov) **42**:253
Engine Trouble (Narayan) **25**:153, 156-57
"Engineer-Private Paul Klee Misplaces an
    Aircraft between Milbertschofen and
    Cambrai, March 1916" (Barthelme) **2**:49,
    54; **55**:42, 84, 119
"Engladia's" (Narayan) **25**:156
"England, My England" (Lawrence) **4**:212-13,
    229, 231-32, 235; **19**:280
England, My England, and Other Stories
    (Lawrence) **4**:202, 230-31, 233-37
"England versus England" (Lessing) **6**:199, 218
"An English Coast Picture" (Gissing) **37**:74
"The English Garden" (Abish) **44**:4-5, 8-9, 12-
    13, 15, 29
"The English Officer" (Moravia)
    See "L'ufficiale inglese"
"The English Spanish Girl" (Cervantes)
    See "La española inglesa"
"English Summer: A Gothic Romance"
    (Chandler) **23**:110-11
"English Writers on America" (Irving) **2**:244,
    254
"The Enigma" (Fowles) **33**:233-34, 236, 238,
    244, 247-48, 257-61, 263-65, 268, 273-75,
    283, 285-86, 289
"Enigmas" (Alcott) **27**:3
"Enjoy Enjoy" (Pohl) **25**:235
"L'enlèvement de la rédoute" (Mérimée) **7**:278,
    280-1, 283, 287-9
"The Enlightenments of Pagett, M. P."
    (Kipling) **5**:261
Enormous Changes at the Last Minute (Paley)
    8:391-92, 397, 407-08, 410-11, 415
"The Enormous Door" (Price) **22**:387
"The Enormous Radio" (Cheever) **1**:106, 109;
    38:52, 61, 66, 84; **57**:8
The Enormous Radio, and Other Stories
    (Cheever) **1**:89, 92, 95, 98-100;
"The Enormous Room" (Ballard) **53**:114, 116,
    123
"The Enormous Space" (Ballard) **53**:67
"Enough" (Turgenev) **7**:323, 325, 336
Enough (Beckett)
    See *Assez*
"Enragée" (Maupassant) **1**:274
"Enrico's Journey" (Appelfeld) **42**:43, 45
"Enter a Dragoon" (Hardy) **2**:215; **60**:182
Enter and Exit (Boell)
    See "Als der Krieg ausbrach"

"Enter Mitchell" (Lawson) **18**:215
"Enter the Fanatic" (Ellison) **14**:103
"Entered as Second-Class Matter" (Perelman)
    32:210
Entering the War (Calvino)
    See *L'entrada en guerra*
Entfernung von der Truppe (Boell) **23**:4, 11, 35
"An Entire Life" (Pilnyak)
    See "Tselaya zhizn"
"The Entomologist" (Cable) **4**:50
L'entrada en guerra (Calvino) **3**:97, 116;
    48:150
"Entrance" (Dybek) **55**:129-30
"The Entrance" (Walser)
    See "Die Einfahrt"
"Entrance to an Unwritten Novel" (Forster)
    27:106, 120
L'entrave (Colette) **10**:257, 272
"Entrevue à Solesmes" (Villiers de l'Isle
    Adam) **14**:386, 396
"Entropy" (Gilchrist) **63**:36
"Entropy" (Pynchon) **14**:308, 312-13, 316-17,
    319-22, 324, 330, 334, 339-44, 347-49
L'envers du music-hall (Colette) **10**:291
"L'Envoi: The Train to Mariposa" (Leacock)
    39:246, 253, 254, 257, 259, 260, 261, 270,
    273, 275
"Envy: or, Yiddish in America" (Ozick) **15**:297-
    301, 304, 309, 312, 314, 316, 321; **60**:312,
    334, 346
"Epaulettes" (Atwood) **46**:75
"Ephemeral Friendships" (Castellanos)
    See "Las amistades efímeras"
"EPICAC" (Vonnegut) **8**:429
L'epidemia: Racconti (Moravia) **26**:162-63, 180
The Epidemic (Moravia)
    See *L'epidemia: Racconti*
"Epifanskie shljuzy" (Platonov) **42**:266
Epifanskie shljuzy (Platonov) **42**:256, 266
Epifany Locks (Platonov)
    See *Epifanskie shljuzy*
The Epigram (Keller)
    See *Das Sinngedicht*
"Epilog to Stifters 'Nachsommer'" (Boell)
    See "Epilog zu Stifters 'Nachsommer'"
"Epilog zu Stifters 'Nachsommer'" (Boell)
    23:19
"Epilogue: The Photographer" (Munro) **3**:332,
    338, 340, 343
"Les epingles" (Maupassant) **1**:263, 286
"Episcopal Justice" (Leskov)
    See "Vladyčnyj sud"
"Episode" (Maugham) **8**:380
"Episode at Gastein" (Sansom) **21**:91, 93, 95
"An Episode in Bachelor Life" (Moore) **19**:343
"An Episode in Married Life" (Moore)
    19:343-44
"Episode in the Life of an Ancestor" (Boyle)
    5:54, 70
"An Episode in the Life of Professor Brooke"
    (Wolff) **63**:260, 263, 282, 284, 287-88,
    290-92, 295-96, 299-300, 314, 336
"An Episode of Cathedral History" (James)
    16:226, 229-30, 232, 240, 244, 246, 248,
    252, 255
"An Episode of War" (Crane) **7**:104, 109-10;
    56:105-10
"An Episode of West Woodlands" (Harte)
    59:308
"Episodes of a Return" (Farrell) **28**:125
"Epitafio" (Arreola) **38**:6-7, 12
"Epitalamio" (Arreola) **38**:5, 9
"Epitaph" (Arreola)
    See "Epitafio"
"Epitaph" (O'Brien) **10**:345, 347
"Epithalamium" (Yamamoto) **34**:348, 350, 358-
    59, 364
"Eppis Bars Boorish Bike Fans as Coaster
    Brakes Roar in Metropolitan Opera"
    (Perelman) **32**:240
"Epstein" (Roth) **26**:231, 238, 251, 257-60,
    265-66

Equator (Aldiss) **36**:18

The Equilibriad (Sansom) **21**:83-4, 98, 127

"Equitable Awards" (Auchincloss) **22**:51

"Det er Dig, Fabelen sigter til" (Andersen) **56**:33

"Erba del nosro orto" (Pirandello) **22**:275

"Das Erdbeben in Chili" (Kleist) **22**:106, 110-14, 116-19, 121, 124, 126, 128, 131-32, 135, 146-48, 150-53

Erections, Ejaculations, Exhibitions, and General Tales of Ordinary Madness (Bukowski)
    See *Life and Death in the Charity Ward*

Eréndira (García Márquez)
    See *La increíble y triste historia de la cándida Eréndira y de su abuela desalmada*

"Eric Hermannson's Soul" (Cather) **2**:96, 100-01, 105, 107; **50**:59, 61, 72, 89, 96-7, 99-100, 104, 133-34, 187-88, 190-91, 193, 197, 245-47, 272-75

"The Erl-King" (Carter) **13**:9, 27-28

Erma bifronte (Pirandello) **22**:275

"Ermolai and the Miller's Wife" (Turgenev)
    See "Yermolai and the Miller's Wife"

"Ermolaj and the Miller's Wife" (Turgenev)
    See "Yermolai and the Miller's Wife"

"Ernestine" (Dreiser) **30**:141-42

"Ernestine ou la Naissance de l'amour" (Stendhal) **27**:247

"Ernesto de Tal" (Machado de Assis) **24**:131, 151

"Ernst in Civilian Clothes" (Gallant) **5**:133, 138

"Eros Rampant" (Updike) **13**:387

"An Erotic Memoir in Six Parts" (Moorhouse) **40**:310

Erotic Tales (Moravia) **26**:171, 173-74

"Um erradio" (Machado de Assis) **24**:128-29

"Errand" (Carver) **8**:43

"Errant Wheat" (Fuentes)
    See "Trigo errante"

"Error" (Singer) **3**:377

"An Error in Chemistry" (Faulkner) **1**:179

"Der erste Schritt" (Walser) **20**:338

"Erstes Leid" (Kafka) **5**:239; **29**:343, 358, 371; **60**:259, 273, 275, 277, 279

Erzählungen (Kleist) **22**:114, 135, 142

Erzählungen 1949-1984 (Lenz) **33**:338

"Es que somos muy pobres" (Rulfo) **25**:245, 249-50, 263-65, 273, 279-80

"Esarhaddon, King of Assyria" (Tolstoy) **9**:380, 388

"Esbjerg, en la costa" (Onetti) **23**:246, 250, 252

"Esbjerg, on the Coast" (Onetti)
    See "Esbjerg, en la costa"

"The Escape" (Appelfeld)
    See "Habrihah"

"Escape" (Galsworthy) **22**:73

"The Escape" (Mansfield) **9**:293

"The Escape" (Moravia) **26**:142, 155

"Escape" (Pirandello) **22**:231, 241, 244

The Escaped Cock (Lawrence)
    See *The Man Who Died*

"Escapement" (Ballard) **1**:68; **53**:10, 41-2

"La escritura del Dios" (Borges) **4**:7, 23, 28-9

"La escuela de noche" (Cortázar) **7**:91

"Eshche o cherte" (Gorky) **28**:187

"Eskimo" (Munro) **3**:347

"The Eskimo Connection" (Yamamoto) **34**:359

"Eskimo Lamps, or The Trials and Tribulations of a Specialist" (Lenz) **33**:337-38

"Eskimo Love" (Apple) **50**:23, 32, 34-9, 45

"Esmé" (Saki) **12**:305, 330-33

"Esmé" (Salinger)
    See "For Esmé—with Love and Squalor"

"La española inglesa" (Cervantes) **12**:3-5, 7-8, 14-16, 18, 35, 44

El espejo de la muerte (Unamuno) **11**:312

"La espera" (Borges) **4**:5, 16, 37-9; **41**:162

Essays and Fiction (Gissing) **37**:79

"Esse est percipi" (Bioy Casares) **17**:75

"Die Essenholer" (Boell) **23**:4

The Essential Ellison: A 25-Year Retrospective (Ellison) **14**:136, 143-47

"Estación de la mano" (Cortázar) **7**:94

"Ester Lucero" (Allende) **65**:26

"La estéril" (Pardo Bazán) **30**:262

"Esther" (Toomer) **1**:445, 450-51, 457, 459; **45**:185, 191, 200-03, 236, 260, 265, 267, 275, 291, 296, 326-27, 335, 360-62, 374, 376-77

"Esther Kreindel the Second" (Singer) **3**:363; **53**:293

"Esther Norn" (Dreiser) **30**:134, 141

"Estos fueron los palacios" (Fuentes)
    See "These Were Palaces"

"The Estuary" (Metcalf) **43**:102, 106-7, 131-33, 137-39

"Et Dona Ferentes" (Wilson) **21**:327, 331, 337, 342, 353, 357, 365

"Et godt Humeur" (Andersen) **56**:37

"Etched in Moonlight" (Stephens) **50**:335-36

Etched in Moonlight (Stephens) **50**:306-07 312-17, 326, 330-32, 335-36

"Eterna" (Lavin) **4**:184, 189

The Eternal Husband (Dostoevsky)
    See *Vechny muzh*

"Eternal Life" (Aleichem)
    See "Oylem-habe"

"The Eternal Moment" (Forster) **27**:69-80, 87-8, 96-7, 100, 102-04, 121-23

The Eternal Moment and Other Stories (Forster) **27**:68-70, 74, 76, 83, 89-90, 06, 114, 124

The Eternal Smile and Other Stories (Lagerkvist) **12**:180-88, 192, 195, 197-98

"The Eternity of Forms" (London) **4**:255-56, 295

"Ethan Brand" (Hawthorne) **3**:159, 179-80, 182; **39**:95, 136

Ethan Frome (Wharton) **6**:415-17, 419, 422, 438-39

"The Ethics of Pig" (Henry) **5**:166

"The Etiquette of Deception" (Moorhouse) **40**:311

"El etnógrafo" (Borges) **41**:152, 154-55

"L'etonnant couple moutonnet" (Villiers de l'Isle Adam) **14**:384

"L'etranger" (Baudelaire) **18**:4-5, 8, 59, 64

"Etude de femme" (Balzac) **5**:31

Etudes analytiques (Balzac) **5**:8-9, 31

Études de moeurs au XIXe siècle (Balzac) **5**:3

Etudes philosophiques (Balzac) **5**:8-9, 12, 31, 48; **59**:4, 22, 25, 33-34, 39

Eugenia (Keller) **26**:97-8

"Eugénie Grandet" (Barthelme) **2**:40

"Euphrasie" (Chopin) **8**:69-70

"Eupompus Gave Splendour to Art by Numbers" (Huxley) **39**:154, 165-66

Eureka: A Prose Poem (Poe) **22**:308, 316

Europe at Love (Morand)
    See *L'Europe galante*

L'Europe galante (Morand) **22**:167-69, 171-72, 182

"Eustacia" (Stuart) **31**:263

"Eva" (Arreola) **38**:9

"Eva está dentro de su gato" (García Márquez) **8**:154-55

"Eva Inside Her Cat" (García Márquez)
    See "Eva está dentro de su gato"

Eva Luna (Allende)
    See *Cuentos de Eva Luna*

"Evan" (Warner) **23**:370

"Evangel in Cyrene" (Garland) **18**:163

"Eva's Visit to Fairy Land" (Alcott) **27**:39

"Evelina's Garden" (Freeman) **47**:84, 103

"Eveline" (Joyce) **3**:205, 226, 231, 234, 247-48; **26**:46-7; **44**:265, 284, 288; **64**:222, 233, 242

"Evelyn and the Rest of Us" (Caldwell) **19**:21, 33

"Even The Devil Can't Save the World" (Moravia) **26**:173-74

"Evening" (Babel) **16**:27-8, 50, 52-3, 54, 56

"Evening at Home" (Boyle) **5**:63-4

"The Evening at Sissy Kamara's" (White) **39**:280, 292-95, 317, 325, 335, 343

"The Evening Gift" (Narayan) **25**:141

"An Evening Meal" (Price) **22**:386, 388

"An Evening Performance" (Garrett) **30**:173

An Evening Performance: New and Selected Short Stories (Garrett) **30**:179-80

"Evening Primrose" (Collier) **19**:99, 102-04, 110, 113-14

"Evening Twilight" (Baudelaire)
    See "Le crépuscule du soir"

"An Evening with Dr. Faust" (Hesse) **9**:230, 236

"An Evening with John Joe Dempsey" (Trevor) **21**:237, 265; **58**:224, 230

"The Evening's at Seven" (Thurber) **1**:417, 425; **47**:378

"An Evening's Entertainment" (James) **16**:231, 234, 237

Evenings on a Farm near Dikanka (Gogol)
    See *Vechera ná khutore bliz Dikanki*

"L'eventail" (Čapek) **36**:109

"Eventide" (Sansom) **21**:90, 96

"Events at Drimaghleen" (Trevor) **21**:246-47, 249-50, 252-53, 260; **58**:298

"Events of That Easter" (Cheever) **1**:93

Eventyr, fortalte for børn (Andersen) **6**:8, 12, 15, 22, 30; **56**:8, 36

"The Everlasting Secret Family" (Moorhouse) **40**:297-300, 305, 307, 309-11, 320, 324

The Everlasting Secret Family and Other Secrets (Moorhouse) **40**:323-24

"Everybody Knew Bubba Riff" (Wideman) **62**:273-74, 278, 286, 288

"Everybody Was Very Nice" (Benét) **10**:142, 144, 153

"An Every-Day Girl" (Jewett) **6**:156-59

"Everything" (Saroyan) **21**:163

"Everything I Know" (Lish) **18**:284

"Everything in Its Right Place" (Andersen) **6**:4, 22-3

"Everything Is Wild" (Thurber) **47**:383

"Everything Stuck to Him" (Carver)
    See "Distance"

"Everything That Rises Must Converge" (O'Connor) **1**:341, 363; **23**:227; **61**:153, 156, 201, 203, 228

Everything That Rises Must Converge (O'Connor) **1**:341-43; **23**:185, 193, 195, 209, 237; **61**:199, 201-2

"Eve's Diary" (Twain) **6**:295

"The Eviction" (O'Flaherty) **6**:277, 280

"Evidence Is High Proof" (Stuart) **31**:265

Det eviga leendet (Lagerkvist) **12**:180-8, 192, 195, 197-8

"An Evil Affair" (Chekhov) **51**:96

"Evil Allures, but Good Endures" (Tolstoy) **9**:388

"The Evil Angel" (Lagerkvist)
    See "Den onda ängeln"

"The Evil Clergyman" (Lovecraft) **52**:291, 309

"The Evil Eye" (Pavese) **19**:375

"The Evil Eye" (Svevo)
    See "Il malocchio"

"The Evil Guest" (Le Fanu) **14**:221, 247

Evil Sagas (Lagerkvist)
    See *Onda sagor*

"The Evil Spirit" (Pirandello) **22**:254

Evil Tales (Lagerkvist)
    See *Onda sagor*

"Evil-Doers" (Gorky) **28**:137

"The Evils of Spain" (Pritchett) **14**:270, 285

"Evolution" (Machado de Assis) **24**:155

"The Evolution of Lorna Treadway" (Auchincloss) **22**:38

"Ex cathedra" (Machado de Assis) **24**:129

"Ex Oblivione" (Lovecraft) **52**:291, 309

"Ex Parte" (Lardner) **32**:133-34, 139-41, 150

"The Exalted Omega" (Machen) **20**:176

"Das Examen" (Lenz) **33**:327, 337-38
"Examen de la obra de Herbert Quain" (Borges) **41**:79
"The Examination" (Pirandello) **22**:243
"An Examination of the Work of Herbert Quain" (Borges)
    See "Examen de la obra de Herbert Quain"
"Excellent People" (Chekhov) **2**:155
"The Excursion" (Andrić)
    See "Ekskurzija"
"Excursion in Reality" (Waugh) **41**:323
"The Executor" (Spark) **10**:362, 366, 368, 370
Exemplary Novels (Cervantes)
    See *Novelas exemplares*
Exemplary Stories (Cervantes)
    See *Novelas exemplares*
Exemplary Tales (Cervantes)
    See *Novelas exemplares*
"Exercises in the Variable Foot" (Williams) **31**:334
"Exhibit Piece" (Dick) **57**:109-10
"Ex-Humans" (Gorky)
    See "Byvshii lyudi"
Exhumations (Isherwood) **56**:205-7
L'éxil et le royaume (Camus) **9**:103-05, 108-11, 118, 122, 125-26, 131, 134
"The Exile" (Moore)
    See "An Deóraidhe"
Exile and the Kingdom (Camus)
    See *L'éxil et le royaume*
"Exile of Eons" (Clarke) **3**:144
"The Exiles" (Bradbury) **29**:47; **53**:199-200, 215
"Exodus" (Hemingway) **63**:125
"An Exorcism" (Malamud) **15**:180, 183, 193-94
Expanded Universe: The New Worlds of Robert A. Heinlein (Heinlein) **55**:229
"The Expansion of the Universe" (Gilchrist) **14**:157
"Expectations" (Galsworthy) **22**:64, 74, 101
"The Expelled" (Beckett)
    See "L'Expulsé"
"Expelled" (Cheever) **57**:9
"Ex-People" (Gorky)
    See "Byvshii lyudi"
"Experience" (Suckow) **18**:417
"Les expériences du Docteur Crookes" (Villiers de l'Isle Adam) **14**:396
Experiences of an Irish R.M. (Somerville & Ross) **56**:339
"The Experiment" (James) **16**:251
"An Experiment in Love" (Kluge)
    See "Ein Liebesversuch"
"An Experiment in Luxury" (Crane) **7**:136, 138
"An Experiment in Misery" (Crane) **7**:102, 108-09, 129, 136, 138, 145; **56**:88
"The Experiment of Professor Rous" (Čapek) **36**:127
"The Experimental World" (Lagerkvist) **12**:195
"The Explanation" (Barthelme) **2**:35, 40-1, 55; **55**:9-10, 18-9, 88, 119
"The Exploit of Choolah, the Chicksaw" (Murfree) **22**:187
Exploits and Opinions of Doctor Faustroll, Pataphysician (Jarry)
    See *Gestes et opinions du Dr. Faustroll, pataphysicien, roman néo-scientifique*
The Exploits of Brigadier Gerard (Doyle) **12**:81-2
"Explorers We" (Dick) **57**:82-83
"Explosive Invention" (Fuentes)
    See "El que inventó la pólvora"
"L'Expulsé" (Beckett) **16**:66, 71, 73-4, 87-8, 90-1
"The Expulsion" (Appelfeld)
    See "Hagerush"
Extracts from Captain Stormfield's Visit to Heaven (Twain) **6**:295, 303, 339
"La extraña muerte del capitancito Candelario" (Ferré) **36**:152
"El extranjero" (Alarcon) **64**:2-4, 28, 30, 38

"The Extraordinary Adventures of a Doctor" (Bulgakov) **18**:92
"Extraordinary Little Cough" (Thomas) **3**:394, 403, 406, 411-12; **44**:324, 351, 360
"The Extravagance of the Dead" (Oe)
    See "Shisha no ogori"
"Extreme Magic" (Calisher) **15**:4-5
Extreme Magic (Calisher)
    See *Extreme Magic: A Novella and Other Stories*
Extreme Magic: A Novella and Other Stories (Calisher) **15**:4-5, 23-7
"Extricating Young Gussie" (Wodehouse) **2**:342
"The Eye" (Bowles) **3**:75, 80
"The Eye" (Powers) **4**:368
"The Eye" (Toomer) **45**:255, 258
"The Eye Altering" (Le Guin) **12**:231, 238
"The Eye of Allah" (Kipling) **5**:283, 285
"The Eye of Apollo" (Chesterton) **1**:121, 136; **46**:132, 149, 152
"Eye of Childhood" (Campbell) **19**:76
The Eye of the Heron (Le Guin) **12**:231, 235
"Eye of the Lynx" (Ligotti) **16**:269-70
"The Eye of the Storm" (White) **39**:325
"The Eye of the Sybil" (Dick) **57**:68
"The Eyelash" (Davie) **52**:8
"The Eyes" (Wharton) **6**:424, 426, 428, 430, 433
"The Eye's Journey" (Nin) **10**:303, 305
"Eyes of a Blue Dog" (García Márquez)
    See "Ojos de perro azul"
Eyes of a Blue Dog (García Márquez) **8**:182
Eyes of Amber (Vinge) **24**:328, 331, 333-35, 337-39, 346-49
"Eyes of Amber" and Other Stories* (Vinge) **24**:338, 343, 345
"The Eyes of the Panther" (Bierce) **9**:87
"The Eyes of the Peacock" (Wilson) **21**:357, 359, 363-64
"The Eyes of the Poor" (Baudelaire)
    See "Les yeux des pauvres"
"Eyes of Zapata" (Cisneros) **32**:7, 10, 37, 39, 48
"Eye-Witness" (Oates) **6**:251-52
"Eyniklekh" (Singer) **53**:322
"An eytse" (Aleichem) **33**:26-8, 35-9, 52
"Ezekiel" (Fisher) **25**:17, 20
"Ezekiel Learns" (Fisher) **25**:17, 20
"The Fabbri Tape" (Auchincloss) **22**:53
"A Fable" (Clarke)
    See "Coll. SS. Trins. Ap. Toron.—A Fable"
"A Fable" (Lavin) **4**:183
"The Fable of the Ant and the Grasshopper" (Hood) **42**:238
"The Fable of the Goat" (Agnon)
    See "Ma'ase ha'Ez"
Fables (Stevenson) **51**:239
Fables and Would-be Tales (Čapek) **36**:130
Fables for Our Time and Famous Poems Illustrated (Thurber) **1**:415, 417, 422, 424, 426-27; **47**:362, 365
"La Fabrique" (Aymé) **41**:11, 18, 21
"La Fabulosa: A Texas Operetta" (Cisneros) **32**:35-6
"The Face" (de la Mare) **14**:79, 82, 84, 86, 89
"The Face and the Image" (Agnon)
    See "Ha-panim la-panim"
"A Face from Atlantis" (Gordimer) **17**:152-53
"The Face in the Desert" (Campbell) **19**:81
"The Face in the Target" (Chesterton) **1**:122
"The Face of Helene Bournow" (Ellison) **14**:118
The Face of Misfortune (Onetti)
    See *La cara de la desgracia*
"A Face of Stone" (Williams) **31**:304, 326, 332-33, 340, 344-45, 351
"The Face of the War" (Wolfe) **33**:370-71
"The Face on the Barroom Floor" (Algren) **33**:88, 108, 110
"Face to Face" (Wolff) **63**:266, 282, 287-88, 290, 292, 295-96, 300, 305, 308-10, 312, 315, 320, 323, 338, 342
Face to Face (Gordimer) **17**:157, 165

Faces (Andrić)
    See *Lica*
"The Faces at Pine Dunes" (Campbell) **19**:66, 73, 92
"The Faces of the Medal" (Cortázar) **7**:63
Facino Cane (Balzac) **5**:26, 31, 33; **59**:3-10
"The Factory Chicken" (Calvino) **48**:147
"Facts" (Galsworthy) **22**:98
"The Facts" (Lardner) **32**:115, 195-96
"Facts concerning the Late Arthur Jermyn and His Family" (Lovecraft) **3**:258, 264; **52**:292-93, 307, 335, 343, 345, 362
"The Facts Concerning the Recent Carnival of Crime in Connecticut" (Twain) **26**:357
"The Facts in the Case of M. Valdemar" (Poe) **1**:379, 385, 400; **34**:250; **54**:170
"The Facts of Life" (Maugham) **8**:380
"The Fad of the Fisherman" (Chesterton) **1**:122
"A Faery Legend" (Hawthorne) **39**:126
Das Fähnlein der sieben Aufrechten (Keller) **26**:109, 114-15
Fahrenheit 451 (Bradbury) **53**:195, 199, 214, 248, 256-62, 264
"The Failed Men" (Aldiss) **36**:5
"Failure" (Chekhov) **51**:77
"The Failure of David Berry" (Jewett) **6**:151
"A Faint Heart" (Dostoevsky) **2**:170-72, 191-92, 195
"Faint Light" (Dazai Osamu)
    See "Hakumei"
"The Fair at Sorochintsy" (Gogol)
    See "Soročinskaja jamarka"
The Fair Egbert (Tieck)
    See *Der blonde Eckbert*
"A Fair Exile" (Garland) **18**:182-83
The Fair Lavinia, and Others (Freeman) **47**:84
"The Fair Young Willowy Tree" (Coppard) **21**:17, 27
"The Fairy Dell" (Alcott) **27**:38
"The Fairy Goose" (O'Flaherty) **6**:261-62, 269-70, 272, 275, 281, 285
"Fairy Pinafores" (Alcott) **27**:43
"The Fairy Spring" (Alcott) **27**:45
"Fairy Tale" (Chesterton) **1**:136
"Fairy Tale for Bored Bar-Flies" (Perelman) **32**:220
"The Fairy Tale of One Who Went Forth to Learn Fear" (Grimm and Grimm) **36**:191, 194
Fairy Tales (Andersen)
    See *Eventyr, fortalte for bøorn*
Fairy Tales (Dazai Osamu)
    See *Otogi zōshi*
"Fairy Tales for Tired Clubmen" (Perelman) **32**:241
"Fairy-Kist" (Kipling) **5**:284
"Fairyland" (Galsworthy) **22**:63, 101
"Faith" (Hammett) **17**:217
"Faith" (Pirandello) **22**:254
"The Faith Cure Man" (Dunbar) **8**:122, 128-29
"Faith, Half Faith and No Faith at All" (Stevenson) **51**:239
"Faith, Hope, and Charity" (McGahern) **17**:299, 309, 317
"Faith in a Tree" (Paley) **8**:408
"Faith in the Afternoon" (Paley) **8**:392, 398, 406, 408
"The Faith of Men" (London) **4**:258-59, 282, 285, 287
Faith of Our Fathers (Dick) **57**:46, 49-50, 91
"The Faith of Wei Cheng" (Akutagawa Ryūnosuke)
    See "Bisei no shin"
"The Faithful Fiancée" (Pardo Bazán) **30**:290
"A Faithful Heart" (Moore) **19**:343
"Faithful John" (Grimm and Grimm) **36**:205
"Faithfulness" (Nin) **10**:306
"The Faithless Wife" (O'Faolain) **13**:296
"Faldum" (Hesse) **9**:235
"Falešné květiny" (Čapek) **36**:110
"Falk" (Conrad) **9**:143, 147, 151-52
"The Fall" (Auchincloss) **22**:44

"The Fall" (Moravia) **26**:138, 141
"The Fall" (Pritchett) **14**:286, 298
"The Fall of a Sparrow" (Auchincloss) **22**:47
"The Fall of Edward Barnard" (Maugham)
    8:370
"The Fall of Joseph Timmins" (O'Flaherty)
    6:262
"The Fall of the House of Usher" (Poe) **1**:377,
    379-80, 383, 385-86, 391, 398-99, 403-07;
    22:288-356; **34**:249, 258, 265, 274, 283;
    35:321, 331, 336; **54**:143, 161, 180, 182,
    185, 209, 231, 240
"The Fall of the House of Voticky" (Čapek)
    See "Pád rodu Votických"
"The Fall River Axe Murders" (Carter) **13**:14-
    18, 20
"Fallen" (Mann)
    See "Gefallen"
"Fallen Star" (Collier) **19**:106, 110, 112
"The Fallguy's Faith" (Coover) **15**:47
"The Falling Dog" (Barthelme) **2**:55; **55**:60,
    62-4, 120
"Falling in Love in Ashton, British Columbia"
    (Oates) **6**:230
"Falling Rocks, Narrowing Road, Cul-de-sac,
    Stop" (O'Faolain) **13**:296
"The Falling Sleet" (Dostoevsky) **2**:165; **33**:162
"Fallings from Us, Vanishings" (Hood) **42**:137,
    144, 180, 196, 198, 200, 225-27, 230, 235
"The False Collar" (Andersen) **6**:7
"False Dawn" (Kipling) **5**:261
False Dawn (The 'Forties) (Wharton) **6**:439-40
"False Face" (Fisher)
    See "The Man Who Passed"
False Gods (Auchincloss) **22**:51
"False-Dmitry Lunacharsky" (Bulgakov) **18**:89
"Fame" (Walker) **5**:412
Famiglia (Ginzburg) **65**:128-29, 134, 137, 143
"The Familiar" (Le Fanu) **14**:221, 223-26, 228,
    233-36, 238-41, 247-48, 250
Familiar Scenes (Peretz)
    See *Bakante bilder*
"The Family" (Pavese) **19**:363, 377, 387
Family (Ginzburg)
    See *Famiglia*
The Family (Mauriac) **24**:159-60, 179
"A Family Affair" (Chopin) **8**:84, 86
"Family Album" (Betts) **45**:12, 27
"Family Album" (Castellanos)
    See "Album de familia"
Family Album (Castellanos)
    See *Album de familia*
"The Family de Cats" (Dinesen) **7**:177
"Family Evening" (O'Hara) **15**:290
"A Family Feud" (Dunbar) **8**:120-21, 131, 140,
    148
Family Happiness (Tolstoy)
    See *Semeinoe schaste*
"Family House" (Davie) **52**:9
"Family in the Wind" (Fitzgerald) **6**:47, 60, 62
"A Family Man" (Pritchett) **14**:299
"The Family of Little Feet" (Cisneros) **32**:30-
    32, 46
A Family Party (O'Hara) **15**:292-93
"Family Portrait" (Andrić)
    See "Porodična slika"
"A Family Reunion" (Naipaul) **38**:333-35
"Family Sins" (Trevor) **21**:262
Family Sins, and Other Stories (Trevor) **21**:258,
    262; **58**:216, 298
Family Ties (Lispector)
    See *Laços de família*
"Family Vitriol" (Zoshchenko) **15**:388
"Family-Peace" (Peretz) **26**:201
"The Famous Gilson Bequest" (Bierce) **9**:87-8
"The Famous Poll at Jody's Bar" (Gilchrist)
    63:10
"The Fan" (Čapek)
    See "L'eventail"
"The Fanatic" (O'Flaherty) **6**:276, 288
*A Fanatic Heart: Selected Stories of Edna
    O'Brien* (O'Brien) **10**:340-41

Fancies and Goodnights (Collier) **19**:102-05
"Fancy Flights" (Beattie) **11**:21, 28
Fancy Goods (Morand)
    See *Tendres stocks*
"The Fancy Woman" (Taylor) **10**:374-77, 386,
    389, 398, 400, 406-07, 415
"Fancy's Friend" (Alcott) **27**:11, 42, 50-7
"Fancy's Show-Box" (Hawthorne) **3**:160,
    190-91
La Fanfarlo (Baudelaire) **18**:9, 11-14, 19-27,
    37, 54
"Fanny and Annie" (Lawrence) **4**:232, 234-35
"Fantaseando" (Pardo Bazán) **30**:294
"Fantasie printaniere" (Norris) **28**:201-03, 207,
    213
The Fantasies of Harlan Ellison (Ellison)
    14:143-47
Fantasiestücke in Callots Manier (Hoffmann)
    13:186, 203, 217
"El fantasma" (Pardo Bazán) **30**:265-66
Fantastic Fables (Bierce) **9**:59, 75
"Fantasticheria" (Verga) **21**:280-81, 285, 300-04
"A Fantasy" (Hawthorne) **39**:126
"Fantasy" (Lenz) **33**:338
Fantomas against the Multinational Vampires
    (Cortázar)
    See *Fantomas contra los vampiros multina-
    cionales*
Fantomas contra los vampiros multinacionales
    (Cortázar) **7**:60
"The Far and the Near" (Wolfe) **33**:369, 386
Far Away from Anywhere Else (Le Guin)
    See *Very Far Away from Anywhere Else*
"The Far Distant Journey" (Bates) **10**:121
"Faraway Image" (Cortázar)
    See "Lejana"
"A Far-Away Melody" (Freeman) **1**:191;
    47:102, 194
"Farce Normande" (Maupassant) **1**:272
"The Farcical History of Richard Greenow"
    (Huxley) **39**:153, 166-67, 172-73
"Fard" (Huxley) **39**:156
"The Fare to the Moon" (Price) **22**:380-81
"Farewell" (Barthelme) **2**:51; **55**:108
"Farewell" (Dybek) **55**:139
"Farewell" (Powers) **4**:381
"A Farewell" (Schnitzler) **61**:306, 308
"Farewell! Farewell! Farewell!" (Aiken) **9**:4,
    12, 14
"The Farewell Murder" (Hammett) **17**:220,
    230-31
"Farewell, My Lovely Appetizer" (Perelman)
    32:211, 214
"Farewell to Earth" (Clarke) **3**:128
Farewell to Maria (Borowski)
    See *Pożegnanie z Maria*
"Farewell to Mary" (Borowski) **48**:3, 6-7
Farewell to Mary (Borowski)
    See *Pożegnanie z Maria*
"A Farewell to Omsk" (Perelman) **32**:222, 234
Farewells (Onetti)
    See *Los adioses*
"Der farkishefter shnayder" (Aleichem) **33**:41-2
"The Farm Murder" (Čapek) **36**:105-06
"The Farmer in the Dell" (Garrett) **30**:174
"The Farmers' Daughters" (Williams) **31**:312,
    314, 333-35
*The Farmers' Daughters: The Collected
    Stories of William Carlos Williams*
    (Williams) **31**:312, 327, 344
"El faro" (Arreola) **38**:9
Fasching (Hauptmann) **37**:241-42, 245
"The Fascination of the Pool" (Woolf) **7**:408,
    410-12
"Fashion" (Galsworthy) **22**:98
"The Fast" (Singer) **3**:355, 361; **53**:294
"Fast and Firm—A Romance at Marseilles"
    (Howells) **36**:399
"Fast Lanes" (Phillips) **16**:335-37
Fast Lanes (Phillips) **16**:332-39
"The Fastest Runner on Sixty-First Street"
    (Farrell) **28**:99

"Fat" (Carver) **8**:3, 29, 42-3, 54
"The Fat Girl" (Dubus) **15**:74, 77, 80, 94
"The Fatal Eggs" (Bulgakov)
    See "Rokovye iaitsa"
"The Fate of Humphrey Snell" (Gissing) **37**:57,
    80
"The Fate of the Forrests" (Alcott) **27**:57-8
"The Fate of the Freiherr von Leisenbohg"
    (Schnitzler)
    See "Das schicksal des Freiherr von Leisen-
    bohg"
"The Father" (Babel) **16**:48-9
"The Father" (Carver) **8**:9, 18, 50-1, 55
"The Father" (Chekhov)
    See "Otec"
"The Father" (Dazai Osamu)
    See "Chichi"
"A Father" (Mukherjee) **38**:238, 240, 242, 252-
    53, 257-59, 265, 270, 273, 279
"The Father" (O'Hara) **15**:290-91
"Father Abraham" (Anderson) **46**:3, 16, 18-19
"Father against Mother" (Machado de Assis)
    See "Pai contra mãe"
"Father Aleksej" (Turgenev)
    See "Rasskaz ottsa Aleksaya"
"Father Alexey's Story" (Turgenev)
    See "Rasskaz ottsa Aleksaya"
"Father and I" (Lagerkvist) **12**:179, 192, 196-97
"Father and Mother" (Howells) **36**:370
"Father and Mother" (Kawabata)
    See "Chichi Haha"
"Father and Son" (Hughes) **6**:109, 119, 121-22,
    141-42
"The Father and Son Cigar" (Algren) **33**:108
"Father Giles of Ballymoy" (Trollope) **28**:320,
    340, 348, 354
"A Father in Sion" (Evans) **43**:10, 12, 30, 32,
    34, 39
"Father of the Stars" (Pohl) **25**:220
"Father Raven" (Coppard) **21**:18, 27
"Father Scothine" (Moore) **19**:311
Father Sergius (Tolstoy)
    See *Otetz Sergii*
"Father Timothy Joyce" (Farrell) **28**:98, 118
"Father versus Mother" (Machado de Assis)
    See "Pai contra mãe"
"Father, Where Are You Going?" (Oe)
    See "Chichi yo, anata wa doko e ikuno ka?"
"Fathering" (Mukherjee) **38**:252, 254, 266-67,
    271
"The Fatherland" (Walser) **20**:357
"The Fathers" (Bradbury) **53**:247-48, 250,
    253-54
"Fathers" (Čapek) **36**:124
"Fathers and Sons" (Hemingway) **1**:212, 216,
    230, 240-42; **40**:251, 258, 260; **63**:103,
    107-8
"The Fathers and the Sons" (Agnon) **30**:11
"The Fathers' Daughters" (Spark) **10**:361, 366
"Father's Help" (Narayan) **25**:141, 153, 156,
    160
"Father's Last Escape" (Schulz)
    See "Ostatnia ucieczka ojca"
"A Father's Story" (Dubus) **15**:76, 87, 93, 98-9
"The Father-Thing" (Dick) **57**:45, 84, 107,
    138-39
"A Father-to-Be" (Bellow) **14**:3, 22-3, 25, 27,
    30-1
"Fatimas and Kisses" (O'Hara) **15**:279, 283
"La fausse monnaie" (Baudelaire) **18**:35, 39-40,
    60
Faust (Turgenev) **7**:320, 323-25, 328, 334-35,
    337; **57**:300, 302, 328-30, 332-34, 336-39
"Le faux policier" (Aymé) **41**:13
"Favors" (Adams) **24**:17-18
"The Favourite" (O'Brien) **10**:330, 332
"Fear" (Chekhov)
    See "Strath"
"Fear" (Galsworthy) **22**:98
"The Fear" (Tanizaki)
    See "Kyofu"
"Fear: Four Examples" (Lish) **18**:266, 268

"Fear Here" (Thomas) **20**:287
"The Fear of Nice" (Nin) **10**:306
"The Fear That Walks by Noonday" (Cather)
　2:100; **50**:77, 91, 184
"A Fearful Responsibility" (Howells) **36**:399
A Fearful Responsibility, and Other Stories
　(Howells) **36**:400
"Fearless Simpleton" (Calvino)
　See "Lo sciocco senza paura"
"The Feast of Crispian" (Ballard) **1**:72
"The Feast of Lugnasa" (Stephens) **50**:334
"The Feast of Nemesis" (Saki) **12**:296, 299
"A Feast of Reason" (Howells) **36**:397
"The Feast of Samhain" (Stephens) **50**:333
"Feathers" (Carver) **8**:24, 31-2, 34-5, 44
"Feathertop" (Hawthorne) **3**:158, 179
"February Mama" (Hood) **42**:191
"Federigo" (Mérimée) **7**:283, 287, 289, 299-
　300
"Fedor Kuzmich" (Tolstoy) **9**:389
"Fedora" (Chopin) **8**:87, 100
"Feed My Lambs" (O'Faolain) **13**:291, 312
"Feizao" (Lu Hsun) **20**:129, 149
"Feldblumen" (Stifter) **28**:299
Felicidade clandestina (Lispector) **34**:231-33,
　235
"Felicità" (Pirandello) **22**:275-76, 285-86
"Felis Catus" (Berriault) **30**:96-7
"Feliz aniversário" (Lispector) **34**:189, 194,
　197, 200, 202
"Fellow-Feeling" (Narayan) **25**:138
"Fellow-Townsmen" (Hardy) **2**:202-03, 207,
　215-16, 228-31
"Female Bandits" (Dazai Osamu) **41**:230, 232
"The Female Body" (Atwood) **46**:75, 99
La femme abandonnée (Balzac) **5**:8, 31
"La femme adultère" (Camus) **9**:103, 105, 108-
　110, 114-16, 119, 126-28,
La femme cachée (Colette) **10**:274-76
"La femme de Paul" (Maupassant) **1**:259, 261
La femme rompue (Beauvoir) **35**:46, 48-50, 54,
　57-8, 64, 67-8, 70-2, 75-9, 81-2, 85, 87
"La femme sauvage et la petite-maîtresse"
　(Baudelaire) **18**:33
"La femme vertueuse" (Balzac) **5**:4, 29
"The Fence" (Cowan) **28**:80
"Fên-chou hu" (P'u Sung-ling) **31**:207
"Fenella" (Warner) **23**:373
"Les fenêtres" (Baudelaire) **18**:6, 9
"Fêng hsien" (P'u Sung-ling) **31**:209
"Fêng San-niang" (P'u Sung-ling) **31**:209
"Feng-po" (Lu Hsun) **20**:136, 140
Feria d'agosto (Pavese) **19**:364-65, 380, 383-
　84, 386
"Las ferias de Madrid" (Alarcon) **64**:2, 10, 13
"Die Fermate" (Hoffmann) **13**:183
Fermé la nuit (Morand) **22**:158, 160-61, 165-
　67, 171-73, 181
"Le fermier" (Maupassant) **1**:274, 285
"Fern" (Stuart) **31**:252
"Fern" (Toomer) **1**:441, 444, 457-58, 460;
　45:174-75, 177-78, 184, 187, 198, 200, 204,
　206, 227, 242, 260, 265, 267, 275, 290, 325,
　330-31, 335, 349-50, 356, 362, 368, 374-
　76, 380-82
"Fernheim" (Agnon) **30**:3-4, 48, 66
"Ferragus" (Balzac) **5**:43-6
"The Ferry of Unfulfillment" (Henry) **5**:158,
　186
"The Ferry; or, Another Trip to Venice"
　(Cortázar) **7**:63
Das Fest zu Kenilworth (Tieck) **31**:272
"Le feste" (Pavese) **19**:384
"The Festival" (Campbell) **19**:81
"The Festival" (Lovecraft) **3**:263, 269, 274,
　292, 294-95; **52**:287-88, 307, 315-16, 336,
　345
"Festival Nights" (Pavese) **19**:387
Festival Nights (Pavese) **19**:363
"Festival with Syphilis" (Bulgakov) **18**:90
"The Festivals" (Pavese)
　See "Le feste"

"Die Festung" (Lenz) **33**:316, 319-20, 328, 330
"The Fetish" (Moravia)
　See "L'automa"
The Fetish, and Other Stories (Moravia)
　See *L'automa*
"A Feud" (Galsworthy) **22**:67, 82, 101
Das Feuerschiff (Lenz) **33**:316, 331
"Fever" (Carver) **8**:26-8, 30, 33-4, 40
"Fever" (Wideman) **62**:258-59, 269, 279-80,
　307-8, 310, 312
"Fever Dream" (Bradbury) **29**:58-9, 62
"Fever Flower" (Grau) **15**:152, 156, 159
Fever: Twelve Stories (Wideman) **62**:258-59,
　268, 272-74, 277, 279, 296, 307-8
"A Few Crusted Characters" (Hardy) **2**:206,
　209, 214-15, 217, 219-20; **60**:180
"A Few Moments of Sleeping and Waking"
　(Barthelme) **55**:108
"A Few Trips and Some Poetry" (O'Hara)
　15:286
Fiabe italiene (Calvino) **3**:105, 119; **48**:52, 79,
　89, 94, 103, 148, 150-51
"An Fiach" (O'Flaherty) **6**:287
"Fiançailles" (Aymé) **41**:11, 19, 22, 26
Ficciones, 1935-1944 (Borges) **4**:15-16, 18-20,
　41; **41**:44, 53, 56, 117, 135-41, 157, 159,
　162
"La ficelle" (Maupassant) **1**:259, 262, 284, 286,
　288
Fictions (Borges)
　See *Ficciones, 1935-1944*
"Fiddle Faddle" (Kazakov) **43**:69
"The Fiddler" (Melville) **1**:304; **17**:361, 363
"The Fiddler of the Reels" (Hardy) **2**:216-22,
　224-25; **60**:180, 185, 193-94, 197
"The Field Devil" (Hesse) **9**:231, 235
"Field Events" (Bass) **60**:9-11, 14-15, 30
"Field Guide to the Western Birds" (Stegner)
　27:195, 198-99, 205-07, 220
"A Field in Space" (Davie) **52**:4, 6, 8-9, 11
"Field of Flowers" (Aiken) **9**:5, 12-13
"The Field of Maize" (Pavese)
　See "Il campo di granturco"
"The Field of Mustard" (Coppard) **21**:8, 16-17,
　19, 25, 28
The Field of Mustard (Coppard) **21**:5-9, 21
"A Field of Snow on a Slope of the
　Rosenberg" (Davenport) **16**:174, 176,
　180-82, 195, 198
"The Field of Vision" (Le Guin) **12**:233
"A Field of Wheat" (Ross) **24**:290, 292, 295,
　297, 301-02, 319
"The Fields at Dusk" (Salter) **58**:194
"Fields of Purple Forever" (Jones) **56**:285
"The Fiend" (Bukowski) **45**:62
"The Fiend" (Pohl) **25**:232
"Fierce, Fine World" (Platonov) **42**:253
"La fiesta del Monstruo" (Bioy Casares) **17**:48,
　50-2
"Fiesta en grande" (Donoso) **34**:3-4, 21, 23, 32,
　49
"Fifteen Years" (Dazai Osamu) **41**:246-50
"The Fifth Quarter" (King) **17**:295
"Fifty Dollars" (Elkin) **12**:103
"Fifty Grand" (Hemingway) **1**:209, 211, 218,
　232, 234-35, 248; **36**:270; **40**:191, 219
"Fifty Grand" (Lardner) **32**:117
"Fifty Pounds" (Coppard) **21**:11, 15, 18
Fifty Stories (Boyle) **5**:65
"A Fifty Year Old Man" (Endō) **48**:210, 212
"Fifty-Seven Views of Fujiyama" (Davenport)
　16:184-85, 188
"The Fig Tree" (Porter) **4**:340, 352-53; **31**:175-
　76; **43**:258-59, 274, 276, 278-79, 281, 307-8
"The Fig Tree" (Pritchett) **14**:263
"The Figgerin' of Aunt Wilma" (Thurber)
　47:376
"The Fight" (Anderson) **1**:31, 50
"The Fight" (O'Flaherty) **6**:269
"The Fight" (Thomas) **3**:402, 406, 411-12;
　44:324, 350-51

"Fight Number Twenty-five" (Stuart) **31**:228,
　265
"Fight Your Own War" (Saroyan) **21**:132
"Fighting for the Rebound" (Mukherjee)
　38:252, 254, 261, 266-67, 283
"Le figlie della luna" (Calvino) **48**:46, 157
"Figura" (Leskov) **34**:110
"The Figure in the Carpet" (James) **8**:265, 280,
　299, 301-02, 304, 306-07; **47**:337
"Filboid Studge, The Story of a Mouse that
　Helped" (Saki) **12**:288, 300
Files on Parade (O'Hara) **15**:264-65
La fille aux yeux d'ors (Balzac) **5**:44, 46-7; **59**:6,
　21-22, 25-30, 50-52
"La Fille du shérif" (Aymé) **41**:16-17, 24
"Les filles de Milton" (Villiers de l'Isle Adam)
　14:387, 390
Les filles du feu (Nerval) **18**:336, 362-64, 379
"Film Preview in the Morning" (Shiga) **23**:346,
　348
"The Film Test" (Moravia) **26**:139
"Filmer" (Wells) **6**:403, 406
"Filming the Hatted Australian" (Moorhouse)
　40:290-91, 303
"Filosofia de um par de botas" (Machado de
　Assis) **24**:130
"Un fils" (Maupassant) **1**:275
"Filthy with Things" (Boyle) **16**:156-57
"La Fin" (Beckett) **16**:72-5, 87-91
"El fin" (Borges) **4**:10; **41**:47
La fin de Chéri (Colette) **10**:255, 257, 260-61,
　264, 267-68, 270-71, 285-87
La fin de la nuit (Mauriac) **24**:168-69, 171,
　180-81
"Fin de una novela" (Alarcon) **64**:4, 31
"A Final Account" (Price) **22**:386
"Final Chapter" (Machado de Assis) **24**:152
Final del juego (Cortázar) **7**:50-1, 53, 62-3, 69-
　70, 79
"The Final Embarrassment" (Williams) **31**:334
"The Final Martyrs" (Endō) **48**:209, 211
The Final Martyrs (Endō) **48**:208-12
The Final Mist (Bombal) **37**:41-42, 44
"A Final Note on Chanda Bell" (Thurber) **1**:421;
　47:383-84
"The Final Problem" (Doyle) **12**:57, 60
"The Final Programme" (Ballard) **53**:124
"Final Request" (Machado de Assis) **24**:140,
　152
"Final Trophy" (Ellison) **14**:127
The Final Years (Dazai Osamu) **41**:249
"A Financial Failure" (Jewett) **6**:158
"A Find" (Gordimer) **17**:184, 187
"Find Me in Fire" (Bradbury) **29**:53
"The Finder" (Spencer) **57**:211, 219, 241-42,
　252-55
"Finding a Girl in America" (Dubus) **15**:76, 87,
　93, 98-9
Finding a Girl in America (Dubus) **15**:74, 78,
　81
"The Finding of Lieutenant Outhwaite"
　(Norris) **28**:203-04
"The Finding of Martha" (Dunbar) **8**:122
"The Finding of Zach" (Dunbar) **8**:122, 128,
　147
"Der Findling" (Kleist) **22**:106, 114, 122, 124-
　28, 131
"Fine Accommodations" (Hughes) **6**:131, 133
"A Fine Beginning" (Thomas) **3**:403; **44**:360
"Fine d'agosto" (Pavese) **19**:375-76, 380
"Fine di una relazione" (Moravia) **26**:179
"Fine Feathers" (Coppard) **21**:8, 16-17, 30
"Fine Furniture" (Dreiser) **30**:152-53, 159
"A Fine Old Firm" (Jackson) **39**:211, 224, 225,
　229
The Finer Grain (James) **8**:276, 302
"The Finest" (Bradfield) **65**:60
"The Finest Diner in the World" (Villiers de
　l'Isle Adam)
　See "Le plus beau dîner du monde"
Finest Short Stories of Seán O'Faoláin
　(O'Faolain) **13**:292, 297, 308

"The Finest Story in the World" (Kipling) **5**:273, 280

"Fingal" (Beckett) **16**:93

"Finger Man" (Chandler) **23**:58, 65-7, 72, 102

"The Finger of Mrs. Knox" (Somerville & Ross) **56**:320, 340

"Fingers and Toes" (Michaels) **16**:302, 311

"Finis" (London) **4**:256

"Finish Good Lady" (Auchincloss) **22**:47

"The Finish of Patsy Barnes" (Dunbar) **8**:122, 125, 128, 137

"Finlandia" (Saroyan) **21**:158, 160

"Finn" (Michaels) **16**:302-03

"Fino a che dura il sole" (Calvino) **48**:46, 154

"The Fir Tree" (Freeman) **47**:163

"Fire and Cloud" (Wright) **2**:361, 363, 365, 368, 371, 373, 375, 379-81, 383-84, 387

"The Fire and the Hearth" (Faulkner) **1**:182; **35**:146, 157

"The Fire Balloons" (Bradbury) **29**:42-3, 46, 48, 53, 81; **53**:213, 216, 247, 254

"Fire by Night" (Fisher) **25**:17-20, 23, 25

"Fire, Fire, Burn Books!" (Bradbury) **29**:53

"A Fire in Fontana" (Yamamoto) **34**:358-59, 381-83

"Fire of the Khans" (Bulgakov) **18**:92, 98

"The Fire Test" (Harris) **19**:162-63

"Fire Worship" (Hawthorne) **3**:182

"The Firebird" (Dazai Osamu) **41**:249

"Firelight" (Wolff) **63**:275-76, 339, 342

"The Fireman" (Bass) **60**:41-42

"The Fireman" (Bradbury) **29**:53

"Fireman Flower" (Sansom) **21**:82, 88, 96, 120, 122, 124

Fireman Flower and Other Stories (Sansom) **21**:82, 84, 92, 94, 97-8, 111, 122-24, 127

"The Fireman's Death" (O'Flaherty) **6**:284

"Fires" (Bass) **60**:16, 20, 36-37

"The Fires" (Shiga) **23**:346

Fires: Essays, Poems, Stories, 1966-1982 (Carver) **8**:18, 30, 32, 40-1, 45, 50, 57-60

Fireship (Vinge) **24**:327

"Firewood" (Banks) **42**:59

"Fireworks" (Ford) **56**:143, 149, 152, 159-60, 175, 194

Fireworks: Nine Profane Pieces (Carter) **13**:2-3, 8-9, 14

First and Last (Lardner) **32**:156

"The First and Second Walls" (Betts) **45**:26

"The First and the Last" (Galsworthy) **22**:61, 75-6, 83, 94, 99, 100-02

"The First Autumn" (Caldwell) **19**:37

"First Blood" (Fitzgerald) **6**:50

"First Breech" (Bulgakov) **18**:86

"First Communion" (Fante) **65**:101

"First Confession" (O'Connor) **5**:364, 366, 386, 389

"The First Countess of Wessex" (Hardy) **2**:204, 208-09; **60**:179

"The First Day in a Gay Town" (Andrić)
See "Prvi dan u radosnom gradu"

"The First Day of School" (Saroyan) **21**:135

"First Day of Winter" (Pancake) **61**:246, 255, 259, 265, 275

"First Encounter" (Clarke) **3**:128

"A First Family of Tasajara" (Harte) **8**:216, 218

"First Foot" (Campbell) **19**:65

The First Forty-Nine Stories (Hemingway) **1**:230, 240

"The First Ivan" (Platonov) **42**:248

"First Love" (Babel) **16**:9, 17, 36, 41, 59

"First Love" (Gorky) **28**:153

"First Love" (Nabokov) **11**:108, 128

"First Love" (Pavese)
See "Primo amore"

"First Love" (Welty) **1**:467-69, 482; **51**:259, 269

First Love (Beckett)
See *Premier amour*

First Love (Turgenev)
See *Pervaya lyubov'*

"First Manhattans" (Gilchrist) **14**:157, 159

"The First Monday in Lent" (Bunin)
See "Chistyi ponedel'nik"

"First Night" (Pirandello) **22**:250

"The First of April" (Barnes) **3**:13

"The First Poet" (London) **4**:256

"The First Report of the Shipwrecked Foreigner to the Kadanh of Derb" (Le Guin) **12**:231, 241

"The First Seven Years" (Malamud) **15**:168, 189, 212, 221

"First Sorrow" (Kafka)
See "Erstes Leid"

"The First Step" (Walser)
See "Der erste Schritt"

"The First Sunday in June" (Jewett) **6**:159

"First Wedding Night" (Pirandello)
See "Prima notte"

"The First Year of My Life" (Spark) **10**:364, 366, 368

"The First-Class Passenger" (Chekhov) **2**:130

"The Fir-Tree" (Andersen) **6**:6, 14, 18, 30, 40

"The Fish" (Banks) **42**:58-60

"Fish for Friday" (O'Connor) **5**:369

"Fish Story" (Lish) **18**:280-82

"The Fish Supper" (Aiken) **9**:14

"The Fish Trap" (Pirandello) **22**:249

"A Fisher of Men" (Galsworthy) **22**:58-9, 98

"The Fisherman" (Banks) **42**:54

"The Fisherman and His Soul" (Wilde) **11**:365, 369, 371, 376, 383-84, 386-87, 394-99, 407-09

"Fishmonger's Fiddle" (Coppard) **21**:4, 9, 15, 27

Fishmonger's Fiddle (Coppard) **21**:4, 8-9, 15, 19-20

"Fishy" (Pritchett) **14**:269

"Fishy Waters" (Rhys) **21**:55-7, 66

"The Fit" (Chekhov) **51**:58

"Fitcher's Bird" (Grimm and Grimm) **36**:198-99

"Fits" (Munro) **3**:347

"Five Acre Virgin" (Jolley) **19**:230, 245

Five Acre Virgin, and Other Stories (Jolley) **19**:221-22, 232, 244-45

"The Five Black Swans" (Warner) **23**:383

"Five Boons of Life" (Twain) **26**:331

"The Five Dollar Guy" (Williams) **31**:358

"The Five Hells of Orion" (Pohl) **25**:230

"Five Incidents Concerning the Flesh and the Blood" (Moorhouse) **40**:302

"Five Incidents Concerning the Flesh and the Blood" (Wilding) **50**:346

"Five Intimate Interviews" (Levi) **12**:275

"Five Loaves of Bread" (Čapek) **36**:84, 130

"The Five Orange Pips" (Doyle) **12**:66, 68, 70, 72-4

"Five Peas from One Pod" (Andersen) **6**:35

"Five Ripe Pears" (Saroyan) **21**:133

Five Tales (Galsworthy) **22**:84, 94-7, 99-102

"The Five White Mice" (Crane) **7**:104, 106, 126, 150

"The Five-Forty-Eight" (Cheever) **1**:100; **38**:66, 84, 87

"Five-Twenty" (White) **39**:301, 303, 306-07, 310-11, 319-20, 324, 326-28, 337, 346, 350-52

Fizzles (Beckett)
See *Foirades*

"The Flag" (Aleichem) **33**:19

"The Flag" (Bates) **10**:116

The Flag of the Seven Upright Ones (Keller) **26**:115

"A Flag on the Island" (Naipaul) **38**:299, 302, 317, 323-24

A Flag on the Island: A Fantasy for a Small Screen (Naipaul) **38**:318-19, 328, 344, 347-49, 353

Flagman Thiel (Hauptmann)
See *Bahnwärter Thiel*

"The Flame" (Bates) **10**:139

"Flanagan and His Short Filibustering Adventure" (Crane) **7**:100-01, 151

Flannery O'Connor: Collected Works (O'Connor) **61**:230, 233, 237-38

Flappers and Philosophers (Fitzgerald) **6**:45-6, 56-8

"Flash" (Arreola) **38**:11, 22-23

"The Flash! Kid" (Bradfield) **65**:59, 61, 65, 69

"Flaskehalsen" (Andersen) **56**:30

"A Flat Country Christmas" (Wilson) **21**:322-23, 333

"A Flat in London" (Waugh) **41**:328

"Flatcar" (Akutagawa Ryūnosuke) **44**:51

"The Flats Road" (Munro) **3**:331-32

"A Flaubert Prose Piece" (Walser) **20**:354

"Flavia and Her Artists" (Cather) **2**:98, 103; **50**:56-7, 81, 107, 109, 121-22, 135, 138, 152-53, 157, 168-69, 194-97, 199-201, 226-27, 230, 236, 238-39, 264

"Flavour of Coconut" (Narayan) **25**:134, 140, 154

"Flavours of Exile" (Lessing) **6**:191, 211; **61**:119, 125

"The Flax" (Andersen) **6**:7

Flèche d'Orient (Morand) **22**:172, 181

"The Fleece of Gold" (Gautier)
See "La chaîne d'or"

"Fleet-Footed Hester" (Gissing) **37**:80-1

"Flesh and the Mirror" (Carter) **13**:4

La fleur de l'age (Colette) **10**:274, 276

"Les fleurs" (Ligotti) **16**:269, 277, 288

"Fleurs de ténèbres" (Villiers de l'Isle Adam) **14**:395-96

"Flick" (Lewis) **40**:276

"Flickerbridge" (James) **47**:203

"Flight" (Grau) **15**:163

"Flight" (O'Hara) **15**:279, 285

"Flight" (Steinbeck) **11**:207-09, 225, 229, 231-34, 236-37, 244

"Flight" (Updike) **13**:367, 370, 384, 388, 392-95

"Flight and Pursuit" (Fitzgerald) **6**:56

Flight into Darkness (Schnitzler)
See *Flucht in die Finsternis*

"The Flight of Pigeons from the Palace" (Barthelme) **2**:37, 40, 55-6; **55**:34, 60, 63-4, 74, 84, 86, 106

"The Flight of Pony Baker" (Howells) **36**:398

"The Flight of the Israelites" (Ballard) **1**:72

"Flights" (Adams) **24**:3-4

Flights of Angels (Gilchrist) **63**:8-9, 28

"The Fling" (Carver) **8**:4, 34; **51**:18

"Flingin' Jim and His Fool-Killer" (Harris) **19**:183

"Flip, a California Romance" (Harte) **8**:253, 255; **59**:306

Flip and Other Stories (Harte) **59**:311

"The Flip of a Coin" (Maugham) **8**:376-77

"Flirts and Their Ways" (Murfree) **22**:221

"The Float" (King) **55**:265

"The Floating Bridge of Dreams" (Tanizaki)
See "Yume no ukihashi"

"The Floating Truth" (Paley) **8**:399

"The Flood" (Anderson) **1**:51

"A Flood" (Moore) **19**:345

"The Flood" (Pavese) **19**:370

"Una flor amarilla" (Cortázar) **7**:52

"Flor de retórica antigua" (Arreola) **38**:11

"Florence Green is 81" (Barthelme) **2**:27; **55**:16, 18, 108

"Flotsam and Jetsam" (Galsworthy) **22**:101

"The Flower" (Pavese) **19**:366

"Flower Days" (Walser) **20**:336

Flower Fables (Alcott) **27**:3, 33, 36, 38-41, 44, 57

"The Flower Garden" (Jackson) **9**:249, 252; **39**:211, 220, 221, 222, 224, 225, 229

"Flowering Judas" (Porter) **4**:329, 339-40, 342, 344, 346, 349-51, 356; **31**:123-81; **43**:175-76, 194, 197-200, 202, 204-5, 222-32, 234-36, 238, 240, 242-44, 246, 253, 258-60, 262, 264, 291-92, 322

Flowering Judas, and Other Stories (Porter) **4**:326-28, 347, 351, 354, 365; **31**:124, 127, 134, 148, 172; **43**:169, 173, 197, 221, 223, 252

"The Flowering of the Strange Orchid" (Wells) **6**:361, 365, 394-96, 404

"The Flowers" (Walker) **5**:402

"Flowers for Marjorie" (Welty) **1**:466, 487-88; **51**:255, 272, 319-21, 323-24, 328

"Flowers of a Clown" (Dazai Osamu) **41**:244

"Flowers of Darkness" (Villiers de l'Isle Adam)
See "Fleurs de ténèbres"

"Flowers of the Abyss" (Ligotti) **16**:282, 284

"The Flower's Story" (Alcott) **27**:44-5

"The Flowers That Bloom in Spring" (Metcalf) **43**:74

"The Flowers that Killed Him" (Ross) **24**:295, 307, 311, 318-19

Flucht in die Finsternis (Schnitzler) **15**:344, 368, 370, 378, 381, 383-84

"Die Flut ist pünktlich" (Lenz) **33**:317, 319

"Flute Dream" (Hesse) **9**:234

"The Flute Player" (O'Flaherty) **6**:281

"Flutter-Duck" (Zangwill)
See "Flutter-duck, A Ghetto Grotesque"

"Flutter-duck, A Ghetto Grotesque" (Zangwill) **44**:371, 388

"The Flutterer" (Chekhov) **51**:58, 61, 63-4, 69, 128

"The Fly" (Dreiser) **30**:128

"The Fly" (Mansfield) **9**:282-84, 307, 312-13; **23**:158; **38**:201-32

"The Fly" (Pirandello) **22**:227-28

"Fly Away Ladybird" (Aiken) **9**:13-14

"A Fly in a Glass of Milk" (Cabrera Infante)
See "La mosca en el vasode leche"

"The Fly in the Coffin" (Caldwell) **19**:14, 28-9

"The Fly in the Ointment" (Pritchett) **14**:271, 298

"Fly Paper" (Hammett) **17**:202, 215-16, 220, 222

"Flyboys" (Wolff) **63**:275-76

"Flying a Red Kite" (Hood) **42**:139, 215, 225-27, 233, 238

Flying a Red Kite (Hood) **42**:137, 139, 142-46, 179-82, 196, 199, 204-05, 213, 224-26, 233, 235

"Flying Carpets" (Millhauser) **57**:189

"The Flying Dutchman" (Bulgakov) **18**:90

"Flying Home" (Ellison) **26**:4, 9-10, 13, 15, 21, 24, 25

"The Flying Man" (Wells) **6**:397-98

"The Flying Stars" (Chesterton) **1**:119, 127, 129; **46**:107, 111, 131, 140, 145, 148, 152

"A Flying Start" (Gallant) **5**:147; **172**:5

"The Flying Trunk" (Andersen)
See "Den flyvende Kuffert"

"Den flyvende Kuffert" (Andersen) **6**:7, 30; **56**:34-5, 37

"FOAM" (Aldiss) **36**:28

"Fog" (Adams) **24**:16

"The Fog Horn" (Bradbury) **29**:59

"The Fog Man" (Boyle) **16**:157

Foirades (Beckett) **16**:100, 123-28

"Fokusniki" (Chekhov) **51**:185

Folks from Dixie (Dunbar) **8**:118-21, 123, 127-29, 131, 140-41, 143, 145-46

"Foma, the Wolf" (Turgenev) **7**:316

"Fonar' umiral" (Gogol) **52**:166

"The Food of the Gods" (Clarke) **3**:133-34

"Fool about a Horse" (Faulkner) **1**:177

"Fooling Marie" (Bukowski) **45**:52

"The Foolish Butterfly" (O'Flaherty) **6**:264, 278-79

"The Foolish Virgin" (Gissing) **37**:64, 81

"Fool's Education" (Price) **22**:365, 369-71, 376-77

"A Fool's Life" (Akutagawa Ryūnosuke)
See "Aru ahō no isshō"

"A Fool's Love" (Tanizaki)
See "Chijin no ai"

The Foot Journey to Amager (Andersen) **6**:4

"Foothold" (Bowen) **3**:40, 44

"The Foothold" (Davie) **52**:3

"The Footprint" (Čapek)
See "Šlépej"

"Footprint II" (Čapek)
See "Šlépeje"

"The Footprints" (Čapek)
See "Šlépeje"

"Footprints in the Jungle" (Maugham) **8**:359, 361, 374-75

"Footsteps in the Footprints" (Cortázar) **7**:63

"The Footwarmer" (Pirandello) **22**:241

"For a Good Purpose" (Levi) **12**:278

For a Nameless Tomb (Onetti)
See *Para una tumba sin nombre*

"For a Place in the Sun" (Grau) **15**:155

"For Altar and Hearth" (Davis) **38**:104

"For Better" (Evans) **43**:16, 19

"For Conscience' Sake" (Hardy) **2**:207, 212, 214-15, 220; **60**:180

"For Dear Life" (Gordimer) **17**:192

"For Esmé—with Love and Squalor" (Salinger) **2**:289, 293-97, 299-300, 303-05, 314, 316-18; **28**:222, 229, 236, 244, 248, 2 61; **65**:294, 304-5, 308-10, 335, 337

"For Good" (Adams) **24**:4

"For Grandmother" (Shiga) **23**:333

"For I'm the Boy Whose Only Joy is Loving You" (Barthelme) **55**:16, 18, 67-68

"For Jeromé—With Love and Kisses" (Lish) **18**:266-68, 284

"For Marse Chouchoute" (Chopin) **8**:89

For Maurice: Five Unlikely Stories (Lee) **33**:307-08, 311-12

"For Rupert—With No Promises" (Lish) **18**:267-68, 284

"For the Duration of the War" (Saki) **12**:285, 326

For the Good of the Cause (Solzhenitsyn)
See *Dlia pol'zy dela*

"For the Love of Brass" (Stuart) **31**:232

"For the Time Being" (Lispector) **34**:215

"For to end yet again" (Beckett) **16**:123, 127, 129

For to end yet again and Other Fizzles (Beckett)
See *Foirades*

"For White Men Only" (Farrell) **28**:121

"The Forbidden" (Barker) **53**:144-45, 154, 156-57, 159, 162

"The Forbidden Buzzards" (Saki) **12**:315, 326

"The Forbidden Lighthouse" (Sansom) **21**:82, 88-9

"Force Majeure" (Levi) **12**:274-75, 277

"The Force of Blood" (Cervantes)
See "La fuerza de la sangre"

"The Force of Circumstance" (Maugham) **8**:372, 375

"Foreign Affairs" (O'Faolain) **13**:322

Foreign Affairs, and Other Stories (O'Faolain) **13**:296, 308, 313-14

Foreign Bodies (Aldiss) **36**:14, 18, 20

"The Foreign Policy of Company 99" (Henry) **5**:197

"Foreign Shores" (Salter) **58**:172, 174-76, 194-95

Foreign Studies (Endō)
See *Ryugaku*

"The Foreigner" (Alarcon)
See "El extranjero"

"The Foreigner" (Jewett) **6**:156, 174-76

"The Foreseeable Future" (Price) **22**:380-81

The Foreseeable Future (Price) **22**:379, 381, 384

"The Forest" (Le Guin) **12**:213, 216, 247-48

"Forest and Steppe" (Turgenev) **57**:284

"Forest Dacha" (Pilnyak) **48**:285-86

"The Forest of the South" (Gordon) **15**:105, 107, 118

The Forest of the South (Gordon) **15**:104, 108, 116, 137

"The Forest Path to the Spring" (Lowry) **31**:41, 44-53, 55-9, 61-3, 66-72, 75-6, 79-83, 86-7

"Forever and the Earth" (Bradbury) **29**:78

Forevermore (Agnon)
See *Ad olam*

"The Forged Coupon" (Tolstoy) **9**:379

"Forgetting" (O'Brien) **10**:343

"Forging Ahead" (Fitzgerald) **6**:50

"Forgiveness in Families" (Munro) **3**:331

"The Forgotten Enemy" (Clarke) **3**:124

"A Forgotten Poet" (Nabokov) **11**:109-10, 112

"The Forks" (Powers) **4**:374, 382

"Form in Wood" (Cowan) **28**:80

"The Form of Space" (Calvino)
See "La forma dello spazio"

"Forma" (Borges)
See "La forma de la espada"

"La forma de la espada" (Borges) **4**:10, 25, 42; **41**:40, 42, 58, 123-30, 148, 180-85

"La forma dello spazio" (Calvino) :92, 109; **48**:46-7, 64, 69-70, 355-576

La formica argentina (Calvino) **3**:91-2, 98, 117; **48**:43, 84, 148, 153, 178-84

"The Forsaken" (Turgenev) **7**:318-19

"Forschungen eines hundes" (Kafka) **5**:206, 229, 238, 241; **29**:345-49, 351, 369, 371; **60**:248, 253

"A Forsyte Encounters the People" (Galsworthy) **22**:71

The Forsyte Saga (Galsworthy) **22**:64-5, 69-71, 81, 84

Forsytes, Pendyces and Others (Galsworthy) **22**:74, 84, 91, 97

"Forsythe and Forsythe" (Gilman) **13**:141

"Fortuna di essere un cavallo" (Pirandello) **22**:270

"Fortuna lo que ha querido" (Fuentes) **24**:32, 56, 58, 74

"Fortune" (Chekhov) **51**:204

"Fortune Always has Her Way" (Fuentes)
See "Fortuna lo que ha querido"

"The Fortune of Arleus Kane" (Auchincloss) **22**:3, 48

"The Fortune Teller" (Spark) **10**:367, 370

"The Fortunes of Martin Waldock" (Scott) **32**:300

"The Fortunes of Sir Robert Ardagh" (Le Fanu) **14**:220-21, 223, 239, 247, 251

"The Fortune-Teller" (Čapek)
See "Věštkyně"

"The Fortune-Teller" (Machado de Assis) **24**:153

Fortunio (Gautier) **20**:3, 7, 14, 26

"40, Still at Home" (Jones) **56**:285

Forty Stories (Barthelme) **2**:56; **55**:67, 76-7, 92, 108, 111-13, 116

"Forty Times Forty" (Bulgakov) **18**:90

"Forty-Five a Month" (Narayan) **25**:132, 137

Forty-Seventeen (Moorhouse) **40**:324

"The Forty-Seventh Saturday" (Trevor) **21**:233, 262; **58**:200, 278

"A Forty-Year-Old Man" (Endō) **48**:192, 210, 212

"La Fosse aux péchés" (Aymé) **41**:11, 13, 17

"The Foster Portfolio" (Vonnegut) **8**:432, 435

"Foster, You=re Dead" (Dick) **57**:91, 107-9

"Le fou et la Vénus" (Baudelaire) **18**:3, 6, 8, 15, 17

"Les foules" (Baudelaire) **18**:31, 38

"The Found Boat" (Munro) **3**:346

Foundations of the River (Appelfeld)
See *Adenei hanahar*

"Foundling" (Grimm and Grimm) **36**:223

"The Foundling" (Kleist)
See "Der Findling"

"The Fountains" (Le Guin) **12**:211, 213, 247-48

"The Four Apples" (Apple) **50**:23

"Four Bottles of Beer" (Williams) **31**:304-05, 333

Four Faultless Felons (Chesterton) **1**:126, 132; **46**:117

"The Four Fists" (Fitzgerald) **6**:58

"Four Generations" (Suckow) **18**:395-96, 405-07, 415

"The Four Lost Men" (Wolfe) **33**:401

"The Four Meetings" (James) **8**:334; **32**:106-09

The Four Million (Henry) **5**:155, 171-72, 192; **49**:196, 200, 205

Four Past Midnight (King) **17**:280-84; **55**:258

"Four Portraits" (Bulgakov) **18**:74, 92

"Four Rupees" (Narayan) **25**:141, 156

"The Four Seasons" (Gallant) **5**:130, 135, 137-38

"Four Stations in His Circle" (Clarke) **45**:87, 94-5

"Four Stories About Lovers" (Beattie) **11**:17

"Four Women" (Garrett) **30**:165, 173

The Four-Dimensional Nightmare (Ballard) **1**:68

"14 Stories" (Dixon) **16**:208-09, 214

14 Stories (Dixon) **16**:204-05, 207-10, 214-15

"The Fourth Alarm" (Cheever) **1**:101, 110; **38**:53

"The Fourth Day Out from Santa Cruz" (Bowles) **3**:61-2, 72

"Fourth Version" (Valenzuela)
See "Cuarta versión"

"The Fox" (Lawrence) **4**:197, 203-04, 210-12, 223-26, 229, 231, 235-36

"The Fox" (Wilson) **21**:364

"The Fox and the Forest" (Bradbury) **29**:49; **53**:216

"Fox Hunters" (Pancake) **61**:248-49, 260, 265, 276

"The Fqih" (Bowles) **3**:68

"The Fragile Age" (Grau) **15**:156

A Fragment of Life (Machen) **20**:165-66, 168, 175, 177, 196, 199, 201

"A Fragment of Stained Glass" (Lawrence) **4**:202

"Fragments of a Hologram Rose" (Gibson) **52**:15

"Fragments: They Dine with the Past" (Waugh) **41**:327

"Frail Vessel" (Lavin) **4**:165, 167, 183-84

"The Frame" (Dixon) **16**:205, 207, 211

"Frame-Tale" (Barth) **10**:40, 42, 48, 79, 81, 84-5, 89, 97

"Francie's Fourpenny Foreigner" (Galsworthy) **22**:71

"The Francis Spaight" (London) **4**:262, 291

"Franciscan Adventures" (Lewis) **34**:160, 170

Frank Norris of "The Wave": Stories and Sketches from the San Francisco Weekly, 1893 to 1897 (Norris) **28**:200-03, 206, 213-15

"Frank Sinatra or Carleton Carpenter" (Lish) **18**:267

"Frankie the Newspaperman" (Williams) **31**:321, 334

"The Franklin Stove" (Dixon) **16**:210, 214-15

"The Franklyn Paragraphs" (Campbell) **19**:86, 90-1

"Franny" (Salinger) **2**:291, 293, 297, 302-03, 305; **28**:221-24, 226-32, 234, 236, 238, 243-44, 2 46, 248-50, 253, 259, 262-63, 265-68; **65**:299, 301-3, 317, 332

Franny and Zooey (Salinger) **2**:297, 304, 318; **28**:220-70; **65**:299-301, 315, 323-29, 332-33

Frau Beate und ihr Sohn (Schnitzler) **15**:344-46; **61**:290, 292-93

"Frau Brechenmacher Attends a Wedding" (Mansfield) **9**:301

"Die Frau des Richters" (Schnitzler) **15**:371

"Frau Holle" (Grimm and Grimm) **36**:214

Frau Regel Amrain und ihr Jüngster (Keller) **26**:107

"Frau Trude" (Grimm and Grimm) **36**:199

Frau von Savern (Arnim) **29**:5

"El fraude" (Arreola) **38**:8

Fräulein Else (Schnitzler) **15**:344-47, 367-69, 375; **61**:290-92, 305

"Fräulein von Posa" (Kluge) **61**:75

"Das Fräulein von Scudéri" (Hoffmann) **13**:181, 205-06, 209, 220, 225-26

"A Freak Melon" (P'u Sung-ling)
See "Gua yi"

"The Freak of a Genius" (Alcott) **27**:29-30, 33, 35-6, 58, 61

Freaks of Genius (Alcott) **27**:32, 34, 36

"Fred" (Anderson) **46**:19

"Free" (Dreiser) **30**:107, 114-16, 122, 127, 144-45

"Free" (O'Hara) **15**:248, 270

"Free Agents" (Apple) **50**:10, 19, 32-4, 37, 39, 45

Free Agents (Apple) **50**:23-4, 27-8, 31-5, 37-9 45-6

Free, and Other Stories (Dreiser) **30**:107-09, 118, 120-27, 153

"The Free Fur Coat" (Davie) **52**:4, 10

Free Joe, and Other Georgian Sketches (Harris) **19**:124, 134, 147, 151

"Free Joe and the Rest of the World" (Harris) **19**:124, 131, 147, 157-58, 173, 177-78, 184

"Free Will" (Pavese) **19**:387

"Free Will and the Commendatore" (Bioy Casares) **17**:73

"Freedom to Breathe" (Solzhenitsyn) **32**:394-95

"Freedom's a Hard-Bought Thing" (Benét) **10**:143, 154, 156

"The Freeholder Ovsyanikov" (Turgenev) **7**:313, 344

"Frei Simão" (Machado de Assis) **24**:131

"Das Fremde Kind" (Hoffmann) **13**:192, 194-95, 199-200

French Girls Are Vicious and Other Stories (Farrell) **28**:105

"French Harvest" (Boyle) **5**:64

"French Life" (Gaskell) **25**:59-60

"The French Poodle" (Lewis) **34**:164, 171

"The French Sympathizer" (Alarcon)
See "El afrancesado"

"The Frenchman Six Foot-Three" (Wescott) **35**:375

Frenzied Fiction (Leacock) **39**:265

"Fresh Air Fiend" (Wilson) **21**:319, 323-24, 327, 329-31, 333, 335, 342, 350-51

"Fresh Well Water" (Platonov) **42**:253

"The Freshest Boy" (Fitzgerald) **6**:49, 58, 80-1, 84-6

"Freud's Room" (Ozick) **15**:318-19

"Ein Freund der Regierung" (Lenz) **33**:318

"Die Freunde" (Tieck) **31**:281

"Freya of the Seven Isles" (Conrad) **9**:142-43, 149

"Friday's Footprint" (Gordimer) **17**:154

Friday's Footprint (Gordimer) **17**:153-54, 165, 168, 184

"The Friend" (Lish) **18**:282

"A Friend and Protector" (Taylor) **10**:382, 418

"A Friend in the Trade" (Trevor) **58**:300-301

"The Friend of Her Youth" (Somerville & Ross) **56**:320, 331, 336, 338

"A Friend of Kafka" (Singer) **3**:384; **53**:301

A Friend of Kafka, and Other Stories (Singer) **3**:370, 373, 375; **53**:325, 329

"A Friend of the Earth" (Thurber) **1**:422, 427; **47**:383

"Friend of the Family" (Boyle) **5**:55

"The Friend of the Family" (McCarthy) **24**:215-16, 225

The Friend of the Family (Dostoevsky) **2**:164, 172, 175-76

"A Friend of the World" (Bowles) **3**:64, 83

"A Friend to Alexander" (Thurber) **47**:381-82

"Friendly Brook" (Kipling) **5**:275, 279

"Friends" (Beattie) **11**:4-5, 7

"The Friends" (Cortázar)
See "Los amigos"

"Friends" (Paley) **8**:409-10

"Friends" (Pavese) **19**:368, 387

"Friends" (Sansom) **21**:110, 126

"Friends and Relations" (Hood) **42**:238

"A Friend's Death" (Dixon) **16**:217

"Friends from Philadelphia" (Updike) **13**:350-51, 354

"Friends of the Family" (O'Connor) **5**:371

"The Friends of the Friends" (James) **8**:270, 316

"A Friendship" (Trevor) **58**:253, 261-62, 275, 277, 286-87

Fritz Kochers Aufsätze (Walser) **20**:332, 338-40, 357

"Fro" (Platonov) **42**:250, 252, 256

"The Frog Prince" (Collier) **19**:104

"The Frog Prince" (Grimm and Grimm) **36**:204, 206, 208

"The Frog Song" (P'u Sung-ling)
See "Wa-ch'u"

"Frog Trouncin' Contest" (Stuart) **31**:234, 260-61

"The Frogs" (Agnon) **30**:68

"Froim grach" (Babel) **16**:27

"The Frolic" (Ligotti) **16**:261, 263, 269, 271, 276, 283, 286, 288

"From a French Prison" (Rhys) **21**:62

"From a Mattress Grave" (Zangwill) **44**:365-66

"From a Mournful Villager" (Jewett) **44**:193

"From a Refugee's Notebook" (Ozick) **15**:306-07

"From a Window in Vartou" (Andersen) **6**:4

"From Bed and Board" (Auchincloss) **22**:48

"From Beyond" (Lovecraft) **52**:264, 267, 308, 335, 362

From Death to Morning (Wolfe) **33**:346-47, 349, 351, 355, 369-72, 376, 382, 397

"From Each according to His Ability" (Henry) **5**:159

"From Lodging to Lodging" (Agnon) **30**:71

"From the Cabby's Seat" (Henry) **5**:158; **49**:197

"From the Childhood of Saint Francis of Assisi" (Hesse) **9**:231, 235

"From the Dark" (Lovecraft) **52**:311

"From the Diary of a New York Lady" (Parker) **2**:278, 286

"From the Fifteenth District" (Gallant) **5**:136-37

From the Fifteenth District (Gallant) **5**:135-37

From the Four Winds (Galsworthy) **22**:57, 72, 80, 84, 90-1, 93, 97

"From the Water Junction" (Sansom) **21**:88

"From Yasukichi's Notebooks" (Akutagawa Ryūnosuke)
See "Yasukichi no techōkara"

"From Your Side to Paradise" (Ferré) **36**:144

"A Front Page Story" (Farrell) **28**:91-2

"The Frontier" (Bates) **10**:116

"Frontiers" (Aldiss) **36**:14, 20

The Frontiersmen (Murfree) **22**:189

"The Frost Is on the Noggin" (Perelman) **32**:235

"The Frost King; or, The Power of Love" (Alcott) **27**:38-9

Frost on the Earth (Appelfeld)
See *Kefor 'al ha'arets*

The Frost-King (Alcott) **27**:44

"A Froward Child" (de la Mare) **14**:82, 86, 89

"The Frozen Fields" (Bowles) **3**:65-6, 79, 84

The Fruit Man, the Meat Man, and the Manager (Hood) **42**:139-40, 148, 175, 183-87, 196, 198, 204-05

"The Fruitful Sleeping of the Rev. Elisha Edwards" (Dunbar) **8**:122, 127

"Fruition at Forty" (Narayan) **25**:132, 155-56

"The Frying Pan" (O'Connor) **5**:371, 389

"Fu hu" (P'u Sung-ling) **31**:208

"The Fuck Machine" (Bukowski) **45**:54, 60

"Fuda-no-Tsuji" (Endō) **48**:191, 212

"El fuego" (Pardo Bazán) **30**:261

"La fuerza de la sangre" (Cervantes) **12**:3, 5, 14-16, 18-22, 33, 36-7, 39-40, 44

"Fuga" (Pirandello) **22**:278

"Fugaku hyakkei" (Dazai Osamu) **41**:240, 245

"Fugitives" (Moore) **19**:305, 312, 333, 336

"Fugue" (O'Faolain) **13**:302-03, 314

"Fuji no Tsudai" (Endō) **48**:192

"Fulano" (Machado de Assis) **24**:128

"Fulfillment" (Dreiser) **30**:122

"The Fulfillment of the Pact" (Howells) **36**:397
"The Full Belly" (White) **39**:301, 303, 305, 308, 319-20, 324-25, 328, 337, 346, 350
"A Full Day" (Price) **22**:386
"Full Employment" (Levi) **12**:278-79
"Full Sun" (Aldiss) **36**:20
"The Fullness of Life" (Wharton) **6**:424
"Fumes" (Pirandello)
    See "Il fumo"
"Fumiko no ashi" (Tanizaki) **21**:182, 210
"Fumiko's Feet" (Tanizaki)
    See "Fumiko no ashi"
"Il fumo" (Pirandello) **22**:241, 244
"A Funeral" (Clarke) **45**:89, 92, 103, 105
"Funeral March" (Machado de Assis) **24**:155
The Funeral of Mama Grand (García Márquez)
    See *Los funerales de la Mamá Grande*
"Los funerales de la Mamá Grande" (García Márquez) **8**:155, 162, 174, 185, 187, 191, 198
Los funerales de la Mamá Grande (García Márquez) **8**:169-70, 183, 185, 187, 189
"Funes" (Borges)
    See "Funes el memorioso"
"Funes el memorioso" (Borges) **4**:19-20, 30; **41**:60, 159, 162, 164
"Funes, His Memory" (Borges)
    See "Funes el memorioso"
"Funes the Memorious" (Borges)
    See "Funes el memorioso"
Der funfzehnte November (Tieck) **31**:274
"Funghi in città" (Calvino) **48**:81-2
"Funhouse" (Barth)
    See "Lost in the Funhouse"
Funhouse (Barth)
    See *Lost in the Funhouse: Fiction for Print, Tape, Live Voice*
Funny Pieces (Leacock) **39**:267
"Fuori dell'abitato di Malbork" (Calvino) **48**:168
"Fur" (Saki) **12**:295
"The Fur Coat" (O'Faolain) **13**:288, 314
"The Fur Hat" (Peretz)
    See "Dos Shtraiml"
"The Fur-Cap" (Peretz)
    See "Dos Shtraiml"
"The Furious Seasons" (Carver) **8**:5, 50
Furious Seasons, and Other Stories (Carver) **8**:4, 30, 32, 34, 46, 50, 57-8; **51**:12, 17-18
"The Furnished Room" (Henry) **5**:156, 171, 174, 180-81, 184, 187-89; **49**:197
"Fürst Ganzgott und Sänger Halbgott" (Arnim) **29**:6-7
Further Confessions of Zeno (Svevo) **25**:334, 338, 340, 342, 349
Further Experiences of an Irish R.M. (Somerville & Ross) **56**:291, 294, 298, 301, 306, 308, 315, 317, 324, 329, 334-5
Further Fables for Our Time (Thurber) **1**:426-28; **47**:362, 364
"Furto in una pasticceria" (Calvino) **48**:80, 147, 162
Futility and Other Animals (Moorhouse) **40**:286-89, 291-94, 297, 301-02, 307-11, 321-25
"The Future, If Any, of Comedy; or, Where Do We Not-Go from Here?" (Thurber) **1**:424
Future Perfect (Abish)
    See *In the Future Perfect*
"Fyrtøjet" (Andersen) **6**:4, 18, 23, 26-7, 30-2, 36-7; **56**:36, 39
G. K. Chesterton: Selected Short Stories (Chesterton) **1**:135
"Gabriel-Ernest" (Saki) **12**:316, 331
"'Gad, Lucy, You're Magnificent!' Breathed the Great Painter" (Perelman) **32**:212
The Gadsbys (Kipling)
    See *The Story of the Gadsbys*
"A Gala Dress" (Freeman) **1**:196, 201; **47**:84-85, 157
"Le galant tireur" (Baudelaire) **18**:6, 18, 36-7

"Galar Dúithche" (Moore) **19**:303, 308, 319-20, 322, 330-31, 333-35
"Galatea" (Thomas) **20**:289, 296, 318
Galaxies like Grains of Sand (Aldiss) **36**:4, 6, 18-19
"Gale" (Schulz) **13**:335
"Galeria póstuma" (Machado de Assis) **24**:129, 133
"A Galician Mother" (Pardo Bazán) **30**:290
Galigaï (Mauriac) **24**:163-64, 167-70, 206
"A Galinha" (Lispector) **34**:185, 189, 195
A Gallery of Women (Dreiser) **30**:110, 122, 133-42, 146-49, 151
"Gallery-going" (Barthelme) **55**:54
"La gallina di reparto" (Calvino) **3**:98; **48**:38-9
Galpa Guccha (Tagore) **48**:337
"Galway Bay" (O'Flaherty) **6**:265, 269, 282
"Galya Ganskaya" (Bunin) **5**:114
"Gambara" (Balzac) **5**:16, 26
"The Gambler, the Nun, and the Radio" (Hemingway) **1**:218, 234; **25**:101; **40**:177, 185, 209, 212, 215, 224, 245, 247, 249, 251
"The Gamblers" (Far) **62**:11, 73
"Gambler's Luck" (Hoffmann)
    See "Spielerglück"
"The Game" (Barthelme) **2**:40
"A Game of Billiards" (Sansom) **21**:90, 92, 95
"A Game of Catch" (Garrett) **30**:173, 180
"A Game of Clue" (Millhauser) **57**:155-57, 180, 185-86
"A game of make-believe" (Kundera) **24**:89
"The Gamekeeper" (Chekhov) **51**:82
"Games without End" (Calvino) **3**:109; **48**:65-6, 132
"Det gamle Egetr[dj]es sidste Drøm" (Andersen) **56**:37
"Gamlet ščigrovskogo uezda" (Turgenev) **7**:316, 344; **57**:259, 266, 278, 282, 297
"Gandhi's Appeal" (Narayan) **25**:137, 140, 153, 156-57
"Ganymede" (du Maurier) **18**:127, 132, 137
"Gaol Birds" (Pavese) **19**:387
The Garbage Wind (Platonov)
    See *Musornyi veter*
"The Garden" (Borges)
    See "El jardín de senderos que se bifurcan"
"The Garden" (Bowles) **3**:64, 68, 80
"The Garden" (Dazai Osamu)
    See "Niwa"
"The Garden at Mons" (Hemingway) **1**:208, 236
"A Garden in Flanders" (Garson)
    See "Tlactocatzine del jardin de Flandes"
"The Garden Lodge" (Cather) **2**:90, 98, 103; **50**:57, 82, 107, 109-10, 122, 138, 198-99, 238, 240, 243, 264, 279
"The Garden of Eden" (Andersen) **6**:30, 37
"The Garden of Eden" (Moore) **19**:311
The Garden of Forking Paths (Borges)
    See *El jardín de senderos que se bifurcan*
The Garden of Krakonoš (Čapek)
    See *Krakonošova zahrada*
"Garden of Paradise" (Andersen) **6**:7
"The Garden of the Forking Paths" (Borges)
    See "El jardín de senderos que se bifurcan"
"The Garden of Time" (Ballard) **1**:71, 74, 77; **53**:9-10, 46
"The Garden Party" (Mansfield) **9**:276, 280, 282, 284, 286, 309-11, 313; **23**:118-77; **38**:230
The Garden Party, and Other Stories (Mansfield) **9**:275-76, 281; **23**:139
"A Garden Story" (Jewett) **6**:156, 158-59
"The Gardener" (Kipling) **5**:276, 279, 282-83, 296-97; **54**:74
"The Gardener" (Lavin) **4**:181
The Gardener (Tagore) **48**:338
"The Gardener and the Family" (Andersen) **6**:15
"Gardens" (Narayan) **25**:138
"Gargantua" (Calisher) **15**:9, 15, 19, 21
Garland for Girls (Alcott) **27**:44

A Garland of Love (Bioy Casares)
    See *Guirnalda con amores*
A Garland of Straw, and Other Stories (Warner) **23**:367-68, 380, 387
"The Garment" (Agnon) **30**:38
"The Garments of the Fairies" (Far) **62**:50
"Gas Stations" (Apple) **50**:5, 7, 9, 16, 20, 25, 29-30, 33, 36, 39
"Gaspar, Melchior, Balthasar" (Thomas) **44**:335
"Gaspar Ruiz" (Conrad) **9**:151, 157, 179, 181
"Gaspard de la nuit" (Donoso) **34**:8, 12-13, 17, 34
Gäst hos verkligheten (Lagerkvist) **12**:180-82, 185, 197
"The Gate of the Hundred Sorrows" (Kipling) **5**:262, 265
"Le gâteau" (Baudelaire) **18**:8, 18
"Le gâteau" (Maupassant) **1**:274, 286
"The Gateman's Gift" (Narayan) **25**:133, 141, 153, 155-56
"The Gatewood Caper" (Hammett) **17**:220, 222
"A Gatherer of Simples" (Freeman) **47**:102
"Gaudissart" (Balzac)
    See "L'illustre Gaudissart"
"The Gauzy Edge of Paradise" (Gilchrist) **14**:153-54
"Gavin O'Leary" (Collier) **19**:106, 110
"A Gay Adventure" (Zoshchenko)
    See "A Gay Little Episode"
"The Gay and Melancholy Flux" (Saroyan) **21**:137, 139
"A Gay Little Episode" (Zoshchenko) **15**:395
"Gazebo" (Carver) **8**:14-15, 19-20; **51**:6, 13, 16
"G.B.S. Interviews the Pope" (Farrell) **28**:94
"G.B.S., Mark V" (Bradbury) **29**:78
"Ge" (P'u Sung-ling) **31**:215
"Ge saku Zammai" (Akutagawa Ryūnosuke) **44**:76-7
"Gedali" (Babel) **16**:8-10, 25, 27-30, 52-3, 55, 57-8
"Gefallen" (Mann) **5**:319, 323, 351-53
Der Geheimnisvolle (Tieck) **31**:270-71
"Gehenna" (Aiken) **9**:10, 12-13, 30
Die Geisterseher (Keller) **26**:110
Der Gelehrte (Tieck) **31**:274, 286
"Das Gelübde" (Hoffmann) **13**:209-11
Die Gemälde (Tieck) **31**:269-70, 286
"Gemcrack" (Phillips) **16**:328
"Das Gemeine" (Dazai Osamu) **41**:244
"The Gemlike Flame" (Auchincloss) **22**:3, 33, 35-7, 53
"The General" (Akutagawa Ryūnosuke)
    See "Shōgun"
"The General" (Head) **52**:209
"The General" (O'Hara) **15**:276-77, 285-86
"The General's Day" (Trevor) **21**:230, 236, 261; **58**:202, 229
"The Generations of America" (Ballard) **1**:82; **53**:53
"The Generous Lover" (Cervantes)
    See "El amante liberal"
"Generous Pieces" (Gilchrist) **14**:150; **63**:10, 23
"Generous Wine" (Svevo)
    See "Vino generoso"
"Genesis" (Stegner) **27**:199, 219, 221, 223
Geneviéve (Gide) **13**:72, 100-05
"The Genial Epoch" (Schulz)
    See "The Age of Genius"
"The Genial Host" (McCarthy) **24**:213, 225
"Das Genie" (Walser) **20**:334
Génitrix (Mauriac) **24**:160, 163, 179-80, 185-86, 188, 206, 208
"The Genius" (Barthelme) **55**:41, 53, 55-6
"The Genius" (O'Connor) **5**:376
"Genkaku Sanbō" (Akutagawa Ryūnosuke) **44**:44, 46, 81-2
"Genkaku's Villa" (Akutagawa Ryūnosuke)
    See "Genkaku Sanbō"
"Gentian" (Freeman) **1**:197; **47**:85, 151
"The Gentle Art" (Gordimer) **17**:161, 184

"Gentle as Flowers Make the Stones" (Metcalf) **43**:73, 81, 85, 91, 102, 111-13, 117, 160-64
"The Gentle Assassin" (Ballard) **53**:10, 42
"The Gentle Boy" (Hawthorne) **3**:164, 167, 181, 185-87
"The Gentle Euphemia; or 'Love Shall Still Be Lord of All'" (Trollope) **28**:316, 347
"A Gentle Ghost" (Freeman) **47**:131-36
The Gentle Grafter (Henry) **5**:155, 162, 172, 182
"The Gentle Insurrection" (Betts) **45**:2, 26-7
The Gentle Insurrection (Betts) **45**:2, 4, 9, 12, 23, 26-7, 35
"The Gentle Lena" (Stein) **42**:274, 280, 282-84, 287, 311, 313-14, 321, 336, 350
"A Gentle Soul" (Lavin) **4**:165-66, 168
"The Gentleman from Cracow" (Singer) **3**:358, 368, 383-84; **53**:301
"The Gentleman from New Orleans" (Chopin) **8**:99
"The Gentleman from San Francisco" (Bunin) **5**:80-3, 85, 87-90, 92, 94-7, 117
The Gentleman from San Francisco (Bunin) **5**:90
"A Gentleman of Bayou Têche" (Chopin) **8**:88, 103
"A Gentleman's Agreement" (Jolley) **19**:233, 245
"A Gentleman's Friend" (Chekhov) **2**:137-39; **51**:49-50, 52
"Gentlemen, Be Seated" (Heinlein) **55**:165-66
"Gentlemen of the Press" (Wolfe) **33**:374
"The Gentry" (O'Hara) **15**:286
"Genuflection in the Sun" (Perelman) **32**:211
"The Geological Spieler" (Lawson) **18**:206, 263
"Geometar i Julka" (Andrić) **36**:66-7
"The Geometry of Love" (Cheever) **1**:97, 101; **38**:53
"George and the Pink House" (Naipaul) **38**:318
George Gissing: Lost Stories from America (Gissing) **37**:79
"George Silverman's Explanation" (Dickens) **17**:124
"George Thurston" (Bierce) **9**:67-9, 76-7
"George Walker at Suez" (Trollope) **28**:318, 331, 335
Georgia Boy (Caldwell) **19**:15, 18, 25, 33, 35-7, 41, 47-55, 57
"Georgia's Ruling" (Henry) **5**:162, 164, 170
"Geraldo" (Cisneros) **32**:4
"The Geranium" (O'Connor) **1**:364
Gerbersau (Hesse) **9**:231
"A Germ Destroyer" (Kipling) **5**:290
"A German Idyll" (Bates) **10**:113
"The German Refugee" (Malamud) **15**:171, 173-74, 176, 213, 216, 221, 235-36
"The German Spy" (Tanizaki)
    See "Dokutan"
"The Gernsback Continuum" (Gibson) **52**:15-16, 27, 35, 42-7
"A Geronimo Story" (Silko) **37**:295-96, 310-11
"Gertrude Talks Back" (Atwood) **46**:75, 99
Gesammelte Erzählungen (Lenz) **33**:333
"Gesammelte Erzählungen und Märchen" (Hoffmann) **13**:217
"Geschäft ist Geschäft" (Boell) **23**:5
Geschichten (Walser) **20**:334
Geschichten aus der Tonne (Storm) **27**:278
Die Gesellschaft auf dem Lande (Tieck) **31**:271, 275, 286
Gestes et opinions du Dr. Faustroll, pataphysicien, roman néo-scientifique (Jarry) **20**:45-7, 49-53, 55-6, 62, 67, 69-70, 77, 82
"Get a Seeing-Eyed Dog" (Hemingway) **40**:192
"Get Thee to a Monastery" (Thurber) **1**:429
"Getting Back on Dave Regan" (Lawson) **18**:233-35
"Getting Funding" (Hood) **42**:235
"Getting into the Set" (Updike) **13**:402
"Getting Lucky" (Michaels) **16**:309, 316

"Getting off the Altitude" (Lessing) **6**:190, 214; **61**:99-100
Getting Through (McGahern) **17**:299, 303-04, 306-09, 322-23
"Getting to Williamstown" (Hood) **42**:186
"Getzel the Monkey" (Singer) **3**:359
Ghetto Comedies (Zangwill) **44**:370, 374-75, 377-79, 381, 389
Ghetto Tragedies (Zangwill) **44**:372, 374-76, 387-88
"The Ghost" (Andersen) **6**:30
"The Ghost and the Bone Setter" (Le Fanu) **14**:216, 219, 221, 239
"Ghost Guessed" (Bradfield) **65**:58, 60, 63
"The Ghost in the Garden Room" (Gaskell)
    See "The Crooked Branch"
"The Ghost of Gideon Wise" (Chesterton) **46**:134-35
"The Ghost of the Crosstrees" (Norris) **28**:198
"The Ghost of the Rose" (Kawabata)
    See "Bara no Yūrei"
Ghost Stories and Mysteries (Le Fanu) **14**:237
Ghost Stories and Tales of Mystery (Le Fanu) **14**:217, 220-21
Ghost Stories of an Antiquary (James) **16**:222, 226-27, 229-31, 237-39, 242, 245, 250-51, 255, 258
"Ghostkeeper" (Lowry) **31**:72, 83
"A Ghostly Chess Game" (London) **4**:294
"The Ghostly Door" (Lawson) **18**:217
"Ghostly Father, I Confess" (McCarthy) **24**:214
Ghostly Tales (Campbell) **19**:63, 86-7, 89
"The Ghost-Maker" (Pohl) **25**:227-28, 230-32, 234-35
Ghosts (Wharton) **6**:426-27, 430
"Ghosts at Jarry" (Hood) **42**:176, 193, 199
"Ghouls" (Toomer) **45**:316, 320
"La giachetta di cuoio" (Pavese) **19**:364, 378, 384, 387
"Giacomo" (Svevo) **25**:329
"The Giant and the Tailor" (Grimm and Grimm) **36**:229-30
"The Giant Mole" (Kafka) **5**:206
"The Giant Wistaria" (Gilman) **13**:128, 130-31, 138-140; **62**:180
"The Giant's House" (Benét) **10**:149
"La giara" (Pirandello) **22**:226, 229, 237-38, 256, 264, 281
"Un giardino incantato" (Calvino) **3**:90, 97, 112; **48**:37
"Gib'ath ha-hol" (Agnon) **30**:20, 54, 66
"The Gift" (Bradbury) **29**:80
"The Gift" (Davie) **52**:4, 6
"The Gift" (Ferré) **36**:147, 150
"The Gift" (Steinbeck) **11**:209-10, 212-13, 232-34, 237
"A Gift from the City" (Updike) **13**:353-54
"Gift of Grass" (Adams) **24**:2, 8
"The Gift of Little Me" (Far) **62**:50-52, 103
"The Gift of the Magi" (Henry) **5**:166, 171-72, 181-82, 184-85, 187-88; **49**:194-207
"The Gift of the Prodigal" (Taylor) **10**:407-08, 418
"Gifts" (Singer) **3**:389
"The Gifts of the Little Folk" (Grimm and Grimm) **36**:229-30
Gigi (Colette) **10**:269-70, 272-74, 293
"Gigolo and Gigolette" (Maugham) **8**:366, 379
"Gilbert's Mother" (Trevor) **58**:252, 261, 287
"The Gilded Six-Bits" (Hurston) **4**:135-36, 138, 151-52
"Gilead" (Henderson) **29**:327
"Gimpel Tam" (Singer) **3**:352, 355, 363, 365-68, 375, 382-84, 389; **53**:279-80, 300-1, 323, 327-30, 342-43
Gimpel Tam und andere Dertseylungen (Singer) **3**:370; **53**:271, 273, 323, 326
"Gimpel the Fool" (Singer)
    See "Gimpel Tam"
Gimpel the Fool, and Other Stories (Singer)
    See *Gimpel Tam und andere Dertseylungen*

"Gin and Goldenrod" (Lowry) **31**:44-6, 48, 51-4, 59, 62, 71-2, 74-5, 81, 86-7
"The Gingerbread House" (Coover) **15**:33, 38, 41, 48
"Giochi senza fine" (Calvino) **48**:47, 69-70
"The Gioconda of the Twilight Noon" (Ballard) **1**:69; **53**:11, 48, 50
"The Gioconda Smile" (Huxley) **39**:155, 162-65, 167-70, 174-75
"Una giornata" (Pirandello) **22**:262, 270
La giornato d'uno scruttatore (Calvino) **48**:34-5, 39, 79, 178, 183-84, 186
"Girl" (Henry) **5**:163, 182
"The Girl" (Oates) **6**:232
"The Girl and the Habit" (Henry) **5**:158, 164
"The Girl Between" (Tagore)
    See "Madhyabartini"
"The Girl from California" (O'Hara) **15**:281
"The Girl from Ciociaria" (Moravia) **26**:139
"The Girl from the Family of Man" (Moorhouse) **40**:286, 302
"A Girl I Knew" (Salinger) **65**:337
"The Girl I Left Behind Me" (Spark) **10**:356
Girl in Gingham (Metcalf) **43**:96, 100, 103, 114-16, 122-23, 142-46, 154
"The Girl in the Bus" (Sansom) **21**:94, 96
"The Girl in the Pink Hat" (Gilman) **13**:126
"A Girl Named Peter" (Bates) **10**:115-16
"A Girl of Modern Tyre" (Garland)
    See "A Stop-Over at Tyre"
"The Girl of My Dreams" (Malamud) **15**:217, 239, 240, 242-43
The Girl on the Baggage Truck (O'Hara) **15**:250-51, 271-72
"The Girl Who Had Been Presented" (O'Hara) **15**:263, 266
"The Girl Who Loved Horses" (Spencer) **57**:206, 210, 215
"The Girl Who Met Simone de Beauvoir in Paris" (Moorhouse) **40**:289, 302
"The Girl Who Sang" (Aldiss) **36**:20
"The Girl Who Trod on the Loaf" (Andersen) **6**:13
"The Girl with a Pimply Face" (Williams) **31**:304-05, 325, 332-33, 340-42, 345, 362
"Girl with Figurines" (Caldwell) **19**:54-5
"The Girl with the Cannon Dresses" (Jewett) **6**:157
"The Girl with the Flaxen Hair" (Grau) **15**:147, 150, 158, 165
"The Girl with the Silver Eyes" (Hammett) **17**:219, 221, 228, 230
"The Girl with the Stoop" (Bowen) **3**:54
"Girls and the Land" (Gilman) **13**:144
"A Girl's Story" (Bambara) **35**:28
"Gitanette" (Colette) **10**:292
"La gitanilla" (Cervantes) **12**:3-4, 6-8, 15-18, 21, 23-5, 33-4, 38-40, 44
"Gitl Purishkevitch" (Aleichem) **33**:19, 26, 38
"Giulia Lazzari" (Maugham) **8**:377
"Give It a Shot" (Clarke) **45**:77-8, 82, 96-7, 108, 113
"Give Us a Prescription, Doctor" (Hemingway) **40**:245, 247, 251, 257
"Give Us This Day: And Forgive Us" (Clarke) **45**:91, 94
"The Given Case" (James) **8**:316
"The Givers" (Freeman) **47**:85-86
The Givers (Freeman) **47**:102
"Giving Birth" (Atwood) **2**:3-4, 6-10, 12, 14, 16; **46**:26-30, 33, 35-6, 58, 62-4, 76-7, 81-2, 84, 87-9
"Giving Blood" (Updike) **13**:373, 386
"Glad Ghosts" (Lawrence) **4**:220, 230
"Glad Yen" (Far) **62**:50
"Gladius Dei" (Mann) **5**:310, 323, 329, 331
"Glamour" (Benét) **10**:142, 144, 154
"The Glamour" (Ligotti) **16**:280
"The Glass Coffin" (Grimm and Grimm) **36**:223, 229-30
"The Glass Mountain" (Barthelme) **2**:34, 40; **55**:34, 57-60, 64-5, 91

"A Glass of Beer" (Stephens) **50**:315, 326
"A Glass of Tea" (White) **39**:280, 291-93, 296-97, 309, 317, 325, 329, 336, 344
"Glass Orchid" (Cowan) **28**:83
"The Glass Scholar" (Cervantes)
    See "El licienciado Vidriera"
"Glazed Tiles" (Chang) **28**:25; 34
"The Glazier's Song" (Baudelaire)
    See "La chanson vitrier"
"A Gleam" (Mann) **5**:322-23
"The Gleaner" (Bates) **10**:113, 128
"Gleanings from Snow Country" (Kawabata) **17**:251, 253, 255, 257
Glenda (Cortázar)
    See *Queremos tanto a Glenda*
"The Glendale People" (O'Hara) **15**:282-83
"Gliding Gulls and Going People" (Sansom) **21**:91, 94, 122-23
"Glinyanyy dom v uyezdnom sadu" (Platonov) **42**:253
"Gloire et malheur" (Balzac) **5**:4, 29
Gloomy People (Chekhov) **2**:146; **51**:81
"Glory in the Daytime" (Parker) **2**:273-74, 280, 283
"The Glory Machine" (Villiers de l'Isle Adam)
    See "La machine à gloire"
"The Glory of His Nostrils" (Betts) **45**:3, 20
"The Glory That Was Sion's" (Evans) **43**:6, 36
"Glossolalia" (Barth) **10**:42-3, 45, 47, 54-5, 80, 90, 94-5, 97-8
"The Gloves" (Walser) **20**:364
"Gluck" (Hoffmann) **13**:225
Glück gibt Verstand (Tieck) **31**:274
"Die Glücksfamilie des Monats" (Lenz) **33**:318, 322-27
"The Gnats" (Pritchett) **14**:299
"Go Back to Your Precious Wife and Son" (Vonnegut) **8**:436
"Go Down, Moses" (Faulkner) **1**:148, 154, 165-67, 173, 180-83; **35**:146, 157, 160
Go Down, Moses and Other Stories (Faulkner) **35**:141, 146, 148-49, 157-58, 160, 164, 170, 173-76, 178, 184, 186-87, 197-98, 206, 210; **42**:107
"Go Forth" (Aleichem)
    See "Lekh-lekh"
"A Goatherd at Luncheon" (Calvino) **3**:116
"The Go-Away Bird" (Spark) **10**:350-56, 358-59, 361, 366, 368, 370
The Go-Away Bird, and Other Stories (Spark) **10**:350-53
"Gobegger Foriu Tostay" (Cabrera Infante) **39**:22
"The Go-Between" (Moravia) **26**:139
"The Goblin and the Hukster" (Andersen)
    See "Nissen hos Spekhøkeren"
"The Goblin at the Grocer's" (Andersen)
    See "Nissen hos Spekhøkeren"
"The Goblins" (Kazakov) **43**:49
"Goblins Who Stole A Sexton" (Dickens) **49**:36
"Gobseck" (Balzac) **5**:18, 22, 24, 28, 31, 33
"God and the Article Writer" (Berriault) **30**:101
"God and the Cobbler" (Narayan) **25**:152, 159
"God Bless the Lonesome Gas Man" (Algren) **33**:108
"God Has Manifested Himself unto Us As Canadian Tire" (Hood) **42**:174-75, 190
"God ikh zhizni" (Pilnyak) **48**:253, 255, 257, 270, 284, 295, 297
"The God of His Fathers" (London) **4**:258, 286-87
The God of His Fathers (London) **4**:264, 282, 285-87
"The God of Restoration" (Far) **62**:50, 58
"The God of the Gongs" (Chesterton) **1**:127; **46**:140
"God Rest You Merry, Gentlemen" (Hemingway) **1**:216; **63**:46, 48, 50
"God Sees the Truth but Waits" (Tolstoy) **9**:382, 386-87; **45**:135
"The Goddess" (Oates) **6**:231

The Goddess and Other Women (Oates) **6**:231, 243
"Godliness" (Anderson) **1**:18, 42, 57
"Godman's Master" (Laurence) **7**:245-46, 249-50, 252-53, 261, 263
"The Godmother" (Chopin) **8**:100
"The Gods" (Pavese) **19**:371
Gods, Demons, and Others (Narayan) **25**:135-36, 152, 166
"The Gods in Flight" (Aldiss) **36**:20, 22
"God's Little Traveling Salesman" (Lagerkvist) **12**:196
"God's Lonely Man" (Wolfe) **33**:374
"God's Own Country" (Kiely) **58**:167-68
"God's Ravens" (Garland) **18**:154, 160, 163
"The God's Script" (Borges)
    See "La escritura del Dios"
"God's Wrath" (Malamud) **15**:217
"The Godson" (Tolstoy) **9**:388
"The Go-Getter" (Wodehouse) **2**:346
"A Goin' to the Buttin'" (Stuart) **31**:254
"Goin' to Town" (Storm)
    See "Going to Town"
"The Going Away of Liza" (Chopin) **8**:71
"Going Blind" (Lawson) **18**:200, 202, 213
"Going Critical" (Bambara) **35**:42
Going Down Slow (Metcalf) **43**:73-5, 82-5, 101-2, 106, 109-10, 116, 120
"Going Home" (Trevor) **21**:244
"Going into Exile" (O'Flaherty) **6**:261, 269, 276-77, 281-82, 284
"Going Out as a Ghost" (Hood) **42**:140, 168, 170-71, 187, 199, 219
"Going Places" (Michaels) **16**:302-03, 311-13
Going Places (Michaels) **16**:301-03, 306-08, 310, 314-16, 322
"Going to Meet the Man" (Baldwin) **10**:3, 5, 7, 10, 17-18, 20
Going to Meet the Man (Baldwin) **10**:2, 4, 6, 8-9, 12, 17; **33**:116, 128, 143
"Going to Naples" (Welty) **1**:476, 484
"Going to the Dogs" (Ford) **56**:140, 143, 152, 158, 175, 194
"Going to the People" (Moravia)
    See "Andare verso il popolo"
"Going to Town" (Kazakov) **43**:58, 67
"Going to Town" (Stegner) **27**:196
Going to Town and Other Stories (Kazakov) **43**:49, 55
"Going Under" (Dubus) **15**:82, 87, 89-90
"The Gold" (Freeman) **47**:84-85
"Gold" (Levi) **12**:256, 258
"Gold and Silver" (Tanizaki) **21**:190, 194
"The Gold at the Starbow's End" (Pohl) **25**:226
"The Gold Belt" (Narayan) **25**:138, 140-41
"The Gold Bug" (Poe) **1**:378, 390; **22**:293, 305; **54**:167-63, 183, 218, 239-41
"The Gold Dress" (Benét) **10**:160
"Gold Is Not Always" (Faulkner) **1**:177
"The Gold of Tomas Vargas" (Allende) **65**:10, 17, 30, 54
"A Gold Slipper" (Cather) **2**:91; **50**:95, 241-43, 247, 275
"The Gold That Glittered" (Henry) **5**:188
"The Gold Watch" (Machado de Assis)
    See "O relógio de ouro"
"The Gold Watch" (McGahern) **17**:304, 309-10, 315, 317, 320-21, 323-24
"The Gold-Children" (Grimm and Grimm) **36**:199, 201
"The Gold Age" (Cheever) **1**:106
"Golden Apple" (Kundera)
    See "The Golden Apple of Eternal Desire"
"The Golden Apple" (Kundera)
    See "The Golden Apple of Eternal Desire"
"The Golden Apple of Desire" (Kundera)
    See "The Golden Apple of Eternal Desire"
"The Golden Apple of Eternal Desire" (Kundera) **24**:86, 88, 91-2, 97, 102-04, 106, 113-14
"The Golden Apples" (Welty) **1**:473-74, 479, 483-85, 492, 494, 497

The Golden Apples (Welty) **51**:264-65, 269-70, 273-75, 277, 279-81, 283, 287-93, 295, 305-7, 310-11, 318-19, 321-23, 329, 332, 338-40
"The Golden Apples of the Sun" (Bradbury) **29**:78, 84; **53**:216
The Golden Apples of the Sun (Bradbury) **29**:44, 48, 52, 78-9; **53**:198
"The Golden Bessie" (Benét) **10**:144, 146
"The Golden Bird" (Grimm and Grimm) **36**:199, 201, 206
"The Golden Bough" (Gilchrist) **63**:36
The Golden Cangue (Chang)
    See *Jin suoji*
"The Golden Death" (Tanizaki)
    See "Konjiki no shi"
"Golden Documents" (Bulgakov) **18**:91
"Golden Gate" (Hughes) **6**:138
"The Golden Goose" (Grimm and Grimm)
    See "The Golden Bird"
"The Golden Graveyard" (Lawson) **18**:239
"The Golden Honeymoon" (Lardner) **32**:114-17, 123, 125, 131-32, 139, 145, 149, 152, 154-55, 166, 195-96
"The Golden Horseshoe" (Hammett) **17**:200, 210, 219, 222-23, 225
"The Golden Kite, the Silver Wind" (Bradbury) **29**:42
"Golden Land" (Faulkner) **1**:167
"The Golden Man" (Dick) **57**:104
"Golden Mirage" (Tagore) **48**:334
The Golden Oriole (Bates) **10**:123-24
The Golden Pot: Fairy Tale of Our Times (Hoffmann)
    See "Der goldene Topf"
"Golden Silks" (Hood) **42**:226
"The Golden Town" (Bulgakov) **18**:90
"Golden Wedding" (Suckow) **18**:389, 396, 398-99, 412
"Der goldene Topf" (Hoffmann) **13**:186, 189, 192-95, 197, 199-205, 208, 215, 218-19, 223, 226
"Goldfish" (Chandler) **23**:59, 63, 87, 107
"The Goldfish" (Pritchett) **14**:297
"Goldfish Bowl" (Heinlein) **55**:214
"Gollan" (Coppard) **21**:10
"Golubaia zhizn" (Gorky) **28**:179, 181-82
"The Gombeen Man" (Stoker) **62**:247
"Gone Away" (Bowen) **3**:53
"Gone Three Days" (Hood) **42**:177, 192, 205
"Goneril, Lear's Daughter" (Čapek) **36**:84-5
"The Gonzaga Manuscripts" (Bellow) **14**:3, 22-3, 25
"Good and Bad Dreams" (Price) **22**:365, 367, 371-72
"The Good Anna" (Stein) **42**:274, 278, 280, 282-84, 287, 289-90, 311-12, 314, 332, 336, 350
Good Bones (Atwood) **46**:74-5, 83, 92, 97, 99
"Good Climate, Friendly Inhabitants" (Gordimer) **17**:181
"The Good Corn" (Bates) **10**:118
"Good Country People" (O'Connor) **1**:335, 343-45, 350, 356, 359-60; **23**:185, 233; **61**:169, 200, 208, 210, 227-28, 230, 234, 241
"Good Deeds" (Moore) **19**:330
"A 'Good Fellow's' Wife" (Garland) **18**:161
"Good Friday" (Dybek) **55**:141
"A Good Game Is Over Quickly" (Calvino) **48**:146
"The Good Girl" (Bowen) **3**:33
"Good Humor" (Andersen) **6**:7
"A Good Job Gone" (Hughes) **6**:109, 121-22, 128, 140, 142
"The Good Listener" (Hood) **42**:192, 205
"A Good Location" (O'Hara) **15**:278-79
"A Good Man Is Hard to Find" (O'Connor) **1**:339, 344, 347-48, 356, 358, 360-63, 371; **23**:178-241; **61**:143, 146-47, 151-56, 169, 172, 186, 188-89, 197, 200, 214-16, 218, 227-30, 232, 234, 240-41

A Good Man Is Hard to Find and Other Stories (O'Connor) **23**:196, 202, 209, 213, 232-33, 236-37; **61**:171, 228
"Good News" (Trevor) **58**:301
"The Good Old Days" (Williams) **31**:334
"Good Pals" (Suckow) **18**:411, 417
"Good Samaritan" (O'Hara) **15**:286
Good Samaritan, and Other Stories (O'Hara) **15**:273, 286
"The Good Soldier" (London) **4**:291
"A Good Temper" (Andersen) **6**:30, 36
"The Good Tenor Man" (Hood) **42**:139, 185
"The Good Trip" (Le Guin) **12**:232
"Good-by, Grandma" (Bradbury) **53**:266
"Good-by, Jack" (London) **4**:269
"Goodbye and Good Luck" (Paley) **8**:388, 391, 394, 396, 398
Goodbye, Columbus (Roth) **26**:228, 230-34, 243, 245-49, 252, 254, 256-57, 260, 265-69
Goodbye, Columbus, and Five Short Stories (Roth) **26**:228, 231, 233, 236, 238, 246-48, 250, 257-60
"Goodbye, Goodbye, Be Always Kind and True" (Garrett) **30**:173
Goodbye Harold, Good Luck (Thomas) **20**:320-23
"Goodbye Marcus, Goodbye Rose" (Rhys) **21**:39-40, 42-3, 51, 55-7, 66, 70
"Goodbye, My Brother" (Cheever) **1**:89, 99, 103-05, 108; **38**:52, 54-5, 66, 84
"Good-Bye, New York" (Morand)
    See "Adieu, New-York!"
Goodbye to Berlin (Isherwood) **56**:200-4, 206-7, 209-14, 216-19, 221-22, 224-26
"Goodbye to Goodbye" (Dixon) **16**:207
Goodbye, Wisconsin (Wescott) **35**:356, 363-65, 367, 375, 377, 379
The Goodbyes (Onetti)
    See *Los adioses*
"Good-for-Nothing" (Andersen)
    See "Hun duede ikke"
"A Goodly Life" (Bunin) **5**:81, 90, 92
"Goodwood Comes Back" (Warren) **4**:387, 389-90, 394, 396; **58**:336, 354, 356
"The Goophered Grapevine" (Chesnutt) **7**:4-6, 9-10, 41; **54**:18, 20, 22-4, 26, 28-31, 33, 35, 43, 46
"Goose Fair" (Lawrence) **4**:197
"The Goose Girl at the Spring" (Grimm and Grimm) **36**:190, 208, 233
"Gooseberries" (Chekhov)
    See "Kryžovnik"
"Gooseberry Winter" (Mason) **4**:6
"Gora" (Leskov) **34**:127
"Gore" (Chekhov) **2**:128; **51**:102, 106, 108, 151, 155
"Gorilla, My Love" (Bambara) **35**:4-5, 8, 32
Gorilla, My Love (Bambara) **35**:2-3, 10, 14-18, 20-5, 28-30, 36, 42
"Gorod Gradov" (Platonov) **42**:257, 266
"Gorod na Neve" (Solzhenitsyn) **32**:352, 354, 394
"The Gospel according to Mark" (Borges) **4**:20, 28, 30; **41**:160
"Gospodjicd" (Andrić) **36**:48
"Gossips' Slope" (Rulfo)
    See "La cuesta de las comadres"
"Got a Letter from Jimmy" (Jackson) **39**:212, 228, 229
La gota de sangre (Pardo Bazán) **30**:277-79
"The Goth" (Page) **23**:288, 307-08
"Gothic Horror" (Ligotti) **16**:287
"Gotterdammerung, in Which Nora Jane and Freddy Harwood Confront Evil in a World They Never Made" (Gilchrist) **63**:36
"A Gourdful of Glory" (Laurence) **7**:245-46, 248-50
"L'gov" (Turgenev) **57**:266, 268
"The Government Bears" (Bass) **60**:8, 39
"Governor of Kentucky" (Stuart) **31**:226, 231, 236

"Governor Warburton's Right-hand Man" (Stuart) **31**:265
"The Go-wa-peu-zi Song" (Silko) **37**:309
"Grabež" (Leskov) **34**:127
"Gracchus the Huntsman" (Kafka)
    See "Der jäger Gracchus"
"La Grâce" (Aymé) **41**:13, 16, 18
"Grace" (Joyce) **3**:202, 205-06, 208, 210-11, 214-15, 225-26, 232-235, 237, 247-48; **26**:46-8, 50; **44**:265; **64**:250, 258-59
"Grace Called" (Dixon) **16**:217
"Grace Calls" (Dixon) **16**:217
"Graduation" (Dubus) **15**:73-4
"Graduation on Market Street" (Borowski) **48**:14
"Graffiti" (Cortázar) **7**:83, 85-6, 91
"Grail" (Ellison) **14**:127
"A Grain as Big as a Hen's Egg" (Tolstoy) **9**:388
"Gramigna's Lover" (Verga)
    See "L'amante di Gramigna"
"Gramigna's Mistress" (Verga)
    See "L'amante di Gramigna"
"Gramma" (King) **55**:250
"Grammar of Love" (Bunin) **5**:89-90, 93, 106
"Grammar's for the Birds" (Cabrera Infante)
    See "Cuando se estudia gramática"
"El gran serafin" (Bioy Casares) **17**:53
El gran serafin (Bioy Casares) **17**:53, 56, 59
"Granada a vista de buho" (Alarcon) **64**:10
"Le Grand Déménagement" (Hood) **42**:151, 217-18, 242
"A Grand Filly" (Somerville & Ross) **56**:317
"The Grand Vizier's Daughter" (O'Connor) **5**:381
"Grandchildren of the Ghetto" (Zangwill) **44**:390
"La grande bretèche" (Balzac) **5**:11-12, 14-15, 18-19, 31, 35-9
"The Grande Malade" (Barnes) **3**:5-6, 9-10, 16, 24-6
"Grandfather and Grandson" (Singer) **3**:374
"Grandfathers" (Bradbury) **53**:247-48
"Grandmother's House" (Barthelme) **55**:26, 113
The Grandmother's Tale (Narayan) **25**:169, 173, 175
The Grandmother's Tale: And Selected Stories (Narayan) **25**:169
"Grandpa Birdwell's Last Battle" (Stuart) **31**:247
"Grandy Devil" (Pohl) **25**:220, 228, 230, 232
"Granella's House" (Pirandello)
    See "La casa del Granella"
"Granit" (Stifter) **28**:292-96
"Granny Weatherall" (Porter)
    See "The Jilting of Granny Weatherall"
"Grantr[dj] et" (Andersen) **56**:37
The Grapes of Paradise (Bates) **10**:121-22
The Grapes of Paradise: Four Short Novels (Bates)
    See *An Aspidistra in Babylon: Four Novellas*
Grass (Pilnyak)
    See *Byl'yo*
"The Grass Fire" (Caldwell) **19**:5-6, 14, 17
"Grass from Our Garden" (Pirandello)
    See "Erba del nosro orto"
The Grass God (Bates) **10**:118
"The Grass Widows" (Trevor) **21**:233, 237, 260; **58**:205-6, 208, 229
Grass-grown (Pilnyak)
    See *Byl'yo*
"The Grasshopper" (Chekhov)
    See "Poprygin'ia"
"Grasshoppers" (Jolley) **19**:246
"Grateful to Life and Death" (Narayan) **25**:167
"The Grave" (Porter) **4**:329-34, 340-42, 344, 352, 354, 365; **31**:160, 175-76; **43**:170-72, 209, 227, 258-59, 266-69, 272-4, 276-85, 305, 314- **15**:343
"The Grave by the Handpost" (Hardy) **2**:210

"The Grave Mound" (Grimm and Grimm) **36**:228
"The Grave of the Famous Poet" (Atwood) **2**:3-5, 7, 10-11, 16; **46**:26, 33-4, 38-40, 49-50, 57-8, 64, 76-7, 93
"The Gravedigger" (Pardo Bazán) **30**:290
"The Gravedigger" (Singer) **3**:378
"Graven Image" (O'Hara) **15**:248-49, 270
"Graveyard Day" (Mason) **4**:7
"The Graveyard Shift" (King) **17**:262; **55**:247
"Gravity" (Beattie) **11**:10, 13
"The Gray Champion" (Hawthorne) **3**:164, 167, 171, 175-76, 178, 186-87
"Gray Days" (Colette) **10**:292
"The Gray Jacket of 'No. 4'" (Page) **23**:284, 292, 295, 328
"The Gray Man" (Jewett) **44**:226
"Gray Matter" (King) **17**:261-62
"The Gray Mills of Farley" (Jewett) **6**:156
"A Gray Moon" (Shiga)
    See "Hai-iro no tsuki"
"The Gray Wolf's Ha'nt" (Chesnutt) **7**:7, 10-11, 40; **54**:39-40, 42
"Greasy Lake" (Boyle) **16**:144-45, 151-52, 156-57
Greasy Lake, & Other Stories (Boyle) **16**:143-46, 148, 153
"The Great American Nude" (Ballard) **53**:105
Great Battles of the World (Crane) **7**:104
"The Great Brown-Pericord Motor" (Doyle) **12**:65, 79
"The Great Carbuncle" (Hawthorne) **3**:157, 159, 181-82, 184-85, 188
"The Great Cat's Tale" (Čapek) **36**:108
"The Great Dark" (Twain) **6**:331-42, 350-53; **26**:324, 329, 332-33
"A Great Day for a Bananafish" (Salinger)
    See "A Perfect Day for Bananafish"
"A Great Day for Bonzo" (Bates) **10**:120
"Great Days" (Barthelme) **55**:29, 89, 113
Great Days (Barthelme) **2**:44, 46; **55**:7, 27-9, 31, 48, 59, 66, 88,-92, 106-9
"The Great Ekbo" (Cabrera Infante)
    See "En el gran ecbó"
"Great Falls" (Ford) **56**:137-38, 143, 152, 154-55, 170, 173, 176-83, 194-95
"The Great God Pan" (Machen) **20**:155, 158, 161-63, 165, 168, 171-73, 182, 185-86, 190-93, 196-201, 204
The Great God Pan and the Inmost Light (Machen) **20**:156-57, 172-73, 175, 177, 190, 194
"A Great God's Angel Standing" (Kiely) **58**:145-46, 157, 167-68
"The Great Good Place" (James) **8**:269, 282, 302, 304, 306-07
"The Great Hallucination" (Bradbury) **53**:253
"A Great Heart" (Pilnyak)
    See "Bol'shoe serdtse"
"The Great Hug" (Barthelme) **55**:88
"The Great Hulabaloo of the Small Folk" (Aleichem)
    See "Digroyse behole fun di kleyne mentshelekh"
"The Great Interrogation" (London) **4**:265, 286
"The Great Keinplatz Experiment" (Doyle) **12**:80
"A Great Mollie" (Suckow) **18**:391, 415
"The Great Mountains" (Steinbeck) **11**:209, 212-14, 232, 237
"The Great Mutation" (Levi) **12**:276
"The Great Panic of the Little People" (Aleichem) **33**:47
"The Great Pine" (Freeman) **47**:107, 163
"Great Poets Die in Steaming Pots of Shit" (Bukowski) **45**:54
"Great Possibilities" (Collier) **19**:110, 113
"The Great Red Drum" (Dazai Osamu) **41**:231
The Great Return (Machen) **20**:163, 166, 181-84, 196, 200
"The Great Road" (Bunin) **5**:87
"A Great Sorrow" (Andersen) **6**:4, 7

"The Great Stone Face" (Hawthorne) **3**:159, 178, 182, 184

"Great Strength" (Dazai Osamu) **41**:228, 232

"The Great Swinglefield Derby" (Benét) **10**:155

"The Great Szarratar Opal" (Norris) **28**:203

"Great Uncle Crow" (Bates) **10**:132

"Great Uncle McCarthy" (Somerville & Ross) **56**:315, 320, 334-5, 338

"A Great Voice Stilled" (Jackson) **39**:224

"The Great Wall of China" (Kafka) **5**:206

The Great Wall of China, and Other Pieces (Kafka)
    See *Beim Bau der Chinesischen Mauer*

The Great Wall of China: Stories and Reflections (Kafka)
    See *Beim Bau der Chinesischen Mauer*

"The Great Wave" (Lavin) **4**:167-68, 174, 184

The Great Wave, and Other Stories (Lavin) **4**:166

"The Great Wildenberg" (Lenz) **33**:337

"The Great Winglebury Duel" (Dickens) **17**:110, 116-17

"The Great World and Timothy Colt" (Auchincloss) **22**:3, 33, 47

"The Greatcoat" (Gogol)
    See "Shinel"

"The Greater Festival of Masks" (Ligotti) **16**:261, 271, 273, 280, 283

The Greater Inclination (Wharton) **6**:413

"Greater Than Love" (Evans) **43**:16, 39

"The Greatest Country in the World" (Saroyan) **21**:163

"The Greatest Love of Don Juan" (Barbey d'Aurevilly)
    See "Le plus bel amour de Don Juan"

"The Greatest Man in the World" (Thurber) **1**:420, 431; **47**:365, 377-78, 382

"The Greatest People in the World" (Bates) **10**:114

The Greatest People in the World, and Other Stories (Bates) **10**:138

"The Greatest Television Show on Earth" (Ballard) **1**:71; **53**:18, 58, 110

"Greatness" (Benét) **10**:154

"The Greek Dancing Girl" (Schnitzler) **15**:343

"Green Atom Number Five" (Donoso)
    See "Atomo verde número cinco"

"The Green Banana" (Powers) **4**:379

"A Green Child" (Hood) **42**:183, 204, 214, 219-21, 240, 243

"Green Christmas" (Benét) **10**:149

"The Green Door" (Henry) **5**:159, 190

"The Green Drake" (Coppard) **21**:17

Green Ginger (Morrison) **40**:329, 333, 349, 369

"The Green Grave and the Black Grave" (Lavin) **4**:166-67, 174, 180, 184

"Green Head" (Davie) **52**:4-6

"Green Hell" (Boyle) **16**:140-42

"A Green Hill Far Away" (Galsworthy) **22**:62-3, 101

"The Green Hills of Earth" (Heinlein) **55**:164, 235

The Green Hills of Earth (Heinlein) **55**:209

"Green Holly" (Bowen) **3**:32, 54; **28**:3

"The Green Isle in the Sea" (Thurber) **1**:417

"The Green Man" (Chesterton) **1**:129; **46**:106

"The Green Morning" (Bradbury) **53**:206, 208, 250

"The Green Room" (Henry) **49**:197

"The Green Room" (de la Mare) **14**:71-2, 83, 86-7, 91

The Green Round (Machen) **20**:166, 177, 194, 196-97

Green Shoots (Morand)
    See *Tendres stocks*

"The Green Spider" (Walser) **20**:348

"Green Tea" (Le Fanu) **14**:222-25, 227, 229, 231-35, 237-38, 240, 242, 249-51

"A Green Thought" (Michaels) **16**:303

"Green Thoughts" (Collier) **19**:98-9, 103, 109

"Green Tunnels" (Huxley) **39**:155, 168, 171, 177-78

Green Water, Green Sky (Gallant) **5**:123, 144, 146

"The Green Wax" (Colette) **10**:292, 295

"Greenie and Yellow" (Naipaul) **38**:300, 318, 322, 328, 345

"Greenleaf" (O'Connor) **1**:343, 358, 360; **23**:205; **61**:169, 186-88, 201, 203, 208, 212

"Green's Book" (Chabon) **59**:83-86

"Greenwich Fair" (Dickens) **17**:125, 134

"Greenwich Time" (Beattie) **11**:12

"Greetings from Earth" (Bradfield) **65**:60-61, 63

Greetings from Earth (Bradfield) **65**:65-69

"Gregory's Island" (Cable)
    See "The Solitary"

"Gregotrimuntan" (Pilnyak) **48**:228

"Greg's Peg" (Auchincloss) **22**:35-6, 47, 52

La grenadière (Balzac) **5**:8, 16

"Gretchen's Forty Winks" (Fitzgerald) **6**:46

"The Grey Angel" (Galsworthy) **22**:62-3, 74, 100-02

"Grey Seagull" (O'Flaherty) **6**:262

"A Grey Sleeve" (Crane) **7**:103, 106; **56**:110

The Grey Wig: Stories and Novelettes (Zangwill) **44**:375, 381-82

"The Grey Woman" (Gaskell) **25**:47-8, 50, 58, 60

"Gribiche" (Colette) **10**:281

Der griechische Kaiser (Tieck) **31**:289

Griechischer Frühling (Hauptmann) **37**:220

"Grief" (Andersen) **6**:26

"Grief" (Chekhov) **51**:46

"Griff" (Clarke) **45**:72-3, 78, 81-2, 88, 97

"Grigia" (Musil) **18**:289, 292-93, 297-99, 302-13, 322, 325

"Den grimme [dJ]lling" (Andersen) **6**:5, 7, 10-11, 18, 30-1, 35, 40; **56**:31, 33-4, 38, 45

Grimm's Fairy Tales (Grimm and Grimm)
    See *Kinder-und Hausmärchen*

Grimscribe: His Lives and Works (Ligotti) **16**:279-80, 282-85, 293, 294, 296

"Grippes and Poche" (Gallant) **5**:147

"Grisha" (Chekhov) **51**:35, 105

"The Grisly Folk" (Wells) **6**:382

"The Grit of the Peagraves" (Perelman) **32**:240

"The Grit of Women" (London) **4**:286, 288

"The Grizzly and the Gadgets" (Thurber) **47**:362

"Grjotgard Ålvesøon and Aud" (Dinesen)
    See "Grjotgard Ålvesøon og Aud"

"Grjotgard Ålvesøon og Aud" (Dinesen) **7**:177

"Grobovshchik" (Pushkin) **27**:129, 145-46, 163, 166, 168-69, 175, 183, 186

"The Grocery Store" (Malamud) **15**:234-35

"La grosse fifi" (Rhys) **21**:62-3

"Der Grosse Wildenberg" (Lenz) **33**:317

Grotesques and Fantasies (Zangwill)
    See *The King of Schnorrers: Grotesques and Fantasies*

A Group of Noble Dames (Hardy) **2**:203-07, 209, 212-13, 220-21; **60**:177, 179, 189-90, 202, 204-9, 216-17

"The Growing Season" (Caldwell) **19**:23-4

"The Growing Stone" (Camus)
    See "La pierre qui pousse"

"Growing Up in Edge City" (Pohl) **25**:236

"The Growtown 'Bugle'" (Jewett) **6**:156, 159

"Groza v gorakh" (Solzhenitsyn) **32**:352

Ein Grünes Blatt (Storm) **27**:278, 284

"Gua yi" (P'u Sung-ling) **31**:215

"El guardagujas" (Arreola) **38**:4, 7-8, 12-20, 23, 26-27, 29-31, 35

"The Guardian" (de la Mare) **14**:79, 85, 89, 91

"The Guardian Angel" (Alarcon)
    See "El ángel de la Guarda"

"Guardian Angel" (Clarke) **3**:149

"Guardian of the Law" (Fisher) **25**:6, 10-12, 16-17, 19-21, 25-6

"Guayaquil" (Borges) **4**:20, 27

"Gubin" (Gorky) **28**:150

"Guduzhe" (Lu Hsun) **20**:140-41, 149-50

"The Güero" (Donoso)
    See "El güero"

"El güero" (Donoso) **34**:3, 21-3, 30-1, 49

Guerra del tiempo (Carpentier) **35**:91, 102, 106, 110, 125

"The Guest" (Aleichem) **33**:70

"The Guest" (Camus)
    See "L'hôte"

"The Guest" (Elkin) **12**:94, 117-18

"The Guest" (Kelly) **50**:286-88, 292

"The Guest" (Pavese) **19**:368

"A Guest at Home" (Jewett) **6**:156, 158-59

Guest of Reality (Lagerkvist)
    See *Gäst hos verkligheten*

"Guests" (Dixon) **16**:217

"Guests" (Taylor) **10**:389-90, 394, 404, 415, 417

"Guests from Gibbet Island" (Irving) **2**:241, 247-48

The Guests of August (Castellanos)
    See *Los convidados de agosto*

"Guests of the Nation" (O'Connor) **5**:369, 375-76, 379-82, 384, 388-89, 393

Guests of the Nation (O'Connor) **5**:363, 370, 375, 377-80, 382, 384, 387, 390-93

"Guests on a Winter Night" (Singer) **53**:302

"The Guests Were Arriving at the Dacha" (Pushkin) **27**:163-64, 175

"The Guide" (Campbell) **19**:77-8

"A Guide to Berlin" (Nabokov) **11**:134

"Guide to Kasrilevke" (Aleichem) **33**:49

Guillotine Party and Other Stories (Farrell) **28**:100-1, 119, 121-2

"Guilt" (Lish) **18**:267-68

"The Guilty Party—An East Side Tragedy" (Henry) **5**:188, 198

Guilty Pleasures (Barthelme) **2**:39, 41

"The Guilty Woman" (Pardo Bazán) **30**:290

"A Guilty Woman" (Wescott) **35**:363, 365, 369, 371-72

"The Guinea Pig Lady" (Banks) **42**:54

Guirnalda con amores (Bioy Casares) **17**:53, 87, 95

"Gulf" (Heinlein) **55**:198, 216, 231, 234

"The Gulf Between" (Calisher) **15**:5, 7, 15, 18

Gulf Coast Stories (Caldwell) **19**:21, 42, 54-6

"Gullible's Travels" (Lardner) **32**:160-62

Gullible's Travels, Etc. (Lardner) **32**:127, 141, 145, 148, 153, 155

"Gulliver" (Wolfe) **33**:369, 380

"The Gully" (Banks) **42**:59-60

"The Gully" (Cowan) **28**:82

"The Gully of Bluemansdyke" (Doyle) **12**:84-5

The Gully of Bluemansdyke and Other Stories (Doyle)
    See *Mysteries and Adventures*

"Gumption" (Hughes) **6**:131, 133

"The Gun" (Dick) **57**:103

"The Gun" (O'Hara) **15**:262

"The Gun and the Hat" (Garrett) **30**:173

"The Gunboat and Madge" (O'Hara) **15**:286

"An Gunna-Phósta" (Moore) **19**:308, 319-20, 322, 324, 328-30, 332, 334

"Guns at Cyrano's" (Chandler) **23**:56, 59, 86, 97, 105-06, 112

"Guo An" (P'u Sung-ling) **31**:214

"Guptadhan" (Tagore) **48**:339-40

"Guru" (Narayan) **25**:174

"Gusev" (Chekhov) **2**:128-29, 143, 147; **28**:58-9; **51**:111, 114-15, 117, 119, 121, 180-82, 184, 186

Gushi xinbian (Lu Hsun) **20**:125, 129, 134, 139-40

Gustav Adolfs Page (Meyer) **30**:186, 188, 213, 249

"The Gutting of Couffignal" (Hammett) **17**:206, 222, 224, 229-30

"The Gut-Wrenching Machine" (Bukowski) **45**:53

"Guxiang" (Lu Hsun) **20**:140-41, 150

"The Guy" (Campbell) **19**:74, 92-4

"Guy de Maupassant" (Babel) 16:4, 5, 15, 20, 36, 42, 59
"Gwilan's Harp" (Le Guin) 12:231
"Gyofukuki" (Dazai Osamu) 41:238, 240, 243, 264-69, 271, 273-74
"The Gypsy Feeling" (Nin) 10:306
"The Gypsy Maid" (Cervantes)
See "La gitanilla"
"A Gypsy Prophecy" (Stoker) 62:253-54
"Ha" (Dazai Osamu) 41:248, 270, 272
"Ha'akhsanya" (Appelfeld) 42:12
"Habakuk Jephson's Statement" (Doyle) 12:85
The Habit of Being: Letters of Flannery O'Connor (O'Connor) 61:199
"The Habit of Loving" (Lessing) 6:218
"An Habitation Enforced" (Kipling) 5:283
"Habrihah" (Appelfeld) 42:9, 12
El hacedor (Borges) 41:53, 148, 157, 159, 163
"La Hachich" (Gautier) 20:23-4, 31
"Hacienda" (Porter) 4:327, 329-30, 346, 351; 31:160, 177; 43:170, 172-74, 183, 194, 222, 227, 234-35, 240, 243-44, 246, 253, 258-60, 262, 292
"Hack Wednesday" (Atwood) 46:79, 98-9
"Hackney Coach Stands" (Dickens) 17:111
"Had a Horse" (Galsworthy) 22:66-7, 69, 79, 101
"Hadgadyah" (Zangwill) 44:368
Hadji Murad (Tolstoy)
See "Khadzi murat"
Hadji Murád (Tolstoy) 9:376, 378, 394-97
"Hadjii murád" (Tolstoy)
See "Khadzi murat"
Hadlaub (Keller) 26:108, 111, 113
"The Hag" (Turgenev) 7:335
"Hagerush" (Appelfeld) 42:7-8, 28
"Der Hagestolz" (Stifter) 28:281, 283, 286-88, 290, 296, 298
"Haguruma" (Akutagawa Ryūnosuke) 44:44, 46, 49, 51, 54-5, 61, 79, 83-4, 89-90
"Haha naru mono" (Endō) 48:191-92, 199, 202-3
"Haha no kouru ki" (Tanizaki) 21:183, 192, 210, 226
"Haha no shi to atarishi haha" (Shiga) 23:334, 346, 354
"Hahishtanut" (Appelfeld) 42:8-9, 12
"Das Haidedorf" (Stifter) 28:290
"Hai-iro no tsuki" (Shiga) 23:352
"Hail Mary" (Fante) 65:74, 95, 99-101
"The Haile Selassie Funeral Train" (Davenport) 16:173-74, 177, 183, 194
"Die Haimatochare" (Hoffmann) 13:187
"The Hair" (Carver) 8:50-1
"Hair" (Faulkner) 1:147, 151
"Hair" (Kelly) 50:290, 293
"Hair Jewellery" (Atwood) 2:3, 5-7, 10-11, 14, 16; 46:26, 33-4, 39-41, 49-50, 58, 76, 80, 93
Hair O' the Chine (Coover) 15:47-8
"The Hair Shirt" (Powers) 4:380
"Hairball" (Atwood) 46:79-80, 98
"Haircut" (Lardner) 32:116-17, 119, 125, 131, 135-36, 139-41, 146, 149, 152-56, 160-61, 169, 1 6, 184-85, 193, 195
"The Hairless Mexican" (Maugham) 8:369, 376
"Haïta the Shepherd" (Bierce) 9:49, 87
"Hakūchyukigo" (Tanizaki) 21:194
"Hakumei" (Dazai Osamu) 41:249
"Hal Irwin's Magic Lamp" (Vonnegut) 8:437
"Halberdier of the Little Rheinschloss" (Henry) 5:181, 196
"Hale Hardy and the Amazing Animal Woman" (Beattie) 11:11, 16, 28
"Half a Grapefruit" (Munro) 3:334, 342
"Half a Lifetime Ago" (Gaskell) 25:55, 58, 72
"Half a Rupee" (Narayan)
See "Half-a-Rupee Worth"
"Half-a-Rupee Worth" (Narayan) 25:135, 139, 157
"The Half-Brothers" (Gaskell) 25:59
"Half-Holiday" (Huxley) 39:157, 162

"The Half-Husky" (Laurence) 7:253, 270
"Halfway to Hell" (Collier) 19:104
"The Hall of Fantasy" (Hawthorne) 3:181
Eine Halligfahrt (Storm) 27:304
"The Halloween Party" (Chabon) 59:71, 73, 77, 79
"The Hallucination" (Oates) 6:250
"A Hamlet of the Scigry District" (Turgenev)
See "Gamlet ščigrovskogo uezda"
"Hamlet of the Shchigrovsky District" (Turgenev)
See "Gamlet ščigrovskogo uezda"
"Hamlet of the Shchigry District" (Turgenev)
See "Gamlet ščigrovskogo uezda"
"Hamlet; or, The Consequences of Filial Piety" (Laforgue)
See "Hamlet; ou, les suites de piété filiale"
"Hamlet; or, The Results of Filial Devotion" (Laforgue)
See "Hamlet; ou, les suites de piété filiale"
"Hamlet; ou, les suites de piété filiale" (Laforgue) 20:86-7, 89, 91, 93-5, 100-4, 106, 114, 119
"Hamlet, Prince of Denmark" (Čapek) 36:114-15, 130
"The Hammer Man" (Bambara) 35:2, 7, 24
"The Hammer of God" (Chesterton) 1:124, 130, 136; 46:109, 149-50
"Hammie and the Black Dean" (Clarke) 45:90
"Hamrick's Polar Bear" (Caldwell) 19:13, 39, 45-6
"Han Fang" (P'u Sung-ling) 31:198
"Han no hanza" (Shiga) 23:332, 341-42, 345-46, 348, 352, 359
"Hana" (Akutagawa Ryūnosuke) 44:41, 45, 49-50, 56-8, 60-1, 73, 75-6, 88-9
"Hand" (Atwood) 2:20
"Hand and Heart" (Gaskell) 25:58-9
"The Hand Car" (Akutagawa Ryūnosuke)
See "Torokko"
"Hand in Glove" (Bowen) 3:54
"The Hand of Emmagene" (Taylor) 10:397-98, 402, 404
"Hand upon the Waters" (Faulkner) 1:179
"Handcarved Coffins: A Nonfiction Account of an American Crime" (Capote) 2:80-2
"The Handkerchief" (Akutagawa Ryūnosuke)
See "Hankechi"
"Hands" (Anderson) 1:32-3, 42, 44, 57; 46:5-6, 21
"The Hands" (Campbell) 19:71
"Hands across the Sea" (Williams) 31:350, 358-60
"Handsome Brown" (Caldwell) 19:17
"Handsome Brown and the Aggravating Goats" (Caldwell) 19:50-1
"Handsome Brown and the Shirt-tail Woodpeckers" (Caldwell) 19:51
"Handsome Is as Handsome Does" (Pritchett) 14:268-69, 291, 298
"The Handsome Lady" (Coppard) 21:3, 12
"The Handsomest Drowned Man in the World: A Tale for Children" (García Márquez)
See "El ahogado más hermoso del mundo"
"The Hanging Stranger" (Dick) 57:106, 109
"Hanka" (Singer) 3:377
"Hankechi" (Akutagawa Ryūnosuke) 44:50, 78
"Hannes" (Hesse) 9:243
"Han's Crime" (Shiga)
See "Han no hanza"
"Hans in Luck" (Grimm and Grimm) 36:188, 193
"Hans My Hedgehog" (Grimm and Grimm) 36:223
"Hans Pfaal" (Poe)
See "The Unparalleled Adventure of One Hans Pfaall"
Hans und Heinz Kirch (Storm) 27:279, 281, 284, 290, 305
"Hansel and Gretel" (Grimm and Grimm) 36:196, 203-05, 208
"Hanz Kuechelgarten" (Gogol) 29:149

"Ha-panim la-panim" (Agnon) 30:21, 37-8
"The Happiest Days" (Metcalf) 43:105-6, 109
"The Happiest I've Been" (Updike) 13:354
"Happily Ever After" (Huxley) 39:153-54, 161-62
"Happiness" (Chekhov) 2:130, 156; 51:58, 70, 74
"Happiness" (Lavin) 4:182, 185
"Happiness" (Pirandello)
See "Felicità"
"Happiness" (Warner) 23:373-74
"Happiness by Conquest" (Norris) 28:213
"Happiness in Crime" (Barbey d'Aurevilly)
See "Le bonheur dans le crime"
"The Happiness of Others" (Price) 22:365, 369, 376-77
"Happy" (Beattie) 11:14
"The Happy Autumn Fields" (Bowen) 3:31-32, 50-51; 28:3, 9-10
"Happy Birthday" (Bambara) 35:4, 32
"Happy Birthday Dear Jesus" (Pohl) 25:223, 230-31
"The Happy Children" (Machen) 20:183
"The Happy Couple" (Maugham) 8:380
"A Happy Death" (Lavin) 4:165, 167
"A Happy Ending" (Chekhov) 51:93-6
"Happy Endings" (Atwood) 2:15, 19-20; 46:98
"The Happy Failure" (Melville) 1:303
"Happy Families" (Huxley) 39:154, 166
Happy Families Are All Alike (Taylor) 10:380, 389, 410
"The Happy Family" (Andersen) 6:18
"A Happy Family" (Trevor) 58:226
"The Happy Farmer" (Thomas) 20:323-25, 327
"Happy Holiday Abroad" (Sansom) 21:84
"Happy Hour" (Johnson) 56:243
"Happy Matrimony" (Chang) 28:25; 31; 34
"The Happy Prince" (Wilde) 11:365, 372, 376-78, 380, 386, 389-90, 394-96, 402-03, 406-08
The Happy Prince, and Other Tales (Wilde) 11:365-66, 375, 377, 381, 386, 390, 393, 402
"Happy Valley" (Taylor) 10:394, 397
"Hapworth 16, 1924" (Salinger) 2:308, 314; 28:269; 65:299-300, 318
"A Harbinger" (Chopin) 8:71
"The Harbinger" (Henry) 5:158
"The Hard Passage" (Hesse) 9:231-32, 234, 236, 243
"A Hard Row to Hoe" (Garrett) 30:165, 172
"Hard Sell" (Boyle) 16:150
"The Hard Sellers" (Levi) 12:279
"Hardball" (Atwood) 46:75
"The Hard-Headed Woman" (Harris) 19:196
"The Hardy Tin Soldier" (Andersen)
See "Den standhaftige Tinsoldat"
"The Hare Chase" (Leskov)
See "Zajačij remiz"
"The Hare Park" (Leskov)
See "Zajačij remiz"
"Hari to Ciarasu to Kiri" (Kawabata) 17:242, 254
"Harischandra" (Narayan) 25:131
"A Harlequin" (Tanizaki)
See "Hokan"
"Harley Talking" (Hood) 42:187
"Harmony" (Lardner) 32:145
"The Harness" (Steinbeck) 11:207, 225, 228, 230, 232-35, 240-41, 243-44; 37:351-52
"The 'Harnt' That Walks Chilhowee" (Murfree) 22:188, 200, 202-03, 205, 207-08, 222
"El haRofe" (Agnon) 30:37-8
"Harper and Wilton" (Spark) 10:356
"Harrington's" (Somerville & Ross) 56:307-8
"The Harris Fetko Story" (Chabon) 59:82-83, 87
"Harrison Barr" (Dreiser)
See "Black Sheep No. Six: Harrison Barr"
"Harrison Bergeron" (Vonnegut) 8:427, 434
"Harry" (Saroyan) 21:132

"Harry and Violet" (Thomas) **20**:295, 298, 312
Harry Heathcote of Gangoil (Trollope) **28**:316, 322, 346
"The Hartleys" (Cheever) **38**:54
"Harv Is Plowing Now" (Updike) **13**:348-49, 375
"Harvest Bugs" (Shiga) **23**:345-46, 348
"Hashire Merosu" (Dazai Osamu) **41**:240, 260, 263, 276
Hasidism (Peretz) **26**:206
"The Hat" (Boyle) **16**:149, 154-55
"The Hat Act" (Coover) **15**:31, 33-4, 48, 59
The Hat on the Bed (O'Hara) **15**:259-60, 282-83
"Hat on the Bedpost" (Caldwell) **19**:55
"The Hated" (Pohl) **25**:220, 232
"Haunted" (Lovecraft) **52**:278
"The Haunted Baronet" (Le Fanu) **14**:220, 223-24, 237, 245
"The Haunted Boy" (McCullers) **9**:330, 332, 343, 345, 354, 356, 358
"The Haunted Dolls' House" (James) **16**:230, 237, 244, 256
"A Haunted House" (Woolf) **7**:369, 374-75, 389-90, 392, 399
A Haunted House, and Other Short Stories (Woolf) **7**:372, 374, 386, 388, 400
"The 'Haunted House' in Royal Street" (Cable) **4**:53, 59, 61, 75-6
The Haunted Man and the Ghost's Bargain (Dickens) **17**:127-32; **49**:7, 41, 45-6, 66, 158, 174
"The Haunted Mind" (Hawthorne) **3**:181
"The Haunter of the Dark" (Lovecraft) **3**:259, 263, 273-75, 279, 284; **52**:278-79, 283, 290, 339
The Haunter of the Dark, and Other Tales of Horror (Lovecraft) **52**:252
"The Haunting of the Tiled House" (Le Fanu) **14**:224, 226
Hauntings (Lee) **33**:302, 304-09
"Hauptstädtisches Journal" (Boell) **23**:8, 10, 21
"Ein Haus aus lauter Liebe" (Lenz) **33**:316, 318-19, 333-36
"Hautot père et fils" (Maupassant) **1**:270, 280, 285, 288
"Have a Wonderful Nice Walk" (Gilchrist) **63**:8
"Have I Got Sun in My Eyes?" (Farrell) **28**:99
"Have You Read Pirandello?" (Bukowski) **45**:58
"De Havilland Hand" (Gilchrist) **14**:163-64
"Having a Wonderful Time" (Ballard) **1**:79; **53**:18, 56, 113
Häwelmann (Storm) **27**:284
"The Hawk" (O'Flaherty) **6**:269, 274, 279
"The Haymaking" (Lavin) **4**:167
"Hazel" (Wideman) **62**:261
"He" (Lovecraft) **3**:259, 262, 283, 289; **52**:292, 336, 346
"He" (Porter) **4**:327-30, 339-40, 349-50, 354, 360; **43**:170, 177-78, 217, 219-20, 222, 237, 247, 253, 292
"He Beats His Women" (Bukowski) **45**:53
"He Couldn't Boogie-Woogie Worth a Damn" (Algren) **33**:108
"He Don't Plant Cotton" (Powers) **4**:368
"He Drank Me" (Lispector)
　　See "El me bebeu"
"He is barehead" (Beckett) **16**:123-24, 126-27
"He Just Adores Her!" (Hood) **42**:139, 179, 200, 225, 231-32
"He of the Assembly" (Bowles) **3**:68, 83-4
"He Ran Off" (Gorky) **28**:160
"He Sings the Epistle" (Pirandello)
　　See "Canta l'epistola"
"He Swung and He Missed" (Algren) **33**:88, 107
"He Thinks He's Wonderful" (Fitzgerald) **6**:47, 49
"He Who Spits at the Sky" (Stegner) **27**:224
"Head and Shoulders" (Fitzgerald) **6**:45, 57, 96-7
"The Head Gardeners Story" (Chekhov) **51**:70
"Head Job" (Bukowski) **45**:59-60

Head o' W-Hollow (Stuart) **31**:224, 230-31, 236, 256
"The Head of Babylon" (Barnes) **3**:19-20
"The Head of Caesar" (Chesterton) **46**:111, 140
"The Head of the Family" (Chekhov) **2**:127
"The Head-Hunter" (Henry) **5**:166
"Heading Home" (Campbell) **19**:75
"Heading Home" (Endō) **48**:212
"The Headless Hawk" (Capote) **2**:61-3, 66, 69, 72, 75-6; **47**:4, 12-14, 16, 28-9, 31, 34-7, 44-7, 53-5
"Heads" (Dixon) **16**:219
"Heads of Houses" (Taylor) **10**:389-90, 404, 415-16
"Heady Wine" (Svevo)
　　See "Vino generoso"
"The Healthiest Girl in Town" (Stafford) **26**:281, 286, 312
"Healthy Landscape with Dormouse" (Warner) **23**:373-74
"Hear O Israel" (Peretz) **26**:204-05
"Hear the Dogs Barking" (Rulfo)
　　See "No oyes ladrar los perros"
"Hear the Nightingale Sing" (Gordon) **15**:107, 118
Hear Us O Lord from Heaven Thy Dwelling Place (Lowry) **31**:40-7, 50-5, 58-61, 63-4, 66-7, 70, 72, 74-6, 82-3, 86-7
"The Heart" (Naipaul) **38**:300, 320, 322, 328, 346
"Heart of a Champion" (Boyle) **16**:140-43, 157
"Heart of a Champion" (Lish) **18**:267
The Heart of a Dog (Bulgakov)
　　See *Sobach'e serdtse*
The Heart of a Goof (Wodehouse) **2**:329, 350
Heart of Darkness (Conrad) **9**:140-41, 143-44, 148-56, 160, 168, 171, 173, 175-76, 178, 188-92, 196-207
"Heart of Elm" (Wilson) **21**:329-31, 333, 355, 357, 365
The Heart of Happy Hollow (Dunbar) **8**:120-22, 127-29, 131-32, 141, 145
"The Heart of John Middleton" (Gaskell) **25**:60, 65, 71-3
The Heart of the West (Henry) **5**:155, 172, 182
"The Heart Sutra" (Chang) **28**:23; 35
"Heartbreak" (Andersen) **6**:30, 32, 35
"Heartburn" (Calisher) **15**:2, 6
"The Hearth and the Salamander" (Bradbury) **29**:53
"Hearts and Crosses" (Henry) **5**:155, 181
"The Heart's Desire" (Far) **62**:50, 55
"Hearts of Oak and Bellies of Brass" (McGahern) **17**:298, 302, 307-09
"Heat" (Dixon) **16**:211
"Heat" (Rhys) **21**:55, 65
"The Heat of the Sun" (O'Faolain) **13**:283, 292, 311
The Heat of the Sun: Stories and Tales (O'Faolain) **13**:290, 307, 313
"Heaven and Earth" (Galsworthy) **22**:101
"Heaven is Not Closed" (Head) **52**:191, 194-95, 202, 205-6, 214, 216, 227, 236-37
"Heaven on a Summer Night" (Beattie) **11**:29
"The Heavenly Animal" (Phillips) **16**:327-28, 330
"A Heavy Husband" (Stephens) **50**:327
"Hê-chien shêng" (P'u Sung-ling) **31**:205
"Hector and Freddie" (Wilding) **59**:349-50
"The Hector Quesadilla Story" (Boyle) **16**:145, 151
"He'd Come Back" (Lawson) **18**:248
"A Hedge of Rosemary" (Jolley) **19**:232, 235
"The Hedgehog" (Saki) **12**:316
"A Hedonist" (Galsworthy) **22**:66, 101
"Heed my Plea" (Dazai Osamu) **41**:263
"Hee-Haw" (Warner) **23**:370
"Heel Number One of the Year" (Saroyan) **21**:163
"Hefker" (Agnon) **30**:34, 69-70
"Heichū, the Amorous Genius" (Akutagawa Ryūnosuke) **44**:50

"A Heifer without Blemish" (Evans) **43**:2, 13
"The Height of the Scream" (Campbell) **19**:75, 84
The Height of the Scream (Campbell) **19**:74, 78, 81, 83-4, 86, 89-90
"Heil!" (Heinlein) **55**:213
Der Heilige (Meyer) **30**:186-89, 192, 195, 204-11
Die heilige Cäcilie; oder, die Gewalt der Musik (Kleist) **22**:109, 115-17, 137, 146
"Heilmann" (Lenz) **33**:337
"Heimkehr" (Kafka) **5**:254
"Heinrich" (Bunin) **5**:114
"Heinrich von ofter dinger" (Hoffmann) **13**:218
"The Heir of the McHulishes" (Harte) **8**:217, 252
"An Heiress of Red Dog" (Harte) **8**:248
The Heiress of Red Dog and Other Tales (Harte) **59**:310
An Heiress on Condition (Gissing) **37**:79
"The Heirs" (Pilnyak) **48**:290
The Heirs in Tail (Arnim)
　　See *Die Majoratsherren*
"Der Heizer" (Kafka) **60**:232, 249
"Hejda" (Nin) **10**:300, 303
"Helbling's Story" (Walser) **20**:336, 350
"Helen, I Love You" (Farrell) **28**:90, 111, 118
"Helen, the Nonexistent Woman" (Andrić)
　　See "Jelena, žena koje nema"
"Helena" (Čapek) **36**:82, 93, 124
Det heliga landet (Lagerkvist) **12**:198
"Hell" (Andrić)
　　See "Pakao"
"Hell Hath No Fury" (Collier) **19**:106
"A Hell of a Good Time" (Farrell) **28**:89
"The Hell Screen" (Akutagawa Ryūnosuke)
　　See "Jigokuhen"
"Hell So Feared" (Onetti)
　　See "El infierno tan temido"
The Hell We Dread (Onetti)
　　See *El infierno tan temido y otros cuentos*
The Hellbound Heart (Barker) **53**:161, 173, 177-79
Hellbox (O'Hara) **15**:250, 255, 257-58, 264-65, 267
"Hello Fine Day Isn't It?" (Oates) **6**:248-50
"Hello Jack" (Michaels) **16**:309
"Hello, Tib" (Aiken) **9**:13
Hellraiser (Barker)
　　See *The Hellbound Heart*
"Hell's Acre" (Stuart) **31**:261
"Hell's Event" (Barker) **53**:137, 143, 156, 158, 161, 163
"Héloïse" (Aymé) **41**:23
"Help" (Apple) **50**:33-4, 45
"Help!" (Čapek)
　　See "Pomoc!"
"Un hemisphère dans une chevelure" (Baudelaire) **18**:5-7, 17
"The Hen" (Saki) **12**:296
"Hêng-niang" (P'u Sung-ling) **31**:205
"Henne Fire" (Singer) **3**:370, 383-84
"Henrietta Marr" (Moore) **19**:296-97, 302, 310-11
"Henry and the Gold Mine" (Benét) **10**:154
Henry Lawson, Fifteen Stories (Lawson) **18**:221
"Henry the Ninth" (Bradbury) **29**:47; **53**:215
"A Hepcat May Look at a King" (Perelman) **32**:234
"Hephaestus God of Newfangled Things" (Auchincloss) **22**:52
"Her Boss" (Cather) **2**:111
"Her Chinese Husband" (Far) **62**:4, 20-21, 50, 75, 77-78, 100, 103
"Her First Ball" (Mansfield) **9**:282-83, 286, 304, 310-11; **23**:137, 153-54, 158, 171-72
"Her Housekeeper" (Gilman) **13**:142, 145
"Her Ladyship's Private Office" (Turgenev) **7**:337
"Her Letters" (Chopin) **8**:92, 98-9, 112-13
"Her Lover" (Gorky)
　　See "Boles"

"Her Loving Husband" (Far) **62**:109

"Her Name Was Amelie" (Caldwell) **19**:42, 54

"Her Name Was Reggina" (Clarke) **45**:95

"Her Need" (Taylor) **10**:404

"Her Own People" (Warren) **4**:389-90, 395, 399; **58**:310, 317, 354

"Her Quaint Honor" (Gordon) **15**:104, 107, 119, 123

"Her Sense of Timing" (Elkin) **12**:119

"Her Ship Came Home" (Wilson) **21**:358, 361

"Her Son" (Wharton) **6**:423-24

"Her Sweet Jerome" (Walker) **5**:402, 405-06, 419

"Her Table Spread" (Bowen) **3**:34-36, 38, 41, 51

"Her Virginia Mammy" (Chesnutt) **7**:16, 23, 33-5, 37; **54**:49, 58, 61, 63-4

"Herakleitos" (Davenport) **16**:162-63, 166, 170

"The Herald" (Kundera) **24**:103

"Herbert West—Reanimator" (Lovecraft) **3**:282, 293-94; **52**:267, 287, 292, 310-14, 341

"The Herder of Storm Mountain" (Murfree) **22**:213, 220

Here and Beyond (Wharton) **6**:422

"Here and Today" (Caldwell) **19**:21

Here Are Ladies (Stephens) **50**:305-06, 312-14, 316, 326-29, 338

"Here Come the Tigers" (Thurber) **1**:429

"Here Comes a Dog" (Kazakov) **43**:59, 61

"Here Comes the Maples" (Updike) **13**:374, 386-87

Here Lies: The Collected Stories of Dorothy Parker (Parker) **2**:274-76

"Here There Be Tygers" (Bradbury) **29**:83

"Here There Be Tygers" (King) **55**:250

"Here to Learn" (Bowles) **3**:75, 79-80

"Here We Are" (Parker) **2**:273-74, 281, 283

"La Herencia de matilde Arcangel" (Rulfo) **25**:257, 265, 272, 275

"Heresy" (Akutagawa Ryūnosuke) **44**:62

The Heretic of Soana (Hauptmann)
   See *Der Ketzer von Soana*

Los heréticos (Valenzuela) **14**:366

The Heretics (Valenzuela)
   See *Los heréticos*

"Heritage" (Galsworthy) **22**:101

"L'héritage" (Maupassant) **1**:256, 259-60, 263, 270, 276, 283

"The Heritage of Dedlow Marsh" (Harte) **8**:254; **59**:307

Hermann Lauscher (Hesse)
   See *Hinterlassene Schriften und Gedichte von Hermann Lauscher*

"Hermes, God of the Self-Made Man" (Auchincloss) **22**:51

"The Hermit" (Gorky) **28**:137

"The Hermit and the Wild Woman" (Wharton) **6**:428

The Hermit and the Wild Woman (Wharton) **6**:420, 435

"The Hermits" (Dinesen) **7**:177

The Hermit's Story (Bass) **60**:41-42

"A Hero" (Narayan) **25**:141, 156

"A Hero in Dingo-Scrubs" (Lawson) **18**:211, 220

"The Hero of Redclay" (Lawson) **18**:234, 240, 250-51

Herod and Mariamne (Lagerkvist)
   See *Mariamne*

"Hérodias" (Flaubert) **11**:37, 46, 50-3, 55-6, 61-5, 70-1, 81-2, 84-7, 91-3, 96-9, 101, 103; **60**:111, 114-16, 124-27, 141-45, 153-54, 159, 171

"The Heroes" (Algren) **33**:87, 108

"The Heroes in the Dark House" (Kiely) **58**:146

"A Heroic Death" (Baudelaire)
   See "Une mort héroïque"

"The Heroine" (Dinesen) **7**:165, 168, 195

"The Heroine" (P'u Sung-ling)
   See "Hsieh-nü"

"L'héroïsme du docteur Hallidonhill" (Villiers de l'Isle Adam) **14**:397

"A Hero's Death" (Lagerkvist) **12**:182, 195

"Herostratus" (Sartre) **32**:255, 257, 259, 261

Der Herr Etatsrat (Storm) **27**:281

Hesitation (Lu Hsun)
   See *P'anghuang*

"Hester's Little Tour" (Galsworthy) **22**:70-1

"He-Who-Intones-the-Epistle" (Pirandello)
   See "Canta l'epistola"

Der Hexensabbath (Tieck) **31**:273, 289-90

"Hey Hey Hey" (Bradfield) **65**:65, 67, 69

"Hey Sailor, What Ship?" (Olsen) **11**:164

"Hey! Taxi!" (Aiken) **9**:4, 12-13

"Hickman Arrives" (Ellison) **26**:11

"Hidden Art" (Maclean) **13**:279

"Hidden Riches" (Tagore)
   See "Guptadhan"

"Hidden Treasure" (Zoshchenko) **15**:395

"Hide and Seek" (Clarke) **3**:124-26, 133, 150

"Hiding Man" (Barthelme) **2**:26, 41-2, 54; **55**:15-16

"Hier ist Tibten" (Boell) **23**:7-8

"La hierba milagrosa" (Pardo Bazán) **30**:270

"The Higgler" (Coppard) **21**:8, 15-16, 18, 20, 24-5, 29

"High" (Oates) **6**:252

"The High Constable's Wife" (Balzac) **5**:19

"High Ground" (McGahern) **17**:306, 311-12, 314-15, 324

High Ground (McGahern) **17**:304-06, 309-12, 322-23

"The High Point" (O'Hara) **15**:252

"The High Road of St. James" (Carpentier) **35**:106, 126

"High School" (Beattie) **11**:26, 29

"High Tea at Mckeown's" (Somerville & Ross) **56**:301

"The High Test" (Pohl) **25**:236

"The High Tide Talker" (Davie) **52**:3

The High Tide Talker and Other Stories (Davie) **52**:3, 7

"High Yaller" (Fisher) **25**:3-4, 7, 14, 17-18, 20-2, 24-5, 27

"The Higher Abdication" (Henry) **5**:180-81

"The Higher Pragmatism" (Henry) **5**:187

"Higher Standards" (Wilson) **21**:323

"The High-heeled Shoes" (Yamamoto) **34**:348-49

"The Highland Widow" (Scott) **32**:286-87, 292, 297, 299-304, 306, 315, 317, 319

"High-Water Mark" (Harte) **8**:210, 232

"The Highway" (Bradbury) **29**:53; **53**:200, 226-27, 234

"El hijo de Andrés Aparicio" (Fuentes) **24**:44, 63

"El hijo de su amigo" (Bioy Casares) **17**:48-52

"Hilda's Wedding" (Jolley) **19**:222, 234, 248

"The Hill Bachelors" (Trevor) **58**:300

The Hill Bachelors (Trevor) **58**:298, 300-301

"The Hill of Sand" (Agnon)
   See "Gib'ath ha-hol"

"The Hill of the Elves" (Andersen) **6**:31

The Hills Beyond (Wolfe) **33**:343, 355, 372-75, 380, 398-99

"Hills Like White Elephants" (Hemingway) **1**:210, 217, 232, 234; **40**:250; **63**:48, 52, 58-59, 118, 124

"The Hilton's Holiday" (Jewett) **6**:152

"Hilufei mishmarot" (Appelfeld) **42**:12

"Him" (Atwood) **2**:20

"Him with His Foot in His Mouth" (Bellow) **14**:40, 42-6

Him with His Foot in His Mouth, and Other Stories (Bellow) **14**:40, 42, 50, 56, 58

"Himitsu" (Tanizaki) **21**:207-08

"Hindus" (Mukherjee) **38**:252, 254, 264-65, 271-72, 277

"The Hint of an Explanation" (Greene) **29**:184-85, 192, 202-04, 209-11, 213, 217

"Hinterlands" (Gibson) **52**:16, 27-9

Hinterlassene Schriften und Gedichte von Hermann Lauscher (Hesse) **9**:229-30, 235, 243

Hinzelmeier (Storm) **27**:284

"Hippie Hat Brain Parasite" (Gibson) **52**:43-7

"Hips" (Cisneros) **32**:14, 42, 44-45

"The Hirelings" (Zangwill) **44**:378-79

"His Apparition" (Howells) **36**:379-80, 382, 386-87, 397

"His Chest of Drawers" (Anderson) **1**:52

"His Chosen Calling" (Naipaul) **38**:327, 350

"His Christmas Miracle" (Murfree) **22**:210

"His Country, After All" (Lawson) **18**:201, 216

"His 'Day in Court'" (Murfree) **22**:209

"His Dead Mother's Portrait" (Norris) **28**:214

"His Excellency" (Maugham) **8**:365, 377

"His Father" (Steinbeck) **11**:246, 252

"His Father's Mate" (Lawson) **18**:197-98, 201-02, 239, 257

"His Father's Son" (Wharton) **6**:421, 424, 435

"His Finest Hour" (Updike) **13**:355

"His General Line of Business" (Dickens) **17**:123

His Last Bow: Some Reminiscences of Sherlock Holmes (Doyle) **12**:50, 64

"His Last Bow: The War Service of Sherlock Holmes" (Doyle) **12**:62

"His Mother" (Gallant) **5**:135, 137

"His Single Blessedness" (Norris) **28**:206

"His Unquiet Ghost" (Murfree) **22**:211

"Hisbrien om en Moder" (Andersen) **6**:6-7, 18-9, 30, 35; **56**:37

"Hissen som gick ner i helvete" (Lagerkvist) **12**:182, 196

L'histoire de Fenni (Voltaire) **12**:341, 343

"Histoire de lunes" (Carpentier) **35**:121-23

Histoire des treize (Balzac) **5**:5, 45-7

L'histoire du Calife Hakem (Nerval) **18**:364

"L'histoire d'une fille de ferme" (Maupassant) **1**:257, 259, 261, 272, 274-75

Histoires insolites (Villiers de l'Isle Adam) **14**:378, 384, 396-97

Historia de cronopios y de famas (Cortázar) **7**:50, 53, 60, 91-2, 94

"La historia de María Griseld" (Bombal) **37**:34, 37-38

"Historia del guerrero y de la cautiva" (Borges) **4**:29

"História interrompida" (Lispector) **34**:229-31, 233-34

"Historia prodigiosa" (Bioy Casares) **17**:59

Historia prodigiosa (Bioy Casares) **17**:58

Historia universal de la infamia (Borges) **4**:4, 17; **41**:39, 53-55, 63-65, 151, 162, 166

Histórias de meia-noite (Machado de Assis) **24**:131-32, 146, 151

Historias desaforados (Bioy Casares) **17**:86-7

Histórias sem data (Machado de Assis) **24**:152

"Historie dirigenta Kaliny" (Čapek) **36**:83, 99, 127

Historietas inverosímiles (Alarcon)
   See *Novelas cortas: Historietas inverosímiles*

"History among the Rocks" (Warren) **58**:309

"History Lesson" (Clarke) **3**:124, 133, 143-44

"The History of a Contraoctave" (Pasternak)
   See "The Story of Counter-Octave"

History of Infamy (Borges)
   See *Historia universal de la infamia*

"The History of Lieutenant Ergunov" (Turgenev)
   See "Istoriya leytenanta Ergunova"

"The History of Rodney" (Bass) **60**:16, 19

"History of the Conductor Kalina" (Čapek)
   See "Historie dirigenta Kaliny"

"The History of the Hardcomes" (Hardy) **2**:215

History of the Manor of Goryukhino (Pushkin) **27**:135

A History of the Village Goryukhino (Pushkin)
   See *Istoriia sela Goriukhino*

"History of the Warrior and the Captive" (Borges)
   See "Historia del guerrero y de la cautiva"

"History of the Young Man with Spectacles" (Machen) **20**:206

"History, or the Four Pictures of Vludka" (Lish) **18**:282
"Hitchhiker" (Betts) **45**:3, 9
"The Hitch-Hikers" (Welty) **1**:466, 468, 481, 487-88, 494; **51**:258, 260, 281, 319, 321, 340
"The Hitchhiking Game" (Kundera) **24**:86-8, 91-2, 94, 97, 103, 106-09, 114, 118, 121-25
"Hizo el bien mientras vivió" (Arreola) **38**:9
"Hjertesorg" (Andersen) **56**:37
"The Hoax" (Svevo)
   See "Una burla riuscita"
"The Hobo and the Fairy" (London) **4**:255
"Hoboes That Pass in the Night" (London) **4**:291
"Der Hochwald" (Stifter) **28**:278, 298-99
Die Hochzeit des Mönchs (Meyer) **30**:186-89, 200, 203-04, 206-11
"Hochzeitsvorbereitungen auf dem Lande" (Kafka) **35**:242, 265
"Hog Pawn" (Faulkner) **1**:178
"Hoist High the Roof Beam, Carpenters" (Salinger)
   See "Raise High the Roofbeam, Carpenters"
La hojarasca (García Márquez) **8**:154-55, 158, 160, 162, 171, 184, 193
"Hokan" (Tanizaki) **21**:194
"Hōkyōnin no shi" (Akutagawa Ryūnosuke) **44**:35
"Hold That Christmas Tiger!" (Perelman) **32**:204
"Holding Her Down" (London) **4**:291
"The Hole" (Dixon) **16**:206, 208
"The Hole" (Hood) **42**:141, 188, 205, 222
"The Hole in the Wall" (Chesterton) **1**:122
"The Holiday" (Machado de Assis) **24**:140, 155
"Holiday" (Porter) **4**:347, 349-50, 355; **43**:177-8, 186-88, 238, 249, 258, 292, 326-34
"Holiday in Texas" (Algren) **33**:113
"A Holiday in the South" (Andrić)
   See "Letovanje na jugu"
"Holiday Romance" (Dickens) **17**:124
"The Holiday Stew" (Aleichem)
   See "Der yontefdiker tsimes"
"Hollow" (Pancake) **61**:248, 263-64, 270, 282
"The Hollow Boy" (Calisher) **15**:10, 14
"The Hollow of the Three Hills" (Hawthorne) **3**:154, 157, 180-81
"Hollywood" (Jones) **56**:272
"The Holy Door" (O'Connor) **5**:365, 367, 371, 384, 390
"The Holy Island" (Somerville & Ross) **56**:324, 333
"The Holy Land" (Lagerkvist) **12**:198
"The Holy Man" (Hood) **42**:165
"The Holy Night" (Čapek) **36**:114, 129
"The Holy Six" (Thomas) **3**:399, 407-08; **44**:329, 332-33, 338, 343, 345-46, 348-49, 354, 357-58
"Holy Wedlock" (Zangwill) **44**:378
"Homage to Che Guevara" (Banks) **42**:66
"Homage to Isaac Babel" (Lessing) **6**:196-99, 214
"Homage to Switzerland" (Hemingway) **1**:211; **40**:221, 231, 245, 256-57
"El hombre" (Rulfo) **25**:245, 249-50, 255, 258, 262, 264-66, 268, 275, 278, 280
"El Hombre de la esquina rosada" (Borges) **4**:10, 14-16; **41**:53-55, 162
"El Hombre en el umbral" (Borges) **4**:4, 40-1; **41**:91, 95, 97
"El hombrecito" (Donoso) **34**:30, 32, 49
"Hombres de las orillas" (Borges)
   See "El Hombre de la esquina rosada"
"Home" (Boyle) **5**:57
"Home" (Chekhov) **51**:35, 46
"Home" (Gordimer) **17**:178, 180, 186, 188, 190-91
"Home" (Grau) **15**:163
"Home" (Hughes) **6**:109, 118-19, 121-22, 133
"Home" (Phillips) **16**:325, 327-28, 330

"Home" (Updike) **13**:397-98
"Home Delivery" (King) **17**:295
A Home for the Highland Cattle (Lessing) **6**:189-91, 195-96
"The Home Front" (Stafford) **26**:274, 276
"Home Is Where" (Adams) **24**:3-4, 13
"Home Life" (Price) **22**:370
"Home Run" (Bukowski) **45**:51
"Home Sickness" (Moore)
   See "Galar Dúithche"
"Home, Sweet Home" (Fante) **65**:74, 83, 95, 97, 99
"Home to Marie" (Beattie) **11**:30-1, 34
"Home to Shawneetown" (Algren) **33**:107
Home Truths: Selected Canadian Stories (Gallant) **5**:138, 141, 143-44, 147
"The Homecoming" (Bradbury) **29**:47, 67, 88; **53**:215
"Homecoming" (Grau) **15**:148, 152
"The Homecoming" (Hesse) **9**:231, 235
"Homecoming" (Kafka)
   See "Heimkehr"
"Homecoming" (Platonov) **42**:254-55
"A Homecoming" (Suckow) **18**:396-97, 401, 409
"The Home-Coming of 'Rastus Smith" (Dunbar) **8**:122, 135
"Homelanding" (Atwood) **46**:74-5, 83
"Um homem célebre" (Machado de Assis) **24**:129
"O homem que apareceu" (Lispector) **34**:209, 215
"Homes on the Mountain" (Kiely) **58**:149, 167
"Hometown" (Dazai Osamu) **41**:249, 252
"Hometown" (Lu Hsun)
   See "Guxiang"
The Homewood Books (Wideman) **62**:275, 277
The Homewood Trilogy (Wideman)
   See *The Homewood Books*
L'homme aux quarante écus (Voltaire) **12**:342, 346
"Un homme d'affaires" (Balzac) **5**:32
"Un homme de lettres" (Mauriac) **24**:183, 196, 199, 203-05, 207
"The Honest Quack" (Chesterton) **1**:133
"An Honest Soul" (Freeman) **1**:198, 201; **47**:106, 153-54, 157-58, 161
"An Honest Thief" (Dostoevsky) **2**:166, 171, 193
"An Honest Woman" (Gilman) **13**:126
"Honey" (Beattie) **11**:33-4
"The Honey Tree" (Jewett) **6**:156, 158
"Honey, We'll Be Brave" (Farrell) **28**:88, 92, 121
"Honeymoon" (Mansfield) **23**:137; **38**:230
"The Honeymoon" (Moravia)
   See "Bitter Honeymoon"
"Honeymoon" (O'Brien) **10**:331, 333
"The Honeymoon" (Pritchett) **14**:298
"Honeymoon at Tramore" (Trevor) **21**:260, 262, 265; **58**:231
"Honolulu" (Maugham) **8**:359, 371-72
"The Honored Dead" (Pancake) **61**:259, 263, 268, 276, 282
Honorine (Balzac) **5**:18, 31, 33
"The Honour of Israel Gow" (Chesterton) **1**:134, 137; **46**:132
"The Honourable Laura" (Hardy) **60**:179
"The Hook" (O'Flaherty) **6**:264, 269
"Hope" (Galsworthy) **22**:98
"The Hope Chest" (Stafford) **26**:301
"Hope for the Unattainable" (Tagore)
   See "Durasa"
"Hopeless" (Atwood) **2**:20
"Hopes Rise" (Boyle) **16**:156-57
"Hop-Frog" (Poe) **1**:408; **22**:305; **35**:306, 317, 344; **54**:180, 189, 192, 196, 200-3
"Hora" (Čapek) **36**:82, 90-1, 110, 121-23, 126
"Horatio Sparkins" (Dickens) **17**:110, 120, 137
"Horatio's Trick" (Beattie) **11**:30-1, 34
"Horibata no sumai" (Shiga) **23**:359
"Horizon" (O'Hara) **15**:267-68

"Le horla" (Maupassant) **1**:259, 262, 265, 269, 273, 283-84, 286-88; **64**:301, 316, 318-21, 326-27, 329, 362
"L'horloge" (Baudelaire) **18**:6
"Horn Came" (Beckett) **16**:123-24, 126
"Horn of Plenty" (Gordimer) **17**:152, 166
"The Horns of the Bull" (Hemingway) **25**:113
"The Horoscope" (Far) **62**:34, 37, 39
"The Horror at Red Hook" (Lovecraft) **3**:258, 262, 289; **52**:292, 334, 336, 346, 354, 362
"The Horror from the Bridge" (Campbell) **19**:79-80, 89-90
"The Horror from the Shadows" (Lovecraft) **52**:311
"Horror House of Blood" (Campbell) **19**:86-7
"The Horror in the Eyes" (Lovecraft) **52**:314
"The Horror in the Museum" (Lovecraft) **3**:279
"Horror Movie" (Dybek) **55**:127, 134
"The Horror of the Heights" (Doyle) **12**:62, 76-7, 79-80
"A Horse and Two Goats" (Narayan) **25**:145, 148, 155, 164, 169, 174-75
A Horse and Two Goats, and Other Stories (Narayan) **25**:135, 137, 139, 145, 152, 155
"A Horse in the Moon" (Pirandello)
   See "Un cavallo nella luna"
The Horse Knows the Way (O'Hara) **15**:262, 283
"Horse Thief" (Caldwell) **19**:19, 23
"The Horse-Dealer's Daughter" (Lawrence) **4**:202-03, 231-33, 235-36, 240
"Horselaugh on Dibber Lannon" (Fante) **65**:94
"A Horseman in the Sky" (Bierce) **9**:50, 55-6, 60, 68
"The Horses" (Stephens) **50**:315, 326
Horses and Men (Anderson) **1**:23, 25, 27, 30, 46, 50
"The Horses and the Sea" (Saroyan) **21**:134
"The Horse's Ha" (Thomas) **3**:409; **44**:329, 359
"A Horse's Name" (Chekhov) **2**:130; **51**:77
"Horses of the Night" (Laurence) **7**:255, 259, 262-63, 270
"A Horse's Tale" (Twain) **6**:303
"Horseshoes" (Lardner) **32**:145, 168
"Horses—One Dash" (Crane) **7**:104, 106, 108, 125-26, 149, 153-54
"The Horse-Stealers" (Chekhov) **2**:130
"Horse-trading Trembles" (Stuart) **31**:265
"Horsie" (Parker) **2**:273-75, 280, 283-84
"The Hoshane Rabe" (Aleichem) **33**:62
"The Hospital Patient" (Dickens) **17**:115
Hospital Sketches (Alcott) **27**:3, 40, 57, 62
"A Host of Furious Fancies" (Ballard) **1**:79; **53**:20-1, 59, 127
"Hostage" (Stegner) **27**:201, 220
"Hostages" (Banks) **42**:58-9
"Hostages" (Wideman) **62**:268, 274
"Hot and Cold" (Sansom) **21**:102
"Hot and Cold Blood" (Fitzgerald) **6**:46
"Hot Ice" (Dybek) **55**:130-34, 136-37, 111-143, 155
Hot Water Music (Bukowski) **45**:50-2, 56-8, 60, 62-3
"Hot-collared Mule" (Stuart) **31**:265
"L'hôte" (Camus) **9**:103, 105, 109-11, 113, 118-19, 120-26, 128, 135
"The Hotel" (Singer) **53**:273
"Hotel Behind the Lines" (Boyle) **5**:74
"Hotel Kid" (O'Hara) **15**:248, 265-66
"The Hotel of the Idle Moon" (Trevor) **21**:261; **58**:252
"Hotel Room in Chartres" (Lowry) **31**:41, 53
"Hot-Foot Hannibal" (Chesnutt) **7**:7, 10-11, 40; **54**:22, 40-2
"The Hound" (Faulkner) **1**:177
"The Hound" (Lovecraft) **3**:258, 262, 274, 276, 282; **52**:268, 281, 283, 291, 293, 313, 341, 343, 359, 362
"The Hounds of Fate" (Saki) **12**:288, 298, 306
"The Hour and the Years" (Gordimer) **17**:151
An Hour Beyond Midnight (Hesse)
   See *Eine Stunde hinter Mitternacht*

"The Hour That Stretches" (Ellison) **14**:128
"The Hours after Noon" (Bowles) **3**:64-6, 80, 82
"The House" (Agnon)
  See "HaBayit"
"The House" (Cowan) **28**:80
"The House" (Le Guin) **12**:213, 248-49
"The House" (de la Mare) **14**:86, 90, 92
"House by the Canal" (Shiga)
  See "Horibata no sumai"
"A House Divided" (Ballard) **53**:131
"House Hunting" (Chabon) **59**:82-87
The House in a Secluded Place (Andrić)
  See *Kuča na osami*
The House in a Secluded Space (Andrić)
  See *Kuča na osami*
"The House in Jail Square" (Kiely) **58**:148
"The House in Turk Street" (Hammett) **17**:218, 220-21
"The House of Asterión" (Borges)
  See "La casa de Asterión"
"The House of Cobwebs" (Gissing) **37**:60, 62-3, 66
The House of Cobwebs, and Other Stories (Gissing) **37**:51-2, 54-7, 79-80
"The House of Eld" (Stevenson) **51**:239
"The House of Fahy" (Somerville & Ross) **56**:308
"House of Flowers" (Capote) **2**:67, 69, 72, 75; **47**:16, 38-40, 45, 57
"The House of Heine Brothers, in Munich" (Trollope) **28**:318, 331
"The House of My Dreams" (O'Brien) **10**:331, 333, 345
"A House of My Own" (Cisneros) **32**:2, 43
A House of Pomegranates (Wilde) **11**:362, 364-65, 375, 376-77, 381, 384, 394, 398, 407-08
The House of Pride, and Other Tales of Hawaii (London) **4**:268-69, 283
The House of Souls (Machen) **20**:155, 172, 185, 194, 198-99, 201
"The House of the Dead Hand" (Wharton) **6**:428
"The House of the Far and Lost" (Wolfe) **33**:347, 353, 376, 386
"The House of the Hundred Grassfires" (Algren) **33**:90, 98
"House of the Sleeping Beauties" (Kawabata)
  See "Nemureru bijo"
House of the Sleeping Beauties, and Other Stories (Kawabata)
  See *Nemureru bijo*
"The House of Usher" (Poe)
  See "The Fall of the House of Usher"
"The House on its Own" (Andrić) **36**:70
The House on Its Own (Andrić)
  See *Kuča na osami*
"The House on Mango Street" (Cisneros) **32**:4, 40
The House On Mango Street (Cisneros) **32**:2-4, 6-9, 11-2, 14-5, 27-30, 32-3, 36, 40, 42, 44-6, 51
"The House on Maple Street" (King) **17**:295
"A House on the Heights" (Capote) **47**:29
"The House on the Hill" (Kazakov) **43**:56
"The House on the Sand" (Onetti)
  See "La casa en la arena"
"A House over a Precipice" (Kazakov) **43**:47
"The House Surgeon" (Kipling) **5**:272, 275, 284-85
"The House Taken Over" (Cortázar)
  See "Casa tomada"
"The House That Johnny Built" (O'Connor) **5**:363, 371
"The House That Was Never Built" (Lawson) **18**:252
"A House under the Hill" (Kazakov)
  See "Dom pod kruchei"
"The House with a Mezzanine" (Chekhov)
  See "Dom s mezoninom"
"The House with an Attic" (Chekhov)
  See "Dom s mezoninom"

"The House with the Blinds" (Norris) **28**:197
"The House with the Lilacs" (Warner) **23**:369-70
"The House with the Loop-Holes" (Lee) **33**:307
"The House with the Maisonette" (Chekhov)
  See "Dom s mezoninom"
"The House with the Mezzanine" (Chekhov)
  See "Dom s mezoninom"
"Houseboat" (Nin) **10**:303-05
"The Housebreaker of Shady Hill" (Cheever) **1**:111; **38**:55, 66, 85-6, 90
The Housebreaker of Shady Hill (Cheever) **38**:84
The Housebreaker of Shady Hill, and Other Stories (Cheever) **1**:89-92, 95, 100; **38**:83-88, 90
"The Household" (Irving) **2**:265
"Household" (Narayan) **25**:141
Household Tales (Grimm and Grimm)
  See *Kinder-und Hausmärchen*
"Housekeeper" (Grau) **15**:163-64
"The Housekeeper" (Lewis) **40**:277
"The Housewife" (Galsworthy) **22**:60, 99
"How 7 Went Mad" (Stoker) **62**:235-37, 251-52
"How a Good Man Went Wrong" (Chesnutt) **7**:14
"How a Witch Was Caught" (Harris) **19**:196
"How about This?" (Carver) **8**:32
"How Andrew Carried the Precinct" (Page) **23**:289
"How Auntie Fedos'ja Chatted with Lenin" (Zoshchenko) **15**:407
"How Brother Fox Was Too Smart" (Harris) **19**:148
"How Brother Parker Fell from Grace" (Dunbar) **8**:122
"How Buton Got Married" (Bulgakov) **18**:90
"How Can I Tell You?" (O'Hara) **15**:260, 291
"How Claeys Died" (Sansom) **21**:90, 95
"How Dasdy Came Through" (Chesnutt) **7**:13
"How Dr. Christopher Evans Landed on the Moon" (Ballard) **53**:8
"How Fear Came" (Kipling) **54**:81-82, 111-13, 121-22, 124, 132
"How He Does It" (Clarke) **45**:78-9, 82, 88, 92, 103, 105-06, 108, 16, 121, 123, 125
"How I Finally Lost My Heart" (Lessing) **6**:197, 200-01, 206, 220
"How I Left Miguel Street" (Naipaul) **38**:335, 343
"How I Went to the Mines" (Harte) **59**:311
"How I Write My Songs" (Barthelme) **2**:52; **55**:81
"How It Is to Be" (Saroyan) **21**:154
"How It Was Done in Odessa" (Babel)
  See "How Things Were Done in Odessa"
"How Lenin Bought a Boy a Toy" (Zoshchenko) **15**:407
"How Lenin Outsmarted the Police" (Zoshchenko) **15**:407
"How Lenin Quit Smoking" (Zoshchenko) **15**:407
"How Lenin Studied" (Zoshchenko) **15**:407
"How Lenin Was Given a Fish" (Zoshchenko) **15**:407
"How Many Midnights" (Bowles) **3**:60, 69, 72, 79
"How Mickey Made It" (Phillips) **16**:335-37, 339
"How Mr. Hogan Robbed a Bank" (Steinbeck) **11**:256-58
"How Mr. Rabbit Was Too Sharp for Mr. Fox" (Harris) **19**:140, 172
"How Much Land Does a Man Need?" (Tolstoy) **9**:377, 388
"How Much Shall We Bet?" (Calvino) **3**:104; **48**:65, 68, 133, 158
"How Old Craney-Crow Lost His Head" (Harris) **19**:194
"How Pearl Button Was Kidnapped" (Mansfield) **9**:302; **23**:174-75

"How Santa Claus Came to Simpson's Bar" (Harte) **8**:223-24, 227, 236, 244; **59**:288, 302
"How She Came By Her Name" (Bambara) **35**:42
"How Six Made Their Way in the World" (Grimm and Grimm) **36**:223, 228-29
"How Sleep the Brave" (Bates) **10**:139
How Sleep the Brave, and Other Stories (Bates) **10**:138
"How Sportsmanship Came to Carver College" (Stuart) **31**:227
"How the Alphabet Was Made" (Kipling) **54**:93
"How the Birds Talk" (Harris) **19**:149
"How the Brigadier Bore Himself at Waterloo" (Doyle) **12**:82
"How the Brigadier Came to the Castle of Gloom" (Doyle) **12**:81
"How the Brigadier Held the King" (Doyle) **12**:82
"How the Brigadier Lost His Ear" (Doyle) **12**:82
"How the Brigadier Played for a Kingdom" (Doyle) **12**:82
"How the Brigadier Slew the Brothers of Ajaccio" (Doyle) **12**:81
"How the Brigadier Slew the Fox" (Doyle) **12**:82
"How the Brigadier Triumphed in England" (Doyle) **12**:82
"How the Brigadier Was Tempted by the Devil" (Doyle) **12**:82
"How the Brigadier Won His Medal" (Doyle) **12**:82
"How the comb gives a meaning to the hair" (Abish) **44**:19
"How the Devil Came Down Division Street" (Algren) **33**:102-04, 109
"How the King Held the Brigadier" (Doyle) **12**:82
"How the Local Committee Bought a Present with an Old Woman's Money" (Bulgakov) **18**:89
"How Things Were Done in Odessa" (Babel) **16**:44-5, 48-9
"How to Become a Pillar of the Establishment" (Machado de Assis)
  See "Teoria do medalhão"
"How to Grow a Wisteria" (O'Brien) **10**:330
"How to Love America" (Updike) **13**:387
"How to Write a Blackwood Article" (Poe) **1**:405; **22**:330
"How to Write a Novel" (Lish) **18**:266, 268
"How to Write a Poem" (Lish) **18**:268
"How to Write a Short Story" (O'Faolain) **13**:296
How to Write Short Stories—With Samples (Lardner) **32**:114-15, 121, 124, 131-33, 150-51, 154
"How We Live Now" (Cheever) **38**:58, 61
"How Whalebone Caused a Wedding" (Harris) **19**:182
"The How, When and Wherefore" (Verga)
  See "Il Come, il Quando, et il Perche"
"How Willie Proudfit Came Home" (Warren) **58**:354
"Howard and the Spinach" (Steinbeck) **11**:203
"Howe's Masquerade" (Hawthorne) **3**:154, 187
"Hsiang-yü" (P'u Sung-ling) **31**:196
"Hsia-nü" (P'u Sung-ling) **31**:196, 204
"Hsiao Ts'ui" (P'u Sung-ling) **31**:207, 209
"Hsieh-nü" (P'u Sung-ling) **31**:192
"Hsien-jen tao" (P'u Sung-ling) **31**:196, 199
"Hsin Shih-ssu niang" (P'u Sung-ling) **31**:196, 206, 209
"Hsü huang-liang" (P'u Sung-ling) **31**:190, 199
"Hu ch'êng yin" (P'u Sung-ling) **31**:204
"Hu hsieh" (P'u Sung-ling) **31**:205
"Hu lien" (P'u Sung-ling) **31**:205
"Hu Ssu-chieh" (P'u Sung-ling) **31**:204
"Hu Ssu-hsiang-kung" (P'u Sung-ling) **31**:205
"Hua pi" (P'u Sung-ling) **31**:217

"Huai-chiu" (Lu Hsun)
   See "Huaijiu"
"Huaijiu" (Lu Hsun) **20**:135, 138, 147-48
"Huang Chiang-chün" (P'u Sung-ling) **31**:201
"Hubert and Minnie" (Huxley) **39**:156
"Huey, the Engineer" (Stuart) **31**:226, 239
"Hugh Monfert" (Moore) **19**:296, 298
"L'Huissier" (Aymé) **41**:12, 17, 22
"The Human Being and the Dinosaur"
   (Thurber) **1**:426, 430
The Human Comedy (Balzac)
   See *La Comédie humaine*
"The Human Element" (Maugham) **8**:357, 366,
   378
"The Human Fly" (Boyle) **16**:154
"Human Habitation" (Bowen) **3**:55
"Human Is" (Dick) **57**:84, 102-3, 107, 139
"Human Lost" (Dazai Osamu) **41**:248
Human Odds and Ends (Gissing) **37**:54-6,
   79-80
"Human Remains" (Barker) **53**:136-37, 139,
   157, 162, 168
"The Human Thing" (O'Faolain) **13**:316
"A Humble Lover" (Leacock) **39**:265
"A Humble Remonstrance" (Stevenson) **51**:232
"A Humble Romance" (Freeman) **1**:196; **47**:83,
   85, 87, 104
A Humble Romance, and Other Stories
   (Freeman) **1**:191, 194-95, 197, 201;
   47:83-4, 101-02, 104-06, 123, 145, 149,
   154, 160, 170, 191-95
"The Humming Birds" (Welty) **51**:278
"The Hummingbird that Lived through the
   Winter" (Saroyan) **21**:154
"A Humorous Southern Story" (Chesnutt) **7**:13
"Humplebee" (Gissing) **37**:55
"Hun duede ikke" (Andersen) **6**:4, 14, 26, 30;
   56:33
"The Hunchback in the Park" (Thomas) **3**:400
A Hundred Camels in the Courtyard (Bowles)
   3:68
"The Hungarian Night" (Morand)
   See "La nuit Hongroise"
"Hunger" (Rhys) **21**:61-2
"Hunger" (Stephens) **50**:316-17, 316
Hunger (Lessing) **6**:190, 192-93, 195-97;
   61:103
"The Hunger Wheel" (Castellanos)
   See "La rueda del hambriento"
"A Hunger-Artist" (Kafka)
   See "Ein Hungerkünstler"
"Hungerford" (Lawson) **18**:215, 261
"Ein Hungerkünstler" (Kafka) **5**:207-09, 220,
   225, 237-40; **29**:331-79; **60**:253, 259, 273-
   75, 278-79
"The Hungry" (Mann) **5**:319, 322-23, 330
The Hungry Ghosts (Oates) **6**:241, 243
"The Hungry Stones" (Tagore)
   See "Kshudhita Pashan"
The Hungry Stones and Other Stories (Tagore)
   48:301, 303, 321
"Hung-yü" (P'u Sung-ling) **31**:198, 209
"Hunktown" (Mason) **4**:8
"The Hunt" (Appelfeld) **42**:45
"The Hunt of the Unicorn" (Vinge) **24**:345-46
"Hunted Down" (Dickens) **17**:124
"Hunter" (Grau) **15**:163
"The Hunter" (Hammett) **17**:217
"The Hunter Gracchus" (Kafka)
   See "Der jäger Gracchus"
"Hunters in the Snow" (Wolff) **63**:282-83, 286-
   88, 290, 295-96, 299-300, 308, 310, 329-
   30, 335
Hunters in the Snow (Wolff)
   See *In the Garden of the North American
      Martyrs*
"A Hunter's Moon" (Thomas) **20**:323-25
Hunter's Sketches (Turgenev)
   See *Zapiski okhotnika*
"The Hunter's Waking Thoughts" (Gallant)
   5:151
"Hunting" (Head) **52**:188, 202-3, 207, 227-28

"Hunting" (Kazakov)
   See "Na oxote"
"Hunting" (Zoshchenko) **15**:407-08
"A Hunting Accident" (Gordimer) **17**:165, 193
"A Hunting Story" (Silko) **37**:309
"The Huntsman" (Chekhov)
   See "Eger"
"The Hurly Burly" (Coppard) **21**:17, 26
"Hurricane Hazel" (Atwood) **2**:21-3; **46**:44, 46,
   49, 52, 78-9, 96-7
"Hurry Kane" (Lardner) **32**:125, 132, 135, 145,
   163
"Hurt Feelings" (Wescott) **35**:375
"The Husband" (Bowles) **3**:80
"The Husband" (Trevor) **58**:252
"The Husband's Revenge" (Pirandello) **22**:265
"Hu-shih" (P'u Sung-ling) **31**:204
"Hvad gamle Johanne fotalte" (Andersen) **56**:35
"Hyacinth" (Saki) **12**:302
"Die Hyänen" (Hoffmann)
   See "Der Vampyrismus"
"The Hyannis Port Story" (Vonnegut) **8**:436
"Hydrogen" (Levi) **12**:259, 262, 264
"The Hyena" (Bowles) **3**:64-5, 68, 80
"The Hyena" (Hoffmann)
   See "Der Vampyrismus"
"Hygeia at the Solito" (Henry) **5**:182
"The Hyland Family" (Farrell) **28**:118-9
"Hymeneal" (O'Faolain) **13**:291, 314
"Hyōfū" (Tanizaki) **21**:207
"Hypnos" (Lovecraft) **52**:268, 276, 283, 312,
   342-43, 351
"The Hypnotist" (Bierce) **9**:75
"The Hypothesis of Failure" (Henry) **5**:184
"Hyrdinden og Skorsteensfeieren" (Andersen)
   56:31-2
"I a mournful God" (Kundera)
   See "I Sad God"
"I Always Wanted You to Admire My Fasting;
   or, Looking at Kafka" (Roth) **26**:251,
   253-54
"I Am a Very Clean Person" (Moorhouse)
   40:292, 309
"I Am Not Now, Nor Have I Ever Been, a
   Matrix of Lean Meat" (Perelman) **32**:222
"I and My Chimney" (Melville) **1**:298, 304,
   322, 326-27; **17**:359, 363
"I Bought a Little City" (Barthelme) **55**:87
I Cannot Get You Close Enough (Gilchrist)
   14:163-65; **63**:20-21
"I Can't Breathe" (Lardner) **32**:135, 139, 141,
   154, 168
"I Can't Put Two and Two Together"
   (Saroyan) **21**:134
"I Could See the Smallest Things" (Carver)
   8:19, 34-5; **51**:4, 13
"I cristalli" (Calvino) **3**:108-09, **48**:47, 65, 105,
   114, 155-56
I den tiden (Lagerkvist) **12**:179
"I dinosauri" (Calvino) **3**:103, 109; **48**:74, 104,
   135, 154, 160
"I due gobbi" (Calvino) **48**:98
"I Gave Up before Birth" (Beckett) **16**:123,
   125-26
"I Hanging on, Praise God" (Clarke) **45**:87
I Have a Thing to Tell You (Wolfe) **33**:347-49,
   376, 392-93
"I Have No Mouth and I Must Scream"
   (Ellison) **14**:97-9, 107, 110, 112-15, 117-
   18, 124-25, 130-31, 138-39, 141, 143-47
I Have No Mouth and I Must Scream (Ellison)
   14:143-47
"I Hope I Shall Arrive Soon" (Dick) **57**:83
"I Killed" (Bulgakov) **18**:86, 89
"I Know Who I Love" (Jackson) **9**:258, 270-71
The I. L. Peretz Reader (Peretz) **26**:212-13
"I Live on Your Visits" (Parker) **2**:283
"I Look Out for Ed Wolfe" (Elkin) **12**:94-5, 99,
   102, 117-18
"I Love Someone" (Stafford) **26**:283, 285, 301
"I Love You, Sophie Western" (Jones) **56**:285
"I Love You Very Dearly" (Aiken) **9**:13-14, 29

"I Maureen" (Spencer) **57**:207-9, 213, 242-44
"I Need a Man to Love Me" (Jones) **56**:282
"I Never Seen Anything Like It" (O'Hara)
   15:265
"I Passed By Your Window" (Pritchett) **14**:299
"I Plinglot Who You?" (Pohl) **25**:230
I racconti (Moravia) **26**:138, 141, 143, 151,
   162, 183, 185
"I Remember Babylon" (Clarke) **3**:131
"I Remember! I Remember!" (O'Faolain)
   13:320-21
I Remember! I Remember! (O'Faolain) **13**:288-
   89, 293, 311
"I Remember Mollie" (Stuart) **31**:252
*I, Rhoda Manning, Go Hunting with My
   Daddy* (Gilchrist) **63**:35-36
"I Ricordi del Capitano d'Arce" (Verga) **21**:294
"I Sad God" (Kundera) **24**:89, 103
"I Sing the Body Electric!" (Bradbury) **29**:46,
   56, 64; **53**:193, 214
I Sing the Body Electric! (Bradbury) **29**:56, 81
"I sogni del pigro" (Moravia) **26**:164
I sogni del pigro: Racconti, miti e allegorie
   (Moravia) **26**:162-63
"I Spend My Days in Longing" (O'Hara)
   15:283
"I Spy" (Greene) **29**:183-84, 193
"I Spy a Stranger" (Rhys) **21**:35, 37-8, 48, 52-4,
   73, 75-6
"I Stand Here Ironing" (Olsen) **11**:163-64, 166,
   171, 177-80, 188, 190, 192-93, 195, 197
"I Used to Live Here Once" (Rhys) **21**:39, 42-3,
   50-1, 55, 64
"I Want to Go Home" (Farrell) **28**:98
"I Want to Know Why" (Anderson) **1**:20, 23,
   27, 35, 37-8, 40, 48-9, 62; **46**:16, 18, 20
"I Want to Live!" (Jones) **56**:274, 279-80, 282,
   285
"I Was a Teenage Grave Robber" (King) **17**:268
"I Will Not Let Thee Go, Except Thou Bless
   Me" (Updike) **13**:358
"I Would Have Saved Them If I Could"
   (Michaels) **16**:307-08, 313, 322
I Would Have Saved Them If I Could
   (Michaels) **16**:305-06, 308, 310-11, 314,
   316
"Iamskaia sloboda" (Platonov) **42**:267
"Ib and Christine" (Andersen) **6**:14
"Ibid" (Lovecraft) **52**:293
"Ibn Hakkan al-Bokhari, Dead in His
   Labryinth" (Borges)
   See "Abencaján el Bojarí, muerto en su la-
      berinto"
"Icarus Montgolfier Wright" (Bradbury) **29**:79
"Ice" (Bambara) **35**:42
"The Ice House" (Gordon) **15**:104, 118, 139
"The Ice Maiden" (Andersen)
   See "Iisjomfruen"
"The Ice Palace" (Fitzgerald) **6**:57-8, 88, 96-7,
   100, 103
"The Ice Wagon Going down the Street"
   (Gallant) **5**:139, 144
"Icebreaker" (Gorky) **28**:150
"Icicles" (Gass) **12**:123, 133, 167, 168
"Iconography" (Atwood) **2**:15, 20
"Ida" (Bunin) **5**:106-07, 116-20
"Ida M'Toy" (Welty) **27**:338
"The Idea" (Carver) **8**:7; **51**:13
"An Ideal Craftsman" (de la Mare) **14**:88
"An Ideal Family" (Mansfield) **9**:282, 284;
   23:158
"The Idealist" (Machen) **20**:199
"The Idealist" (Nin) **10**:306
"Idéis de canário" (Machado de Assis)
   24:128-29
"Idenborough" (Warner) **23**:380
"The Idiots" (Conrad) **9**:179
"Idiots First" (Malamud) **15**:171-75, 195, 197;
   204-05, 214, 216, 219-20, 225, 243
Idiots First (Malamud) **15**:170-72, 174, 188,
   197, 213-14, 220, 225, 227, 235

"An Idiot's Love" (Tanizaki)
  See "Chijin ai ai"
"An Idle Fellow" (Chopin) 8:73, 78, 98
"The Idol" (Pavese) 19:364, 377, 387
"The Idol of the Cyclades" (Cortázar)
  See "El ídolo de las cícladas"
"El ídolo" (Bioy Casares) 17:87
"El ídolo de las cícladas" (Cortázar) 7:57-8, 69-70, 76, 78
"The Idyl of Red Gulch" (Harte) 8:210, 217, 236-37, 246; 59:286-87, 290, 292, 301, 338-39
"An Idyll of North Carolina Sand-Hill Life" (Chesnutt) 7:14
"Une idylle" (Maupassant) 1:256, 270
"If Grant Had Been Drinking at Appomatox" (Thurber) 47:377
"'If I Forget Thee, O Earth'" (Clarke) 3:124, 126, 143
"If I Should Open My Mouth" (Bowles) 3:64, 68-9, 80, 83, 85
"If I Were a Man" (Gilman) 13:126
"If Not Higher" (Peretz) 26:201-02, 213-14
"If One Green Bottle. . ." (Thomas) 20:293, 322
"If Only: Only If..." (Clarke) 45:79, 82, 87-8, 103, 109
"If Such be Nature's Holy Plan..." (Lewis) 40:281
"If the Bough Breaks" (Clarke) 45:109-10
"If the River Was Whiskey" (Boyle) 16:146-48, 150, 152, 154, 156
If the River Was Whiskey (Boyle) 16:146, 148-49, 153-54
"If There Were No Benny Cemoli" (Dick) 57:46, 54-55
"If They Knew Yvonne" (Dubus) 15:69, 71, 90, 100
"If They Say He's Crazy—Believe It!" (Peretz)
  See "Az men zogt meshuge—gleyb!"
"If This Goes On —" (Heinlein) 55:168-70, 184, 187-90, 198-200, 210-11, 216
"If You Don't Want to Live I Can't Help You" (Calisher) 15:5
"If You Must Use Profanity" (Algren) 33:113
"If You Touched My Heart" (Allende) 65:7, 23, 34
"Ignat" (Bunin) 5:100
"Ignaz Denner" (Hoffmann) 13:183, 186, 209
"Igra" (Andrić) 36:49-50
"A igreja do diabo" (Machado de Assis) 24:127-30, 152
"Igur and the Mountain" (Aldiss) 36:20
"Iisjomfruen" (Andersen) 6:12, 19, 26, 34-5, 37; 56:31
"Ike and Nina" (Boyle) 16:144-45, 151
"Ikkai no tsuchi" (Akutagawa Ryūnosuke) 44:46, 53, 81
"Il bosco degli animali" (Calvino) 48:41
"Il bosco sull'autostrada" (Calvino) 48:82
Il castello dei destini incrociati (Calvino) 3:99-102, 106, 114, 116, 118
"Il cielo di pietra" (Calvino) 48:155, 160
"Il coccodrillo" (Moravia) 26:164
"Il Come, il Quando, et il Perche" (Verga) 21:280
"Il concorrenza" (Moravia) 26:164
"Il Conde" (Conrad) 9:151, 160, 179, 184
"Il coniglio velenoso" (Calvino) 48:83
"Il gatto e il poliziotto" (Calvino) 48:80
"Il guidatore notturno" (Calvino) 48:48
"Il malocchio" (Svevo) 25:336, 360
"Il mare" (Moravia) 26:164
"Il mio ozio" (Svevo) 25:329-30, 360-61
"Il mostro" (Moravia) 26:165
"Il naso" (Moravia) 26:164
"Il negro e il vecchio dalla roncola" (Moravia) 26:151, 163
"Il niente e il poco" (Calvino) 48:152, 155, 157, 160
"Il nome il naso" (Calvino) 3:119; 48:128, 174

"Il Peccato di Donna Santa" (Verga) 21:294-96, 298
"Il pensatore" (Moravia) 26:174-76, 178
"Il piccione comunale" (Calvino) 48:82
"Il reverendo" (Verga) 21:292
"Il sangue, il mare" (Calvino) 3:109-10; 48:47, 78, 106, 114, 167, 173
"Il sesto giorno" (Levi) 12:279
"Il Tramonto di Venere" (Verga) 21:294
Il vecchione (Svevo) 25:334, 350-53, 361
"Il viaggio di nozze" (Moravia) 26:182
"Il viccolo di Madama Lucrezia" (Mérimée) 7:283-4, 290, 295-6, 306-07
"The Iliad of Sandy Bar" (Harte) 59:339
"Ilias" (Tolstoy) 45:131
"I'll Be Waiting" (Chandler) 23:89, 110
"I'll Not Look for Wine" (Bradbury) 53:246, 253
"Ill Omens" (Akutagawa Ryūnosuke)
  See "Kyō"
Ill Seen Ill Said (Beckett)
  See *Mal vu mal dit*
"The Illegality of the Imagination" (Moorhouse) 40:299
The Ill-Tempered Clavichord (Perelman) 32:245
"The Illuminated Man" (Ballard) 1:69
"Les illuminés; ou, Les précurseurs de socialisme" (Nerval) 18:328
"Illusion" (Rhys) 21:54, 61
"An Illusion in Red and White" (Crane) 7:104
The Illustrated Man (Bradbury) 29:52, 57, 62, 77, 79-82; 53:199, 253
"L'illustre Gaudissart" (Balzac) 5:18, 26
"The Illustrious Gaudissart" (Balzac)
  See "L'illustre Gaudissart"
"The Illustrious Kitchen Maid" (Cervantes)
  See "La ilustre fregona"
"The Illustrious Serving Wench" (Cervantes)
  See "La ilustre fregona"
"La ilustre fregona" (Cervantes) 12:4, 6-8, 15, 17-18, 36-7, 40
"I'm a Fool" (Anderson) 1:23, 25, 27, 30, 37-8, 40, 48-50; 46:16, 20
"I'm Being Good" (Selby) 20:275
"I'm Crazy" (Salinger) 65:312-13
"I'm Dancing Frences" (Farrell) 28:111
"Im Lande der Rujuks" (Boell) 23:6, 34
"I'm Not Desperate!" (Hood) 42:147, 237
Im Schloss (Storm) 27:279-81
"The Image" (Narayan) 25:135
The Image, and Other Stories (Singer) 3:384-86; 53:316-27, 330
The Image of Misfortune (Onetti)
  See *La cara de la desgracia*
"An Image of Success" (Gordimer) 17:154
"The Image of the Lost Soul" (Saki) 12:285, 305
"The Image Trade" (Pritchett) 14:300, 305
"Images" (Munro) 3:326, 338, 343-44
"The Imaginary Assassin" (Mukherjee) 38:255, 271-72
"The Imagination of Disaster" (Gordon) 59:231, 237, 260, 263-64
"An Imaginative Woman" (Hardy) 2:215, 220, 223, 225; 60:180, 184-86, 188-89
"Imagine a Day at the End of Your Life" (Beattie) 11:30, 33-4
Imagine Kissing Pete (O'Hara) 15:250, 272
"Imagined Scenes" (Beattie) 11:2, 18, 21
"The Imbroglio" (Moravia) 26:138
L'imbroglio: Cinque romanzi brevi (Moravia) 26:162
"Imenimy" (Chekhov) 51:174, 177-78
"A imitação da rosa" (Lispector) 34:185, 193, 195, 197, 199, 201-02, 205
Immaculate Man (Gordon) 59:239-46, 248-54, 258-59, 269, 272, 274
Immensee (Storm) 27:282, 284, 286, 301-03, 308
"The Immigrant Story" (Paley) 8:406, 409
"The Immortal" (Borges)
  See "El inmortal"

The Immortal Bartfuss (Appelfeld) 42:19, 39
"Immortality" (Platonov)
  See "Bessmertie"
"The Immortality Crew" (Aldiss) 36:19
"The Immortals" (Bioy Casares) 17:75
"Imogayu" (Akutagawa Ryūnosuke) 44:50, 57, 76
"Imogene" (Moorhouse) 40:324
"Imogene Continued" (Moorhouse) 40:299-300, 307, 324
"Imp Among Aunts" (Lish) 18:284
"The Imp and the Crust" (Tolstoy) 9:377, 388; 45:149
"The Imp of the Perverse" (Poe) 22:348; 34:241, 251, 281; 35:307-11, 315, 343; 54:174, 198
"Impasse" (Banks) 42:69
"Impasse" (Stegner) 27:197, 205, 220
"Impatience" (Sansom) 21:93
"Impatience de la foule" (Villiers de l'Isle Adam) 14:381, 388, 394
"The Impatient Mob" (Villiers de l'Isle Adam)
  See "Impatience de la foule"
"An Imperfect Conflagration" (Bierce) 9:75
"The Impertinent Curiosity" (Cervantes)
  See "El curioso impertinente"
"Impertinent Daughters" (Lessing) 6:215
"Implosion" (Calvino)
  See "L'implosione"
"L'implosione" (Calvino) 48:151, 160
"The Importance of Healing Ernest" (Perelman) 32:213, 229
"The Important Houses" (Gordon) 59:261, 267-68
"The Impossible Man" (Ballard) 1:75-7; 53:11, 56
"The Impossible Marriage" (O'Connor) 5:372, 374
"Impostor" (Dick) 57:52, 78-81, 84-8, 88, 88, 118, 138, 151
"The Impresario" (Singer) 3:389
"The Impressions of a Cousin" (James) 8:316
"Impressions of a Journey Through the Tomaszow Region in the Year 1890" (Peretz) 26:213
"The Improbable Tale of the Archibishop of Canterbridge" (Greene) 29:221
"Impulse" (Aiken) 9:6, 13, 24-5, 27, 32
"In a Café" (Lavin) 4:183, 185, 189
"In a Café" (Rhys) 21:39, 42-3, 62
"In a Dry Season" (Lawson) 18:210, 261
"In a Far Country" (London) 4:264, 267-68, 279, 281-82, 284-86, 290; 49:340, 342
"In a Flemish Garden" (Fuentes)
  See "Tlactocatzine del jardin de Flandes"
"In a Free State" (Naipaul) 38:300, 305, 313, 354
In a Free State (Naipaul) 38:300-01, 303, 310-11, 314-15, 317-18, 323-24, 328, 353, 355
In a German Pension (Mansfield) 9:284, 288, 301; 23:137, 139
In a Glass Darkly (Le Fanu) 14:214, 225, 230, 234-35, 239-41, 243-45, 248-49
"In a Grove" (Akutagawa Ryūnosuke)
  See "Yabu no naka"
"In a Grove" (O'Hara) 15:251
"In a Mexican Patio" (Porter) 43:227
"In a Public Place" (Oates) 6:237
"In a Shaken House" (Warner) 23:372
"In a Strange Country" (Ellison) 26:10-12, 21
"In a Strange Town" (Anderson) 1:50
"In a Thicket" (Wescott) 35:363-64, 368, 370-72, 380, 382-83
"In a Thousand Years' Time" (Andersen) 6:30
In a Vision (Peretz) 26:205
"In a Wet Season" (Lawson) 18:210
"In Amalfi" (Beattie) 11:30-3
"In Ambush" (Kipling) 54:96
"In an Elevator" (Clarke) 45:112
"In and Out of Old Nachitoches" (Chopin) 8:103, 105, 113

"In Another Country" (Hemingway) **1**:209, 230-32, 234; **40**:177; **63**:50, 55, 91
"In at the Birth" (Trevor) **21**:230, 262; **58**:252
"In Autumn" (Bunin) **5**:114
"In Bed One Night" (Coover) **15**:47
In Bed One Night and Other Brief Encounters (Coover) **15**:46
In Black and White (Kipling) **54**:121
"In Business" (Morrison) **40**:330, 337, 364, 367
"In Butterfly Time" (Freeman) **47**:145, 148
"In Camp" (Andrić)
  See "In the Camp"
"In Court" (Chekhov) **51**:77
"In Defense of Tigolobia" (Fuentes)
  See "En defensa de la Trigolibia"
"In der Finsternis" (Boell) **23**:5
"In der Strafkolonie" (Kafka) **5**:218, 223-24, 229-30, 235-36, 240, 249-52; **29**:346, 372; **35**:217, 224, 239, 264; **60**:237, 248-51, 255-57, 296, 298-99
"Um in endio" (Machado de Assis) **24**:155
"In Exile" (Chekhov)
  See "V ssylke"
"In Fear of Death" (Stoker) **62**:252
"In Flight Sadism" (Moorhouse) **40**:304
"In Football Season" (Updike) **13**:367, 375, 404
"In Front of the Rio-Niterói Bidge" (Lispector)
  See "Antes da ponte Rio-Niterói"
"In Greenwich There are Many Gravelled Walks" (Calisher) **15**:2, 10
"In Heat" (Crace) **61**:30
"In High Places" (Aleichem) **33**:54
"In Honour Bound" (Gissing) **37**:54
"In Isfahan" (Trevor) **21**:233, 237
"In Kew Gardens" (Malamud) **15**:235
"In le Havre" (Lowry) **31**:41-2
"In Lilliput" (O'Faolain) **13**:308, 314
In Love and Trouble: Stories of Black Women (Walker) **5**:401-03, 405, 407, 411-12, 418-19, 422
"In Love with Ariadne" (Trevor) **21**:265
"In Memoriam" (Arreola) **38**:6, 21
"In Memory of Ann Jones" (Thomas)
  See "After the Funeral: In Memory of Anne Jones"
"In Memory of Judith Cortright" (Caldwell) **19**:42, 54
"In Memory of L. I. Shigaev" (Nabokov) **11**:124, 126, 145
In Minor Keys (Moore) **19**:339, 341, 345
In Mr. Knox's Country (Somerville & Ross) **56**:297, 301, 307, 309, 315, 318, 320, 324, 329, 334-35
"In My Life" (Dubus) **15**:70, 77, 79, 81
"In No Man's Land" (Gissing) **37**:54
"In Northern Waters" (Williams) **31**:334
In Old Plantation Days (Dunbar) **8**:120-22, 127-29, 132, 134, 141, 145, 148
In Ole Virginia, or Marse Chan and Other Stories (Page) **23**:283-86, 289, 291-93, 296-97, 299-300, 302-05, 314, 316-17, 319-23, 325-29
In Our Time (Hemingway) **1**:206-08, 212, 214-15, 234-36, 238, 243-45; **25**:85; **36**:251; **40**:156, 194, 209, 220-21, 230; **63**:39-40, 42, 45, 55, 65, 67-68, 72-75, 78-84, 98, 125
"In paese straniero" (Moravia) **26**:147
"In Paris" (Bunin) **5**:114
In Peace as in War (Cabrera Infante)
  See *Así en la paz como en la guerra*
In Praise of Darkness (Borges)
  See *Elogio de la sombra*
"In Reserve" (Platonov)
  See "Vprok"
"In Ruth's Country" (Bass) **60**:5
"In Sabine" (Chopin) **8**:90, 99, 103
"In Search of the Rattlesnake Plantain" (Atwood) **46**:51-2, 78, 96
"In Serenella" (Svevo) **25**:329
"In Shadow" (Jewett) **6**:150, 168
In Single Strictness (Moore) **19**:296-98, 310, 344

"In So Many Words" (Abish) **44**:5, 8-9, 12, 29
In St. Jürgen (Storm) **27**:286, 307
"In St. Valentine's Church" (Babel) **16**:25, 53, 55, 57-8
"In Stone" (Appelfeld) **42**:45
In That Time (Lagerkvist)
  See *I den tiden*
"In the Absence of Angels" (Calisher) **15**:5
In the Absence of Angels (Calisher) **15**:2, 4-5
"In the Abyss" (Wells) **6**:366, 389, 403, 408-09
"In the Alley" (Elkin) **12**:94
"In the Autumn of the Year" (Oates) **6**:247
"In the Avu Observatory" (Wells) **6**:361
"In the Bag" (Campbell) **19**:87
"In the Basement" (Babel) **16**:13, 15, 22, 36, 41, 59
"In the Beauty of the Lillies" (Auchincloss) **22**:35, 45, 50
"In the Black Hills" (Lowry) **31**:71
"In the Black Mill" (Chabon) **59**:82-83, 85-86
"In the Bleak Mid-Winter" (Thomas) **20**:289, 298, 305
"In the Bosom of the Country" (O'Faolain) **13**:283, 295, 322
"In the Briar Patch" (Garrett) **30**:165, 172
In the Briar Patch (Garrett) **30**:172
In the Cage (James) **8**:302-05, 329, 331; **47**:207, 337-38
"In the Camp" (Andrić) **36**:45
"In the Carquinez Woods" (Harte) **8**:216, 223, 227, 233, 244, 251
"In the Cart" (Chekhov) **2**:156-58; **51**:85
"In the City of Slaughter" (Appelfeld) **42**:6
"In the Clay" (Moore) **19**:312-14, 317, 319-20, 322-23, 330-31, 333, 336
"In the Corner of a Small Sqauare" (Pushkin) **27**:163-64
In the Days When the World Was Wide, and Other Verses (Lawson) **18**:262
"In the Direction of the Beginning" (Thomas) **3**:396, 402, 407, 409; **44**:357
"In the Dry" (Pancake) **61**:248, 255-56, 259-60, 263, 275, 282, 284, 429
"In the Family" (Pavese) **19**:368
In the Fertile Valley (Appelfeld)
  See *Bagai' haporeh*
"In the Fifties" (Michaels) **16**:308
"In the Flesh" (Barker) **53**:140, 144-45, 157-58, 161-62, 168
In the Flesh: Tales of Terror (Barker) **53**:140-1, 143-45, 174
"In the Fog" (Kazakov) **43**:49
"In the Forest" (de la Mare) **14**:81-2, 87-8
"In the Forests of the North" (London) **4**:265, 280
"In the Future Perfect" (Abish) **44**:9, 13
In the Future Perfect (Abish) **44**:4-5, 10, 12-13, 19-21, 24, 26, 29, 38
"In the Gallery" (Kafka)
  See "Auf der Galerie"
"In the Garden" (Thomas) **44**:348
"In the Garden of the North American Martyrs" (Wolff) **63**:282, 295-96, 298-301, 303, 305, 318-19, 338, 341
In the Garden of the North American Martyrs (Wolff) **63**:260, 262-64, 266, 271-72, 277, 281-82, 284-301, 305, 309, 319-21
"In the Garrett" (Alcott) **27**:4
"In the Green Tree" (Lewis) **40**:272, 275-77
"In the Groove" (Thomas) **20**:324
"In the Guest House" (Andrić) **36**:55, 78
"In the Heart of the Heart of the Country" (Gass) **12**:123-24, 128-29, 133-35, 141, 152, 157-66, 171, 173
In the Heart of the Heart of the Country, and Other Stories (Gass) **12**:123
"In the Hills, the Cities" (Barker) **53**:136-37, 141, 143, 154-55, 162, 168-69
"In the Hour of Our Death" (Warner) **23**:368
"In the Hours of Darkness" (O'Brien) **10**:333
"In the House of Suddhu" (Kipling) **5**:265

"In the Land of Dreamy Dreams" (Gilchrist) **63**:10, 12
In the Land of Dreamy Dreams (Gilchrist) **14**:150-55, 158-59, 161-62; **63**:2-3, 5, 8-12, 14-17, 19-20, 22-24, 27-31
"In the Land of the Free" (Far) **62**:13, 17-19, 50-52, 54, 57, 59, 75
"In the Land of the Rujuks" (Boell)
  See "Im Lande der Rujuks"
In the Land of Youth (Stephens) **50**:311-12, 317, 326, 330, 333-35
"In the Loyal Mountains" (Bass) **60**:16-17, 19-21, 23, 27, 36, 38
"In the Luxembuxg Gardens" (Rhys) **21**:61
"In the Maelstrom" (Pirandello) **22**:255
"In the Mail Coach" (Peretz) **26**:212-13
"In the Market" (Davis) **38**:114-15
"In the Matter of a Private" (Kipling) **5**:260
"In the Maze" (Sansom) **21**:82, 86, 88
"In the Middle of the Fields" (Lavin) **4**:183, 185
In the Middle of the Fields, and Other Stories (Lavin) **4**:172
In the Midst of Life (Bierce)
  See *Tales of Soldiers and Civilians*
"In the Miro District" (Taylor) **10**:395, 397, 400-02, 408-09, 411
In the Miro District, and Other Stories (Taylor) **10**:397-99, 404
"In the Mist" (O'Hara) **15**:262
"In the Morning" (Sansom) **21**:82
"In the Morning Sun" (O'Hara) **15**:248, 265-66
"In the Night" (Tagore)
  See "Nisithe"
"In the Orchard" (Woolf) **7**:411
"In the Park" (Wolfe) **33**:355
"In the Penal Colony" (Kafka)
  See "In der Strafkolonie"
"In the Penny Arcade" (Millhauser) **57**:187
In the Penny Arcade (Millhauser) **57**:154, 156, 158, 167, 172-73, 175
"In the Picture" (Campbell) **19**:85
"In the Presence" (Kipling) **54**:77
"In the Pride of His Youth" (Kipling) **5**:274
In the Prime of Her Life (Agnon) **30**:81-2, 87, 89-92
"In the Problem Pit" (Pohl) **25**:226
"In the Ravine" (Chekhov)
  See "V ovrage"
"In the River" (Chekhov)
  See "V ovrage"
"In the Rue de l'Arrivée" (Rhys) **21**:62
"In the Rukh" (Kipling) **5**:287; **54**:90, 119, 121, 123-25, 129, 131-32, 136-37
"In the Same Boat" (Kipling) **5**:284-85
"In the Shadow of Another World" (Ligotti) **16**:277-78, 284
"In the Spring" (Chekhov) **51**:71
"In the Spring" (Fante) **65**:78-79
"In the Square" (Bowen) **3**:31
"In the Stadium" (Andrić)
  See "U Stadionu"
"In the Steppe" (Gorky)
  See "V Stepi"
In The Tennessee Mountains (Murfree) **22**:185, 188, 197-98, 200-01, 203-05, 207, 209, 213, 215-17
"In the Time of the Great Dying" (Bradfield) **65**:69
"In the Train" (Davie) **52**:4-5
"In the Train" (O'Connor) **5**:364, 371, 376-77, 381-82, 388, 395
"In the Trees" (Campbell) **19**:75, 77, 87
"In the Tules" (Harte) **8**:244
"In the Tunnel" (Gallant) **5**:130-31, 144
"In the Twilight" (Chekhov) **51**:81, 96
"In the Twilight" (Stegner) **27**:194, 196-97
"In the Valley of the Thundering Hooves" (Boell) **23**:7, 10
"In the Vault" (Lovecraft) **3**:262; **52**:320
"In the Voyeur's Gaze" (Ballard) **53**:114
"In the Walls of the Eyrx" (Lovecraft) **52**:277

"In the Warehouse" (Oates) **6**:232
"In the White Night" (Beattie) **11**:25-6, 28
"In The Wilderness" (Appelfeld) **42**:45
"In the Wineshop" (Lu Hsun)
　See "Zai jiulou shang"
"In the Zoo" (Stafford) **26**:278, 281, 283-88,
　307
In This World (Hesse) **9**:230
"In Time" (Dixon) **16**:217-18
"In Time Which Made a Monkey of Us All"
　(Paley) **8**:403
"In Transit" (Gallant) **5**:150
In Transit: Twenty Stories (Gallant) **5**:150
"In Youth Is Pleasure" (Gallant) **5**:128-29, 134,
　143, 148
"The Incarnation of Krishna Mulvaney"
　(Kipling) **5**:259, 262
"Incendiaries" (Hood) **42**:188
"Incest" (Updike) **13**:355
"An Inch and a Half of Glory" (Hammett)
　17:217
"The Incident" (Chekhov) **51**:35
"An Incident" (Shiga) **23**:336-37, 339, 345-46
"An Incident at Krechetovka Station"
　(Solzhenitsyn) **32**:330, 333, 335-37, 339,
　357, 361, 364, 387, 395, 397
"An Incident at Yanagiyu" (Tanizaki) **21**:194
"Incident in a Far Country" (Aldiss) **36**:20, 22
"Incident in Azania" (Waugh) **41**:323, 340
"An Incident in Practice" (Chekhov)
　See "Sluaj iz praktiki"
"An Incident in the Park" (Oates) **6**:248-49
"An Incident on the Volga" (Zoshchenko)
　15:404
"Incipit vita nova" (Hesse) **9**:231
"El incivil maestro de ceremonias Kotsuké no
　Suké" (Borges) **41**:39
"L'inconnue" (Villiers de l'Isle Adam) **14**:379-
　81, 393
"The Inconsolable" (Pavese) **19**:368
"Incontro di vecchi amici" (Svevo) **25**:360
*The Incredible and Sad Story of Innocent
　Eréndira and Her Heartless
　Grandmother* (García Márquez)
　See *La increíble y triste historia de la cán-
　dida Eréndira y de su abuela desalmada*
"The Incredible and Sad Tale of Innocent
　Eréndira and Her Heartless Grandmother"
　(García Márquez)
　See *La increíble y triste historia de la cán-
　dida Eréndira y de su abuela desalmada*
The Incredulity of Father Brown (Chesterton)
　1:128; **46**:111, 116, 130, 133-34, 141
*La increíble y triste historia de la cándida
　Eréndira y de su abuela desalmada*
　(García Márquez) **8**:167, 169-72, 182,
　186, 198-200
"The Incurable" (Zangwill) **44**:366, 375, 387
"The Independence of Silas Bollender"
　(Dunbar) **8**:127, 134
"An Independent Thinker" (Freeman) **1**:196;
　47:147-49, 161, 191
"The Index" (Ballard) **53**:67
"The Indian" (Updike) **13**:348, 387
"Indian Camp" (Hemingway) **1**:214, 219, 234,
　240-41, 244-45; **25**:125; **36**:251, 291;
　40:209, 211, 249; **63**:50, 52-53, 55, 65-69,
　79, 81, 83-84, 97-98, 103-6, 125
"The Indian Sign" (Thurber) **1**:425
"Indian Summer" (Barnes) **3**:12, 22
"Indian Summer" (Caldwell) **19**:37
"Indian Summer" (Spencer) **57**:207, 211-12,
　215-18, 242-43
"Indian Summer: A Hsiao's Autumnal Lament"
　(Chang) **28**:26; 28; 31; 34-35
"The Indian Summer of a Forsyte"
　(Galsworthy) **22**:83-4, 95-6, 99-100
"The Indian Summer of Dry Valley Johnson"
　(Henry) **5**:162
"The Indian Uprising" (Barthelme) **2**:35-6, 38,
　42, 46, 53; **55**:23, 38, 47, 67-8, 70, 72, 74,
　96-103, 120

"Indifference" (Aldiss) **36**:14
"Indignities" (Gilchrist) **63**:10, 20
"An Indiscreet Journey" (Mansfield) **9**:303,
　317; **38**:230
"The Indiscretion of Elsbeth" (Harte) **59**:308,
　310-11
"Indisposed" (Banks) **42**:52
The Indulgent Husband (Colette) **10**:261-62,
　269-70
"El indulto" (Pardo Bazán) **30**:272, 295
"The Inevitable White Man" (London) **4**:266
"The Inexperienced Ghost" (Wells) **6**:400
Infamy (Borges)
　See *Historia universal de la infamia*
The Infant Prodigy (Mann)
　See *Das Wunderkind*
"Infatuation" (Shiga) **23**:352
"The Inferior Man" (Far) **62**:50, 56
"The Inferior Woman" (Far) **62**:7, 48, 50-51,
　74, 96-97
"The Infernal Parliament" (Saki) **12**:322
"El infierno tan temido" (Onetti) **23**:250, 258,
　260
El infierno tan temido y otros cuentos (Onetti)
　23:248, 258
"The Infinite Passion of Expectation"
　(Berriault) **30**:103
The Infinite Passion of Expectation (Berriault)
　30:98-100, 105
"Influenza" (Shiga) **23**:344, 346
"An Influx of Poets" (Stafford) **26**:298, 307,
　312
El informe de Brodie (Borges) **4**:17-20, 26-7;
　41:117-18, 131, 157, 159, 161-62, 167
"The Informer" (Conrad) **9**:157, 179, 182-86
L'Ingénu (Voltaire) **12**:338-39, 341-43, 362,
　364-68, 394
L'ingénue libertine (Colette) **10**:257, 262
"An Ingènue of the Sierra" (Harte) **8**:244, 252
"The Ingrate" (Dunbar) **8**:122-23, 128-29, 136,
　142-43, 149
"The Inhabitant of the Lake" (Campbell) **19**:72,
　90
*The Inhabitant of the Lake and Less Welcome
　Tenants* (Campbell) **19**:61-2, 66, 71-2,
　81-6, 89-90, 92
Inhale and Exhale (Saroyan) **21**:132-33, 136-
　37, 143, 152-53, 161-62
"The Inherited Clock" (Bowen) **3**:31-2; **28**:3
"The Inhuman Condition" (Barker) **53**:156-57,
　162, 168
The Inhuman Condition: Tales of Terror
　(Barker) **53**:141-43, 169, 172
"Initiation" (Clarke) **45**:114
The Injustice Collectors (Auchincloss) **22**:2-3,
　9, 29, 33, 35-6, 38, 46-7, 50-1
"Inkalamu's Place" (Gordimer) **17**:157
"La inmiscusión terrupta" (Cortázar) **7**:95
"El inmortal" (Borges) **4**:7-8, 10-12, 14, 18-20,
　26-7; **41**:59, 74, 88, 90
"The Inmost Light" (Machen) **20**:158, 165, 173,
　182, 190-93, 196, 199, 201, 204-05
"The Inn" (Appelfeld)
　See "Ha'akhsanya"
"The Inn" (Turgenev) **7**:315, 320, 323, 325,
　337, 359
The Innermost Man (Platonov)
　See *Sokrovennyi chelovek*
"Innocence" (Bates) **10**:113
"Innocence" (McGahern) **17**:321
"The Innocence of Father Brown" (Chesterton)
　46:148-49
The Innocence of Father Brown (Chesterton)
　1:119-21, 124-25; **46**:116, 130, 132, 142,
　151
"The Innocence of Reginold" (Saki) **12**:321,
　328
"The Innocent" (Greene) **29**:185, 193, 195, 198
The Innocent and the Guilty (Warner) **23**:375,
　380

Innocent Eréndira, and Other Stories (García
　Márquez)
　See *La increíble y triste historia de la cán-
　dida Eréndira y de su abuela desalmada*
"An Innocent Gamester" (Freeman) **47**:102,
　106, 193
"Inochi no Ki" (Kawabata) **17**:246
"Inquest" (Williams) **31**:315, 334
"L'inquiéteur" (Villiers de l'Isle Adam) **14**:382
"The Inquisition" (O'Flaherty) **6**:264, 284
"The Insane Ones" (Ballard) **53**:11, 49
"The Inscription" (Čapek)
　See "Nápis"
"The Insect World" (Rhys) **21**:56, 69-70
"Insectíada" (Arreola) **38**:7
"Insects and Birds" (Shiga) **23**:346
"The Insects from Shaggai" (Campbell) **19**:72,
　90
"Inside and Outside" (Hesse) **9**:230-32, 236
Inside Kasrilevke (Aleichem) **33**:53
"Inside Norman Mailer" (Apple) **50**:3-5, 16,
　22, 30, 32, 48
"Inside Out" (Abish) **44**:12, 37
"An Inside Outside Complex" (O'Faolain)
　13:296, 309, 320
"The Insoluble Problem" (Chesterton) **1**:128;
　46:141
"Insomnia" (Lardner) **32**:156
"Insomnia" (Pavese) **19**:378
"Insomnie" (Mauriac) **24**:185, 196, 199-200,
　204-06
"L'insonnia insieme" (Moravia) **26**:148
"The Inspector" (Sansom) **21**:92
"Inspector General with a Kicking Out"
　(Bulgakov) **18**:74, 90
"Inspector General with an Ejection"
　(Bulgakov)
　See "Inspector General with a Kicking Out"
"An Inspiration" (Gissing) **37**:54, 80
"Inspired People" (Platonov) **42**:254
"Installation # 6" (Beattie) **11**:30-1
"Instant of the Hour After" (McCullers) **9**:342,
　344-45, 354, 359-60
"Instrucciones para John Howell" (Cortázar)
　7:62
"Instructions for the Third Eye" (Atwood) **2**:16-
　17; **46**:98
"Instructions on How to Dissect a Ground
　Owl" (Cortázar) **7**:92
"Instrument of Destruction" (Spencer) **57**:241
"The Insult" (Čapek) **36**:124
"The insulting master of etiquette Kotsuké no
　Suké" (Borges)
　See "El incivil maestro de ceremonias Kot-
　suké no Suké"
Insurrections (Stephens) **50**:316
Intangibles Inc., and Other Stories (Aldiss)
　36:18
"Intensive Care Unit" (Ballard) **1**:79; **53**:18, 58,
　109-11, 115
"Intercession" (Updike) **13**:355
"L'interdiction" (Balzac) **5**:8, 16, 26
"An Interest in Life" (Paley) **8**:389-90, 396-99,
　415-18
"An Interesting Point" (Moorhouse) **40**:322
"The Interference of Patsy Ann" (Dunbar)
　8:122, 132
"Interim" (Bradbury) **53**:207, 253
"The Interior Castle" (Stafford) **26**:274-75, 277,
　283, 291-96, 312-13
The Interior Castle (Stafford) **26**:291
"The Interloper" (Borges) **41**:159, 162, 164
"The Interloper" (Campbell) **19**:90
"The Interlopers" (Saki) **12**:285, 317
"Interlopers at the Knap" (Hardy) **2**:203, 205,
　207, 216, 229-31; **60**:178
"An Interlude" (Sansom) **21**:84, 89
"Interlude in a Book Shop" (Powers) **4**:368-69
"Interlude: Lea I" (Henderson) **29**:327
"Intermission" (Coover) **15**:60-1
"An International Episode" (James) **8**:299, 302;
　32:90

"Interpretation" (Akutagawa Ryūnosuke) **44**:50
"Interpretation of a Dream" (Collier) **19**:110, 112
"The Interpreter" (Aldiss) **36**:5
"The Interrupted Class" (Hesse) **9**:229-30, 232-33, 235-36
"Interruption" (Lewis) **40**:271
"L'intersigne" (Villiers de l'Isle Adam) **14**:377, 379, 381-82, 394-96, 403-04, 407-11, 413, 415
"The Intervention of Peter" (Dunbar) **8**:121, 127, 140
"Interview" (Arreola) **38**:9, 25
"An Interview" (Čapek) **36**:130
"An Interview" (Colette) **10**:292
"The Interview" (Singer) **3**:387
"The Interview" (Thurber) **1**:420; **47**:384
"Interview with a Lemming" (Thurber) **1**:417
"Intimacy" (Carver) **8**:43
"Intimacy" (Sartre)
    See "Intimité"
Intimacy, and Other Stories (Sartre)
    See *Le mur*
"The Intimate Disclosures of a Wronged Woman" (Leacock) **39**:266
"Intimations" (Michaels) **16**:302-03
"Intimité" (Sartre) **32**:250-53, 255, 258-59, 261, 281
"Into Egypt" (Benét) **10**:154-56
"Into the Comet" (Clarke) **3**:147
"The Intoxicated" (Jackson) **39**:209, 210-214, 227
The Intoxicated (Jackson) **39**:223
"Intoxication" (Oates) **6**:252
"Intracom" (Le Guin) **12**:235
"The Introducers" (Wharton) **6**:424, 437-38
"Introduction" (Andrić)
    See "Uvod"
"The Introduction" (Woolf) **7**:381, 390-91, 393, 395, 397, 399
"The Introspections of J. P. Powers" (Trevor) **21**:261
"The Intruder" (Borges)
    See "La intrusa"
"The Intruder" (Dixon) **16**:204, 214
"An Intruder" (Gordimer) **17**:158, 181
"Intruder" (Pavese) **19**:387
"Intruders" (Abe) **61**:9
"La intrusa" (Borges) **4**:14-15, 20, 37, 40-1; **41**:114-15, 117, 119, 162
"L'inutile beauté" (Maupassant) **1**:273, 275, 286-87
La invención de Morel (Bioy Casares) **17**:53-61, 64-7, 75, 83-5, 90, 94-5
The Invention of Morel, and Other Stories (from "La trama celeste") (Bioy Casares)
    See *La invención de Morel*
"The Invention of Photography in Toledo" (Davenport) **16**:169, 174, 179, 194
"The Invention of Robert Herendeen" (Millhauser) **57**:158, 161-62, 187
"The Invention of the Horse Collar" (Updike) **13**:360
"The Inventor" (Čapek) **36**:130
"Inverno di malato" (Moravia) **26**:138, 163, 179, 182-83, 186
"The Inverted Forest" (Salinger) **2**:309
"Investigations of a Dog" (Kafka)
    See "Forschungen eines hundes"
"The Investiture" (Banks) **42**:56-7, 64
"The Invincible Slave-Owners" (Dinesen) **7**:177, 196
"Invisible Boy" (Bradbury) **29**:65
"The Invisible Dove Dancer of Strathpheen Island" (Collier) **19**:98, 110, 114
"The Invisible Giant" (Stoker) **62**:251
"The Invisible Japanese Gentlemen" (Greene) **29**:200-01, 229
The Invisible Knight (Calvino)
    See *Il cavaliere inesistente*
"The Invisible Man" (Chesterton) **1**:130, 134, 136, 142; **46**:108, 148-49

"L'invitation au voyage" (Baudelaire) **18**:5-6, 8, 17, 35-6
"Invitation to a Dance" (Warren) **58**:354
"Invite" (O'Hara) **15**:253
"The Invited" (Sansom) **21**:83
"Invulnerable" (Ellison) **14**:127
"Ionitch" (Chekhov)
    See "Iony"
"Iony" (Chekhov) **2**:128, 131-32, 155; **51**:76, 117, 121, 129-30, 139-40, 200, 209, 211-12
Iounn the Weeper (Bunin) **5**:90
Iowa Interiors (Suckow) **18**:389-90, 395, 405, 418, 421-22
"¡Por qué era rubia?" (Alarcon) **64**:3, 8
"Irina" (Gallant) **5**:128-32, 137
"Iris" (Hesse) **9**:234, 243; **49**:211, 245-46, 248
Irish Fairy Tales (Stephens) **50**:306-09, 318-19, 325-26
"An Irish Problem" (Somerville & Ross) **56**:317
"Irish Revel" (O'Brien) **10**:341
The Irish R.M. and His Experiences (Somerville & Ross) **56**:320, 331, 335
"Iron" (Levi) **12**:256-57, 259, 262
"Iron Hans" (Grimm and Grimm) **36**:200-01
"The Iron Khiva" (Garland) **18**:147, 179
"The Iron Man and the Tin Woman" (Leacock) **39**:266
The Iron Man and the Tin Woman (Leacock) **39**:240
"Iron Mills" (Davis)
    See "Life in the Iron Mills"
"An Iron Will" (Leskov)
    See "Železnaja volja"
"The Ironbark Chip" (Lawson) **18**:217, 263
"The Iron-Man" (Grimm and Grimm) **36**:201
"An Irrelevant Death" (Abe) **61**:9, 11
"An Irrevocable Diameter" (Paley) **8**:390
Irrlichter (Hauptmann) **37**:249, 251
"Is There a Writer in the House?" (Perelman) **32**:235
"Is There Nowhere Else Where We Can Meet?" (Gordimer) **17**:159, 168, 172
"Is Your Name Joe?" (Algren) **33**:88, 107
"Isaac" (Michaels) **16**:303
Isabella of Egypt (Arnim)
    See *Isabella von Ägypten, Kaiser Karl des Fünften erste Jugendliebe*
Isabella von Ägypten, Kaiser Karl des Fünften erste Jugendliebe (Arnim) **29**:10-11, 15-25
Isabelle (Gide) **13**:42-3, 68-70, 72-3, 77-8, 94-9
"Ishui hsiu-ts'ai" (P'u Sung-ling) **31**:199
Isis (Nerval) **18**:338, 362
"Isis in Darkness" (Atwood) **46**:79-80, 98
"La isla a mediodía" (Cortázar) **7**:55-6, 61
"The Island" (Čapek)
    See "Ostrov"
"The Island" (Cheever) **38**:56
"The Island" (Cowan) **28**:76
"The Island" (Pavese) **19**:369
"The Island at Noon" (Cortázar)
    See "La isla a mediodía"
"The Island Dream" (Hesse) **9**:229-33, 235
Island Nights' Entertainments (Stevenson) **51**:232-33, 236, 239-40, 248
"The Island of Fairies" (P'u Sung-ling)
    See "Hsien-jen tao"
Island of Sakhalin (Chekhov)
    See "Ostrov Sakhalin"
"An Island Princess" (Bates) **10**:123
Island Tales (London)
    See *On the Makaloa Mat*
"The Island Ven" (Berriault) **30**:104
"The Islands of St. George" (Appelfeld)
    See "The Isles of St. George"
"Las islas nuevas" (Bombal) **37**:3, 9, 33, 38, 45
"The Isle of Voices" (Stevenson) **11**:269, 283; **51**:247-48
"The Isles of St. George" (Appelfeld) **42**:45, 48
"Isolated Incidents" (Mukherjee) **38**:252-53, 264-65, 272-73, 277
"The Isolation Booth" (Hood) **42**:237

The Isolation Booth (Hood) **42**:236, 238
"Ispoved" (Andrić) **36**:33, 37-8
"Ispoved" (Gorky) **28**:174
"The Istanbul Papers" (Abish) **44**:3, 11
"Istoriia moei golubiatni" (Babel) **16**:9, 15, 17, 20, 36, 41, 59
Istoriia sela Goriukhino (Pushkin) **27**:129-30, 133, 162-63, 171-72, 183
"Istorija lejtenanta Ergunova" (Turgenev)
    See "Istoriya leytenanta Ergunova"
"Istoriya leytenanta Ergunova" (Turgenev) **7**:316, 321, 326, 337, 358-59
"Iswaran" (Narayan) **25**:138, 153, 155
"It Always Breaks Out" (Ellison) **26**:11
"It Grows on You" (King) **17**:295
"It Happened Like This" (Caldwell) **19**:39
"It Helps If You Sing" (Campbell) **19**:77
"It Is Parallels That Are Deadly" (Dreiser)
    See "Tabloid Tragedy"
"It Isn't the Heat, It's the Cupidity" (Perelman) **32**:222, 231
"It May Never Happen" (Pritchett) **14**:263-65, 286, 301, 305
It May Never Happen, and Other Stories (Pritchett) **14**:270
"It Must Have Been Spring" (O'Hara) **15**:266
"It Was the Devil's Work" (O'Flaherty) **6**:259
"It Wouldn't Break Your Arm" (O'Hara) **15**:248, 263, 266
"The Italian Banditti" (Irving) **2**:251, 261
Italian Chronicles (Stendhal)
    See *Chroniques italiennes*
Italian Fables (Calvino)
    See *Fiabe italiene*
Italian Folktales (Calvino)
    See *Fiabe italiene*
"Italian Robber" (Irving) **2**:255
"Italian Sunshine" (Babel) **16**:27-8, 52-3, 55-7
"Itansha no kanashimi" (Tanizaki) **21**:193
"Itchy" (Hammett) **17**:218
"Ithaka" (Davenport) **16**:178-79, 185, 194-95
"It's a Dirty World" (Bukowski) **45**:51, 63
"It's a Young World" (Pohl) **25**:232
"It's about Your Daughter, Mrs. Page" (Jolley) **19**:233
"It's Cold in the Alps" (Farrell) **28**:111
"It's Great to Be Back" (Heinlein) **55**:164-65
Its Image on the Mirror (Gallant) **5**:122-23, 135, 140, 148-49
"It's Just Another Day in Big Bear City, California" (Beattie) **11**:11, 15, 21
"It's Just the Way It Is" (Bates) **10**:114, 137, 139
"It's Nothing Serious" (Pirandello) **22**:229, 264
"It's Perfectly True" (Andersen) **6**:30
"Its Wavering Image" (Far) **62**:20, 50, 62-64, 78, 80, 101, 109, 111-12, 114-17
"Ivan and Mary" (Pilnyak) **48**:285
"Ivan Federovič Špon'ka and His Aunt" (Gogol)
    See "Ivan Federovič Špon'ka i ego tetsuška"
"Ivan Federovič Špon'ka i ego tetsuška" (Gogol) **4**:105, 117, 121; **29**:149; **52**:110, 121, 136, 143, 146, 151
Ivan Ilyitch (Tolstoy) **30**:299; **45**:132
"Ivan the Fool" (Tolstoy) **9**:377, 380-81, 388
"Ivan Zhokh" (Platonov) **42**:266
"The Ivanov Family" (Platonov)
    See "Homecoming"
"I've Got It Made" (Metcalf) **43**:106
"¡Viva el Papa!" (Alarcon) **64**:2, 28, 30-31, 38
"Ivory, Apes, and People" (Thurber) **1**:426
"The Ivory Woman" (Andrić)
    See "Žena iz slonove kosti"
"L'ivrogne" (Maupassant) **1**:274
"Ivy Day in the Committee Room" (Joyce) **3**:201, 205-06, 210-11, 214, 218-21, 225-26, 228, 231, 234, 237, 240, 242, 248; **26**:39-40, 46, 50, 79; **44**:265; **64**:231, 233, 244, 250, 258
"Ivy Gripped the Steps" (Bowen) **3**:31-2, 38, 41, 48, 51; **28**:3-4

Ivy Gripped the Steps (Bowen)
See *The Demon Lover and Other Stories*
"Iya na yatsu" (Endō) **48**:193-95
Izbrannye rasskazy (Pilnyak) **48**:254
"Izerghil the Crone" (Gorky)
See "Starukha Izergil"
"The Izu Dancer" (Kawabata)
See "Izu no Odoriko"
"Izu no Odoriko" (Kawabata) **17**:240-43, 249-50, 252
"Izvozchik" (Gorky) **28**:162
"Jachid and Jechidah" (Singer) **3**:357, 363, 375; **53**:294
"Jack and Gill of the Sierras" (Harte) **8**:214
"Jack in the Box" (Campbell) **19**:76
"The Jack Kerouac Wake" (Moorhouse) **40**:285
"Jack of Diamonds" (Spencer) **57**:224, 229, 242
Jack of Diamonds and Other Stories (Spencer) **57**:220-26, 228-31, 238-39, 242-44
"Jack of the Straw" (Kipling) **54**:77
"Jack the Giant Killer" (Grimm and Grimm) **36**:194
"Jack-a-Boy" (Cather) **50**:75, 104, 106, 187-88, 190, 193, 199, 257
"The Jackdaw" (Hesse) **9**:243-44
"Jack-in-the-Box" (Bradbury) **29**:42, 67, 88-9
Jackpot: The Short Stories of Erskine Caldwell (Caldwell) **19**:16, 25, 37-8, 50
"Jacob and the Indians" (Benét) **10**:143-44, 154
"Jacob and the Other" (Onetti)
See "Jacob y el otro"
Jacob Pasinkov (Turgenev)
See *Yakov Pasynkov*
"Jacob Pasynkov" (Turgenev)
See "Stepnoy Korol 'Lir"
"Jacob: The Faith-Healing Priest" (Head) **52**:189-92, 196, 199, 205-7, 211-12, 222, 227
"Jacob y el otro" (Onetti) **23**:258
"Jacqueline Ess: Her Will and Testament" (Barker) **53**:136, 19, 143, 159, 162, 173, 175-76
"Die Jagd" (Goethe) **38**:189
"Jäger des Spotts" (Lenz) **33**:317-19, 327
Jäger des Spotts (Lenz) **33**:316, 318, 328-29, 331
"Der jäger Gracchus" (Kafka) **5**:210; **29**:349
"Jakov, drug iz detinjstva" (Andrić) **36**:66-7
"Jakov, the Childhood Friend" (Andrić)
See "Jakov, drug iz detinjstva"
"The Jama" (O'Hara) **15**:278, 285
"James Francis and the Star" (O'Hara) **15**:278, 284-85
"Jamesie" (Powers) **4**:368, 371-72
"Jan Godfrey" (Frame) **29**:101, 115-16
"Jan the Unrepentant" (London) **4**:286
"Jane" (Maugham) **8**:356, 378-79
"Janice" (Jackson) **9**:266
"O Jantar" (Lispector) **34**:191, 193
"January" (Barthelme) **55**:76-7, 112
"January Offensive" (Borowski) **48**:6
"Janus" (Beattie) **11**:25-7
"Japanese in Warsaw" (Endō) **48**:211-12
"The Japanese Quince" (Galsworthy) **22**:58, 77, 85-6, 98
"The Jar" (Bradbury) **29**:67, 75, 86, 88; **53**:245
"The Jar" (Pirandello)
See "La giara"
"El jardín" (Borges)
See "El jardín de senderos que se bifurcan"
"El jardín de senderos que se bifurcan" (Borges) **4**:5, 8, 10-11, 13, 16, 18-19, 28; **41**:59, 91, 135-38, 140-41
El jardín de senderos que se bifurcan (Borges) **4**:4, 18; **41**:59, 79, 87, 138, 157-59
"Jasmine" (Mukherjee) **38**:235-37, 245, 252, 254, 267-68, 273, 279-80, 283, 286
Jasmine (Mukherjee) **38**:294
"Jasmine Tea" (Chang) **28**:23; 25; 35
"Jasnovidec" (Čapek) **36**:96, 98, 102, 127
"The Jaunt" (King) **17**:276; **55**:250
"Jazz" (Cabrera Infante) **39**:22

"A Jazz Age Clerk" (Farrell) **28**:119
"Jazz, Jive and Jam" (Hughes) **6**:143-44, 146
"Je ne parle pas français" (Mansfield) **9**:280, 284, 295-96, 310
"Je Suis le Plus Malade des Surréalistes" (Nin) **10**:303-04, 306
"Je suis perdu" (Taylor) **10**:380-81, 416
"Jealous" (Ford) **56**:150, 160-61, 164-66, 177, 195
"The Jealous Extremaduran" (Cervantes)
See "El celoso extremeño"
"The Jealous Hens" (O'Flaherty) **6**:262, 280
"The Jealous Hidalgo" (Cervantes)
See "El celoso extremeño"
"A Jealous Husband" (Adams) **24**:3-4
"Jealousy" (Dreiser)
See "The Shadow"
"Jean Beicke" (Williams) **31**:305, 318, 325, 332-34, 346, 348, 351, 362
Jean Rhys: The Collected Short Stories (Rhys) **21**:67
"Jean-ah Poquelin" (Cable) **4**:67-70, 72-3
"Jean-Pierre" (Spencer) **57**:224, 229-31, 243
"Jeeves and the Dog MacIntosh" (Wodehouse) **2**:355-56
"Jeeves and the Greasy Bird" (Wodehouse) **2**:344
"Jeeves and the Yuletide Spirit" (Wodehouse) **2**:356
"Jeff Brigg's Love Story" (Harte) **8**:216; **59**:311
"Jeffty Is Five" (Ellison) **14**:124-25
"Jehla" (Čapek) **36**:98-9, 127
"Jelena, the Woman Who Does not Exist" (Andrić)
See "Jelena, žena koje nema"
"Jelena, the Woman Who Was Not" (Andrić)
See "Jelena, žena koje nema"
"Jelena, žena koje nema" (Andrić) **36**:51
"Jeli il pastore" (Verga) **21**:283, 286, 295, 298-99, 301
"Jeli, the Shepard" (Verga)
See "Jeli il pastore"
"The Jelly-Bean" (Fitzgerald) **6**:58-9
"Jemima, the Mountain Girl" (Fitzgerald) **6**:45, 58
Jemmy (Nerval) **18**:334, 362
"Jenny Garrow's Lovers" (Jewett) **6**:156-58, 166
"Jericho's Brick Battlements" (Laurence) **7**:252, 259, 267
"Jerry and Molly and Sam" (Carver) **8**:12
"Jesse and Meribeth" (Munro) **3**:347, 349
"The Jest of Jests" (Barnes) **3**:18
Jests of Death and Life (Pirandello)
See *Beffe della morte e della vita*
"Die Jesuiterkirche in G." (Hoffmann) **13**:183
"Jesus Christ in Flanders" (Balzac)
See "Jésus-Christ en Flandre"
"Jesus Said to Watch for 28 Signs" (Moorhouse) **40**:289, 291
Jesus' Son (Johnson) **56**:233-40, 242-46, 249, 251, 253-57, 260-65, 267
"Jesus upon Honshu" (Updike) **13**:360
"Jesusa" (Pardo Bazán) **30**:263, 269
"Jésus-Christ en Flandre" (Balzac) **5**:14, 16-17, 23
"The Jet Set" (O'Hara) **15**:283, 287-88
Jettatura (Gautier) **20**:6-8, 16-17, 19, 21, 31, 33
"Le jeu des grâces" (Villiers de l'Isle Adam) **14**:387
"La Jeune; or, Actress and Woman" (Alcott) **27**:31
Les jeunes-France, romans goguenards (Gautier) **20**:7, 9-11, 13, 22
"The Jew" (Turgenev) **7**:316, 320, 324, 359; **57**:287, 291-92
"The Jew from Babylon" (Singer) **3**:389; **53**:273
"The Jew Who Became a Bird" (Aleichem) **33**:79
"The Jewbird" (Malamud) **15**:171, 173-75, 189, 195, 197-99, 200-02, 204, 220, 235, 240

"The Jewel of Jeopardy" (Coppard) **21**:10
"The Jewels of the Cabots" (Cheever) **1**:101; **38**:54
"The Jewess" (Babel) **16**:35
"The Jewish Refugee" (Malamud)
See "The German Refugee"
"The Jewish Trinity" (Zangwill) **44**:367, 378, 390
"Jigokuhen" (Akutagawa Ryūnosuke) **44**:44-5, 47, 51-4, 56, 65, 68, 72, 76-8, 78, 81
"Jigyô" (Abe) **61**:27
"The Jilting of Granny Weatherall" (Porter) **4**:327-28, 340, 348, 356-58; **43**:177, 179, 235-36, 238, 249, 253-56, 292, 318-19, 325
"The Jilting of Jane" (Wells) **6**:360, 392
"Jim Blaine and His Grandfather's Old Ram" (Twain) **6**:310; **34**:308
"Jim O'Neill" (Farrell) **28**:118-9, 122
"Jim Pemberton and His Boy Trigger" (Saroyan) **21**:156
"Jim Smiley and His Jumping Frog" (Twain)
See "The Celebrated Jumping Frog of Calaveras County"
"Jim Sullivan's Adventures in the Great Show" (Le Fanu) **14**:219
"Jimmy and the Desperate Woman" (Lawrence) **4**:219, 238
"Jimmy Goggles the God" (Wells) **6**:360
"Jimmy Rose" (Melville) **1**:303-04, 325-26; **17**:359, 363
"Jim's Big Brother from California" (Harte) **8**:254
"Jim's Probation" (Dunbar) **8**:122, 127
"Jimsella" (Dunbar) **8**:119, 121, 127, 129, 143, 146
Jin suoji (Chang) **28**:21, 23, 26-28, 31, 34-35, 41-42, 44-47
"Jivitra O Mrita" (Tagore) **48**:327, 339
"Jo" (O'Connor) **5**:382
"The Job" (Saroyan) **21**:142
"The Job Appication" (Walser) **20**:336, 349
"The Jockey" (McCullers) **9**:322, 332, 347, 358; **24**:232
"Joe Craddock's Old Woman" (Caldwell) **19**:43
Joe Wilson and His Mates (Lawson) **18**:202-05, 208-09, 213, 221, 252, 261-62
"Joe Wilson's Courtship" (Lawson) **18**:202-03, 210, 228-29, 232, 252, 258, 262
"Joe's Absence" (Wilding) **50**:347
"Johanna" (Walser) **20**:364
"Johannes-Wassersprung and Caspar-Wassersprung" (Grimm and Grimm) **36**:187
"John and I" (Leacock) **39**:265, 266
"John Archer's Nose" (Fisher) **25**:13, 20
"John Barleycorn Lives" (Boyle) **16**:142-43
"John Barrington Cowles" (Doyle) **12**:85-6
"John Bull" (Irving) **2**:244, 251, 253
"John Bull on the Guadalquivir" (Trollope) **28**:318, 328-29, 331, 340, 348, 354
"John Carter of Mars" (Bradbury) **53**:245
"John Charles Tapner" (Davenport) **16**:180, 193
The John Fante Reader (Fante) **65**:111-12
"John Hitchcock" (Farrell) **28**:96, 124, 127
"John Inglefield's Thanksgiving" (Hawthorne) **3**:189
"John Lamar" (Davis) **38**:133-37, 139
"John Napper Sailing through the Universe" (Gardner) **7**:214, 216-17, 222, 233, 235, 238
"John Nicholson's Predicament" (Stevenson)
See "The Misadventures of John Nicholson"
"John Redding Goes to Sea" (Hurston) **4**:136-38, 149, 153
"Johnnie Brewer" (Warner) **23**:374
"Johnny" (Dreiser)
See "Black Sheep No. One: Johnny"
"Johnny Bear" (Steinbeck)
See "The Ears of Johnny Bear"
"Johnny Mnemonic" (Gibson) **52**:17, 22, 27, 29, 41, 62

"Johnny Pye and the Fool-Killer" (Benét) **10**:142-44, 148, 154, 156-57, 159-60
"The Johnson Girls" (Bambara) **35**:3, 21, 23-4, 35
"Johnsonham, Jr." (Dunbar) **8**:135, 148
"Joining Charles" (Bowen) **3**:30, 47
Joining Charles and Other Stories (Bowen) **3**:30, 33, 40; **28**:4
"Jo-Jo" (Farrell) **28**:119, 122
"Joke" (Dixon) **16**:207
"The Joke on Eloise Morey" (Hammett) **17**:218, 222
"A Joker" (Baudelaire)
    See "Un plaisant"
"The Joker's Greatest Triumph" (Barthelme) **2**:28, 34; **55**:24
"The Jokers of New Gibbon" (London) **4**:266
"Jolene from Moline" (Hood) **42**:235
"The Jolly Corner" (James) **8**:296, 304, 306, 308-09, 326-29; **47**:210, 294
"Jonas ou l'artiste au travail" (Camus) **9**:103, 105, 108-09, 119, 129-35
"Jones's Alley" (Lawson) **18**:238
"Le Jongleur de Taillebois" (Norris) **28**:204, 212
"The Jongleur of Taillebois" (Norris)
    See "Le Jongleur de Taillebois"
"Jon's World" (Dick) **57**:107, 128
"Jordan" (Henderson) **29**:326, 328-29
"Jordan's End" (Glasgow) **34**:57-8, 62-3, 66-7, 75-6, 78, 81, 92, 95-7, 103-04
"Jorinda and Jorindel" (Gallant) **5**:138, 141-44
"Josefina, Take Good Care of the Señores" (Cabrera Infante) **39**:18, 23
"Joseph and His Brother" (Thomas) **20**:290, 292, 319
"Joseph the Dreamer" (Zangwill) **44**:366, 370, 373
"Joseph Yates' Temptation" (Gissing) **37**:67-8
"Josephine" (O'Flaherty) **6**:264
"Josephine de Montmorenci" (Trollope) **28**:321, 340
"Josephine, die Sängerin oder Das Volk der Mäuse" (Kafka) **5**:231, 240, 242; **29**:349-50; **60**:227, 259, 275
"Josephine the Chanteuse" (Kafka)
    See "Josephine, die Sängerin oder Das Volk der Mäuse"
"Josephine, the Mouse" (Kafka)
    See "Josephine, die Sängerin oder Das Volk der Mäuse"
"Josephine the Singer, or the Mouse Folk" (Kafka)
    See "Josephine, die Sängerin oder Das Volk der Mäuse"
"Josephine the Songstress" (Kafka)
    See "Josephine, die Sängerin oder Das Volk der Mäuse"
"Joseph's House" (Evans) **43**:20
"Joshua" (Grau) **15**:156, 168, 164
"Le joueur généreux" (Baudelaire) **18**:19, 41
"Le joujou du pauvre" (Baudelaire) **18**:33-4, 47-51, 53
"Journal" (Michaels) **16**:314, 317
"The Journal of a Superfluous Man" (Turgenev)
    See "Dnevnik lišnego čeloveka"
"The Journal of J. P. Drapeau" (Ligotti) **16**:277, 283, 286
Journal of Katherine Mansfield (Mansfield) **9**:281, 294
"Journey" (Cowan) **28**:76
"A Journey" (Gordimer) **17**:177, 180, 183, 187-88, 190
"The Journey" (Irving) **2**:244, 265
"A Journey" (O'Brien) **10**:333
"The Journey" (Peretz) **26**:214
"The Journey" (Pirandello)
    See "Il viaggio"
"The Journey" (Porter) **4**:352, 358, 363
"A Journey" (Wharton) **6**:423

"Journey Across a Crater" (Ballard) **53**:19, 61, 65
"The Journey and the Dream" (Saroyan) **21**:163
"Journey Back to the Source" (Carpentier)
    See "Viaje a la semilla"
"Journey into Smoke" (Sansom) **21**:124
"Journey into the Woodland" (Turgenev) **57**:305
"The Journey of Alija Djerzelez" (Andrić)
    See "Put Alije Djerzeleza"
"The Journey to Hanford" (Saroyan) **21**:171
"The Journey to Panama" (Trollope) **28**:320, 323, 349-52
"Journey to Polessie" (Turgenev) **7**:335
Journey to the East (Hesse)
    See *Die Morgenlandfahrt*
"Journey to the Heartland" (Aldiss) **36**:10-11, 23, 26-7
"A Journey to the Seven Streams" (Kiely) **58**:150, 167, 169
A Journey to the Seven Streams: Seventeen Stories (Kiely) **58**:144, 154
"The Journeyman's Secret" (Howells) **36**:398
Les jours et les nuits: Roman d'un déserter (Jarry) **20**:46, 50-2, 58-9, 61, 67, 75, 77-9, 82
"Joy" (Singer) **3**:360, 363-64, 368
"Joy of Life" (Galsworthy) **22**:58
"The Joy of Mooching" (Perelman) **32**:235
"The Joy of Nelly Deane" (Cather) **2**:98, 104; **50**:105, 201, 206-7, 246-7, 254
"The Joy of the Just" (Gardner) **7**:226-28
"Joyce" (Gilchrist) **63**:20
"The Joyous Comrade" (Zangwill) **44**:366
"J's Marriage" (Coover) **15**:33, 35, 48, 59
"Juan Manso" (Unamuno) **11**:312
"Juan Muraña" (Borges) **4**:19-20
"Juanita" (Chopin) **8**:98, 110-11
"Judas" (O'Connor) **5**:368-69, 378, 381
"The Judas Tree" (Moravia) **26**:159, 161
"The Judge" (Tagore) **48**:326-28
"Judge Lu" (P'u Sung-ling)
    See "Lu p'an"
"The Judgement" (Kafka)
    See "Das Urteil"
"Judgement Day" (O'Connor) **1**:343, 365
"Judges" (Evans) **43**:18
"The Judge's House" (Stoker) **62**:238, 242-43, 253
"The Judge's Wife" (Allende) **65**:3-4, 6, 18, 20
"The Judge's Wife" (Schnitzler)
    See "Die Frau des Richters"
"The Judgment" (Kafka)
    See "Das Urteil"
"A Judgment in the Mountains" (Benét) **10**:156
"The Judgment of Dungara" (Kipling) **5**:262
"A Judgment of Paris" (Dunbar) **8**:122, 128, 136
"Judith" (Coppard) **21**:12, 17, 29
Judith, and Other Stories (Farrell) **28**:112-3, 116
"Judith Kane" (Spencer) **57**:97-98, 241
"Judy's Service of Gold Plate" (Norris) **28**:201-02, 207
"Jug and Bottle" (Ross) **24**:291, 293, 307, 311
"Jug of Silver" (Capote) **2**:63, 65-6, 70; **47**:4, 10-11, 17, 45, 53-5, 58
"Juggernaut" (Bass) **60**:4, 8-9
"The Juggler Pamphalon" (Leskov)
    See "Skomorox Pamfalon"
The Jules Verne Steam Balloon (Davenport) **16**:198-200
Julia Bride (James) **8**:311-13, 343-45, 347-51
"Julia Cahill's Curse" (Moore) **19**:305, 317, 319, 322, 347-49
"Juliani Kichisuke" (Akutagawa Ryūnosuke) **44**:62
Julie de Carneilhan (Colette) **10**:269-70
"Julip" (Harrison) **19**:216-17
Julip (Harrison) **19**:215-17
"July Storm" (Platonov) **42**:253
"July the Fifteenth, 1988" (Lish) **18**:286
"Jumbo" (Saroyan) **21**:132

"Jumbo's Wife" (O'Connor) **5**:390
"Jump" (Gordimer) **17**:178, 181-82, 185, 187, 190-91
"A Jump Ahead" (Warner) **23**:375
Jump, and Other Stories (Gordimer) **17**:177-89, 191
"Jump to Chicago" (Farrell) **28**:112
"June Recital" (Welty) **1**:474, 480, 483, 485, 495, 497; **51**:265-68, 270, 283, 287, 289, 292-93, 295-300, 302, 304-5, 311, 318-19, 322, 330, 332, 330, 332, 335, 338-40
"Juneteenth" (Ellison) **26**:11
Der junge Tischlermeister (Tieck) **31**:269, 275, 282-83, 287, 290-91
Die Jungfrau als Ritter (Keller) **26**:92, 99, 108
Die Jungfrau und der Teufel (Keller) **26**:107
Die Jungfrau und die Nonne (Keller) **26**:99, 108
"The Jungle" (Bowen) **3**:30, 33, 49
The Jungle Books (Kipling) **5**:277, 279, 282, 285, 287-88, 292-94; **54**:80-3, 88-90, 92-3, 109-16, 119, 121-27, 129, 131-32
"Junior" (Lewis) **34**:163, 165
"The Juniper-Tree" (Grimm and Grimm) **36**:233
"Jupiter Doke, Brigadier-General" (Bierce) **9**:96, 98-100
"Jupiter Five" (Clarke) **3**:124, 129, 134-35, 149
Jürg Jenatsch (Meyer) **30**:186-87, 200, 204, 249
"Jurge Dulrumple" (O'Hara) **15**:282
"Jūrokusai no Nikki" (Kawabata) **17**:248
"A Jury Case" (Anderson) **1**:50
"A Jury of Her Peers" (Glaspell) **41**:278-307
"The Juryman" (Čapek)
    See "Porotce"
"The Juryman" (Galsworthy) **22**:61, 74, 78, 95, 99-100, 102
"Just a Little One" (Parker) **2**:281
"Just Before the War with the Eskimos" (Salinger) **2**:300; **28**:221; **65**:294-95, 304-5, 307-8, 314, 321
"Just Him and Her" (Suckow) **18**:409
"Just like Little Dogs" (Thomas) **3**:403, 406, 411-12; **44**:325, 350-51, 360
"A Just Man in Sodom" (Evans) **43**:29
"Just Meat" (London) **4**:253-54, 262-63, 291
"Just One More Time" (Cheever) **1**:100; **38**:54
"The Just Ones" (Shiga) **23**:336
Just So Stories (Kipling) **5**:273, 279, 287, 293; **54**:89, 91-3, 98
"Just Tell Me Who It Was" (Cheever) **1**:90; **38**:87
"Just Two Old Men" (Metcalf) **43**:108, 141
"A Just Verdict" (P'u Sung-ling)
    See "Che yü"
"Just Waiting" (Campbell) **19**:92
"A Justice" (Faulkner) **1**:147, 177, 181
"Justice" (Galsworthy) **22**:98
"Justice" (O'Hara) **15**:287-88
"The Justice and the Vagabond" (Gissing) **37**:55
"Justicia?" (Pardo Bazán) **30**:264
Jyotaro (Tanizaki) **21**:195, 225
"Kaa's Hunting" (Kipling) **54**:84, 105, 110-13, 122, 131
"The Kabbalists" (Peretz) **26**:206
Kabe-S. Karuma shi no hansai (Abe) **61**:9-10, 21, 25
"Kabiasy" (Kazakov) **43**:59, 69
"Kabnis" (Toomer) **1**:440, 442-44, 446-48, 451-54, 457, 459-60; **45**:181, 191, 196, 209, 211, 214, 233, 242, 260, 265-67, 270, 272, 275, 277-79, 287, 289, 293-94, 297, 304, 316, 333, 336-41, 349, 351, 355-57, 359, 361, 370, 372, 379, 384, 386-87, 390
"Kacheli" (Bunin) **5**:113
"Kaika no satsujin" (Akutagawa Ryūnosuke) **44**:78
"Kain and Artyom" (Gorky)
    See "Kain i Artem"
"Kain i Artem" (Gorky) **28**:137, 159, 190
"Eine Kaiserliche Botschaft" (Kafka) **60**:300-301

"Kak zazhglas' lampa Il'icha" (Platonov) **42**:267

"Kaleidoscope" (Bradbury) **29**:42, 48, 79, 80; **53**:215

"Kalkstein" (Stifter) **28**:283-84, 286, 288-90, 298-99

Kamienny świat (Borowski) **48**:8, 10-11, 13, 15, 18, 26

Kämpande ande (Lagerkvist) **12**:179

"Der Kampf der Sänger" (Hoffmann) **13**:182,212

"The Kanaka Surf" (London) **4**:257, 266

"Kankal" (Tagore) **48**:340

"K'ao-pi ssu" (P'u Sung-ling) **31**:198

Kapitanskaya-dochka (Pushkin) **27**:130-33, 154-62, 164, 175-76, 178-81, 185-86, 188

"Karain" (Conrad) **9**:143

"Karamora" (Gorky) **28**:137, 161-62

"Karataev" (Turgenev) **57**:266

"Karenoshō" (Akutagawa Ryūnosuke) **44**:44, 64, 75, 88-90

"Karintha" (Toomer) **1**:441, 452, 455-56, 459; **45**:175, 181-83, 197, 203-04, 206, 209, 223, 228, 236, 260-67, 277, 285, 325, 334, 348-49, 358-59, 361, 369, 373-75, 380, 386

"Kärleken och döden" (Lagerkvist) **12**:195

"Karl-Yankel" (Babel) **16**:13, 16, 22

"Kartofel'nyy el'f" (Nabokov) **11**:117, 137, 139-40

"Kashtánka" (Chekhov) **2**:130; **51**:52

"Kas'ian of the Beautiful Lands" (Turgenev) **7**:343-45

"Kas'jan of Fair Strath" (Turgenev) **57**:266

"Kata Ucle" (Kawabata) **17**:235, 240-41, 246-47

"Katastrofa" (Nabokov) **11**:131, 133

"Katchen's Caprices" (Trollope) **28**:317, 333

"Kate Lancaster's Plan" (Jewett) **6**:167

"Kate McCloud" (Capote) **47**:65-7

"Kathleen's Field" (Trevor) **21**:246-47, 260, 262, 265, 270, 273-74

"Kathy" (Caldwell) **19**:54

"Katz" (Algren) **33**:106

"Katzenzilber" (Stifter) **28**:298-99, 303, 305-07

"Kazimír Stanislávovich" (Bunin) **5**:81

"Keel and Kool" (Frame)
   See "Keel, Kool"

"Keel, Kool" (Frame) **29**:100-01, 107

"Keela, the Outcast Indian Maiden" (Welty) **1**:468, 470, 497; **27**:338, 352-53; **51**:314, 318

Keep It Crisp (Perelman) **32**:205-06

"Keep Your Pity" (Boyle) **5**:55

"The Keeper of Conscience" (Zangwill) **44**:375, 387

"A Keeper of the Doors" (Evans) **43**:13, 18

"Keeping Fit" (Gordimer) **17**:177, 185, 187-88, 190

"Keesh, the Son of Keesh" (London) **4**:287-88

Kefor 'al ha'arets (Appelfeld) **42**:3, 6, 45, 48

"Keiserens nye Kl[dj]der" (Andersen) **6**:10-11, 13, 16, 18, 26, 30; **56**:33, 36, 38

The Képi (Colette)
   See *Le képi*

Le képi (Colette) **10**:274, 281, 292-93, 295

"The Kerchief" (Agnon)
   See "HaMitpahat"

"Kerfol" (Wharton) **6**:426-28, 431-32

"kesa and Mórito" (Akutagawa Ryūnosuke) **44**:51, 63

Der Ketzer von Soana (Hauptmann) **37**:195, 202, 204-7

"Kew Gardens" (Woolf) **7**:368, 370-71, 374-76, 378, 382-83, 385, 387-88, 392, 398-99, 404-07

Kew Gardens (Woolf) **7**:382

"Kewpie Doll" (Algren) **33**:113

"The Key" (Welty) **1**:468; **51**:260-61, 318, 321

"The Key to My Heart" (Pritchett) **14**:268

"Keys and Watercress" (Metcalf) **43**:72

"The Keystone" (Powers) **4**:376, 381

"Kezia and Tui" (Mansfield) **9**:282

"Kgotla" (Head) **52**:200, 212, 227

"Khadzi murat" (Tolstoy) **9**:376, 378, 394-97; **45**:143, 155, 158

"The Khan and His Son" (Gorky) **28**:144

"Khat" (Dreiser) **30**:113, 115

"A Kholem" (Peretz) **26**:222-23

"Khor and Kalinych" (Turgenev)
   See "Chor' i Kalinyč"

"Khoziain" (Gorky) **28**:189

"Khozyaika" (Dostoevsky) **2**:163, 170-71, 173-74, 181, 191, 193; **44**:98

Khozyain i rabotnik (Tolstoy) **9**:368, 372, 377, 382-86; **45**:128-66; **54**:313-15, 319

"The Kid Nobody Could Handle" (Vonnegut) **8**:432

"A Kidnaping in the Family" (Fante) **65**:86, 95-97, 111

"Kidnapped" (Kipling) **5**:274

"The Kidnapping of President Lincoln" (Harris) **19**:125, 133

"The Kid's Whistling" (Updike) **13**:355

"Kierkegaard Unfair to Schlegel" (Barthelme) **2**:31, 38-9, 54; **55**:14-15, 26, 28, 75-6, 88, 92, 119

"Kiev—a Town" (Bulgakov) **18**:91

"The Kill" (Boyle) **5**:64

"Killed at Resaca" (Bierce) **9**:67, 75-7

"Killer in the Rain" (Chandler) **23**:58, 65-8, 72, 80-2, 85, 87, 92, 98, 102, 104-07

Killer in the Rain (Chandler) **23**:67-8

"The Killers" (Bukowski) **45**:53

"The Killers" (Hemingway) **1**:211, 218-19, 234-36, 242; **25**:84; **40**:166, 184, 191, 209, 211; **63**:56-57

"Killing" (Updike) **13**:402-03, 409

"The Killing Ground" (Ballard) **1**:76; **53**:57

"Killings" (Dubus) **15**:75, 88, 94, 96-7, 100-01

"Kimyōna shigoto" (Oe) **20**:214, 229

"Kin" (Welty) **1**:475-76, 487; **51**:318

Kindergeschichten (Stifter)
   See *Bunte Steine*

"Kinderseele" (Hesse) **9**:218

Kinder-und Hausmärchen (Grimm and Grimm) **36**:175-241

"The Kindest Thing to Do" (Gordimer) **17**:166-67

"The King" (Babel) **16**:17-18, 42-4, 48-9, 59

"The King" (Kipling) **54**:100

"King Bee" (Boyle) **16**:148, 155

"The King Business" (Hammett) **17**:222

"King Gregor and the Fool" (Gardner) **7**:234

"A King Lear of the Steppes" (Turgenev)
   See "Stepnoy Korol 'Lir"

King Leopold's Soliloquy (Twain) **26**:354

"A King Listens" (Calvino) **3**:119

"The King of Folly Island" (Jewett) **6**:154

The King of Folly Island and Other People (Jewett) **6**:154

"The King of Greece's Tea Party" (Hemingway) **1**:208

"The King of Jazz" (Barthelme) **55**:90, 94, 107-8

"King of Schnorrers" (Zangwill) **44**:384

The King of Schnorrers: Grotesques and Fantasies (Zangwill) **44**:366-68, 370, 375, 377-78, 380-81, 384-86, 388-89

"King of the Bingo Game" (Ellison) **26**:3, 10, 13, 19-23, 25

"The King of the Cats" (Benét) **10**:143-44, 158

"The King of the Desert" (O'Hara) **15**:248-49, 270

"The King of the Foxes" (Doyle) **12**:64

"The King of the Golden Mountain" (Grimm and Grimm) **36**:189

"King of the Grey Spaces" (Bradbury)
   See "R Is for Rocket"

"King of the Mountain" (Garrett) **30**:163

King of the Mountain (Garrett) **30**:164-65, 172

"The King of the Trenches" (Lewis) **34**:164, 171

"King Pest" (Poe) **1**:406; **22**:300, 306; **35**:317

"The King Set Free" (Pirandello) **22**:229

"King Thrushbeard" (Grimm and Grimm) **36**:190

"The King Who Lived on Air" (Bates) **10**:112

"King Yu" (Hesse) **9**:244

"Kingdom City to Cairo" (Algren) **33**:107, 109

"The Kingdom of Cards" (Tagore) **48**:301

The Kingdoms of Elfin (Warner) **23**:378-80, 382-85

"King's Ankus" (Kipling) **5**:293; **54**:84, 105, 112-13, 122

"The King's Bride" (Hoffmann)
   See "Königsbraut"

"The King's Favor" (Crane) **56**:95

"The King's in Yellow" (Chandler) **23**:59, 65, 72, 88, 109-10

The King's Indian: Stories and Tales (Gardner) **7**:213-21, 226, 228-29, 235

"The King's Shilling" (Kiely) **58**:145, 154

"Kinjū" (Kawabata) **17**:235, 240-41

"Kinkies" (Trevor) **21**:233

"Kinosaki nite" (Shiga) **23**:344, 346, 348, 352, 359-60

"A Kinsman of His Blood" (Wolfe) **33**:374

"Kiosk Encounter" (Davie) **52**:4-7

Die Kirchenordnung (Arnim) **29**:6

"Kirilka" (Gorky) **28**:161

"Kirin" (Tanizaki) **21**:195, 206-08

"The Kiss" (Babel) **16**:16, 59

"The Kiss" (Carter) **13**:17

"The Kiss" (Chekhov)
   See "Poceluj"

"The Kiss" (Chopin) **8**:72, 111-12

"The Kiss" (Sansom) **21**:83

"The Kiss" (Trevor) **58**:252

"Kiss Me Again, Stranger" (du Maurier) **18**:126, 138

Kiss Me Again, Stranger: A Collection of Eight Stories, Long and Short (du Maurier)
   See *The Apple Tree: A Short Novel and Some Stories*

"The Kiss of Moses" (Peretz) **26**:194

The Kiss to the Leper (Mauriac)
   See *Le baiser au lépreux*

"Kissing the President" (Barthelme) **55**:112

"The Kitchen" (O'Faolain) **13**:311, 320

"The Kitchen Child" (Carter) **13**:17-18

"The Kitchen Colonel" (Freeman) **47**:85, 161

"A Kitchen Knife" (Warner) **23**:370-71

"Kitchenware, Notions, Lights, Action, Camera!" (Perelman) **32**:211

"The Kite" (Maugham) **8**:380

"Kitty" (Appelfeld) **42**:43-45

"Kitty" (Bowles) **3**:76, 80

"Kitty Partners" (Apple) **50**:23, 33-4

"Kitty the Wren" (O'Faolain) **13**:309

"Kj[dj]restefolkene" (Andersen) **56**:30

"Klara Milič" (Turgenev)
   See "Klara Milich"

"Klara Milich" (Turgenev) **7**:321, 324, 326-28, 334, 338, 362

"Klara Milich. After Death" (Turgenev)
   See "Klara Milich (Posle smerti)"

"Klara Milich (Posle smerti)" (Turgenev) **57**:305, 311, 315, 338, 380

Klassik Komix #1" (Millhauser) **57**:156-57

Die Klausenburg (Tieck) **31**:286

"Klee Dead" (Coover) **15**:33, 37, 41

Kleider machen Leute (Keller) **26**:96, 100, 107, 127

"Klein and Wagner" (Hesse) **49**:245-47, 249-51, 253

Klein und Wagner (Hesse) **9**:218, 227, 236-40; **49**:283-84, 286

Klein Zaches gennant Zinnober (Hoffmann) **13**:192-93, 195, 197, 199, 200, 218-19

"Kleine Fabel" (Kafka) **5**:254; **29**:348

"Eine Kleine Frau" (Kafka) **60**:273

Der kleine Herr Friedemann (Mann) **5**:319, 323, 327, 332, 334, 336

"Die Kleine Komödie" (Schnitzler) **15**:377

"Eine Kleine Mothmusik" (Perelman) **32**:213

Kleine Prosa (Walser) **20**:334

"Kleist in Thun" (Walser) **20**:336-37
Kleyne mentshelekh mit kleyne hasoges
　(Aleichem) **33**:6
Klingsohr (Hesse)
　See *Klingsors letzter Sommer*
Klingsohrs letzter Sommer (Hesse)
　See *Klingsors letzter Sommer*
Klingsor (Hesse)
　See *Klingsors letzter Sommer*
"Klingsor's Last Summer" (Hesse) **9**:218, 220,
　227, 240-41; **49**:235, 246-47, 251
Klingsor's Last Summer (Hesse)
　See *Klingsors letzter Sommer*
Klingsors letzter Sommer (Hesse) **9**:219, 227,
　238-39; **49**:211-13, 230, 232-33, 245, 281-
　86, 311-12
"Klods-Hans" (Andersen) **6**:11; **56**:33
"Klokken" (Andersen)
　See "The Bell"
Das Kloster bei Sendomir (Grillparzer) **37**:160
"Kneel to the Rising Sun" (Caldwell) **19**:7, 9,
　17-23, 33, 38, 43, 45-6
Kneel to the Rising Sun, and Other Stories
　(Caldwell) **19**:9, 12, 18-19, 21, 25, 35,
　37-8, 57
"The Knife and the Naked Chalk" (Kipling)
　5:284, 292
"Knife Blows" (Mauriac)
　See "Coups de couteaux"
"The Knife of the Times" (Williams) **31**:302,
　324, 334, 350-51, 357, 359-62
The Knife of the Times (Williams) **31**:302-03,
　320, 324, 330-32, 357-59, 361-62, 365
"The Knife Thrower" (Boell)
　See "Der Mann mit den Messern"
"The Knife Thrower" (Millhauser) **57**:189
"A Knife to Cut Corn Bread With" (Caldwell)
　19:13-14, 38-9
"A Knight" (Galsworthy) **22**:74, 79, 91-4, 97
"A Knight-Errant of the Foothills" (Harte) **8**:249
Knights and Dragons (Spencer) **57**:196-97, 199,
　202-4, 207-12, 214, 219-20, 228, 232, 234-
　37, 240-244
"Knight's Gambit" (Faulkner) **1**:178-81
Knight's Gambit (Faulkner) **1**:151, 178-79
Kniha apokryfů (Čapek) **36**:94, 111-15, 117-18,
　128, 130
"Der Knirps" (Walser) **20**:339
"Knjiga" (Andrić) **36**:37
"The Knock at the Manor Gate" (Kafka) **5**:206;
　60:235-36
"Knock, Knock" (Wilding) **50**:364, 367-68
"Knock...Knock...Knock" (Turgenev)
　See "Stuk...stuk...stuk"
"Knots upon Knots" (Agnon) **30**:38
"Knowledge" (Lish) **18**:275, 283
"Knox" (Ellison) **14**:102, 104-05
Knulp (Hesse) **49**:211, 226
"Kochergà" (Zoshchenko) **15**:398
"Kod kazana" (Andrić) **36**:33, 38, 45, 56
"Kod lekara" (Andrić) **36**:51-2
"Kohkababur Pratyabartan" (Tagore) **48**:310-11
Kohlhaas (Kleist)
　See *Michael Kohlhaas*
"The Kolkhoz Rucksack" (Solzhenitsyn) **32**:394
"Kolymen' City" (Pilnyak) **48**:290
"The Komarov Case" (Bulgakov) **18**:91
"Kometa" (Schulz) **13**:330, 335
Konarmiia (Babel) **16**:2-7, 9-21, 23-7, 29-31,
　35-36, 42, 49-54, 56-60
"Kong Yiji" (Lu Hsun) **20**:149
"Königsbraut" (Hoffmann) **13**:192, 195-96,
　198-200, 223, 226
"Konjiki no shi" (Tanizaki) **21**:196, 209
"Konkin" (Babel) **16**:50
"Konkin's Prisoner" (Babel) **16**:26, 28
"Konovalov" (Gorky) **28**:156, 178, 189
"Koolau the Leper" (London) **4**:269
"Korea" (McGahern) **17**:298, 322
"Korrespondent" (Turgenev)
　See "Peripiska"
"Kosa" (Andrić) **36**:45, 47

"Koster i murav'i" (Solzhenitsyn) **32**:354
"Kotin and Platonida" (Leskov)
　See "Kotin doilec"
"Kotin doilec" (Leskov) **34**:108, 118
"Ko-yi" (P'u Sung-ling) **31**:197
"Kozo no kamisama" (Shiga) **23**:352, 354, 360
Krakonošova zahrada (Čapek) **36**:92, 109
"Krasavets" (Leskov) **34**:131
"Krasavicy" (Chekhov) **51**:175
Krasnoe derevo (Pilnyak) **48**:216, 230, 233-37,
　240, 247-54, 295-97
"Der Kreisel" (Kafka) **60**:297
"Kreisler's Certificate" (Hoffmann) **13**:212
Kreitserova sonata (Tolstoy) **9**:363, 377-78,
　396, 403-06; **30**:298-343; **45**:157; **54**:268
The Kreutzer Sonata (Tolstoy)
　See *Kreitserova sonata*
"Krøblingen" (Andersen) **6**:13; **56**:37
"Kroy Wen" (Boyle) **5**:55
"Krushniker Delegation" (Aleichem) **33**:82
"Kryžovnik" (Chekhov) **2**:136-37, 139, 141-43,
　155-57; **28**:48-72; **51**:130-31, 147-48,
　209-10
"Kshudhita Pashan" (Tagore) **48**:302, 341-45,
　347
"Księga" (Schulz) **13**:328, 334-36, 338
Ku shih hsin pien (Lu Hsun)
　See *Gushi xinbian*
"Ku Yum and the Butterflies" (Far) **62**:4, 53
"Ku Yum's Little Sister" (Far) **62**:20, 36, 38,
　55
"K'uang-jen jih-chi" (Lu Hsun)
　See *Kuangren riji*
Kuangren riji (Lu Hsun) **20**:125-26, 128, 141,
　144, 148, 151
Kuča na osami (Andrić) **36**:63-8, 78-9
"Kudo" (Endō) **48**:206
"Kuei-li" (P'u Sung-ling) **31**:200
"Kuma" (Shiga) **23**:346, 348
"Kumonoito" (Akutagawa Ryūnosuke) **44**:52,
　59-60, 75-6
"Kung-sun Chiu-niang" (P'u Sung-ling) **31**:200
"Kung-sun Hsia" (P'u Sung-ling) **31**:192
"Kuniko" (Shiga) **23**:346-48, 352
"Der Kuntsenmakher" (Peretz) **26**:198, 217
"Kuo shêng" (P'u Sung-ling) **31**:205
"Kupón" (Čapek) **36**:96, 128
"Kurōdiasu no nikki" (Shiga) **23**:339, 345-46,
　348, 361-64
"Kusatsu Spa" (Shiga) **23**:349
"Der Kuss von Sentze" (Stifter) **28**:299
"Kuyarka enitsja" (Chekhov) **51**:104
"Kylin" (Akutagawa Ryūnosuke) **44**:54
"The Kylin" (Tanizaki)
　See "Kirin"
"Kyō" (Akutagawa Ryūnosuke) **44**:80
"Kyofu" (Tanizaki) **21**:193
"De la grafología como ciencia aplicada"
　(Cortázar) **7**:95
"Labour Day Dinner" (Munro) **3**:346
"The Labyrinth" (Nin) **10**:317, 319
Labyrinths (Borges)
　See *Labyrinths: Selected Stories, and Other
　Writings*
*Labyrinths: Selected Stories, and Other
　Writings* (Borges) **41**:49-52, 56-64, 66,
　77, 132, 135-37, 140, 148-49, 157, 162-63,
　165, 168
"A Lack of Passion" (Hemingway) **40**:191
"Os Laços de família" (Lispector) **34**:194-95
Laços de família (Lispector) **34**:184-85, 187-
　97, 201-02, 211, 213-18
"The Ladder" (Pritchett) **14**:296
Ladies and Escorts (Thomas) **20**:287-90, 292,
　317, 319-20
"Ladies and Gentleman" (Spark) **10**:356
"Ladies and Gentlemen, into the Gas Please"
　(Borowski)
　See "This Way for the Gas, Ladies and
　Gentlemen"
"Ladies in Spring" (Welty) **51**:318
"Ladies' Shoes" (Walser) **20**:356

"El lado de la sombra" (Bioy Casares) **17**:95
El lado de la sombra (Bioy Casares) **17**:87, 95
"The Lady" (Andrić)
　See "Gospodjicd"
"A Lady" (Donoso)
　See "Una señora"
"The Lady and the Masters of History"
　(Farrell) **28**:126
"The Lady and the Pedlar" (Agnon) **30**:40
"The Lady Bandit" (Pardo Bazán) **30**:290
"The Lady Cornelia" (Cervantes)
　See "La Señora Cornelia"
"Lady Eleanore's Mantle" (Hawthorne) **3**:184
"The Lady from Guatemala" (Pritchett) **14**:268
"The Lady from Lucknow" (Mukherjee)
　38:238-41, 250, 252-55, 265, 271-73, 278
"The Lady from the Land" (Thurber) **1**:424
Lady Godiva and Other Stories (Moravia)
　See *Un'altra vita*
"The Lady Iceway" (Hardy) **2**:205; **60**:180,
　207-8
"The Lady in the Lake" (Chandler) **23**:65, 67,
　72, 82-3, 88-9, 109-10
"The Lady in the Looking-Glass: A Reflection"
　(Woolf) **7**:375-76, 378-80, 388, 392, 399,
　407-12
"The Lady Knight-Errant" (P'u Sung-ling)
　See "Hsia-nü"
"Lady Lucifer" (O'Faolain) **13**:300-02, 304-07
"A Lady Macbeth of the Mtsensk District"
　(Leskov)
　See "Ledi Makbet Mcenskogo uezda"
"Lady Mottisfont" (Hardy) **2**:208; **60**:179-80,
　205, 207
"A Lady of Bayou St. John" (Chopin) **8**:72, 84,
　87, 91, 106, 110
"The Lady of Beasts" (Pavese)
　See "La belva"
"The Lady of Launay" (Trollope) **28**:311, 322-
　23, 334, 344, 355, 357
"The Lady of Moge" (Le Guin) **12**:211, 213
"The Lady of the House of Love" (Carter) **13**:9,
　28
"The Lady of the Lake" (Malamud) **15**:168,
　178, 181, 217, 220
"The Lady of the Monor" (Chekhov)
　See "Barnja"
"The Lady of the Sagas" (O'Connor) **5**:371
"The Lady on 142" (Thurber) **47**:374-75, 382,
　389-90
"The Lady on the Gray" (Collier) **19**:104
"The Lady Penelope" (Hardy) **2**:209; **60**:180
"Lady Perkins" (Lardner) **32**:148
"The LAdy Roku-no-miya" (Akutagawa
　Ryūnosuke) **44**:50
"A Lady Slipper" (Dunbar) **8**:122
"Lady Tal" (Lee) **33**:304
"The Lady Turned Peasant" (Pushkin)
　See "Baryshnia-krest'ianka"
The Lady Who Sold Furniture (Metcalf) **43**:72,
　75, 79-80, 101-2, 105, 107-10, 114, 120,
　125, 127-28, 131, 140-42
"Lady with a Lamp" (Parker) **2**:273-74, 280,
　285
"Lady with a Little Dog" (Chekhov)
　See "Dama s sobačkoj"
"A Lady with Pearls" (Gilchrist) **63**:8
"The Lady with the Dog" (Chekhov)
　See "Dama s sobačkoj"
"The Lady With the Pet Dog" (Chekhov)
　See "Dama s sobačkoj"
"The Lady with the Pet Dog" (Oates) **6**:234
"The Ladybird" (Lawrence) **4**:219, 231, 238-39
"The Lady-Peasant" (Pushkin)
　See "Baryshnia-krest'ianka"
"Lady's Dream" (Wolff) **63**:325-26, 337
"The Lady's Maid" (Mansfield) **9**:303, 311;
　23:139
"The Lady's Maid's Bell" (Wharton) **6**:427
"The Lady's Walk" (Oliphant) **25**:209
"The Lagoon" (Conrad) **9**:143-44, 152
"The Lagoon" (Frame) **29**:99-101, 105

The Lagoon and Other Stories (Frame) **29**:99-103, 105-08, 110, 111, 115

"Lágrimas de Xerxes" (Machado de Assis) **24**:128-29

"Laila min haLelot" (Agnon) **30**:38

"The Lake" (Bradbury) **29**:84-5, 88; **53**:245

"The Lake" (Cowan) **28**:78

"The Lake" (Pavese) **19**:369

The Lake (Moore) **19**:316, 318, 332, 334-39, 353-60

"Lake Greifen" (Walser) **20**:352, 364

"A Lake of Home-brew" (Bulgakov) **18**:92

"The Lake of Peace" (Bass) **60**:17

"Lake Segden" (Solzhenitsyn)
    See "Ozero Segden"

The Lamb (Mauriac)
    See *L'angeau*

"The Lame Shall Enter First" (O'Connor) **1**:343-45, 356, 365; **61**:156, 202-5

"The Lament" (O'Flaherty) **6**:276

"The Lamentable Comedy of Willow Wood" (Kipling) **5**:261

"Lamentations" (Evans) **43**:43

Laments for the Living (Parker) **2**:272, 274

"The Lamias" (Wells) **6**:380

"The Lamp" (Agnon)
    See "ha-Panas"

"The Lamp at Noon" (Ross) **24**:289-93, 295, 302, 309, 311, 319

The Lamp at Noon, and Other Stories (Ross) **24**:294, 300, 304, 306, 312, 319-20

"A Lamp in the Window" (Capote) **2**:80

"The Lamp of Psyche" (Wharton) **6**:424, 427

"The Lamplighter" (Dickens) **17**:124

"Lance" (Nabokov) **11**:108

"Lance Jack" (Lewis) **40**:271, 276

"The Land and the Water" (Grau) **15**:161

"A Land Beyond the River" (Stuart) **31**:227, 263

"The Land Ironclads" (Wells) **6**:374, 380, 403

The Land of Darkness, along with Some Further Chapters in Experience of the Little Pilgrim (Oliphant) **25**:185-86, 196

"Land of Exile" (Pavese)
    See "Terra d'esilio"

"The Land of Promise" (Zangwill) **44**:375, 387

"The Land of the Free" (Far)
    See "In the Land of the Free"

The Land of the Spirit (Page) **23**:307-08, 312

"The Land They Gave Us" (Rulfo)
    See "Nos han dado la tierra"

"Land Where My Fathers Died" (Dubus) **15**:81, 86

"The Land Where There Is No Death" (Benét) **10**:160

"Ein landarzt" (Kafka) **5**:213, 216, 230, 246; **29**:345, 349, 369; **60**:231, 234-38, 289, 291-92

"The Landauers" (Isherwood) **56**:200, 204, 210, 224-27

"The Landing" (O'Flaherty) **6**:264, 269, 273, 276-77

"Landing in Luck" (Faulkner) **1**:177

"The Landlady" (Dostoevsky)
    See "Khozyaika"

"A Landlocked Sailor" (Jewett) **6**:156

"The Landlord" (Pritchett) **14**:255, 296

A Landlord's Morning (Tolstoy) **9**:376, 399

"The Landmarker" (Auchincloss) **22**:9, 12

"The Landowner" (Turgenev) **7**:313

"Land's End" (Welty) **51**:274

"The Landscape Chamber" (Jewett) **6**:154; **44**:226

"Landsend" (Selby) **20**:258, 261, 263, 265, 281

Der Landvogt von Greifensee (Keller) **26**:94, 109, 111, 113, 115

"Der Längere Arm" (Lenz) **33**:317-18, 333-36

"The Langhe Hills" (Pavese) **19**:377

The Langoliers (King) **17**:280, 282-84

The Langston Hughes Reader (Hughes) **6**:122-23

"The Language of Flowers" (Warner) **23**:368, 387

Lantern Slides (O'Brien) **10**:345-46

"Le lapin" (Maupassant) **1**:263, 274

"Lappin and Lapinova" (Woolf) **7**:376-77, 388, 393-94, 398

"L'Lapse" (Barthelme) **2**:40

"A Lapse of Judgment" (Tagore)
    See "Durbuddhi"

"Laquelle des deux? Histoire perplexe" (Gautier) **20**:13

"Laquelle est la vraie?" (Baudelaire) **18**:6

"La larga historia" (Onetti) **23**:247

"The Largest Theme Park in the World" (Ballard) **53**:35, 67, 113

"Las Vegas Charley" (Yamamoto) **34**:348-49, 352-53, 359-60

"The LaSalle Hotel in Chicago" (Saroyan) **21**:149

"The Last" (Dixon) **16**:217

The Last Address (Lowry)
    See *Lunar Caustic*

"The Last Adventure of the Brigadier" (Doyle) **12**:83

"The Last Anniversary" (Caldwell) **19**:54

"The Last Asset" (Wharton) **6**:424-25

"The Last Austrian Who Left Venice" (Trollope) **28**:319, 323

"The Last Bus" (Agnon)
    See "Ha'Autobus ha'Aharon"

"The Last Cab Driver, and the First Omnibus Cad" (Dickens) **17**:121, 125

"The Last Carousel" (Algren) **33**:98, 111, 114

The Last Carousel (Algren) **33**:95-8

The Last Circle (Benét) **10**:160

"The Last Crop" (Jolley) **19**:245

"The Last Day" (Verga) **21**:298, 300

"The Last Day in the Field" (Gordon) **15**:120, 128, 142

"The Last Day of Shraft" (Somerville & Ross) **56**:318, 331

Last Days (Oates) **6**:254

"Last Days in Deephaven" (Jewett) **6**:167

"The Last Demon" (Singer) **3**:383; **53**:294

"Last Descent to Earth" (Lish) **18**:283

"The Last Dream of the Old Oak" (Andersen) **6**:18, 40

"The Last Escapade" (Alarcon)
    See "La última calaverada"

Last Exit to Brooklyn (Selby) **20**:253-57, 264-65, 267-68, 273-75, 277-79

"The Last Feast of Harlequin" (Ligotti) **16**:274, 277-80, 282-83, 287, 289, 297

"The Last Fiddling of Mordaunts Jim" (Dunbar) **8**:122, 149

"The Last Flight of Father" (Schulz)
    See "Ostatnia ucieczka ojca"

"The Last Flower" (Thurber) **47**:366

"The Last Galley" (Doyle) **12**:80

"The Last Gas Station" (Grau) **15**:148-49, 152, 154, 160

"The Last Gift" (Freeman) **47**:103

"The Last Illusion" (Barker) **53**:154, 161-62

The Last Inspection (Lewis) **40**:271-72, 275-77, 280-82

"The Last Judgment" (Čapek)
    See "Poslední soud"

"The Last Kiss" (Gordimer) **17**:154

"The Last Laugh" (Lawrence) **19**:277-79

The Last Laugh (Perelman) **32**:235-38

"The Last Leaf" (Henry) **5**:185; **49**:203

"The Last Leaf" (Porter) **4**:339, 352-53, 358, 361; **43**:306-7

"The Last Letter of a Litterateur" (Schnitzler)
    See "Derletzebrief eines literaten"

"The Last Man That Time" (Bradfield) **65**:66

"Last May" (Dixon) **16**:203

"The Last Mohican" (Malamud) **15**:169, 171, 175, 179, 181-82, 187, 192-93, 195-96, 211-12, 219, 222

"The Last News" (Price) **22**:386

"The Last Night in the Old Home" (Bowen) **3**:41

"The Last of a Long Correspondence" (Price) **22**:388

The Last of Chéri (Colette)
    See *La fin de Chéri*

"The Last of the Belles" (Fitzgerald) **6**:46-8, 100, 103; **31**:33

"The Last of the Legions" (Benét) **10**:143, 154

"The Last of the Masters" (Dick) **57**:70, 104

"The Last of the Spanish Blood" (Garrett) **30**:173, 180

"Last Orders" (Aldiss) **36**:19, 24-5

Last Orders, and Other Stories (Aldiss) **36**:18-20, 23-27

"The Last Pearl" (Andersen) **6**:36

"The Last Refuge" (Appelfeld) **42**:43

"The Last Resort" (Dixon) **16**:215-16

"The Last Ride" (Sansom) **21**:116

Last Round (Cortázar)
    See *Ultimo round*

"Last Rung on the Ladder" (King) **55**:250

The Last Summer (Pasternak)
    See *Povest*

"Last Supper" (Endō) **48**:209, 212

Last Tales (Dinesen) **7**:162, 166, 171, 175-76, 180-81, 191, 198, 200

"The Last Tea" (Parker) **2**:274, 285

"The Last Term" (Kipling) **54**:96

"The Last Things of Man" (Čapek)
    See "Poslední věci člověka"

"The Last Throw" (Pritchett) **14**:273

"The Last Trolley Ride" (Calisher) **15**:11

The Last Trolley Ride (Calisher) **15**:5

"The Last Visit" (Aiken) **9**:13, 29-30

"The Last Voyage of the Ghost Ship" (García Márquez)
    See "El último viaje del buque fantasma"

"Last Wishes" (Trevor) **21**:262

"The Last Word" (Greene) **29**:217, 223, 229

"A Last Word" (Sansom) **21**:93, 112

The Last Word and Other Stories (Greene) **29**:216-17, 223-30

Last Words (Crane) **7**:103

"The Last World of Mr. G." (Ballard) **53**:9

The Last Worthless Evening (Dubus) **15**:81, 85-6, 96

"A Late Encounter with the Enemy" (O'Connor) **1**:356; **23**:192, 205, 237-38

"The Late Henry Conran" (O'Connor) **5**:369, 371, 398

"Late, Late Show" (O'Hara) **15**:278-79

Late Prose (Hesse) **9**:230

"The Late Sir Glamie" (Warner) **23**:384

"A Late Supper" (Jewett) **6**:166

"Late 299" (Galsworthy) **22**:78, 101

"Late-Blooming Flowers" (Chekhov)
    See "Cvety zapozdalye"

"The Latehomecomer" (Gallant) **5**:130, 133, 136-37

Later the Same Day (Paley) **8**:412, 419

"The Latin Scholar" (Hesse) **9**:230-32, 235

"La lattaia regina" (Calvino) **48**:97

"Das Läufer" (Lenz) **33**:317-18, 329

"A Laugh and a Look" (Alcott) **27**:31-2

Laughable Loves (Kundera)
    See *Směsné lásky*

"The Laughing Man" (Salinger) **2**:293, 296, 299, 313-14, 316; **65**:294, 304-5, 307-9, 316

"Laughing Sam" (Saroyan) **21**:135

Laughing to Keep from Crying (Hughes) **6**:111-12, 116, 119, 121-22, 127, 131, 133

"Laughter" (Dybek) **55**:139, 154

"Laughter" (O'Connor) **5**:390-91

"Laughter and Grief" (Leskov) **34**:127

"The Laughter of Akiva" (Ozick) **60**:307, 311

"The Laughter of Gioia" (Moravia) **26**:150-51

"Laura, Immortal" (Saroyan) **21**:139, 143

"Lauth" (Norris) **28**:204, 208-10, 212

"Lavana" (Narayan) **25**:131

"Lavin" (McGahern) **17**:302, 322

"Lavinia: An Old Story" (Paley) **8**:412

"The Law Breaker" (O'Hara) **15**:283
"The Law of Life" (London) **4**:287-89, 292
"The Law of the Jungle" (Cheever) **1**:99
"The Law of the Jungle" (Kipling) **54**:83
"Lawley Road" (Narayan) **25**:139, 157, 174
Lawley Road, and Other Stories (Narayan) **25**:132-35, 137, 139, 152, 155
"The Lawn Party" (Beattie) **11**:6-7
"El lay de Aristotle" (Arreola) **38**:6
"Layaways" (Dixon) **16**:206, 208
"Lazarus" (Dybek) **55**:126
A Lazy Man's Dreams (Moravia)
     See *I sogni del pigro: Racconti, miti e allegorie*
"Lazy Sons" (Calvino) **3**:112; **48**:146
"Léa" (Barbey d'Aurevilly) **17**:9-11
"Lead" (Levi) **12**:264, 268, 281
"The Leader of the People" (Steinbeck) **11**:207-10, 212-13, 217-18, 220-21, 233, 236, 242; **37**:330, 333-34, 336, 340, 342, 351, 354, 356-57, 359-60
"Leaf" (Porter) **43**:307
"A Leaf From the Sky" (Andersen) **6**:6
"Leaf Season" (Updike) **13**:401
Leaf Storm (García Márquez)
     See *La hojarasca*
"The Leaf Sweeper" (Spark) **10**:356, 366
"The League of Old Men" (London) **4**:265, 287
"Leander's Light" (Page) **23**:307, 312
"The Leaning Tower" (Porter) **4**:331, 339-40; **31**:124, 126-27, 161, 173, 177, 182, 186, 188, 190, 228, 234, 253, 292
The Leaning Tower, and Other Stories (Porter) **4**:331, 347, 352; **31**:124; **43**:139, 182, 343
"The Leap" (Barthelme) **2**:45, 55; **55**:29, 90
"The Leap" (Oates) **6**:250, 252
"The Leap Frog" (Andersen) **6**:7, 10
"A Lear of the Steppes" (Turgenev)
     See "Stepnoy Korol 'Lir"
"Learnin'" (Fisher)
     See "The South Lingers On"
Learning Processes with a Deadly Outcome (Kluge)
     See *Lernprozesse mit tödlichem Ausgang*
"Learning to Be Dead" (Calvino) **3**:113
"Learning to Fall" (Beattie) **11**:10, 13, 22-3, 29
"Learning's Little Tribute" (Wilson) **21**:322, 333, 346, 356-57
"The Leather Funnel" (Doyle) **12**:65-6, 76
"The Leather Jacket" (Pavese)
     See "La giachetta di cuoio"
"Leaves" (Dazai Osamu)
     See "Ha"
"Leaves" (Updike) **13**:375-77, 379
"Leaving School" (Gordimer) **17**:166
"Leaving the Yellow House" (Bellow) **14**:22-3, 25-6, 32-3, 35, 37
"Leaving This Island Place" (Clarke) **45**:72, 81, 87, 94
Das Lebens Überfluss (Tieck) **31**:286-87, 291
Lebensläufe (Kluge) **61**:49-55, 57, 74-76, 78-80, 82-83
"Lección de cocina" (Castellanos) **39**:30, 45, 47, 51, 52, 53, 60, 62, 75, 76, 80, 82
"Lechery" (Phillips) **16**:325, 327-28, 337
"Lecturer in Morphology" (James) **16**:251
"Ledi Makbet Mcenskogo uezda" (Leskov) **34**:108, 116, 118, 128, 130-34
"Ledokhod" (Pilnyak) **48**:249
"Leela's Friend" (Narayan) **25**:138
"The Lees of Happiness" (Fitzgerald) **6**:45, 58-9
The Left Bank, and Other Stories (Rhys) **21**:33, 39, 44, 48, 58, 61-3, 65, 68-71
"The Left-handed Craftsman" (Leskov)
     See "Levša"
"The Left-Handed Smith and the Steel Flea" (Leskov)
     See "Levša"
"The Lefthander" (Leskov)
     See "Levša"
"Legacy" (Vinge) **24**:328-29, 332, 334-36, 338

"The Legacy" (Woolf) **7**:376-77, 388, 393-95
"The Legend" (Wharton) **6**:429, 437
"Legend of Khalif Hakem" (Nerval)
     See *L'histoire du Calife Hakem*
"The Legend of Lapwater Hall" (Morrison) **40**:365
"The Legend of Madame Krasinska" (Lee) **33**:310
"The Legend of Miss Sasagawara" (Yamamoto) **34**:348-49, 352, 355, 357-58, 360-62, 379
"The Legend of Pig-Eye" (Bass) **60**:16, 19
"Legend of Prince Ahmed Al Kemel, or The Pilgrim of Love" (Irving) **2**:267
"The Legend of Saamstadt" (Harte) **8**:250
The Legend of Saint Julien Hospitaller (Flaubert)
     See *La légende de Saint-Julien l'Hospitalier*
The Legend of Saint Julien the Hospitator (Flaubert)
     See *La légende de Saint-Julien l'Hospitalier*
"The Legend of Sleepy Hollow" (Irving) **2**:239, 241, 243-51, 253, 255, 259-60; **37**:265-84
"Legend of the Arabian Astrologer" (Irving) **2**:267
"The Legend of the Moor's Legacy" (Irving) **2**:246, 254, 268
"Legend of the Rose of Alhambra" (Irving) **2**:246, 268
"The Legend of the Scribe" (Agnon) **30**:8-9, 11, 66
"Legend of the Three Beautiful Princesses" (Irving) **2**:267
"La légende de l'éléphant blanc" (Villiers de l'Isle Adam) **14**:397
La légende de Saint-Julien l'Hospitalier (Flaubert) **11**:37-9, 42, 45, 53, 55, 61, 63, 65, 70, 78-9, 81, 84, 89-92; **60**:110-16, 125-26, 130-31, 154, 158-60, 171
"La légende du Mont-Saint-Michel" (Maupassant) **1**:285, 288
"Légende poldève" (Aymé) **41**:11, 12-13, 17
"Legends" (Adams) **24**:9
"The Legends of Henry Everett" (Auchincloss) **22**:48
"Legends of the Fall" (Harrison) **19**:201-02, 204-06, 209
Legends of the Fall (Harrison) **19**:204-07, 209-11, 213-15
A legião estrangeira (Lispector) **34**:187-91, 231, 235
Das Leiden eines Knaben (Meyer) **30**:188-90, 204, 219-20
"Leil zeva'ah" (Peretz) **26**:223-24
"Lejana" (Cortázar) **7**:52, 56-7, 81
"Lekh-lekh" (Aleichem) **33**:8
"The Lemon" (Thomas) **3**:396, 399, 407-08; **44**:345, 354
"Lemonade" (Lavin) **4**:166
"Lêng shêng" (P'u Sung-ling) **31**:205, 207
"Lenin and the Firewood" (Zoshchenko) **15**:407
"Lenin and the Sentry" (Zoshchenko) **15**:407, 409
"Lenin and the Stovemaker" (Zoshchenko) **15**:407
Lenin in Zurich (Solzhenitsyn) **32**:399-400, 403, 406
"The Lenton Croft Robberies" (Morrison) **40**:349
"Leon, dvoreckij syn" (Leskov) **34**:108, 112, 125
"Un león en el bosque de Palermo" (Bioy Casares) **17**:95
"Leon the Butler's Son" (Leskov)
     See "Leon, dvoreckij syn"
"Leonard" (O'Hara) **15**:278
"The Leonardo" (Nabokov) **11**:117
"Leopard George" (Lessing) **6**:186, 190; **61**:131
"Leopard in a Temple" (Lish) **18**:275
"The Leper's Helix" (Coover) **15**:59
Lernprozesse mit tödlichem Ausgang (Kluge) **61**:54-57, 63, 71, 74, 76, 80-81, 83

"Less Delicate than the Locust" (Bukowski) **45**:52
Lessness (Beckett)
     See *Sans*
"The Lesson" (Bambara) **35**:2, 4-6, 32
"The Lesson" (O'Hara) **15**:290
"A Lesson in Pets" (Stoker) **62**:252
"The Lesson of the Master" (James) **8**:279, 282, 302
"Lest the Traplock Click" (Algren) **33**:113
"Let It Go" (Empson) **40**:215
"Let the Ants Try" (Pohl) **25**:227, 230-32, 234-35
"Let the Old Dead Make Room for the Young Dead" (Kundera) **24**:86, 88-9, 91-2, 101, 103, 107-08, 116-18, 121
"Let Them Call It Jazz" (Rhys) **21**:49-50, 53, 65
"Let There Be Honour" (Boyle) **5**:56; **121**:33
"Let There Be Light" (Clarke) **3**:130
"Let There be Light" (Heinlein) **55**:207, 216-17
"Let Us Now Praise Stupid Women" (Atwood) **46**:75-5, 83, 99
Let Your Mind Alone! and Other More or Less Inspirational Pieces (Thurber) **1**:414, 422-23, 426
"Letanía de la orquídea" (Fuentes) **24**:38, 54-5
"Letovanje na jugu" (Andrić) **36**:51-2
"Let's Beat Down the Poor" (Baudelaire)
     See "Assommons les pauvres"
"Let's Get Organized" (Čapek) **36**:130
"The Letter" (Agnon)
     See "HaMikhtav"
"A Letter" (Babel) **16**:27-8, 50
"A Letter" (Chekhov) **28**:62-3
"The Letter" (Chekhov)
     See "Pis'mo"
"Letter" (Clarke)
     See "Letter of the Law of Black"
"The Letter" (Maugham) **8**:359, 361, 367, 373-74, 382
"The Letter" (Oates) **6**:236
"The Letter" (O'Flaherty) **6**:262, 265, 276, 280
"A Letter from 1920" (Andrić)
     See "Pismo iz 1920 godine"
"Letter from His Father" (Gordimer) **17**:169, 171
"A Letter from Home" (Lessing) **6**:199
"Letter from the Year 1920" (Andrić)
     See "Pismo iz 1920 godine"
"Letter of the Law of Black" (Clarke) **45**:110
"A Letter That Never Reached Russia" (Nabokov) **11**:132
"The Letter That Was Never Mailed" (Barnes) **3**:13
"Letter to a Young Lady in Paris" (Cortázar)
     See "Carta a un senorita en París"
"A Letter to Peachtree" (Kiely) **58**:165
A Letter to Peachtree and Nine Other Stories (Kiely) **58**:165-67
"A Letter to Rome" (Moore) **19**:320, 332, 347, 350, 352
"The Letter Writer" (Singer) **3**:360, 384
"The Letters" (Wharton) **6**:424-25, 427, 436
"The Letters" (White) **39**:280-81, 286, 289, 292, 294, 299, 312, 316-17, 323, 325, 327-28, 344
"Letters from the Earth" (Twain) **26**:330
Letters from the Underworld (Dostoevsky)
     See *Zapiski iz podpol'ya*
"Letters from Tula" (Pasternak)
     See "Pis'ma iz Tuly"
"Letters in the Wind" (Dazai Osamu) **41**:239
"Letters to an Ex-wife Concerning a Reunion in Portugal" (Moorhouse) **40**:323
"Letters to an Old Garibaldian" (Chesterton) **46**:120
"Letters to the Editore" (Barthelme) **2**:40
"The Letters to Twiggy" (Moorhouse) **40**:290, 303, 322
"Letting Go" (Grau) **15**:161-62

"Letting in the Jungle" (Kipling) 54:84, 105, 112, 123, 131, 134-36
"Un letto di passaggio" (Calvino) 3:112; 48:80, 147
"Lettre d'un fou ou Qui sait?" (Maupassant) 64:316
Lettre d'un Turc (Voltaire) 12:359
"Lettura di un'onda" (Calvino) 48:120, 123
"Letty Coe" (Gissing) 37:63, 79
Der letzte Betrug ist ärger als der erste (Tieck) 31:274
Die Leute von Seldwyla (Keller) 26:89, 102, 106, 108, 115, 117, 125, 127
"Leutnant Gustl" (Schnitzler) 61:290, 292-93
Leutnant Gustl (Schnitzler) 15:345, 351-53, 375; 61:298
"The Level Crossing" (Warner) 23:368
"The Level-Crossing" (Narayan) 25:141, 154
"Leviathan" (Wolff) 63:263, 301, 316, 319-20, 338
"Levitation" (Ozick) 15:307, 318; 60:308, 315
Levitation: Five Fictions (Ozick) 15:306, 312, 318-19
"Levša" (Leskov) 34:112, 116, 123-25
"Liadin and Curithir" (Moore) 19:311
"Liaisons Dangereuses" (Zoshchenko) 15:399
Liao-chai chih-i (P'u Sung-ling) 31:183-88, 193-206, 211-21
Liaozhai zhiui (P'u Sung-ling)
  See Liao-chai chih-i
Liaozhai's Records of the Strange (P'u Sung-ling)
  See Liao-chai chih-i
"The Liar" (Faulkner) 1:177
"The Liar" (James) 8:275, 296, 318, 320-21
"The Liar" (Wolff) 63:260, 282, 298-301, 303, 305, 310, 319-21, 341
The Liar (James) 47:202
"Liars" (O'Faolain) 13:312
"The Liars" (Pritchett) 14:285-86, 296
"The Libation" (Jolley) 19:223, 234, 242
"Libbie Marsh's Three Eras" (Gaskell) 25:46, 54, 58
"The Liberal Lover" (Cervantes)
  See "El amante liberal"
"The Liberation" (Stafford) 26:278, 283, 286-87, 312
"The Liberation of Jake Hanley" (Oates) 6:230
"Libertà" (Verga) 21:312
"Libertad" (Arreola) 38:4
"Libertarianism" (Wilding) 50:374
"The Libertine" (Bulgakov) 18:89
"Liberty" (Arreola)
  See "Sinesio de Rodas"
"Liberty" (O'Faolain) 13:296, 322-23
"Liberty Hall" (Lardner) 32:117, 135-36, 139-40, 145, 159
"The Library Horror" (Gardner) 7:226
"The Library of Babel" (Borges)
  See "La biblioteca de Babel"
"The Library of Byzantium" (Ligotti) 16:278-80
The Library Policeman (King) 17:282-84; 55:250, 260, 263
"The Library Window" (Oliphant) 25:186, 193, 196, 203
Libro que no muerde (Valenzuela) 14:366, 368
"El libro talonario" (Alarcon) 64:3-4, 9
"Lica" (Andrić) 36:63
Lica (Andrić) 36:46, 50, 63
"Licciu papa" (Verga) 21:292
"Lice" (Akutagawa Ryūnosuke) 44:42, 50, 57-8;
"The License" (Pirandello)
  See "La patente"
"Lichen" (Munro) 3:347-49
"El licienciado Vidriera" (Cervantes) 12:4, 8, 14-15, 17, 36, 38-40
"A Lickpenny Lover" (Henry) 5:163, 171, 186
"Lída" (Čapek) 36:92, 121-24
"The Lie" (Banks) 42:56, 65-6
"The Lie" (Carver) 8:34

"Die Liebesgeschichte des Kanzlers Schlick und der schonen Sienerin" (Arnim) 29:27
"Ein Liebesversuch" (Kluge) 61:50, 75, 79
Liebeswerben (Tieck) 31:286
"Lieblingsspeise der Hyänen" (Lenz) 33:317
"Lien-hsiang" (P'u Sung-ling) 31:209
"Lien-hua kung-chu" (P'u Sung-ling) 31:190
"Lies" (Endō) 48:209
"Lies and Lilies" (Stoker) 62:251
"Lieutenant" (O'Hara) 15:248-49
"Lieutenant Boulanger" (Kluge) 61:50, 75
"The Lieutenant Died Last" (Greene) 29:223, 225
Lieutenant Gustl (Schnitzler)
  See Leutnant Gustl
"Lieutenant Yergunov's Story" (Turgenev)
  See "Istoriya leytenanta Ergunova"
"Life" (Davis) 38:106-07, 110, 113
"Life" (Endō) 48:212
"Life" (Head) 52:192, 196, 199, 204, 208, 212, 216, 227, 236-37
"Life" (Machado de Assis) 24:153
"Life" (O'Flaherty) 6:260, 269, 271, 277-78, 280
The Life Adventurous and Other Stories (Farrell) 28:119
"Life along the Passaic River" (Williams) 31:304, 324, 332, 350, 362
Life along the Passaic River (Williams) 31:300, 306, 318, 320, 324, 332, 340, 343, 345-46, 351, 357, 362-65
"Life among the Oilfields" (Yamamoto) 34:351, 359
"The Life and Adventures of Matthew Pavlichenko" (Babel)
  See "The Life Story of Pavlichenko"
Life and Death in the Charity Ward (Bukowski) 45:47, 49, 52, 56-8, 60
"The Life and Death of God" (Ballard) 53:18, 58
"Life and Letters" (Saroyan) 21:160
"The Life and Work of Professor Roy Millen" (Warren) 4:387, 389-90, 395, 400; 58:354
"A Life at Angelo's" (Benét) 10:144
"Life, Death" (Sansom) 21:94, 103, 105, 108, 110-11, 118, 126
"Life Everlastin'" (Freeman) 1:192, 195; 47:147
"Life Hutch" (Ellison) 14:112-15, 117
"Life in Death" (Poe) 54:157-60, 227
"Life in Its Nakedness" (Pirandello)
  See "La vita nuda"
"Life in the Iron Mills" (Davis) 38:96, 98-106, 116-19, 123, 125, 127, 129, 131, 133-35, 142-45, 150
"Life Is Better than Death" (Malamud) 15:173-75, 223
"Life Is No Abyss" (Stafford) 26:302, 308
"Life Is Not to Be Taken too Seriously" (Rulfo)
  See "La vida no es muy seria en sus cosas"
"Life Isn't a Short Story" (Aiken) 9:9, 13-14, 32, 40
"The Life of a Bum" (Bukowski) 45:62, 64-8
"The Life of a Certain Idiot" (Akutagawa Ryūnosuke)
  See "Aru ahō no isshō"
"Life of a Peasant Woman" (Leskov)
  See "Zhitié odnói báby"
"The Life of Death" (Barker) 53:157, 159, 162, 168
The Life of Death: Tales of Terror (Barker) 53:141
"The Life of Imagination" (Gordimer) 17:158, 172
"Life of Ma Parker" (Mansfield) 9:281, 310, 313-14
"A Life of Matter and Death" (Aldiss) 36:28
"The Life of Nancy" (Jewett) 6:152
"The Life of Pavlichenko" (Babel)
  See "The Life Story of Pavlichenko"

"The Life of Tadeo Isidoro Cruz" (Borges)
  See "Biografía de Tadeo Isidoro Cruz (1829-1874)"
"Life on the Earth" (Gilchrist) 14:162
"A Life Spent at Frivolous Writing" (Akutagawa Ryūnosuke)
  See "Ge saku Zammai"
"Life Story" (Barth) 10:43, 47-8, 51-5, 73-4, 77-80, 83, 85-7, 91, 97-8, 100
"The Life Story of Pavlichenko" (Babel) 16:28, 51-2
"The Life to Come" (Forster) 27:92, 96, 103, 105, 106, 111, 123, 124
The Life to Come, and Other Stories (Forster) 27:89-90, 102, 104, 106-09, 115, 117, 124
"Life Uniforms" (Abish) 44:20
"Life Vanquished" (Lagerkvist) 12:187
"Life with Freddie" (Wodehouse) 2:344
"The Life You Save May Be Your Own" (O'Connor) 1:343-44, 348-49, 356, 359-60; 23:184, 210-11, 227, 237; 61:227-29, 231
"The Lifeguard" (Beattie) 11:16
"Lifeguard" (Updike) 13:348, 350, 398-99; 27:323
"Lifeline" (Heinlein) 55:159-61, 206, 216, 227, 229, 233
"The Life-Ration" (Aymé) 41:5
Life's Handicap (Kipling) 5:274, 291
Life's Little Ironies (Hardy) 2:205-08, 210, 212, 214-16, 220, 222-23; 60:177, 180-81, 184-85, 192
"The Lift" (Doyle) 12:78, 80
"The Lift That Went Down into Hell" (Lagerkvist)
  See "Hissen som gick ner i helvete"
"Ligeia" (Poe) 1:377, 379-80, 385, 393-97, 399; 22:290, 299, 305-06, 308, 318, 325, 330, 351; 34:274; 35:321, 331; 54:161, 166, 180, 184-85, 198, 209
"Light" (O'Flaherty) 6:265, 280
"The Light at Birth" (Berriault) 30:105
"A Light Breath" (Bunin)
  See "Light Breathing"
"Light Breathing" (Bunin) 5:81, 93, 104
"Light Can Be Both Wave and Particle" (Gilchrist) 14:162
Light Can Be Both Wave and Particle (Gilchrist) 14:161-62; 63:4, 7, 16, 20-21, 27-28
The Light in the Piazza (Spencer) 57:193-95, 198-204, 208-9, 212, 219-21, 223, 228, 231-37, 240, 247
"The Light of the World" (Hemingway) 1:242, 245; 40:257; 63:103
"Light Shining Out of Darkness" (Hood) 42:183, 214-17, 222, 242
"The Lighter When Needed" (O'Hara) 15:252
"The Lighthouse" (Bates) 10:115-17
"Lightning" (Barthelme) 2:51; 55:93, 110-11
"The Lightning-Rod Man" (Melville) 1:298, 303-04; 17:361
"Lights" (Chekhov) 41:190; 51:164, 166
"Lights" (Dybek) 55:130
"The Light-Years" (Calvino) 3:104; 48:154, 157
"Den liile Idas Blomster" (Andersen) 6:3-4, 6, 23, 30; 56:36
"Den liile pige med Svovlstikkerne" (Andersen) 56:37
"Like a Bad Dream" (Boell) 23:6
"Like a Lover" (Wescott) 35:357, 363, 365, 368-72
"Like a Queen" (Anderson) 1:31, 52-3
"Like All Other Men" (McGahern) 17:321
"Like Glass" (Beattie) 11:13
"Like Mother Used to Make" (Jackson) 9:272; 39:211, 214, 215, 217, 223, 227
"Like Old Times" (O'Hara) 15:250
"Like That" (McCullers) 9:342, 345, 354-55
"Like the Night" (Carpentier) 35:106
"Like the Sad Heart of Ruth" (Taylor) 10:376, 410

"Like the Sun" (Narayan) **25**:140
"Like Yesterday" (Sansom) **21**:127
"Liking Men" (Atwood) **2**:20
"Lilacs" (Chopin) **8**:72, 87, 108-10, 112
"Lilacs" (Lavin) **4**:171
"Liliana llorando" (Cortázar) **7**:62-3
"Liliana Weeping" (Cortázar)
    See "Liliana llorando"
"The Lilies" (Chopin) **8**:93
Lilít e altri racconti (Levi) **12**:260, 263, 272-73, 276, 280
"Lilith" (Nin) **10**:317, 319
"Lilith, and Other Stories" (Levi)
    See *Lilít e altri racconti*
"Lilith's" (Campbell) **19**:76
"Det lilla fälttåget" (Lagerkvist) **12**:179, 182, 195
"Lille Claus og Store Claus" (Andersen) **6**:4, 11, 13, 16, 18, 26, 30, 37; **56**:33, 36-40
"Den Lille Havfrue" (Andersen) **6**:6-7, 11-13, 18, 26-30, 36-7, 40-1; **56**:3-4, 6-7, 12, 31, 36, 38
"Lily Bell and Thistledown" (Alcott) **27**:39
"Lily Daw and the Three Ladies" (Welty) **1**:470, 482, 497
"The Lily's Quest" (Hawthorne) **3**:181
"Limbo" (Huxley) **39**:161
"Limbo" (Lavin) **4**:167
Limbo (Huxley) **39**:153-54, 162, 166-67, 171-73
"Limestone" (Stifter)
    See "Kalkstein"
Limestone and Other Stories (Stifter) **28**:283, 285
Limits and Renewals (Kipling) **5**:278, 283; **54**:77
"The Limits of Fantasy" (Campbell) **19**:85
"The Limpet" (du Maurier) **18**:128
"The Limping Lady" (Coppard) **21**:10
"Lin John" (Far) **62**:33, 39, 41, 50, 75
"Linda" (Pardo Bazán) **30**:293
Linda Tressel (Trollope) **28**:317, 323
"The Lindy Hop" (Fisher) **25**:10-11, 16-19, 22
"Line and Colour" (Babel)
    See "Colour and Line"
"The Line of Apelles" (Pasternak)
    See "Il tratto di Apelle"
"Lines" (Davie) **52**:4
Lines of Life (Mauriac)
    See *Destins*
"The Linesman" (Frame) **29**:98
"Lingering Love" (Chang) **28**:26-27; 31; 33-34
"A língua do 'p'" (Lispector) **34**:211
"The Linguister" (Murfree) **22**:189
"Linha reta e linha curva" (Machado de Assis) **24**:132, 151
"Linoleum Roses" (Cisneros) **32**:42
"Lion" (Faulkner) **1**:182; **35**:147-48, 161
"Lion" (Garrett) **30**:166
"The Lion and the Lizard" (Thurber) **47**:362
"The Lion at Morning" (Wolfe) **33**:374
"The Lion Hunter" (Garrett) **30**:165, 172
The Lion of Comarre (Clarke) **3**:145, 148
"A Lion on the Freeway" (Gordimer) **17**:164, 191-92
"Lionizing" (Poe) **35**:336
"The Lion's Den" (Pritchett) **14**:271
"Lions, Harts, Leaping Does" (Powers) **4**:371, 377-78, 380, 384
"The Lion's Skin" (Maugham) **8**:379
"The Lippia Lawn" (Stafford) **26**:284, 296
"Lips to Lips" (Nabokov) **11**:117
"Lisa" (Beauvoir) **35**:60, 62-4, 66, 68-71
"Lisheen Races, Second-Hand" (Somerville & Ross) **56**:294, 316, 318, 320, 331, 336
"Lispet, Lispett & Vaine" (de la Mare) **14**:60, 80, 85
"Lispeth" (Kipling) **5**:262
"La Liste" (Aymé) **41**:16
Listen to the Mockingbird (Perelman) **32**:245
"Listening" (Paley) **8**:420
"Le Lit" (Maupassant) **64**:329
"Le lit 29" (Maupassant) **1**:274; **64**:340, 343

Literary Lapses (Leacock) **39**:264, 266
"The Literary Life of Laban Goldman" (Malamud) **15**:235
"Literary Talk" (Michaels) **16**:316
"The Literature Teacher" (Chekhov)
    See "Uitel' Slovesnosti"
"The Litigants" (Singer) **3**:385
"Litter" (Campbell) **19**:75
"A Little Album" (Dazai Osamu)
    See "Chiisai arubamu"
"Little Annie's Dream" (Alcott) **27**:39
"The Little Berliner" (Walser) **20**:336
"Little Bessie" (Twain) **6**:339
"The Little Bishop" (Kiely) **58**:147
"The Little Black Box" (Dick) **57**:70
"The Little Black Goat" (Pirandello) **22**:252
"The Little Blond Fellow" (Farrell) **28**:92, 118
"The Little Boy and His Dogs" (Harris) **19**:196
"A Little Boy Lost" (Coppard) **21**:17
"Little Briar-Rose" (Grimm and Grimm) **36**:204-05, 208
"Little Brother" (Wideman) **62**:258-59, 269
"The Little Brown Girl" (Spencer) **57**:208, 210, 215
"Little Bud" (Alcott) **27**:39
"Little Bull" (Cortázar)
    See "Torito"
"Little Caruso" (Saroyan) **21**:167
"A Little Child Shall Lead Them" (Harper) **15**:371
Little Children (Saroyan) **21**:134, 143, 153, 158, 175
"The Little Chill" (Boyle) **16**:148, 155
"Little Claus and Big Claus" (Andersen)
    See "Lille Claus og Store Claus"
"A Little Cloud" (Joyce) **3**:205, 209-10, 226, 231, 234, 245, 248; **26**:46-7; **44**:263, 284, 288; **64**:222, 230-37, 242-43, 258
"The Little Comedy" (Schnitzler)
    See "Die Kleine Komödie"
The Little Comedy, and Other Stories (Schnitzler) **15**:371
"A Little Companion" (Wilson) **21**:325, 329, 332, 337, 339, 346-47, 356-57
"Little Compton" (Harris) **19**:124, 131, 174, 178
"The Little Countess" (Čapek) **36**:128
"The Little Cousins" (Taylor) **10**:383-84
"Little Curtis" (Parker) **2**:274, 280-81, 283
"Little Darby" (Page) **23**:284, 291, 296-98, 307, 328
"Little Did I Know" (Calisher) **15**:7
The Little Disturbances of Man (Paley) **8**:388, 391, 395, 407, 410, 414
"Little Dog" (Hughes) **6**:109, 121-23, 129-30, 142
"The Little Dog Laughed to See Such Sport" (Saroyan) **21**:162
"Little Dramas of the Curbstone" (Norris) **28**:199, 213-14
The Little Dream (Galsworthy) **22**:60
"Little Fable" (Kafka)
    See "Kleine Fabel"
"The Little Fan" (Pirandello)
    See "Il ventaglino"
"The Little Farm" (Bates) **10**:116
"The Little Fat One" (Far) **62**:50
"The Little Fears" (Sansom) **21**:88
"The Little Fir Tree" (Andersen)
    See "The Fir-Tree"
"A Little Free Mulatto" (Chopin) **8**:105
"Little French Mary" (Jewett) **6**:155
"The Little Girl" (Mansfield) **9**:281, 284, 315-16; **38**:204
The Little Girl, and Other Stories (Mansfield) **9**:281, 301
"The Little Girl Continues" (Barnes)
    See "The Grande Malade"
"The Little Girl in Green" (Leacock) **39**:265
"A Little Girl Tells a Story to a Lady" (Barnes)
    See "Cassation"

"The Little Girl's Room" (Bowen) **3**:33, 43
"Little Girls Wiser than Men" (Tolstoy) **9**:388
"The Little Glass Bottle" (Lovecraft) **52**:262
"The Little Governess" (Mansfield) **9**:283
"The Little Gray Goat" (Zoshchenko) **15**:407-09
"Little Gulliver" (Alcott) **27**:41
"The Little Heidelberg" (Allende) **65**:33
"The Little Hero" (Dostoevsky) **2**:171, 189-90
Little Herr Friedemann (Mann)
    See *Der kleine Herr Friedemann*
"The Little Hours" (Parker) **2**:274, 281
"The Little House" (Bowles) **3**:76
"The Little House" (Jackson) **9**:270-71
"Little Ida's Flowers" (Andersen)
    See "Den liile Idas Blomster"
"Little Imber" (Forster) **27**:115, 117-18
"The Little Kingdom" (Tanizaki) **21**:218
The Little Kingdom of J. Franklin Payne (Millhauser) **57**:172-73, 175-76
Little Kingdoms (Millhauser) **57**:172-74, 176
"Little Klaus and Big Criticism" (Andersen)
    See "Lille Claus og Store Claus"
"The Little Knife" (Chabon) **59**:73-74, 76, 79
"Little Lizzy" (Mann) **5**:322-23, 327, 331, 334-36
"A Little Local Color" (Henry) **5**:191
"The Little Madonna" (Pirandello) **22**:254
"The Little Maid at the Door" (Freeman) **47**:134-36
"A Little Maid at the Door" (Freeman) **47**:86, 104, 132
The Little Man, and Other Stories (Galsworthy) **22**:59-60, 97, 99
"The Little Man in Black" (Irving) **2**:242
"The Little Match Girl" (Andersen) **6**:18-9, 25-6, 30, 41; **56**:38
"The Little Match Seller" (Andersen)
    See "The Little Match Girl"
"Little Memento" (Collier) **19**:109
"The Little Mermaid" (Andersen)
    See "Den Lille Havfrue"
"Little Mexican" (Huxley) **39**:156, 161-62
Little Mexican (Huxley) **39**:156, 168, 171, 173, 175-76
"Little Miracles, Kept Promises" (Cisneros) **32**:16, 23, 25, 35-36, 38
The Little Misery (Mauriac)
    See *La sagouin*
"Little Miss Universe" (Saroyan) **21**:134
"The Little Mistress" (Coppard) **21**:21, 28
"The Little Mother" (O'Connor) **5**:371-72
Little Novels (Schnitzler) **15**:342-43
Little Novels of Sicily (Verga)
    See *Novelle rusticane*
"A Little of Chickamauga" (Bierce) **9**:99
"Little Old Spy" (Hughes) **6**:131
Little People with Little Minds (Aleichem)
    See *Kleyne mentshelekh mit kleyne hasoges*
"The Little Photographer" (du Maurier) **18**:127, 138
"The Little Pilgrim Goes Up Higher" (Oliphant) **25**:185
A Little Pilgrim in the Unseen (Oliphant) **25**:180, 185
"A Little Place off the Edgware Road" (Greene) **29**:193, 217
Little Poems in Prose (Baudelaire)
    See *Petits poèmes en prose: Le spleen de Paris*
"The Little Pot" (Aleichem)
    See "Dos tepl"
"A Little Prep." (Kipling) **54**:97
"The Little Prince" (Lavin) **4**:165-67, 183
"A Little Ramble" (Walser) **20**:364
"The Little Red Book" (Pirandello) **22**:252
"The Little Red Hen Tells All" (Atwood) **46**:83, 99
"Little Red Riding Hood" (Grimm and Grimm) **36**:184, 203, 208
"Little Red-Cap" (Grimm and Grimm)
    See "Little Red Riding Hood"

"The Little Regiment" (Crane) **7**:102, 106; **56**:109

The Little Regiment, and Other Episodes of the American Civil War (Crane) **7**:102

"A Little Respect" (Selby) **20**:275

"The Little Room" (Sansom) **21**:83, 89, 124

"The Little Sailor" (Sansom) **21**:102

"The Little Sea-Maid" (Andersen)
See "Den Lille Havfrue"

"The Little Shoemakers" (Singer) **3**:356, 375, 378, 383-84; **53**:301, 323

The Little Stepmother (Storm)
See *Viola tricolor*

"Little Tembi" (Lessing) **6**:191, 197

"Little Things in Bishops' Lives" (Leskov) **34**:127

"The Little Tree" (Walser) **20**:364

"Little Tuk" (Andersen) **6**:3-4

"The Little Virgin" (Hughes) **6**:127

"The Little Voice" (Campbell) **19**:87

"The Little White Dog" (O'Flaherty) **6**:280

"Little Willie" (Gordimer) **17**:154

"A Little Woman" (Kafka) **5**:239; **29**:358

"The Little Wrens and Robins" (Kiely) **58**:145, 147, 157

Little Zack (Hoffmann)
See *Klein Zaches gennant Zinnober*

"Liu Liang-ts'ai" (P'u Sung-ling) **31**:205

"Live? Our Computers Will Do That for Us" (Aldiss) **36**:19, 26

"Liver Pâté" (Čapek) **36**:130

"Lives" (Andrić)
See "Životi"

Lives of Girls and Women (Munro) **3**:323, 325-28, 330-33, 335-36, 338-46

"The Lives of the Poets" (Atwood) **2**:3-4, 6, 10-11; **46**:34, 39, 57, 63, 72-3

"Lives of the Poets" (Stafford) **26**:285

"Lives of the Saints" (Berriault) **30**:103

"Living" (Cowan) **28**:80

"The Living" (Lavin) **4**:167

"Living" (Paley) **8**:391, 408-09, 416

"Living and Dead" (Tagore)
See "Jivitra O Mrita"

"The Living and the Dead" (Saroyan) **21**:146, 168

Living at Home (Gordon) **59**:239-43, 245-46, 248-54, 259, 269, 272

"The Living Flame" (Čapek) **36**:82

"Living or Dead?" (Tagore) **48**:301-2

"A Living Relic" (Turgenev) **7**:321-22, 326, 337; **57**:264, 266, 317-18

"Living Relics" (Turgenev)
See "A Living Relic"

"Livingstone's Companions" (Gordimer) **17**:157, 173

Livingstone's Companions (Gordimer) **17**:157-58, 168, 181, 186, 189

"Livvie" (Welty) **1**:467, 469, 471; **27**:338; **51**:265, 319

"Lizabeth: The Caterpillar Story" (Wideman)
See "Lizbeth: The Caterpillar Story"

"Lizards in Jamshyd's Courtyard" (Faulkner) **1**:177

"Lizbeth: The Caterpillar Story" (Wideman) **62**:261, 275-76

"Lizer's First" (Morrison) **40**:366

"Lizerunt" (Morrison) **40**:328, 330, 335-36, 338, 343, 355, 365-67, 370, 378

"Lizzie Leigh" (Gaskell) **25**:46, 54, 59, 65, 70-2

"Ljubav u kasabi" (Andrić) **36**:34-5, 48

"Ljubka the Cossack" (Babel) **16**:48

"Ljuvabi" (Andrić) **36**:67-8

"El llano en llamas" (Rulfo) **25**:250, 262, 264-65, 267-68

El llano en llamas, y otros cuentos (Rulfo) **25**:244, 247-49, 251, 253, 256, 265, 270-73, 277-80

"Lo" (Faulkner) **35**:159

"A Loaded Bag" (Davie) **52**:8

"The Loaded Dog" (Lawson) **18**:201, 206, 217, 242, 244-45, 248, 262-63

"The Loan" (Malamud) **15**:169, 212, 216, 220, 234

"Local Customs" (Thomas) **20**:320-21

"Lo-ch'a hai-shih" (P'u Sung-ling) **31**:200

"Loco de amor" (Arreola) **38**:6

"Locomotive 38, the Ojibway" (Saroyan) **21**:169

"The Locum Tenens" (Warner) **23**:372

"The Locusts" (Bradbury) **53**:207, 253-54

"The Lodger in Maze Pond" (Gissing) **37**:52, 65

"A Lodging for the Night: A Story of François Villon" (Stevenson) **11**:269, 279, 284-86; **51**:218-19, 236, 248

"Lofty" (Beattie) **11**:29

"Lofty" (O'Connor) **5**:382

"Logarithms" (Singer) **3**:388

"Logging and Pimping and 'Your Pal, Jim'" (Maclean) **13**:260, 270-71

"Logic of Empire" (Heinlein) **55**:199, 208-10, 237

"Lohengrin, fils de Parsifal" (Laforgue) **20**:86, 89, 91-2, 101, 105, 114-6

"Lohengrin, Son of Parsifal" (Laforgue)
See "Lohengrin, fils de Parsifal"

"Lohengrin's Tod" (Boell) **23**:5

"Lois the Witch" (Gaskell) **25**:37-8, 47, 55-7, 60, 72-3

"Lokis" (Mérimée) **7**:276-7, 283, 285-6, 296-9

"The Lombardy Poplar" (Freeman) **47**:163, 193

"London Hospital" (Morrison) **40**:354, 365

"The London Times of 1904" (Twain) **26**:331

"The Lone Charge of Francis B. Perkins" (Crane) **7**:108

"The Lone Charge of William B. Perkins" (Crane) **56**:110

"Lone Wolf's Old Guard" (Garland) **18**:147

"The Loneliest Man in the U.S. Army" (Boyle) **5**:55

"Loneliness" (Anderson) **1**:30, 44

"Loneliness" (Bukowski) **45**:54

"Loneliness" (Schulz) **13**:330

"The Lonely Day" (Caldwell) **19**:20

"The Lonely One" (Grau) **15**:155

"A Lonely Ride" (Harte) **8**:210

"Lonely Rock" (O'Connor) **5**:371-72

"The Lonely Track" (Lawson) **18**:225

"The Loner" (Kazakov) **43**:47

"The Loner" (Lu Hsun)
See "Guduzhe"

"Lonesome Ben" (Chesnutt) **54**:45

"Lonesome Road" (Berriault) **30**:97

"The Long Affair" (Onetti)
See "La larga historia"

"Long After Bedtime" (Leacock) **39**:240

Long after Midnight (Bradbury) **29**:78, 81-2

"The Long Arm" (Freeman) **47**:102-03, 123, 170-74, 177

The Long Arm (Freeman) **47**:103

"Long Black Song" (Wright) **2**:360-63, 365, 367, 369, 371, 374, 376, 379-81, 387

"The Long Day" (Gordon) **15**:104, 106, 119, 139-40

"The Long Distance Runner" (Paley) **8**:397-98, 408-09, 415

"The Long Dress" (Pirandello)
See "La veste lunga"

"The Long Exile" (Tolstoy)
See "God Sees the Truth but Waits"

"A Long Fourth" (Taylor) **10**:374-77, 379, 387-88, 397-400, 402

A Long Fourth, and Other Stories (Taylor) **10**:375-76, 381, 384-86, 395

"Long Live the Pope!" (Alarcon)
See "¡Viva el Papa!"

"Long, Long Ago" (Bunin) **5**:82

"The Long, Long Day" (Betts) **45**:26

The Long March (Styron) **25**:283, 285-88, 291-94, 296, 300, 305-6, 308-12, 316, 319-21, 323, 325

"The Long Night" (Bambara) **35**:27-8, 40-1

"Long Night" (Price) **22**:384

"A Long Night" (Warner) **23**:375

"The Long Rain" (Bradbury) **29**:80

"The Long Road to Ummera" (O'Connor) **5**:362-65, 378, 380, 383, 388-89, 397-98

"The Long Run" (Wharton) **6**:418, 424-25, 436

"The Long Sheet" (Sansom) **21**:82-3, 88, 92, 100

"The Long Thoughts" (Dybek) **55**:126, 142

"The Long Tongue" (Chekhov) **51**:109

The Long Valley (Steinbeck) **11**:207-08, 210, 221, 225-27, 229-34, 236, 239-40, 244-45, 249

"The Long Walk to Forever" (Vonnegut) **8**:424

"The Long Watch" (Heinlein) **55**:166, 200

"The Long Years" (Bradbury) **53**:193-96, 210-11, 246, 248-49, 251, 259

"A Long-ago Affair" (Galsworthy) **22**:101

"The Longest Day of the Year" (Beattie) **11**:30, 34

"The Longest Science Fiction Story Ever Told" (Clarke) **3**:133

"Longing for Mother" (Tanizaki)
See "Haha no kouru ki"

"Look at All Those Roses" (Bowen) **3**:55; **28**:4

Look at All Those Roses (Bowen) **3**:33, 39, 41, 28

"Look Homeward, Jeannie" (Thurber) **47**:368

"Look How the Fish Live" (Powers) **4**:368, 373-74, 376-77

Look How the Fish Live (Powers) **4**:375-76, 380-82

Look Who's Talking! (Perelman) **32**:202, 205

Looking Backwards (Colette) **10**:293

"Looking Down from Above" (Hood) **42**:151, 183, 203, 214-15, 218-19, 221-22, 239-40, 242

"Looking 'Em Over" (Farrell) **28**:90, 92, 119, 121

"Looking for a Rain God" (Head) **52**:188, 191, 200, 204, 211, 227-28

"Looking for Mr. Green" (Bellow) **14**:3, 22-3, 25, 27-8, 30-2

"The Looking Glass" (de la Mare) **14**:66, 84, 87, 90

"The Looking Glass" (Machado de Assis)
See "O espelho"

"Looking Out" (Campbell) **19**:75

"A Looking-Glass for Saint Luke" (Coppard) **21**:8

"The Loons" (Laurence) **7**:255, 259, 270

"Loophole" (Clarke) **3**:125, 148-50

"Loopy Ears" (Bunin)
See "Petlistye ushi"

"Loose Ends" (Mukherjee) **38**:252-53, 261-62, 266, 273, 283, 285

"Loppen og Professoren" (Andersen) **56**:34-35

"Lord Arthur Savile's Crime: A Study of Duty" (Wilde) **11**:362, 366-69, 371, 373, 375-77, 394, 399-402

Lord Arthur Savile's Crime, and Other Stories (Wilde) **11**:407

"Lord Curzon's Benefit Day" (Bulgakov) **18**:90, 110

"Lord Douglas" (Lawson) **18**:243

"Lord Emsworth Acts for the Best" (Wodehouse) **2**:346, 348

"Lord Emsworth and the Girl Friend" (Wodehouse) **2**:346-49

"The Lord Knows" (Greene) **29**:222

Lord Love Us (Sansom) **21**:84, 102, 111, 118, 125

"Lord Mountdrago" (Maugham) **8**:369, 380

"The Lord of the Dynamos" (Wells) **6**:361, 365-67, 375-76, 381-82, 396-97

"Lord Susanoo" (Akutagawa Ryūnosuke) **44**:49

"The Lord's Day" (Powers) **4**:380-81

"Lorelei of the Roads" (Sansom) **21**:94, 102

"The Los Amigos Fiasco" (Doyle) **12**:81

"De los reyes futuros" (Bioy Casares) **17**:54

"Lose With a Smile" (Lardner) **32**:120

Lose with a Smile (Lardner) **32**:116-17, 129

"A Losing Game" (Powers) **4**:370

"Loss" (Oates) 6:236
"The Loss of a Friend by Cablegram"
　　(Moorhouse) 40:306
"Loss of Breath" (Poe) 1:407; 22:334; 54:166,
　　191, 228-30
"The Lost" (Boyle) 5:57, 74-6
"The Lost" (Campbell) 19:62-3, 74, 83
"The Lost" (Dazai Osamu) 41:240, 245
"Lost" (Dybek) 55:130
"The Lost Art of Twilight" (Ligotti) 16:269,
　　271, 273
"Lost Ball" (Bates) 10:123
"The Lost Blend" (Henry) 5:163
"The Lost Boy" (Wolfe) 33:340, 342-45, 355-
　　57, 360-64, 372-75, 386, 399, 401
"Lost Cat" (Adams) 24:18
"Lost City of Mars" (Bradbury) 29:81
"Lost Dog" (Freeman) 47:164
"A Lost Dog" (Galsworthy) 22:98
"Lost Face" (London) 4:265, 289
Lost Face (London) 4:265, 283, 288
"The Lost Ghost" (Freeman) 47:112, 132,
　　136-37
"Lost Ground" (Trevor) 58:239-42, 253-54,
　　261, 263, 273, 276
"A Lost Halo" (Baudelaire)
　　See "Perte d'auréole"
"Lost Hearts" (James) 16:230, 232-33, 236-39,
　　241-42, 245, 250-51, 255-56
*The Lost Honor of Katharina Blum: How
　　Violence Develops and Where It Can
　　Lead* (Boell)
　　See *Die verlorene Ehre der Katharina
　　Blum: oder, Wie Gewalt entstehen und
　　wohin sie führen kann*
"Lost in the Funhouse" (Barth) 10:35, 37, 39,
　　41-3, 46-8, 52-4, 57, 61, 63, 65, 67, 80,
　　84-5, 88-9, 95, 97-100
*Lost in the Funhouse: Fiction for Print, Tape,
　　Live Voice* (Barth) 10:38-43, 45, 48-50,
　　52-60, 63-5, 67, 73-85, 87-91, 94-5, 97-9,
　　100-03
"The Lost Jewels" (Tagore)
　　See "Manihara"
"The Lost Leg" (Čapek) 36:128
"Lost Legacy" (Heinlein) 55:215
"Lost Legion" (Heinlein) 55:215-16
"The Lost Legion" (Kipling) 5:272-75, 285
"The Lost Leonardo" (Ballard) 53:10, 42
"The Lost Letter" (Gogol)
　　See "Propavšaja gramotax"
"The Lost Love Blues" (Fisher) 25:17-19
"A Lost Lover" (Jewett) 6:156, 159, 166
"Lost Luggage" (Adams) 24:13, 15, 19, 21, 23
"A Lost Masterpiece" (Moore) 19:341
"The Lost Novel" (Anderson) 1:31
"Lost on Dress Parade" (Henry) 5:158, 189;
　　49:197
The Lost Ones (Beckett)
　　See *Le dépeupleur*
"The Lost Phoebe" (Dreiser) 30:107, 112, 114-
　　16, 122, 145
"The Lost Reflection" (Hoffmann)
　　See "Das Verlorene Spiegelbild"
The Lost Smile (Keller)
　　See *Das Verlorene Lachen*
"Lost Sons" (Salter) 58:174, 182, 193
"Lost Souls" (Barker) 53:148-50, 154, 158, 163
Lost Stories from America (Gissing)
　　See *George Gissing: Lost Stories from
　　America*
"The Lost Track" (de la Mare) 14:80, 84
"The Lost Turkey" (Jewett) 6:156
"The Lost Way" (Čapek) 36:89-90, 122
"The Lost World" (Chabon) 59:71, 73, 75,
　　77-78
"A Lot You Got to Holler" (Algren) 33:106
"La lotería en Babilonia" (Borges) 4:5-7, 11-
　　12, 14; 41:61-62, 137, 147, 166
"Una lotta" (Svevo) 25:357, 362
"Lotta Schmidt" (Trollope) 28:319, 323

Lotta Schmidt and Other Stories (Trollope)
　　28:319, 322-23, 332, 339, 342, 350
"The Lottery" (Jackson) 9:249-52, 254-55, 258,
　　261, 264-70; 39:182-235
"The Lottery in Babylon" (Borges)
　　See "La lotería en Babilonia"
"The Lottery of Babylon" (Borges)
　　See "La lotería en Babilonia"
*The Lottery; or, The Adventures of James
　　Harris* (Jackson) 9:249; 39:209, 210, 212,
　　213, 214, 216, 217, 219, 220, 222, 223, 224,
　　225, 226, 227, 228, 230, 231
"Lottery Ticket" (Chekhov) 51:37
"The Lottery Ticket" (Greene) 29:223, 224
"The Lotus" (Rhys) 21:52, 64, 69
"The Lotus-Eater" (Maugham) 8:379
"Lou and Liz" (Gissing) 37:63, 80
"Lou, the Prophet" (Cather) 2:96, 100, 105;
　　50:59-60, 73, 89, 91, 184
"The Loudest Voice" (Paley) 8:388
"Louisa" (Freeman) 1:196; 47:104, 108, 149-
　　50, 152
"Louisa, Please Come Home" (Jackson) 9:267,
　　272
"Louise" (Saki) 12:322
"Loulou; or, The Domestic Life of the
　　Language" (Atwood) 2:18, 21, 23; 46:49,
　　79, 96
"Lounge Suit" (Somerville & Ross) 56:318
"Le Loup" (Aymé) 41:15
"Love" (Bowen) 3:33, 41
"Love" (Cowan) 28:75
"Love" (Dreiser)
　　See *Chains*
"Love" (Paley) 8:419
"Love" (Zoshchenko) 15:399
Love (Saroyan) 21:156
"Love seventy-seven" (Cortázar) 7:93
"The Love Affair" (Bradbury) 53:247-49
"Love among the Haystacks" (Lawrence) 4:197
"Love Among the Ruins" (Waugh) 41:311
Love Among the Ruins (Waugh) 41:313-17
"Love and Death" (Lagerkvist)
　　See "Kärleken och döden"
"Love and Death" (Oates) 6:225, 254
"Love and Lethe" (Beckett) 16:68, 72, 93
"Love and Napalm: Export USA" (Ballard)
　　See "The Atrocity Exhibition"
Love and Napalm: Export USA (Ballard)
　　See *The Atrocity Exhibition*
"Love and Russian Literature" (Maugham)
　　8:378
Love and Will (Dixon) 16:211, 216-19
"Love at First Sight" (Sansom) 21:115
"Love Day" (Styron) 25:312-15, 317-18
"Love, Death, Sacrifice, and So Forth"
　　(Saroyan) 21:132
"Love for $17.50" (Bukowski) 45:55
"Love. Friendship." (Oates) 6:227-28
Love Goes Visiting (Jarry)
　　See *L'amour en visites*
"Love Has Its Own Action" (Dixon) 16:204,
　　210, 214
Love, Here Is My Hat (Saroyan) 21:153, 155,
　　158, 161, 167
"Love in a Colder Climate" (Ballard) 53:67
"Love in a Wych Elm" (Bates) 10:133
"Love in the Casbah" (Andrić)
　　See "Ljubav u kasabi"
"Love in the Fallen City" (Chang) 28:25; 27;
　　31-32; 35-36
"Love in the Kasaba" (Andrić)
　　See "Ljubav u kasabi"
"Love in the Slump" (Waugh) 41:323, 328-29
"Love in the Spring" (Stuart) 31:227-28, 244,
　　249
"Love is for Lovers" (Lavin) 4:166
"Love Life" (Mason) 4:9
Love Life (Mason) 4:28
"Love Love Love Alone" (Naipaul) 38:341
"A Love Match" (Warner) 23:375

"The Love Nest" (Lardner) 32:116, 124-25,
　　127, 133-34, 137-38, 140, 147, 149, 152-
　　56, 160, 162, 168, 182-83, 195
The Love Nest, and Other Stories (Lardner)
　　32:119, 131-33, 139, 149, 151, 190
The Love Object (O'Brien) 10:330, 341
"The Love of Elsie Barton: A Chronicle"
　　(Warren) 4:389-91, 394; 58:310, 354, 356
"Love of Life" (London) 4:253, 265, 272-73,
　　278, 288-89, 291-92; 49:328, 335, 342
Love of Life, and Other Stories (London) 4:252,
　　264-65, 282, 285, 288-89
"Love of My Life" (Gilchrist) 63:6
"The Love of Parson Lord" (Freeman) 47:103
The Love of Parson Lord, and Other Stories
　　(Freeman) 47:83-84, 101, 103, 105
"The Love of Three Pomegranates" (Calvino)
　　48:102
"Love on the Bon-Dieu" (Chopin) 8:89
"The Love Song of the Conquering Lovers"
　　(Turgenev)
　　See "Pesn' torzhestvuyushchey lyubvi"
"The Love Song—Lída II" (Čapek) 36:92,
　　121-22
"A Love Story" (Bowen) 3:41, 54
"A Love Story" (Lawson) 18:239
"The Love Story of Chancellor Schlick and the
　　Beautiful Sienese" (Arnim)
　　See "Die Liebesgeschichte des Kanzlers
　　Schlick und der schonen Sienerin"
"A Love Story of Our Time" (Farrell) 28:125
"A Love Story of the Orient" (Far) 62:11
"Love Suicides" (Kawabata) 17:258
Love without Love (Pirandello)
　　See *Amori senza amore*
The Loved and the Unloved (Mauriac)
　　See *Galigaï*
"Lovelessness" (Pasternak)
　　See "Bezlyub'e"
"The Lovely April" (Grau) 15:153
"The Lovely Lady" (Lawrence) 4:220
The Lovely Lady, and Other Stories
　　(Lawrence) 4:230, 238
"The Lovely Leave" (Parker) 2:277, 280,
　　285-86
"The Lovely Myfwanny" (de la Mare) 14:69
"The Lovely Troubled Daughters of Our Old
　　Crowd" (Updike) 13:403
"Loveman's Comeback" (Campbell) 19:88
"Love-o'-Women" (Kipling) 5:266, 276, 279;
　　54:74, 78
"The Love-Philtre of Ikey Schoenstein"
　　(Henry) 5:182; 49:197
"The Lover" (Bowen) 3:40
"The Lover" (Walker) 5:413-14
The Lover (Duras)
　　See *L'amant*
"The Lovers" (Andersen) 6:7
"The Lovers" (Head) 52:209
"Lovers" (O'Flaherty) 6:282
"Lovers of the Lake" (O'Faolain) 13:288, 295,
　　297
"Lovers of Their Time" (Trevor) 21:258, 262;
　　58:200, 212-13, 216, 230
Lovers of Their Time, and Other Stories
　　(Trevor) 21:262; 58:200, 209, 212, 256
"Loves" (Andrić)
　　See "Ljuvabi"
"The Loves of Lady Purple" (Carter)
　　See "The Loves of the Lady Purple"
"The Loves of the Lady Purple" (Carter) 13:3-5
"Love's Young Dream" (O'Faolain) 13:315,
　　319-20
"Loving Memory" (Lavin) 4:166, 168
"Low Sunday, 1950" (Trevor) 58:300-301
"The Lowboy" (Cheever) 1:112; 38:55
"Low-Flying Aircraft" (Ballard) 1:73-4, 83;
　　53:18-19, 61
Low-Flying Aircraft, and Other Stories
　　(Ballard) 1:71-3; 53:18, 118
"Low-Lands" (Pynchon) 14:308, 310, 312, 321-
　　22, 324, 329, 334-35, 340-42, 344, 347-48

"The Loyal Traitors" (Chesterton) **46**:125
"Lu p'an" (P'u Sung-ling) **31**:190
"Luani of the Jungle" (Hughes) **6**:127
"Luc and His Father" (Gallant) **5**:147
Luca (Moravia)
  See *La disubbidienza*
"Lucas, His Modesty" (Cortázar)
  See "Lucas, sus pudores"
"Lucas, His Partisan Arguments" (Cortázar)
  See "Lucas, sus discusiones partidarias"
"Lucas, sus discusiones partidarias" (Cortázar)
  7:94
"Lucas, sus pudores" (Cortázar) **7**:94
"Lucerne" (Tolstoy) **9**:376, 389-91, 393; **30**:332
"The Luceys" (O'Connor) **5**:371, 378, 381-83,
  389
"An Luchóg" (O'Flaherty) **6**:287
"Lucifer" (Akutagawa Ryūnosuke) **44**:62
"Lucilla" (Pirandello) **22**:286
"The Luck of Jad Peters" (Thurber) **47**:382-83
"The Luck of Roaring Camp" (Harte) **8**:208,
  210, 219, 225-26, 228, 231-32, 237-39, 241,
  243-44, 245, 249, 251-52, 255, 257; **59**:286-
  87, 290, 292, 296, 300, 302, 313-17, 319-
  20, 325, 336-41
*The Luck of Roaring Camp, and Other
  Sketches* (Harte) **8**:219, 229, 236, 238,
  255-56; **59**:291, 294, 313, 318, 323-24, 331,
  337, 340
"The Luckiest Man in Kodny" (Aleichem)
  33:62
"The Lucksmith" (Benét) **10**:148
"The Lucky Fist" (Benét) **10**:147-48
"The Lucky Pair" (Lavin) **4**:173, 183
"Lucretia Burns" (Garland) **18**:173, 182
"Lucy" (Freeman) **47**:102
"Lucy" (de la Mare) **14**:69, 87
"Lucy Friend" (Cisneros) **32**:8
"Lucy Grange" (Lessing) **6**:191
Ludwig Tieck's Schriften (Tieck) **31**:282-84
"Luella Miller" (Freeman) **47**:110
"The Luftbad" (Mansfield) **9**:307
The Luftmensch (Zangwill) **44**:378
"The Luggage Store" (Bradbury) **53**:199, 209,
  249, 253, 259
"Lui?" (Maupassant) **1**:265-66, 281; **64**:329
"Luís Soares" (Machado de Assis) **24**:131
"Lukas, Sanftmütiger Knecht" (Lenz) **33**:317-
  18, 331
"The Lull" (Saki) **12**:295-96, 299, 306, 324
"Lullaby" (Gorky) **28**:137
"Lullaby" (Silko) **37**:294, 303, 307
"Lulu" (Hesse) **9**:243
Lulu's Library (Alcott) **27**:44
"The Lumber Room" (Saki) **12**:293, 297, 308-
  09, 320
"Il lume dell'altra casa" (Pirandello) **22**:231,
  233
"Lumìe di Sicilia" (Pirandello) **22**:269
"The Luminous Depths" (Čapek) **36**:87-8
Luminous Depths (Čapek)
  See *Zářivé hlubiny*
"A Lump of Sugar" (Walser) **20**:335-56
"La luna come un fungo" (Calvino) **48**:46, 157
"Luna de miel" (Arreola) **38**:11, 25
"Luna e GNAC" (Calvino) **3**:97; **48**:38
Lunar Caustic (Lowry) **31**:41, 43-4, 50, 66-70,
  73, 83, 86-7
"Lunch" (Bowen) **3**:40
"Lunch in Winter" (Trevor) **58**:213-14
"La lune de pluie" (Colette) **10**:281
"Lung-fei hsiang kung" (P'u Sung-ling) **31**:191
"Luosha haishi" (P'u Sung-ling) **31**:213
"La Lupa" (Verga) **21**:283-84, 286, 301, 305
"The Lurking Fear" (Lovecraft) **3**:258, 260,
  281; **52**:267, 292-93, 313, 340-41, 345-46
"Luther on Sweet Auburn" (Bambara) **35**:42
"Luvina" (Rulfo) **25**:247, 249-50, 255-56, 258,
  262, 265, 267, 277-79
"Luxury" (Coppard) **21**:11-12, 19, 28
"The Lynching of Jube Benson" (Dunbar)
  8:121-22, 126, 128-30, 132, 136

"The Lynching of Nigger Jeff" (Dreiser)
  See "Nigger Jeff"
"Lynx Hunting" (Crane) **7**:104
"The Lyrical Thief" (Čapek)
  See "O lyrickém zloději"
"Lysene" (Andersen) **56**:37
"Ma Chieh-fu" (P'u Sung-ling) **31**:205, 207
"Ma femme" (Maupassant) **1**:280
"Ma'ame Pélagie" (Chopin) **8**:87, 105
"Ma'ase ha'Ez" (Agnon) **30**:4, 39
"Maata" (Mansfield) **23**:153
"Mac in Love" (Dixon) **16**:203, 209-10, 213
"Macacos" (Lispector) **34**:189
"Macario" (Rulfo) **25**:245, 249, 263-65, 267,
  273, 275-76, 279
"The Macbeth Murder Mystery" (Thurber)
  1:426
"La machine à gloire" (Villiers de l'Isle Adam)
  14:377, 379, 383, 396
"The Machine Gun" (Wilding) **50**:346
"The Machine Stops" (Forster) **27**:68-9, 72,
  74-5, 81, 83, 87, 101, 103-04, 114-15,
  122-23
"The Machine-Gun Corps in Action"
  (O'Connor) **5**:369, 371, 390-91
"The Machineries of Joy" (Bradbury) **29**:82;
  53:215
The Machineries of Joy (Bradbury) **29**:48, 58-
  60, 82
"Mackintosh" (Maugham) **8**:359, 370, 372
"Mackintosh Willy" (Campbell) **19**:75, 88
"The Mad Convalescent at Fort Rattonneau"
  (Arnim)
  See "Der Tolle Invalide auf dem Fort Ra-
  tonneau"
"The Mad Idler" (Peretz)
  See "Der meshugener batlen"
"The Mad Laundress of Ding Dong
  Daddyland" (Algren) **33**:96, 98
"The Mad Lomasneys" (O'Connor) **5**:363, 370-
  71, 378, 383, 389
"Mad Night of Atonement" (Ligotti) **16**:276-77,
  288, 292, 295, 297
"The Mad Talmudist" (Peretz)
  See "Der meshugener batlen"
"The Mad Wizards of Mars" (Bradbury) **53**:248
"Madam Cluck, and Her Family" (Alcott) **27**:42
"Madame Celestine's Divorce" (Chopin)
  8:72-3, 84, 91
"Madame de Mauves" (James) **32**:108
"Madame Délicieuse" (Cable) **4**:48, 56, 67,
  69-71
Madame Delphine (Cable) **4**:48, 51-2, 56-7, 67,
  75-8
"Madame Dodin" (Duras) **40**:3, 8-9, 65
"Madame Zilensky and the King of Finland"
  (McCullers) **9**:322, 330, 332, 347, 357-
  58; **24**:232
"Made in Goatswood" (Campbell) **19**:63, 74
"Made in Heaven" (Updike) **13**:404
"The Madeline Wherry Case" (O'Hara) **15**:262,
  283, 287-88, 290
"Mademoiselle Bistouri" (Baudelaire) **18**:15-
  16, 19, 36, 38, 42
Mademoiselle Coeur-Brisé (West)
  See *Miss Lonelyhearts*
"Mademoiselle O" (Nabokov) **11**:108, 113, 128
"Mademoisselle Fifi" (Maupassant) **1**:256, 259,
  274, 287
"Madhyabartini" (Tagore) **48**:317-20
"A Madman's Diary" (Gogol)
  See "Diary of a Madman"
"The Madness of Ortheris" (Kipling) **5**:260
"The Madonna" (Barker) **53**:146-47, 157, 159,
  162, 173-76
"Madonna, Madonna" (Clarke) **45**:94
"A Madonna of the Trenches" (Kipling) **5**:271;
  54:73-5, 77-8
"La madre" (Ginzburg) **65**:116, 119-20, 123-25
"Le madre" (Svevo) **25**:328, 335-36, 352-53,
  357-58

"Una Madre" (Svevo) **25**:352
"Madre gallega" (Pardo Bazán) **30**:272
"Mae West's Reduction Mammoplasty"
  (Ballard) **53**:19
"Maelstrom II" (Clarke) **3**:129, 147
"The Maenads" (Cortázar) **7**:69-70
"Un maestro de antaño" (Alarcon) **64**:13
"The Magazine" (Singer) **3**:374
"Maggie Meriwether's Rich Experience"
  (Stafford) **26**:312
"Maggie of the Green Bottles" (Bambara)
  35:7-8, 23, 33
"Magi" (Henry)
  See "The Gift of the Magi"
"Magic" (Greene) **29**:219-20
"Magic" (Porter) **4**:327-30, 339-40, 360;
  43:177, 180, 236, 238, 253
"The Magic Barrel" (Malamud) **15**:168, 170,
  172, 176, 186, 188, 192, 195-96, 211, 213,
  217, 221, 227-34, 239, 241-43
"Magic Fishbone" (Dickens) **17**:124
Magic, Inc. (Heinlein) **55**:171, 176, 179-80,
  186, 197, 207-9, 215-17
The Magic of Shirley Jackson (Jackson) **9**:252
"The Magic Poker" (Coover) **15**:31, 38, 41-2,
  48, 50, 53-6
The Magic Striptease (Garrett) **30**:167-69
"The Magic Table, the Gold Donkey, and the
  Club in the Sack" (Grimm and Grimm)
  36:206, 229-30
"The Magician" (Peretz)
  See "Der Kuntsenmakher"
"The Magician" (Singer) **3**:375
"The Magician's Wife" (Gordon) **59**:230, 263
Magie noire (Morand) **22**:169, 172, 174-75,
  182
"Magna Mater" (Oates) **6**:232
"Magna . . . Reading" (Dixon) **16**:217
"Magna Takes the Calls" (Dixon) **16**:207
"Magnetism" (Fitzgerald) **6**:61
"Magnetisme" (Maupassant) **64**:316, 321
"Magnolia Flower" (Hurston) **4**:136
"Mags" (Trevor) **21**:263
"Mahatma Joe" (Bass) **60**:9-11, 15
"The Mahatma's Little Joke" (London) **4**:294
Mahogany (Pilnyak)
  See *Krasnoe derevo*
"The Maid of Saint Phillippe" (Chopin) **8**:71
"The Maiden" (Stafford) **26**:274, 276, 285
"The Maiden and Death" (Gorky) **28**:144
"Maiden in a Tower" (Stegner) **27**:197, 207,
  220
"Maiden, Maiden" (Boyle) **5**:56, 65
"Maiden Voyage" (Wolff) **63**:260, 282, 290,
  292, 296, 300, 303, 318-19
"Maiden's Leap" (Kiely) **58**:157-58
"The Maid's Shoes" (Malamud) **15**:173, 175
"Maidstone Comfort" (Gilman) **13**:144
"La main" (Maupassant) **1**:281
"The Main Death" (Hammett) **17**:213
"La main d'ecorché" (Maupassant) **1**:281
"Main Road" (Pritchett) **14**:269, 286, 298
"Main Street" (Hawthorne) **39**:120-22
Main-Travelled Roads (Garland) **18**:142-46,
  148, 150, 155-56, 158-75, 177, 180-81, 183,
  186, 191-94
"Mais dois bêbedos" (Lispector) **34**:230, 233,
  236
La maison de Claudine (Colette) **10**:278-79
"La maison du bonheur" (Villiers de l'Isle
  Adam) **14**:384, 387, 390, 396
"La maison du chat-qui-pelote" (Balzac) **5**:21-2,
  29, 31-3
La maison nucingen (Balzac) **5**:31
"La maison Tellier" (Maupassant) **1**:256-57,
  259-60, 263, 266, 271-72, 274, 276, 282-
  83, 287; **64**:329, 331-33; **64**:333
"The Maja" (Nin) **10**:326
"Maja Thurup" (Bukowski) **45**:60
"Majesty" (Fitzgerald) **6**:47
"The Majesty of the Law" (O'Connor) **5**:364-
  66, 369, 371, 377, 381, 389, 395, 398

"Major Bruce and Mrs. Conway" (Warner) **23**:369

"The Major of Hussars" (Bates) **10**:117

Die Majoratsherren (Arnim) **29**:5, 11-15

"Majskaja noč, ili Vtoplennica" (Gogol) **4**:118-19; **29**:132, 171; **52**:123, 146

"Majutah" (Fisher)
See "The South Lingers On"

"Makar Chudra" (Gorky) **28**:134, 136, 144, 148, 152-53, 178, 183-84, 186-88

Make Light of It (Williams) **31**:326, 333, 347-48

The Maker (Borges)
See *El hacedor*

The Maker of His Fortune (Keller)
See *Der Schmied seines Glückes*

"The Make-Up Artist" (Leskov)
See "Tupejnyi xudožnik"

"Making a Change" (Gilman) **13**:126, 141-42; **62**:190-91

"Making a Man" (Atwood) **46**:75, 99

"Making a Night of It" (Dickens) **17**:116, 122

"Making Arrangements" (Bowen) **3**:54

"Making Changes" (Michaels) **16**:301-02, 311-12

"Making Love" (Pohl) **25**:229

"The Making of a Master" (Platonov)
See "Proischozhdenie mastera"

"The Making of a New Yorker" (Henry) **5**:194

"The Making of a Statesman" (Harris) **19**:184

The Making of a Statesman (Harris) **19**:183

The Making of Ashenden (Elkin) **12**:93, 95, 106-07, 110, 114-16; **91**:97

"Making Poison" (Atwood) **2**:17

"Making Westing" (London) **4**:263

Le mal (Mauriac) **24**:160-62, 171, 174, 180, 206-08

"Mal di mestiere" (Pavese) **19**:384

Mal vu mal dit (Beckett) **16**:129-30, 132, 134-37

"Malachi" (Lawson) **18**:200

"Malachi's Cove" (Trollope) **28**:316-17, 319, 322, 324, 334, 349, 357

"Malan'ja—golova baran'ja" (Leskov) **34**:108

"Malaria" (Verga) **21**:292, 298, 300

"Maldito amor" (Ferré) **36**:159

Eine Malerarbeit (Storm) **27**:282-83, 305, 307, 314

Malgudi Days (Narayan) **25**:137-38, 152, 157, 159, 165, 170

"The Malice of Inanimate Objects" (James) **16**:251

"The Maltese Cat" (Kipling) **5**:279; **54**:69, 72

"Malva" (Gorky) **28**:136, 148, 178, 184-85, 190

"Mam Lyddy's Recognition" (Page) **23**:311

Mama Grande's Funeral (García Márquez)
See *Los funerales de la Mamá Grande*

"Mama's Little Girl" (Caldwell) **19**:6

"Mame" (Suckow) **18**:389, 396, 398, 405, 407

"Mamma" (Lardner) **32**:129

"Mamma Mia" (Sansom) **21**:117

"Mamma's Plot" (Alcott) **27**:22

"Mammon and the Archer" (Henry) **5**:195; **49**:197, 202

"Mammy Peggy's Pride" (Dunbar) **8**:121, 128, 131

"Mamouche" (Chopin) **8**:93

"The Man" (Bradbury) **29**:46, 48, 53, 81; **53**:213, 216

"A Man" (Bukowski) **45**:55

"A Man" (Clarke) **45**:78-9, 83, 87, 92, 103, 106, 108, 113, 116-17, 121-23, 125

"The Man" (Clarke) **45**:73, 76, 79, 85, 88-9, 96-7

"The Man" (Rulfo)
See "El hombre"

"Man About Town" (Henry) **49**:197

"A Man Alone at Lunch" (Aiken) **9**:14

"A Man and a Woman" (Caldwell) **19**:13, 17-18, 33

"Man and Daughter in the Cold" (Updike) **13**:361

"A Man and His Dog" (Mann) **5**:312

"A Man and Some Others" (Crane) **56**:71

"The Man and the Darwinian Theory" (Svevo)
See "L'uomo e la teoria darwiniana"

"The Man and the Snake" (Bierce) **9**:53, 88

"A Man and Two Women" (Lessing) **6**:198, 200-01, 203, 205, 208, 218, 220

A Man and Two Women (Lessing) **61**:93-94

"A Man by the Name of Ziegler" (Hesse) **9**:230, 235

"The Man Child" (Baldwin) **10**:4, 7-8, 10, 17

"The Man from Archangel" (Doyle) **12**:85-8

"A Man from Fort Necessity" (Benét) **10**:151, 154

"A Man from Glasgow" (Maugham) **8**:380

"The Man from Kilsheelan" (Coppard) **21**:3, 17-18

"The Man from Mars" (Atwood) **2**:3, 5-7, 10-11, 14, 21; **46**:33, 38, 41, 44, 57, 77, 92

"The Man from Shorrox" (Stoker) **62**:233, 249

"The Man Higher Up" (Henry) **5**:166, 193; **49**:206

"The Man in a Case" (Chekhov)
See "Čelovek v futljare"

"The Man in a Shell" (Chekhov)
See "Čelovek v futljare"

"The Man in the Brooks Brothers Shirt" (McCarthy) **24**:213, 215, 218

"The Man in the Brown Coat" (Anderson) **1**:21, 27

"Man in the Drawer" (Malamud) **15**:189, 191, 216

"The Man in the Passage" (Chesterton) **1**:136; **46**:137, 152

"The Man in the Rorschach Shirt" (Bradbury) **29**:47; **53**:215

"The Man in the Tree" (Porter) **43**:286-87

"The Man in the Underpass" (Campbell) **19**:88

"A Man is Born" (Gorky)
See "The Birth of a Man"

"Man Not Overboard" (Lardner) **32**:135, 138, 140-41

"The Man of Adamant" (Hawthorne) **3**:171, 185; **39**:114

"Man of All Work" (Wright) **2**:388

"A Man of Devon" (Galsworthy) **22**:58, 74-5, 82, 89-90, 93, 97

A Man of Devon (Galsworthy) **22**:57-8, 88-9, 91-4, 97, 99, 102

"Man of Letters" (Dixon) **16**:210, 215

"The Man of No Account" (Harte) **8**:236

The Man of Slow Feeling: Selected Short Stories (Wilding) **50**:358

"The Man of the Crowd" (Poe) **1**:379; **34**:243, 246-7; **54**:163, 180, 185-87

"The Man of the Family" (Bowen) **3**:45

"The Man of the Family" (Suckow) **18**:395, 410

"The Man of the Forests" (Hesse) **9**:243

"The Man of the House" (O'Connor) **5**:371

"A Man of the World" (Hemingway) **40**:191-96

"The Man of the World" (O'Connor) **5**:386

"Man on an Island of History" (Farrell) **28**:126

"The Man on the 99th Floor" (Ballard) **53**:11, 43, 49

"Man on the Pink Corner" (Borges)
See "El Hombre de la esquina rosada"

"The Man on the Threshold" (Borges)
See "El hombre en el umbral"

"The Man on the Tractor" (O'Hara) **15**:259, 283

"Man Orchid" (Williams) **31**:356

"The Man That Came to Buy Apples" (Somerville & Ross) **56**:316, 333

"The Man That Corrupted Hadleyburg" (Twain) **6**:293-95, 301-03, 305-09, 325, 334-35, 345; **26**:351; **34**:340

"The Man That Stopped" (O'Connor) **5**:371

"The Man That Was Used Up" (Poe) **1**:407-08; **22**:330; **34**:245; **35**:336; **54**:183

"A Man to Be Trusted" (O'Hara) **15**:286

"The Man to Send Rainclouds" (Silko) **37**:309

"The Man Upstairs" (Bradbury) **29**:67, 88

The Man Upstairs, and Other Stories (Wodehouse) **2**:347

"The Man Who Appeared" (Lispector)
See "O homem que apareceu"

"The Man Who Ate the World" (Pohl) **25**:223, 232

"The Man Who Became a Woman" (Anderson) **1**:30, 37, 48-50; **46**:20

"The Man Who Could Not Shake Hands" (King) **17**:266

"The Man Who Could Work Miracles: A Pantoum in Prose" (Wells) **6**:367, 375, 383, 389, 404-06

"The Man Who Couldn't Sleep" (Čapek)
See "Muž, který nemohl spát"

"The Man Who Died" (Lawson) **18**:215

The Man Who Died (Lawrence) **4**:212, 220-21, 226, 238

"The Man Who Gave Up His Name" (Harrison) **19**:201-06, 209

"The Man Who Got Fat" (Saroyan) **21**:135

"The Man Who Had to Talk to Somebody" (O'Hara) **15**:265-66

"The Man Who Hated Moonbaum" (Thurber) **47**:377, 382

"The Man Who Invented Sin" (O'Faolain) **13**:293, 301, 306, 314, 318

"The Man Who Kept His Form" (Galsworthy) **22**:67, 79, 101

"The Man Who Kept His Money in a Box" (Trollope) **28**:318, 330-32, 335, 347

"The Man Who Kicked Cancer's Ass" (Gilchrist) **14**:163

"The Man Who Killed a Shadow" (Wright) **2**:366, 385-86

The Man Who Knew Too Much (Chesterton) **1**:121-22, 125-26; **46**:117, 145

"The Man Who Liked Dickens" (Waugh) **41**:328-29, 334, 340

"The Man Who Liked Dogs" (Chandler) **23**:65, 67, 72, 82, 86, 106-07, 109

"The Man Who Lived Underground" (Wright) **2**:364, 366, 370, 373-74, 377, 379, 387-88

"The Man Who Loved His Kind" (Woolf) **7**:373, 376, 381, 388

"The Man Who Loved Islands" (Lawrence) **4**:197, 212-17, 221, 230, 233, 238

"The Man Who Passed" (Fisher) **25**:17-19, 21

"The Man Who Ploughed the Sea" (Clarke) **3**:134

"The Man Who Saw the Flood" (Wright) **2**:366

The Man Who Sold the Moon (Heinlein) **55**:209

"The Man Who Stole the Eiffel Tower" (Greene) **29**:223, 226-27

"The Man Who Traveled in Elephants" (Heinlein) **55**:167

"The Man Who Turned into a Statue" (Oates) **6**:224

The Man Who Turned into a Stick (Abe)
See *Bo ni natta otako*

"The Man Who Walked on the Moon" (Ballard) **53**:65, 67

"The Man Who Was" (Kipling) **5**:293

"The Man Who Was Almos' a Man" (Wright) **2**:366, 376, 388

"The Man Who was Drowned" (Lawson) **18**:242, 255

"The Man Who Was Unlucky With Women" (Lewis) **34**:163, 165

"The Man Who Was Very Homesick for New York" (Cheever) **38**:43

"The Man Who Watched" (Moravia)
See "L'uomo che guarda"

"The Man Who Would Be King" (Kipling) **5**:262, 264, 273, 278, 282, 291, 299; **54**:87-8

"The Man Whom Women Adored" (Oates) **6**:255

"A Man with a Conscience" (Maugham) **8**:379

"Man with a Thermometer" (Bulgakov) **18**:90

"The Man with Clam Eyes" (Thomas) **20**:320, 322

The Man with Forty Ecus (Voltaire)
   See *L'homme aux quarante écus*
"The Man with His Heart in the Highlands"
   (Saroyan) **21**:143, 168, 175
"The Man with the Broken Arm" (O'Hara)
   15:252
"The Man with the French Postcards"
   (Saroyan) **21**:132
"The Man with the Knives" (Boell)
   See "Der Mann mit den Messern"
"The Man with the Moon in Him" (Sansom)
   21:113
"The Man with the Twisted Lip" (Doyle) **12**:51,
   59, 68, 70, 74-5
"The Man With Two Beards" (Chesterton)
   46:111, 135
The Man with Two Left Feet (Wodehouse) **2**:327
"The Man Within" (Greene) **29**:184
"Man without a Fig Leaf" (Garrett) **30**:166, 174
"The Man without a Temperament"
   (Mansfield) **9**:284, 314
"The Management of Grief" (Mukherjee)
   38:238, 242, 252-53, 266, 271, 287, 290,
   292
"The Manager" (O'Hara) **15**:283
"Mañanas de abril y mayo" (Alarcon) **64**:7, 25,
   27, 30
"The Manchester Marriage" (Gaskell) **25**:55,
   58
"The Mandarin" (Betts) **45**:7-8, 28, 30
"The Mandarin" (Fuentes) **24**:61-2
"Mandarin Oranges" (Akutagawa Ryūnosuke)
   44:50
"Mandarin's Jade" (Chandler) **23**:59, 65, 67-8,
   72, 80, 82, 87, 98, 108, 110
"Mandorf" (Kluge) **61**:74
"Manfred Schmidt" (Kluge) **61**:74
"The Mangler" (King) **17**:262
"Mango Says Goodbye Sometimes" (Cisneros)
   32:43
Mango Street (Cisneros)
   See *The House On Mango Street*
"Manhole 69" (Ballard) **1**:68; **53**:11, 47, 50
"Man-hunt" (Narayan) **25**:156
Manhunt (Carpentier)
   See *El acoso*
"The Maniac" (Oates) **6**:243
"Manihara" (Tagore) **48**:341, 343
"Manikin" (Michaels) **16**:301, 303, 311-12
"Man'ka" (Kazakov) **43**:58, 67, 69
Man'ka (Kazakov) **43**:50
"Mankind" (Pavese) **19**:370, 389
"Der Mann mit den Messern" (Boell) **23**:12
"Manna" (Galsworthy) **22**:63, 78, 101
"Mannequin" (Rhys) **21**:62
The Manor (Singer) **53**:273
"Man's Fate" (Dubus) **15**:88
"The Man's Story" (Anderson) **1**:39, 52
"The Mantle of Whistler" (Parker) **2**:273, 283
"Manual for Sons" (Barthelme) **55**:68, 108, 114
"Manuel" (Lewis) **40**:275
"Manuscript Found in a Pocket" (Cortázar)
   See "Manuscrito hallado en un bolsillo"
"Manuscrito de um sacristão" (Machado de
   Assis) **24**:129-30
"Manuscrito hallado en un bolsillo" (Cortázar)
   7:61-2, 69
"Many Are Disappointed" (Pritchett) **14**:255,
   259, 269, 271, 282, 284, 297
Many Inventions (Kipling) **5**:266, 273, 283,
   287; **54**:74, 129
"The Map of Love" (Thomas) **3**:399, 402, 407;
   44:322, 332, 338, 349, 354, 357
The Map of Love (Thomas) **3**:410; **44**:321, 324-
   25, 336, 350
"A Map of the World" (Davie) **52**:11
"El mapa de objetos perdidos" (Arreola) **38**:11,
   26-28
"The Mapmakers" (Pohl) **25**:224, 227, 229-31,
   234-35
"Die Mappe meines Urgrossvaters" (Stifter)
   28:285, 298-99

"The Mappined Life" (Saki) **12**:290, 297, 305,
   310, 313, 321, 323
"El mar del tiempo perdido" (García Márquez)
   8:155, 167-68, 172
"Mar, mar, enemigo" (Cabrera Infante) **39**:22
"Mara milosnica" (Andrić) **36**:30, 34-5, 37-8,
   45, 48, 59-62, 65, 67
"Mara the Concubine" (Andrić)
   See "Mara milosnica"
Les marana (Balzac) **5**:8, 26, 31
"Maravillosas ocupaciones" (Cortázar) **7**:92
"A Marble Woman; or, The Mysterious Model"
   (Alcott) **27**:4, 45-50, 58-60
"The Marble Works" (Hesse) **9**:230-31, 234-35
"Marcelie" (Beauvoir) **35**:60, 62-65, 67-9, 71
"The March" (McCullers) **9**:332, 354, 360
"The March Hare" (Leskov)
   See "Zajačij remiz"
"The March of Progress" (Chesnutt) **7**:27-8, 37;
   54:59-60, 63
"Das Märchen" (Hauptmann) **37**:246-47
Märchen (Hesse) **9**:244
"Ein Märchen aus der neuen Zeit" (Hoffmann)
   13:218-19
Das Märchen von blonden Eckbert (Tieck)
   See *Der blonde Eckbert*
"Marching through Boston" (Updike) **13**:386
"The Marchioness of Stonehenge" (Hardy)
   2:204, 217; **60**:179, 205, 208-9
"Marcia" (Davis) **38**:104-05, 119-20
Marcovaldo: or, The Seasons in the City
   (Calvino)
   See *Marcovaldo ouvero le stagioni in citta*
Marcovaldo ouvero le stagioni in citta
   (Calvino) **3**:106-07; **48**:83, 149-50, 163
"Il mare" (Pavese) **19**:365, 384
"The Mares" (Pavese) **19**:365-66
Marginalia (Poe) **22**:304, 312, 325
"Margins" (Barthelme) **55**:16, 24
"Marguerite" (Beauvoir) **35**:60, 62-4, 66, 68,
   71
Maria and Some Other Dogs (Somerville &
   Ross) **56**:313
"María Concepción" (Porter) **4**:326, 328, 330,
   339-40, 346, 349; **43**:170, 193, 221-23, 234,
   237, 240, 253, 292, 344
"Maria Cora" (Machado de Assis) **24**:134
"Maria-Fly" (de la Mare) **14**:86-7
Marianne (Lagerkvist) **12**:198-99, 201-03
"Mariana" (Machado de Assis) **24**:128, 134,
   145, 153, 155
"Marianno" (Svevo) **25**:329
"Marie" (Barthelme) **55**:16, 25
"Marie, Marie, Hold On Tight" (Barthelme)
   2:34, 40; **55**:22, 47
"Marie Rogêt" (Poe)
   See "The Mystery of Marie Rogêt"
Marilee (Spencer) **57**:209, 212, 215
"Marina and the Lion" (Ferré)
   See "Marina y el leon"
"Marina y el leon" (Ferré) **36**:157, 160
"The Marine Excursion of the Knights of
   Pythias" (Leacock) **39**:269
"A Marine Merry-Making" (Alcott) **27**:43
Mario and the Magician (Mann)
   See *Mario und der Zauberer*
Mario und der Zauberer (Mann) **5**:310-12, 337,
   340-41, 353-59
"The Mariposa Bank Mystery" (Leacock)
   39:270
"The Mark" (Pancake) **61**:246, 249, 259-60,275
"The Mark of Apelles" (Pasternak)
   See "Il tratto di Apelle"
"A Mark of Distinction" (Betts) **45**:27
"The Mark of the Beast" (Kipling) **5**:271, 273-
   74, 280, 299
"The Mark on the Wall" (Woolf) **7**:368, 370-
   71, 378, 382-83, 385-88, 392, 397-98, 405,
   409
The Mark on the Wall (Woolf) **7**:382
Mark Twain's Sketches, New and Old (Twain)
   34:336

*Mark Twain's "Which Was the Dream?" and
   Other Symbolic Writings of the Later
   Years* (Twain) **6**:331
"The Marker" (Coover) **15**:37
"Market" (Walser) **20**:355
"The Markets of Madrid" (Alarcon)
   See "Las ferias de Madrid"
"Markheim" (Stevenson) **11**:266, 268-69, 276,
   278-79, 281-82, 292, 297; **51**:216-50
"Marklake Witches" (Kipling) **5**:285
"Marley's Chain" (Auchincloss) **22**:51
"Marlowe Takes on the Syndicate" (Chandler)
   23:110
"Marmalade" (O'Faolain) **13**:322
The Marmalade Bird (Sansom) **21**:115-19, 127
El marqués de Lumbría (Unamuno) **11**:313,
   323-24
"Die Marquise de la Pivadière" (Hoffmann)
   13:188
The Marquise of —— and Other Stories
   (Kleist) **22**:136
"Die Marquise von O..." (Kleist) **22**:105-08,
   110, 116, 125-26, 128, 130-32, 134-35, 142
"Marrakesh" (Munro) **3**:346
"Marriage à la mode" (Mansfield) **9**:279, 310
"The Marriage Contract" (Auchincloss) **22**:41-2
"The Marriage Feast" (Lagerkvist) **12**:179, 196
"The Marriage of Phaedra" (Cather) **2**:98, 103;
   50:57, 80, 82, 107, 112, 122, 138, 196-97,
   200-01, 203, 239, 263-65, 267-68, 270-71
The Marriage of the Monk (Meyer)
   See *Die Hochzeit des Mönchs*
"Marriage—For One" (Dreiser) **30**:112, 114,
   122, 145-46, 156
"The Marriages" (James) **47**:203
Marriages and Infidelities (Oates) **6**:224, 234,
   254
"Married" (Dreiser) **30**:122, 142-43
"The Married Couple" (Kafka) **5**:206-07
"Married Life" (Leacock) **39**:266
The Married Lover (Colette)
   See *Duo*
"A Married Man's Story" (Mansfield) **9**:282,
   311
"Marroca" (Maupassant) **1**:257
"The Marry Month of May" (Henry) **5**:163
"Marrying Damian" (Trevor) **58**:261, 273, 276,
   287
"Mars by Moonlight" (Pohl) **25**:232
"Mars Is Heaven" (Bradbury) **29**:55; **53**:201,
   203, 246, 248, 252, 254
"Mars Jeems's Nightmare" (Chesnutt) **7**:7-8,
   10, 40; **54**:33-5, 37, 40-3, 46
"Marse Chan" (Page) **23**:284, 287-93, 295-98,
   300-02, 305-06, 308, 311-12, 314, 316-17,
   320-21, 323, 325-26, 328
"The Marsh King's Daughter" (Andersen)
   See "Dynd-Kongens Datter"
"Marsh Rosemary" (Jewett) **6**:150
"Marshall's Capture" (Garland) **18**:167
"Marshall's Dog" (Beattie) **11**:18, 20-3
"The Marshland" (Akutagawa Ryūnosuke)
   44:64
Marshlands (Gide)
   See *Paludes*
"Martha" (Thomas) **44**:337
"Martha and Mary" (Čapek) **36**:85, 117, 129
"Martha Jean" (Caldwell) **19**:18, 38, 42, 46
"Martha Preston" (Gaskell) **25**:72
Marthe und ihre Uhr (Storm) **27**:283
"The Martian" (Bradbury) **53**:187-90, 195, 205,
   207-9, 222, 247-48, 250
The Martian Chronicles (Bradbury) **29**:38-40,
   46, 49-52, 55, 60-1, 64, 75, 79, 87; **53**:186-
   91, 193-96, 198-213, 220-23, 225, 227, 244-
   45, 247-57, 259-62, 264
"The Martian Stargazers" (Pohl) **25**:225
"Martians Come in Clouds" (Dick) **57**:107-8
Martin Hewitt, Investigator (Morrison) **40**:332,
   349
"Martin Martir" (Arnim) **29**:6, 7
"Martina" (Pardo Bazán) **30**:264

"Martin's Close" (James) **16**:232, 237, 252, 256
"El martirio de Sor Bibiana" (Pardo Bazán) **30**:262
"Martwy sezon" (Schulz) **13**:326-27, 334
"The Martydom of Solomon" (Coppard) **21**:8
"The Martyr" (Akutagawa Ryūnosuke)
    See "Hōkyōnin no shi"
"The Martyr" (Auchincloss) **22**:44
"The Martyr" (Farrell) **28**:98-9, 122, 125
"The Martyr" (Peretz) **26**:215-16
"The Martyr" (Porter) **31**:178; **43**:221, 238, 253, 292
"The Martyr's Corner" (Narayan) **25**:134, 139-41
"Maruja" (Harte) **8**:216, 244, 251; **59**:306-7
"The Marvelous Girl" (Pritchett) **14**:261
"Marvelous Pursuits" (Cortázar)
    See "Maravillosas ocupaciones"
"Marvels and Miracles-Pass It On!" (Bradbury) **29**:76
"Mary" (Collier) **19**:104, 109
"Mary" (Mansfield) **9**:284
"Mary" (O'Hara) **15**:266
"Mary and Norma" (O'Hara) **15**:252, 281
"Mary Button's Principles" (Gilman) **13**:141
"Mary Gresley" (Trollope) **28**:321, 324, 335, 340, 348
"Mary O'Reilley" (Farrell) **28**:118, 122
"Mary Osaka, I Love You" (Fante) **65**:92
"Mary Postgate" (Kipling) **5**:279, 281-83; **54**:108
"Mary Winosky" (Hughes) **6**:117-19
"Maryelle" (Villiers de l'Isle Adam) **14**:378, 381-82, 384, 393, 396
"Mary's Piece" (Dixon) **16**:210
"Más allá" (Pardo Bazán) **30**:264
"Mas vai chover" (Lispector) **34**:211
"Mascarada" (Onetti) **23**:249, 252
"The Masculine Principle" (O'Connor) **5**:366, 371-72, 381, 388-89
"Masculine Protest" (O'Connor) **5**:387
Mashi and Other Stories (Tagore) **48**:302-3, 321-22
"The Mask of the Bear" (Laurence) **7**:254, 259, 263
The Masked Days (Fuentes)
    See *Los días enmascarados*
"Le masque" (Maupassant) **1**:274, 286
"The Masque of the Red Death" (Poe) **1**:379, 389-90, 398, 406; **22**:305, 307; **35**:322; **54**:209
"The Masquerade" (Banks) **42**:56-7, 66
"Masquerade" (Onetti)
    See "Mascarada"
Masquerade, and Other Stories (Walser) **20**:354-56, 363, 365-66
"Masquerade of a Dead Sword" (Ligotti) **16**:269, 273, 277-78
The Masquerade of Souls (Lagerkvist)
    See *Själarnas maskerad*
Mass Death in Venice (Kluge) **61**:58, 60-61, 63-65, 68, 71-72
"The Mass Island" (O'Connor) **5**:372
"Massensterben in Venedig" (Kluge) **61**:56
"Masses of Men" (Caldwell) **19**:9, 38-9
"Massimilla doni" (Balzac) **5**:16
"Mastarmasay" (Tagore)
    See "Mastarmashai"
"Mastarmashai" (Tagore) **48**:317, 340-41
"Master" (Carter) **13**:4
Master and Man (Tolstoy)
    See *Khozyain i rabotnik*
Master Flea (Hoffmann)
    See *Meister Floh: Ein Märchen in seiben Abenteuern zweier Freunde*
"Master Glass" (Cervantes)
    See "El licenciado Vidriera"
"Master Hynek Ráb of Kufštejn" (Čapek) **36**:95, 117
"Master John Horseleigh, Knight" (Hardy) **2**:210

"Master Misery" (Capote) **2**:63-5, 72-3, 75, 78; **47**:3, 11, 28-9, 31, 35, 37, 44, 48, 50, 53, 55, 58
The Master of Ballantrae: A Winter's Tale (Stevenson) **51**:218, 232-33, 236, 240, 248-49
"The Master of Lenses" (Zangwill) **44**:364
"The Master Thief" (Grimm and Grimm) **36**:199, 235
"The Masters" (Le Guin) **12**:223, 232-33, 241
Mat' syra zemlya (Pilnyak) **48**:216, 235-37, 239, 254, 264, 268-70, 295-97
"The Maternal Instinct" (Naipaul) **38**:326, 341, 350
"Mathewson" (Dreiser) **30**:149-51
Matilda's England (Trevor) **21**:235, 260; **58**:209, 212-13, 228
"The Mating of Marjorie" (Caldwell) **19**:34, 46
Matrena's House (Solzhenitsyn)
    See "Matryonin Dvor"
"Matryona's Home" (Solzhenitsyn)
    See "Matryonin Dvor"
"Matryonin Dvor" (Solzhenitsyn) **32**:330-33, 337-39, 342, 359, 361-65, 370-75, 377, 379-86, 394-95, 397, 409
Matteo Falcone (Mérimée) **7**:278, 280-1, 283, 285, 287-9, 300-01
"A Matter of Chance" (Nabokov) **11**:123-24, 126
"A Matter of Doctrine" (Dunbar) **8**:122
"A Matter of Prejudice" (Chopin) **8**:93
"A Matter of Principle" (Chesnutt) **7**:16, 23, 33-6; **54**:11-13, 48, 58
"A Matter of Taste" (Collier) **19**:108
"Mauá Square" (Lispector)
    See "Praça Mauá"
"Maud Island" (Caldwell) **19**:17
"Maude" (Auchincloss) **22**:3, 30, 47
"Maupassant" (Babel)
    See "Guy de Maupassant"
"Le Mauvais Jars" (Aymé) **41**:6, 14-15
"Le mauvais vitrier" (Baudelaire) **18**:6, 16, 18, 34, 45, 60-1, 63
"Le Mauvaises fivres" (Aymé) **41**:11
"The Mavericks" (Auchincloss) **22**:5, 53
"May Day" (Fitzgerald) **6**:45, 57-9, 74-6, 96-101
"A May Night; or, The Drowned Maiden" (Gogol)
    See "Majskaja noč, ili Vtoplennica"
"May We Borrow Your Husband" (Greene) **29**:201, 213
May We Borrow Your Husband? and Other Comedies of the Sexual Life (Greene) **29**:200-02, 212-13, 217, 221, 223, 228, 230
"May you learn to open the door to go out to play" (Cortázar)
    See "que sepa abrir la puerta para ir a jugar"
"The Mayor" (O'Hara) **15**:260
"The Mayor of Lapeza" (Alarcon) **64**:38
"La mayorazga de Bouzas" (Pardo Bazán) **30**:272
"The Mayor's Committee" (Farrell) **28**:125
"The Maypole of Merry Mount" (Hawthorne) **3**:164-67, 180-81, 183-84, 187, 188
"May-Ry" (Calisher) **15**:15-16
Mayses far yidishe kinder (Aleichem) **33**:5, 16
"The Maysville Minstrel" (Lardner) **32**:117, 128, 135-36, 138, 174-76
"Mazes" (Le Guin) **12**:230, 235
"A M[dj]cenas of the Pacific Slope" (Harte) **8**:216, 255
"McEwen of the Shining Slave Makers" (Dreiser) **30**:115, 122-23, 127-30, 132
"Me and Miss Mandible" (Barthelme) **2**:26-7, 35, 47, 49, 53; **55**:16, 21, 26, 32, 44, 108
"El me bebeu" (Lispector) **34**:215
"Me Cago en la Leche (Robert Jordan in Nicaragua)" (Boyle) **16**:151
"Mearbhall" (O'Flaherty) **6**:287-89
"The Measurements" (Moravia) **26**:142,155

"Meccana d'amore" (Levi) **12**:276
"Un mécène" (Villiers de l'Isle Adam)
    See "Le tueur de cygnes"
"El mechón blanco" (Pardo Bazán) **30**:294
"Mety" (Chekhov) **28**:56; **51**:107-8
"Le médaillon" (Villiers de l'Isle Adam)
    See "Antonie"
"The Medals" (Pirandello) **22**:235
"The Medals, and Other Stories" (Pirandello) **22**:234, 236
"Meddlance Tersplat" (Cortázar)
    See "La inmiscusión terrupta"
"Meddlesome Curiosity" (Cervantes)
    See "El curioso impertinente"
"Meddlesome Jack" (Caldwell) **19**:6, 23, 39, 44
"Media Man" (Vinge)
    See "Mediaman"
"Mediaman" (Vinge) **24**:338
"Las medias rojas" (Pardo Bazán) **30**:272
"Medicine" (Lu Hsun)
    See "Yao"
A Medicine for Melancholy (Bradbury) **29**:58, 61, 78, 80-1, 83; **53**:191, 196
"The Medicine Man" (Caldwell) **19**:6, 21, 25-6
"Medicine Men of Civilisation" (Dickens) **17**:123
"A Medieval Romance" (Twain) **34**:343
El medio pollito (Ferré) **36**:146, 149
"Meditations in Monmouth Street" (Dickens) **17**:115, 117, 121
"Medley" (Bambara) **35**:11, 18, 27
"Medusa" (Campbell) **19**:85
"The Medusa" (Ligotti) **16**:274, 294, 297
Meet Mr. Mulliner (Wodehouse) **2**:325, 338
"Meet the Girls" (Farrell) **28**:121
"The Meeting" (Borges) **4**:20
"The Meeting" (Cortázar)
    See "Reunión"
"The Meeting" (Dixon) **16**:210
"The Meeting" (Galsworthy) **22**:58, 98
"A Meeting" (O'Faolain) **13**:293-95, 309, 316
"The Meeting" (Turgenev)
    See "Svidanie"
"Meeting a Moscow Acquaintance in the Detachment" (Tolstoy) **9**:389-90
"Meeting Aline" (Dixon) **16**:212-13
"A Meeting in Middle Age" (Trevor) **21**:254, 260; **58**:200, 269, 271
"A Meeting in Rauch" (Bioy Casares) **17**:95-6
"A Meeting in Space" (Gordimer) **17**:158
"A Meeting South" (Anderson) **1**:37, 52-3
"Meeting the Author" (Campbell) **19**:77-8
"A Meeting with Medusa" (Clarke) **3**:128, 130, 132, 135-36, 138-40, 146
"The Megalopolis Millennia" (Aldiss) **36**:19
"Megh o Roudra" (Tagore) **48**:315-16, 321, 331
"Meh Lady: A Story of the War" (Page) **23**:284, 286-87, 289, 291-93, 297, 302-03, 307-08, 311, 314, 316-18, 320, 322-23, 325, 327-28
"Mein Onkel Fred" (Boell) **23**:5
"Mein teures Bein" (Boell) **23**:34
"Mein verdrossenes Gesicht" (Lenz) **33**:316-18, 320, 331
"Meine Bemühungen" (Walser) **20**:332
"Mei-nü" (P'u Sung-ling) **31**:198
"Meiosi" (Calvino) **3**:109; **48**:58-9, 65, 67, 106-7, 142-44
"Meiosis" (Calvino)
    See "Meiosi"
Meister Floh: Ein Märchen in seiben Abenteuern zweier Freunde (Hoffmann) **13**:186, 192, 195, 197-200, 218-19, 225
Meister Martin (Hoffmann) **13**:182
"Mejdoub" (Bowles) **3**:68
Los Mejores cuentos de Donoso (Donoso)
    See *Cuentos*
"The Melancholy Hussar of the German Legion" (Hardy) **2**:214-15, 220; **60**:177, 189

"Melanctha—Each One as She May" (Stein) **42**:274-76, 279-80, 282-87, 292-95, 298-99, 301-02, 305-08, 310-11, 313-19, 321, 323, 326-30, 332-36, 338-41, 343-52, 354-57, 359-60, 362
"Melhor do que order" (Lispector) **34**:215
"Mellonta Tauta" (Poe) **1**:401, 406
"Melmoth Converted" (Balzac)
　　See "Melmoth réconcilié"
"Melmoth réconcilié" (Balzac) **5**:12, 31
"Melos, Run!" (Dazai Osamu)
　　See "Hashire Merosu"
"A Member of the Family" (Spark) **10**:364, 367
"The Memento" (Henry) **5**:185
"Memento Mori" (Farrell) **28**:110-11
Memnon; ou, La sagesse humaine (Voltaire) **12**:340-42, 357, 379-81, 383, 392-94, 396-97, 399-401
"A Memoir" (Suckow) **18**:396
Memoires (Flaubert)
　　See *Les mémoires d'un fou*
Les mémoires d'un fou (Flaubert) **11**:71
"Memoirs" (Balzac) **5**:11
Memoirs from Underground (Dostoevsky)
　　See *Zapiski iz podpol'ya*
The Memoirs of a Billiard-Marker (Tolstoy) **9**:375
Memoirs of a Madman (Tolstoy)
　　See *Zapiski sumasshedshego*
The Memoirs of a Sportsman (Turgenev)
　　See *Zapiski okhotnika*
The Memoirs of Sherlock Holmes (Doyle) **12**:49-51, 59
"Memorandum of Sudden Death" (Norris) **28**:198-99
"La memoria del mondo" (Calvino) **48**:48, 156, 160
La memoria del mondo (Calvino) **48**:46, 48, 131, 147, 149-50, 158
"Memorial" (Munro) **3**:331
"Memorial" (Wolff) **63**:323-25
"Memorial Eve" (Suckow) **18**:414, 422, 424
"Memories" (Dazai Osamu)
　　See "Omoide"
"Memories of a Yellow Dog" (Henry) **49**:197
"Memories of D. H. Lawrence" (Thurber) **1**:414
"Memories of the Space Age" (Ballard) **53**:22-24, 35-36, 64-65, 117-18
"Memories of Youghal" (Trevor) **21**:262
"Memories of Yugashima" (Kawabata)
　　See "Yugashima no Omoide"
"A Memory" (Lavin) **4**:178-79, 182-83
"A Memory" (Welty) **1**:466, 469-70, 472; **51**:254, 263, 314-18
"The Memory of Martha" (Dunbar) **8**:122
"The Memory of the World" (Calvino)
　　See "La memoria del mondo"
Memory of the World (Calvino)
　　See *La memoria del mondo*
"A Memory of Yamashina" (Shiga) **23**:352
"Memphis" (Gilchrist) **14**:159; **63**:4
"Memphis" (Mason) **4**:10
"Men At Sea" (Atwood) **46**:75
"Men in the Storm" (Crane) **7**:108, 110, 136-37, 145
"The Men of Forty Mile" (London) **4**:267, 282, 284, 286
"Men of the Mountains" (Stuart) **31**:252
Men of the Mountains (Stuart) **31**:231-32
"The Men with Bowler Hats" (Wilson) **21**:358, 360-63
"Men with Their Big Shoes" (Jackson) **9**:270; **39**:212, 227, 229, 231
Men without Women (Ford) **56**:150
Men without Women (Hemingway) **1**:209-12, 214, 216-17; **63**:61
"Az men zogt meshuge—gleyb!" (Peretz) **26**:224
"The Menace" (du Maurier) **18**:127-28
"Menaces in May" (Thurber) **47**:373, 378-79, 383-84
"Mendel and His Wife" (Farrell) **28**:89, 122

"Mendel Breines" (Peretz) **26**:201
"Le Mendiant" (Aymé) **41**:13
"The Mendicant" (Kazakov) **43**:56
"Menelaiad" (Barth) **10**:39, 43, 47-51, 54, 58, 60-1, 75-6, 80, 90, 97-8, 100-02
"Meng-lang" (P'u Sung-ling) **31**:197
"A Menor Mulher do Mundo" (Lispector) **34**:194-96, 200
"A mensagem" (Lispector) **34**:188, 229, 231-34
"mensuro Zoili" (Akutagawa Ryūnosuke) **44**:64
"A Mental Suggestion" (Chopin) **8**:72, 100
"Menudo" (Carver) **8**:43
"Menuet" (Maupassant) **1**:278
"Meola's Defence" (Pirandello) **22**:254
"A Mercenary" (Ozick) **15**:302, 304, 316-17, 333-35; **60**:308-9, 317
"The Merchant Bartfuss" (Appelfeld) **42**:14
"The Merchant of Heaven" (Laurence) **7**:245-46, 249-50, 255, 260
"The Merchants of Venus" (Pohl) **25**:226, 230
"Mercury" (Levi) **12**:264, 268, 281
"A Mercury of the Foothills" (Harte) **8**:214, 249
"The 'Mercy' of God" (Dreiser) **30**:158-59
"La Mère aux monstres" (Maupassant) **64**:357, 364
"La Mère Bauche" (Trollope) **28**:316-18, 323, 327-28, 330, 333, 343, 349, 357
"A Mere Formality" (Pirandello) **22**:241, 245
"A Mere Interlude" (Hardy) **2**:211, 215; **60**:183
"Mère Pochette" (Jewett) **6**:156
"La mère sauvage" (Maupassant) **1**:277-78
"Merle" (Marshall) **3**:317
Merle: A Novella, and Other Stories (Marshall)
　　See *Reena, and Other Stories*
"Mermaid Sea" (Dazai Osamu) **41**:229
"The Merman" (Hesse) **9**:242-43
"Merrittsville" (Suckow) **18**:393, 413, 422, 424
"The Merry Blind-man" (Far) **62**:50
"The Merry Chase" (Lish) **18**:278
"Merry May" (Campbell) **19**:76
"The Merry Men" (Stevenson) **11**:268, 281-82, 303, 306
"Mes vingt-cinq jours" (Maupassant) **1**:274
"Der meshugener batlen" (Peretz) **26**:218-20, 223-24
"Der meshulekh" (Peretz) **26**:218, 223-24
"Mesiras Nefesh" (Peretz) **26**:197
"Mesmeric Revelation" (Poe) **1**:401; **34**:250; **54**:166-67
"A Mess of Pottage" (Dunbar) **8**:122, 124, 128
"Le message" (Balzac) **5**:8, 31, 40-1, 43
"The Message" (Boell)
　　See "Die Botschaft"
"Message in a Bottle" (Gordimer) **17**:156
"Messages" (Abish) **44**:19
Messaline, roman de l'acienne Rome (Jarry) **20**:50, 63-8
"La messe de l'athée" (Balzac) **5**:16, 26, 31
"The Messenger" (Peretz)
　　See "Der meshulekh"
"The Messiah" (Bradbury) **29**:82; **53**:195
"Metamorphoses" (Cheever) **1**:94, 100
"Metamorphosis" (Agnon)
　　See "Panim aherot"
"The Metamorphosis" (Appelfeld)
　　See "Hahishtanut"
"Metamorphosis" (Dazai Osamu)
　　See "Gyofukuki"
"Metamorphosis" (Moravia) **26**:136
"The Metamorphosis" (Oates) **6**:225, 234
The Metamorphosis (Kafka)
　　See *Die verwandlung*
"Metel" (Pilnyak) **48**:264
"Metel" (Pushkin) **27**:129, 141-45, 163, 166, 168, 171, 183, 186-87
"Metel" (Tolstoy) **45**:136, 143, 156, 161; **54**:315
"Methinks the Lady Doth Propel too Much" (Perelman) **32**:235
"Methuseleh, a Jewish Horse" (Aleichem) **33**:20
"Metropolitan Journal" (Boell) **23**:34

"Metzengerstein" (Poe) **1**:379; **22**:300, 331, 334; **54**:205, 209
"The Mex Would Arrive at Gentry's Junction at 12:10" (Coover) **15**:43-6
"The Mexican" (London) **4**:291
"The Mexican" (Moravia) **26**:151
"The Mexican General" (Bellow) **14**:37-8, 40
"Mexican Movies" (Cisneros) **32**:8
"Mexico" (Bass) **60**:4-6, 8, 30
"Mexico" (Gilchrist) **14**:161-63; **63**:16, 21-22
"The Mezzotint" (James) **16**:232, 237, 240, 243-44, 251-52, 255, 257
"Mi suicidio" (Pardo Bazán) **30**:264
"Michael Egerton" (Price) **22**:363, 384, 388
Michael Kohlhaas (Kleist) **22**:106, 109-10, 117, 119-21, 125-26, 128-29, 132-37, 139, 141-42
"Michael's Wife" (O'Connor) **5**:377
"Michel Siniagin" (Zoshchenko) **15**:399
"Mick the Devil" (Stoker) **62**:252-53
Micromégas (Voltaire) **12**:341, 343, 390-94
"The Midas Plaque" (Pohl) **25**:212-13, 220, 223
"The Middle Drawer" (Calisher) **15**:7, 15, 19-21
"The Middle of Nowhere" (Pohl) **25**:232
"The Middle One" (Tagore) **48**:327-29
The Middle Years (James) **8**:291, 299-300
The Middle-Aged Man on the Flying Trapeze: A Collection of Short Pieces (Thurber) **1**:413, 420, 423
"A Middle-Class Education" (Oates) **6**:246
"The Middleman" (Mukherjee) **38**:245, 254, 260, 265-66, 272, 279, 283, 285, 292
The Middleman, and Other Stories (Mukherjee) **38**:235, 238-39, 241-45, 247, 250, 255, 257, 260, 262-63, 269-70, 273, 278-79, 281, 287, 291-92, 294
"A Middling Type" (Moravia) **26**:159-60
"The Midget" (Walser)
　　See "Der Knirps"
"Midnight at Tim's Place" (Thurber) **1**:429
"Midnight Blue" (Collier) **19**:109-11
"A Midnight Clear" (Jones) **56**:285-86
"Midnight Magic" (Mason) **4**:11
"Midnight Mass" (Bowles) **3**:75, 80
"Midnight Mass" (Machado de Assis) **24**:139, 154-55
Midnight Mass (Bowles) **3**:75-6, 79-80
"Midnight Meat Train" (Barker) **53**:136-37, 139-41, 163
Midnight Tales (Stoker) **62**:246
"Midsummer" (Machen) **20**:200
"A Midsummer Knight's Dream" (Henry) **5**:184
"Midsummer Madness" (Galsworthy) **22**:70
"Midsummer Night Madness" (O'Faolain) **13**:295, 301-02, 304, 309, 314-15
Midsummer Night Madness, and Other Stories (O'Faolain) **13**:284, 292, 308, 312-13, 316-17
"Midsummer Passion" (Caldwell) **19**:34, 39, 46
"Mid-western Primitive" (Suckow) **18**:391, 412, 416
"The Midwinter Guest" (Caldwell) **19**:17
"La migala" (Arreola) **38**:9, 25
"Miggles" (Harte) **8**:209-10, 236, 254; **59**:291, 294, 319-20, 322, 325, 338
Miguel Street (Naipaul) **38**:305-06, 311, 315-20, 322-28, 330, 335-37, 339-45, 347-50, 352
"Mikan" (Akutagawa Ryūnosuke) **44**:80, 87-90
"HaMikhtav" (Agnon) **30**:22, 37
"Mila and Prelac" (Andrić) **36**:43
"El milagro secreto" (Borges) **4**:29-30, 37; **41**:52, 57-58, 91, 164
"A Mild Attack of Locusts" (Lessing) **6**:191
"Mildred Lawson" (Moore) **19**:341
"Miles City, Montana" (Munro) **3**:347-48
"Milford Junction, 1939: A Brief Encounter" (Coover) **15**:61
"Militona" (Gautier) **20**:3, 7
"Milk Is Very Good for You" (Dixon) **16**:204, 210, 214

"Milking Time" (O'Flaherty) **6**:262, 277

"The Milkmaid of Samaniago" (Coover) **15**:36

"The Milkmaid Queen" (Calvino)
     See "La lattaia regina"

"Milkman 2" (King)
     See "Big Wheels: A Tale of the Laundry
         Game"

"The Mill" (Bates) **10**:126, 130-31, 133

"La Mille et deuxieme nuit" (Gautier) **20**:15

"The Millennium, and What They Can Do
     With It" (Perelman) **32**:230

"A Miller of Dee" (Galsworthy) **22**:58, 93

"Millie" (Mansfield) **9**:302

"Un Million" (Maupassant) **64**:285-86, 290-91

"A Millionaire of Rough and Ready" (Harte)
     8:254

"Millionaires" (Chabon) **59**:71-77

"Million-Dollar Brainstorm" (Algren) **33**:107

"The Million-Year Picnic" (Bradbury) **29**:50,
     61; **53**:189-90, 195-201, 205-6, 208, 210-
     12, 246-47, 249, 261

"Mina de Vanghel" (Stendhal) **27**:251-53, 259

"Mind and Body" (Williams) **31**:303, 312, 324,
     331, 352-53, 359-60

"Minds Meet" (Abish) **44**:2, 18, 20-21

Minds Meet (Abish) **44**:2-4, 11, 17, 19-20, 24-
     26, 28, 30

"Mine" (Carver) **8**:30, 34

"Mine" (Wideman) **62**:301-2

"Mine Field" (Calvino) **48**:149

"Mingo: A Sketch of Life in Middle Georgia"
     (Harris) **19**:131, 149, 174-75, 178, 184

Mingo, and Other Sketches in Black and White
     (Harris) **19**:134, 146-47, 151, 173, 176,
     181

"Mingtian" (Lu Hsun) **20**:128, 141

"Minister Dragon's Flight" (P'u Sung-ling)
     See "Lung-fei hsiang kung"

"The Minister's Black Veil" (Hawthorne) **3**:154,
     159-60, 164, 171, 177-78, 184, 186-87;
     39:86-150

"The Minister's Books" (Benét) **10**:154, 160

"Ministers of Grace" (Saki) **12**:334

"A Mink of One's Own" (Capote) **47**:44-6, 50

Minne (Colette) **10**:257

"A Minor Mood" (Dybek) **55**:140-41

"The Minority Committee" (Dunbar) **8**:127

"The Minority Report" (Dick) **57**:142-45, 147,
     150-51

"Minotaur" (Walser) **20**:356

"Minus One" (Ballard) **53**:9, 44

"Mio marito" (Ginzburg) **65**:115, 131-32, 138

"The Miracle" (Auchincloss) **22**:47

"Miracle" (Kipling) **54**:121

"The Miracle" (O'Connor) **5**:388

"The Miracle at Ballinspittle" (Boyle) **16**:148,
     151-2, 154-55

"The Miracle at Olovo" (Andrić)
     See "Čudo u Olovu"

"Le Miracle des roses" (Laforgue) **20**:86, 88-9,
     91, 100-2, 114

"The Miracle in Olovo" (Andrić)
     See "Čudo u Olovu"

"Miracle Joyeaux" (Norris) **28**:200

"The Miracle of Moon Crescent" (Chesterton)
     46:111, 113, 134-35

"The Miracle of Purun Bhagat" (Kipling) **5**:295

"The Miracle of Tepayac" (Steinbeck)
     11:249-51

"The Miracle of the Roses" (Laforgue)
     See "Le Miracle des roses"

"Miracles" (Singer) **3**:385-86

"The Miracles of Jamie" (Bradbury) **29**:47;
     53:214

"La mirada" (Pardo Bazán) **30**:284-86, 289-90

"The Mirage" (Akutagawa Ryūnosuke)
     See "Shinkirō"

"Miranda over the Valley" (Dubus) **15**:69-70,
     85, 87

Mirgorod (Gogol) **4**:86-7, 117; **29**:142

"Miriam" (Capote) **2**:61-2, 64, 66, 69, 73-5,
     78-9, 83; **47**:3, 11-13, 16, 29-31, 35, 44-5,
     47, 53-5, 58-9

"Le miroir" (Baudelaire) **18**:16, 49

"The Mirror" (Machado de Assis)
     See "O espelho"

"The Mirror" (O'Flaherty) **6**:260, 265, 276-77,
     279

"The Mirror" (Singer) **3**:364, 368, 375; **53**:329

The Mirror Maker (Levi)
     See *Terza pagina: Racconti e Saggi*

"The Mirror of Ink" (Borges) **41**:65

"The Mirror of the Magistrate" (Chesterton)
     46:125, 135

"The Misadventures of a Matrimonial
     Swindler" (Čapek) **36**:128 .

"The Misadventures of John Nicholson"
     (Stevenson) **11**:269, 282, 303, 305-06

"The Misanthrope" (Lu Hsun)
     See "Guduzhe"

Miscellaneous Papers (Machado de Assis)
     See *Papéis avulsos*

"A Miscellany of Characters That Will Not
     Appear" (Cheever) **1**:93, 100; **38**:61; **57**:9

"A Misdeal" (Somerville & Ross) **56**:334

"The Miser" (O'Connor) **5**:371

"Misery" (Chekhov)
     See "Toska"

"Misfit" (Heinlein) **55**:161-62, 206-7, 213

"A Misfortunate Girl" (Turgenev)
     See "Neschastnaya"

"The Misfortunes of Frederick Pickering"
     (Trollope)
     See "The Adventures of Frederick Picker-
         ing"

"The Misogamist" (Dubus) **15**:75

"Miss Algrave" (Lispector) **34**:205, 212-14

"Miss Baker" (Pritchett) **14**:269

"Miss Brill" (Mansfield) **9**:287, 299, 307, 309,
     312-13

"Miss Chauncey" (Jewett) **6**:168

"Miss Chia-no" (P'u Sung-ling)
     See "Ying-ning"

"Miss Crystal Confronts the Past" (Gilchrist)
     63:8

"Miss Cynthie" (Fisher) **25**:5, 7, 11, 16-17, 19-
     21, 24-6

"Miss Dangerlie's Roses" (Page) **23**:328

"Miss Dollar" (Machado de Assis) **24**:151

"Miss Duveen" (de la Mare) **14**:68, 83-4, 87

"Miss Gibson" (Frame) **29**:104

"Miss Godwin's Inheritance" (Page) **23**:288,
     307

"Miss Harriet" (Maupassant) **1**:259, 271, 274,
     280, 285-87

"Miss Huan-niang" (P'u Sung-ling) **31**:192

"Miss Jemima" (de la Mare) **14**:69

"Miss Leonora When Last Seen" (Taylor)
     10:390, 401, 406, 407, 409, 415

Miss Lonelyhearts (West) **16**:345-49, 351-52,
     354, 356-57, 359-60, 362, 364, 366-67, 369,
     375-81, 383-86, 389-90, 394-402, 404, 407-
     08, 411, 415, 417

"Miss Manning's Minister" (Jewett) **6**:156, 159

"Miss Mary Pask" (Wharton) **6**:431

"Miss Miller" (de la Mare) **14**:87

"Miss Ophelia Gledd" (Trollope) **28**:319, 323,
     348

"Miss Parker Possessed" (Betts) **45**:8, 27

"Miss Parker's Possession" (Betts) **45**:8

"Miss Pinkerton's Apocalypse" (Spark) **10**:350,
     355, 359, 366

"Miss Plarr" (Ligotti) **16**:280

"Miss Puss's Parasol" (Harris) **19**:183

"Miss Rodney's Leisure" (Gissing) **37**:56

"Miss Sarah Jack, of Spanish Town, Jamaica"
     (Trollope) **28**:318, 329

"Miss Slattery and her Demon Lover" (White)
     39:280, 283, 286-87, 291-92, 298-99, 312,
     316, 328, 335, 344

"Miss Smith" (Trevor) **21**:246-47, 262

"Miss Sydney's Flowers" (Jewett) **6**:157, 166,
     168

"Miss Tempy's Watcher's" (Jewett) **6**:151, 156

"Miss W." (O'Hara) **15**:258

"Miss Willie Lou and the Swan" (Benét) **10**:148

"Miss Winchelsea's Heart" (Wells) **6**:391

"Miss Witherwell's Mistake" (Chopin) **8**:84, 86

"Miss Yellow Eyes" (Grau) **15**:158, 164

Die Missbrauchten Liebesbriefe (Keller) **26**:107

"Missed Connection" (Campbell) **19**:75

"Missed Vocation" (Pavese)
     See "Mal di mestiere"

"Missing" (Campbell) **19**:74

"Missing" (de la Mare) **14**:70, 80, 83, 87-8, 92

"The Missing Eye" (Bulgakov) **18**:86-7

"The Missing Line" (Singer) **3**:389

"Missing Mail" (Narayan) **25**:138, 140, 153,
     155

"The Missing Person" (Wolff) **63**:273, 301, 303,
     305, 307-8, 310, 312, 315, 318-20

"The Mission of Jane" (Wharton) **6**:424-25

"The Mission of Mr. Scatters" (Dunbar) **8**:122,
     132, 137, 147

"Mississippi" (Bass) **60**:3, 5, 38

"Mississippi" (Gilchrist) **63**:9

"Mississippi, Ham Rider" (Bambara) **35**:24

"Mrs. Moysey" (Bowen) **3**:30, 33, 40, 42

"Mrs. Windermere" (Bowen) **3**:40, 54

The Mist (Bombal) **37**:43

The Mist (King) **17**:265, 268-71, 273-76, 283;
     55:250-52

"The Mistake" (Gorky) **28**:159

"A Mistake" (Zoshchenko)
     See "A Slight Mistake"

"The Mistake of the Machine" (Chesterton)
     1:131; **46**:110, 133, 152

"A Mistaken Charity" (Freeman) **47**:105, 162,
     193

"The Mistaken Milliner" (Dickens) **17**:135

"Mr. Andrews" (Forster) **27**:69, 75-6, 86, 97,
     100, 114, 122, 123

"Mr. Higginbotham's Catastrophe"
     (Hawthorne) **3**:154

"Mr. Kempe" (de la Mare) **14**:70, 80, 85, 90

"Mr. Lyon" (Carter)
     See "The Courtship of Mr. Lyon"

Mr. (Calvino)
     See *Palomar*

"Mister Palomar in the City" (Calvino) **3**:113,
     115

"Mister Palomar's Vacation" (Calvino) **3**:113

"Mister Toussan" (Ellison) **26**:7-9, 11, 21, 28-9

"Mistério em São Cristóvão" (Lispector)
     34:194-96

"The Mistletoe Bough" (Sansom) **21**:110, 126

"The Mistletoe Bough" (Trollope) **28**:318, 326,
     331, 333, 340, 346, 349, 355

"The Mistress" (Berriault) **30**:95, 97-8

The Mistress and Other Stories (Berriault)
     30:95-8

"Mistress into Maid" (Pushkin)
     See "Baryshnia-krest'ianka"

"Mistris Lee" (Arnim) **29**:29-30

"A Misunderstanding" (Farrell) **28**:99

"Misunderstood" (Far) **62**:50, 54

"Mitchell on Matrimony" (Lawson) **18**:250-51

"Mitchell on the 'Sex,' and Other 'Problems'"
     (Lawson) **18**:250

"Mitchell on Women" (Lawson) **18**:250

"Mitosis" (Calvino) **3**:109-10; **48**:106-7, 114-5,
     142

"HaMitpahat" (Agnon) **30**:4, 35-6

Mitsou (Colette) **10**:257, 271-74

"A Mixed Bag" (Sansom) **21**:102, 127

"Mixing Cocktails" (Rhys) **21**:68-9

The Mixture as Before (Maugham) **8**:379

"Mizu kara waga namida o nuguitamo hi" (Oe)
     20:220-21, 223, 225, 227-32, 234, 237-44,
     246-47, 249-50

"M'Liss: An Idyl of Red Mountain" (Harte)
     8:210, 219, 222, 224-25, 231-32, 234;
     59:300, 332

"Mlle de Scudèry" (Hoffmann) 13:202
"The Mnemogogues" (Levi) 12:279
"Mobile" (Ballard) 1:68; 53:81, 128
"Mobiles" (Cowan) 28:78; 80
Mobiles (Cowan) 28:80; 83
The Mocassin Ranch (Garland) 18:182
"The Mock Auction" (Lavin) 4:183
"Mock Battle" (Kiely) 58:165
"The Mocking-Bird" (Bierce) 9:64, 67-8, 96
"The Model" (Nin) 10:326
A Model for Death (Bioy Casares)
    See *Un modelo para la muerte*
"A Model Millionaire: A Note of Admiration"
    (Wilde) 11:362, 399, 401, 407
"The Model of Sorrows" (Zangwill) 44:378,
    389
"A Model World" (Chabon) 59:71
A Model World and Other Stories (Chabon)
    59:69-78, 81-83, 85, 87
Un modelo para la muerte (Bioy Casares)
    17:48, 74; 48:42
"The Moderate Murderer" (Chesterton) 1:132
Moderato cantabile (Duras) 40:2-3, 10-17, 21,
    25, 31, 33-34, 36-38, 40-50, 53-54, 58-61,
    66-68, 75, 77-79, 82, 84-95, 106, 114, 136-
    40, 142
"A Modern Brutus" (Page)
    See "The Outcast"
"Modern Children" (Aleichem) 33:8
A Modern Comedy (Galsworthy) 22:70-1
"A Modern Dragon" (Freeman) 47:101, 182
"Modern Love" (Boyle) 16:148, 154-56
A Modern Lover (Lawrence) 4:230
"A Modern Scribe in Jerusalem" (Zangwill)
    44:368
"A Modest Proposal" (Stafford) 26:274-76, 285,
    299, 307, 312
"Modesta Gómez" (Castellanos) 39:58, 73
"Modrá chryzantéma" (Čapek) 36:99, 102, 128
"Moebius Strip" (Cortázar) 7:69
"Mohammed Fripouille" (Maupassant) 1:275
"The Mohican" (Nin) 10:303
"Moja izn" (Chekhov) 51:170, 175-76
"Mojave" (Capote) 2:79-80; 47:44, 49-50, 64-6
"La molle luna" (Calvino) 3:94, 108-09; 48:46,
    65, 68, 155, 157
"Molly" (Dubus) 15:86, 90-1
"Molly Cottontail" (Caldwell) 19:46
"Molly's Dog" (Adams) 24:11, 14
"Mom Bi: Her Friends and Enemies" (Harris)
    19:146, 157, 180
"The Moment" (Aiken) 9:5, 13-14, 41
"The Moment before the Gun Went Off"
    (Gordimer) 17:178, 187, 189-90
The Moment of Eclipse (Aldiss) 36:18, 25
"The Moment of Truth" (Greene) 29:223, 228
"Moments of Being: 'Slater's Pins Have No
    Points'" (Woolf) 7:375, 388-89, 391-92,
    398, 408-10
Moments of Reprieve (Levi)
    See *Lilít e altri racconti*
"Momma's Boy" (Apple) 50:33
"Mōmoku monogatari" (Tanizaki) 21:181, 188-
    89, 191, 198, 210-11, 224
"Mon Ami, Emile" (Kiely) 58:147
"Mon oncle Jules" (Maupassant) 1:277
"Mon oncle Sosthène" (Maupassant) 1:263, 272
"A Monastery Legend" (Pilnyak) 48:287-88
The Monastery of Sendomir (Grillparzer)
    See *Das Kloster bei Sendomir*
"A Monday Dream at Alameda Park"
    (Thomas) 20:317
"Monday Is Another Day" (Farrell) 28:120-1
"Monday or Tuesday" (Woolf) 7:371, 374-75,
    390, 392, 397-98, 402
Monday or Tuesday (Woolf) 7:367-69, 371,
    374, 392, 398-401, 404
"Money" (Čapek) 36:92-3, 124
"Money" (Galsworthy) 22:98
Money and Other Stories (Čapek)
    See *Trapné providky*
"The Money Diggers" (Irving) 2:251, 261-62

"The Money Juggler" (Auchincloss) 22:9, 34,
    49-50
"Mongan's Frenzy" (Stephens) 50:319
"The Mongoose" (Grimm and Grimm) 36:190
"Monk" (Faulkner) 1:165, 179
"Monk Eastman" (Borges) 41:164
"The Monkey" (Dinesen) 7:163, 167, 170, 173,
    200-01, 203
"The Monkey" (Freeman) 47:164
"The Monkey" (King) 17:274-75, 290-91, 293;
    55:250-51, 254, 280-82
"The Monkey Garden" (Cisneros) 32:31-32
"The Monkey Island" (Dazai Osamu)
    See "Sarugashima"
"Monkey Nuts" (Lawrence) 4:231, 234-35
"Monkey-Faced Youngster" (Dazai Osamu)
    41:244
"The Monkey's Grave" (Dazai Osamu) 41:228,
    232, 234
"The Monkey's Mound" (Dazai Osamu) 41:276
"Monólogo del insumiso" (Arreola) 38:9
Monologue (Beauvoir) 35:46-50, 53-4, 74-5,
    79, 81-6
"Monologue of an Old Pitcher" (Farrell) 28:112
"Monologue of Isabel Watching It Rain in
    Macondo" (García Márquez) 8:194
"Monrovia" (Toomer) 45:218-21
"Monsieur les deux chapeaux" (Munro) 3:348
"Monsieur Parent" (Maupassant) 1:259-60, 283
"The Monster" (Bradfield) 65:68
"The Monster" (Crane) 56:88, 91-99, 101-5,
    110-14, 116-20, 124-26, 128, 130-31
"The Monster" (Moravia)
    See "Il mostro"
The Monster (Crane) 7:103-05, 107, 114, 116,
    131, 134, 138, 146-48; 56:88, 111
The Monster, and Other Stories (Crane) 7:104
"Monte Cristo" (Calvino)
    See "The Count of Monte Cristo"
Monte Verità (du Maurier) 18:126, 137
A Month by the Lake, and Other Stories
    (Bates) 10:122, 139-40
"Le Monument" (Aymé) 41:24
"A Monument of French Folly" (Dickens)
    17:124
"The Monumental Arena" (Saroyan) 21:163
"The Moon and GNAC" (Calvino)
    See "Luna e GNAC"
"The Moon and Six Guineas" (Auchincloss)
    22:49
"The Moon in Letters" (Bierce) 9:78
"The Moon in the Mill-Pond" (Harris) 19:173
"The Moon in the Orange Street Skating Rink"
    (Munro) 3:348-49
"Moon Lake" (Welty) 1:474, 486; 51:269-70,
    272, 275, 283, 303, 305, 315, 322
"The Moon Lens" (Campbell) 19:72, 81
"The Moon of the Arfy Darfy" (Algren) 33:95,
    97, 108
"Moon Rocket" (Spencer) 57:213
"The Moon-Bog" (Lovecraft) 52:310, 343
"Moon-Face" (London) 4:252, 258-59
Moon-Face, and Other Stories (London) 4:252
"A Moon-Light Effect" (Stoker) 62:252
"A Moonlight Fable" (Wells) 6:376
"Moonlight on the Snow" (Crane) 7:108;
    56:79-81
The Moons of Jupiter (Munro) 3:346-47
"Moonshine Lake" (Bulgakov) 18:74
"The Moonshiners of Hoho-Hehee Falls"
    (Murfree) 22:211
"Moon-Watcher" (Clarke) 3:127-28
The Moor of Peter the Great (Pushkin)
    See *Arap Petra Velikogo*
Moorland Cottage (Gaskell) 25:31, 47, 58, 60,
    65, 71-2
"Moors and Christians" (Alarcon)
    See "Moros y cristianos"
"A Moral Exigency" (Freeman) 47:102, 147
"The Moral Reformers" (Kipling) 54:99-100,
    107

Moral Tales (Laforgue)
    See *Moralités légendaires*
Moralités légendaires (Laforgue) 20:85-6, 88-
    91, 93-5, 97-100, 102, 104-6, 108, 114,
    122-3
"A Morality" (Forster)
    See "What Does It Matter? A Morality"
"A Morality" (Hawthorne) 39:126
"Mordecai and Cocking" (Coppard) 21:3
"The Mordivinian Sarafin" (Bunin)
    See "Mordovskiy sarafan"
"Mordovskiy sarafan" (Bunin) 5:82, 106-08
"More about the Devil" (Gorky)
    See "Eshche o cherte"
"More Alarms at Night" (Thurber) 1:428
"More Birds" (Hood) 42:235
"More by George" (Abish) 44:2
"More Friend Than Lodger" (Wilson) 21:320-
    21, 337, 339
"More Geese than Swans" (Garrett) 30:166,
    174
More Ghost Stories of an Antiquary (James)
    16:231, 238, 251-52, 255, 258
"More Joy in Heaven" (Warner) 23:380
"The More Little Mummy in the World"
    (Thomas) 20:287, 308, 317
The More New Arabian Nights (Stevenson)
    51:232, 236
More Pricks than Kicks (Beckett) 16:64-8, 70-2,
    76, 78, 87, 92-4, 106, 108
More Roman Tales (Moravia)
    See *Nuovi racconti romani*
"More Stately Mansions" (Updike) 13:402, 409
"More Stately Mansions" (Vonnegut) 8:433
More Stories by Frank O'Connor (O'Connor)
    5:371
"More Than Human" (Chabon) 59:70, 73-74,
    76, 79
"Morella" (Poe) 22:299, 329; 35:336; 54:161
Die Morgenlandfahrt (Hesse) 9:227-29, 240-41,
    244-45; 49:241, 255, 274
"Morning" (Barthelme) 2:45, 55; 55:89, 113
"Morning" (Dazai Osamu) 41:251
"The Morning" (Updike) 13:375
"The Morning after the Ball" (Tolstoy)
    See "After the Ball"
"Morning Calm" (Kazakov) 43:59-60
"The Morning Mare" (Davie) 52:6
"Morning, Noon, Evening" (Shiga) 23:344, 346,
    348
"The Morning of a Landed Proprietor"
    (Tolstoy)
    See *A Landlord's Morning*
"A Morning Walk" (Chopin) 8:98
Morning-Glories and Other Stories (Alcott)
    27:11, 41-3
"Morning-Glory" (Freeman) 47:87
"Mornings in April and May" (Alarcon)
    See "Mañanas de abril y mayo"
"Moros y cristianos" (Alarcon) 64:3, 9, 44
"Morphine" (Bulgakov) 18:86, 89
"Morris in Chains" (Coover) 15:31, 50-1
"Mort and Mary" (O'Hara) 15:248
"Une mort héroïque" (Baudelaire) 18:15-16,
    18, 27, 29-30, 34, 60
"The Mortal Coil" (Lawrence) 4:235
Mortal Coils (Huxley) 39:155-56, 163, 165,
    167, 171, 174-75, 177
"Mortality and Mercy in Vienna" (Pynchon)
    14:308, 310, 312, 320, 322-25, 328, 342-43,
    347-49
"Mortals" (Wolff) 63:275
"Una morte" (Svevo)
    See "La morte"
"La morte" (Svevo) 25:330-32, 336-37, 351,
    360
"La morte addosso" (Pirandello) 22:281, 283
"La morte amoureuse" (Gautier) 20:3-4, 6-8,
    13, 17-20, 31-2, 38, 41
The Mortgaged Heart (McCullers) 9:341-44,
    355-57, 359
"The Mortification of the Flesh" (Dunbar) 8:127

"Mortmain" (Greene) **29**:200, 202
"Morton Hall" (Gaskell) **25**:48-9, 59-60, 73
Mosaïque (Mérimée) **7**:287-8, 290, 300
"Mosby's Memoirs" (Bellow) **14**:22, 24-5
Mosby's Memoirs, and Other Stories (Bellow) **14**:22-3, 25, 56
"La mosca en el vasode leche" (Cabrera Infante) **39**:23
"Moscas y arañas" (Bioy Casares) **17**:87-9
"Moscow of the Twenties" (Bulgakov) **18**:92
"The Moslem Wife" (Gallant) **5**:135-38
"Mosquitoes" (Jones) **56**:273, 279
"The Moss People" (Alcott) **27**:43
Mosses from an Old Manse (Hawthorne) **3**:155, 160, 174, 180, 185
"The Most Beautiful Woman in Town" (Bukowski) **45**:58
"The Most Extraordinary Thing" (Andersen) **6**:11
"Most na Žepi" (Andrić) **36**:30, 35, 37, 40, 43, 45-7, 52, 78-9
"The Most Noble Conquest of Man" (Norris) **28**:205
The Most of S. J. Perelman (Perelman) **32**:209, 215, 219, 227-28, 234
"The Most Profound Caress" (Cortázar) See "La caricia más profunda"
"Mostovi" (Andrić) **36**:50
"Motel Architecture" (Ballard) **1**:79; **53**:18-19, 58-9, 114-15
"The Moth" (Wells) **6**:383
"The Mothball Fleet" (Barthelme) **55**:109
"Mother" (Anderson) **1**:33, 44
"Mother" (Barnes) **3**:22, 26
"A Mother" (Galsworthy) **22**:59, 98
"A Mother" (Joyce) **3**:205, 210-11, 234, 237, 245, 247, 249; **26**:46, 50; **64**:246-47, 249-51
"The Mother" (Pavese) **19**:366, 368, 389
"The Mother" (Saroyan) **21**:134
"The Mother" (Svevo) See "Le madre"
"Mother and Child" (Hughes) **6**:119, 142
Mother and Child (Vinge) **24**:327-28, 331, 333-35, 337, 345
"Mother and Daughter" (Lawrence) **4**:205, 220; **19**:267
"Mother and Son" (Narayan) **25**:135, 137, 153, 156, 159
"Mother and Son" (O'Flaherty) **6**:262
"The Mother Bit Him" (Narayan) **25**:135
Mother Earth, and Other Stories (Pilnyak) See *Mat' syra zemlya*
"The Mother Hive" (Kipling) **5**:279
"Mother Matilda's Book" (O'Faolain) **13**:293, 297
"Mother Nature" (Chekhov) **51**:122
"The Mother of a Queen" (Hemingway) **1**:211
The Mother of Captain Shigemoto (Tanizaki) See *Shōshō Shigemoto no haha*
"The Mother of the Child in Question" (Lessing) **61**:123
"The Mother Stone" (Galsworthy) **22**:101
"The Mother Trip" (Pohl) **25**:236
"Motherhood" (Anderson) **1**:27
"Mothering Sunday" (Thomas) **20**:321-22
"The Mother-in-Law" (Betts) **45**:26, 30, 32
"A Mother-in-Law" (Pirandello) **22**:236
"Mothers" (Endō) See "Haha naru mono"
"Mother's Day" (Fuentes) **24**:61, 75-8
"Mother's Death and the New Mother" (Shiga) See "Haha no shi to atarishi haha"
"Mother's Sense of Fun" (Wilson) **21**:319, 321, 323, 330-31, 333, 337-38, 342-43, 351, 364
"A Mother's Vision" (Peretz) **26**:205
"The Motive" (Cortázar) **7**:69-70
"The Motive" (du Maurier) **18**:125, 138
A Motley (Galsworthy) **22**:58-60, 97-100
"The Motor Car" (Clarke) **45**:72, 86, 111
Mottel, the Cantor's Son (Aleichem) **33**:7, 57, 83
"The Motto" (Čapek) **36**:89-90

"Mouche" (Maupassant) **1**:273, 284
"The Mound" (Lovecraft) **3**:270-71, 274, 279
"Mount Yoshino" (Dazai Osamu) **41**:232, 236
"The Mountain" (Čapek) See "Hora"
"The Mountain" (Leskov) See "Gora"
"The Mountain" (Pavese) **19**:368, 390
"The Mountain Day" (Stafford) **26**:289
"The Mountain Tavern" (O'Flaherty) **6**:277-78, 281, 284
The Mountain Tavern, and Other Stories (O'Flaherty) **6**:262-65, 278, 283
"Mountjoy" (Irving) **2**:242
Mourner at the Door (Lish) **18**:275, 277-78, 280-83
"The Mourners" (Malamud) **15**:203, 205, 214, 217-18, 222-23, 225, 227
"The Mourners" (Naipaul) **38**:317, 321, 328, 331, 334, 344
"The Mourning" (Trevor) **58**:290, 299
"The Mouse" (Lavin) **4**:167, 182
"The Mouse" (Nin) **10**:299-303, 319
"The Mouse and the Woman" (Thomas) **3**:399-402, 408; **44**:322, 325, 344-45, 349, 354-57, 359
"Mouse Performance" (P'u Sung-ling) See "Shu'hsi"
"Mouses" (Jones) **56**:285
"La moustache" (Maupassant) **1**:274
Mouth (Ellison) See *I Have No Mouth and I Must Scream*
"Le Mouton" (Aymé) **41**:15
"The Moviemaker" (Dixon) **16**:211
"Movies" (Dixon) **16**:206, 208, 214
Movies (Dixon) **16**:205-08, 211, 214-15
"The Moving Finger" (King) **17**:294
"The Moving Finger" (Wharton) **6**:414
"Moving Spirit" (Clarke) **3**:134
"The Mower" (Bates) **10**:124, 131-32
"Mowgli's Brothers" (Kipling) **5**:293; **54**:81, 83-4, 110, 112, 121-22
"Moxon's Master" (Bierce) **9**:72, 88
"Mr and Mrs Dove" (Mansfield) **9**:305
"Mr. and Mrs. Elliot" (Hemingway) **1**:208; **63**:55, 83
"Mr. and Mrs. Fix-It" (Lardner) **32**:117, 134-36, 139, 141, 145, 158-59
"Mr. Arcularis" (Aiken) **9**:5-6, 9, 12-13, 15, 18-19, 33-41
"Mr. Auerbach in Paris" (Wescott) **35**:375-76
"Mr. Austin" (Farrell) **28**:114, 116
"Mr. Bruce" (Jewett) **6**:157, 166
"Mr. Cass and the Ten Thousand Dollars" (O'Hara) **15**:248
"Mr. Coffee and Mr. Fixit" (Carver) **8**:18-19, 32-3, 59-60; **51**:7, 13
"Mr. Cornelius Johnson, Office Seeker" (Dunbar) **8**:122, 125, 128, 131, 141, 144
"Mr. Durant" (Parker) **2**:274
"Mr. F. is Mr. F." (Ballard) **53**:9, 42
Mr. Featherstone Takes a Ride (Bates) **10**:124
"Mr. Foolfarm's Journal" (Barthelme) **2**:40
"Mr. Fox Gets into Serious Business" (Harris) **19**:171
"Mr. Frisbie" (Lardner) **32**:117, 146
"Mr. Groby's Slippery Gift" (Dunbar) **8**:122
"Mr. Harrington's Washing" (Maugham) **8**:369, 377, 383
"Mr. Harrison's Confessions" (Gaskell) **25**:32-3, 55, 66-7, 73
"Mr. Havlena's Verdict" (Čapek) **36**:127
"Mr. Humphreys and His Inheritance" (James) **16**:230-32, 234, 245, 252-53, 258
"Mr. Icky" (Fitzgerald) **6**:58
"Mr. Jack Hamlin's Mediation" (Harte) **8**:248-49
"Mr. Janík's Cases" (Čapek) See "Případy pana Janíka"
"Mr. Jones" (Wharton) **6**:426-27
"Mr. Justice Harbottle" (James) **16**:238

"Mr. Justice Hartbottle" (Le Fanu) **14**:223-25, 232-34, 236-38, 240-41, 248
"Mr. Know-All" (Maugham) **8**:366
"Mr. Lightfoot in the Green Isle" (Coppard) **21**:19
"Mr. Loveday's Little Outing" (Waugh) **41**:311, 323, 330
Mr Loveday's Little Outing and Other Sad Stories (Waugh) **41**:322, 328, 330-31
"Mr. MacGlowrie's Widow" (Harte) **59**:307
"Mr. McMillen" (Spencer) **57**:211
"Mr. McNamara" (Trevor) **21**:247; **58**:227, 230, 278
"Mr. Minns and His Cousin" (Dickens) **17**:121, 125; **49**:164
Mr. Mulliner Speaking (Wodehouse) **2**:338
"Mr. Pale" (Bradbury) **29**:66; **53**:267
"Mr. Peebles' Heart" (Gilman) **13**:126
"Mr. Pietro" (Pavese) **19**:378
"Mr. Potter Takes a Rest Cure" (Wodehouse) **2**:355-56
"Mr. Powers" (Gordon) **15**:143
"Mr. Preble Gets Rid of His Wife" (Thurber) **1**:418
"Mr. Prokharchin" (Dostoevsky) **2**:170, 191-94
"Mr. Rabbit Grossly Deceives Mr. Fox" (Harris) **19**:172, 194
"Mr. Rabbit Nibbles Up the Butter " (Harris) **19**:195
"Mr. S. Karuma's Crime" (Abe) See "S. Karuma-shi no hanzai"
"Mr. Shawn and Father Scott" (Betts) **45**:2, 8, 26-7
"Mr. Skelmersdale in Fairyland" (Wells) **6**:391-92
"Mr. Smellingscheck" (Lawson) **18**:215
"Mr. Taylor's Funeral" (Chesnutt) **7**:18
"Mr. Thompson's Prodigal" (Harte) **59**:338
"Mr Tritas on the Roofs" (Thomas) **44**:336
"Mr. U" (Morand) **22**:178-80
"Mr. Wolf Makes a Failure" (Harris) **19**:171
"Mrs. Acland's Ghosts" (Trevor) **21**:262; **58**:230
"Mrs. Bathurst" (Kipling) **5**:266, 278-79, 281; **54**:72, 75, 78
"Mrs. Billingsby's Wine" (Taylor) **10**:392, 401-02
"Mrs. Bonny" (Jewett) **6**:150, 168
"Mrs. Box" (Chabon) **59**:82-83, 85-87
"Mrs. Brown" (O'Hara) **15**:248
"Mrs. Brumby" (Trollope) **28**:321, 335, 348, 353
"Mrs. Bullfrog" (Hawthorne) **3**:180
"Mrs. Cassidy's Last Year" (Gordon) **59**:230, 236-38, 263-64
"Mrs. Dalloway in Bond Street" (Woolf) **7**:381-82
Mrs. Dalloway's Party (Woolf) **7**:381-82, 388, 392
"Mrs. Fay Dines on Zebra" (Calisher) **15**:3, 7
"Mrs. Frola and Her Son-in-Law, Mr. Ponza" (Pirandello) See "La Signora Frola e il signor Ponza, suo genero"
"Mrs. Galt and Edwin" (O'Hara) **15**:248, 266
Mrs. Gaskell's Tales of Mystery and Horror (Gaskell) **25**:37
"Mrs. General Talboys" (Trollope) **28**:317-18, 330, 332, 336, 347, 357
"Mrs. Gunton of Poughkeepsie" (James) **8**:311
"Mrs. Hofstadter on Josephine Street" (Parker) **2**:283
"Mrs. Hospitality" (Dazai Osamu) **41**:240, 242
"Mrs. Johnson" (Howells) **36**:399
"Mrs. Kemper" (Suckow) **18**:393, 409
"Mrs. M" (Williams) **31**:329
"Mrs. Mean" (Gass) **12**:123, 134,138-9
"Mrs. Merrill's Duties" (Gilman) **13**:141
"Mrs. Mobry's Reason" (Chopin) **8**:71
"Mrs. Parkins's Christmas Eve" (Jewett) **6**:156, 159
"Mrs. Partridge Has a Fit" (Harris) **19**:195

"Mrs. Paulatim" (Calvino) 48:147, 149
"Mrs. Peckover's Sky . . ." (Wilson) 21:358, 362
"Mrs. Powers' Duty" (Gilman) 13:141
"Mrs. Reinhardt" (O'Brien) 10:333
Mrs. Reinhardt, and Other Stories (O'Brien) 10:333
"Mrs. Rinaldi's Angel" (Ligotti) 16:280, 292, 294-95, 297
"Mrs. Ripley's Trip" (Garland) 18:143, 159, 162-63, 165-67, 172, 192
"Mrs. Silly" (Trevor) 21:233; 58:200, 207-8, 252
"Mrs. Skagg's Husbands" (Harte) 8:234, 244; 59:301, 331
"Mrs. Spring Fragrance" (Far) 62:18, 48-52, 56, 70, 73, 75, 94-95, 97
Mrs. Spring Fragrance (Far) 62:4, 6, 10-11, 13, 46-50, 52-54, 56-60, 62, 64, 70, 72-73, 75-76, 78, 80, 82, 92, 96, 109, 111, 117-18
"Mrs. Stratton of Oak Knoll" (O'Hara) 15:252, 280
"Mrs. Todd's Shortcut" (King) 17:275; 55:250
"Mrs. Vane's Charade" (Alcott) 27:32, 60
"Mrs. Vincent" (Bates) 10:117
"Mrs. Vogel and Ollie" (Suckow) 18:394-95, 413, 416, 422-23
"Mrs. Whitman" (O'Hara) 15:264
"MS. Found in a Bottle" (Poe) 1:379, 391-92, 398; 35:310; 54:234-35
"Mt. Pisgah's Christmas Possum" (Dunbar) 8:121, 127, 131, 136
"Muddler on the Roof" (Perelman) 32:231
"The Mudfog Association" (Dickens) 17:121
"Muerte constante más allá der amor" (García Márquez) 8:167, 169-72, 186
"La muerte del tigre" (Castellanos) 39:47, 48, 56
"La muerte y la brújula" (Borges) 4:4, 10, 16, 19-24, 28-30, 35-6; 41:64-65, 69-72, 75-76, 152, 164, 166
"El muerto" (Borges) 4:4-5, 8-9, 23, 37-9; 41:114-17, 119
"Les muets" (Camus) 9:103, 105, 108, 110, 116, 119, 121-22, 125
"The Muffled Ship" (Galsworthy) 22:62, 101
"La mujer alta" (Alarcon) 64:8, 28-31, 45
"Una mujer amaestrada" (Arreola) 38:10-11
"Mule in the Yard" (Betts) 45:29
"Mule in the Yard" (Faulkner) 1:177
Mules and Men (Hurston) 4:133-36, 139-49, 153, 155-56, 158-59
"A mulher de preto" (Machado de Assis) 24:132
Mulliner Nights (Wodehouse) 2:338
A Multitude of Sins (Ford) 56:184, 196-97
"Mulvihill's Memorial" (Trevor) 21:262
"Mummy to the Rescue" (Wilson) 21:337, 346, 348, 354-55
The Mummy's Tale (Gautier)
    See *Le Roman de la momie*
"Mumu" (Turgenev) 7:315, 320, 323, 326, 352-57, 363
Munchmeyer (Thomas) 20:286-87, 313-16, 320
"El mundo" (Pardo Bazán) 30:272
"El Mundo Nuevo" (Alarcon) 64:10
"La muñeca menor" (Ferré) 36:142-43, 148, 150-51, 156, 159-60, 163-67
"La muñeca reina" (Fuentes) 24:29, 31, 44, 51, 56, 58, 61-3, 70, 73, 82
Una muñeca rusa (Bioy Casares) 17:94, 96
"El Muñeco" (Fuentes) 24:37
"A Municipal Report" (Henry) 5:156, 165, 171-72, 179, 182, 192; 49:205
"Munitions of War" (Machen) 20:200
"Le Mur" (Sartre) 32:255, 261, 264-67, 273-74, 276, 278-82
Le mur (Sartre) 32:254-55, 265, 267-68, 270, 272
"The Murder" (Boell) 23:38
"The Murder" (Chekhov) 2:150; 51:26, 83-4
"Murder" (Sansom) 21:94, 125

"The Murder" (Steinbeck) 11:207, 210, 225, 229-33, 235, 244, 247, 254; 37:330, 357
"Murder as Text" (Kelly) 50:291
"Murder at Cobbler's Hulk" (O'Faolain) 13:296
"Murder at Full Moon by Peter Pym" (Steinbeck) 11:254-55
"A Murder during the Age of Enlightenment" (Akutagawa Ryūnosuke)
    See "Kaika no satsujin"
"Murder for the Wrong Reason" (Greene) 29:216-17, 223
Murder in the Dark (Atwood) 2:15, 17-20; 46:37, 75, 92, 99
"Murder on Belpoggio Street" (Svevo)
    See *L'assassinio di via Belpoggio*
"The Murdered Cousin" (Le Fanu)
    See "A Passage in the Secret History of an Irish Countess"
"The Murderer" (Bulgakov) 18:101
"The Murderer Guest" (Gordon) 59:231, 264-65, 267
"Murderers" (Michaels) 16:306, 308-11, 316, 321
"The Murders in the Rue Morgue" (Poe) 1:378, 387, 389, 395, 406; 22:293, 303, 306; 35:307-08; 54:159, 162-67, 169-78, 185, 187, 192, 195-202, 235-37, 239-43, 245
"Muriel" (Gardner) 7:234
Murke's Collected Silences (Boell)
    See *Doktor Murkes gesammeltes Schweigen, und andere Satiren*
"The Muse as Fluffball" (Atwood) 46:74
"The Muse of the Coming Age" (Andersen) 6:7
"The Muses" (Pavese) 19:370-71, 390
"The Muse's Tragedy" (Wharton) 6:414, 428
"The Museum of Cheats" (Warner) 23:370
The Museum of Cheats (Warner) 23:369, 380
"Museums and Women" (Updike) 13:348, 375
Museums and Women, and Other Stories (Updike) 13:356-61, 366-68
"Mushrooms" (Bradbury) 29:58-9
"Mushrooms in the City" (Calvino)
    See "Funghi in città"
"Music" (Gilchrist) 14:154; 63:17-18, 30-31
"Music" (de la Mare) 14:92
"Music" (Nabokov) 11:122, 125
"Music" (Trevor) 21:246, 248; 58:270, 279
"Music for Chameleons" (Capote) 2:80
Music for Chameleons (Capote) 2:79-81; 47:59, 63-4
"Music from Spain" (Welty) 1:474, 495; 51:260, 271-72, 283, 305, 310, 319, 321-25, 327, 329, 339
"The Music Lesson" (Cheever) 1:100
"The Music Lover" (Gardner) 7:223, 225-26, 238
"The Music of Erich Zann" (Lovecraft) 3:269; 52:255, 266, 290-93, 304-6, 312, 320, 336, 344-45, 359
"The Music of the Moon" (Ligotti) 16:278
"The Music on the Hill" (Saki) 12:288, 315, 331, 334
"The Music School" (Updike) 13:348, 375
The Music School (Updike) 13:352, 354, 356, 366-67, 374-76, 378, 380
"The Music Teacher" (Cheever) 1:106; 38:47
"The Musician" (Selby) 20:275
"The Musicians" (Bradbury) 53:207, 209
Musikalische Leiden und Freuden (Tieck) 31:271, 286
"The Musk Ox" (Leskov)
    See "Ovcebyk"
Musornyi veter (Platonov) 42:254
"Mustafa Madjar" (Andrić) 36:30, 33, 38, 52
"The Mutability of Literature" (Irving) 2:251, 254
"Mute" (Atwood) 2:16
"The Mute Companions" (Narayan) 25:134, 138, 140, 154
"Mutimer's Choice" (Gissing) 37:63
"Muttsy" (Hurston) 4:136, 138, 151
"Muž, který nemohl spát" (Čapek) 36:98

"Muž, který se nelíbil" (Čapek) 36:97, 101-02, 105, 128
"Muza" (Bunin) 5:114
"Muiki" (Chekhov) 51:27, 58, 60, 72, 82, 102, 112, 131, 200-6, 211
"My Aquatic Uncle" (Calvino)
    See "Lo zio acquativo"
"My Aunt" (Irving) 2:242
"My Aunt Gold Teeth" (Naipaul) 38:300, 318, 320, 328, 334, 344
"My Aunt Margaret's Mirror" (Scott) 32:319
"My Belongings" (Endō)
    See "Watakushi no mono"
My Boys (Alcott)
    See *Aunt Jo's Scrap-Bag: My Boys*
"My Brother Elye's Drink" (Aleichem) 33:83
"My Brother Paul" (Dreiser) 30:112, 114
"My Clerical Rival" (Gissing) 37:79
"My Cousin Dickran, The Orator" (Saroyan) 21:172
"My Cousin Dikran, the Orator" (Saroyan)
    See "My Cousin Dickran, The Orator"
"My Cousin Fanny" (Page) 23:284, 326, 328
"My Cousins who could eat cooked turnips" (Frame) 29:106
"My Da" (O'Connor) 5:388
"My Daily Horse" (Valenzuela) 14:366
"My Daughter's Admirers" (Murfree) 22:221
My Day (Rhys) 21:48
"My Disciple" (Lewis) 34:157
My Dog Stupid (Fante) 65:75, 106, 108-11
"My Dream of Flying to Wake Island" (Ballard) 53:21, 61, 129
"My Entry into the War" (Calvino)
    See *L'entrada en guerra*
"My Expensive Leg" (Boell)
    See "Mein teures Bein"
"My Father" (Michaels) 16:321
"My Father Is an Educated Man" (Stuart) 31:232-33, 266
"My Father Joins the Fire Brigade" (Schulz) 13:335
"My Father Leaves Home" (Gordimer) 17:177, 182-85
"My Father's Best Suit" (Frame) 29:106
"My Father's Cough" (Boell) 23:34
"My Father's God" (Fante) 65:100
"My Fellow-Traveler to Oxford" (Lewis) 34:157
"My Fellow-Traveller" (Gorky) 28:136, 148, 158
"My Financial Career" (Leacock) 39:261
"My First and Only House" (Adams) 24:15
"My First Goose" (Babel) 16:9, 10, 16, 28, 30, 53-4, 57-8
"My First Protestant" (O'Connor) 5:386-87
"My First Rehearsal" (Gissing) 37:79
My First Rehearsal and My Clerical Rival (Gissing) 37:79
"My First Two Women" (Gordimer) 17:152
"My French Master" (Gaskell) 25:67
"My Friend Naboth" (Page) 23:311-12
"My Friend the Doctor" (Page) 23:288, 307
"My Girls" (Alcott) 27:9
My Girls (Alcott) 27:43
"My Great-Grandfather's Papers" (Stifter)
    See "Die Mappe meines Urgrossvaters"
"My Heart Is Broken" (Gallant) 5:141
My Heart Is Broken (Gallant) 5:122-23, 130, 139-41
My House in Umbria (Trevor)
    See *Two Lives: Reading Turgenev; My House in Umbria*
"My Hundredth Tale" (Coppard) 21:10, 12, 17, 28
"My Husband Is Right" (Wilson) 21:357, 363
"My Kinsman, Major Molineux" (Hawthorne) 3:164-65, 167, 171, 175-76, 179-80, 182-83, 186-87, 189; 39:100, 128, 135
"My Lady Brandon and the Widow Jim" (Jewett) 6:154
"My Lady Greensleeves" (Pohl) 25:223-24

My Lady Ludlow (Gaskell) **25**:34-6, 41, 54-5, 57-9, 66, 73

"My Last Duchess" (Lardner) **32**:133

"My Last Journey" (Pirandello) **22**:236

"My Last Story" (Frame) **29**:103, 110, 115

"My Life" (Chekhov) **2**:128, 130-32, 135-36, 145, 155, 157; **28**:60; **41**:202; **51**:26, 75-6, 79, 83, 130-31, 136, 192, 195, 199-202, 206, 211-12, 214

My Life and Hard Times (Thurber) **1**:413-14, 419, 421-24, 426-28, 435; **47**:369-70, 373

"My Life as a Bat" (Atwood) **46**:75, 99

"My Life with R. H. Macy" (Jackson) **9**:252, 267; **39**:211, 216, 217, 222

"My Little Robins" (Sansom) **21**:91, 93

"My Lost Opportunities" (Leacock) **39**:262

"My Love, My Umbrella" (McGahern) **17**:302, 308-09, 318, 323

"My Lucy Friend Who Smells Like Corn" (Cisneros) **32**:4

"My Man Bovanne" (Bambara) **35**:18, 24, 33

"My Metamorphosis" (Harte) **8**:254

"My Molly" (Lavin) **4**:167

"My Mother's Death and the Coming of My New Mother" (Shiga)
See "Haha no shi to atarishi haha"

My Mother's House (Colette)
See *La maison de Claudine*

"My Mother's Life" (Lessing) **6**:216

"My Mother's Mother" (O'Brien) **10**:334

"My Name" (Cisneros) **32**:32, 41, 46

My Name is Aram (Saroyan) **21**:146-47, 153, 156, 169, 173-75

"My Name is Everyone" (Vonnegut) **8**:433, 437

"My Name is Jacob" (Betts) **45**:26

"My Neighbor" (Kafka) **5**:206

"My Neighbor Radilov" (Turgenev) **57**:266

My Neighbours (Evans) **43**:15-16, 18, 20, 24, 36, 39

"My Nurse Above All Others" (Kundera) **24**:103

"My Object All Sublime" (Heinlein) **55**:214

"My Oedipus Complex" (O'Connor) **5**:368-69, 378, 386-87

"My Old Home" (Lu Hsun)
See "Guxiang"

"My Old Man" (Caldwell) **19**:17-18, 41, 47, 50

"My Old Man" (Hemingway) **1**:208, 219, 234, 245; **36**:280

"My Old Man" (Lardner) **32**:117

"My Old Man and Pretty Sooky" (Caldwell) **19**:50-1

"My Old Man and the Gypsy Queen" (Caldwell) **19**:51

"My Old Man Hasn't Been the Same Since" (Caldwell) **19**:50-2

"My Old Man's Baling Machine" (Caldwell) **19**:51

"My Old Man's Political Appointment" (Caldwell) **19**:50-1

"My Own True Ghost-Story" (Kipling) **5**:272-73

"My Pal with the Long Hair" (Boell) **23**:11

My People (Evans) **43**:2-4, 6, 9-10, 12-18, 20, 22-3, 26, 29, 33-4, 36-43, 45

"My Picture in the Paper" (Saroyan) **21**:137

"My Picture Left in Scotland" (Garrett) **30**:166, 174

"My Plan for the Assassination of Jacqueline Kennedy" (Ballard) **53**:68, 95

"My Platonic Sweetheart" (Twain) **26**:330

"My Pretty Birdie, Birdie in My Cage" (Garrett) **30**:174

"My Pretty Pony" (King) **17**:294

"My Professions" (Zoshchenko) **15**:400

"My Real Estate" (Apple) **50**:3, 5, 9, 20, 29-30, 43

"My Roomy" (Lardner) **32**:115-16, 128-29, 131, 142-43, 145, 148, 154-55, 164-65

"My Sad Face" (Boell) **23**:11-12

"My Sengalese Birds and Siamese Cats" (Thurber) **47**:368

"My Side of the Matter" (Capote) **2**:61-2, 65, 70, 83-5; **47**:10, 17, 52-4, 59-61, 63

"My Son Austin" (O'Faolain) **13**:284

"My Tears" (Oe)
See "Mizu kara waga namida o nuguitamo hi"

"My Tocaya" (Cisneros) **32**:9, 35-36

"My Travelling Companion" (Gorky)
See "My Fellow-Traveller"

"My Tree" (Sansom) **21**:85

"My Uncle John" (Irving) **2**:242

My Uncle Silas (Bates) **10**:117, 130-31

"My Unforgettable Character" (Cabrera Infante) **39**:24

"My Vocation" (Lavin) **4**:167

"My Warszawa:1980" (Oates) **6**:255

My World—And Welcome to It (Thurber) **1**:420

"My Youngest Child" (Shiga) **23**:349

"Myra" (Berriault) **30**:97-8

"Myra Meets His Family" (Fitzgerald) **6**:56, 96

"Myself upon the Earth" (Saroyan) **21**:132, 135, 141, 143

Mystères de Province (Balzac) **59**:4

Mysteries and Adventures (Doyle) **12**:58-9

"The Mysterious Key" (Alcott) **27**:57

"Mysterious Kôr" (Bowen) **3**:31-32, 39, 41-42, 44, 53; **28**:3-4, 9

"The Mysterious Lodger" (Le Fanu) **14**:238

"The Mysterious Ship" (Lovecraft) **52**:290

"The Mysterious Stranger" (Twain) **6**:331

The Mysterious Stranger (Twain) **6**:294-99, 301-02, 305-06, 312-16, 322-25, 331, 334, 345-50, 353; **26**:318-64

"The Mystery" (Pavese) **19**:365, 370

"The Mystery of Dave Regan" (Lawson) **18**:217, 238-39

"A Mystery of Heroism" (Crane) **7**:102, 106, 109; **56**:105-10

"The Mystery of Marie Rogêt" (Poe) **1**:386, 388, 400, 406; **35**:306; **54**:162-67, 169-70, 236-37, 240, 242-43

"The Mystery of Sasassa Valley, a South African Story" (Doyle) **12**:84

"The Mystery of the Graveyard" (Lovecraft) **52**:262

"The Mystery of the Time Piece" (Moorhouse) **40**:324

"The Mystery of Witch-Face Mountain" (Murfree) **22**:196, 212

"The Mystic Journal" (Auchincloss) **22**:45, 50

"The Mystics of Muelenburg" (Ligotti) **16**:263, 267, 276, 278, 283-84, 286-87, 295

"Mystification" (Poe) **22**:300

"Myten om människorna" (Lagerkvist) **12**:181

"The Myth of Mankind" (Lagerkvist)
See "Myten om människorna"

"The Myths of Bears" (Bass) **60**:23-25, 40

"Myths of the Near Future" (Ballard) **1**:78-9; **53**:22-3, 26-7, 64-5, 117-18

Myths of the Near Future (Ballard) **1**:78-9, 82; **53**:18, 35, 67, 109, 114, 117-18

"My-to ne umrem" (Solzhenitsyn) **32**:353, 395

"N" (Machen) **20**:177, 186-87, 196

"Na arca" (Machado de Assis) **24**:128-29, 132

"N.A. Bugrov" (Gorky) **28**:182

"Na drugi dan Božića" (Andrić) **36**:47, 52

"Na kamenu u Počitelju" (Andrić) **36**:50

"Na kraj sveta" (Bunin) **5**:98

"Na kraju sveta" (Leskov) **34**:108, 114, 129

"Na obali" (Andrić) **36**:47

"Na ostrove" (Kazakov) **43**:49, 52, 58, 62, 65-66, 68

"Na oxote" (Kazakov) **43**:52

"Na plotakh" (Gorky) **28**:144, 159, 178, 190

"Na Podvode" (Chekhov) **51**:58, 61, 70-1, 74, 204

"Na polustanke" (Kazakov) **43**:54

Na polustanke (Kazakov) **43**:50, 62-3, 66-7

"Na xutore" (Bunin) **5**:98

"Nabo: The Black Man Who Made the Angels Wait" (García Márquez) **8**:154-55, 157-58, 183, 185

Nabokov's Dozen (Nabokov) **11**:108, 110, 126-28, 130

"Nabonides" (Arreola) **38**:13

"Nachkommenschaften" (Stifter) **28**:299

Nachstücke (Hoffmann) **13**:180, 182, 186-88, 234

"Die Nacht im Hotel" (Lenz) **33**:318

"Der Nachtzug" (Hauptmann) **37**:258

Nada menos que todo un hombre (Unamuno) **11**:313-14, 320-22, 324-25, 327, 345, 351-52

"Naga" (Narayan) **25**:170

Nahan (Lu Hsun) **20**:125-26, 136, 138-39, 141-42, 144, 146, 148

"The Nail" (Alarcon)
See "El clavo"

The Nail and Other Stories (Alarcon) **64**:39, 45

"The Nails in Mr. Caterer" (Hammett) **17**:224

"Le Nain" (Aymé) **41**:18-19, 22

"Los naipes del Tahur" (Borges) **41**:65

La naissance du jour (Colette) **10**:262, 274, 278-79, 285

"Naked" (Michaels) **16**:311

"Naked in the River" (Dazai Osamu) **41**:229

Naked Life (Pirandello)
See *La vita nuda*

"Naked Nude" (Malamud) **15**:171, 173-75, 183, 192-94, 222

"The Naked Truth" (Pirandello) **22**:227

The Naked Truth (Pirandello) **22**:226, 228

"Nakedness" (Pavese)
See "Nudismo"

"Nakedness" (Updike) **13**:387

"Nala" (Narayan) **25**:131

"Namanjur Galpa" (Tagore) **48**:316

"The Name" (Pavese) **19**:376, 387

The Name of the World (Johnson) **56**:248-54, 262

"The Name, the Nose" (Calvino)
See "Il nome il naso"

"The Name-Day" (Saki) **12**:317

"The Name-Day Party" (Chekhov) **2**:128, 130-31, 133, 149, 155-56; **51**:25, 84, 129, 157

"The Nameless City" (Lovecraft) **3**:262-63, 269, 274, 276; **52**:267, 283, 307, 309-10, 313, 335, 343-44, 351, 359

A Nameless Tomb (Onetti)
See *Para una tumba sin nombre*

"Names" (Dixon) **16**:204

"The Names and Faces of Heroes" (Price) **22**:361, 375, 382-84, 387

The Names and Faces of Heroes (Price) **22**:359-60, 363-64, 367, 374, 384-85

"The Namesake" (Cather) **2**:97, 103-04, 113; **50**:74, 80, 106, 200-01

"Namgay Doola" (Kipling) **5**:262

"The Naming of Names" (Bradbury)
See "Dark They Were, and Golden-Eyed"

"Nancy Culpepper" (Mason) **4**:13

"Nanette: An Aside" (Cather) **2**:101; **50**:80, 82, 94-5, 156, 184

Nanji mo mata (Endō) **48**:204-5, 207-8

"Nanni Volpe" (Verga) **21**:298

"Nanny" (Dick) **57**:108-9

"The Nap" (Banks) **42**:64

"The Nap" (de la Mare) **14**:70, 79, 83, 86, 88

"Napier Court" (Campbell) **19**:62, 87

"Nápis" (Čapek) **36**:111, 122

"Naprostý dukaz" (Čapek) **36**:96, 102

Narcissa, and Other Fables (Auchincloss) **22**:35, 47, 51

"Narcissus" (Dazai Osamu)
See "Suisen"

Der Narr auf Manegg (Keller) **26**:92, 108, 113

The Narrative (Pasternak)
See *Povest*

Narrative of ARthur Gordon Pym (Poe)
See *The Narrative of Arthur Gordon Pym, of Nantucket*

The Narrative of Arthur Gordon Pym, of Nantucket (Poe) **54**:236

"Die Narrenburg" (Stifter) **28**:290, 299

"A Narrow Heart: The Portrait of a Woman"
(Gordon) **15**:122-23, 126
"Nashtanir" (Tagore) **48**:317, 319-20
"A Nasty Type" (Bulgakov) **18**:89
Natasqua (Davis) **38**:96
"Nathalie" (Bunin) **5**:87, 113, 115
Natica Jackson (O'Hara) **15**:278, 284-85
"A Nation of Wheels" (Barthelme) **2**:40
"The National Debt" (Apple) **50**:23
"The National Pastime" (Cheever) **1**:100
"Native of Winby" (Jewett) **6**:155
"Native's Return" (Farrell) **28**:112
"Nattergalen" (Andersen) **6**:7, 16, 27, 30, 32-4,
37, 40; **56**:34, 37
"Natural Boundaries" (Oates) **6**:248-50
"A Natural History of the Dead" (Hemingway)
1:211
Natural Stories (Levi)
See *Storie naturali*
Natural Supernaturalism (Abrams) **20**:289,
295-96, 298, 317, 319
"Nature" (Machen) **20**:159
"Nature" (Turgenev) **7**:335
The Nature of Love (Bates) **10**:117-21
"Las náufragas" (Pardo Bazán) **30**:271-72
"The Naughty Boy" (Andersen) **6**:30, 32
"A Naughty Boy" (Chekhov)
See "Zloj mal'ik"
"A Naval Mutiny" (Kipling) **54**:78
"The Navigator Returns to His Country" (Bioy
Casares) **17**:94
"Nazis" (Borowski) **48**:4, 7
Neanderthal Planet (Aldiss) **36**:18
"Near the Shore" (Appelfeld)
See "Ahar hahatunah"
"Necessity's Child" (Wilson) **21**:333, 346, 348,
354, 359
"The Necklace" (Maupassant)
See "La parure"
"The Necklace" (Pritchett) **14**:280, 299, 305
"The Necktie" (Aiken) **9**:5, 9, 13-14
"Nedda" (Verga) **21**:284-86, 301-04, 308
"A Need for Something Sweet" (Gordimer)
17:193-94
"The Needle" (Čapek)
See "Jehla"
"Needle and Glass and Fog" (Kawabata)
See "Hari to Ciarasu to Kiri"
"The Needlecase" (Bowen) **3**:41
"Der Neger" (Walser) **20**:341
"A Neglected Class" (Page) **23**:311
"Negriero" (Moravia) **26**:144
"The Negro" (Walser)
See "Der Neger"
"The Negro and the Old Man with the Knife"
(Moravia)
See "Il negro e il vecchio dalla roncola"
"The Negro in the Drawing Room" (Hughes)
6:121-22
"The Negro in the Well" (Caldwell) **19**:14
The Negro of Peter the Great (Pushkin)
See *Arap Petra Velikogo*
"The Neighbor" (Banks) **42**:56, 64-5
"The Neighborhood" (Gordon) **59**:265, 267-68
"The Neighborhood" (O'Hara) **15**:279
"Neighborhood Drunk" (Dybek) **55**:126, 136,
141
"The Neighboring Families" (Andersen) **6**:7
"Neighbors" (Carver) **8**:4-6, 9-10, 34, 42, 47,
54
"The Neighbors" (Chekhov)
See "Sosedi"
"Neighbors" (Singer) **3**:384
Neighbors (Hesse) **9**:230
"A Neighbor's Landmark" (James) **16**:236, 252,
254
"Neighbour Rosicky" (Cather) **2**:105, 115-17;
50:59, 65, 116, 126-29, 131, 141-42, 144,
208-10, 212, 229, 249-50
"Neighbours" (Andrić)
See "Susedi"
"The Neighbours" (Galsworthy) **22**:58, 80, 82

"Neighbours" (de la Mare) **14**:87
"Neighbours" (Pritchett) **14**:277
"Neighbour's Help" (Narayan) **25**:138
"Neil MacAdam" (Maugham) **8**:376
"Neither the Most Terrifying nor the Least
Memorable" (Valenzuela) **14**:367
"Nell" (Ross) **24**:297, 306, 310
"Nelse Hatton's Revenge" (Dunbar) **8**:119, 121,
127, 140, 143
"Nelse Hatton's Vengeance" (Dunbar)
See "Nelse Hatton's Revenge"
*Nelson Algren's Own Book of Lonesome
Monsters* (Algren) **33**:89
"Nelson Redline" (Hammett) **17**:217
"Nemirna godina" (Andrić) **36**:34
"Nemureru bijo" (Kawabata) **17**:235-41, 243-45
Nemureru bijo (Kawabata) **17**:234, 240, 246
"Nenashin Side" (Pilnyak) **48**:293
"Neo-Einstein Stirs Savants!" (Perelman)
32:240
The Neon Wilderness (Algren) **33**:87-9, 99, 101-
02, 107-11, 113
"Neron tiple o el calvario de un inglé"
(Unamuno) **11**:312
"HaNerot" (Agnon) **30**:37
"Nerot" (Singer) **53**:322
"Nervous" (Walser) **20**:349
"A Nervous Breakdown" (Chekhov)
See "An Attack of Nerves"
Nervous People, and Other Stories
(Zoshchenko) **15**:405-07
"Nesčastnaja" (Turgenev)
See "Neschastnaya"
"Neschastnaia" (Turgenev)
See "Neschastnaya"
"Neschastnaya" (Turgenev) **7**:321, 324, 326,
336-38, 358-59; **57**:272-77
"Nesselrode to Jeopardy" (Perelman) **32**:211
"Nest, Door, Neighbours" (Cabrera Infante)
39:24
"Nest Egg" (Stuart) **31**:233, 263
"The Nest of Nightingales" (Gautier) **20**:3
"Nestor and Kir" (Kazakov) **43**:67
Net of Jewels (Gilchrist) **63**:33
"Nethescurial" (Ligotti) **16**:284, 293
*Neue Geschichten. Hefte 1-18: Unheimlichkeit
der Zeit* (Kluge) **61**:63, 83
"Neutron Tide" (Clarke) **3**:133
"Nevada Gas" (Chandler) **23**:56, 59, 85, 104,
106-07, 109
"Never Bet the Devil Your Head" (Poe) **1**:407
"Never Marry a Mexican" (Cisneros) **32**:10,
15-17, 20-21, 23, 25, 34, 36-37, 39
"Never, Never—Never, Never" (Trollope)
28:317, 333
"Nevermore Without End" (Sansom) **21**:122
"Nevesta" (Chekhov) **2**:131, 139, 143, 149,
151; **51**:58, 70, 79-80, 126-27, 129-30, 141,
144, 194, 214
"Nevskij Avenue" (Gogol) **4**:95, 122, 124-25,
128; **29**:135, 152; **52**:92, 96, 104-5, 108,
113, 121-23, 129-31, 155
"Nevsky Prospect" (Gogol) **4**:95, 122, 124-25,
128; **29**:135, 152
"The New Accelerator" (Wells) **6**:367, 391, 393,
404, 406
The New Arabian Nights (Stevenson) **11**:268-
70, 280; **51**:218, 227, 232-33, 236, 248
New Arrivals, Old Encounters (Aldiss) **36**:13-
14, 18
"The New Atlantis" (Le Guin) **12**:220
"The New Automaton Theatre" (Millhauser)
57:189
"The New Catacomb" (Doyle) **12**:49
"The New Century's Muse" (Andersen)
See "Den ny Aarhundredes Musa"
"New Country" (Hood) **42**:191
"The New Dacha" (Chekhov)
See "Novaja doa"
"New Day" (O'Hara) **15**:248
"A New Departure in Art" (Stoker) **62**:252

"The New Dress" (Woolf) **7**:373, 376, 381-82,
387, 393, 395
"New Dresses" (Mansfield) **9**:281; **38**:204
"A New England Nun" (Freeman) **1**:192, 197,
199; **47**:85, 87, 89-90, 101, 104, 108, 116,
119, 125, 150, 161, 167, 186
A New England Nun, and Other Stories
(Freeman) **1**:191, 194-95, 197; **47**:83-5,
93, 95, 97, 102-06, 123, 133-34, 145, 149,
154, 160, 170, 188, 190-94
"A New England Prophet" (Freeman) **1**:197
"The New Englander" (Anderson) **1**:27, 30, 39,
46-7, 53, 55
"New Eve and Old Adam" (Lawrence) **4**:220
"The New Father Christmas" (Aldiss) **36**:20
"The New Fruit" (Kelly) **50**:290
"The New House" (Bowen) **3**:40, 54
"The New House" (Greene) **29**:222-23
New Islands and Other Stories (Bombal) **37**:41
"The New Lebanon Agent" (Page) **23**:307,
311-12
"The New Life" (Kelly) **50**:291
"The New Man" (Lessing) **6**:191, 198
"A New Melody" (Peretz) **26**:206
"The New Member" (Barthelme) **55**:119-21
"A New Method of Book Distribution"
(Bulgakov) **18**:90
"The New Moon Party" (Boyle) **16**:143-44, 146
"New Murders in the Rue Morgue" (Barker)
53:138-39, 143, 154, 162
"The New Music" (Barthelme) **2**:55; **55**:30, 66,
68, 72, 88-9, 107-8, 113
"The New Owner" (Barthelme) **55**:111-12
"A New Refutation of Time" (Borges)
See "Nueva refutación del tiempo"
"New Rose Hotel" (Gibson) **52**:22, 41
New Stories (Andersen)
See *Eventyr, fortalte for bøorn*
New Stories (Kluge) **61**:76
"A New Stretch of Woods" (Price) **22**:387
"The New Suit" (O'Flaherty) **6**:287
New Tales of the Provinces (Dazai Osamu)
41:247
"The New Teacher" (O'Connor)
See "The Cheapjack"
"The New Villa" (Chekhov)
See "Novaja doa"
"The New World" (Banks) **42**:52
"A New World" (Jolley) **19**:234
The New World (Banks) **42**:52-53
"The New Year" (Dickens) **17**:116; **49**:164
"New Year's Bells" (Dreiser)
See "When the Old Century Was New"
New Year's Eve (The 'Seventies) (Wharton)
6:439-40, 442
"The New Year's Sacrifice" (Lu Hsun)
See "Zhufu"
"New York by Campfire Light" (Henry) **5**:159
"New York Lady" (Parker)
See "From the Diary of a New York Lady"
New York Quartet (Wharton)
See *Old New York*
"New York to Detroit" (Parker) **2**:274, 280, 285
"Newborn Thrown in Trash and Dies"
(Wideman) **62**:274, 286, 292, 294-95
"The Newel Vignettes" (Ford) **56**:194
"News for the Church" (O'Connor) **5**:371, 383,
385, 389
"News from Chelsea" (Sansom) **21**:102
"The News from Ireland" (Trevor) **21**:247-48,
250, 252-53, 262, 267-68; **58**:235, 242, 249-
51, 295
The News from Ireland, and Other Stories
(Trevor) **21**:246, 262; **58**:200, 212-13,
245-48
"News from the Sun" (Ballard) **1**:78-9; **53**:22-3,
63-5, 89-90
"The News in English" (Greene) **29**:217, 223,
225-26
"The Newspaper" (Wolfe) **33**:401
The Newspaper of Claremont Street (Jolley)
19:221, 229, 233, 237, 242, 244-46

"A New-Wave Format" (Mason) 4:14
"Next Door" (Wolff) 63:282, 285-88, 290, 292, 296, 298-300, 305, 315, 318, 320, 323
"The Next in Line" (Bradbury) 29:41, 66, 88
"The Next Tenants" (Clarke) 3:135
"The Next Time" (James) 8:281, 317
"Next Time You'll Know Me" (Campbell) 19:77-8
"Nice Day at School" (Trevor) 21:231, 233
"Nice Girl" (Anderson) 1:52
"The Nice Old Man and the Pretty Girl" (Svevo)
   See "La novella del buon vecchio e della bella fanciulla"
The Nice Old Man and the Pretty Girl, and Other Stories (Svevo)
   See *La novella del buon vecchio e della bella fanciulla*
"A Nice Old-Fashioned Romance with Love Lyrics and Everything" (Saroyan) 21:172
"A Nice Quiet Place" (Fitzgerald) 6:80
"Nicht nur zur Weihnachtzeit" (Boell) 23:38
The Nick Adams Stories (Hemingway) 1:240; 63:125
"Nickel" (Levi) 12:268, 280
"Un nido de gorrionesen un toldo" (Cabrera Infante) 39:24
"Nieh Hsiao-ch'ien" (P'u Sung-ling) 31:192
"Nien yang" (P'u Sung-ling) 31:205
"Niente" (Moravia) 26:148
"El nieto del Cid" (Pardo Bazán) 30:272, 290
"The Nigger" (Barnes) 3:5, 10-11, 14, 22
"Nigger Jeff" (Dreiser) 30:114-22, 126-27, 129, 131-33
The Nigger of Peter the Great (Pushkin)
   See *Arap Petra Velikogo*
"The Night" (Agnon)
   See "Laila min haLelot"
"The Night" (Bradbury) 29:63, 65; 53:238-39, 241-43
"Night" (Bunin) 5:100, 108, 114
"Night" (Kazakov) 43:48
"Night" (O'Brien) 10:345
"Night" (Pirandello)
   See "Notte"
"A Night among the Horses" (Barnes) 3:5-7, 10, 14, 16, 22-4
"Night and Silence" (Price) 22:384
"A Night at Greenway Court" (Cather) 2:100; 50:68, 91, 184
"A Night at the Fair" (Fitzgerald) 6:49
A Night at the Movies, or You Must Remember This (Coover) 15:57, 61, 63
"The Night before Prohibition" (Aiken) 9:12, 14
"Night Call, Collect" (Bradbury) 29:56
"The Night Came Slowly" (Chopin) 8:98, 110-11
"The Night Club in the Woods" (Calisher) 15:5, 8
"A Night Conversation" (Bunin) 5:81, 90-1
"The Night Driver" (Calvino) 3:109; 48:86-88, 113-15, 117, 147, 156
"The Night Face Up" (Cortázar)
   See "La noche boca arriba"
"The Night Flier" (King) 17:295
"A Night for Love" (Vonnegut) 8:433
"Night Games" (Schnitzler) 61:307-8
Night Games and Other Stories and Novellas (Schnitzler) 61:306-7, 309-10
"The Night He Was Left Alone" (Rulfo)
   See "La noche que lo dejaron solo"
A Night in Acadie (Chopin) 8:66-8, 77, 84, 93-4, 97, 110-14
"A Night in June" (Williams) 31:304-05, 325, 332-33, 340, 342, 344-45, 347-48
"A Night in New Arabia" (Henry) 5:184
"The Night in Question" (Wolff) 63:275-77
The Night in Question (Wolff) 63:276-78, 280-81, 337, 339
"A Night in the Alhambra" (Andrić)
   See "Noc u Alhambri"

"A Night in the Woods" (Barnes) 3:18
"Night Journey" (Lewis) 40:278-79
"Night Meeting" (Bradbury) 53:205-6, 208-9, 247-48, 250
"The Night My Old Man Came Home" (Caldwell) 19:14, 49-50, 52
"The Night Ocean" (Lovecraft) 52:293
"A Night of Cyclone" (Narayan) 25:138, 155-56
"The Night of Denial" (Bunin) 5:82
"A Night of Horror" (Peretz)
   See "Leil zeva'ah"
"A Night of Nothing" (Saroyan) 21:134
"Night of Six Days" (Morand)
   See "La nuit de seis jours"
"The Night of the Curlews" (García Márquez)
   See "La noche de los alcaravanes"
The Night of the Funny Hats and Other Stories (Davie) 52:3, 12
"Night of the Great Season" (Schulz)
   See "Noc wielkiego sezonu"
"The Night of the Numbers" (Calvino) 48:146-47
"A Night on the Divide" (Harte) 8:216, 253
"Night Out, 1925" (Rhys) 21:55-6
"Night Owls" (Leskov)
   See "Polunoščniki"
Night Pieces after the Manner of Callot (Hoffmann)
   See *Phantasiestüeke in Callots Manier*
"Night Report" (Jolley) 19:234
Night Run to the West (Bates) 10:119
Night Shift (King) 17:261-62, 273-76, 294; 55:249-51, 260
"Night Sketches" (Hawthorne) 3:189, 191; 39:111
"Night Surf" (King) 17:269
"The Night the Bed Fell" (Thurber) 1:428; 47:369
"The Night the Favorite Came Home" (Gordimer) 17:161
"The Night the Ghost Got In" (Thurber) 1:428, 432
"The Night the Prowler" (White) 39:301, 303, 306, 309-11, 319, 324, 327, 329, 337, 345
"The Night They Left Him Alone" (Rulfo)
   See "La noche que lo dejaron solo"
Night Visions 3 (Campbell) 19:87
"The Night Watchman's Occurrence Book" (Naipaul) 38:321, 328, 346-47
"The Night We Rode with Sarsfield" (Kiely) 58:157
"Night! Youth! Paris! and the Moon!" (Collier) 19:101-02, 110, 114-15
"The Night-Born" (London) 4:266, 291
Nightbreed (Barker) 53:179-80
"Nighthawks" (Dybek) 55:130, 133-34, 154
"The Nightingale" (Andersen)
   See "Nattergalen"
"The Nightingale and the Rose" (Wilde) 11:372, 375-76, 378-79, 386-87, 389, 393, 395, 402-04, 406-09
Nightlines (McGahern) 17:298, 301-03, 306-09, 320, 322
"A Nightmare" (Chekhov) 51:90
"The Nightmare Child" (Galsworthy) 22:63, 74, 79, 101
"Nightmares" (Cortázar)
   See "Pesadillas"
Nightmares and Dreamscapes (King) 17:293-96
"Nightpiece with Figures" (O'Connor) 5:382, 385, 391-92
"Nights in Europe's Ministeries" (Cortázar)
   See "Noches en los ministerios de Europa"
"Nights in the Gardens of Spain" (Berriault) 30:96-8, 104
"The Nights of Goliadkin" (Bioy Casares)
   See "Las noches de Goliadkin"
"The Nights of the UNPA" (Calvino)
   See "Le notti dell'UNPA"

Nights with Uncle Remus: Myths and Legends of the Old Plantation (Harris) 19:130, 133-34, 144, 146, 148, 151, 156, 160-64, 166, 169, 187, 189, 193-96
"A Night's Work" (Gaskell)
   See "A Dark Night's Work"
"Night-Sea Journey" (Barth) 10:41-3, 45-8, 53-4, 56-7, 60-1, 75-6, 80, 90, 97-8, 80, 84, 87, 89, 91, 97-100
"The Night-Worker" (Pritchett) 14:297
"Nikishkin's Secrets" (Kazakov)
   See "Nikishkiny tainy"
"Nikishkiny tainy" (Kazakov) 43:52, 54, 67
"Nilushka" (Gorky) 28:150
"N'importe où hors du monde" (Baudelaire) 18:5, 40
"Nimram" (Gardner) 7:223-27, 235, 238, 241
Nina Balatka (Trollope) 28:317
"La niña mártir" (Pardo Bazán) 30:263, 271
"Niña perversa" (Allende) 65:37, 39-41, 43
"The Nine Billion Names of God" (Clarke) 3:134-35, 137, 145
"Nine Dollars Worth of Mumble" (Caldwell) 19:44
Nine Fairy Tales (Čapek) 36:84, 108
"Nine Hours Alone" (Price) 22:386
"Nine Lives" (Le Guin) 12:231-33
Nine Men Who Laughed (Clarke) 45:75-6, 78-83, 88, 91-3, 100, 102-05, 107, 109-10, 116, 124-25
Nine Stories (Salinger) 2:289-91, 299, 312-13, 316, 318-19; 28:261; 65:294, 297-98, 303-6, 311, 316-18, 321
Nine Women (Grau) 15:161-64
"Ninepenny Flute" (Coppard) 21:17, 29
"Nineteen Fifty-Five" (Walker) 5:412, 414
Nineteen Stories (Greene) 29:182-86, 190, 213, 224-25
"1957, a Romance" (Gilchrist) 14:150; 63:9-10, 13-14, 16-19, 22
"1940: FALL" (Adams) 24:16
"1944" (Gilchrist) 14:150; 63:10-11, 19
"1934" (Phillips) 16:326, 328, 337
"1939" (Taylor) 10:381-82, 385, 416
"Ninety Minutes Away" (O'Hara) 15:259
The 99: New Meaning (Abish) 44:12, 37-38
"Ningyo no nageki" (Tanizaki) 21:197
"El niño de San Antonio" (Pardo Bazán) 30:262
"The Nipples of Venus" (Metcalf) 43:155-56
"Nirvana Small by a Waterfall" (Perelman) 32:211
"Nisithe" (Tagore) 48:341, 343
"Nissen hos Spekhøkeren" (Andersen) 6:30, 34, 41; 56:33-4
"Nitrogen" (Levi) 12:255, 265, 268
"Niwa" (Dazai Osamu) 41:247-48
"Nixey's Harlequin" (Coppard) 21:28
Nixey's Harlequin (Coppard) 21:10, 12
"The Nizhni Novgorod Otkos" (Pilnyak) 48:296
"No Country for Old Men" (O'Faolain) 13:314
"No Crime in the Mountains" (Chandler) 23:65, 67-8, 72, 82, 89, 110
"No Cure for It" (Wolfe) 33:374, 398-99, 401
"No Different Flesh" (Henderson) 29:327
"No Dogs Bark" (Rulfo) 25:269-70
No Door (Wolfe) 33:347-49, 351-54, 367, 369-70, 376
"No Friend Like a New Friend" (Auchincloss) 22:43
"No Haid Pawn" (Page) 23:283, 292, 300, 303, 314-16, 320, 325
"No Harm Trying" (Fitzgerald) 6:69-70
"No Hero" (Stuart) 31:228, 265
"No Man's Laughter" (Algren) 33:108
"No More Rivers" (Wolfe) 33:401
"No More the Nightingales" (Bates) 10:116-17
"No Morning After" (Clarke) 3:149
"No Motive" (du Maurier)
   See "The Motive"
No Name (Onetti)
   See *Para una tumba sin nombre*
"No Neck and Bad as Hell" (Bukowski) 45:54

"No, No, Go Not to Lethe" (Aiken) 9:6, 9, 14, 41
"No One Will Laugh" (Kundera) 24:87-8, 90-3, 96-7, 103, 106, 109, 111-4, 121
No One Writes to the Colonel (García Márquez)
  See *El colonel no tiene quien le escribe*
"No Other Way" (Ross) 24:291-92, 306, 309-10
"No oyes ladrar los perros" (Rulfo) 25:246, 249-50, 263, 265, 269, 274, 276, 278
"No Particular Night or Morning" (Bradbury) 29:42, 80
"No Petty Thief" (Stuart) 31:229
"No Place for a Woman" (Lawson) 18:252
"No Place for You, My Love" (Welty) 1:476, 479, 484, 493; 51:281, 319
"No Place Like" (Gordimer) 17:158
No Relief (Dixon) 16:203, 209-10, 213, 215
"No Starch in the Dhoti, s'il vous plaît" (Perelman) 32:222
"No te dejes" (Cortázar) 7:95
No Time like Tomorrow (Aldiss) 36:6, 18
"No Trespassing" (Gordon) 59:274
"No Use to Talk to Me" (Le Guin) 12:231
"No Witchcraft for Sale" (Lessing) 6:186, 190-91
"A No-Account Creole" (Chopin) 8:90, 103
"Noah's Ark" (Zangwill) 44:375, 387-89
"Nobody Knows" (Anderson) 1:34, 45
"Nobody Knows the Rubble I've Seen/Nobody Knows but Croesus" (Perelman) 32:225, 231
"Nobody Said Anything" (Carver) 8:54
"Nobody Will Laugh" (Kundera)
  See "No One Will Laugh"
"Nobody's Going Anywhere!" (Hood) 42:138-39, 146, 179, 189, 205, 225, 231-32
"Noč pered roždestvom" (Gogol) 4:86, 118; 29:135; 52:105, 107
"Noc u Alhambri" (Andrić) 36:46
"Noc wielkiego sezonu" (Schulz) 13:327, 334, 344
"La noche boca arriba" (Cortázar) 7:52, 54, 57, 64, 69-71, 81
"La Noche Buena en el Limbo" (Pardo Bazán) 30:263
"La noche de los alcaravanes" (García Márquez) 8:154-55, 159, 183
"La noche de Mantequilla" (Cortázar) 7:89, 91
"La noche que lo dejaron solo" (Rulfo) 25:245, 249-50, 258-59, 265, 268
"Las noches de Goliadkin" (Bioy Casares) 17:70, 74
"Noches en los ministerios de Europa" (Cortázar) 7:94
"Nochi na ville" (Gogol) 52:169, 172
Noctuary (Ligotti) 16:291, 292, 294, 296-97
"Nocturnal Games" (Hesse) 9:244
"Noget" (Andersen) 56:36
"Noise of Footsteps" (Lispector)
  See "Ruído de passos"
"Noise of Strangers" (Garrett) 30:168, 179
"Noisy Flushes the Birds" (Pritchett) 14:305
"Noite de almirante" (Machado de Assis) 24:129
"No-Man's-Mare" (Barnes) 3:11-12, 22
"Non approfondire" (Moravia) 26:144
"Non sanno parlare" (Moravia) 26:144
"Non ti senti meglio?" (Moravia) 26:148
"Nona" (King) 17:274; 55:250-51
None but the Brave (Schnitzler)
  See *Leutnant Gustl*
"None Genuine Without This Signature" (Hood) 42:175, 193, 205
None Genuine without This Signature (Hood) 42:174, 190-94, 205, 213
"None of That" (Lawrence) 4:219, 230
The Nonexistent Knight (Calvino)
  See *Il cavaliere inesistente*
"Nonsense Novels" (Leacock) 39:240
"Non-Site" (Abish) 44:11
"Noon" (Apple) 50:4-5, 9, 29-30, 43, 48

"Noon Street Nemesis" (Chandler) 23:106
"Noon Wine" (Porter) 31:147
Noon Wine (Porter) 4:327-30, 339-40, 347, 349-52, 355-56, 359-60; 43:173, 177-79, 194-95, 206-8, 235, 238, 246-47, 253, 260, 292
"Noon Wine: The Sources" (Porter) 43:178, 207, 246
"Noonday Dark Enfolding Texas" (Saroyan) 21:162
"Nora" (Gordon) 59:265, 267
"Nora" (Lardner) 32:140-41
Nora Jane and Company (Gilchrist) 63:8
"The Nordic Night" (Morand)
  See "La nuit Nordique"
"Norman Allen" (Farrell) 28:110
"Norman and the Killer" (Oates) 6:224, 226
"Un normand" (Maupassant) 1:288
"Noroma Puppets" (Akutagawa Ryūnosuke) 44:64
"North of the Abyss" (Aldiss) 36:28
"Northern Pass" (Rulfo)
  See "El pasa del norte"
"Nos Anglais" (Maupassant) 1:263
"Nos han dado la tierra" (Rulfo) 25:244, 246, 249-50, 255, 258, 262, 264-65, 273, 278-79
"The Nose" (Akutagawa Ryūnosuke)
  See "Hana"
"The Nose" (Gogol) 4:82-4, 91-5, 97, 124-25, 127-29; 29:120, 149, 152, 167, 172, 175, 177; 52:79-185
"A Nose" (de la Mare) 14:69
"The Nose" (Moravia)
  See "Il naso"
"Nostalgia" (Mukherjee) 38:238-39, 252-55, 270-71
I nostri antenati (Calvino) 3:91-2, 106, 117; 48:34-5, 39, 43-5, 47, 79, 89, 148-50, 164
"Not a Leg to Stand On" (Boyle) 16:144-45
"Not a Love Story" (Howells) 36:396
"Not a Very Nice Story" (Lessing) 6:188, 197, 220
"Not After Midnight" (du Maurier) 18:129
Not after Midnight (du Maurier) 18:128, 130, 133
"Not By Its Cover" (Dick) 57:138
"Not by Rain Alone" (Ross) 24:289, 292-93, 295, 297, 300, 302, 319-20
"Not Charles" (Dixon) 16:206, 208, 214
"Not for Publication" (Gordimer) 17:155
Not for Publication, and Other Stories (Gordimer) 17:154, 168, 181, 183
"Not for the Sabbath" (Singer) 3:381
"Not If I Know It" (Trollope) 28:317, 322, 325, 339, 345, 348, 356
"Not Quite Bernadette" (Bukowski) 45:52
"Not Sixteen" (Anderson) 1:52
"Not So Old, But Oh So Professional" (Clarke) 45:111-12
"The No-Talent Kid" (Vonnegut) 8:431
"Notch" (Gorky)
  See "Zazubrina"
"A Note on the Russian War" (Frame) 29:104
"Notebook" (Tagore) 48:327
Notebook (Thomas)
  See *Red Notebook*
"Notes by Flood and Field" (Harte) 8:210
"Notes for a Case History" (Lessing) 6:198, 200, 208, 218
"Notes From Nowhere" (Ballard) 53:91, 96
Notes from the Underground (Dostoevsky)
  See *Zapiski iz podpol'ya*
Notes from Underground (Dostoevsky)
  See *Zapiski iz podpol'ya*
Notes of a Dirty Old Man (Bukowski) 45:51-3, 56, 58
Notes of a Hunter (Turgenev)
  See *Zapiski okhotnika*
"Notes of a Madman" (Gogol)
  See "Diary of a Madman"
Notes of a Madman (Tolstoy)
  See *Zapiski sumasshedshego*

The Notes of a Young Doctor (Bulgakov)
  See *Zapiski iunogo vracha*
"Notes on the Cuffs" (Bulgakov) 18:75, 92, 100
"Notes on the Writing of Horror: A Story" (Ligotti) 16:269, 271, 277-78, 284, 286-87, 293, 295
"Notes Toward a Mental Breakdown" (Ballard) 53:63, 67
"Nothing at All" (Walser) 20:336
"Nothing But the Tooth" (Perelman) 32:231, 234
"Nothing Could Be Finer Than To Dine From Manny's China in the Mornin'" (Perelman) 32:234
Nothing Ever Breaks Except the Heart (Boyle) 5:63
"The Nothing Machine" (O'Hara) 15:282
"Nothing Missing" (O'Hara) 15:248, 270
Nothing Serious (Wodehouse) 2:345
Nothing So Monstrous (Steinbeck) 11:206
"Notizbuchauszug" (Walser) 20:334
"Notte" (Pirandello) 22:249-50, 282
"Le notti dell'UNPA" (Calvino) 48:37, 150
Nouveaux contes cruels (Villiers de l'Isle Adam) 14:378, 396, 398
Nouvelles (Beckett) 16:72-5, 87
Nouvelles complètes (Morand) 22:181
"Novaia dacha" (Chekhov)
  See "Novaja doa"
"Novaja doa" (Chekhov) 2:131, 156, 51:50, 80, 145-6, 194, 206
"A Novel in Nine Letters" (Dostoevsky) 2:170
"A Novel in One Chapter" (Aldiss) 36:28
"The Novel of the Black Seal" (Machen) 20:156, 162-63, 165, 174, 182-83, 186, 198-99, 203-04
"Novel of the Dark Valley" (Machen) 20:173, 199
"The Novel of the Iron Maid" (Machen) 20:199
"The Novel of the White Powder" (Machen) 20:156, 162, 165, 168, 172, 182-83, 190-92, 199, 201, 203-04
"Novela natural" (Alarcon) 64:3, 6, 29
Novelas (Alarcon) 64:27
Novelas cortas: Cuentos amartorios (Alarcon) 64:2-3, 5-6, 8, 28, 38-39
Novelas cortas: Historietas inverosímiles (Alarcon) 64:3-4, 9, 28, 38-39
Novelas cortas: Historietas nacionales (Alarcon) 64:3, 9, 28, 30, 38-39
Novelas ejemplares (Cervantes)
  See *Novelas exemplares*
Novelas exemplares (Cervantes) 12:2-3, 5, 16, 29-34, 36-40, 44
"The Novelist of Manners" (Auchincloss) 22:39-40, 48-9, 53
"La novella del buon vecchio e della bella fanciulla" (Svevo) 25:329-31, 333, 335-37, 351-52, 357, 359-60, 362-63
La novella del buon vecchio e della bella fanciulla (Svevo) 25:328
Novelle (Goethe) 38:156-98
Novelle per un anno (Pirandello) 22:226, 231-34, 256, 270, 274-75, 277-78
Novelle rusticane (Verga) 21:293-95, 300, 308, 312
Novels and Stories (Stevenson) 11:287
"November Night" (Hesse) 9:230-31, 234
Novembre: Fragments de style quelconque (Flaubert) 11:71
"La novia fiel" (Pardo Bazán) 30:266
"La novia robada" (Onetti) 23:252, 275, 280
"Now and Then" (Lardner) 32:128, 133-34, 139-41, 145, 149
"Now I Am Married" (Gordon) 59:231, 260, 266, 268
"Now I Lay Me" (Hemingway) 1:220, 241, 247; 40:155, 166, 184, 209, 212, 214; 63:86, 89, 91
"Now Sleeps the Crimson Petal" (Bates) 10:123
"Now Wakes the Sea" (Ballard) 53:9-10, 48, 50
"Now We Know" (O'Hara) 15:248, 265, 270

"Now: Zero" (Ballard) **1**:68; **53**:11, 43
"The Nowaks" (Isherwood) **56**:200, 204, 210, 222-27, 229
"Nube de paso" (Pardo Bazán) **30**:280
"Nudismo" (Pavese) **19**:385-86
"Nueva refutación del tiempo" (Borges) **4**:5
"The Nuisance" (Lessing) **6**:186, 217
"La nuit Catalane" (Morand) **22**:160, 166, 172, 176, 178
"La nuit de Babylone" (Morand) **22**:160, 166, 173
"La nuit de Charlottenburg" (Morand) **22**:158, 160, 166
"Une nuit de Clèopâtre" (Gautier) **20**:5-6, 8, 14, 17, 22, 24, 28-9
"La nuit de Portofine Kulm" (Morand) **22**:159-60, 166, 173
"La nuit de Putney" (Morand) **22**:167, 176
"La nuit de seis jours" (Morand) **22**:160, 163, 166, 173, 178
"La nuit des Six Hours" (Morand) **22**:160
"La nuit du borreau de soi-même" (Mauriac) **24**:205
"La nuit Hongroise" (Morand) **22**:160, 166, 173
"La nuit Nordique" (Morand) **22**:160, 166, 173
"La nuit Romaine" (Morand) **22**:166, 173, 176
"La nuit Turque" (Morand) **22**:159-60, 166
Les nuits d'Octobre (Nerval) **18**:334-35, 350, 373
"Numancia" (Arreola) **38**:10
"Number 13" (James) **16**:230, 232, 248, 250-52
"No. 13: The Elpit-Rabkommun Building" (Bulgakov) **18**:72, 74, 92, 98-9
"No. 16" (Bowen) **3**:41
"The Nun" (Alarcon)
　　See "La Comendadora"
"A Nun No More" (Fante) **65**:95-96
"Nung-jên" (P'u Sung-ling) **31**:204
"Nuns at Luncheon" (Huxley) **39**:155, 159, 161, 168-69, 171, 174-76
"The Nuns of Crith Gaille" (Moore) **19**:293, 311
Nuovi racconti romani (Moravia) **26**:144, 149-50, 152-53, 164, 175, 180
"Nur auf Sardinien" (Lenz) **33**:317-18
"The Nurse" (Pardo Bazán) **30**:290
Nursery and Household Tales (Grimm and Grimm)
　　See *Kinder-und Hausmärchen*
"A Nursery Tale" (Nabokov) **11**:123, 125
Nursery Tales (Dazai Osamu) **41**:238, 244
"Nurse's Stories" (Dickens) **17**:123
"A Nurse's Story" (Alcott) **27**:28-30, 33-6, 57, 59, 61
"Nutcracker" (Hoffmann) **13**:192, 194-95, 197, 199-200, 213
La nuvola di smog (Calvino) **3**:98, 111-12, 117; **48**:35, 83-5, 146-48, 153-54, 164, 178, 181-83
"Den ny Aarhundredes Musa" (Andersen) **56**:11
"Nyarlathotep" (Lovecraft) **3**:269, 273
"O alienista" (Machado de Assis) **24**:128-30, 132
"O caso de vara" (Machado de Assis) **24**:128, 133, 139, 145
"O cherte" (Gorky) **28**:187
"O chizhe, kotoryi lgal, i o diatle liubitele istiny" (Gorky) **28**:136, 187
"O City of Broken Dreams" (Cheever) **1**:89, 107; **38**:53
"O cônego" (Machado de Assis) **24**:129
"The O. D. and Hepatitis Railroad or Bust" (Boyle) **16**:151
"O di uno o di nessuno" (Pirandello) **22**:245-46
"O dicionário" (Machado de Assis) **24**:129
"O enfermeiro" (Machado de Assis) **24**:129
"O espelho" (Machado de Assis) **24**:128, 135, 138, 152
"O Fat White Woman" (Trevor) **21**:231, 262, 265
"O Happy Melodist" (Hood) **42**:137, 145, 148, 225-27, 230

"O How She Laughed!" (Aiken) **9**:6, 9, 14
"The O in Jose" (Aldiss) **36**:20
"O lapso" (Machado de Assis) **24**:128, 133
"O Lasting Peace" (Gallant) **5**:124, 133
"O ljubvi" (Chekhov) **2**:139, 141, 143, 157; **28**:54-6, 65-6, 68-72; **51**:58, 93, 147-48, 208-11
"O lyrickém zloději" (Čapek) **36**:101-02, 127
"O machete" (Machado de Assis) **24**:134
"O relógio de ouro" (Machado de Assis) **24**:131, 151
"O Russet Witch!" (Fitzgerald) **6**:45, 59, 91-3
"O segrêdo de Augusta" (Machado de Assis) **24**:131
"O segrêdo do bonzo" (Machado de Assis) **24**:128-29, 152
"O starim i mladim Pamukovicima" (Andrić) **36**:59-60, 62
"O vrede filosofii" (Gorky) **28**:181-82
"O Yam—A Sketch" (Far) **62**:17, 36-37
"O Yes" (Olsen) **11**:164-66
"O Youth and Beauty!" (Cheever) **1**:90, 110; **38**:47, 51, 54, 60, 84-6; **57**:35
"The Oar" (O'Flaherty) **6**:262, 265, 274, 276-77
The Oasis (McCarthy) **24**:214-15, 217, 219, 221-22, 227, 28
"The Obelisk" (Forster) **27**:94, 06, 104-05, 107, 119
Obituaries (Saroyan) **21**:173
"An Object of Love" (Freeman) **47**:145, 147, 164
"The Object of the Attack" (Ballard) **53**:59
"Oblako, ozero, bashnia" (Nabokov) **11**:108-09, 127
"Obligation" (Dazai Osamu) **41**:229-30, 233
"La obra" (Bioy Casares) **17**:95
Obras completas (Alarcon) **64**:2-3, 7, 15, 25-28, 38
Obras completas (Borges) **41**:39-42, 137-38, 144, 149, 157, 163, 180, 184
Obscure Destinies (Cather) **2**:92, 115, 117-18; **50**:64, 80, 176, 130-31, 141, 143-46, 208, 210, 212, 249-52, 254-56
"Obstruction on the Line" (Davie) **52**:6
"Obyčejná vražda" (Čapek) **36**:98
"Obyvateli" (Chekhov) **51**:192
"Očarovannyj strannik" (Leskov) **34**:109-10, 113-16, 118, 120-21, 123, 129-30, 135-36, 138, 141
"The Occasional Garden" (Saki) **12**:311-12, 325
"Occasional Licenses" (Somerville & Ross) **56**:333
"L'occhio del padrone" (Calvino) **3**:97; **48**:37
"Occidentals" (Ford) **56**:150, 160-61, 167, 169, 187
"Occult Memories" (Villiers de l'Isle Adam)
　　See "Souvenirs occulte"
"An Occurrence at Owl Creek Bridge" (Bierce) **9**:49-50, 53-6, 60-1, 75, 77-82, 85-6, 89, 92, 95
"The Ocean" (Cheever) **1**:94, 111; **38**:47, 50, 52-3
"The Ocean" (Mason) **4**:15
"Ocean Avenue" (Chabon) **59**:69, 71-73, 76-77, 87
"Ocean Springs" (Gilchrist) **63**:9
"The O'Conors of Castle Conor, County Mayo" (Trollope) **28**:318, 328, 340, 348
"Ocracoke Island" (Adams) **24**:16
Octaedro (Cortázar) **7**:60
"The Octascope" (Beattie) **11**:6, 14
Octavie: L'illusion (Nerval) **18**:362, 369-70
"October and June" (Henry) **5**:182
The October Country (Bradbury) **29**:65-8, 75, 88-92
"The October Man" (Bradbury) **53**:247-48
October Nights (Nerval)
　　See *Les nuits d'Octobre*
"Odalie Misses Mass" (Chopin) **8**:93
"Das öde Haus" (Hoffmann) **13**:185
An Ode to Truth (Gissing) **37**:81
"Odessa" (Babel) **16**:35, 59

The Odessa Stories (Babel)
　　See *The Odessa Tales*
The Odessa Tales (Babel) **16**:5, 9, 13, 17-18, 20-2, 35, 42, 44, 49
Odin den' Ivana Denisovicha (Solzhenitsyn) **32**:330-34, 337-41, 344-50, 355-56, 361, 367-70, 372-74, 376, 387, 395, 402
"Odnazhdy osen'iu" (Gorky) **28**:137, 145, 161, 190
"The Odor of Sanctity" (Benét) **10**:146-47
"An Odor of Verbena" (Faulkner) **1**:171; **35**:159
"The Odour of Chrysanthemums" (Lawrence) **4**:197-98, 202, 220, 230
"Odour of Eucalyptus" (Wilding) **50**:346-47
"Odrazy" (Čapek) **36**:89, 111, 122
"The Odyssey of a Wop" (Fante) **65**:84, 86-87, 93, 95, 97-99
"An Odyssey of the North" (London) **4**:251, 258, 278, 282-84, 289, 291
"Oedipus at Colonus" (Forster) **27**:96
"The Oedipus Complex" (Pritchett) **14**:271, 285
Oeuvres (Nerval) **18**:379
Oeuvres complètes (Baudelaire) **18**:9, 20, 32, 35, 37-8, 52, 63-4
"Of Birds and Beasts" (Kawabata)
　　See "Kinjū"
"Of Course" (Jackson) **39**:212, 226
"Of Emelya, the Fool" (Bunin) **5**:82
Of Intimate Things (Čapek) **36**:84
"Of Love: A Testimony" (Cheever) **1**:88, 99
"Of Our Young People and Our Elders" (Agnon) **30**:68
"Of Sanctity and Whiskey" (O'Faolain) **13**:291
"Of the Cloth" (Trevor) **58**:298-99, 301
"Una of the Hill Country" (Murfree) **22**:213
"The Off Season" (Bradbury) **29**:50, 61; **53**:199, 207, 209-10, 246, 251
"The Offended Man" (Čapek) **36**:93
"An Offering" (Apple) **50**:23, 46
"An Offering to the Dead" (Campbell) **19**:81
"Offerings" (Mason) **4**:16
"Offerings" (O'Flaherty) **6**:262, 264, 281
Off-Hours (Cortázar)
　　See *Deshoras*
"The Office" (Munro) **3**:322, 325, 340, 343
"Office Romances" (Trevor) **21**:233, 237; **58**:231
"An Official Position" (Maugham) **8**:379
"The Offshore Pirate" (Fitzgerald) **6**:45, 56, 58-9, 96-7
"Oft in a Stilly Night" (O'Brien) **10**:345-46
"Ogata Ryōsais Affidavit" (Akutagawa Ryūnosuke) **44**:53, 62
"Gli oggetti" (Moravia) **26**:148
"Ogni" (Chekhov) **51**:169, 177
"Oh, Love! Oh, Fire!" (Somerville & Ross) **56**:301, 317, 333
"Oh, My Name Is William Kidd" (Benét) **10**:154
"Oh, To Be a Blobel!" (Dick) **57**:54, 75, 77
Oh What a Paradise It Seems (Cheever) **1**:108, 113-15;
"Oh Whistle and I'll Come to You, My Lad" (James) **16**:225, 228, 230, 232-33, 235-37, 240, 251-54, 256-57
"O'Halloran's Luck" (Benét) **10**:154, 158-59
"An Ohio Pagan" (Anderson) **1**:27, 30, 39
Ohio Pastorals (Dunbar) **8**:127, 134
"Oifig an Phoist" (O'Flaherty) **6**:280, 287, 289
"Ojos de perro azul" (García Márquez) **8**:154, 157
"Los ojos negros" (Alarcon) **64**:2, 8, 28, 30-31
"O.K. Baby, This Is the World" (Saroyan) **21**:143, 163
"Oke of Okehurst" (Lee) **33**:302, 305, 308
"Ol' Bennet and the Indians" (Crane) **7**:103
"Ol' Pap's Flaxen" (Garland) **18**:163
"Olalla" (Stevenson) **11**:269, 282, 296, 298; **51**:219, 229, 233, 236-77, 240, 248
"Old Abe's Conversion" (Dunbar) **8**:122, 146
"The Old Adam" (Lawrence) **4**:220

"Old Age" (Akutagawa Ryūnosuke)
See "Rōnen"
"Old Age" (Galsworthy) 22:98
"The Old Age Pensioner" (Schulz)
See "Emeryt"
"The Old Apple Dealer" (Hawthorne) 3:189
"An Old Arithmetician" (Freeman) 47:104, 134, 192
"The Old Army Game" (Garrett) 30:166, 174
"Old Aunt Peggy" (Chopin) 8:89
"The Old Bachelor's Nightcap" (Andersen) 6:12
"The Old Bascom Place" (Harris) 19:147, 149, 180
"The Old Beauty" (Cather) 2:93-4; 50:85-7, 105, 154, 156-57, 213, 249, 254-57
The Old Beauty and Others (Cather) 2:93; 50:80, 84-7, 235-36, 254-55
"The Old Bird, a Love Story" (Powers) 4:368, 371, 373
"Old Bones" (Narayan) 25:132, 138, 141, 154
"An Old Boot" (Lavin) 4:165, 168
"The Old Bucket" (Solzhenitsyn)
See "Staroe vedro"
"Old Bugs" (Lovecraft) 52:264
"The Old Chevalier" (Dinesen) 7:163, 165-66, 169, 175
"The Old Chief Mshlanga" (Lessing) 6:186, 189, 196-97, 213; 61:100, 102, 135-36
"Old Clothes" (Campbell) 19:77, 87
"Old Country Advice to the American Traveler" (Saroyan) 21:170
Old Creole Days (Cable) 4:47, 49-58, 60-2, 64-8, 75-6, 78
"Old Daddy Deering" (Garland)
See "Daddy Deering"
"Old Dick" (Stuart) 31:227
"Old Doc Rivers" (Williams) 31:303-04, 312-13, 324, 331, 357, 359-60
"Old Earth" (Beckett) 16:123, 126
"Old Esther Dudley" (Hawthorne) 3:186
"The Old Faith" (O'Connor) 5:369, 372, 385, 398
"Old Fellows" (O'Connor) 5:366, 389
"Old Folks Christmas" (Lardner) 32:134-37, 141, 163
"The Old Forest" (Taylor) 10:403, 409-10, 416, 418-20, 424
The Old Forest (Taylor) 10:410
"An Old Friend" (Kiely) 58:156
"Old Friends" (Endō) 48:192
"The Old Friends" (Gallant) 5:124, 133
Old Friends and New (Jewett) 6:165-66, 168
"Old Friends Meet" (Svevo)
See "Incontro di vecchi amici"
"Old Garbo" (Thomas) 3:403-06, 410-12; 44:324-25, 343, 351-53, 360
"The Old Gentleman of the Black Stock" (Page) 23:284, 298, 307, 313
"The Old Guys" (Kazakov) 43:56
"The Old Horns" (Campbell) 19:63-4, 74
"The Old House" (Andersen) 6:4, 25
"The Old Hunter" (O'Flaherty) 6:264, 280
"Old Hunting Grounds" (Kazakov) 43:69
"Old Izergil" (Gorky)
See "Starukha Izergil"
"Old John's Place" (Lessing) 6:186, 190, 211, 213-14, 217
Old Lady Mary (Oliphant) 25:180, 182, 184-86, 196, 204, 209
"Old Love" (Singer) 3:376, 384; 53:304
Old Love and Other Stories (Singer) 3:380-82; 53:325-26
The Old Maid (The 'Fifties) (Wharton) 6:439-41
"An Old Maid's Triumph" (Gissing) 37:64
"The Old Man" (Akutagawa Ryūnosuke) 44:56
"The Old Man" (Coover) 15:46
"The Old Man" (du Maurier) 18:138
"Old Man" (Faulkner) 1:159-61, 167-68
"The Old Man" (Naipaul) 38:332, 334-35
"The Old Man" (Shiga) 23:332-33
"The Old Man" (Singer)
See "A Zokn"

"Old Man Alone" (Sansom) 21:102, 127
The Old Man and the Sea (Hemingway) 1:222-24, 226-28, 238-39, 247-50; 36:242-347; 40:156-57; 63:39, 101
"Old Man at the Bridge" (Hemingway) 1:234
"Old Man of the Temple" (Narayan) 25:132, 154
"The Old Man with a Wen" (Dazai Osamu) 41:238
"An Old Man's Confessions" (Svevo)
See "Le confessioni del vegliardo"
"An Old Man's Memory" (Greene) 29:223, 229-30
"The Old Manse" (Hawthorne) 3:159, 174, 184; 39:105
"The Old Master" (O'Faolain) 13:284, 287, 300, 309
"An Old Mate of Your Father's" (Lawson) 18:200, 215, 262
"Old Men" (Kazakov)
See "Stariki"
"The Old Men" (McCarthy) 24:216
"The Old Morality" (Fuentes)
See "Vieja moralidad"
"Old Mortality" (Gilchrist) 14:151
"Old Mortality" (Porter) 31:161
Old Mortality (Porter) 4:327, 329-34, 338, 340-42, 346-52, 361-65; 43:173, 228, 238, 253, 258, 260, 262-63, 271, 274, 280, 283-85, 292, 294-95, 298, 302, 305, 308, 312, 315-17, 337-78, 342
"Old Mr. Marblehall" (Welty) 1:466, 471, 498; 51:306, 319
"Old Mrs. Crosley" (Gilman) 13:143
"Old Mrs. Harris" (Cather) 2:97, 102, 115-17; 50:74, 79, 128-29, 131, 141, 143-45, 200-210, 214, 229, 249-50, 252, 280
"The Old Murder" (Akutagawa Ryūnosuke) 44:53
"The Old Neighborhood" (Dreiser) 30:122
Old New York (Wharton) 6:439-40, 442
"Old News" (Hawthorne) 3:174
"The Old Nun" (Warner) 23:372
"The Old Nurse's Story" (Gaskell) 25:37-8, 41, 47, 55, 72
"Old Oak Tree's Last Dream" (Andersen)
See "The Last Dream of the Old Oak"
The Old, Old Man (Svevo)
See *Il vecchione*
"Old, Old Message" (Wilson) 21:333
"The Old Ones" (Bradbury) 53:207, 253
"The Old Order" (Porter) 4:339-40, 348, 350-54, 358, 361-62, 365; 31:178
Old Order: Stories of the South (Porter) 43:253, 256-58, 263, 274-76, 280-81, 283-86, 292, 302-3, 305, 309, 315-17
"The Old People" (Faulkner) 35:141, 145-46, 157, 164-65, 178, 181-82, 197, 200-02, 210
"The Old Planters" (Page) 23:309, 312
"Old Portraits" (Turgenev)
See "Starye portrety"
"Old Red" (Gordon) 15:106, 119-21, 129-30, 141, 143
Old Red, and Other Stories (Gordon) 15:116, 131, 137
"Old Rogaum and His Theresa" (Dreiser) 30:107, 122, 152-53
"The Old School" (Campbell) 19:77-8
"Old Sid's Christmas" (Garland) 18:167
"The Old Stock" (Calisher) 15:14-15, 18-19
"The Old Street Lamp" (Andersen) 6:4, 7
"The Old System" (Bellow) 14:22, 24-5, 27
Old Tales Newly Collected (Lu Hsun)
See *Gushi xinbian*
Old Tales Retold (Lu Hsun)
See *Gushi xinbian*
"Old Tar" (Mansfield) 9:301
"Old Things" (Mason) 4:17
"Old Ticonderoga" (Hawthorne) 3:174
"An Old Time Christmas" (Dunbar) 8:122, 125, 128, 133, 144
"An Old Time Indian Attack" (Silko) 37:292

"An Old Time Raid" (Williams) 31:302-03, 324, 359, 361
"Old Unhappy Faroff Things..." (Lewis) 40:280
"The Old Venerable" (Coppard) 21:5, 7, 9, 12, 17
"The Old Woman" (O'Flaherty) 6:277-78, 280
"An Old Woman and Her Cat" (Lessing) 61:93
"The Old Woman in the Forest" (Grimm and Grimm) 36:223
"The Old Woman Izergil" (Gorky)
See "Starukha Izergil"
"Old Woman Magoun" (Freeman) 47:102-03, 151
"The Old Woman of Iron" (Platonov) 42:253
"The Old Woman's Despair" (Baudelaire)
See "Le désespoir de la vieille"
"Old-Age Pensioners" (O'Connor) 5:369
"Oldfashioned" (McGahern) 17:304-05, 308, 311, 317-18, 320, 323
"Old-Fashioned Landowners" (Gogol)
See "Starosvetskie Pomeščiki"
An Old-Fashioned Thanksgiving (Alcott) 27:43
The Oldster (Svevo)
See *Il vecchione*
"Old-World Landowners" (Gogol)
See "Starosvetskie Pomeščiki"
"Ole Luköie" (Andersen) 6:12
"Ole 'Stracted" (Page) 23:284, 297, 303, 307, 322-23, 325
"Ole Underwood" (Mansfield) 9:278, 302
Olinger Stories: A Selection (Updike) 13:350, 354, 366, 368-69, 404
"Olive" (O'Hara) 15:264
"Olive and Camilla" (Coppard) 21:21-2, 28
"Olive Brand" (Dreiser) 30:139, 142
"The Olive Garden" (Gordon) 15:118, 138, 142-43
"Olujaci" (Andrić) 36:34, 38, 48, 66
"Omar James" (Farrell) 28:96
"Omnibus" (Cortázar) 7:50, 54, 56
"Omnibuses" (Dickens) 17:112, 137
"Omo" (Thomas) 20:290-92, 317
"Omoide" (Dazai Osamu) 41:238, 240, 247, 256-57, 259, 263, 266, 268, 271-76
"Omphale ou la Tapisserie amoureuse, histoire rococo" (Gautier) 20:5, 13, 16, 33
"On a Field, Rampant" (Elkin) 12:94-6, 99, 101, 118
"On a Mountain" (Bierce) 9:61
"On A Wagon" (Singer) 3:375
"On Account of a Hat" (Aleichem) 33:22
"On an Amateur Beat" (Dickens) 17:124
"On Angels" (Barthelme) 2:32, 38; 55:5, 53, 55-6, 74
"On Approval" (Saki) 12:314
"On Aspects of the Familiar World as Perceived in Everyday Life and Literature" (Abish) 44:11
"On Ballistics" (Arreola)
See "De balística"
"On Being Courteous when Compelled to Break the Law" (Boell) 23:36
"On Blackwell Pier" (Morrison) 40:335, 352
"On Clothes" (Dazai Osamu) 41:244
"On for the Long Haul" (Boyle) 16:146
On Forsyte 'Change (Galsworthy) 22:69-70, 74, 84, 92, 97
"On Graphology As an Applied Science" (Cortázar)
See "De la grafología como ciencia aplicada"
"On Greenhow Hill" (Kipling) 5:260
"On Guard" (Waugh) 41:323, 329-31
"On His Back under the Night" (Cortázar)
See "La noche boca arriba"
"On His Hands" (O'Hara) 15:248, 263, 266
"On Keeping a Dog" (Dazai Osamu) 41:244
"On Leprechauns" (Wolfe) 33:374
"On Living for Others" (Warner) 23:272
"On Neutral Ground" (Harris) 19:183
"On Not Shooting Sitting Birds" (Rhys) 21:55-6

"On Official Business" (Chekhov)
  See "Po delam sluzhby"
"On Official Duty" (Chekhov) **2:**128
"On One Leg" (Clarke) **45:**75, 77, 82, 84, 88, 97
"On Parables" (Kafka) **35:**241
"On Persisting as a Writer" (Apple) **50:**39
"On Ruegen Island" (Isherwood) **56:**200, 204, 210, 222, 227, 229
"On Sparrows" (Shiga) **23:**346
"On Stony Ground" (Sansom) **21:**93-4
"On Style in Literature Its Technical Elements" (Stevenson) **51:**240
"On Taxes" (Agnon) **30:**68
"On the car" (Frame) **29:**110
"On the Cart" (Chekhov)
  See "Na Podvode"
"On the City Wall" (Kipling) **5:**265
"On the Confederate Side" (Harris) **19:**183
"On the Dark Mountains" (Oliphant) **25:**185-86
"On the Deck" (Barthelme) **55:**94
"On the Divide" (Cather) **2:**96-7, 100-01, 105-07; **50:**59, 61, 73, 89-91, 184, 186, 230
"On the Downhill Side" (Ellison) **14:**115
On the Edge (de la Mare) **14:**70-2, 74, 83, 89
"On the Edge of the Cliff" (Pritchett) **14:**263, 267, 272-73, 291
On the Edge of the Cliff, and Other Stories (Pritchett) **14:**263, 290, 292, 299
"On the Edge of the Plain" (Lawson) **18:**211, 213, 239, 261
"On the Gate" (Kipling) **5:**271, 283
"On the Great Wall" (Kipling) **5:**292
On the Ground Floor (Appelfeld)
  See *Bekomat hakarka*
"On the Gulf" (Spencer) **57:**241-42
"On the Gulls' Road" (Cather) **2:**99, 104; **50:**201, 205-06
"On the Island" (Kazakov)
  See "Na ostrove"
"On the Makaloa Mat" (London) **4:**266
On the Makaloa Mat (London) **4:**256-57, 266, 270
"On the Quai at Smyrna" (Hemingway) **1:**244; **63:**78-81, 84
"On the Question of Apparel" (Dazai Osamu) **41:**276
"On the Rafts" (Gorky)
  See "Na plotakh"
"On the Road" (Adams) **24:**18
"On the Road" (Agnon) **30:**4
"On the Road" (Hughes) **6:**122, 131-32
"On the Rock in Počitelj" (Andrić)
  See "Na kamenu u Počitelju"
"On the Run" (Boyle) **5:**70, 72
"On the Seashore" (Akutagawa Ryūnosuke) **44:**52-53, 64
"On the Shore" (Andrić)
  See "Na obali"
"On the Slab" (Ellison) **14:**138
"On the Stairs" (Morrison) **40:**328, 337, 355, 367
"On the Steps of the Conservatory" (Barthelme) **55:**89, 108
"On the Telephone" (Bulgakov) **18:**89
On the Track and Over the Sliprails (Lawson) **18:**208, 250, 252
"On the Union Side" (Harris) **19:**183
"On the Usefulness of Alcoholism" (Bulgakov) **18:**90
"On the Veldt" (Galsworthy) **22:**90
"On the Walpole Road" (Freeman) **1:**201; **47:**153-58
On the Way (Kazakov)
  See *Po doroge*
"On the Way Back: A Work Not in Progress" (Greene)
  See "An Appointment with the General"
"On the Way Home" (Hughes) **6:**119, 121-23, 132-33

"On the Western Circuit" (Hardy) **2:**206-07, 214, 220, 222-23; **60:**181, 184-86, 188-89, 193, 195-96, 198-200
"On the Wind River in Wyoming" (Gilchrist) **63:**36
On the Wing of Occasions (Harris) **19:**125
"On Time" (O'Hara) **15:**265, 270
"On Writing" (Hemingway) **1:**240, 243; **63:**125
"Once in Autumn" (Gorky)
  See "Odnazhdy osen'iu"
"Once More" (Galsworthy) **22:**59, 74, 78, 99
"Once There was a King" (Tagore) **48:**301
"Once Upon a Time" (Gordimer) **17:**177, 183, 185, 187, 190-91
"Den onda ängeln" (Lagerkvist) **12:**179, 195
Onda sagor (Lagerkvist) **12:**179
"Onde estivestes de noite" (Lispector) **34:**233, 235
Onde estivestes de noite? (Lispector) **34:**203, 233, 235
"Den onde Fryste" (Andersen) **56:**37
"One Afternoon at Utah Beach" (Ballard) **53:**21
"One against Thebes" (Gordon) **15:**119, 123, 126, 138-39
"One Among Them" (Clarke) **45:**95
"The One and the Other" (Warner) **23:**384
"One Arm" (Kawabata)
  See "Kata Ucle"
"One Autumn Evening" (Gorky)
  See "Odnazhdy osen'iu"
"One Christmas at Shiloh" (Dunbar) **8:**122, 138, 146
"One Christmas Eve" (Hughes) **6:**109
"One Dash—Horses" (Crane)
  See "Horses—One Dash"
"One Day After Saturday" (García Márquez)
  See "A Day after Saturday"
One Day in the Life of Ivan Denisovich (Solzhenitsyn)
  See *Odin den' Ivana Denisovicha*
"One Day of Happiness" (Singer) **3:**385-86
"One Day of Oishiuchi Kuranosuke" (Akutagawa Ryūnosuke) **44:**63-4
"One for Cupid" (Metcalf) **43:**106
"One Friday Morning" (Hughes) **6:**111-12, 119, 121
"One Good Time" (Freeman) **1:**198; **47:**84, 86, 105
"One Holy Night" (Cisneros) **32:**34, 38
"$106,000 Blood Money" (Hammett) **17:**200, 202, 215, 219-220, 222, 224, 230
"One Hundred Views of Mount Fuji" (Dazai Osamu)
  See "Fugaku hyakkei"
"One Interne" (Fitzgerald) **6:**47-8
"One is a Wanderer" (Thurber) **1:**417, 420, 425, 427, 435; **47:**379-80, 383-84
"One Is One and All Alone" (Thomas) **20:**290, 292, 317
"One Kind of Officer" (Bierce) **9:**52, 61
"One Life Furnished in Early Poverty" (Ellison) **14:**109-10, 115
"One Man, One Boat, One Girl" (O'Faolain) **13:**322
"One Man's Fortune" (Dunbar) **8:**120, 122, 125, 128, 131, 136, 145, 150
One More for the Road: A New Story Collection (Bradbury) **53:**267
"One More Thing" (Carver) **8:**17, 19, 38, 53; **6:**8, 16
"One More Time" (Gordon) **15:**106, 120, 130
"One Night in Bed" (Moorhouse) **40:**293
"One Night in Turin" (O'Faolain) **13:**288, 320, 322
"One Night Together" (Tagore)
  See "Ekatri"
"One of Cleopatra's Nights" (Gautier)
  See "Une nuit de Clèopâtre"
"One of the Chosen" (Calisher) **15:**14
"One of the Family" (Spark) **10:**369
"One of the Girls in Our Party" (Wolfe) **33:**380
"One of the Lost Tribe" (Stuart) **31:**224

"One of the Missing" (Bierce) **9:**53, 55-6, 61-2, 65-8, 76-7, 87
"One of the Three Is Still Alive" (Calvino) **48:**149
"One of Them" (Powers) **4:**375-76
"One of Three Others" (Suckow) **18:**394-95, 413-14, 416, 422-23
"One of Us" (Fante) **65:**73-74
"One Off the Short List" (Lessing) **6:**197, 199, 200, 203-08, 214, 218; **61:**105-11
"One Officer, One Man" (Bierce) **9:**53, 55, 57, 64, 67-8
"One Ordinary Day, with Peanuts" (Jackson) **9:**267
"One Out of Many" (Naipaul) **38:**301, 303-04, 309, 311, 323, 353-54
"One Reader Writes" (Hemingway) **1:**211
"One Size Fits All" (Thomas) **20:**320, 322
"One Summer" (Grau) **15:**159, 165
"One Summer" (Lavin) **4:**173, 183
"One Sunday Morning" (Boyle) **5:**64
"One Sunny Afternoon" (Sansom) **21:**85
One Thing Leading to Another, and Other Stories (Warner) **23:**381
"One Thousand Dollars" (Henry) **5:**184
"$1,000 a Week" (Farrell) **28:**94-5, 119
$1,000 a Week, and Other Stories (Farrell) **28:**121
"£1000 for Rosebud" (O'Faolain) **13:**295, 318, 320, 322
"One Trip Abroad" (Fitzgerald) **6:**61, 100, 104
"One Trip Across" (Hemingway) **25:**113
"One True Friend" (O'Faolain) **13:**288
"1,2,3,4,5,6,7,8" (Saroyan) **21:**136, 140, 142, 148, 164
"One Warm Saturday" (Thomas) **3:**394-95, 398, 403, 410-12; **44:**324, 350-53, 360
"One Way North and South" (Hood) **42:**182, 219-20
"One Way of Happiness" (Gissing) **37:**80
"The One Who Waits" (Bradbury) **29:**60, 81; **53:**196
"The One-Armed Giant" (Narayan) **25:**137
"One-Eyed Dogs" (Lawson) **18:**233
"Oneiric Horror" (Ligotti) **16:**288
"The £1,000,000 Bank-Note" (Twain) **6:**303, 328-30
"One's a Heifer" (Ross) **24:**290, 292, 295, 307-08, 310-11, 317-19
"The Ones Who Walk Away From Omelas" (Le Guin) **12:**234, 239-41
"Only a Daisy" (Glasgow) **34:**61, 65
"Only a Subaltern" (Kipling) **5:**272
"The Only Rose" (Jewett) **6:**169
"The Only Son" (Farrell) **28:**118, 120-1
"An Only Son" (Jewett) **6:**152-53
"The Only Son of the Doctor" (Gordon) **59:**230, 260, 263-64
"Only the Dead Know Brooklyn" (Wolfe) **33:**350, 367, 369-70, 380, 382, 386
"Onnagata" (Mishima) **4:**313, 315, 318, 322-23
"Onuphrius ou les Vexations fantastiques d'un admirateur d'Hoffmann" (Gautier) **20:**4, 10, 31
"Oogawa no mizu" (Akutagawa Ryūnosuke) **44:**90
"Ooh Baby Baby" (Jones) **56:**276
Open All Night (Morand)
  See *Ouvert la nuit*
"The Open Boat" (Crane) **7:**100-01, 103-04, 107-13, 116-18, 120, 140, 142-43, 145, 148-49, 151-53; **56:**58, 60, 60-6, 82-4, 88-9, 105
The Open Boat, and Other Tales of Adventure (Crane) **7:**102, 104
The Open Door (Oliphant) **25:**180, 182, 193, 208-09
Open Door (Valenzuela) **14:**365-66
"Open House" (Gordimer) **17:**157, 160, 186
"The Open Window" (Saki) **12:**315, 318-19, 321, 324
"L'Opera del Divino Amore" (Verga) **21:**294-95

Opere, raccolte e ordinate dall'autore (Ginzburg) **65**:145

"The Opinions of Leander" (Norris) **28**:202

"Oplatka's End" (Čapek)
 See "Oplatkuv konec"

"Oplatkuv konec" (Čapek) **36**:97-8, 105, 128

"An Optimistic Story" (Boell) **23**:38

"Optimists" (Ford) **56**:137-38, 144, 146, 152, 154-55, 172, 177, 194

The Optimist's Daughter (Welty) **51**:318

"Orache" (Nabokov) **11**:133

"The Oracle of the Dog" (Chesterton) **1**:133-34, 136

"Oral Confession" (Čapek) **36**:83

"Oral History" (Gordimer) **17**:163, 191-92

"Orange" (Kelly) **50**:290

"The Orange Grove" (Lewis) **40**:272, 274, 278-79

"The Orange Moth" (Aiken) **9**:3-4, 13-14

The Orange Tree (Fuentes) **24**:78-80

"The Oranges" (Saroyan) **21**:134, 143

"The Oranging of America" (Apple) **50**:4-9, 14, 17, 20, 25, 29, 38, 41-2, 45-6

The Oranging of America, and Other Stories (Apple) **50**:2-5, 8, 10, 23-4, 27-34, 36-9, 41-3, 47-8

"The Orator" (Chekhov) **51**:77

"The Oratory Contest" (Farrell) **28**:89, 118, 122

"Orazio Cima" (Svevo) **25**:360

"Orbiting" (Mukherjee) **38**:244-47, 250, 252-54, 261, 266-67, 282-83, 286

"The Orchards" (Thomas) **3**:396, 399-402, 407-08; **44**:322, 330, 336-38, 354-57, 359

"The Orchestra" (Agnon)
 See "HaTizmoret"

"Orchid Litany" (Fuentes)
 See "Letanía de la orquídea"

"L'orco con le penne" (Calvino) **48**:95-6

"The Ordeal" (Fitzgerald) **6**:58

"The Ordeal at Mt. Hope" (Dunbar) **8**:118, 120-21, 127, 131, 146

"Ordeal in Space" (Heinlein) **55**:166, 239

"Order of Illusion" (Ligotti) **16**:276

"Order of Insects" (Gass) **12**:123-4, 133, 139, 152, 156-7

"The Orderly" (Alarcon) **64**:38

"An Ordinary Murder" (Čapek)
 See "Obyčejná vražda"

Les oreilles du comte de Chesterfield (Voltaire) **12**:341-43

"The Organizer's Wife" (Bambara) **35**:17-18, 26, 28-9, 34, 39-40

The Orgy (Fante) **65**:75, 106-8

"The Orgy: An Idyll" (de la Mare) **14**:72, 74, 87-8

"Orientation of Cats" (Cortázar) **7**:69, 71

"Origin of a Broken Nose" (Far) **62**:40, 55

"The Origin of the Birds" (Calvino)
 See "L'origine degli Uccelli"

"The Origin of the Hatchet Story" (Chesnutt) **7**:14-15

"The Origin of the Ocean" (Harris) **19**:195

"The Original Sins of Edward Tripp" (Trevor) **21**:269; **58**:231, 233, 236

"L'origine degli Uccelli" (Calvino) **3**:108-10, **48**:48, 58, 63, 67-8, 76, 132, 135, 157, 160

Origins of a Master Craftsman (Platonov)
 See *Proiskhozhdenie mastera*

"The Orlov Couple" (Gorky) **28**:149, 151, 157

"Orlov Married Couple" (Gorky)
 See "The Orlov Couple"

"The Orlovs" (Gorky)
 See "The Orlov Couple"

"The Ormolu Clock" (Spark) **10**:353, 361-63

Ornaments in Jade (Machen) **20**:159-60, 177, 196, 199-200

"The Orphanage" (McCullers) **9**:342, 345, 354-55

"The Orphaned Swimming Pool" (Updike) **13**:367

"The Orphans" (Verga) **21**:298

"Orphan's Progress" (Gallant) **5**:138

"Orpheus" (Dybek) **55**:126

"Orpheus and His Lute" (O'Connor) **5**:377, 382

Orsinian Tales (Le Guin) **12**:212-19, 222-23, 231, 234, 245-48, 250

"Osan" (Dazai Osamu) **41**:240-41, 249, 251-52, 254-56

"Osatičani" (Andrić) **36**:47-9, 72

Osatičans (Andrić)
 See "Osatičani"

"Oscar" (Barnes) **3**:2-4

"Oscar et Erick" (Aymé) **41**:24

"Osen v dubovykhlesakh" (Kazakov) **43**:51, 53, 58-9, 61

"Osen' v dubovyx lesax" (Kazakov) **43**:62, 64-6

"Osenju" (Chekhov) **51**:102

"Ostatnia ucieczka ojca" (Schulz) **13**:328-29, 334

"Ostras interrogadas" (Cabrera Infante) **39**:24

"Ostrov" (Čapek) **36**:82, 87, 110

"Ostrov Sakhalin" (Chekhov) **51**:30

"Otbornoje zerno" (Leskov) **34**:112, 114, 141

"Otchayanny" (Turgenev) **7**:324, 337, 362-63

"Otec" (Chekhov) **51**:109

Otetz Sergii (Tolstoy) **9**:377-78, 397; **30**:317, 320-22, 339-40, 342-43; **45**:143

"The Other" (Updike) **13**:402

"The Other Boat" (Forster) **27**:90-1, 95-6, 102-07, 110-11, 119-21, 124-25

"The Other Death" (Borges)
 See "La otra muerte"

"The Other Foot" (Bradbury) **53**:199, 248

"The Other Gods" (Lovecraft) **3**:274; **52**:285-86, 299-300, 335, 359-61

"Other Kingdom" (Forster) **27**:72, 74, 76, 81-83, 85-6, 99, 102-03, 112-13, 122

"The Other Labrynth" (Bioy Casares)
 See "El otro labertino"

Other Main-Travelled Roads (Garland) **18**:148, 180, 182

"The Other Man" (Johnson) **56**:234

"The Other Man" (Kipling) **5**:274

"The Other Miller" (Wolff) **63**:275-76, 321-23

The Other One (Colette)
 See *La seconde*

"The Other Paris" (Gallant) **5**:125-26, 148

Other People's Ambitions (Suckow) **18**:400-03

"Other People's Stories" (Ozick)
 See "Usurpation (Other People's Stories)"

"The Other Rib of Death" (García Márquez)
 See "La otra costilla de la muerte"

"The Other Room" (Thurber) **47**:379, 382

"The Other Side" (Campbell) **19**:77

"The Other Side" (Lardner) **32**:118

"The Other Side of Death" (García Márquez)
 See "La otra costilla de la muerte"

"The Other Side of the Border" (Greene) **29**:183

"The Other Side of the Hedge" (Forster) **27**:74, 76-7, 86-87, 97, 114-15, 122-23

"The Other Side of the Lake" (Aldiss) **36**:20

The Other Side of the Sky (Clarke) **3**:125, 131-32

"The Other Son" (Pirandello) **22**:226, 229, 272

"The Other Two" (Wharton) **6**:421, 424-26

Other Voices, Other Rooms (Capote) **47**:2-5, 8-11, 13, 16-17, 19, 23, 26, 28-9, 31, 34, 37, 45, 50, 52-3, 55-6, 58-9, 64, 66, 68-79

"The Other Way" (Grau) **15**:149, 160

"Other Weapons" (Valenzuela)
 See "Cambio de armas"

Other Weapons (Valenzuela)
 See *Cambio de armas*

"The Other Woman" (Anderson) **1**:42

"The Other Woman" (Campbell) **19**:84

"The Other Woman" (Gordon) **59**:262

"Other Women's Households" (O'Hara) **15**:255

"Others' Dreams" (Oates) **6**:234

"Ōtō" (Dazai Osamu) **41**:240, 249, 256

Otogi zōshi (Dazai Osamu) **41**:226, 247, 260, 276

"La otra costilla de la muerte" (García Márquez) **8**:154-56, 182

"La otra muerte" (Borges) **4**:35, 37, 42-4; **41**:46-47

"Otrazhenie v vode" (Solzhenitsyn) **32**:351

"El otro cielo" (Cortázar) **7**:55, 57, 59, 61-2

"El otro labertino" (Bioy Casares) **17**:75-9, 81-2

Otrochestvo (Tolstoy) **9**:375; **30**:331

"Otschchepenets" (Kazakov) **43**:51

Ōtsu junkichi (Shiga) **23**:339, 344, 352-54, 362-63

"The Ottawa Valley" (Munro) **3**:337

Ottilie (Lee) **33**:301, 306

Our Ancestors (Calvino)
 See *I nostri antenati*

"Our Bovary" (Gordimer) **17**:154

"Our Demeanor at Wakes" (Cortázar)
 See "Conducta en los velorios"

"Our English Watering-Place" (Dickens) **17**:124

"Our Eunuch Dreams" (Thomas) **44**:334

"Our Exploits at West Poley" (Hardy) **2**:214, 216, 221; **60**:183

"Our Fearful Innocence" (O'Faolain) **13**:292, 312, 322

"Our Feathered Friends" (Betts) **45**:26

"Our French Watering-Place" (Dickens) **17**:124

"Our Friend Judith" (Lessing) **6**:201-02, 218-20

"Our Humble Notice" (Oe) **20**:231

"Our Lady of the Easy Death of Alferce" (Oates) **6**:237

"Our Lady of the Massacre" (Carter) **13**:16-19

"Our Lady's Child" (Grimm and Grimm) **36**:196-98, 200

"Our Little Brown Brothers the Filipinos" (Saroyan) **21**:133-34, 137

"Our Oldest Friend" (Pritchett) **14**:255, 298

"Our Pipes" (Lawson) **18**:261

"Our School" (Dickens) **17**:124

"Our Secret" (Allende) **65**:34, 47-50

"Our Story Begins" (Wolff) **63**:263, 315, 317, 320, 342

"Our Story of Ah Q" (Lu Hsun)
 See "Ah Q zheng zhuan"

"Our Trip (A Diary)" (Bioy Casares) **17**:95

"Our Wall" (Oates) **6**:255

"Our Wife" (Pritchett) **14**:273

"Our Work and Why We Do It" (Barthelme) **55**:86, 105, 108

"Out in the Midday Sun" (Thomas) **20**:288, 290, 294, 296-97, 318

"Out of Boredom" (Gorky)
 See "Boredom"

"Out of Business" (Narayan) **25**:132, 153

"Out of Copyright" (Campbell) **19**:70

"Out of Depth" (Waugh) **41**:323, 329, 340

"Out of Hand" (Davie) **52**:7

"Out of My Generation" (Updike) **13**:387

"Out of Nowhere into Nothing" (Anderson) **1**:21, 27, 30, 39, 46-7, 53

"Out of Order" (Davie) **52**:4, 7

"Out of Season" (Gordimer) **17**:187

"Out of Season" (Hemingway) **1**:245; **36**:334; **63**:78, 124

"Out of the Deep" (de la Mare) **14**:65, 68, 80, 86-7, 92

"Out of the Earth" (Machen) **20**:158, 183, 198, 200

"Out of the Eons" (Lovecraft) **3**:279

"Out of the Fray" (Gordon) **59**:231, 262, 268

"Out of the Sun" (Clarke) **3**:132, 135-36

"Out on Bail" (Johnson) **56**:234, 241, 258-60, 266

"The Outcast" (Agnon) **30**:9-11

"The Outcast" (Page) **23**:307-09, 312

"The Outcasts" (O'Flaherty) **6**:262, 264, 284

"The Outcasts of Poker Flat" (Harte) **8**:209-10, 219, 223, 226-27, 232-33, 236, 244, 250-51, 254-55, 257; **59**:286-87, 290, 292, 300, 331, 338, 341

The Outcasts of Poker Flat and Other Tales (Harte) **59**:290

The Outcry (Lu Hsun)
 See *Nahan*

"The Outing" (Baldwin) **10**:2-4, 6-9

"The Outlaw" (Ross) **24**:290, 295-96, 304, 310-11, 316-19, 323-24
"Outlink to Uncle's Place" (Jolley) **19**:230
The Outpost of Progress (Conrad) **9**:143-44, 163
Outros contos (Machado de Assis) **24**:151, 155
Outros relíquias (Machado de Assis) **24**:151
"Outside the Cabinet-Maker's" (Fitzgerald) **6**:51
"Outside the Machine" (Rhys) **21**:50, 65
"Outside the Ministry" (Lessing) **6**:199
"Outside the Zenana" (Norris) **28**:205
"The Outsider" (Kazakov) **43**:58, 60-1, 67-8
"The Outsider" (Lovecraft) **3**:258, 260, 262, 264, 274; **52**:252, 254, 266, 281, 287, 290, 300, 304, 324-26, 328-32, 334-36, 342-43, 354, 359
The Outsider and Others (Lovecraft) **52**:252, 266
"The Outstation" (Maugham) **8**:357, 359, 361, 366-67, 372
"Outtakes" (Dybek) **55**:130, 133
"Outward and Visible Signs" (Norris) **28**:212
Ouvert la nuit (Morand) **22**:158-67, 171-73, 178, 180-82
"Ovadia the Cripple" (Agnon) **30**:66-7, 71
"The Oval Portrait" (Poe) **1**:392; **22**:305; **54**:157, 159-61, 227-28, 230-31
"Ovcebyk" (Leskov) **34**:128
"Oven Gloves" (Davie) **52**:12
"Over" (O'Brien) **10**:330-31, 333
"Over Insurance" (Collier) **19**:107, 109
"Over on the T'other Mounting" (Murfree) **22**:188, 202, 207-09, 213, 222
"Over the Brandy-Still" (Andrić) **36**:56
"Over the Green Mountains" (Caldwell) **19**:5, 37, 44
"Over the River and through the Wood" (O'Hara) **15**:252-54, 264-65
"The Overcoat" (Agnon) **30**:71
"The Overcoat" (Gogol)
  See "Shinel"
"The Overcoat II" (Boyle) **16**:143, 145, 151
Overhead in a Balloon: Stories of Paris (Gallant) **5**:147
The Overloaded Man (Ballard) **1**:73-7; **53**:11-12, 46
"The Over-Night Bag" (Greene) **29**:200-01
"Overnight to Many Distant Cities" (Barthelme) **55**:111, 116-17
Overnight to Many Distant Cities (Barthelme) **2**:50-1, 56; **55**:92-5, 108-12, 115-17
"An Oversight" (Pirandello) **22**:236
"The Overtone" (Lawrence) **4**:238-39
"Overture and Beginners Please" (Rhys) **21**:55-6
"Overture and Incidental Music for A Midsummer Night's Dream" (Carter) **13**:17-18
"O ovo e a galinha" (Lispector) **34**:189
"Ovsianko the Freeholder" (Turgenev)
  See "The Freeholder Ovsyanikov"
"Ovskyanikov the Freeholder" (Turgenev)
  See "The Freeholder Ovsyanikov"
Owarishi michi no shirube ni (Abe) **61**:12, 19, 21, 26
Owen Tudor (Arnim) **29**:5-7
"Owen Wingrave" (James) **8**:270
"Oweneen the Sprat" (Somerville & Ross) **56**:317
"An Owl's Letter" (Dazai Osamu) **41**:246
"An Owl's View of Granada" (Alarcon)
  See "Granada a vista de buho"
Own Your Own Home (Lardner) **32**:127
The Owners of the Entail (Arnim)
  See *Die Majoratsherren*
"The Ox" (Bates) **10**:131, 133
"Oyb Nish Noch Hecher" (Peretz) **26**:191
"Oyf der elter" (Singer) **53**:322
"Oyfn oylemhatoye" (Singer) **53**:323
"Oylem ha-be" (Peretz) **26**:222
"Oylem-habe" (Aleichem) **33**:68, 82-3
"Oysgetreyslt" (Aleichem) **33**:41

"Oysters" (Chekhov)
  See "Ustricy"
"Oysters Helping with Their Inquiry" (Cabrera Infante)
  See "Ostras interrogadas"
"Ozème's Holiday" (Chopin) **8**:94, 113
"Ozero Segden" (Solzhenitsyn) **32**:352
"P. & O." (Maugham) **8**:359, 366, 372, 375
"P. S. What's Octagon Soap?" (Garrett) **30**:174
"Pablo" (Arreola) **38**:8
"The Pace of Youth" (Crane) **7**:149
"The Pack" (Galsworthy) **22**:58, 75
"The Package" (Vonnegut) **8**:437
"The Package Store" (Dixon) **16**:207
"Packed Dirt, Churchgoing, A Dying Cat, A Traded Car" (Updike) **13**:370, 388, 397
"Un pacto con el diablo" (Arreola) **38**:8
"Pád rodu Votických" (Čapek) **36**:102, 121, 127
"Los padres de un santo" (Pardo Bazán) **30**:272
"The Pagan Rabbi" (Ozick) **15**:297-98, 300-01, 311-13, 315, 335, 337-39; **60**:315, 333
The Pagan Rabbi, and Other Stories (Ozick) **15**:297-98, 304, 306, 311-12, 314, 328, 331
"The Page" (Atwood) **2**:15, 17; **46**:83, 98
"Page and Monarch" (Pritchett) **14**:296
The Page of Gustavus Adolphus (Meyer)
  See *Gustav Adolfs Page*
"A Pageant of Birds" (Welty) **27**:338, 353
"Pages from Cold Point" (Bowles) **3**:59, 61-2, 66, 69, 73, 76-7, 85
Páginas recolhidas (Machado de Assis) **24**:154
"Pai contra mãe" (Machado de Assis) **24**:133, 139, 145, 155
"Pai kuang" (Lu Hsun)
  See "Bai guang"
"Pain maudit" (Maupassant) **1**:263
"A Painful Case" (Joyce) **3**:203, 205, 209-11, 234-35, 246, 249; **26**:40, 46-7; **44**:263, 268-69, 279-80, 284; **64**:196, 242, 252, 259
Painful Stories (Čapek)
  See *Trapné provídky*
"Paingod" (Ellison) **14**:106-07, 118
"Paint Me a Pinion Immortal, Limner Dear" (Perelman) **32**:229
"The Painted Door" (Ross) **24**:289-93, 295, 297, 299, 303, 319-20
"The Painted Skin" (P'u Sung-ling)
  See "Hua pi"
"The Painted Woman" (O'Flaherty) **6**:262, 264
"The Painter" (Hesse) **9**:243
"The Painter's Adventure" (Irving) **2**:262
A Painter's Work (Storm)
  See *Eine Malerarbeit*
"The Painting of an Autumn Mountain" (Akutagawa Ryūnosuke) **44**:51
"A Pair" (Singer) **3**:377, 384
"A Pair of Eyes" (Alcott) **27**:33, 58, 60
"A Pair of Patient Lovers" (Howells) **36**:394-95, 397-98
A Pair of Patient Lovers (Howells) **36**:394, 400
"A Pair of Silk Stockings" (Chopin) **8**:72
"A Pair of Vikings" (Aiken) **9**:7, 13
"Pairen" (Vinge) **24**:338
"La paix du ménage" (Balzac) **5**:5, 29, 31
"Pakao" (Andrić) **36**:47, 55
Pal Joey (O'Hara) **15**:263
"La palabra asesino" (Valenzuela) **14**:361-62, 364-65
"Palata No. 6" (Chekhov) **2**:126, 131-32, 143, 152, 157; **51**:114-15, 130, 136, 169, 171, 177, 180-82, 185-89, 192, 196, 201-2, 207
"A Pale and Perfectly Oval Moon" (Adams) **24**:2, 4-5, 8
"Pale Hands I Loathe" (Perelman) **32**:222
"Pale Horse, Pale Rider" (Porter) **31**:160, 179
Pale Horse, Pale Rider (Porter) **4**:327, 329, 331-35, 339-41, 347, 349, 361, 364-65; **43**:173, 180, 194, 212, 216, 227, 238, 253, 258, 260, 262-64, 270-71, 273, 280, 283-85, 292, 298, 302, 305, 312, 314, 336-40, 342,44

Pale Horse, Pale Rider: Three Short Novels (Porter) **4**:327-28, 331, 339
"The Pale Pink Roast" (Paley) **8**:389, 397, 414-16
Palm-of-the-Hand Stories (Kawabata)
  See *Tanagokoro no Shōsetsu*
The Palm-Sized Stories (Kawabata)
  See *Tanagokoro no Shōsetsu*
"La paloma negra" (Pardo Bazán) **30**:271
Palomar (Calvino) **3**:113-18
Paludes (Gide) **13**:52-3, 56-7, 59, 61-5, 70, 72, 80, 86-9, 91-5, 99, 101
"Pamfalon the Clown" (Leskov)
  See "Skomorox Pamfalon"
"Pan and the Syrinx" (Laforgue)
  See "Pan et la Syrinx"
"Pan Apolek" (Babel) **16**:6-7, 26, 28, 30-1, 50, 53, 55, 58-9
"Pan et la Syrinx" (Laforgue) **20**:86, 89, 91, 93-4, 101-2, 105
"ha-Panas" (Agnon) **30**:85
"La panchina" (Calvino) **3**:97; **48**:38, 81, 83-4
"Pandora" (James) **8**:310-12
Pandora (Nerval) **18**:346-48, 350-52, 354, 362, 369-72
Pandora's Papers (Ferré)
  See *Papeles de Pandora*
Pandor's Roles (Ferré)
  See *Papeles de Pandora*
"Panel Game" (Coover) **15**:32, 37
P'anghuang (Lu Hsun) **20**:125-26, 138-44, 146, 148
"Panim aherot" (Agnon) **30**:3-4, 16-18, 20, 47-9, 52, 54, 66
"Panixida" (Chekhov) **2**:130, 155; **51**:53, 89, 107, 109
"The Panjandrum" (Trollope) **28**:320, 335-37, 340, 348, 354
Pankraz, der Schmoller (Keller) **26**:106, 108, 125, 127
"Pantaloon in Black" (Faulkner) **1**:148, 174, 183; **35**:157, 192
"Pantera en jazz" (Fuentes) **24**:31, 37
"Panther in Jazz" (Fuentes)
  See "Pantera en jazz"
"The Panther of Jolton's Ridge" (Murfree) **22**:187, 203
"El pañuelo" (Alarcon) **64**:13
"Pao Chu" (P'u Sung-ling) **31**:188
"Le Paon" (Aymé) **41**:8, 15
"Le papa de Simon" (Maupassant) **1**:261, 271; **64**:329
"Papa Sisto" (Verga) **21**:294-95
Papéis avulsos (Machado de Assis) **24**:132, 144, 152
Papeles de Pandora (Ferré) **36**:135, 137, 146-47, 153-54, 156, 159, 162-63, 169
"Paper Children" (Jolley) **19**:240
The Paper Door and Other Stories (Shiga) **23**:352, 360
"The Papers" (James) **8**:321
Para una tumba sin nombre (Onetti) **23**:247, 252, 260-61, 272-73
"Parábola del trueque" (Arreola) **38**:10-11
"Parachutes" (McGahern) **17**:308, 310-15, 318-19, 323
"The Parade Song of the Camp Animals" (Kipling) **54**:83
"Paradise" (Lagerkvist) **12**:179, 195
"Paradise" (O'Brien) **10**:330, 341, 343
Paradise, and Other Stories (Moravia)
  See *Il paradiso*
"The Paradise Lounge" (Trevor) **21**:262, 265
"The Paradise of Bachelors" (Melville) **17**:359
"The Paradise of Bachelors and the Tartarus of Maids" (Melville) **1**:298, 303-05, 323; **49**:393-94
"The Paradise of Thieves" (Chesterton) **46**:133, 151
"Paradise Park" (Millhauser) **57**:189
"Paradise Retained?" (Hood) **42**:185
"Paradisets Have" (Andersen) **56**:36

Il paradiso (Moravia) **26**:161-63, 165

"The Paradoxes of Mr. Pond" (Chesterton) **46**:115

The Paradoxes of Mr. Pond (Chesterton) **1**:125, 139; **46**:117

"The Paragon" (O'Connor) **5**:371-72

"Paragraph" (Lish) **18**:286

"Paraguay" (Barthelme) **2**:35, 38, 41; **55**:28, 36, 91-2, 119

"The Parakeet and the Cat" (Bradfield) **65**:66, 68

"Le parapluie" (Maupassant) **1**:286

"A Parasita Azul" (Machado de Assis) **24**:146-51

"Pardner" (O'Hara) **15**:250

"The Pardon" (Pardo Bazán) **30**:290

"Un parecido" (Pardo Bazán) **30**:265

"Pari" (Chekhov) **51**:77, 137

"Paris" (Gilchrist) **63**:5, 7

"Paris at Nightfall" (Baudelaire)
See "Le crépuscule du soir"

Paris Spleen (Baudelaire)
See *Petits poèmes en prose: Le spleen de Paris*

The Parisian Prowler (Baudelaire)
See *Petits poèmes en prose: Le spleen de Paris*

"The Park" (Frame) **29**:108-09, 118

"Parker Adderson, Philosopher" (Bierce) **9**:60, 68, 84-5

"Parker's Back" (O'Connor) **1**:344-45, 357, 359, 368-70; **61**:168, 173, 225

"The Parking Lot" (Beattie) **11**:17-18, 20, 22

Parlor, Bedlam, and Bath (Perelman) **32**:206, 219

"La Parola Mamma" (Moravia) **26**:144

"Le parole e la notte" (Moravia) **26**:148

"Parrón" (Alarcon) **64**:4

"The Parrot" (Bowen) **3**:37, 55

"The Parrot" (Freeman) **47**:164-65

"The Parrot" (Singer) **3**:358

"A Parrot Story" (Narayan) **25**:138

"The Parshley Celebration" (Jewett) **6**:156

"The Parsley Garden" (Saroyan) **21**:155

"The Parson's Daughter of Oxney Colne" (Trollope) **28**:318, 331-33, 349

A Part of the Institution (Suckow) **18**:400, 403

"Parted" (Moore) **19**:343

Parti-colored Stories (Chekhov) **2**:130

"Une partie de campagne" (Maupassant) **1**:260-61

"A Parting" (Galsworthy) **22**:58, 98

"The Parting" (O'Flaherty) **6**:265, 281, 286, 288

"A Parting and a Meeting" (Howells) **36**:398

"Parting Shot" (Abish) **44**:9, 16, 20, 29

The Partners (Auchincloss) **22**:22, 26, 28, 33-4, 38, 40-1, 46-50

"The Partridge Festival" (O'Connor) **1**:356; **61**:225

"Parturient montes" (Arreola) **38**:10-11

"The Party" (Barthelme) **2**:39, 55; **55**:15, 34, 41, 75, 82, 86

"The Party" (Chekhov)
See "The Name-Day Party"

"Party" (Cowan) **28**:74

The Party at Jack's (Wolfe) **33**:348-49, 368, 376

"A Party for the Girls" (Bates) **10**:131

"La parure" (Maupassant) **1**:273, 278, 280, 284, 286, 288; **64**:305, 329, 352

"Pas de Deux" (Sansom) **21**:89, 126

"El pasa del norte" (Rulfo) **25**:246, 249, 265, 270

"Paseo" (Donoso) **34**:4-6, 22, 25, 29-31, 34-9, 41-2, 49, 50-1

"The Pasha's Concubine" (Andrić)
See "Mara milosnica"

The Pasha's Concubine, and Other Stories (Andrić) **36**:44-5

"El Paso" (Phillips) **16**:326-28, 330, 337

"Los paso en las huellas" (Cortázar) **7**:62

"A Passage in the Life of Mr. John Oakhurst" (Harte) **8**:233; **59**:331

"Passage in the Life of Mr. Watkins Tottle" (Dickens) **17**:110, 138

"A Passage in the Secret History of an Irish Countess" (Le Fanu) **14**:220, 221, 237

Passaic (Williams)
See *Life along the Passaic River*

"Le passe muraille" (Aymé) **41**:10-13, 18, 21-25

"The Passenger" (Calisher) **15**:9

"The Passenger" (Nabokov) **11**:134

"Passengers" (Wolff) **63**:282, 288-90, 296, 299-300, 307-8, 318, 320, 323, 338

"The Passenger's Story" (Twain) **6**:337

"A Passer in the Storm" (Lovecraft) **52**:314

"Passer-By" (Clarke) **3**:134

"Passing" (Galsworthy) **22**:91

"Passing" (Hughes)
See "Who's Passing for Who?"

"The Passing of Ambrose" (Wodehouse) **2**:356

"The Passing of Black Eagle" (Henry) **5**:158

"The Passing of Enriquez" (Harte) **8**:228

"The Passing of Grandison" (Chesnutt) **7**:16, 19, 22-3, 25-6; **54**:14-16, 50-1

"A Passing Storm" (Lu Hsun) **20**:148

"The Passing Years" (Bradbury) **53**:248, 250

"The Passion" (Barnes) **3**:5, 24-7

"Une passion" (Maupassant) **1**:274

"Passion" (O'Faolain) **13**:294-95

"Une passion dans le désert" (Balzac) **5**:12-14, 31

"A Passion for Snakes" (P'u Sung-ling)
See "She pi"

"A Passion in the Desert" (Balzac)
See "Une passion dans le désert"

The Passionate North (Sansom) **21**:84, 114

"A Passionate Pilgrim" (James) **8**:302

"Passions" (Singer) **3**:378

Passions, and Other Stories (Singer) **3**:376-77, 381, 384; **53**:325-26

"Passport to Eternity" (Ballard) **53**:7, 39, 49

"The Past" (Glasgow) **34**:56, 61-2, 68, 74, 79-80, 82, 88-90, 95, 101

"The Past" (Lu Hsun)
See "Huaijiu"

"Past Carin'" (Lawson) **18**:210, 225

"Past One at Rooney's" (Henry) **5**:198

The Past through Tomorrow (Heinlein) **55**:229, 236-37

"Pastel rancio" (Fuentes) **24**:31, 37

Pastime Stories (Page) **23**:289, 292

"Pastor Dowe at Tacaté" (Bowles) **3**:59, 61-3, 66-7, 69, 79

"The Pastor of Six Mile Bush" (Lavin) **4**:169

"Pastoral" (Anderson) **1**:52

"Pastoral" (Carver) **8**:5, 30, 50

"Pastoral Care" (Gardner) **7**:217, 219-22, 229, 232

The Pastoral Symphony (Gide)
See *La Symphonie pastorale*

"Pastorale" (Aymé) **41**:16-17, 20

"Pastorale" (Sansom) **21**:91, 94-6

The Pastures of Heaven (Steinbeck) **11**:202-03, 206-07, 225, 233, 242, 244, 246; **37**:354

"Pat and Pan" (Far) **62**:7, 19, 50, 60, 62-63, 109, 111-12, 114, 117

"Pat Collins" (O'Hara) **15**:282

"Pat Hobby's Christmas Wish" (Fitzgerald) **6**:69-70

"Pat Shlema" (Agnon) **30**:4, 22, 24, 26, 37-9, 71

"The Patagonia" (James) **8**:299, 311

"Patchwork" (Moore) **19**:304

"Patent Pending" (Clarke) **3**:133-34

"La patente" (Pirandello) **22**:254, 257

"The Patented Gate and the Mean Hamburger" (Warren) **4**:387, 390, 394, 396, 399; **58**:314, 317, 336, 354-56

"The Path of the Moon's Dark Fortnight" (Gordimer) **17**:154

"The Path through the Wood" (Stifter)
See "Der Waldsteig"

"Paths" (Andrić)
See "Staze"

"The Pathways of Desire" (Le Guin) **12**:235

"A Patient Waiter" (Freeman) **1**:201; **47**:105, 149, 195

"Patra o Patri" (Tagore) **48**:317

"The Patriarch" (Grau) **15**:149, 152, 160-61

"The Patriarch" (O'Connor) **5**:393-94

"Patricia, Edith, and Arnold" (Thomas) **3**:402, 405, 410, 412; **44**:324, 351-52, 359-60

"Patricide" (Oates) **6**:237

"Patrick Day's Hunt" (Somerville & Ross) **56**:295

"The Patriot" (Galsworthy) **22**:79

"The Patriot" (O'Faolain) **13**:286, 314, 316

"The Patriot Son" (Lavin) **4**:167, 172, 183

The Patriot Son, and Other Stories (Lavin) **4**:165

"The Patriotic Honeymoon" (Waugh) **41**:328, 340

"A Patriotic Short" (Fitzgerald) **6**:70-1

"Patriotism" (Mishima) **4**:313-15, 317-23

"The Patron" (Phillips) **16**:330

"La patronne" (Maupassant) **1**:256

"La patronne" (Maupassant) **1**:256

"La Patte du chat" (Aymé) **41**:7, 15

"The Pattern" (Campbell) **19**:84, 87

"Patty-Cake, Patty-Cake ... A Memoir" (Apple) **50**:3, 30, 42

"Paul Blecker" (Davis) **38**:96

"Pauline's Passion and Punishment" (Alcott) **27**:3, 12, 23, 33, 57, 60, 62

"Paul's Case" (Cather) **2**:90-1, 94, 103, 113, 118, 121-22; **50**:52, 56, 58, 83, 106-7, 112-16, 119, 123, 135-36, 138-39, 153, 170-74, 176-77, 179, 181-82, 199-201, 205-07, 229, 236-41, 247, 260-61, 276, 283

"The Pavilion on the Links" (Stevenson) **11**:265, 268-69, 280, 296-97, 303, 306; **51**:237, 248-49

"Le Pavillon sur l'eau" (Gautier) **20**:16

"The Pawnbroker's Shop" (Dickens) **17**:115

"The Pawnbroker's Wife" (Spark) **10**:350, 354, 359, 363

"Pay for the Printer" (Dick) **57**:104, 108, 110

"Payable Gold" (Lawson) **18**:220

Peace, It's Wonderful (Saroyan) **21**:144, 153, 158, 160, 162-63

"The Peace Meeting" (Galsworthy) **22**:62, 101

"Peace of Mind" (Boyle) **16**:148, 153, 155

"The Peace of Mowsle Barton" (Saki) **12**:288

"The Peace of Utrecht" (Munro) **3**:321, 326

"The Peacelike Mongoose" (Thurber) **1**:426

"Peaches" (McGahern) **17**:298, 303, 309, 319

"The Peaches" (Thomas) **3**:394, 396, 402, 404-05, 410-12; **44**:324, 351-52, 359

"The Peach-house Potting Shed" (Sansom) **21**:88, 100

"The Peach-Tree" (Bates) **10**:112

"Peacock" (Carver) **8**:39

"The Peacock Cry" (Galsworthy) **22**:71

"The Peacock Lantern" (Far) **62**:50, 53

"Pear Tree Dance" (Jolley) **19**:233

"The Pearl" (Dinesen) **7**:165, 167-68, 198

"The Pearl" (Mishima) **4**:313, 317-18, 322

"The Pearl of Love" (Wells) **6**:376

"Pearls Are a Nuisance" (Chandler) **23**:72, 88-9, 97, 110

"The Peasant Marey" (Dostoevsky) **2**:166

"Peasant Women" (Chekhov)
See "Baby"

"Peasants" (Chekhov) **2**:126, 131, 156

"The Peasants" (Chekhov)
See "Muiki"

"Peasants" (O'Connor) **5**:371, 377-78, 389, 394-95, 398

La peau de chagrin (Balzac) **59**:22

"Pecheneg" (Chekhov) **2**:155; **28**:60

"Peddler's Apprentice" (Vinge) **24**:337, 344

"The Pedersen Kid" (Gass) **12**:123-24, 126, 129, 131-32, 137, 139, 152-53, 156, 166, 168-73

"A Pedestrian Accident" (Coover) **15**:32

"Pedro Salvadores" (Borges) **4**:14-17
"The Pegnitz Junction" (Gallant) **5**:124, 127, 132-34, 143
The Pegnitz Junction (Gallant) **5**:124, 127, 130-32
"Le Pelerin enchante" (Leskov) **34**:114
"The Pelican" (Wharton) **6**:413, 423, 428-29
"The Pemberton Thrush" (Bates) **10**:121
"Pen and Inkstand" (Andersen) **6**:7
"The Penance" (Saki) **12**:302
"The Pencil" (Chandler) **23**:89, 110
"Los pendientes" (Pardo Bazán) **30**:274-77
"The Pendulum" (Henry) **5**:158-59, 163, 188
"La penitencia de Dora" (Pardo Bazán) **30**:262
"The Penknife" (Aleichem)
    See "Dos meserl"
"A Penny for Your Thoughts" (Selby) **20**:282
"The Pension Beaurepas" (James) **8**:299
"I pensionati della memoria" (Pirandello) **22**:232
"The Pensioners of Memory" (Pirandello)
    See "I pensionati della memoria"
"The Penthouse Apartment" (Trevor) **21**:261
"Pentolaccia" (Verga) **21**:286
"The Penultimate Puritan" (Auchincloss) **22**:46, 50
"Peony" (Freeman) **47**:163
The People, and Uncollected Short Stories (Malamud) **15**:234-35
"People Marching" (Borowski) **48**:5-6
The People: No Different Flesh (Henderson) **29**:319-20
"The People of Osatica" (Andrić)
    See "Osatičani"
The People of Seldwyla (Keller)
    See *Die Leute von Seldwyla*
"People That Once Were Men" (Gorky)
    See "Byvshii lyudi"
"The People v. Abe Lathan, Colored" (Caldwell) **19**:38
"The People Who Walked On" (Borowski) **48**:8, 10, 13
"The People, Yes and Then Again No" (Saroyan) **21**:163
"The People's Choice" (Caldwell) **19**:6, 11-12
"The People's Saviour" (Zangwill) **44**:366
"Pepperoni" (Barthelme) **55**:92
"Un pequeño paraíso" (Cortázar) **7**:93
Per le vie (Verga) **21**:291, 297
"Percy" (Cheever) **38**:50, 52
"Le père" (Maupassant) **1**:275
"Le père amable" (Maupassant) **1**:259, 284
"Le Père Canet" (Balzac)
    See *Facino Cane*
"Père Raphaël" (Cable) **4**:51, 77-9
Perelman's Home Companion: A Collector's Item (The Collector Being S. J. Perelman) of Thirty-Six Otherwise Unavailable Pieces by Himself (Perelman) **32**:208
"Perepiska" (Turgenev)
    See "Peripiska"
"Pereval" (Bunin) **5**:98
"The Perfect Couple" (Banks) **42**:53
"A Perfect Day for Bananafish" (Salinger) **2**:290-93, 295, 297-99, 303, 305, 308, 312, 314, 318; **28**:229, 236-38, 243, 263, 265-66; **65**:292, 294, 304-6, 308-10, 318, 321, 335, 337-38
"The Perfect Life" (Fitzgerald) **6**:47, 49
"The Perfect Murder" (Barnes) **3**:13
"The Perfect Night" (Hood) **42**:236-38
"The Perfect Setting" (Warner) **23**:376
"The Perfect Tenants" (Naipaul) **38**:322, 328, 336, 345
The Perfecting of a Love (Musil)
    See "Vollendung der Liebe"
"Perfection" (Nabokov) **11**:123
"The Performance" (Jolley) **19**:220, 234, 243-44
"The Performing Child" (Narayan) **25**:135, 140, 156

"The Perfume Sea" (Laurence) **7**:245, 248-50, 256
"Perhaps We Are Going Away" (Bradbury) **29**:59
"Pericoloso" (Gordon) **59**:274
"The Peril in the Streets" (Cheever) **1**:99
"Perilous Play" (Alcott) **27**:59-60
"Perils of the Nile" (Gilchrist) **63**:10, 16, 19, 21, 31
"Period Piece" (Waugh) **41**:323, 328-29, 331-32
The Periodic Table (Levi)
    See *Il sistema periodico*
"Peripiska" (Turgenev) **57**:297, 299, 303
"The Perishing of the Pendragons" (Chesterton) **1**:131, 138; **46**:110, 113, 133
"El perjurio de la nieve" (Bioy Casares) **17**:59, 85
"The Perjury of the Snow" (Bioy Casares)
    See "El perjurio de la nieve"
"La perla rosa" (Pardo Bazán) **30**:264-65
"Perlmutter at the East Pole" (Elkin) **12**:94-5, 117-18
Permanent Errors (Price) **22**:366-70, 372, 376, 384-85
"Permutations Among the Nightingales" (Huxley) **39**:155
"Pero Venceremos" (Algren) **33**:88, 108
"Perpetua" (Barthelme) **2**:55; **55**:111
Perronik the Fool (Moore) **19**:309
"Persecution" (Andrić) **36**:71-2
"Persecution Mania" (O'Faolain) **13**:297
"Persée et Andromède" (Laforgue) **20**:86, 90-4, 99-103, 122-3
"El perseguidor" (Cortázar) **7**:50-1, 58, 61, 67-8, 70
"Perseid" (Barth) **10**:44, 51, 55-6, 66-9, 71, 91, 93, 101-02, 104
"Pershing or Ten Eyck, Ten Eyck or Pershing" (O'Hara) **15**:253
"The Persistence of Desire" (Updike) **13**:391-92
"The Persistence of Memory" (Ballard) **53**:98
"A Person of Accomplishment" (Wilding) **50**:346
"Perte d'auréole" (Baudelaire) **18**:35, 49
Pervaia liubov (Turgenev)
    See *Pervaya lyubov'*
Pervaja ljubov (Turgenev)
    See *Pervaya lyubov'*
Pervaya lyubov' (Turgenev) **7**:321, 323-24, 327-29, 332-34, 337-39, 341, 352; **57**:302-3, 340-42, 344-49, 351, 358-61, 374-78, 385
"Pesadillas" (Cortázar) **7**:91
Pescara'a Temptation (Meyer)
    See *Die Versuchung des Pescara*
"Peschanaia uchitel'nitsa" (Platonov) **42**:267
"Pesci grossi, pesci piccoli" (Calvino) **3**:96; **48**:33, 36-7, 162
"The Peseta with the Hole in the Middle" (Algren) **33**:109
"Pesn' toržestvujuščej liubvi" (Turgenev)
    See "Pesn' torzhestvuyushchey lyubvi"
"Pesn' torzhestvennoi liubvi" (Turgenev)
    See "Pesn' torzhestvuyushchey lyubvi"
"Pesn' torzhestvuyushchey lyubvi" (Turgenev) **7**:321, 323, 337-38, 362; **57**:302, 311, 314, 380-85
"Pesnia o burevestnike" (Gorky) **28**:178
"Pesnia o sokole" (Gorky) **28**:144, 178, 187-88
"Pet Milk" (Dybek) **55**:130-31, 133, 143
"Pete and Emil" (Stegner) **27**:214
"Pete and the Ox" (Calvino)
    See "Cecino e il bue"
"Peter" (Cather) **2**:96-7, 100, 105; **50**:59, 68, 73, 89, 91, 132-34, 151-52, 184, 230
"Peter and the Wolf" (Carter) **13**:14, 17-18
"Peter Atherley's Ancestors" (Harte) **8**:215
"Peter Goldthwaite's Treasure" (Hawthorne) **3**:183, 185
"Le petit coq noir" (Aymé) **41**:15
"Le petit fût" (Maupassant) **1**:259, 284
"Petit soldat" (Maupassant) **1**:259

"La petite danceuse de quatorze ans" (Beattie) **11**:6, 17
"La petite rogue" (Maupassant) **1**:275, 283, 288; **64**:293, 298
"Petition" (Barth) **10**:38, 41-3, 46, 52, 54, 56-7, 59-60, 76, 79, 84, 91, 95, 97
Petits poèmes en prose: Le spleen de Paris (Baudelaire) **18**:3, 6-8, 14-16, 19, 22-5, 27-9, 31-4, 38, 44-8, 50, 52-4, 59, 61-5
"Petlistye ushi" (Bunin) **5**:81, 101-04, 110-13
Petlistye ushi i drugie rasskazy (Bunin) **5**:101
"The Petrified Man" (Welty) **1**:465, 467, 469, 471, 482, 490, 493-95, 497; **27**:332, 340; **51**:282, 305-9, 314, 318, 321, 330-32
"The Petrified Woman" (Gordon) **15**:119-20, 123, 139
"The Petrol Dump" (Pritchett) **14**:296
"Petunias" (Walker) **5**:413
"Petushkov" (Turgenev) **57**:287, 292-93
"Le peuple des etoiles filantes" (Morand) **22**:175
"La peur" (Maupassant) **1**:265, 288; **64**:316
"Der Pförtner im Herrenhause" (Stifter)
    See "Tourmaline"
"The Phallic Forest" (Wilding) **50**:349, 373
Phantasiestüeke in Callots Manier (Hoffmann) **13**:179, 188-90
"Les Phantasmes de M. Redoux" (Villiers de l'Isle Adam) **14**:397
"Phantasms" (Turgenev)
    See "Prizraki. Fantaziya"
Phantasus (Tieck) **31**:282, 286, 289
"Phantom Gold" (Dreiser) **30**:112
"The Phantom Lover" (Jackson) **39**:212, 213
"A Phantom Lover" (Lee) **33**:308
"The Phantom of the Movie Palace" (Coover) **15**:57, 59, 63, 65
"The Phantom of the Opera's Friend" (Barthelme) **2**:31, 35, 52, 54; **55**:5
"Phantom Palace" (Allende) **65**:54
"The Phantom 'Rickshaw" (Kipling) **5**:261, 265, 271-75, 297-99; **54**:79
The Phantom 'Rickshaw (Kipling) **5**:272-73
"Phantoms" (Turgenev)
    See "Prizraki. Fantaziya"
"The Phantoms of the Foot-Bridge" (Murfree) **22**:212
"The Pheasant" (Carver) **8**:53
"Philander unter den streifenden Soldaten und Zigeunern im Dreissigjahrigen Kreige" (Arnim) **29**:9
"Philanthropy" (Galsworthy) **22**:101
"Philip and Margie" (Jewett) **6**:156
"Philip Marlowe's Last Case" (Chandler) **23**:110
"Philippa's Foxhunt" (Somerville & Ross) **56**:301, 316, 339
"A Philistine in Bohemia" (Henry) **5**:190, 196
"The Philistines" (Chekhov)
    See "Obyvateli"
"The Philosopher's Stone" (Andersen) **6**:26, 34
Philosophic Studies (Balzac)
    See *Etudes philosophiques*
Philosophie's (Voltaire) **12**:364
"The Philosophy Lesson" (Stafford) **26**:286-87, 289, 307
"The Philter" (Stendhal)
    See "Le Phitre"
"Le Phitre" (Stendhal) **27**:247-48, 259
"Phoebe" (Gissing) **37**:63, 75, 79
"Phoenix in the Ashes" (Vinge) **24**:328, 330, 332, 334-35, 337-38, 343, 345
Phoenix in the Ashes (Vinge) **24**:343, 345
"Phosphorus" (Levi) **12**:256
"The Photograph Album" (Onetti) **23**:280
"Phyladda, or the Mind/Body Problem" (Gilchrist) **63**:9
"Physic" (de la Mare) **14**:80, 83
"The Physician and the Saratoga Trunk" (Stevenson) **51**:247
"Piano" (Saroyan) **21**:144
"Piano Fingers" (Mason) **4**:18

"The Piano Player" (Barthelme) **55**:16, 18, 30
"The Piano Tuner's Wives" (Trevor) **58**:253, 261-63, 273, 278, 287
"The Piazza" (Melville) **1**:303
The Piazza Tales and Other Prose Pieces, 1839-1860 (Melville) **1**:295-97; **46**:157
"El pichon" (Rulfo) **25**:268
"Picking Cotton" (Caldwell) **19**:6
"Pickman's Model" (Lovecraft) **3**:261-62; **52**:254-56, 269-70, 320, 324, 330, 361
"Pickpocket" (Jones) **56**:275
"Pick-Up on Noon Street" (Chandler) **23**:80, 86, 106
"The Picnic" (de la Mare) **14**:83-4
"Picnic" (Lewis) **40**:277
"Pico Rico Mandorico" (Ferré) **36**:147, 151
Pictor (Hesse)
    See *Piktors Verwandlungen*
"Pictor's Metamorphoses" (Hesse) **9**:221, 242, 244-45
Pictor's Metamorphoses, and Other Fantasies (Hesse)
    See *Piktors Verwandlungen*
Pictor's Transformations (Hesse)
    See *Piktors Verwandlungen*
"The Picture" (de la Mare) **14**:83-4
"A Picture History of the War" (Barthelme) **55**:78
"The Picture in the House" (Lovecraft) **3**:262, 275-76, 292-95; **52**:265-66, 281, 287-88, 295-96, 320, 335, 343-44, 346-47
A Picture-Book without Pictures (Andersen) **6**:4, 15, 30
"The Pictures" (Frame) **29**:109
"Pictures" (Mansfield) **9**:304, 307, 311
"Pictures in the Fire" (Collier) **19**:106, 110
Pictures in the Fire (Collier) **19**:105
"Pictures of Corruption" (Moorhouse) **40**:323
"Pictures of Fidelman" (Malamud) **15**:186-87
Pictures of Fidelman: An Exhibition (Malamud) **15**:178, 181, 184, 190, 192-93, 195, 211, 218, 220, 236, 240-41
"Pictures of the Artist" (Malamud) **15**:185, 193-94
"The Picture-Well" (Aymé) **41**:3-4
"A Piece of Advice" (Aleichem)
    See "An eytse"
"A Piece of Advice" (Singer) **3**:368
"The Piece of Glass" (Peretz) **26**:216
"A Piece of Land" (Harris) **19**:177, 181
"A Piece of News" (Welty) **1**:468, 478, 487, 496; **51**:260, 281
"A Piece of Steak" (London) **4**:253, 262-63, 291
"A Piece of String" (Maupassant)
    See "La ficelle"
"Le Pied de la momie" (Gautier) **20**:15
"Pied Piper" (Heinlein) **55**:214
"Pierre Grassou" (Balzac) **5**:18
"Pierre Menard, Author of the Quixote" (Borges)
    See "Pierre Menard, autor del Quixote"
"Pierre Menard, autor del Quijote" (Borges)
    See "Pierre Menard, autor del Quixote"
"Pierre Menard, autor del Quixote" (Borges) **4**:15, 26, 30, 34-5; **41**:55, 66, 103-13, 158, 163, 165-66
"La pierre qui pousse" (Camus) **9**:103, 106, 108-110, 118-19, 131-34
"Pierrette" (Balzac) **5**:9
"Pierrot" (Maupassant) **1**:277-78
"La pietanziera" (Calvino) **48**:82
Pietro von Abano oder Petrus Apone, Zaubergeschichte (Tieck) **31**:271-72, 286
"The Pig" (Lessing) **6**:196-97, 212-17; **61**:131
"The Pig" (O'Hara) **15**:291
"Pig Blood Blues" (Barker) **53**:137; 139, 141, 158, 162-63
"Pig Hoo-o-o-o-ey!" (Wodehouse) **2**:346, 348
"Pig Latin" (Lispector)
    See "A língua do 'p'"

"Pigen, som traadte paa Brødet" (Andersen) **56**:37
"The Pigeon" (Oe) **20**:219
"Pigeon Feathers" (Updike) **13**:370-71, 388, 395, 397, 404, 407
Pigeon Feathers, and Other Stories (Updike) **13**:356, 366, 389-90, 392, 400, 404; **27**:321, 323-24
"Pigtails, Ltd." (de la Mare) **14**:68, 85, 87
Pikovaya dama (Pushkin) **27**:130, 133-34, 146-54, 164-65, 172-75, 176-78, 184-88; **55**:286-351
Piktors Verwandlungen (Hesse) **9**:244; **49**:245-48, 256, 265
"Pilate's Creed" (Čapek) **36**:113, 117
"The Pilgrim" (Betts) **45**:3
"A Pilgrim and a Stranger" (Suckow) **18**:409, 414
Pilgrim at Sea (Lagerkvist) **12**:188, 191, 194, 198
The Pilgrim Hawk: A Love Story (Wescott) **35**:357-65, 372, 376, 378-79
"A Pilgrimage" (Galsworthy) **22**:58
Pilgrimage: The Book of the People (Henderson) **29**:320
"The Pilgrims" (Kiely) **58**:148, 154
Pilgrims in a Foreign Land (Evans) **43**:22, 25, 35, 38
"Pillar of Fire" (Bradbury) **29**:90-1
"Pillar of Salt" (Jackson) **9**:252, 258; **39**:210, 212, 227
"The Pillars of Sion" (Evans) **43**:18
"Pillow of Stone" (Grau) **15**:148, 160
"A Pimp's Revenge" (Malamud) **15**:183-84, 192, 194
"Piña" (Pardo Bazán) **30**:295
"A Pinch of Salt" (Jewett) **6**:158
"The Pincian Gate" (Spencer) **57**:240-41
"The Pine Tree" (Andersen) **6**:12, 40-1
"The Pines" (Bunin) **5**:100
Ping (Beckett)
    See *Bing*
"Pink and Blue" (Williams) **31**:303, 324, 331, 333, 359, 361
The Pink and the Green (Stendhal)
    See *Le rose et le vert*
"The Pink Corner Man" (Borges)
    See "El Hombre de la esquina rosada"
"Pink May" (Bowen) **3**:31-2, 41; **28**:3-4
"The Pioneer Hep-Cat" (O'Hara) **15**:280
"Pioneers, Oh, Pioneers" (Rhys) **21**:50, 55-6, 65
"The Pious Cat" (Peretz) **26**:201
"The Pipe" (Akutagawa Ryūnosuke) **44**:42
"La Pipe d'opium" (Gautier) **20**:23-5
Pipe Night (O'Hara) **15**:248-50, 262, 264-65, 267, 269
"The Piper" (Bradbury) **53**:245, 247
"Pisces" (Agnon) **30**:68
"Pish-Tush" (Lewis) **34**:165
"Pis'ma iz Tuly" (Pasternak) **31**:98, 105, 108, 111, 116-18
"Pis'mo" (Chekhov) **28**:62-3; **51**:48, 91, 109
"Pismo iz 1920 godine" (Andrić) **36**:35, 43, 47, 79
The Pit (Onetti)
    See *El pozo*
"The Pit and the Pendulum" (Poe) **1**:405-06; **22**:305; **34**:249-50, 259, 263; **35**:310, 320, 345
"The Pitcher" (Dubus) **15**:83, 100
"The Pitcher" (Hood) **42**:141, 188
"Pity for Living Creatures" (Aleichem) **33**:18
"The Pixy and the Grocer" (Andersen)
    See "Nissen hos Spekhøkeren"
"Pizza Time" (Apple) **50**:36,
"A Place in the Heart" (Bates) **10**:119
"The Place of the Gods" (Benét)
    See "By the Waters of Babylon"
"A Place to Lie Down" (Algren) **33**:113
"The Place with No Name" (Ellison) **14**:109, 118, 120, 138

"Places I've Never Been" (Hood) **42**:187, 205
"Les plagiaires de la foudre" (Villiers de l'Isle Adam) **14**:397
"Plagiarized Material" (Oates) **6**:237, 242
"The Plague-Cellar" (Stevenson) **11**:304
"The Plague-Daemon" (Lovecraft) **52**:311
"The Plain Girl" (Kazakov) **43**:69
"The Plain in Flames" (Rulfo)
    See "El llano en llamas"
The Plain in Flames (Rulfo)
    See *El llano en llamas, y otros cuentos*
"The Plain Man" (Galsworthy) **22**:60, 99
Plain of Fire (Rulfo)
    See *El llano en llamas, y otros cuentos*
Plain Tales (Kipling)
    See *Plain Tales from the Hills*
Plain Tales from the Hills (Kipling) **5**:273-74, 278, 288; **54**:72, 80
"The Plain, the Endless Plain" (Aldiss) **36**:20, 22
"Un plaisant" (Baudelaire) **18**:17-18, 32, 60
Plan de evasión (Bioy Casares) **17**:53-5, 61, 63-4, 94
A Plan for Escape (Bioy Casares)
    See *Plan de evasión*
"Plan: Great White Africa" (Kluge) **61**:56
"Planchette" (London) **4**:265, 294-95
Planet Stories (Bradbury) **29**:90
"The Planets of the Years" (O'Faolain) **13**:291, 318-19
"A Plantation Witch" (Harris) **19**:140, 195
"The Planter of Malata" (Conrad) **9**:147
"Plants and Girls" (Lessing) **6**:217; **61**:131
"Platte River" (Bass) **60**:9, 11, 40
Platte River (Bass) **60**:9-10, 13, 15-17, 20-21, 27
"The Plattner Story" (Wells) **6**:359, 364-66, 394, 405
The Plattner Story, and Others (Wells) **6**:366-67, 380, 388
Plautus im Nonnenkloster (Meyer) **30**:187, 227, 236
The Play, and Other Stories (Dixon) **16**:215
Play Days (Jewett) **6**:165-66
"Playback" (Beattie) **11**:11, 22
"The Playhouse Called Remarkable" (Spark) **10**:359, 361, 370
"A Play-House in the Waste" (Moore)
    See "San n-Diothramh Dubh"
"Playing the Game" (Campbell) **19**:76, 78, 90
"Playing With Fire" (Doyle) **12**:64
"Playing with Punjab" (Bambara) **35**:24-5
"Please Don't Talk About Me When I'm Gone" (Algren) **33**:106
"Pleasure" (Lessing) **6**:197
"Pleasure" (O'Hara) **15**:248, 265
"The Pleasure of Plain Rice" (Yamamoto) **34**:58
"The Pleasure-Cruise" (Kipling) **5**:284
"The Pleasures of Solitude" (Cheever) **1**:88
"The Pleasure-Seeker" (Čapek) **36**:130
"Pledges, Vows and Pass this Note" (Moorhouse) **40**:312-18
Plongées (Mauriac) **24**:183-84, 196, 203, 206, 208
"The Plot" (Borges) **41**:176
"Plots and Counterplots" (Alcott)
    See "V.V.: or Plots and Counterplots"
"The Ploughman" (Dinesen) **7**:177
"Plowshare in Heaven" (Stuart) **31**:245, 251-52
Plowshare in Heaven (Stuart) **31**:226-27, 235-36, 245, 255
"Plumbing" (Updike) **13**:348
"A Plunge into Real Estate" (Calvino)
    See "La speculazione edilizia"
A Plunge into Real Estate (Calvino)
    See *La speculazione edilizia*
"Le plus beau dîner du monde" (Villiers de l'Isle Adam) **14**:377
"Le plus bel amour de Don Juan" (Barbey d'Aurevilly) **17**:7, 11-14, 19-20, 42-4
"Plus Ultra!" (Machado de Assis) **24**:152
"Plutarco Roo" (Warner) **23**:368

"Po delam sluzhby" (Chekhov) **51**:80, 131, 206, 211

Po doroge (Kazakov) **43**:50

"Po povodu Krejcerovoj sonaty" (Leskov) **34**:108

"Po' Sandy" (Chesnutt) **7**:5-7, 10, 13, 42; **54**:26, 31-3, 35, 37, 40-2, 46

"Poaching" (Wolff) **63**:282, 297, 300, 320, 323, 326

"Poceluj" (Chekhov) **2**:126, 156; **28**:56; **51**:42, 110, 117-18, 120-23, 159, 193

Pocket Stories (Čapek)
   See *Tales from Two Pockets*

"Pocock Passes" (Pritchett) **14**:271, 285-86, 297

"Pod prazdnik obideli" (Leskov) **34**:108

Podrostok (Dostoevsky) **44**:93, 96, 98, 112

"A Poem as the Corpus Delicti" (P'u Sung-ling)
   See "Shih-yen"

Poems and Stories (Harte) **59**:291

Poems in Prose from Charles Baudelaire (Baudelaire)
   See *Petits poèmes en prose: Le spleen de Paris*

"The Poet" (Čapek)
   See "Básník"

"The Poet" (Dinesen) **7**:167-68, 180, 203, 209

"The Poet" (Hesse) **9**:234

The Poet and the Lunatics (Chesterton) **1**:124-26, 132; **46**:117

"The Poet and the Peasant" (Henry) **5**:194

"The Poet at Home" (Saroyan) **21**:155

"The Poet of Sierra Flat" (Harte) **59**:319, 324-25

"The Poetess" (Freeman) **47**:84, 105, 108, 134, 145-48, 151, 184-85, 194

"The Poetess of Clap City" (Davis) **38**:120-21, 123

"A Poetics for Bullies" (Elkin) **12**:94-7, 99, 117-18

"A Poetizing Thief" (Čapek)
   See "O lyrickém zloději"

Poetry and Tales of Edgar Allan Poe (Poe) **54**:236-37, 239, 241-45

"The Poetry of Modern Life" (Greene) **29**:218

"Poet's Ashes" (Solzhenitsyn)
   See "Prakh poeta"

"The Poet's Portmanteau" (Gissing) **37**:64

"Pogassee delo" (Leskov) **34**:109

Pohlstars (Pohl) **25**:235

"A Point at Issue!" (Chopin) **8**:70, 73

"A Point in Morals" (Glasgow) **34**:57-9, 65, 67, 77-8, 97, 99

"The Point of a Pin" (Chesterton) **46**:134

"The Point of It" (Forster) **27**:69, 71, 74, 76-7, 83, 86, 96, 100, 114-15

"A Point of Law" (Faulkner) **1**:177

"Poison" (Mansfield) **9**:310-11

The Poisoned Kiss (Oates) **6**:236, 241-43

"The Poisoned Pastries" (Donoso) **34**:21

"The Poisoned Story" (Ferré) **36**:151, 156

"Poisson d'Avril" (Somerville & Ross) **56**:318, 323, 329, 332, 339

"Poker Night" (Updike) **13**:409

"Polar Bears and Others" (Boyle) **5**:54

"Polaris" (Lovecraft) **3**:288; **52**:264, 285, 356-57

"Polarities" (Atwood) **2**:2-5, 7-8, 10, 13-14; **46**:26, 28, 30, 33, 36-9, 40, 49, 58, 76-7, 81-2, 92

"The Polatski Man" (Dybek) **55**:125, 127-28, 134, 136, 139-40, 142-43, 151, 157

"Poldi" (McCullers) **9**:342, 345, 357

"The Pole" (Lewis) **34**:166-67, 177, 179

Pole Poppenspäler (Storm) **27**:279, 282, 284

"Polen'ka" (Chekhov) **51**:59-60

"The Police Band" (Barthelme) **55**:4, 52-3

"The Policeman's Ball" (Barthelme) **2**:31, 45; **55**:53, 82

"The Policy of the Closed Door" (Somerville & Ross) **56**:317

Polikushka (Tolstoy) **9**:376, 389, 393-94, 399, 403

"Polinka" (Chekhov) **51**:49

"Polite Conversation" (Stafford) **26**:297, 312

"A Political Boy Is Now Dead" (Oe)
   See "Seiji shonen shisu"

"Political Director of Divine Worship" (Bulgakov) **18**:90

"Politics" (Bukowski) **45**:55

"Pollock and the Porroh Man" (Wells) **6**:388

"Polly: A Christmas Recollection" (Page) **23**:283-84, 297, 303-04

Polly Ongle (Metcalf) **43**:152-56, 165-66

"Polunoščniki" (Leskov) **34**:109, 112, 125, 127

"Polydore" (Chopin) **8**:93

"Polyhymnia Muse of Sacred Song" (Auchincloss) **22**:51

"Polzunkov" (Dostoevsky) **2**:170, 192-93

"Pomegranate Seed" (Wharton) **6**:426-27, 431-32

"The Pomegranate Trees" (Saroyan) **21**:150, 168, 172, 174

"Un pomeriggio Adamo" (Calvino) **3**:97, 112; **48**:37, 146, 162

"Pomoc!" (Čapek) **36**:91-2, 110, 122, 125

"Pomorka" (Kazakov) **43**:53, 58, 67

"Pompeii" (Lowry)
   See "Present Estate of Pompeii"

The Ponder Heart (Welty) **1**:474, 477, 483, 494-95, 497; **51**:265, 312

"Ponto de vista" (Machado de Assis) **24**:151

"Poodle" (Lardner) **32**:129

The Poodle Springs Story (Chandler) **23**:111

"The Pool" (du Maurier) **18**:127-28

"The Pool" (Maugham) **8**:369-71

"The Pool of Narcissus" (Calisher) **15**:15, 17

"The Poor and the Rich" (Saroyan) **21**:166

"The Poor Are Always with Us" (Wolff) **63**:266, 301, 306-8, 310, 318-20

"The Poor Benefactor" (Stifter)
   See "Der Arme Wohltäter"

"The Poor Bird" (Andersen) **6**:4

"The Poor Boy" (Peretz) **26**:201

"The Poor Child's Toy" (Baudelaire)
   See "Le joujou du pauvre"

"The Poor Clare" (Gaskell) **25**:41, 54-5, 60

"The Poor Fiddler" (Grillparzer)
   See *Der Arme Spielmann*

Poor Folk (Dostoevsky)
   See *Bednye lyudi*

"A Poor Gentleman" (Gissing) **37**:53, 56

"A Poor Girl" (Chopin) **8**:69

"The Poor Heart" (Saroyan) **21**:162

"Poor John" (Andersen) **6**:4

"Poor Koko" (Fowles) **33**:233, 235-36, 244, 246-48, 257-61, 263-65, 272, 275, 288-89

"Poor Little Black Fellow" (Hughes) **6**:118, 121-22, 134

"Poor Little Rich Town" (Vonnegut) **8**:436

"The Poor Man" (Coppard) **21**:3, 15, 17, 27

"A Poor Man's Got His Pride" (Dazai Osamu) **41**:264, 276

"Poor Man's Pennies" (Algren) **33**:105, 109

"Poor Man's Pudding and Rich Man's Crumbs" (Melville) **1**:303, 323

"Poor Mary" (Warner) **23**:370

The Poor Musician (Grillparzer)
   See *Der Arme Spielmann*

"Poor People" (O'Flaherty) **6**:262, 264, 280, 283

"A Poor Stick" (Morrison) **40**:368

"The Poor Thing" (Powers) **4**:368, 372-73

"Poor Thumbling" (Andersen) **6**:4, 7

"Pop Goes the Alley Cat" (Stegner) **27**:218, 220

"Pope Jacynth" (Lee) **33**:310

Pope Jacynth, and Other Fantastic Tales (Lee) **33**:303, 307, 309

"Pope Zeidlus" (Singer) **3**:364

"Poppy Seed and Sesame Rings" (Jolley) **19**:241

"Poprygin'ia" (Chekhov) **2**:126; **51**:42, 90-1, 93, 112, 182-83, 194

"Popsy" (King) **17**:295

"Popular Mechanics" (Carver) **8**:14, 18, 26, 30, 44-5; **51**:20

Popular Stories (Grimm and Grimm)
   See *Kinder-und Hausmärchen*

"Por boca de los dioses" (Fuentes) **24**:30, 38, 40, 43-4, 54-5

"Por enquanto" (Lispector) **34**:208, 215

"Por qué ser así?" (Unamuno) **11**:312

"Porcelain and Pink" (Fitzgerald) **6**:59

"Porcupines at the University" (Barthelme) **2**:56; **55**:106, 108

"Porn" (Walker) **5**:412-14

"Porodična slika" (Andrić) **36**:48

"Porotce" (Čapek) **36**:102

"Le port" (Baudelaire) **18**:6

"Le port" (Maupassant) **1**:264

"Port of Embarkation" (Spencer) **57**:242

"Port Swettenham" (Lowry) **31**:41

Portable Kipling (Kipling) **54**:79

The Portable Ring Lardner (Lardner) **32**:131, 156

"Porte cochère" (Taylor) **10**:379, 407

"The Porter's Son" (Andersen) **6**:11-12

"The Portly Gentleman" (O'Hara) **15**:284

"The Portobello Road" (Spark) **10**:350-53, 355, 357-58, 360, 365-66, 368, 370-71

"Portrait" (Boyle) **5**:54

"A Portrait" (Galsworthy) **22**:58, 74-5, 98, 100

"The Portrait" (Gogol)
   See "Portret"

"The Portrait" (Huxley) **39**:156, 175

"The Portrait" (Oliphant) **25**:196, 209

"The Portrait" (Wharton) **6**:414

"Portrait of a Literary Critic" (Wolfe) **33**:401

"A Portrait of Aunt Ida" (Thurber) **47**:376

A Portrait of Bascom Hawke (Wolfe) **33**:345-49, 357, 359-60, 375

"A Portrait of Shunkin" (Tanizaki)
   See "Shunkin shō"

Portrait of the Artist as a Young Dog (Thomas) **3**:394-97, 399, 402-04, 410-13; **44**:321, 323-25, 341-42, 348-52, 359-60

"Portrait of the Intellectual as a Yale Man" (McCarthy) **24**:213

"Portraits de maîtresses" (Baudelaire) **18**:18, 25, 37

"Portret" (Gogol) **9**:102-03, 116, 122, 125; **29**:128, 135, 172; **52**:122, 128, 130, 150, 164

Die Portugiesin (Musil) **18**:292-93, 297-303, 322

The Portuguese Lady (Musil)
   See *Die Portugiesin*

"The Porush and the Bear" (Peretz) **26**:216

"Poseidon and Company" (Carver) **8**:50-1

"Poseidon's Daughter" (Sansom) **21**:86-7, 124

"Poseshchenie muzeia" (Nabokov)
   See "The Visit to the Museum"

"Posesión" (Pardo Bazán) **30**:274-76

"Posle teatre" (Chekhov) **51**:177

"Poslední soud" (Čapek) **36**:83, 98, 106, 128

"Poslední věci člověka" (Čapek) **36**:98

"The Possessed" (Clarke) **3**:132, 135, 143-44, 148

"Possession of Angela Bradshaw" (Collier) **19**:98, 101, 110, 114

"The Possibility of Evil" (Jackson) **9**:256

"Posson Jone'" (Cable) **4**:48, 56, 58, 62, 64-5, 67, 77-80

"The Post" (Chekhov) **2**:130, 156

"The Post Card" (Boell)
   See "Die Postkarte"

"Post Modernism" (Apple) **50**:23-4, 33

"The Post Office" (O'Flaherty)
   See "Oifig an Phoist"

"The Post Office Crime" (Čapek)
   See "Zločin na poště"

"The Postcard" (Dixon) **16**:217

"Postcard" (Munro) **3**:322

The Posthumous Writings and Poems of Hermann Lauscher (Hesse)
See *Hinterlassene Schriften und Gedichte von Hermann Lauscher*
"Post-Impressionist Daddy" (Perelman) **32**:202
"Die Postkarte" (Boell) **23**:8
"Postmastar" (Tagore) **48**:310, 315
"The Postmaster" (Pushkin)
See "Stantsionnyi smotritel"
"The Postmaster" (Tagore)
See "Postmastar"
"The Postoffice and the Serpent" (Coppard) **21**:10
Post-Stage Master (Pushkin) **55**:288-89, 296
"Posy" (Lavin) **4**:166
"The Pot" (Aleichem)
See "Dos tepl"
"The Pot of Gold" (Cheever) **1**:89, 99; **38**:55
"The Pot of Gold" (O'Flaherty) **6**:271
"Potassium" (Levi) **12**:257
"The Potato Dealer" (Trevor) **58**:253-54, 262, 276-77
"The Potato Elf" (Nabokov)
See "Kartofel'nyy el'f"
"Potatoes" (Naipaul) **38**:331-34
"The Pot-Boiler" (Wharton) **6**:435
"Potential" (Campbell) **19**:73, 84, 92-3
"Potshack" (Jones) **56**:276
"Pottage" (Henderson) **29**:326-27
"The Potted Princess" (Kipling) **54**:92-93
"Potter" (Gallant) **5**:136-37
The Potter's House (Stegner) **27**:194, 216-17
Pour finir encour et Autres Foirades (Beckett)
See *Foirades*
"Poverty" (Zoshchenko) **15**:404
Povest (Pasternak) **31**:98, 105-06, 110, 114-17, 120-21
Povest' nepogašennoj luny (Pilnyak) **48**:216, 218-22, 224-31, 237, 239, 249, 254-55, 258, 265, 268, 270, 272-73, 295-97
"Povest nepogašhennoy luny" (Pilnyak) **48**:230
Povesti Belkina (Pushkin) **27**:129, 134-35, 141-46, 148-49, 163-67, 176, 181-83, 185-87
Povídky z druhé kapsy (Čapek) **36**:83, 96, 98, 100, 103, 105, 120-21, 126
Povídky z jedné kapsy (Čapek) **36**:83, 96, 98, 100, 104, 120-21, 126
"Powder" (Wolff) **63**:275-76
"The Powder Blue Dragon" (Vonnegut) **8**:432-33
"The Powder of the Angels and I'm Yours" (Phillips) **16**:325, 328
"Powder-White Faces" (Hughes) **6**:118, 122
"Power in Trust" (Auchincloss) **22**:4
"The Power of Appointment" (Auchincloss) **22**:4
"The Power of Literature" (Farrell) **28**:127
"The Power of Words" (Poe) **22**:320
"A Power Struggle" (Head) **52**:188
"Powerhouse" (Bradbury) **29**:42, 48; **53**:215
"Powerhouse" (Welty) **1**:466, 488, 494; **27**:338; **51**:305-6; 317
"Powers" (Singer) **3**:360
Powers of Attorney (Auchincloss) **22**:4-7, 9, 17-19, 33-4, 37, 46-50
"A Pox on You, Mine Goodly Host" (Perelman) **32**:201-02
Pożegnanie z Maria (Borowski) **48**:3, 16
El pozo (Onetti) **23**:244, 246, 248-49, 251-52, 258-61, 264, 273-74
"El pozo de la vida" (Pardo Bazán) **30**:261
"Praça Mauá" (Lispector) **34**:207, 215
"The Practice of the Craft" (Metcalf) **43**:73-4, 85, 89, 113
Prairie Folks (Garland) **18**:144-45, 148, 150, 160, 174-77, 182, 194
"A Prairie Heroine" (Garland) **18**:163, 166, 173
"Prakh poeta" (Solzhenitsyn) **32**:352-53
"Pranzo con un pastore" (Calvino) **3**:97; **48**:36
"Pravaya kist" (Solzhenitsyn) **32**:386, 392
"Prayaschitta" (Tagore) **48**:312, 327-28
"Prayer to the Pacific" (Silko) **37**:309

"Preacher's Legend" (Capote) **47**:45, 51-2
"A Preacher's Love Story" (Garland) **18**:148, 160
"Precinct Captain" (Farrell) **28**:90
"Preciosidade" (Lispector) **34**:194-97, 200-02, 217, 224-25
"The Precipice" (Oates) **6**:247
"A Predestined Disaster" (Aleichem) **33**:26, 48
"A Predicament" (Poe) **1**:405-06; **22**:330
"Predictions of Ice" (Hood) **42**:182, 203, 221, 242
"Prelude" (Mansfield) **9**:279-80, 282-84, 286, 288-91, 298, 300-01, 303, 305, 307, 309, 311, 313, 316; **23**:139, 153, 158
"Prelude to a Parking Lot" (Spencer) **57**:209, 211
"Prelude to an American Symphony" (Saroyan) **21**:134
"A Premature Autobiography" (Oates) **6**:232
"The Premature Burial" (Poe) **1**:407; **22**:330, 334; **54**:218
Premier amour (Beckett) **16**:73-4, 87-8, 90-1, 97
"Premier prix decomédie" (Aymé) **41**:24
"The Pre-Persons" (Dick) **57**:102-3, 107, 109
"The Presence" (Gordon) **15**:116, 121, 131
"The Presence of Grace" (Powers) **4**:370, 381
The Presence of Grace (Powers) **4**:372-73
"Present Estate of Pompeii" (Lowry) **31**:44-5, 47-8, 51, 59-60, 62, 72-4, 81, 86
"A Present for a Good Girl" (Gordimer) **17**:167
Presenting Moonshine (Collier) **19**:98, 103, 105
"Presents" (Spencer) **57**:241
"Presents" (Wideman) **62**:269
"Preservation" (Carver) **8**:26, 32
"The Preserving Machine" (Dick) **57**:52
The Preserving Machine (Dick) **57**:114, 137
"The President" (Barthelme) **2**:31; **55**:4, 49
"The President of the Louisiana Live Oak Society" (Gilchrist) **14**:151-52, 155; **63**:10-12
"El Presidente de Méjico" (Algren) **33**:106, 113
"Press Clippings" (Cortázar)
See "Recortes de prensa"
"The Presser" (Coppard) **21**:9, 28
"The Pretender" (Gordimer)
See "My First Two Women"
"The Pretender" (O'Connor) **5**:386, 390
"The Pretty Girl" (Dubus) **15**:76, 87-9, 91, 93-4, 96, 101
"Pretty Maggie Moneyeyes" (Ellison) **14**:107-08, 115
"Pretty Mouth and Green My Eyes" (Salinger) **2**:290, 293, 298, 300; **65**:294, 296, 304-5, 308-9, 311
"Pretty Poll" (de la Mare) **14**:85
"Previous Condition" (Baldwin) **10**:3, 5, 7, 9-10, 17
"Previous Days" (Algren) **33**:96
"The Previous Tenant" (Campbell) **19**:83, 87
"Las previsiones de Sangiácomo" (Bioy Casares) **17**:68-70
"Prey" (O'Flaherty) **6**:281
"Příběh o kasaři a žháři" (Čapek) **36**:101
"Příběhy sňatkového podvodníka" (Čapek) **36**:97, 101
"Priča" (Andrić) **36**:65-6, 78
"Priča iz Japana" (Andrić) **36**:32
"Priča o soli" (Andrić) **36**:38
"Priča o vezirovom slonu" (Andrić) **36**:33-6, 37-8, 46-7, 78
"The Price of the Harness" (Crane) **7**:104
"Price's Always Open" (O'Hara) **15**:255-56
Pricksongs and Descants (Coover) **15**:34-5, 37-41,43, 45, 47, 49-50, 53, 56, 58, 63
"The Pride of the Cities" (Henry) **5**:159, 194
"The Pride of the Village" (Irving) **2**:240-41, 245, 251
"The Priest of Shiga Temple and His Love" (Mishima) **4**:313, 315-17, 322-23
"Priestly Fellowship" (Powers) **4**:376, 381-82
"The Priestly Prerogative" (London) **4**:282

"The Priests" (Bradbury) **53**:248-50
"Prikliucheniia obez'iany" (Zoshchenko)
See "Adventures of a Monkey"
"Priklyuchenie" (Platonov) **42**:257
"Prima Belladonna" (Ballard) **1**:68; **53**:7, 72, 75-7, 79, 81, 131
"Prima notte" (Pirandello) **22**:231
"Prime Leaf" (Warren) **4**:387-90, 393, 395, 400; **58**:308, 317, 344, 346, 354
"O primeiro beijo" (Lispector) **34**:231, 233-34
"Primer amor" (Pardo Bazán) **30**:265
"Primo amore" (Pavese) **19**:375, 378, 384, 387
"Primo rapporto sulla terra dell' Inviato speciale dalla luna" (Moravia) **26**:164
"The Primrose Path" (Lawrence) **4**:234-37
"Prince Alberic and the Snake Lady" (Lee) **33**:302, 309
"The Prince and the Pauper" (Auchincloss) **22**:14, 50, 53
"Un Prince de la Bohème" (Balzac) **5**:31-3
"Prince Hamlet of Shehrigov Province" (Turgenev)
See "Gamlet ščigrovskogo uezda"
"The Prince of a 100 Soups" (Lee) **33**:300
"Prince of Darkness" (Powers) **4**:370, 383
Prince of Darkness and Other Stories (Powers) **4**:369-71
"The Prince Who Was a Thief" (Dreiser) **30**:113, 115
"The Princess" (Chekhov) **2**:130, 144; **51**:112, 182
"The Princess" (Kluge) **61**:74
"The Princess" (de la Mare) **14**:80
The Princess (Lawrence) **4**:238-40, 242; **19**:251
"The Princess and All the Kingdom" (Lagerkvist) **12**:195
"The Princess and the Pea" (Andersen) **6**:7, 13, 18, 26, 30; **56**:38-9, 49, 51-4
"The Princess and the Zucchini" (Thomas) **20**:320, 322
"The Princess Baladina—Her Adventure" (Cather) **2**:100; **50**:77, 93-4
"The Princess Bob and Her Friends" (Harte) **8**:216
Princess Brambilla (Hoffmann)
See *Prinzessin Brambilla: Ein Capriccio nach Jakob Callot*
"Princess Lotus Bloom" (P'u Sung-ling)
See "Lien-hua kung-chu"
"Princess Margaret's Facelift" (Ballard) **53**:19
"The Princess on the Pea" (Andersen)
See "The Princess and the Pea"
The Princess, the Dwarf, and the Dungeon (Millhauser) **57**:172-75
La princesse de Babylon (Voltaire) **12**:341-42
"Prinzessin Brambilla" (Hoffmann) **13**:192, 198, 218-19
Prinzessin Brambilla: Ein Capriccio nach Jakob Callot (Hoffmann) **13**:183-84
"Případ dra Mejzlíka" (Čapek) **36**:96, 102, 121
"Případ s dítětem" (Čapek) **36**:83, 127
"Případ Selvinuv" (Čapek) **36**:96, 99, 128
"Pripadok" (Chekhov) **51**:115, 171
"Případy pana Janíka" (Čapek) **36**:96, 98, 102, 128
"Prischepa's Revenge" (Babel) **16**:7, 24-5
"Priscilla" (Calvino) **3**:95-6; **48**:106, 134, 136, 138-39, 161, 167, 173
"Priscilla and Emily Lofft" (Moore) **19**:301, 310-11, 344-45
"Prishchepa" (Babel) **16**:50
"The Prison" (Malamud) **15**:175
"The Prison Window" (Auchincloss) **22**:13, 53
"The Prisoner" (Galsworthy) **22**:58, 82, 98
"The Prisoner of the Caucasus" (Tolstoy) **9**:382, 386-87; **45**:135
"Prisoner of the Coral Deep" (Ballard) **53**:9-10, 42
"Prisoner Who Wore Glasses" (Head) **52**:209, 222, 224
"The Prisoners" (Lewis) **40**:272
"Pristupaia ko dniu" (Solzhenitsyn) **32**:353

"Privacy" (Ford) **56**:196
"Private Jones" (Lewis) **40**:271, 277
"Private Lies" (Mason) **4**:19
"Private Life" (Arreola)
　　See "La vida privada"
"The Private Life" (James) **8**:280-81
"The Private Life of Mr. Bidwell" (Thurber)
　　1:419
Private Parts: A Memoir (Metcalf) **43**:101, 103,
　　115-16, 123-25, 146-50, 154
"Private Property" (Sill) **37**:37, 315
"A Private Room" (Davie) **52**:7, 11
"Private Theatres" (Dickens) **17**:117, 122
"Privilege" (Munro) **3**:334
"The Privy Councilor" (Chekhov) **2**:130; **51**:35
"The Prize China Baby" (Far) **62**:50-52, 59,
　　97-98
"The Prize Lodger" (Gissing) **37**:56, 64
Prize Stock (Oe)
　　See *Shiiku*
"Prizes" (Frame) **29**:97
"Prizraki. Fantaziya" (Turgenev) **7**:321, 323,
　　325, 334-35, 338
"Pro Aris et Focis" (Davis) **38**:104
"Problem No. 4" (Cheever) **1**:99
"The Problem of Art" (Gardner) **7**:226
"The Problem of Thor Bridge" (Doyle) **12**:52,
　　63-4
"Le Problème" (Aymé) **41**:8
Problems, and Other Stories (Updike) **13**:383,
　　385-86, 388
"Problems of Adjustment in Survivors of
　　Natural/Unnatural Disasters" (Oates)
　　6:225
"A Process of Time" (Metcalf) **43**:105-6, 109
"The Procession of Life" (Hawthorne) **3**:181,
　　190
"The Procession of Life" (O'Connor) **5**:381,
　　393
"A procura de uma dignidade" (Lispector)
　　34:233
"The Prodigal Children" (Benét) **10**:156
"Prodigal Father" (Gallant) **5**:138
"The Prodigal Father" (London) **4**:256
"The Prodigies" (Cather) **50**:81, 94-5, 153, 184,
　　279
"La prodigiosa tarde de Baltazar" (García
　　Márquez) **8**:185, 187-91
"El prodigioso miligramo" (Arreola) **38**:7
"The Prodigy" (Singer) **3**:374
"The Prodigy of Dreams" (Ligotti) **16**:277-79,
　　295, 297
"Proditoriamente" (Svevo) **25**:329-30, 336, 360
"The Professional Instinct" (Glasgow) **34**:62,
　　65-6, 69-71, 78, 81
"The Professor" (Farrell) **28**:89, 92
"Professor" (Hughes) **6**:112, 118, 122, 131-32
Professor Bernhardi (Schnitzler) **61**:309
"Professor Bingo's Snuff" (Chandler) **23**:64,
　　111
"Professor Nobody's Little Lectures on
　　Supernatural Horror" (Ligotti) **16**:261,
　　269, 284-85, 293
"Professor Rado" (Tanizaki) **21**:218
"Il Professor Terremoto" (Pirandello) **22**:278
"The Professor's Commencement" (Cather)
　　2:99, 103, 113; **50**:81, 104-05, 146-47, 149-
　　50, 187, 190-91, 193
"The Professor's Escape" (Aiken) **9**:14
"The Profile" (Cather) **2**:98, 103-04; **50**:202-03
"Progeny" (Dick) **57**:84
"Progress" (Galsworthy) **22**:98
"The Progress of Love" (Munro) **3**:347, 349
The Progress of Love (Munro) **3**:346-48
"Prohibition" (Wescott) **35**:357, 364, 366-67,
　　369-72
"Proischozhdenie mastera" (Platonov) **42**:257
Proiskhozhdenie mastera (Platonov) **42**:256
"Project Earth" (Dick) **57**:107
"Les projets" (Baudelaire) **18**:6-7
"Prokhodimets" (Gorky) **28**:156, 189

Prokleta avlija (Andrić) **36**:31, 33, 36, 38, 43,
　　46-8, 57, 77-8
"A Prologue to America" (Wolfe) **33**:401
"Prologue to an Adventure" (Thomas) **3**:399,
　　401; **44**:335, 354, 357
"Prologue to Ask the Dust" (Fante) **65**:92
"La prolongada busca de Tai An" (Bioy
　　Casares) **17**:70
"Promenade" (Maupassant) **1**:260, 274;
　　64:304-6, 308-12
Prométhée (Gide) **13**:52-57, 67
Le Prométhée mal enchaîné (Gide) **13**:59, 61,
　　65, 72, 79-81, 86
Prometheus Illbound (Gide)
　　See *Le Prométhée mal enchaîné*
Prometheus Misbound (Gide)
　　See *Le Prométhée mal enchaîné*
"Prometheus' Punishment" (Čapek) **36**:85, 113,
　　129
"Promise" (Davie) **52**:10
"The Promise" (Steinbeck) **11**:209-10, 212-13,
　　232
"The Promise of America" (Wolfe) **33**:401
"Promise of Rain" (Taylor) **10**:417
"The Promised Land" (Fisher) **25**:5, 9-10, 14,
　　16, 19-21, 25, 27
"The Promoter" (Dunbar) **8**:122, 147
"Proof of the Pudding" (Henry) **5**:165
"Proof Positive" (Čapek) **36**:128
"Proof Positive" (Greene) **29**:184, 193
"The Propagation of Knowledge" (Kipling)
　　54:96
"Propavšaja gramotax" (Gogol) **4**:117, 121
"The Proper Respect" (Allende) **65**:14, 17
"The Properties of Love" (O'Hara) **15**:252
"Property" (Head) **52**:222
"Property" (Singer) **3**:374
"Property" (Verga) **21**:298, 300
"The Property of Colette Nervi" (Trevor)
　　21:246-47, 262, 270; **58**:223, 280, 282
"The Prophecy" (Schnitzler) **15**:343
"The Prophet Peter" (Chesnutt) **7**:17
"The Prophetic Pictures" (Hawthorne) **3**:158,
　　181, 185-86, 190-91
"Proprietors of the Olden Time" (Gogol)
　　See "Starosvetskie Pomeščiki"
Prose and Poetry (Crane) **56**:111
"Prose Piece" (Walser) **20**:364-65
Prose Poems (Baudelaire)
　　See *Petits poèmes en prose: Le spleen de
　　Paris*
Prose Works of Henry Lawson (Lawson) **18**:202
"Prosody" (Arreola) **38**:13
A Prospect of the Orchards (Bates) **10**:121-22
"A Prospect of the Sea" (Thomas) **3**:394, 399,
　　401, 407-09; **44**:326, 338, 345, 347, 354,
　　356-57
Prospero on the Island (Thomas) **20**:286-87,
　　313, 315-17
"Le protecteur" (Maupassant) **1**:280
"A Protégée of Jack Hamlin's" (Harte) **8**:249;
　　59:301, 331
"A Protest against the Sun" (Millhauser) **57**:154
"The Proud and the Virtuous" (Betts) **45**:28
The Proverb, and Other Stories (Aymé) **41**:5
"Providence and the Guitar" (Stevenson)
　　11:280; **51**:218-19, 319
"La provinciale" (Moravia) **26**:163
Provintzreise (Peretz) **26**:191
"The Prowler in the City at the End of the
　　War" (Ellison) **14**:115
Proxopera (Kiely) **58**:159, 161, 163
"The Prussian Officer" (Lawrence) **4**:197-99,
　　210, 212, 214-18, 235; **19**:268
The Prussian Officer, and Other Stories
　　(Lawrence) **4**:196-98, 202, 230, 235-36
"Prvi dan u radosnom gradu" (Andrić) **36**:50
"A Psalm" (Bulgakov) **18**:74, 92
"Psiren" (Vinge) **24**:337, 344
"The Psoriasis Diet" (Lish) **18**:284
"P-s-s-t, Partner, Your Peristalsis Is Showing"
　　(Perelman) **32**:201-02

"Psyche" (Andersen) **6**:36, 38; **56**:19, 21-7
Psyche (Storm) **27**:314
"Psyche and the Pskyscraper" (Henry) **5**:162
"Psychiatric Services" (Oates) **6**:232
"The Psychiatrist" (Machado de Assis) **24**:136-
　　38, 140, 152
The Psychiatrist and Other Stories (Machado
　　de Assis) **24**:135
"Psychology" (Machen) **20**:200
"Psychology" (Mansfield) **9**:280, 284, 310
"The Psychophant" (Levi) **12**:279
"Ptaki" (Schulz) **13**:327, 333-34
"The Public Career of Mr. Seymour
　　Harrisburg" (O'Hara) **15**:248
"A Public Example" (Lu Hsun)
　　See "Shizhong"
"Public Opinion" (O'Connor) **5**:374
"Public Speech" (Saroyan) **21**:163
"Publicity Campaign" (Clarke) **3**:134, 150
"Puck of Pook's Hill" (Kipling) **5**:271-73, 292
Puck of Pook's Hill (Kipling) **54**:94
"Pueblerina" (Arreola) **38**:5, 7, 9, 13, 23
"La puerta cerrada" (Donoso) **34**:143, 23, 25,
　　31, 49
"The Pugilist at Rest" (Jones) **56**:272-73,
　　279-82
The Pugilist at Rest (Jones) **56**:272, 274-78,
　　285-86
"The Pug-Nosed Fox" (Somerville & Ross)
　　56:302, 317-18
Le Puits aux images (Aymé) **41**:10
"Punctum Indifferens Skibet Gaar Videre"
　　(Lowry) **31**:41
"Punin and Baburin" (Turgenev)
　　See "Punin i Baburin"
"Punin i Baburin" (Turgenev) **7**:321, 323-24,
　　326, 337, 358, 360
"The Punishment" (Lenz) **33**:337
"Punishment" (Tagore)
　　See "Shasti"
"The Punishment of Prometheus" (Čapek)
　　See "Prometheus' Punishment"
Punta de Plata (Arreola) **38**:12, 30
"The Pupil" (James) **8**:291, 316; **47**:252
"The Puppeteer" (Akutagawa Ryūnosuke) **44**:57
"The Puppets and the Puppy" (Norris) **28**:202,
　　214-18
"Puppy" (Ford) **56**:196-97
"The Puppy" (Solzhenitsyn) **32**:395
Le pur et l'impur (Colette) **10**:262
The Purcell Papers (Le Fanu) **14**:217, 221, 245
"A Purchase of Some Golf Clubs" (O'Hara)
　　15:270
The Pure and Impure (Colette)
　　See *Le pur et l'impur*
"Pure as the Driven Snow" (Aiken) **9**:6, 14
"The Pure Diamond Man" (Laurence) **7**:245
"A Pure Soul" (Fuentes)
　　See "Un alma pura"
"The Purim Feast" (Aleichem) **33**:16
"Purl and Plain" (Coppard) **21**:27
"The Purloined Letter" (Poe) **1**:387-88; **35**:306,
　　308-10, 322; **54**:162-67, 169-70, 185, 210,
　　218, 235-36, 241-45
"The Purple Envelope" (Forster) **27**:97, 103
"The Purple Hat" (Welty) **1**:468-69, 471, 479
"The Purple of the Balkan Kings" (Saki) **12**:322
"The Purple Pileus" (Wells) **6**:360, 383, 389,
　　404
"The Purple Wig" (Chesterton) **1**:131; **46**:110,
　　133
A Purse of Coppers (O'Faolain) **13**:284, 286,
　　293, 301-02, 309, 312-13, 316
"The Pursuer" (Cortázar)
　　See "El perseguidor"
"A Pursuit Race" (Hemingway) **1**:216, 219;
　　40:166
"Purun Bhagat" (Kipling)
　　See "The Miracle of Purun Bhagat"
"Put Alije Djerzeleza" (Andrić) **36**:30, 32, 43,
　　45-7, 54, 56, 65-6

"Put Down Two and Carry One" (Somerville & Ross) 56:301, 307

"Put Yourself in My Shoes" (Carver) 8:9, 13, 20, 46, 49

"Puteshestvuia vdol' Oki" (Solzhenitsyn) 32:352-53

"The Putney Night" (Morand)
    See "La nuit de Putney"

"Puttermesser and Xanthippe" (Ozick) 15:307-08, 319-23, 325, 327; 60:314-15

"Puttermesser: Her Work History, Her Ancestry, Her Afterlife" (Ozick) 15:307, 320, 322, 326

"Pyetushkov" (Turgenev) 7:320

"Pylades and Orestes" (Machado de Assis) 24:155

Pym (Poe)
    See *The Narrative of Arthur Gordon Pym, of Nantucket*

"The Pyrotechnicist" (Naipaul) 38:349

"The Pyrrhon of Elis" (Davenport) 16:198-99

"Pythias" (Pohl) 25:227, 229-31

"Pytor Petrovich Karataev" (Turgenev) 7:313

q1The Bright Graves" (Kiely) 58:145-46

Q.E.D. (Stein)
    See *Things As They Are*

"Quality" (Galsworthy) 22:74, 79

"The Quality of Mercy" (Warner) 23:376

Quand prime le spirituel (Beauvoir) 35:61-2, 64-5, 67-8, 71-3, 76, 78

Quand'ero matto (Pirandello) 22:231, 259, 275

"Quant'è caro" (Moravia) 26:145

"Quanto scommettiamo" (Calvino) 3:92; 48:69-71

"The Quare Gander" (Le Fanu) 14:219-20

"The Quarrel of Two Ivans" (Gogol)
    See "The Tale of How Ivan Ivanovich Quarrelled with Ivan Nikiforovich"

"Quarter, Half, Three-Quarter, and Whole Notes" (Saroyan) 21:160

"The Quartette" (Gautier) 20:3

"El que inventó la pólvora" (Fuentes) 24:38, 54-5

"Lo que se oye desde una silla del Prado" (Alarcon) 64:8, 13

"que sepa abrir la puerta para ir a jugar" (Cortázar) 7:95

"The Queen Bee" (Grimm and Grimm) 36:188-89, 206, 208

"The Queen Doll" (Fuentes)
    See "La muñeca reina"

"Queen Elizabeth's Rhinoplasty" (Ballard) 53:19

"Queen for a Day" (Banks) 42:59

"The Queen Is Dead" (Selby) 20:253, 260, 262-67, 273, 278

"Queen Louisa" (Gardner) 7:233

The Queen of Spades (Pushkin)
    See *Pikovaya dama*

The Queen of Spain Fritillary (Bates) 10:119

Queen of Terrors (Kelly) 50:292

"Queen of the Night" (Oates) 6:246

"Queen Ysabeau" (Villiers de l'Isle Adam)
    See "La reine Ysabeau"

"The Queen's Twin" (Jewett) 6:152

"The Queer Feet" (Chesterton) 1:119, 125, 127, 130; 46:109, 140, 144-45, 148

"A Queer Heart" (Bowen) 3:33, 41, 43, 49-50

"A Queer Job" (Oe)
    See "Kimyōna shigoto"

"A Queer Streak" (Munro) 3:347

"Quenby and Ola, Swede and Carl" (Coover) 15:38, 48, 51

Queremos tanto a Glenda (Cortázar) 7:64, 68, 71-2, 79, 90

"The Quest" (Saki) 12:299

"A Quest for the Night" (Agnon) 30:48

"The Quest of Iranon" (Lovecraft) 3:274; 52:281, 285, 299-300, 335, 359

"Question and Answer" (Sansom) 21:90-1

"A Question of Re-Entry" (Ballard) 1:68; 53:8, 43

"The Question of the Existence of Waring Stohl" (Auchincloss) 22:39, 49

Questionable Shapes (Howells) 36:360-61, 365, 386-89, 400

"Quetzalcoatl Lite" (Boyle) 16:143

"Qui sait?" (Maupassant) 1:273

"The Quick and the Dead" (Pirandello) 22:226, 229

"The Quick One" (Chesterton) 46:136

"Quick Returns" (Lardner) 32:148

"Quicksand" (Jones) 56:276, 281

"The Quicksand" (Wharton) 6:424

"Quidquid volueris" (Flaubert) 11:71-3, 75-6; 60:146-49, 151-53

"The Quiet City" (Levi) 12:273

The Quiet One (Bates) 10:124

"A Quiet Spot" (Turgenev) 7:328

"The Quiet Woman" (Coppard) 21:15

"The Quince Tree" (Saki) 12:295

"The Quincunx" (de la Mare) 14:84, 91

"A Quinta História" (Lispector) 34:189

"Quitclaim" (Agnon)
    See "Hefker"

Quite Contrary: The Mary and Newt Story (Dixon) 16:204-05, 210, 214-15

Quite Early One Morning (Thomas) 3:392; 44:354

"Quitters, Inc" (King) 17:262

"R Is for Rocket" (Bradbury) 29:77, 85; 53:245

R Is for Rocket (Bradbury) 29:75, 83

"The R. K. K." (Bulgakov) 18:89

"The Rabbi" (Babel) 16:9, 25-6, 28-30

"The Rabbi's Daughter" (Calisher) 15:4, 7, 12, 15, 19

"The Rabbi's Son" (Babel) 16:16, 26, 28, 30-1, 52, 55-6

"The Rabbit" (Barnes) 3:6-7, 22-4

"Rabbit" (Shiga) 23:348

"The Rabbit-Pen" (Anderson) 1:52

"The Rabbit's Revenge" (Dazai Osamu) 41:238

"The Rabbits Who Caused All the Trouble" (Thurber) 1:431

I racconti (Calvino) 3:96-7, 116; 48:33-7, 39, 79-85, 145-52

I racconti Romani (Moravia) 26:139, 143-46, 150, 152-53, 155, 156, 160, 162, 164, 174-75, 180

Racconti surrealistici e satirici (Moravia) 26:179

"The Race" (Ross) 24:309-11, 323

The Race and Other Stories (Ross) 24:309, 319

"The Race Question" (Dunbar) 8:122, 147

"Rachel" (Caldwell) 19:5

"Radilov" (Turgenev)
    See "My Neighbor Radilov"

"Radio" (O'Hara) 15:265, 267-68, 270

"Rafaela Who Drinks Coconut and Papaya Juice on Tuesdays" (Cisneros) 32:41

"Rafferty's Reasons" (Pohl) 25:223-24, 227-28, 230-32, 234

"The Raffle" (Naipaul) 38:300, 320, 328, 345

"The Raft" (King) 17:274-75; 55:250-51, 254-55, 265-72

"La ragazza mela" (Calvino) 48:98

"Rags and Bones" (Gordimer) 17:169, 171

"Rags Martin-Jones and the Pr-nce of W-les" (Fitzgerald) 6:46, 56

"Ragtime" (Nin) 10:299, 301, 303, 305

"Rahamim" (Agnon) 30:18

"The Raid" (Bulgakov) 18:74, 90

"Raid" (Faulkner) 1:170

"The Raid" (Lewis) 40:276, 278

"The Raid" (Steinbeck) 11:207-08, 225, 232-33, 239-40

"The Raid" (Tolstoy) 9:375

Railroad Stories (Aleichem) 33:25, 29, 61-4, 74

"Railway Accident" (Mann) 5:323-24, 330, 348-50

"The Railway Police" (Calisher) 15:5, 11

The Railway Police (Calisher) 15:5-6, 21-3

"Rain" (Maugham) 8:356-61, 371, 373, 375, 377, 381-84

"The Rain Child" (Laurence) 7:246, 248, 250, 253, 272

"The Rain Gutter" (Boell) 23:38

"Rain in May" (Moravia) 26:139

"Rain in the Heart" (Taylor) 10:374-76, 385, 387

"Rain in the Sierra" (Pritchett) 14:268, 273, 285

"Rain on Tanyard Hollow" (Stuart) 31:228, 260-61

"Rainbow Villa" (Warner) 23:369

"Rain-Queen" (Gordimer) 17:158

"The Raintree Street Bar and Washataria, A Fable" (Gilchrist) 63:6-7

"The Rainy Moon" (Colette)
    See "La lune de pluie"

"Rainy Season" (King) 17:295

"The Rainy Station" (Kawabata) 17:251

"Raise High the Roofbeam, Carpenters" (Salinger) 2:291-93, 298, 307, 314; 28:221-24, 243, 245, 248, 262, 265, 269; 65:299-300, 315, 318

Raise High the Roofbeam, Carpenters and Seymour: An Introduction (Salinger) 2:318; 28:265, 269; 65:316

"The Raising of Elvira Tremlett" (Trevor) 21:247, 259; 58:230, 241, 283

"Raisins" (Saroyan) 21:134

"The Rajah's Diamond" (Stevenson) 51:248

"Rajtika" (Tagore) 48:316, 329

"The Rakshas and the Sea Market" (P'u Sung-ling)
    See "Luosha haishi"

Ralph and Tony (Forster) 27:115-117

"Ralph Ringwood" (Irving) 2:241

"A Ramble among the Hills" (Irving) 2:266

"Rambling Boy" (Moorhouse) 40:325

"Ramkanai's Folly" (Tagore) 48:333

"Rancid Pastry" (Fuentes)
    See "Pastel rancio"

"Rancors Aweigh" (Perelman) 32:231

"Le rang" (Mauriac) 24:185, 196-98, 203, 205, 208

"Rangta" (Narayan) 25:137

"Rank" (Mauriac)
    See "Le rang"

"Ranocchi Sulla Luna" (Levi) 12:276

"The Ransom of Red Chief" (Henry) 5:193; 49:206

"Rape Fantasies" (Atwood) 2:3-4, 6-8, 10-12; 46:26, 33, 35, 40, 76, 94

"The Rape of Persephone" (Dybek) 55:126

"The Rape of the Drape" (Perelman) 32:247

"Rappaccini's Daughter" (Hawthorne) 3:159, 171, 173-74, 179-80, 189, 191-92; 39:91, 100, 125

"Rapunzel" (Grimm and Grimm) 36:204, 208

"Rapunzel" (Thomas) 20:287, 290, 292, 294, 317

"Rapunzel, Rapunzel" (Rhys) 21:51, 56, 59, 65

"Rara Avis" (Boyle) 16:146

"Rare Bit of Coolidgeana Bobs Up; Quickly Bobs Down Again" (Perelman) 32:240

"Rashad" (Wideman) 62:262, 315

"Rashmonir Chele" (Tagore) 48:312-14

"Rashmoni's Son" (Tagore)
    See "Rashmonir Chele"

"Rashōmon" (Akutagawa Ryūnosuke) 44:41-42, 45, 49-50, 56-58, 60-61, 63, 73-75

Rashomon, and Other Stories (Akutagawa Ryūnosuke) 44:42, 57

"Raspberry Jam" (Wilson) 21:318, 322-27, 332, 336, 343, 346, 348-49, 352-54, 359, 361, 363, 365

"Raspberry Spring" (Turgenev) 7:341; 57:266

"Raspberry Waters" (Turgenev)
    See "Raspberry Spring"

"Rasplësnutoe vremja" (Pilnyak) 48:248

Rasplyosnutoye vremya (Pilnyak)
    See "Rasplësnutoe vremja"

"Rasskaz neizvestnogo eloveka" (Chekhov) **51**:83, 169-71, 173, 175-77, 191-93, 196
"Rasskaz o geroe" (Gorky) **28**:184
"Rasskaz otca Alekseja" (Turgenev)
See "Rasskaz ottsa Aleksaya"
"Rasskaz ottsa Aleksaya" (Turgenev) **7**:324, 338, 361-62; **57**:380
"Rasskazy kstati" (Leskov) **34**:109
"Rat Krespel" (Hoffmann) **13**:200, 202, 205-06
"Ratbird" (Aldiss) **36**:28
"Un rato de tenmeallá" (Cabrera Infante) **39**:18, 22
"Rats" (James) **16**:236, 245, 251, 254, 256
"Rats" (Lawson) **18**:218, 240-41, 245
The Rats (Hauptmann)
See *Die Ratten*
"The Rats in the Walls" (Lovecraft) **3**:258, 262, 267, 269, 275, 277; **52**:253, 259, 290-91, 300-1, 304, 312, 316, 319, 336, 346, 354
Die Ratten (Hauptmann) **37**:258
"Rattlesnake Creek" (Cather) **2**:106
"Rattling Wheels" (Turgenev) **57**:266
"Rautavaara's Case" (Dick) **57**:84, 116, 118
"The Ravages of Spring" (Gardner) **7**:214-15, 218, 222, 228-29, 232-33
"The Raven" (Bunin)
See "Voron"
"Raw Materials" (Atwood) **2**:17-19
A Raw Youth (Dostoevsky)
See *Podrostok*
The Raw Youth (Dostoevsky)
See *Podrostok*
"Rawdon's Roof" (Lawrence) **4**:220
"Rawhead Rex" (Barker) **53**:136, 138, 140-41, 145-47, 158-59, 163, 174-76
"Ray Taite" (Farrell) **28**:112
"Rayme" (Phillips) **16**:336-37, 339
"Raymond Bamber and Mrs. Fitch" (Trevor) **21**:262, 265, 270; **58**:203, 206, 208
"Raymond's Run" (Bambara) **35**:7, 9-10, 18, 22, 33, 36-7
"Razaranja" (Andrić) **36**:48
"Razbojnik" (Leskov) **34**:109
"Razgovor predveče" (Andrić) **36**:65
"Razgovori sa Gojom" (Andrić) **36**:50, 56
"The Razor" (Shiga) **23**:333-34, 345-46, 351
"Razzle-dazzle in the Rib Room" (Perelman) **32**:229
"Un re in ascolto" (Calvino) **48**:129-30
"The Reach" (King) **17**:275; **55**:250-, 255-56, 275, 277-78
Reach for Tomorrow (Clarke) **3**:124, 129
"Read Only Memory" (Abish) **44**:15
"The Reader" (Gorky)
See "Chitatel"
"Reading a Wave" (Calvino) **3**:113
"A Reading Problem" (Stafford) **26**:279, 286, 309-10
"The Reading Public: A Book Store Study" (Leacock) **39**:263
Reading the Signs (Wilding) **50**:358-59, 364, 367
Reading Turgenev (Trevor)
See *Two Lives: Reading Turgenev; My House in Umbria*
"A Real Discovery" (Chesterton) **1**:140
The Real Dope (Lardner) **32**:144
"Real Impudence" (Calisher) **15**:9
"Real Mothers" (Thomas) **20**:295-96, 298, 312, 319
Real Mothers (Thomas) **20**:288-90, 295, 305, 307, 309-10, 318-20
"The Real Thing" (James) **8**:296-98, 302; **47**:226
The Real Thing (Lessing) **61**:114, 120, 123, 125
"The Reality of Dream" (Pirandello)
See "La realtà del sogno"
"Really, Doesn't Crime Pay?" (Walker) **5**:401, 405, 408-09, 419
"Realpoltik" (Wilson) **21**:319, 324, 330, 332-33, 344, 350, 364

"La realtà del sogno" (Pirandello) **22**:285
"The Reaping Race" (O'Flaherty) **6**:264, 281
"A Reasonable Facsimile" (Stafford) **26**:278-280
"A Reasonable Man" (Beattie) **11**:12, 15-17,
"Reassurance" (O'Hara) **15**:281
"Rebecca" (Barthelme) **55**:94
The Rebecca Notebook and Other Memories (du Maurier) **18**:130
"Rebel Families" (P'u Sung-ling)
See "Tao-hu"
The Rebellion in the Cévennes (Tieck)
See *Der Aufruhr in den Cevennen*
"Recent Photograph" (Bowen) **3**:40
"Rechute" (Aymé) **41**:22, 26-28
"Reci" (Andrić) **36**:47, 71-2
"The Reckoning" (Wharton) **6**:425-26
"A Recluse" (de la Mare) **14**:72-3, 80-1, 83, 85, 88, 90
"The Recluse" (Stifter)
See "Der Hagestolz"
"The Recognition" (Ballard) **53**:9
"Recollection of a Young King" (Boell) **23**:35
"A Recollection of Childhood" (Mansfield) **9**:282
"Recollections" (Dazai Osamu)
See "Omoide"
"Recollections of a Billiard Marker" (Tolstoy) **9**:375
"The Recollections of Captain Wilkie" (Doyle) **12**:88
"Recollections of Mortality" (Dickens) **17**:123
"Recollections of My Mother's Death and of Her Tabi" (Shiga) **23**:336
"Recollections of the Gas Buggy" (Thurber) **1**:431
"Recollections of the Works Department" (Hood) **42**:138-39, 179, 200, 225-27, 229-31
Reconciliation (Shiga)
See *Wakai*
"Record" (Čapek)
See "Rekord"
"A Record As Long As Your Arm" (Garrett) **30**:172, 174
"Record of a Transformation" (Abe) **61**:9, 11
"The Record of Badalia Herodsfoot" (Kipling) **5**:261
"A Record of Longing for Mother" (Tanizaki)
See "Haha no kouru ki"
"Recorded" (Galsworthy) **22**:101
Records of the Strange (P'u Sung-ling)
See *Liao-chai chih-i*
"Recortes de prensa" (Cortázar) **7**:69, 71, 83, 87, 91
"The Recovery" (Chopin) **8**:99
"The Recovery" (Wharton) **6**:414, 420, 423, 428-29
"The Recrudescence of Imray" (Kipling)
See "The Return of Imray"
"The Recruit" (Galsworthy) **22**:82, 101-02
"The Recruiting Officer" (McGahern) **17**:302, 307, 309, 323
"Red" (Gorky) **28**:137
"Red" (Maugham) **8**:370
"Red Barbara" (O'Flaherty) **6**:260, 262, 271, 277-78, 285
"A Red Carnation" (Warner) **23**:368, 387
Red Cavalry (Babel)
See *Konarmiia*
"Red Clowns" (Cisneros) **32**:32
"The Red Cocoon" (Abe)
See "Akai mayu"
"The Red Cow Group" (Morrison) **40**:328, 338, 366-67
"Red Crown" (Bulgakov) **18**:91
"The Red Devil" (Gorky) **28**:146
"Red Dog" (Kipling) **54**:83-84, 113-14
"The Red Hand" (Machen) **20**:165, 186, 197-99, 201
"The Red Head" (Williams) **31**:334

"The Red Inn" (Balzac)
See *L'Auberge rouge*
"Red Jacket: The Knocking Spirit" (Stuart) **31**:226, 245, 256
"Red Leaves" (Faulkner) **1**:147, 162, 168-70, 180
"The Red Mark" (Zangwill) **44**:378
"The Red Moon of Meru" (Chesterton) **1**:129; **46**:107, 135
Red Notebook (Thomas) **44**:330-38
"The Red Petticoat" (O'Flaherty) **6**:271
The Red Pony (Steinbeck) **11**:204, 207, 209-10, 212-14, 217, 220, 225, 232-33; 359
"The Red Room" (Wells) **6**:366, 383, 388
"Red Roses and White Roses" (Chang) **28**:28; 35
"The Red Shoes" (Andersen) **6**:4, 7, 34, 37-8
"The Red Stockade" (Stoker) **62**:249
"Red Story" (Čapek)
See "Červená povídka"
The Red Triangle (Morrison) **40**:332, 349
"Red Wind" (Chandler) **23**:59, 88, 108, 110, 112
"The Red-Backed Spiders" (Cowan) **28**:80
"Redemption" (Evans) **43**:37
"Redemption" (Gardner) **7**:224-27, 235-36, 238, 240-41
"Redfish" (Bass) **60**:4-5, 8, 30-31
"Red-Headed Baby" (Hughes) **6**:109, 118-19, 121, 123-25, 129-30, 141
"The Red-Headed League" (Doyle)
See "The Adventure of the Red-Headed League"
"Red-Herring Theory" (Updike) **13**:387
"Red-Stoned Moscow" (Bulgakov) **18**:90
"Reduced" (Bowen) **3**:33
The Reed Cutter (Tanizaki) **21**:224-27
"The Reed Flute" (Chekhov)
See "Svirel'"
"The Reed Pipe" (Chekhov)
See "Svirel'"
"Reena" (Marshall) **3**:300, 303, 308, 310, 313, 315, 317
Reena, and Other Stories (Marshall) **3**:313, 315-17
"The Reference" (Barthelme) **2**:55; **55**:88
"The Refined Man" (Dazai Osamu) **41**:231
"Reflection in the Water" (Solzhenitsyn)
See "Otrazhenie v vode"
"Reflections" (Čapek)
See "Odrazy"
"Reflections" (Carter) **13**:2, 4
"Reflections" (Solzhenitsyn) **32**:395
"The Refuge of the Derelicts" (Twain) **6**:339
"A Refusal to Mourn" (Thomas)
See "A Refusal to Mourn the Death, by Fire, of a Child in London"
"A Refusal to Mourn the Death, by Fire, of a Child in London" (Thomas) **44**:336
"The Regal" (Narayan) **25**:135, 156
Die Regentrude (Storm) **27**:278, 284
Regina (Keller) **26**:102-03, 110
"Reginald" (Saki) **12**:286-87, 322, 327-28, 332
Reginald in Russia, and Other Stories (Saki) **12**:287, 322, 328, 331
"Reginald on Besetting Sins" (Saki) **12**:322, 328
"Reginald on House Parties" (Saki) **12**:325, 327, 329
"Reginald on Tariffs" (Saki) **12**:328
"Reginald's Choir Treat" (Saki) **12**:329
"Reginald's Christmas Revel" (Saki) **12**:303, 324
"The Region Between" (Ellison) **14**:146
"Regret" (Chopin) **8**:72-3, 84, 93, 111
"Regret for the Past" (Lu Hsun)
See "Shang shi"
Regretful Parting (Dazai Osamu) **41**:247
"Regulus" (Kipling) **54**:97, 99
"The Rehearsal" (Dixon) **16**:211
"The Reign of the Doll" (Freeman) **47**:102
"Reina" (Dreiser) **30**:146

"The Reincarnation of Smith" (Harte) 8:254
"La reine Ysabeau" (Villiers de l'Isle Adam) 14:378, 382, 396
"Reisekammeraten" (Andersen) 6:18-19, 30-1, 35; 56:36, 39
Die Reisenden (Tieck) 31:270
"The Rejected Gift" (Castellanos)
    See "El don rechazado"
"The Rejected Story" (Tagore)
    See "Namanjur Galpa"
"Rejuvenation through Joy" (Hughes) 6:109, 128
"Reka Potudan" (Platonov) 42:252
Reka Potudan (Platonov) 42:249-50, 256
"Rekord" (Čapek) 36:102, 127
"Relato con un fondo de agua" (Cortázar) 7:58
Los Relatos (Cortázar) 7:91
"Relics" (Thomas) 20:321-22
"Relics of General Chassé" (Trollope) 28:318, 323, 328, 335, 348
Réliquas de casa velha (Machado de Assis) 24:155
"Rella" (Dreiser) 30:141
"The Reluctant Orchid" (Clarke) 3:133-34
"Rem the Rememberer" (Pohl) 25:235
"The Remarkable Case of Davidson's Eyes" (Wells) 6:364-66, 376, 393-95, 405
"The Remarkable Rocket" (Wilde) 11:365, 375-76, 380, 386, 395, 407-09
"The Rembrandt" (Wharton) 6:414
"Rembrandt's Hat" (Malamud) 15:187-88, 190, 221
Rembrandt's Hat (Malamud) 15:188, 190, 197-98, 220
"The Remedy: Geography" (Pirandello)
    See "Rimedio: La geografia"
"Remember" (Rulfo)
    See "Acuérdate"
"Remember the Alamo" (Cisneros) 32:35
Remembering Laughter (Stegner) 27:194-95, 215-17, 219-21
"Remembrances of the Past" (Lu Hsun)
    See "Huaijiu"
"Reminders of Bouselham" (Bowles) 3:66
"The Reminiscence of Dr. Samuel Johnson" (Lovecraft) 52:293
"Reminiscence of My Beloved Mother" (Tanizaki)
    See "Haha no kouru ki"
"Reminiscences" (Dazai Osamu)
    See "Omoide"
"The Remission" (Gallant) 5:135-38
"Remnants" (Singer) 3:385, 387
"Remordimiento" (Pardo Bazán) 30:268-69
"Remorse" (Gilchrist) 63:36
"The Remount Officer" (Babel) 16:7, 27, 50, 53
"Removal" (Davie) 52:8
"Le remplacant" (Maupassant) 1:256
"Rena Walden" (Chesnutt) 7:19, 21, 33, 35; 54:25-7, 47
Renate (Storm) 27:283, 286, 307
"Le rendez-vous" (Colette) 10:274-75
"The Rendezvous" (du Maurier) 18:136
The Rendezvous and Other Stories (du Maurier) 18:130, 136
"The Renegade" (Camus)
    See "Le renégat"
"The Renegade" (Farrell) 28:122, 126
"Renegade" (Jackson) 9:252, 266; 39:209, 211, 217, 219, 220, 221, 226, 229, 231
"The Renegade" (Kazakov)
    See "Otschchepenets"
"Renegade to Autumn" (Kazakov) 43:54
"Le renégat" (Camus) 9:106-07, 109, 116-17, 119, 130-31
"Renner" (Powers) 4:368, 370, 372-73
"Renters" (Suckow) 18:396, 398
"Renunciation" (Barnes) 3:16
"The Renunciation" (Tagore) 48:330-32
"A Repartição dos Pães" (Lispector) 34:191
"'Repent, Harlequin!' Said the Ticktockman" (Ellison) 14:105, 112-15, 117, 124, 134-36

"The Repentant Sinner" (Tolstoy) 9:387
"Repitition" (Moravia)
    See "La ripetizione"
"Replies to an Enquiry" (Thomas) 44:344
"Report" (Barthelme) 55:72
"A Report" (Gallant) 5:138
"Report from Normalia" (Hesse) 9:244
"Report on an Unidentified Space Station" (Ballard) 53:123
"Report on the Barnhouse Effect" (Vonnegut) 8:428-29
"Report on the Threatened City" (Lessing) 6:188; 61:93
"A Report to an Academy" (Kafka)
    See "Ein Beriht für eine Akademie"
Reprinted Pieces (Dickens) 17:124
"The Reptile Enclosure" (Ballard) 1:68-9; 53:36, 48, 50, 110
"Una reputación" (Arreola) 38:7, 10, 21-23
"The Reputation of Pascual Humfortas" (Kelly) 50:291
"Repy Guaranteed" (Campbell) 19:83
"Requa" (Olsen) 11:187-89, 191, 193-97
"The Requiem" (Chekhov)
    See "Panixida"
"Requiem" (Cowan) 28:80
"Requiem" (Heinlein) 55:161-62, 202, 207
"Requiescat" (Bowen) 3:40
"Le réquisitionnaire" (Balzac) 5:16
"De rerum natura" (Boyle) 16:143
"Resaca" (Cabrera Infante) 39:18
"Rescue" (Pardo Bazán) 30:290
"The Rescue" (Pritchett) 14:272, 288-89
"Rescue Party" (Clarke) 3:124-26, 135-36, 148-49
"The Rescuer" (Conrad) 9:206
"The Rescuer" (Dixon) 16:216
"The Rescuer" (Wescott) 35:375
"Reservations: A Love Story" (Taylor) 10:417
"The Reservoir" (Frame) 29:96, 100
The Reservoir: Stories and Sketches (Frame) 29:95-7, 103, 112-13, 115
"The Reshaping of Rossiter" (Campbell) 19:82
"The Residence at Whitminster" (James) 16:230, 232, 234, 237, 246, 255-56
"Residents and Transients" (Mason) 4:20
Residua (Beckett) 16:135
"Respectability" (Anderson) 1:18, 53, 58
"A Respectable Place" (O'Hara) 15:248, 270
"A Respectable Woman" (Chopin) 8:72, 96-7, 110, 113
"The Resplendent Quetzal" (Atwood) 2:3, 5, 7, 10-11, 15-16, 19, 22; 46:26, 33-4, 38-9, 41, 46, 49-51, 56-63, 77, 93
"Responsable" (Pardo Bazán) 30:263
"Rest Cure" (Boyle) 5:55
"The Rest Cure" (Huxley) 39:159, 162, 172-74, 176
"The Rest of Life" (Gordon) 59:239-40, 243, 245, 248-49, 252-53, 255, 269-73, 275
The Rest of Life (Gordon) 59:239-46, 248-54, 258-59, 261, 269, 271-73, 276
"The Restoration of Whiskers: A Neglected Factor in the Decline of Knowledge" (Leacock) 39:262
"Resurrection" (Cather) 50:77, 92, 184-87, 191, 193-94
"Resurrection" (Lish) 18:280
"The Resurrection" (Suckow) 18:396, 405, 408, 415
"Resurrection of a Life" (Saroyan) 21:143
"The Resurrection of Father Brown" (Chesterton) 1:129, 137-38; 46:107, 114, 134
A Retelling of the Tales from the Provinces (Dazai Osamu) 41:226, 228-30, 232-33
"The Reticence of Lady Anne" (Saki) 12:296, 315
"Retired" (Suckow) 18:395-97, 409, 414
"The Retired Man" (Schulz)
    See "Emeryt"
"Le retour" (Maupassant) 1:285

"Retreat" (Faulkner) 1:170-71; 35:159
"The Retreat" (Mason) 4:21
"Retreat from Earth" (Clarke) 3:148
"Retreat Syndrome" (Dick) 57:116
"Retreating Figures" (Endō) 48:193
"A Retrieved Reformation" (Henry) 5:158, 170, 193; 49:203, 206
"The Return" (Anderson) 1:31, 39, 50
"The Return" (Bowen) 3:40, 53
"The Return" (Conrad) 9:151-52
"Return" (Henderson) 29:328
"The Return of a Private" (Garland) 18:142, 144, 150, 154, 159, 168, 170, 172, 176, 192
"The Return of Chorb" (Nabokov) 11:131, 133
"The Return of Imray" (Kipling) 5:262, 273-75, 285
"The Return of Khokababu" (Tagore)
    See "Kohkababur Pratyabartan"
The Return of Sherlock Holmes (Doyle) 12:51, 60, 62-3
"Return of the Native" (Thurber) 1:424
"The Return of the Prodigal" (Wolfe) 33:374
"Return to Lavinia" (Caldwell) 19:14
"Return Trip Tango" (Cortázar) 7:69
"Return Trips" (Adams) 24:14
Return Trips (Adams) 24:11-15
Returning (O'Brien) 10:334
"Returning Home" (Trollope) 28:318, 323, 331, 349, 357
"Reunion" (Cheever) 1:100
"Reunion" (Clarke) 3:133
"The Reunion" (Coover) 15:35, 43, 45-6
"Reunión" (Cortázar) 7:83, 89-90
"Reunion" (Ford) 56:184
"Reunion" (Lardner) 32:134-35, 138, 145
"The Reunion" (Lewis) 40:278
"The Reunion" (Nabokov) 11:133
"Reunion Abroad" (Farrell) 28:112, 126
"Reunión con un círculo rojo" (Cortázar) 7:85
"Reunion in the Avenue" (Boell)
    See "Wiedersehen in der Allee"
"Rêve d'enfer" (Flaubert) 11:71
Le rêve et la vie (Nerval) 18:328, 330, 337
"Rêveil" (Maupassant) 1:274
"Revelation" (O'Connor) 1:341-42, 344; 61:192
"Revelations" (Barker) 53:142-43, 154, 159, 162-63, 172
"Revelations" (Mansfield) 9:313
"A Revenant" (de la Mare) 14:80, 83, 86-7, 90, 93
"Revenge" (Allende) 65:18, 21-22, 54
"Revenge" (Balzac)
    See "La vendetta revenge"
"Revenge" (Gilchrist) 14:150-51, 159; 63:3, 10, 13-14, 19, 24, 30
"The Revenge" (Gogol) 4:85
"Revenge" (Harrison) 19:201-06, 209, 214
"Revenge" (O'Hara) 15:248
"Revenge for the Dog" (Pirandello) 22:251
"The Revenge of Lard Ass Hogan" (King) 17:272, 279, 285, 290
"Revenge of Truth" (Dinesen) 7:177, 180
"The Revenges of Mrs Abercrombie" (Auchincloss) 22:4
"Reverend Father Gilhooley" (Farrell) 28:92, 118-9
"Reversal" (Dixon) 16:208
"The Reversed Man" (Clarke)
    See "Technical Error"
"A Reversion to a Type" (Galsworthy) 22:82
"A Reversion to Type" (Norris) 28:197, 199, 207, 214
"Reves" (Maupassant) 64:316, 321
"Revival" (Fisher)
    See "The South Lingers On"
"The Revolt at Brocéliande" (Warner) 23:379
"Revolt at Roger's" (Galsworthy) 22:71
"The Revolt of 'Mother'" (Freeman) 1:192, 196-97, 200; 47:84-5, 87, 97-100, 105, 108, 118, 120-22, 126-30, 147, 150, 161, 168, 188, 192

"The Revolutionist" (Hemingway) 1:244; 63:79-80

"Revolving Lantern of Romance" (Dazai Osamu) 41:244

Rewards and Fairies (Kipling) 5:273, 283, 285, 292; 54:92

"Rex Imperator" (Wilson) 21:330-32, 354

"El rey negro" (Arreola) 38:25

"El rey se divierte" (Alarcon) 64:2, 30

"Rhapsody: A Dream Novel" (Schnitzler)
    See *Traumnovelle*

"A Rhinoceros, Some Ladies, and a Horse" (Stephens) 50:316

"Rhobert" (Toomer) 1:445, 450, 458-59; 45:206, 208-09, 224-25, 232, 236, 240, 253-54, 260, 265, 268, 286, 381

Rhoda: A Life in Stories (Gilchrist) 63:28

"Rhythm" (Lardner) 32:136-38, 149, 151

"Rich" (Gilchrist) 14:151; 63:10-11, 13, 23

"Rich and Rare Were the Gems She Wore" (Kiely) 58:145, 154

"The Rich Boy" (Fitzgerald) 6:46-7, 76, 86-9, 95, 100-03

"The Rich Brother" (Wolff) 63:267, 301, 318-20

"Rich in Russia" (Updike) 13:380

"Rich Man's Crumbs" (Melville)
    See "Poor Man's Pudding and Rich Man's Crumbs"

"Richard Greenow" (Huxley)
    See "The Farcical History of Richard Greenow"

"The Richard Nixon Freischütz Rag" (Davenport) 16:168, 173-74, 177, 191

"Riches in Custody" (Tagore)
    See "Sampatti-Samarpan"

Die Richterin (Meyer) 30:187-90, 195, 199, 223, 227

"The Riddle" (Grimm and Grimm) 36:223

"The Riddle" (de la Mare) 14:67, 74, 76-9, 80, 82, 90

The Riddle, and Other Stories (de la Mare) 14:65-7, 90, 92

"The Riddle of the Rocks" (Murfree) 22:210

"The Ride" (Ross) 24:324

"A Ride across Palestine" (Trollope) 28:318, 330, 333, 335, 340, 347-48

"A Ride with Olympy" (Thurber) 1:431

"Le rideau cramoisi" (Barbey d'Aurevilly) 17:7-8, 10-14, 19, 21, 24-6, 40-1, 43-4

"Riders in the Chariot" (White) 39:288-89

Ridiculous Loves (Kundera)
    See *Směsné lásky*

"The Riding of Felipe" (Norris) 28:198, 207

"Riding Pants" (Malamud) 15:235

"The Right Eye of the Commander" (Harte) 8:245-46; 59:340

"The Right Hand" (Solzhenitsyn)
    See "Pravaya kist"

"Right of Sanctuary" (Carpentier) 35:106, 125-30

"The Right Side" (Collier) 19:101

"The Righteous" (Shiga) 23:347

"Righteous Anger" (Stephens)
    See "A Glass of Beer"

"Rikki-Tikki-Tavi" (Kipling) 5:293

"Rimedio: La geografia" (Pirandello) 22:281

"Rinconete y Cortadillo" (Cervantes) 12:3-4, 6-8, 14, 16, 23, 26-7, 35

"The Ring" (Kawabata) 17:256-57

The Ring Lardner Reader (Lardner) 32:156

"The Ring of Thoth" (Doyle) 12:85-6

The Ring of Truth (Bates) 10:124

"Ring the Bells of Heaven" (Coppard) 21:27

"The Ring with the Green Stone" (Freeman) 47:87

"Ringtail" (Fisher) 25:4, 8-9, 17-18, 20-1, 25, 27

"El rinoceronte" (Arreola) 38:5, 7, 9

"El río" (Cortázar) 7:59, 70, 79, 81-3

"Rip Flip" (Hood) 42:235

"Rip Van Winkle" (Irving) 2:239-51, 253, 256-60, 262-64; 37:273-74, 276, 280

"Ripe Figs" (Chopin) 8:93

The Ripening Seed (Colette) 10:276-77

"La ripetizione" (Moravia) 26:142, 149, 155

"Ripped Off" (Adams) 24:3

"Ripple the Water Spirit" (Alcott) 27:40

"The Rise of Capitalism" (Barthelme) 2:37, 39, 47; 55:28, 47

"The Rise of the Middle Class" (Banks) 42:52-3

Risibles Amours (Kundera)
    See *Směsné lásky*

"Risiko für Weihnachtsmänner" (Lenz) 33:316, 318, 321-26

The Rising Gorge (Perelman) 32:212-13, 230, 236

"Rising Wolf—Ghost Dancer" (Garland) 18:178

Rita Hayworth and Shawshank Redemption (King) 17:262-65, 271; 55:243-44

"Ritorno al mare" (Moravia) 26:138, 163

"Ritter Glück" (Hoffmann) 13:203, 217-18

"Rituals of Rejection" (Valenzuela)
    See "Ceremonias de rechazo"

"The Rivals" (Garrett) 30:163, 172

"The River" (Cortázar)
    See "El río"

"The River" (Dybek) 55:139

"The River" (O'Connor) 1:344-45, 356; 23:237; 61:171-76, 179, 181

"The River behind Things" (Hood) 42:182, 203, 214, 221-22, 240-42

"River Driftwood" (Jewett) 44:193

"River of the Naked" (Dazai Osamu) 41:230, 233

"The River Potudan" (Platonov)
    See "Reka Potudan"

The River Potudan (Platonov)
    See *Reka Potudan*

"River Rising" (Oates) 6:227-28, 230, 249-50

A River Runs Through It (Maclean) 13:260-63, 265-67, 270-72, 274-76, 278-80

A River Runs Through It, and Other Stories (Maclean) 13:260-63, 265-67, 270-72, 274-76, 278-80

"The Road" (Babel)
    See "Doroga"

"The Road" (Pavese) 19:368

"The Road East" (Le Guin) 12:213, 249-50

"The Road from Colonus" (Forster) 27:70-72, 74-8, 80-1, 87-88, 91, 98-99, 103-04, 112, 114-15, 118, 121-22

"The Road North" (Allende) 65:7

"Road Number One" (Stuart) 31:265

"The Road of Ali Djerzelez" (Andrić)
    See "Put Alije Djerzeleza"

The Road Sign at the End of the Road (Abe)
    See *Owarishi michi no shirube ni*

The Road Sign at the End of the Street (Abe)
    See *Owarishi michi no shirube ni*

"The Road to Brody" (Babel) 16:25, 27, 29, 31, 54-8

"The Road to Hell" (Fante) 65:78, 94-95, 97

The Road to Miltown; or, Under the Spreading Atrophy (Perelman) 32:209, 229

The Road to the City (Ginzburg)
    See *La strada che va in città*

"The Road to the Sea" (Clarke) 3:135-36

Road to Within (Hesse)
    See *Der Weg nach Innen*

"The Roads Must Roll" (Heinlein) 55:199, 206, 212

"Roads of Destiny" (Henry) 5:163

"The Roads Round Pisa" (Dinesen) 7:164, 167-68, 171, 175, 179-80, 182, 187, 198, 208

"The Robber Bridegroom" (Grimm and Grimm) 36:199, 203, 206, 208

The Robber Bridegroom (Welty) 1:471-72, 483, 489-90, 496; 51:260, 262, 281, 297, 318

"Robbers!" (Aleichem) 33:20

"A Robbery" (Leskov)
    See "Grabež"

"Robert" (Toomer)
    See "Rhobert"

Robert (Gide) 13:72, 100, 104-05

"Robert Aghion" (Hesse) 9:231-32, 235

Robert Aghion (Hesse) 49:233

"Robert Kennedy Saved from Drowning" (Barthelme) 2:31, 36, 42, 46-7; 55:4, 6-7, 26, 34-6, 41, 55-7, 64

Robert Louis Stevenson: Tales from the Prince of Storytellers (Stevenson) 51:248

"Robert, Standing" (Metcalf) 43:107

"The Robing of the Bride" (Ballard) 53:97

"Robinja" (Andrić) 36:66-7

"Robins and Hammers" (Freeman) 47:161

"The Robin's House" (Barnes) 3:12

"Robot" (Davenport) 16:162, 165-66, 170

"The Robot Millennia" (Aldiss) 36:19

"The Rock" (Cowan) 28:76

"The Rock" (Forster) 27:98-99, 103

"The Rock" (Jackson) 9:254

"Rock, Church" (Hughes) 6:133

"Rock Crystal" (Stifter)
    See "Bergkristall"

Rock Crystal (Stifter)
    See *Bergkristall*

"Rock God" (Ellison) 14:118

"Rock River" (Wideman) 62:269

"Rock Springs" (Ford) 56:143, 148-49, 152, 158, 173-75, 194

Rock Springs (Ford) 56:136-37, 141-43, 145-49, 151-52, 160-61, 164, 170, 172, 174-77, 185-86, 188, 193-95

"The Rocket" (Bradbury) 29:47; 53:215

"The Rocket Man" (Bradbury) 29:77-8

"Rocket Man" (Jones) 56:273-74, 277, 280

"Rocket Summer" (Bradbury) 53:201-5, 210-12, 246, 248, 252

"Rocketfire Red" (Jones) 56:278

"The Rockfish" (O'Flaherty) 6:260-61, 267-69, 280

"The Rocking Chair" (Gilman) 13:128-30; 62:180

"The Rocking-Horse Winner" (Lawrence) 4:200-01, 206, 212, 221, 229-30, 233, 238; 19:250-91

"The Rockpile" (Baldwin) 10:4, 7-9, 17

Rococo (Morand) 22:169

"The Rod of Justice" (Machado de Assis)
    See "O caso de vara"

"De røde Sko" (Andersen) 56:37

"Rodina elektrichestva" (Platonov) 42:267

"Rofe' 'o chole?" (Peretz) 26:224

"Roger Malvin's Burial" (Hawthorne) 3:157, 164, 166-67, 171, 185-86, 189; 39:105

"Rogue's Gallery" (McCarthy) 24:213

"Le Roi candaule" (Gautier) 20:5-6, 8, 15, 17, 26, 28-9

"Rokovye iaitsa" (Bulgakov) 18:69, 72-6, 78, 81-2, 93-9, 105, 108-13

Rolling All the Time (Ballard) 1:72

"A Rolling Stone" (Gorky)
    See "Prokhodimets"

Le Roman de la momie (Gautier) 20:3, 7, 20-1, 29

"Roman Fever" (Wharton) 6:423-24

"Roman Figures" (Bates) 10:119

"A Roman Holiday" (Sansom) 21:84

"The Roman Image" (Narayan) 25:138, 155, 160

"The Roman Legions" (Čapek) 36:129

"The Roman Night" (Morand)
    See "La nuit Romaine"

Roman Tales (Moravia)
    See *I racconti Romani*

"Romance and Sally Byrd" (Glasgow) 34:65-67, 72, 76, 78, 81, 103-04

"Romance Lingers, Adventure Lives" (Collier) 19:110, 115

"The Romance of a Bouquet" (Alcott) 27:32

"The Romance of a Busy Broker" (Henry) 5:158, 181-82, 194; 49:197

The Romance of a Mummy (Gautier)
See *Le Roman de la momie*
"The Romance of Madrono Hollow" (Harte) **8**:225
"A Romance of Real Life" (Howells) **36**:397
"The Romance of Sunrise Rock" (Murfree) **22**:188, 203, 206-08, 218
"Romance of the Crossing" (Howells) **36**:398-99
"A Romance of the Equator" (Aldiss) **36**:14, 20
The Romance of the Swag (Lawson) **18**:208, 217, 233, 235
"Romance of the Thin Man and the Fat Lady" (Coover) **15**:32-4, 51
"The Romancers" (Saki) **12**:296
Romances (Chang)
See *Chuanqi*
"Le Romancier Martin" (Aymé) **41**:18, 20, 23
"Romanesque" (Dazai Osamu)
See "Romanesuku"
"Romanesuku" (Dazai Osamu) **41**:240
Romans et Contes (Gautier) **20**:7, 23
Romans et contes philosophiques (Balzac) **5**:22-3, 31
"The Romantic Adventures of a Milkmaid" (Hardy) **2**:211, 215-18, 221, 224; **60**:183
"The Romantic Egoists" (Auchincloss) **22**:38
The Romantic Egoists (Auchincloss) **22**:3-4, 7-9, 17, 33, 36-7, 46-8, 50, 53
"A Romantic Interlude in the Life of Willie Collins" (Farrell) **28**:99
"A Romantic Young Lady" (Maugham) **8**:380
Romantische Dichtungen (Tieck) **31**:282
"Rome" (Gogol) **4**:83; **52**:104
"Romeo and Juliet" (Čapek) **36**:85
Romeo und Julia auf dem Dorfe (Keller) **26**:89, 90-1, 106, 116-19, 121-23, 125
"Romolo e Remo" (Moravia) **26**:180
"Rondone e rondinella" (Pirandello) **22**:253, 269
"Rōnen" (Akutagawa Ryūnosuke) **44**:73
"Roof Beam" (Salinger)
See "Raise High the Roofbeam, Carpenters"
"The Roof, the Steeple and the People" (Ellison) **26**:11
"Roog" (Dick) **57**:69, 151
"The Rookers" (Mason) **4**:22
"A Room" (Lessing) **6**:200-01; **61**:93, 96-97
"The Room" (Sartre)
See "La chambre"
"A Room Forever" (Pancake) **61**:248, 255, 257, 276
"A Room in Linden" (Kiely) **58**:156-57
"The Room in the Castle" (Campbell) **19**:70, 72, 86, 90
"The Room in the Dragon Volant" (Le Fanu) **14**:214, 216, 225, 237-39, 243
"A Room of Photos" (Davie) **52**:7
Room Service (Moorhouse) **40**:324
"Root Cause" (Campbell) **19**:75
"The Root of All Evil" (Greene) **29**:201
"Roots" (Thomas) **20**:325, 328
"The Rope" (Baudelaire)
See "La corde"
"Rope" (Porter) **4**:327-28, 339-40, 342; **43**:177, 181-2, 222-23, 253, 292
"Rope Enough" (Collier) **19**:98, 104, 109, 112
"Rosa" (Ozick) **15**:327; **60**:307-11, 316-21, 324, 333-37, 340, 346-49, 354-57
"La rosa" (Pirandello) **22**:240-41, 245, 271-72
Rosa (Ozick) **60**:325, 327, 331-32
"Rosalie" (Harris) **19**:178, 181
"Rosalie Prudent" (Maupassant) **1**:286
"The Rosary" (Kelly) **50**:296
"Rosa's Tale" (Alcott) **27**:43
"Rose" (Dubus) **15**:86, 89, 91, 95-6, 101
"The Rose" (Pirandello)
See "La rosa"
Die Rose (Walser) **20**:333, 335, 344
"The Rose Elf" (Andersen) **6**:12, 30
Le rose et le vert (Stendhal) **27**:251-53, 259

"A Rose for Emily" (Faulkner) **1**:147-52, 158, 162, 165, 180-81; **35**:172; **42**:73-135
"The Rose Garden" (James) **16**:229-30, 240, 244, 249, 252-53, 256
"The Rose Garden" (Machen) **20**:180
A Rose in the Heart (O'Brien) **10**:333, 342, 344
"The Rose of Dixie" (Henry) **5**:159, 171
"A Rose of Glenbogie" (Harte) **8**:217, 222, 252
"The Rose of Jutland" (Dinesen) **7**:169
"The Rose of New York" (O'Brien) **10**:340
"Rose of the Ghetto" (Zangwill) **44**:371
"The Rose of Tuolumne" (Harte) **8**:223, 233
"The Rose Prince" (Stoker) **62**:251
"Roselily" (Walker) **5**:401-02, 405, 408-09
"Rosendo Juarez" (Borges) **41**:46
"Rosendo's Tale" (Borges) **4**:18, 20
"Roses, Rhododendron" (Adams) **24**:2-3, 5-6, 13, 16
"Le rosier de Madame Husson" (Maupassant) **1**:280
"Rosso malpelo" (Verga) **21**:283-84, 300-01, 313
"Rosy's Journey" (Alcott) **27**:44
"The Rot" (Lewis) **34**:153, 163
"The Rot-Camp" (Lewis) **34**:158
"Rothschild's Fiddle" (Chekhov)
See "Skripka Rotsil'da"
"Rothschild's Violin" (Chekhov)
See "Skripka Rotsil'da"
"Rotkäppchen" (Grimm and Grimm) **36**:184-85
Rotting Hill (Lewis) **34**:148-49, 151-53, 157-58, 163-64, 180
"Rouge High" (Hughes) **6**:112, 118
"The Rough Crossing" (Fitzgerald) **6**:61, 100, 103-04
"A Rough Shed" (Lawson) **18**:215
"La rouille" (Maupassant) **1**:256, 272, 274
"Round by Round" (Aiken) **9**:13, 40
"The Round Dozen" (Maugham) **8**:364, 378-79
Round the Red Lamp: Being Facts and Fancies of Medical Life (Doyle) **12**:88-9
Round Up (Lardner) **32**:122-23, 132-33, 149, 194-95, 197
"The Rout of the White Hussars" (Kipling) **5**:260
"A Royal Command" (Somerville & Ross) **56**:301, 339
"The Royal Man" (P'u Sung-ling)
See "Wang-che"
"Der roye veeyne-nire" (Singer) **53**:323
"A Rude Awakening" (Chopin) **8**:88, 103
"Rue de l'Évangile" (Aymé) **41**:4
"La rueda del hambriento" (Castellanos) **39**:29, 49, 57
"The Ruffian" (Dickens) **17**:124
"The Rug" (Andrić)
See "Ćilim"
"Ruído de passos" (Lispector) **34**:213
"Las ruinas circulares" (Borges) **4**:5, 10, 18-19, 28-9, 33, 35-6; **41**:49-50, 56, 58, 64, 87, 152, 161, 166
"The Rule of Names" (Le Guin) **12**:225, 231-32
"Rules and Practices for Overcoming Shyness" (Moorhouse) **40**:322
"Rummy" (Coppard) **21**:19
"The Rumor" (Caldwell) **19**:44
"Rumpelstiltskin" (Grimm and Grimm) **36**:204, 208
"Run of Luck" (Harris) **19**:182
"A Run through the Jungle" (Ford) **56**:285
"Run to Seed" (Page) **23**:297-98
"The Runaway" (Caldwell) **19**:38
"The Runaway" (Ross) **24**:293, 295, 305, 319-23
"Runaways" (Vonnegut) **8**:433
"The Runaways" (Wescott) **35**:363, 366-67, 370-72
The Runenberg (Tieck) **31**:276
"Runners to Nowhere" (Singer) **53**:272
"The Running Amok of Synge Sahib" (Galsworthy) **22**:90
"Running Dreams" (Beattie) **11**:10, 23

"Rupert Beersley and the Beggar Master of Sivani-Hotta" (Boyle) **16**:143, 145
"A Rural Community" (Suckow) **18**:395-97, 405, 408
"Rural Life in England" (Irving) **2**:244
"Rus in Urbe" (Henry) **5**:191
"Rusia" (Bunin) **5**:113
Russia Laughs (Zoshchenko) **15**:387-88
"A Russian Beauty" (Nabokov) **11**:116
A Russian Beauty, and Other Stories (Nabokov) **11**:116
"A Russian Doll" (Bioy Casares) **17**:94, 96
A Russian Doll, and Other Stories (Bioy Casares)
See *Una muñeca rusa*
"A Russian Hamlet" (Turgenev)
See "Gamlet ščigrovskogo uezda"
"A Russian Husband" (Moore) **19**:340
Russian Life in the Interior (Turgenev)
See *Zapiski okhotnika*
"Russian Tales" (Kelly) **50**:290-91
"The Russian Who Did Not Believe in Miracles and Why" (Nin) **10**:306
"Rusya" (Bunin)
See "Rusia"
"Ruth and Bertram" (Farrell) **28**:106
"Ruthy and Edie" (Paley) **8**:411
Ryazan Apples (Pilnyak) **48**:235-36
"Ryder by Gaslight" (Waugh) **41**:333-35, 337
Ryugaku (Endō) **48**:196, 204-8
"Rzavski bregovi" (Andrić) **36**:33-5
"S Angel" (Chabon) **59**:69, 71, 73-74, 76, 81
S Is for Space (Bradbury) **29**:75, 82, 90
"S. Karuma-shi no hanzai" (Abe) **61**:9, 11, 13, 22-23, 25
"The Sabbath Breaker" (Zangwill) **44**:375, 387
"Sabbath in Gehenna" (Singer) **3**:389; **53**:271, 273
"Sabbath in Portugal" (Singer) **3**:376
"The Sabbath Question in Sudminster" (Zangwill) **44**:378
"Les sabines" (Aymé) **41**:23
"The Sack of Lights" (Pritchett) **14**:269, 297
"The Sack Race" (Sansom) **21**:126
"Sacks" (Carver) **8**:14-15, 18, 20-1, 37-8; **51**:5, 18
Sacred Families; Three Novellas (Donoso)
See *Tres novelitas burguesas*
"The Sacred Marriage" (Oates) **6**:254
Sacred Water (Silko) **37**:314
"The Sacrifice" (Auchincloss) **22**:13-14, 50
"Sacrifice" (Tagore) **48**:335
"A Sacrifice Hit" (Henry) **5**:184
"A Sacrifice unto Sion" (Evans) **43**:36
The Sacrilege of Alan Kent (Caldwell) **19**:6, 8, 11-13, 23-4, 29-33, 40-1, 50
Sad as She Is (Onetti)
See *Tan triste como ella*
"A Sad Fall" (Wilson) **21**:323-24
"The Sad Fate of Mr. Fox" (Harris) **19**:195
"The Sad Horn Blowers" (Anderson) **1**:23, 27, 30
"A Sad Tale's Best for Winter" (Spark) **10**:359, 362
"Sadhana" (Tagore) **48**:335
Sadness (Barthelme) **2**:37-40, 46-7, 49; **55**:5, 7, 10, 12, 15, 27-30, 32-4, 41, 55, 63, 66-8, 82-8, 106, 11, 119
"Safe" (Gordon) **59**:230-31, 238, 264, 266-67
"Safe Houses" (Gordimer) **17**:178, 182, 184, 186-87
"Saffercisco" (O'Hara) **15**:253
"Saga y Agar" (Pardo Bazán) **30**:266
Sagittario (Ginzburg) **65**:118-19, 122-23, 145-47
La sagouin (Mauriac) **24**:173, 181, 206
"Said" (Dixon) **16**:216-17
"Saigo Takamori" (Akutagawa Ryūnosuke) **44**:62
"Sailing down the Chesapeake" (Saroyan) **21**:154

"The Sailor" (Pritchett) **14**:263, 269, 271, 281, 286, 299, 304-05
"The Sailor" (Wescott) **35**:357, 363-64, 366-67, 371-73
"The Sailor and the Steward" (Hughes) **6**:131
"Sailor Ashore" (Hughes) **6**:122, 132
"The Sailor Boy's Tale" (Dinesen) **7**:199
The Sailor, Sense of Humour, and Other Stories (Pritchett) **14**:256, 267, 271
"The Sailor's Son" (Williams) **31**:302, 324, 331, 351, 360-61
"The Saint" (Pritchett) **14**:256, 263-64, 267, 269, 271, 292, 298, 305
The Saint (Meyer)
　　See *Der Heilige*
"The Saint and the Goblin" (Saki) **12**:305
"Saint Cecilia" (Kleist)
　　See *Die heilige Cäcilie; oder, die Gewalt der Musik*
Saint Emmanuel the Good, Martyr (Unamuno)
　　See *San Manuel Bueno, mártir*
"St. John's Eve" (Gogol)
　　See "Večer nakanune Ivana Kupala"
"Saint Joseph in the Forest" (Grimm and Grimm) **36**:224
"Saint Julien" (Flaubert)
　　See *La légende de Saint-Julien l'Hospitalier*
"Saint Katy the Virgin" (Steinbeck) **11**:225-26, 232-33, 245-46
Saint Katy the Virgin (Steinbeck) **11**:207
St. Mawr (Lawrence) **4**:205, 211-12, 238-29, 241-42
"Saints" (Mukherjee) **38**:252-54, 271
"Saints" (Trevor) **21**:247; **58**:292-94
Saints and Strangers (Carter)
　　See *Black Venus*
"Lo Sakhmod" (Peretz) **26**:196
"The Salad of Colonel Cray" (Chesterton) **1**:131; **46**:110
"A Sale" (Maupassant) **1**:262
"Sales Pitch" (Dick) **57**:108-9
"The Saliva Tree" (Aldiss) **36**:20
The Saliva Tree and Other Strange Growths (Aldiss) **36**:18
"Sally" (Cisneros) **32**:32
Sally Bowles (Isherwood) **56**:200, 202, 204, 207, 209-10, 212, 222, 226-28, 230
Salmagundi (Irving) **2**:241, 250-53
"Salomé" (Laforgue) **20**:85-6, 89, 91-2, 100-2, 104-7, 111, 119
Salome (Keller) **26**:104
"Salome Müller, the White Slave" (Cable) **4**:49, 59
"Salon des refusés" (Thomas) **20**:310, 318
"Salon Episode" (Walser) **20**:354
"Salt" (Babel) **16**:27-8, 51, 53
"Salt and Sawdust" (Narayan) **25**:175
"The Salt Garden" (Atwood) **2**:21; **46**:38, 43, 49-50, 96
"Salta pro Nobis (A Variation)" (Galsworthy) **22**:101
"Les Saltimbanques" (Lewis) **34**:177
"The Saltmine" (Gorky) **28**:150
"La salud de los enfermos" (Cortázar) **7**:61
The Salutation (Warner) **23**:380
"La salvación de don Carmelo" (Pardo Bazán) **30**:262, 290
"Salvador, Late or Early" (Cisneros) **32**:8
"The Salvation of a Forsyte" (Galsworthy) **22**:59, 69, 74, 89, 91-4
"The Salvation of Me" (Pancake) **61**:247, 257, 259-61, 265, 276
"The Salvation of Swithin Forsyte" (Galsworthy) **22**:88-90, 97
"Salvatore" (Maugham) **8**:366
"The Same as Twenty Years Ago" (Saroyan) **21**:144
The Same Door (Updike) **13**:350-52, 354, 356, 366, 395, 404
Sämmtliche Werke (Tieck) **31**:282
"Samooborona" (Zangwill) **44**:378, 381, 390
"Sampatti-Samarpan" (Tagore) **48**:339

"Samson" (Aymé) **41**:13, 22
"Samson and Delilah" (Lawrence) **4**:202, 232-36
"Samuel" (London) **4**:254-55
"Samuel Naked" (Kelly) **50**:286-88, 296, 302
"San bega Karčića" (Andrić) **36**:52
San Manuel Bueno, mártir (Unamuno) **11**:320, 322, 327, 329-30, 339-44, 351-56, 58
"San n-Diothramh Dubh" (Moore) **19**:310, 319, 322, 330, 347-50, 352
"Sanatorium" (Maugham) **8**:369, 380
Sanatorium pod klepsydra (Schulz) **13**:330, 333-38, 343, 344
Sanatorium under the Sign of the Hourglass (Schulz)
　　See *Sanatorium pod klepsydra*
Sanatorium under the Water Clock (Schulz)
　　See *Sanatorium pod klepsydra*
"San-ch'ao Yüan-lao" (P'u Sung-ling) **31**:201
"Sanctuary" (Dreiser) **30**:110, 122, 153
"The Sand Castle" (Lavin) **4**:178-81
"The Sand Hill" (Agnon)
　　See "Gib'ath ha-hol"
"The Sandman" (Andersen)
　　See "Ole Luköie"
"The Sandman" (Barthelme) **2**:52; **55**:11-12, 27, 73, 78, 80, 83
"The Sandman" (Hoffmann)
　　See "Der Sandmann"
"Der Sandmann" (Hoffmann) **13**:179-181, 190, 200, 204-05, 214-15, 219-20, 223-25, 234-39, 242-47, 250-52
"Sandy the Christ" (Babel) **16**:25, 29-31, 50, 53, 55
"The Sanitary Fair" (Alcott) **27**:4
"Sanity" (Wolff) **63**:271, 275-76
Sans (Beckett) **16**:76-9, 83-6, 88, 94, 100, 123
"Santa Claus vs. S.P.I.D.E.R." (Ellison) **14**:104, 133
"Santa Claus's Partner" (Page) **23**:285
"Santa Lucia" (Galsworthy) **22**:101
"Santana Mysli" (Platonov) **42**:266
"Santelices" (Donoso) **34**:4-7, 14-15, 22-3, 25, 31, 35-6, 39-40, 42, 49, 50-1
"El sapo" (Arreola) **38**:7
"Sapore sapere" (Calvino) **48**:161, 174
"A Sappho of Green Springs" (Harte) **8**:247-48, 255
"Sarah" (Lavin) **4**:167, 184
"Sarah Bas Tovim" (Peretz) **26**:198, 215-16
"Sarah Cole: A Type of Love Story" (Banks) **42**:59
"Sarah Gwynn" (Moore) **19**:296, 303, 311
"Sarah Walker" (Harte) **59**:310
"Saratoga, Hot" (Calisher) **15**:9
Saratoga, Hot (Calisher) **15**:9, 23-5, 27
"Saratoga Rain" (Hughes) **6**:112
"The Sardonic Star of Tom Dooley" (Hammett) **17**:218
Sardonic Tales (Villiers de l'Isle Adam)
　　See *Contes cruels*
Sarrasine (Balzac) **5**:33-4
"The Sartorial Revolution (I)" (Bioy Casares) **17**:74, 86
"Sarugashima" (Dazai Osamu) **41**:240, 245
"Sasaki's Case" (Shiga) **23**:347
"Sashka the Christ" (Babel)
　　See "Sandy the Christ"
"Satan" (Tanizaki)
　　See "Akuma"
Satan in Goray (Singer)
　　See *Shoten an Goray*
"Satan Mekatrig" (Zangwill) **44**:366, 375-76, 387
"Satarsa" (Cortázar) **7**:91
"Satisfaction" (Phillips) **16**:328
"The Satisfaction of a Gentleman" (Kipling) **54**:96-97
"The Satisfactory" (Pritchett) **14**:281, 285, 297
"Saturday" (Gallant) **5**:141

"Saturday Afternoon" (Caldwell) **19**:16-17, 25, 38, 43
"Saturday Lunch" (O'Hara) **15**:288-89
"Saturday Night" (Calisher) **15**:5
"Saturday Night" (Farrell) **28**:118-9
"Saturday Night" (Ross) **24**:307, 311
"A Saturday Night in America" (Farrell) **28**:111
"Saturday Night on the Farm" (Garland) **18**:160, 177
"Saturn, November 11th" (Ellison) **14**:127
"Saturn Rising" (Clarke) **3**:132
"Saturnalia" (Wilson) **21**:319, 322, 326, 330, 332-33, 338-39, 342, 344, 349-50
"The Satyr Shall Cry" (Garrett) **30**:168
"Sauce for the Gander" (Perelman) **32**:204
"Sauerkraut Soup" (Dybek) **55**:126, 128, 136-37, 142
"Savages" (O'Brien) **10**:341
"Savannah River Payday" (Caldwell) **19**:38, 46
"Saved from the Dogs" (Hughes) **6**:121
"A Saving Grace" (Sansom) **21**:86, 91, 95, 124
"Saviour John" (Lagerkvist) **12**:179, 196
"Savitri" (Narayan) **25**:131
"Saw Gang" (Stegner) **27**:200-02, 204, 206, 220
"Say Goodbye to the Wind" (Ballard) **53**:7, 55, 72, 79, 128-29
"Say Yes" (Wolff) **63**:264, 305-6, 315, 320, 325-26, 329-30, 332-33
"Sbírka známek" (Čapek) **36**:98-9, 127
"Scandal" (Cather) **50**:95
"A Scandal and the Press" (Čapek) **36**:87
"The Scandal Detectives" (Fitzgerald) **6**:49
"A Scandal in Bohemia" (Doyle) **12**:49, 51-3, 57-8, 66, 68, 70, 72-3
"The Scandal of Father Brown" (Chesterton) **46**:115
The Scandal of Father Brown (Chesterton) **1**:128, 139; **46**:116, 131, 136, 141
"A Scandalous Woman" (O'Brien) **10**:332, 340-41, 344
A Scandalous Woman, and Other Stories (O'Brien) **10**:330, 332
"The Scapegoat" (Dunbar) **8**:122, 129, 132, 137, 141-43
"The Scapegoat" (Pritchett) **14**:286, 299
"Scape-Goats" (Barker) **53**:137-38, 159, 162
"The Scar" (Campbell) **19**:62, 71, 74, 82, 87-8
"The Scarecrow" (Farrell) **28**:87, 112, 118
Scared Stiff (Campbell) **19**:69-70, 74, 76, 84-5, 87-8
"Scarlet Ibis" (Atwood) **2**:18, 22; **46**:45-6, 50
"The Scarlet Letter" (Stafford) **26**:310
"The Scarlet Moving Van" (Cheever) **38**:47-8, 53
Scarmentado (Voltaire) **12**:340, 342, 357
"Scars" (Price) **22**:376
"An Scáthán" (O'Flaherty) **6**:289
"Scatter-Brains" (Moravia) **26**:142
"Scenario" (Perelman) **32**:204, 209, 222
"A Scenario for Karl Marx" (Saroyan) **21**:143
"Scene" (Howells) **36**:399
"Scene for Winter" (Coover) **15**:36, 58
"Scenes and Characters No. 10 Christmas Festivities" (Dickens) **49**:164
Scènes de la vie de campagne (Balzac) **5**:9
Scènes de la vie de province (Balzac) **5**:3, 5, 7-9, 13
Scènes de la vie militaire (Balzac) **5**:7-9
Scènes de la vie orientale (Nerval)
　　See *Voyage en Orient*
Scènes de la vie Parisienne (Balzac) **5**:3, 5, 7-9
Scènes de la vie politique (Balzac) **5**:7-9, 13
Scènes de la vie privée (Balzac) **5**:3-4, 7, 9, 21-2, 25, 28-31
Scenes from Russian Life (Turgenev)
　　See *Zapiski okhotnika*
"Scenes from the Life of a Double Monster" (Nabokov) **11**:110, 113, 128
Scenes of Country Life (Balzac)
　　See *Scènes de la vie de campagne*

Scenes of Parisian Life (Balzac)
See *Scènes de la vie Parisienne*
Scenes of Political Life (Balzac)
See *Scènes de la vie politique*
Scenes of Private Life (Balzac)
See *Scènes de la vie privée*
Scenes of Provincial Life (Balzac)
See *Scènes de la vie de province*
Scenic Drive (Wilding) **50**:351
"A Scent of Sarsaparilla" (Bradbury) **29**:63
"The Schartz-Metterklume Method" (Saki) **12**:296, 311, 324, 329-30
"Scherzi di Ferragosto" (Moravia) **26**:150
"Scherzo e gelosia" (Moravia) **26**:149
"Das schicksal des Freiherr von Leisenbohg" (Schnitzler) **15**:346
Der Schimmelreiter (Storm) **27**:274, 284-91, 293, 296, 304-07
Schlachtbeschreibung (Kluge) **61**:52-53, 55-57, 80, 83
Der Schlimm-heilige Vitalis (Keller) **26**:99-100, 108
Der Schmied seines Glückes (Keller) **26**:107, 121
"Schneeweisschen und Rosenrot" (Grimm and Grimm) **36**:208, 212
"Scholar with a Hole in his Memory" (Cortázar) **7**:59
"The Scholarship" (Mansfield) **9**:282
"The School" (Barthelme) **2**:53; **55**:106, 108, 119, 121
"School" (O'Hara) **15**:262
"The School by Night" (Cortázar)
See "La escuela de noche"
"The School for Witches" (Thomas) **3**:399, 408-09; **44**:329, 345-46, 354, 357-58
The School for Wives (Gide)
See *L'école des femmes*
"A School Story" (James) **16**:233, 245-46, 256
"A School Story" (Trevor) **21**:230, 262
"Schoolgirl" (Dazai Osamu) **41**:244-45
"The Schoolmaster's Vision" (Gissing) **37**:65
"The Schoolmistress" (Chekhov) **2**:128
"The Schoolteacher's Guest" (Allende) **65**:28, 30
"Schooner Fairchild's Class" (Benét) **10**:144, 152, 154
Schriften (Tieck)
See *Ludwig Tieck's Schriften*
"Schrödinger's Cat" (Le Guin) **12**:227-30, 236, 241
"Der Schuß von der Kanzel" (Meyer) **30**:187-88, 195-96, 199-200, 207-11, 213
Der Schutzgeist (Tieck) **31**:272
"Schwallinger's Philanthropy" (Dunbar) **8**:122, 132, 137, 147
"Die schwarzen schafe" (Boell) **23**:6, 11
"Schwierige Trauer" (Lenz) **33**:317-18, 320, 330
"Scialle nero" (Pirandello) **22**:233
"The Science Club Meets" (Moorhouse) **40**:298
"Lo sciocco senza paura" (Calvino) **48**:96
"Scissors" (Pardo Bazán) **30**:290
"The Scorched Face" (Hammett) **17**:203, 219, 222-23, 225
"The Scorn of Women" (London) **4**:286
"The Scorpion" (Bowles) **3**:59, 61, 68, 70-2, 79
Scott-King (Waugh)
See *Scott-King's Modern Europe*
Scott-King's Modern Europe (Waugh) **41**:309, 311, 314-16
"The Scoutmaster" (Taylor) **10**:374-76
"Scram You Made the Pants Too Short" (Perelman) **32**:238
"A Scrap and a Sketch" (Chopin) **8**:98
Scrap-Bag (Alcott)
See *Aunt Jo's Scrap-Bag*
The Scrapbook of Katherine Mansfield (Mansfield) **9**:281, 309
"The Scrapper" (Pancake) **61**:260, 264-65, 276
"The Scream" (Oates) **6**:248-49
"The Scream of the Dead" (Lovecraft) **52**:311

"The Scream on Fifty-Seventh Street" (Calisher) **15**:3
"The Screaming Potato" (White) **39**:347-49
"The Screen Game" (Ballard) **53**:7, 71-3, 76, 79, 127, 129
"The Scrupulous Father" (Gissing) **37**:53
"The Sculptor's Funeral" (Cather) **2**:90, 94-5, 98, 100, 103, 105; **50**:54, 57-9, 72, 79, 81-2, 106-08, 116-19, 122, 135, 137-39, 197, 239, 241, 254, 264
"The Sculptor's Garden" (Cather) **50**:239
"Scum Grief" (Bukowski) **45**:52
"Scylla and Charybdis" (Lavin) **4**:183
"The Scythe" (Andrić)
See "Kosa"
"The Sea" (Dazai Osamu) **41**:244
"The Sea" (Pavese)
See "Il mare"
"The Sea Birds Are Still Alive" (Bambara) **35**:17, 40-1
The Sea Birds Are Still Alive: Collected Stories (Bambara) **35**:15-18, 20, 25, 28-30, 38, 40-2
"The Sea Change" (Hemingway) **40**:166; **63**:117, 122
"The Sea Changes" (Cabrera Infante)
See "Mar, mar, enemigo"
"Sea Constables" (Kipling) **5**:270
"Sea Foam" (Pavese) **19**:368
The Sea in Being (Hemingway)
See *The Old Man and the Sea*
"The Sea of Hesitation" (Barthelme) **2**:51; **55**:94, 109, 115
"The Sea of Lost Time" (García Márquez)
See "El mar del tiempo perdido"
"The Sea Raiders" (Wells) **6**:361, 365, 367, 389, 393, 406
"Sea Travel" (Kipling) **54**:121
"The Seacoast of Bohemia" (Garrett) **30**:163-65, 172
"The Sea-Farmer" (London) **4**:254
"The Seagull" (Auchincloss) **22**:51
The Seagull (Chekhov)
See *Chayka*
"Seagulls" (Dazai Osamu) **41**:238
"The Seal" (O'Flaherty) **6**:282
"The Sealed Angel" (Leskov)
See "Zapečatlennyj angel"
"The Sealed Room" (Doyle) **12**:65
"The Séance" (Singer) **3**:369
The Séance, and Other Stories (Singer) **3**:362, 369-70, 373; **53**:325
"The Search for J. Kruper" (Berriault) **30**:99, 103
Searches and Seizures (Elkin) **12**:92-3, 95, 106-07, 110, 114
Searching for Survivors (Banks) **42**:55-57, 63, 65, 70
"Searching for Survivors II" (Banks) **42**:56-7, 70
"Searching for Survivors—I" (Banks) **42**:56-7, 68
"Searchlight" (Heinlein) **55**:167
"The Searchlight" (Woolf) **7**:377, 390, 392, 396
"The Sea's Green Sameness" (Updike) **13**:359-61, 376
"A Seashore Drama" (Balzac)
See "Un drame au bord de la mer"
"The Seaside Houses" (Cheever) **1**:100, 105; **38**:51, 60; **57**:7
"A Season of Calm Weather" (Hood) **42**:237
"Season of Disbelief" (Bradbury) **29**:86
"The Season of Divorce" (Cheever) **1**:99; **38**:53-4
"Season of Mists" (Collier) **19**:104
"Season of the Hand" (Cortázar)
See "Estación de la mano"
Seasons in Flight (Aldiss) **36**:18, 20-22
"Seaton's Aunt" (de la Mare) **14**:65-6, 68, 71, 80-1, 84-5, 87, 89-91
"Sebunchin" (Oe)
See "Sevuntiin"

"The Secession" (Bowen) **3**:40
"Der sechste Geburtstag" (Lenz) **33**:320-26, 333, 335-36
"The Second" (Schnitzler)
See "Der sekundant"
"Second Best" (Lawrence) **4**:197
Second Book of Laughable Loves (Kundera) **24**:103
"Second Chance" (Auchincloss) **22**:14, 42, 49
"Second Chance" (Campbell) **19**:75
Second Chance: Tales of Two Generations (Auchincloss) **22**:12-14, 17, 21, 28, 34, 42, 50
"The Second Choice" (Dreiser) **30**:107, 122, 134, 143-44, 153
"Second Coming" (Pohl) **25**:236
"Second Dawn" (Clarke) **3**:131, 135, 144, 150
"The Second Death" (Greene) **29**:184
"The Second Generation" (Crane) **56**:110
"Second Hand" (Lavin) **4**:167, 183
"The Second Hut" (Lessing) **6**:186, 189, 191; **61**:100
The Second Jungle Book (Kipling) **5**:287, 295; **54**:81-4, 102, 110, 113
"The Second Leg" (Abish) **44**:2-3, 11, 28
"A Second Life" (Machado de Assis) **24**:152
"Second Opinion" (Narayan) **25**:159, 174
"Second Sight" (Campbell) **19**:77
"The Second Swimming" (Boyle) **16**:143
"Second Time Around" (Cortázar)
See "Segunda vez"
"Second Trip" (Cortázar)
See "Segundo viaje"
"Second Variety" (Dick) **57**:40, 52-53, 103, 143-44, 151
"Second-Class Matter" (Perelman) **32**:204, 229
La seconde (Colette) **10**:254, 261-62, 267-69, 272
"The Second-Story Angel" (Hammett) **17**:218
"The Secret" (Frame) **29**:99, 107
"The Secret" (Singer) **3**:385-86
"Secret" (Tanizaki)
See "Himitsu"
"The Secret Cause" (Machado de Assis)
See "A causa secreta"
"The Secret Cave" (Lovecraft) **52**:290
"The Secret Chamber" (Oliphant) **25**:193-96, 204-05
"Le secret de la belle Ardiane" (Villiers de l'Isle Adam) **14**:386
"Le secret de l'ancienne musique" (Villiers de l'Isle Adam) **14**:395
"Le secret de l'échafaud" (Villiers de l'Isle Adam) **14**:389, 397
"The Secret Garden" (Chesterton) **1**:119, 134, 137; **46**:108, 131, 143, 146-47, 153
"The Secret Heart" (Machado de Assis) **24**:139, 153
The Secret History of the Lord of Musashi (Tanizaki)
See *Bushūkō hiwa*
"The Secret History of World War III" (Ballard) **53**:35, 56, 67, 110
"The Secret Integration" (Pynchon) **14**:308, 315, 320, 322, 332, 335, 340-42, 344-48
"The Secret Life of Houses" (Bradfield) **65**:61
The Secret Life of Houses (Bradfield) **65**:58-61, 65
The Secret Life of the Lord of Musashi (Tanizaki)
See *Bushūkō hiwa*
"The Secret Life of Walter Mitty" (Thurber) **1**:420, 422, 424, 427, 431-32, 435; **47**:365, 373-75, 385-86, 388-90
"The Secret Miracle" (Borges)
See "El milagro secreto"
"The Secret Mirror" (Oates) **6**:237
"The Secret of Father Brown" (Chesterton) **1**:128, 131; **46**:110
The Secret of Father Brown (Chesterton) **46**:114, 116, 131, 135, 141

"The Secret of Flambeau" (Chesterton) **1**:126; **46**:135, 139
"A Secret of Telegraph Hill" (Harte) **8**:233
"The Secret of the Growing Gold" (Stoker) **62**:234, 243, 253-54
"The Secret of the Old Music" (Villiers de l'Isle Adam)
　See "Le secret de l'ancienne musique"
"The Secret of the Pyramids" (Mason) **4**:23
"The Secret Sharer" (Conrad) **9**:141-45, 147-51, 156-61, 166, 171-74, 191, 205
"The Secret Sin of Septimus Brope" (Saki) **12**:335
Secret Stories of the Lord of Musashi (Tanizaki)
　See *Bushūkō hiwa*
The Secret Tales of the Lord of Musashi (Tanizaki)
　See *Bushūkō hiwa*
"Secret Weapons" (Cortázar)
　See "Las armas secretas"
Secret Window, Secret Garden (King) **17**:281-83
"A secreto agravio" (Pardo Bazán) **30**:264-65
Secrets and Surprises (Beattie) **11**:4-6, 8, 12-13, 15-16, 22, 27, 29, 32
"Les secrets de la Princesse de Cadignan" (Balzac) **5**:31
"Secrets of Alexandria" (Saroyan) **21**:134, 140
"Secrets of Lord Bushu" (Tanizaki)
　See *Bushūkō hiwa*
"The Sect of the Idiot" (Ligotti) **16**:264-65, 267, 276, 282-83, 286-87
"The Sect of the Phoenix" (Borges)
　See "La secta del Fénix"
"La secta del Fénix" (Borges) **41**:85, 124, 133
"Security" (Davie) **52**:8
"The Security Guard" (Dixon) **16**:204
"Sedile sotto il vecchio cipresso" (Pirandello) **22**:270
"The Seductress" (Campbell) **19**:76
"Seduta spiritica" (Moravia) **26**:180-82
"See the Moon?" (Barthelme) **2**:35, 42-3, 53; **55**:35, 120
"The Seed of Faith" (Wharton) **6**:422
"Seeds" (Anderson) **1**:20, 27, 46
"Seeing the World" (Campbell) **19**:70-1, 88
"Der seelische Ratgeber" (Lenz) **33**:317-18
"Seen from Afar" (Levi) **12**:279
Sefer ha-Maasim (Agnon) **30**:3, 21-2, 36-40, 58, 69
"Un segno nello spazio" (Calvino) **3**:92, 104, 109; **48**:59-61, 66, 69-71, 75-6, 127, 129-30, 137, 156, 160
"Segunda vez" (Cortázar) **7**:83-5, 90-1
"Segundo viaje" (Cortázar) **7**:89
"Seibei's Gourds" (Shiga) **23**:332, 340, 342, 346
"Seiji shonen shisu" (Oe) **20**:215, 231-32, 234
Seis problemas para Don Isidro Parodi (Bioy Casares) **4**:25; **17**:48, 60, 67-8, 71-2, 74
"Los seis velos" (Alarcon) **64**:3, 8, 23, 28-30, 39
Seize the Day (Bellow) **14**:3-7, 11, 13-18, 21-3, 26, 32, 34, 46, 49-56, 59
"Der sekundant" (Schnitzler) **15**:377; **61**:306, 308
"A Select Party" (Hawthorne) **3**:181
Selected Prose (Bulgakov) **18**:86
The Selected Short Stories of John O'Hara (O'Hara) **15**:252
Selected Stories (Coppard) **21**:23
Selected Stories (Debus) **15**:94-5, 100-01
Selected Stories (Gordimer) **17**:158, 160, 162, 165, 169, 172, 181, 184, 189, 191
Selected Stories (Lavin) **4**:163, 186
Selected Stories (Metcalf) **43**:131
Selected Stories (Peretz) **26**:209
Selected Stories (Pritchett) **14**:260, 272
Selected Stories (Walser) **20**:349, 356, 360, 364
Selected Stories and Poems (Harte) **59**:291
Selected Stories of Philip K. Dick (Dick) **57**:151

The Selected Stories of Siegfried Lenz (Lenz) **33**:337-38
Selected Works of Djuna Barnes (Barnes) **3**:5, 7, 13, 20, 22
The Selected Works of Henry Lawson (Lawson) **18**:201
Selected Works of Stephen Vincent Benét (Benét) **10**:143, 156
Selected Writings (Capote) **47**:30-8
Selected Writings of Truman Capote (Capote) **2**:72, 74
"Selection" (Le Guin) **12**:237
"Selections of Lovecraft" (Ligotti) **16**:287
"Selections of Poe" (Ligotti) **16**:287
"The Selector's Daughter" (Lawson) **18**:250
"Self Defense" (Zangwill)
　See "Samooborona"
"The Selfish Giant" (Wilde) **11**:365, 372, 375-76, 379, 386, 388, 390-93, 396, 401-02, 408
"The Selfishness of Amelia Lamkin" (Freeman) **47**:139-144
"A Self-Made Man" (Crane) **7**:108-09
"Self-Portrait" (Dixon) **16**:207, 215
"Self-Portrait" (Evans) **43**:16
"Self-Sacrifice" (Peretz)
　See "Mesiras Nefesh"
"Selina's Parable" (de la Mare) **14**:83
"Selling Out" (Apple) **50**:9, 29
"Selma" (Caldwell) **19**:56
"Das seltsame Mädchen" (Walser) **20**:333
"The Selvin Case" (Čapek)
　See "Případ Selvinuv"
Semeinoe schaste (Tolstoy) **9**:376, 389, 391-92, 403
"Semejante a la noche" (Carpentier) **35**:91
"Seminar" (Cowan) **28**:80
"Semley's Necklace" (Le Guin) **12**:219, 224-28, 231-32
"Semper Idem" (London) **4**:263
"Sem'ya Ivanova" (Platonov) **42**:256
"El sencillo don Rafael, cazador y tresillista" (Unamuno) **11**:312-13
"Send Round the Hat" (Lawson) **18**:206, 218, 245, 257
"Uma senhora" (Machado de Assis) **24**:128
"A senhora do Galvão" (Machado de Assis) **24**:128
"Senility" (Lavin) **4**:182
"The Senior Partner's Ghosts" (Auchincloss) **22**:9, 37
"Senior Prom" (Farrell) **28**:111
"The Sennin" (Akutagawa Ryūnosuke) **44**:71
"Un Señor muy viejo con unas alas enormes" (García Márquez) **8**:1609, 167-70, 182, 186
"Señor Ong and Señor Ha" (Bowles) **3**:59, 61, 69, 79
"Una señora" (Donoso) **34**:3, 21, 25-28, 30, 49
"La Señora Cornelia" (Cervantes) **12**:4-5, 8, 34, 36-7
"Sense of Humour" (Pritchett) **14**:259, 269, 271, 276, 281, 301-02, 305
"A Sense of Proportion" (Frame) **29**:103, 115, 117
A Sense of Reality (Greene) **29**:187-90, 195, 211, 213, 215
"A Sense of Responsibility" (O'Connor) **5**:372
"A Sense of Shelter" (Updike) **13**:388, 392-94
"The Sensible Thing" (Fitzgerald) **6**:46
"The Sentence" (Barthelme) **2**:38, 41, 44; **55**:39, 74, 109, 117
"Sentences" (Lish) **18**:286
"Sentiment" (Parker) **2**:273-74, 280, 285
A Sentimental Education (Oates) **6**:246-47
"Sentimental Journey" (Oates) **6**:251-52
"A Sentimental Soul" (Chopin) **8**:72, 95, 108, 110, 112
Sentimental Tales (Zoshchenko) **15**:395, 403
"Sentimentalisme" (Villiers de l'Isle Adam) **14**:378, 381, 384, 396
"Sentimentality" (Villiers de l'Isle Adam)
　See "Sentimentalisme"

"The Sentimentality of William Tavener" (Cather) **2**:101; **50**:89, 99-100, 104, 187
"The Sentinel" (Clarke) **3**:124, 127, 135, 145-46, 149-50
"The Sentinels" (Campbell) **19**:92
"The Sentry" (Leskov)
　See "Chelovék na chasákh"
"The Sentry" (O'Connor) **5**:369, 372
"Senza colori" (Calvino) **3**:92, 104, 108-9; **48**:47, 61, 65-6, 71, 103-4, 133, 155
"Separate Flights" (Dubus) **15**:71, 77, 80, 82, 87, 90
Separate Flights (Dubus) **15**:69-70, 72, 75-7, 81, 91
"Separating" (Updike) **13**:374, 387
"Separation" (Gordon) **59**:261, 265
"Sepi Jingan" (Hemingway) **63**:104
"The Sepia Postcard" (Millhauser) **57**:183
"September Dawn" (O'Connor) **5**:385, 391-92
"September Snow" (Ross) **24**:290, 295, 302-03, 320
Septuagenarian Stew (Bukowski) **45**:56, 62-4
"Ser kurster fraytik" (Singer) **53**:290-92, 323, 338
"The Seraph and the Zambesi" (Spark) **10**:354, 356, 358-359, 361, 366, 370
Séraphita (Balzac) **59**:41-47
"The Serapion Brothers" (Hoffmann)
　See *Die Serapions Brüder*
Die Serapions Brüder (Hoffmann) **13**:191-92, 195, 202, 217, 228
"La Serata della Diva" (Verga) **21**:294
"Serenade" (Benét) **10**:150
"A se600íssima República" (Machado de Assis) **24**:128-30
"The Sergeant" (Barthelme) **2**:53
"Sergeant Carmichael" (Bates) **10**:114
"Sergeant Major Hans Peickert" (Kluge) **61**:74, 76
"Sergeant Prishibeev" (Chekhov) **2**:155
"Serious Need" (Price) **22**:387
"A Serious Person" (Gordon) **59**:261
"A Serious Question" (Pritchett) **14**:297
"A Serious Talk" (Carver) **8**:14, 18-19, 53; **51**:2, 15
Sermons and Soda Water (O'Hara) **15**:251, 271
"Serowe Weddings" (Head) **52**:227
"The Serpent of Fire" (Bunin) **5**:87
"Serpents and Doves" (Betts) **45**:2, 27
"La Serre" (Maupassant) **64**:286, 290-91
"The Servant" (Levi) **12**:278-79
"Servants of the Queen" (Kipling) **54**:83
"A Service of Love" (Henry) **5**:171, 185; **49**:197
"A Session with the Analyst of Colors" (Kelly) **50**:290
A Set of Six (Conrad) **9**:147, 151, 157, 179
A Set of Variations (O'Connor) **5**:373-74, 378
"A Set of Variations on a Borrowed Theme" (O'Connor) **5**:373
"Šetnja" (Andrić) **36**:47
"Setteragic On" (Warner) **23**:369
"The Setting of Venus" (Verga)
　See "Il Tramonto de Venere"
"The Settlers" (Bradbury) **53**:201, 205-7, 250, 252, 257
"The Settling In" (Bradbury) **53**:248
"Settling on the Land" (Lawson) **18**:201, 215
Sevastopol (Tolstoy)
　See *Tales of Sevastopol*
"Sevastopol in August, 1855" (Tolstoy) **9**:375; **30**:311, 317-19, 323-24
"Sevastopol in December 1854" (Tolstoy) **9**:375
"Sevastopol in May, 1855" (Tolstoy) **9**:374-75, 389; **30**:332
"The Seven Bridges" (Mishima) **4**:313, 315, 317, 322
Seven by Five: Stories 1926-61 (Bates) **10**:125
"The Seven Deadly Sins of Today" (Waugh) **41**:339
"The Seven Deadly Virtues" (Pohl) **25**:232
Seven Gothic Tales (Dinesen) **7**:161, 166, 170, 172, 175, 180, 191, 196-98, 200-03, 208-09

Seven Japanese Tales (Tanizaki) **21**:180
"The Seven League Boots" (Aymé) **41**:4
Seven Legends (Keller)
    See *Sieben Legenden*
"The Seven Ravens" (Grimm and Grimm) **36**:225-26, 233
Seven Tales and Alexander (Bates) **10**:111
"Seven Types of Ambiguity" (Jackson) **39**:210, 211, 212, 225, 227
"Seven Years of Plenty" (Peretz)
    See "Zibn Gite Yor"
"The Seven-Ounce Man" (Harrison) **19**:215-18
"Seventeen" (Farrell) **28**:92
"Seventeen" (Oe)
    See "Sevuntiin"
"Seventeen" (Saroyan) **21**:161
"Seventeen Syllables" (Yamamoto) **34**:348, 350, 352, 355, 357-61, 365-67, 369, 371-79, 387, 389-90
Seventeen Syllables and Other Stories (Yamamoto) **34**:356, 364, 374, 381
Seventeen Syllables: Five Stories of Janpanese American Life (Yamamoto) **34**:352
"The Seventh House" (Narayan) **25**:139-40, 153, 156, 160
"The Seventh Pullet" (Saki) **12**:301
"Seventh Street" (Toomer) **1**:443, 450, 458; **45**:223-25, 228, 231-32, 236, 238, 240, 253-54, 260, 264-65, 268, 276, 286, 288, 319-20, 356, 362, 380
"Seventy Thousand Assyrians" (Saroyan) **21**:132, 146, 156-57, 165, 174
76 Short Stories (Saki) **12**:314
"Sevuntiin" (Oe) **20**:215-16, 231, 234-38, 240-42
"Sex, Death, and Starshine" (Barker) **53**:137-39, 141, 154, 157, 162
"Sex Ex Machina" (Thurber) **1**:431
"The Sexes" (Parker) **2**:273, 281, 283
"Seymour: An Introduction" (Salinger) **2**:296, 307-09; **65**:299-300, 303, 315, 317-18, 330-32, 338
Seymour: An Introduction (Salinger)
    See *Raise High the Roofbeam, Carpenters and Seymour: An Introduction*
"La sfida al labirinto" (Calvino) **48**:130, 160
"Shabbes nakhamu" (Babel) **16**:34
"Shabby-Genteel People" (Dickens) **17**:111, 116, 133
"Shabos nahamu" (Babel)
    See "Shabbes nakhamu"
The Shackle (Colette)
    See *L'entrave*
"The Shades of Spring" (Lawrence) **4**:197-98, 219
"The Shadow" (Andersen)
    See "Skyggen"
"The Shadow" (Dreiser) **30**:114, 146
"A Shadow" (Narayan) **25**:135
"Shadow, a Parable" (Poe) **1**:379
"The Shadow at the Bottom of the World" (Ligotti) **16**:280, 289
"The Shadow Builder" (Stoker) **62**:251
"The Shadow Line" (Conrad) **9**:151
"The Shadow of a Crib" (Singer) **3**:361
"The Shadow of the Glen" (Le Fanu) **14**:219-20
"The Shadow of the Shark" (Chesterton) **1**:124
"The Shadow on the Chimney" (Lovecraft) **52**:313
"The Shadow out of Time" (Lovecraft) **3**:258-61, 263, 266, 268, 271-72, 274-75, 279, 290; **52**:252-53, 255, 276-77, 280, 287, 305, 320-21, 333, 338-39
"The Shadow over Innsmouth" (Lovecraft) **3**:259, 263, 271-77, 291; **52**:261, 273, 281, 290, 296, 299, 308, 316, 322, 335, 338, 350
"The Shadow-Children" (Alcott) **27**:41
"Shadows" (Endō) **48**:208, 210-12
"The Shadows on the Wall" (Freeman) **47**:85-6, 110
"The Shadowy Crown" (Benét) **10**:147
"The Shadowy Land" (Grau) **15**:155

"The Shadowy Third" (Bowen) **3**:54
"The Shadowy Third" (Glasgow) **34**:56, 58-9, 62, 70, 73, 79, 82, 87-90, 93-97, 100
The Shadowy Third, and Other Stories (Glasgow) **34**:56-64, 70- 78, 82, 85, 88, 92, 97, 103-04
"Shadrach" (Styron) **25**:312-13, 315, 317
"Shake Hands with Birdey Doggett" (Thurber) **47**:383
"The Shaker Bridal" (Hawthorne) **3**:185-86
Shakespeare's Memory (Borges) **41**:157, 160
"Shakuntala" (Narayan) **25**:131
"Shame" (Crane) **7**:104
"A Shameful Affair" (Chopin) **8**:71, 86
"Shampadak" (Tagore) **48**:314
"Shang shi" (Lu Hsun) **20**:140
"Shao nü" (P'u Sung-ling) **31**:207
"The Shape of the Sword" (Borges)
    See "La forma de la espada"
"The Shape of Things" (Capote) **2**:65; **47**:10, 44, 50
"Sharing Joys and Sorrows" (Grimm and Grimm) **36**:229-30
"The Sharks" (O'Hara) **15**:280
"Sharon" (Spencer) **57**:212, 215-16, 218, 241, 243
"Sharper Than a Ferret's Tooth" (Somerville & Ross) **56**:318
"Shasti" (Tagore) **48**:304-6, 308, 321, 325, 327
"Shatterday" (Ellison) **14**:124
Shatterday (Ellison) **14**:125-26
"Shattered Like a Glass Goblin" (Ellison) **14**:115
"The Shattered Star" (Porter) **43**:271-72
"The Shawl" (Ozick) **15**:327; **60**:307-11, 313-14, 316-17, 320-27, 333, 335-37, 339-40, 345-49, 354-57, 360
The Shawl: A Story and a Novella (Ozick) **15**:327-28; **60**:307-61
The Shawshank Redemption (King)
    See *Rita Hayworth and Shawshank Redemption*
She (Peretz) **26**:205
"She and the Other Fellow" (Norris) **28**:205
"She Chiang-chün" (P'u Sung-ling) **31**:201
"The She Devil" (Lawson) **18**:255
"She Kept Her Distance" (Stuart) **31**:251
"She Married Her Double, He Married Himself" (Perelman) **32**:202
"She pi" (P'u Sung-ling) **31**:215
"She Walks in Beauty—Single File, Eyes Front and No Hanky-Panky" (Perelman) **32**:229
"She Was Good for Nothing" (Andersen)
    See "Hun duede ikke"
"She Was No Good" (Andersen)
    See "Hun duede ikke"
"She Was Rosa" (Platonov) **42**:254
"She Yawned" (Chekhov) **51**:84
"The Shearing of the Cook's Dog" (Lawson) **18**:201, 244
"The Shed" (Jolley) **19**:243-44
The She-Dragoon (Jarry)
    See *La dragonne*
"Sheep" (Oe) **20**:210-11, 213
"The Sheep" (Saki) **12**:316
"Shell Game" (Dick) **57**:92-96
"The Shelter" (Narayan) **25**:140, 156
"Shemesh shel horef" (Appelfeld) **42**:14
"The Shepard on the Roof" (Jolley) **19**:222, 245
"Shepherd, Lead Us" (Fisher)
    See "The South Lingers On"
"The Shepherd Who Watched by Night" (Page) **23**:308
"The Shepherdess and the Chimney Sweep" (Andersen) **6**:6, 18, 36
"The Shepherdess and the Sheep" (Andersen)
    See "Hyrdinden og Skorsteensfeieren"
"The Shepherd's Pipe" (Chekhov) **2**:130, 156
"The Sheridans" (Mansfield) **9**:286-87; **38**:205
"The Sheriff of Kona" (London) **4**:269

"The Sheriff's Children" (Chesnutt) **7**:13, 16, 18-19, 21-6, 29, 32-5, 37; **54**:3-4, 6-7, 11, 27, 48-9, 54, 58, 60
"The Sherrington Theory" (Ballard) **53**:11
The Sherwood Anderson Reader (Anderson) **46**:5
"The She-Wolf" (Saki) **12**:307, 323
"The She-Wolf" (Verga) **21**:298, 305-07
"Shifting" (Beattie) **11**:4, 7-8, 15, 17
"Shih Ch'ing-hsü" (P'u Sung-ling) **31**:191, 197
"Shih-chung" (Lu Hsun)
    See "Shizhong"
"Shih-yen" (P'u Sung-ling) **31**:190
Shiiku (Oe) **20**:214-16
"The Shilling" (O'Flaherty) **6**:271
"Shiloh" (Mason) **4**:299-03, 307, 309
Shiloh, and Other Stories (Mason) **4**:299-03, 306-07, 309
"Shin Bones" (London) **4**:256, 270
"Shindō" (Tanizaki) **21**:205
"Shinel" (Gogol) **4**:82-3, 87-91, 93, 106-08, 110-11, 113-17, 127, 129-30; **29**:119-79; **52**:82, 103-10, 112-15, 126, 133, 151, 156
"Shingles for the Lord" (Faulkner) **1**:178
Shining Deeps (Čapek)
    See *Zářivé hlubiny*
"The Shining Houses" (Munro) **3**:321, 336, 343
"The Shining Ones" (Clarke) **3**:132
"The Shining Pyramid" (Machen) **20**:158, 169, 182-83, 197-98
The Shining Pyramid: Tales and Essays (Machen) **20**:166, 194
"The Shining Slave Makers" (Dreiser)
    See "McEwen of the Shining Slave Makers"
"Shinkirō" (Akutagawa Ryūnosuke) **44**:52-54, 83
Ship Island, and Other Stories (Spencer) **57**:197-98
"Ship Island: The Story of a Mermaid" (Spencer) **57**:197, 207, 211, 240, 243
"The Ship of '49" (Harte) **59**:310
"The Ship That Found Herself" (Kipling) **5**:279
"Ship that Saw a Ghost" (Norris) **28**:198
"A Ship-Load of Crabs" (Calvino) **3**:116
"The Shipwreck" (Dickens) **17**:123
"The Shipwrecked Buttons" (Jewett) **6**:157
"Shir-hashirim: a yugnt-roman in fir teyl" (Aleichem) **33**:41-2
"The Shirt" (Dixon) **16**:211
"The Shirt Collar" (Andersen) **6**:30, 32, 35
"The Shirts" (Čapek) **36**:92-3, 124-25
"Shisei" (Tanizaki) **21**:181-82, 190-92, 195-96, 200, 206-08
"Shisha no ogori" (Oe) **20**:214
"Shisha no Sho" (Kawabata) **17**:247
"Shiso" (Akutagawa Ryūnosuke) **44**:90
"Shit" (Lish) **18**:275, 282
"Shizhong" (Lu Hsun) **20**:137, 147
"Shock Tactics" (Saki) **12**:303-04, 323, 325
"A Shocking Accident" (Greene) **29**:201
"The Shocks of Doom" (Henry) **5**:182, 184
"Shoes: An International Episode" (Bowen) **3**:30, 49
"Shōgun" (Akutagawa Ryūnosuke) **44**:50, 78
"Shōkonsai Ikkei" (Kawabata) **17**:248-49
"Shōnen" (Tanizaki) **21**:206-08
"The Shooting" (Caldwell) **19**:39
"The Shooting" (Dubus) **15**:73, 88
"The Shooting of Judge Price" (Caldwell) **19**:42
"The Shooting of Shinroe" (Somerville & Ross) **56**:331
"The Shooting of the Cabinet Ministers" (Hemingway) **1**:208, 238
"The Shooting Party" (Woolf) **7**:375, 390, 392
"The Shopboy's God" (Shiga)
    See "Kozo no kamisama"
"Shoppe Keeper" (Ellison) **14**:126
"Shops and Their Tenants" (Dickens) **17**:117
"The Shore" (Bradbury) **53**:207-9, 252-53
"The Shore and the Sea" (Thurber) **1**:430

"The Shore House" (Jewett) **6**:150, 157, 167, 170

"A Short Acquaintance" (Clarke) **45**:78-9, 81, 92, 103-04

"Short Easterly Squall, With Low Visibility and Rising Gorge" (Perelman) **32**:222

"Short Feature" (Cortázar)
　See "Cortísimo metraje"

Short Fiction of Sarah Orne Jewett and Mary Wilkins Freeman (Freeman) **47**:108-09

"Short Friday" (Singer) **3**:355, 360, 363-64, 383

Short Friday, and Other Stories (Singer) **3**:357, 370, 373, 376; **53**:293, 324, 345, 350, 353

"The Short Happy Life of Cash Bentley" (Cheever) **38**:47

"The Short Happy Life of Francis Macomber" (Hemingway) **1**:217, 230, 232, 234; **25**:79-80, 87, 89, 92, 97, 99-100, 102; **36**:251; **40**:155, 191, 208-09, 214-15; **63**:100-102

Short Novels of Colette (Colette) **10**:266-67, 269

The Short Novels of Thomas Wolfe (Wolfe) **33**:375-76

Short Prose Poems (Baudelaire)
　See *Petits poèmes en prose: Le spleen de Paris*

"Short Sentimental Journey" (Svevo)
　See "Corto Viaggio sentimentale"

"A Short Sentimental Journey" (Svevo)
　See *Corto viaggio sentimentale e altri racconti inediti*

"A Short Sleep in Louisiana" (Caldwell) **19**:23

Short Stories (Pirandello) **22**:242, 244

Short Stories in Prose and Verse (Lawson) **18**:220, 240, 256, 258

The Short Stories of Conrad Aiken (Aiken) **9**:6, 24, 28

The Short Stories of Ernest Hemingway (Hemingway) **40**:166, 173, 181, 184, 204, 245, 247; **63**:66, 103, 107-8, 112, 114-15

The Short Stories of James T. Farrell (Farrell) **28**:90

The Short Stories of Saki (Saki) **12**:296, 307, 309

The Short Stories of Thomas Hardy (Hardy) **2**:212

"A Short Trip Home" (Fitzgerald) **6**:47-8, 60, 62

Shorter Novels of Herman Melville (Melville) **46**:335

"The Shortest Way Home" (Kiely) **58**:149

"The Short-Short Story of Mankind: An Improbable Allegory of Human History Compressed for a Very Small Time Capsule" (Steinbeck) **11**:257-58

"Shorty Stack, Pugilist" (Norris) **28**:199, 207, 213

Shōshō Shigemoto no haha (Tanizaki) **21**:182, 186, 188-89, 191, 198, 223-25

"The Shot" (Pushkin)
　See "Vystrel"

The Shot from the Pulpit (Meyer)
　See "Der Schuß von der Kanzel"

Shoten an Goray (Singer) **53**:273, 299-301, 323-24, 327-30, 338, 373

"Shots" (Ozick) **15**:307, 318-19

"Should Wizard Hit Mommy?" (Updike) **13**:400

"A Shower of Gold" (Barthelme) **2**:27-8, 38, 42, 52, 55; **55**:14, 16, 23-4, 26, 28

"Shower of Gold" (Welty) **1**:483, 485, 493; **27**:332; **51**:266, 271, 288-89, 322-23, 329

"Showin' Off" (Crane) **56**:111

"Shprintse" (Aleichem) **33**:7

"The Shrine" (Lavin) **4**:183

The Shrine, and Other Stories (Lavin) **4**:181

"The Shrink Flips" (Pynchon) **14**:308

The Shrouded Woman (Bombal)
　See *La amortajada*

"Shuang teng" (P'u Sung-ling) **31**:207

"Shu-chih" (P'u Sung-ling) **31**:196-97

Shuffle (Michaels) **16**:314, 316-21

"Shu'hsi" (P'u Sung-ling) **31**:192

"Shuju no kotoba" (Akutagawa Ryūnosuke) **44**:80

"Shumpū shūu roku" (Tanizaki) **21**:205

"Shunkin shō" (Tanizaki) **21**:180, 182-83, 185, 188-91, 195, 198, 200-04, 219, 224, 227

"The Shunned House" (Lovecraft) **3**:262, 276, 282; **52**:268, 282, 288, 292, 322, 336, 345

"Shut a Final Door" (Capote) **2**:61-2, 64, 66, 69, 72-6, 83; **47**:13, 16, 28-9, 31, 34-5, 44-5, 47, 53, 55, 58-9, 66

Shut Up, He Explained (Lardner) **32**:156

"Shūzan zu" (Akutagawa Ryūnosuke) **44**:64, 72

"Shy Neighbourhoods" (Dickens) **17**:123

"Si dorme come cani" (Calvino) **3**:112; **48**:80, 147

"Sibi" (Narayan) **25**:131

The Sibyl (Lagerkvist) **12**:185-92, 194, 198

"Sicilian Honor" (Pirandello) **22**:235-36, 265-66

"Sicilian Tangerines" (Pirandello) **22**:236

"Sicilian Vespers" (White) **39**:302-03, 307, 310, 319-20, 324-25, 329, 337, 345

"A Sick Boy's Winter" (Moravia)
　See "Inverno di malato"

"A Sick Collier" (Lawrence) **4**:202

"The Sickness of Lone Chief" (London) **4**:287

"Sictransit" (Auchincloss) **22**:51

Siddharta (Hesse)
　See *Siddhartha, eine indische Dichtung*

Siddhartha: An Indic Poem (Hesse)
　See *Siddhartha, eine indische Dichtung*

Siddhartha, eine indische Dichtung (Hesse) **9**:211-15, 217, 221-26, 231, 234, 240, 246; **49**:211-322

"The Side Effects of Orthonovin G" (Ballard) **53**:19

"The Sidi" (Rhys) **21**:62

Sido (Colette) **10**:278-79, 285

"Sidonie" (Dreiser) **30**:148

Sieben Legenden (Keller) **26**:97, 100, 102, 106-07, 115

"The Siege" (Davie) **52**:2

"Siegfried et la Limousin" (Morand) **22**:158

"Sierra Leone" (McGahern) **17**:307, 309, 316-17, 321, 323

"La sierva ajena" (Bioy Casares) **17**:83

"Siestas" (Cortázar) **7**:57

"Sieur George" (Cable) **4**:50, 52, 65-7

"The Sight of a Dead Body" (Wescott) **35**:375-76

"Sigismund" (Lewis) **34**:170, 178-79

"The Sign" (Villiers de l'Isle Adam)
　See "L'intersigne"

"A Sign in Space" (Calvino)
　See "Un segno nello spazio"

"The Sign of Apelles" (Pasternak)
　See "Il tratto di Apelle"

"A Sign of Blood" (Price) **22**:367-68

"Sign of Space" (Calvino)
　See "Un segno nello spazio"

"The Sign of the Broken Sword" (Chesterton) **1**:127, 136-37, 142; **46**:132, 140

"The Sign of the Potent Pills" (Hammett) **17**:226

"Signatures" (Dixon) **16**:207

"Significant Experience" (Wilson) **21**:322, 331, 351, 365

"Significant Moments in the Life of My Mother" (Atwood) **2**:17, 21-3; **46**:38, 43-4, 46, 50-1, 78-9, 96-7

"Signor Formica" (Hoffmann) **13**:183

"La Signora Frola e il signor Ponza, suo genero" (Pirandello) **22**:245, 247, 270

"Signs" (Moravia) **26**:161

"Signs" (Wideman) **62**:274, 277, 285-86, 294-95

"Signs along the Road" (Andrić)
　See "Znakovi pored puta"

"Signs and Symbols" (Nabokov) **11**:109, 117-18, 120-22, 129, 135-36, 140, 144, 147-48, 150-51, 153, 157-60

Signs by the Roadside (Andrić)
　See "Znakovi pored puta"

"Silas Jackson" (Dunbar) **8**:122, 128, 133, 135, 147

"Silence" (Borowski) **48**:9

"Silence" (Freeman) **47**:84, 104

"The Silence" (Galsworthy) **22**:92, 97

"Silence, a Fable" (Poe) **1**:379; **22**:330; **54**:154, 156

Silence, and Other Stories (Freeman) **47**:83-4, 86, 103-04, 106, 134

"The Silence of the Valley" (O'Faolain) **13**:288, 293, 297-98, 302, 305, 312, 314, 318

"Silence Please" (Clarke) **3**:133

"The Silences of Mr. Palomar" (Calvino) **3**:113

"El silencio de Dios" (Arreola) **38**:8

"Silent Bontche" (Peretz)
　See "Bontsye Shvayg"

"The Silent Eaters" (Garland) **18**:147, 177-79, 186, 188-89

"Silent in Gehenna" (Ellison) **14**:102-03

"The Silent Men" (Camus)
　See "Les muets"

The Silent Mr. Palomar (Calvino)
　See *Palomar*

"Silent Pianist" (Wilson) **21**:359

"Silent Samuel" (Dunbar) **8**:122, 128

"Silent Snow, Secret Snow" (Aiken) **9**:5-7, 9, 12, 20, 22, 30-40, 42-4

"The Silent Towns" (Bradbury) **53**:201, 210, 248, 259

Silhouettes of American Life (Davis) **38**:95

"Silver" (Levi) **12**:268

"Silver Bugles, Cymbals, Golden Silks" (Hood) **42**:137, 139, 180, 200, 225-31

"Silver Circus" (Coppard) **21**:29

Silver Circus (Coppard) **21**:7, 9, 15

"The Silver Crown" (Malamud) **15**:190, 195, 197-99, 220

"A Silver Dish" (Bellow) **14**:43

"Silver Jemmy" (Benét) **10**:151-52

"The Silver Key" (Lovecraft) **3**:258, 262, 276, 286; **52**:270, 284, 286, 337, 360-62

"The Silver Leaves" (Far) **62**:50

"Silver Throat" (Bulgakov)
　See "Steel Throat"

"Silver Wig" (Chandler) **23**:107

"Silvester-Unfall" (Lenz) **33**:317-26

"Silvia" (Cortázar) **7**:57

"Sim Burns's Wife" (Garland) **18**:154-55, 160, 176, 184

"A Similarity" (Pardo Bazán)
　See "Un parecido"

"Simmering" (Atwood) **2**:19-20; **46**:97

The Simple Art of Murder (Chandler) **23**:67

"A Simple Enquiry" (Hemingway) **1**:216

A Simple Heart (Flaubert)
　See *Un coeur simple*

"Simple Maria" (Allende) **65**:15, 17, 47, 50, 52

"Simple Simon" (Andersen) **6**:30

"Simple Simon" (Coppard) **21**:3

Simple Speaks His Mind (Hughes) **6**:110-11, 113, 137

Simple Stakes a Claim (Hughes) **6**:143

Simple Takes a Wife (Hughes) **6**:113

"A Simple Tale" (Galsworthy) **22**:99

"Simulacra" (Cortázar)
　See "Simulacros"

"Simulacros" (Cortázar) **7**:92

"The Sin Eater" (Atwood) **2**:15, 18, 22; **46**:44-5, 50, 76-8, 94-5

"Sin un cuarto" (Alarcon) **64**:3, 5, 7, 29-30

"Sinbad" (Barthelme) **55**:112

"Since It's Not Raining" (Pirandello) **22**:253-54

"Sinesio de Rodas" (Arreola) **38**:12-13, 22

"Sinesius of Rhodes" (Arreola)
　See "Sinesio de Rodas"

"Sing a Song of Sixpence" (Gissing) **37**:55

"Sing the Epistle" (Pirandello)
　See "Canta l'epistola"

"The Singapore Hotel" (Hood) **42**:185

"The Singers" (Turgenev) **7**:316; **57**:266, 284

"A Singer's Romance" (Cather) **2**:101; **50**:81, 95, 100, 156, 187

"The Singing Lesson" (Mansfield) **9**:280

"The Singing Statues" (Ballard) **53**:43, 72, 77, 128, 131

"A Single Daring Act" (Salter) **58**:178

"Single Gents Only" (Metcalf) **43**:154-55, 159-60, 164, 166

"A Single Lady" (Lavin) **4**:166

A Single Lady, and Other Stories (Lavin) **4**:164

"The Single Reader" (Auchincloss) **22**:4, 37, 48, 52

"The Sing-Song of Old Man Kangaroo" (Kipling) **5**:287

"The Sing-Song Woman" (Far) **62**:24, 35, 38-40, 50-51, 55, 64, 76-77, 79

"Singular ocorrência" (Machado de Assis) **24**:129, 152

"Le Sinistre de Tonbridge" (Moore) **19**:341

"The Sinking House" (Boyle) **16**:153, 155

"The Sinking Ship" (Stevenson) **51**:239

"The Sinner" (O'Flaherty) **6**:277, 280

"Sinners" (O'Faolain) **13**:284, 287-88, 302

Das Sinngedicht (Keller) **26**:95, 102-06, 109-10, 121

"El sino" (Pardo Bazán) **30**:261

"Sins and Virtues" (Crace) **61**:30, 32-33

"The Sins of Prince Saradine" (Chesterton) **46**:109, 111, 145, 149, 153

"The Sins of the Fathers" (Gissing) **37**:79

The Sins of the Fathers (Gissing) **37**:67, 72, 79

"The Sins of the Mother" (Fante) **65**:92

"Sins of the Third Age" (Gordimer) **17**:169, 171, 193

"Sir Dominick's Bargain" (Le Fanu) **14**:223, 228

"Sir Hercules" (Huxley) **39**:162

"Sir Rabbit" (Welty) **1**:474, 480, 486, 495

"The Sire de Malétroit's Door" (Stevenson) **11**:269-72, 279, 281, 296-97

La sirena negra (Pardo Bazán) **30**:262-63, 267, 270

"The Siren's Story" (Forster)
See "The Story of the Siren"

"Sis' Becky's Pickaninny" (Chesnutt) **7**:7, 10, 40, 42; **54**:37, 40

"The Siskin Who Lied and the Truth-Loving Woodpecker" (Gorky)
See "O chizhe, kotoryi lgal, i o diatle liu-bitele istiny"

Il sistema periodico (Levi) **12**:255-57, 259-61, 263-69, 274-76, 279-81

"Sister" (Farrell) **28**:113

"Sister" (Wolff) **63**:263, 301, 310, 312, 316, 318, 338

Sister Benvenuta and the Christ Child (Lee) **33**:307, 310

"Sister Imelda" (O'Brien) **10**:334, 341, 345

"Sister Liddy" (Freeman) **1**:199-200; **47**:102, 105, 154, 157-58

"Sister Peacham's Turn" (Jewett) **6**:156

"Sister Superior" (Wilson) **21**:330, 332, 354, 360

"The Sisters" (Joyce) **3**:201, 205-06, 208, 211-12, 216-17, 225, 230, 232, 234-35, 237, 244-47, 249; **26**:46-8, 50; **44**:262-63, 265, 279-80, 284, 288, 291-97, 299; **64**:204-5, 231, 241

"The Sisters" (O'Connor) **5**:392

"Sisters of the Golden Circle" (Henry) **49**:197, 200

"Sittin' up with Grandma" (Stuart) **31**:251

"Siwash" (London) **4**:286

Six Feet of the Country (Gordimer) **17**:152-3, 187

"Six Inches" (Bukowski) **45**:54

Six Moral Tales from Jules Laforgue (Laforgue)
See *Moralités légendaires*

Six Problems for Don Isidro Parodi (Bioy Casares)
See *Seis problemas para Don Isidro Parodi*

"The Six Servants" (Grimm and Grimm) **36**:190

"Six Shots By Moonlight" (Lovecraft) **52**:311

Six Stories Written in the First Person Singular (Maugham) **8**:356, 364, 378

"The Six Swans" (Grimm and Grimm) **36**:225-26

Six Trees (Freeman) **1**:194; **47**:87, 105, 107, 132, 160, 162, 193

"The Six Veils" (Alarcon)
See "Los seis velos"

"Six Weeks at Heppenheim" (Gaskell) **25**:49-50, 59

"Six Years After" (Mansfield) **9**:282; **38**:228

"The Six-Day Night" (Morand)
See "La nuit de seis jours"

"Sixpence" (Mansfield) **9**:282, 310-11

"The Sixth Day" (Levi)
See "Il sesto giorno"

The Sixth Day (Levi)
See "Il sesto giorno"

The Sixth Day, and Other Stories (Levi)
See *The Sixth Day and Other Tales*

The Sixth Day and Other Tales (Levi) **12**:278-81

"A Sixties Romance" (Adams) **24**:16, 19

"Sixty Acres" (Carver) **8**:3, 10, 34

"The 60 Minute Zoom" (Ballard) **53**:20, 57, 59, 91

Sixty Stories (Barthelme) **2**:46, 51, 56; **55**:26, 66-8, 81, 108-9, 111-15

"A Sixty Year Old Man" (Endō) **48**:209-12

"Sixty-six" (Aleichem) **33**:26, 29

Själarnas maskerad (Lagerkvist) **12**:179, 181-2, 197

"The Skater" (Spencer) **57**:224, 226, 229, 242

"The Skeleton" (Aldiss) **36**:14

"Skeleton" (Bradbury) **29**:43, 68, 88

"The Skeleton" (Pritchett) **14**:268, 285, 297, 299, 305

"The Skeleton" (Tagore)
See "Kankal"

"Skeleton Crew" (Aldiss) **36**:7, 20

Skeleton Crew (King) **17**:273-76, 290, 294; **55**:250-56, 280

"Skeleton Fixer" (Silko) **37**:288, 293

"The Skeleton in the Closet" (Alcott) **27**:59

"Skeletons" (Beattie) **11**:29

"The Skeletons" (O'Hara) **15**:279, 283

"Sketch" (Walser)
See "Skizze"

The Sketch Book (Irving)
See *The Sketch Book of Geoffrey Crayon, Gent.*

The Sketch Book of Geoffrey Crayon, Gent. (Irving) **2**:238-46, 250-55, 257-59, 262, 265, 267; **37**:265-66, 269, 271, 274

Sketches and Stories (Gorky) **28**:186, 188

Sketches by Boz of Every-Day Life and Every-Day People (Dickens) **17**:109, 111, 113, 115-17, 120-22, 124-26, 132-34, 139; **49**:34, 36, 71, 111, 120, 164-65

Sketches from a Hunter's Album (Turgenev)
See *Zapiski okhotnika*

"Sketches from Memory" (Hawthorne) **3**:157

"Sketches of Life in an English Manufacturing Town" (Gissing) **37**:70-2

"Sketches of the Nineteen Seventies" (Auchincloss) **22**:35, 51

"A Sketching Trip" (Welty) **1**:480

Skin Trade (Thomas)
See *Adventures in the Skin Trade, and Other Stories*

Skinny Island (Auchincloss) **22**:30, 42-3

"The Skins of the Fathers" (Barker) **53**:136, 138-39, 143, 158, 168, 174, 178-79

"The Skipping Shoes" (Alcott) **27**:44

"Skirmish at Sartoris" (Faulkner) **1**:170-71

"Skizze" (Walser) **20**:343, 364

"Skoler Rebbetzin" (Peretz) **26**:191

"Skomorox Pamfalon" (Leskov) **34**:130

"Skripka Rotsil'da" (Chekhov) **2**:157-58; **28**:61-3; **51**:79, 92, 177, 191

"Skunaja istorija" (Chekhov) **51**:45, 78, 114-15, 124, 130, 134, 179, 182, 193

"Skull Hunters" (Bulgakov) **18**:89

"The Sky" (Cowan) **28**:83

The Sky Blue Life and Selected Stories (Gorky) **28**:179

"Sky Lift" (Heinlein) **55**:166

"Sky Line" (Taylor) **10**:375-76, 385-87

"The Sky, the Stars, the Wilderness" (Bass) **60**:26

The Sky, the Stars, the Wilderness (Bass) **60**:20, 23-25, 27, 40

"The Sky-blue Life" (Gorky) **28**:139, 180-81

"Skyggen" (Andersen) **6**:7, 24, 30, 35, 41; **56**:33

"The Skylight Room" (Henry) **49**:197

"The Slashers" (Kipling) **5**:277-78

"Slater's Pins Have No Points" (Woolf)
See "Moments of Being: 'Slater's Pins Have No Points'"

"The Slaughterer" (Singer) **3**:358, 384; **53**:301, 325

"Slave" (Phillips) **16**:327-28

"The Slave Girl" (Andrić)
See "Robinja"

"Slave on the Block" (Hughes) **6**:119, 121-22, 128, 134

"Slaves of the Lamp" (Kipling) **54**:96

"Slaves of the Lamp, Part II" (Kipling) **54**:96, 98-99

"The Sledding Party" (Millhauser) **57**:154

"A Sleep and a Forgetting" (Howells) **36**:365-66, 368-70, 396-97, 399

"Sleep in Unheavenly Peace" (Saroyan) **21**:166

"Sleep it Off, Lady" (Rhys) **21**:51, 53-5, 58, 63-4, 69

Sleep It Off, Lady (Rhys) **21**:39-40, 42, 48, 50-2, 54, 56, 58, 61, 63-7, 69-71

"Sleeping Beauty" (Clarke) **3**:134

"Sleeping Beauty" (Collier) **19**:99, 107-09, 115

"Sleeping Beauty" (Ferré)
See "La bella durmiente"

"Sleeping Beauty" (Grimm and Grimm) **36**:177-79

"The Sleeping Beauty" (Perelman) **32**:241

"The Sleeping Beauty in the Fridge" (Levi) **12**:278

"Sleeping like Dogs" (Calvino)
See "Si dorme come cani"

"Sleepy" (Chekhov)
See "Spat' xoetsja"

"Sleepy Hollow" (Irving)
See "The Legend of Sleepy Hollow"

"Šlépej" (Čapek) **36**:89, 97, 110-11, 121-24

"Šlépeje" (Čapek) **36**:97, 104-06, 121, 126, 128

"Slice Him Down" (Chekhov)
See "Spat' xoetsja"

"A Slice of Life" (Wodehouse) **2**:347

"Slick Gonna Learn" (Ellison) **26**:7-8, 21-2, 29

"A Slight Maneuver" (Stafford) **26**:303-04, 306

"A Slight Mistake" (Zoshchenko) **15**:388-89, 407-08

"The Slim Syrens" (Stoker) **62**:252

"A Slip under the Microscope" (Wells) **6**:360, 381, 384, 393

"The Slipover Sweater" (Stuart) **31**:234

"A Slippery Floor" (Nin) **10**:306

"A Slip-Up" (McGahern) **17**:309, 317

"Slooter's Vengeance" (Pritchett) **14**:298

"A Sloppy Story" (Dixon) **16**:217

"Slouch" (Farrell) **28**:99

"Slow Death" (Caldwell) **19**:37-8

"A Slow Death" (Clarke) **45**:76, 81, 83, 89, 96-7

Slow Learner: Early Stories (Pynchon) **14**:333-34, 340-42, 346-49

"The Slow of Despond" (Thomas) **20**:325-27

"Sluaj iz praktiki" (Chekhov) **2**:127, 156-58; **51**:58, 70, 78-9, 84, 131, 145, 194, 204, 212

"Sluchai iz praktiki" (Chekhov)
See "Sluaj iz praktiki"

"The Small Assassin" (Bradbury) **29**:65, 75, 87-9

"Small Avalanches" (Oates) 6:231
"Small Bear" (Dixon) 16:206, 211
"A Small Bequest" (Lavin) 4:167
"A Small Day" (Caldwell) 19:13, 23
"Small Fry" (Chekhov) 51:38
"A Small, Good Thing" (Carver) 8:19-26, 30, 39, 56-9
"A Small Incident" (Lu Hsun)
    See "Yijian xiaoshi"
"Small Island Republics" (Apple) 50:18, 23, 33-4
"The Small Lady" (O'Faolain) 13:314
"A Small Paradise" (Cortázar)
    See "Un pequeño paraíso"
"A Small Piece of Spite" (Twain) 34:327
"The Small Rain" (Pynchon) 14:327, 334, 340, 342-43, 347-49
"A Small Star in the East" (Dickens) 17:123-24
"The Small Stones of Tu Fu" (Aldiss) 36:14, 20
"Small Town" (Dick) 57:109-10
"Small Town Affair" (Arreola) 38:13
"The Small Town Lovers" (O'Brien) 10:333
"A Small World" (Sansom) 21:88
"Small-Bore in Africa" (Perelman) 32:229
"Small-Town Taxi Cab Driver" (Farrell) 28:112
"A Smart Cookie" (Cisneros) 32:46
"Smart-Aleck Kill" (Chandler) 23:58, 80, 102, 106
"The Smell" (Clarke) 45:78-9, 81-2, 92, 101, 103
"The Smell of Bread" (Kazakov) 43:58, 67, 69
"The Smell of Death and Flowers" (Gordimer) 17:153, 160
Smert Ivana Ilyicha (Tolstoy) 9:368-69, 373-74, 377, 382-83, 394, 396-97; 45:129, 131, 136-37, 142-43, 156-59, 161, 165; 54:253, 259-61, 269, 272, 276, 283-91, 295, 297-300, 304, 307-8, 310, 312-20, 323-25, 327-31, 333
"Smert starika Arkhipova" (Pilnyak) 48:258
"Smerti" (Pilnyak) 48:254, 284, 286-87
Směsné lásky (Kundera) 24:86-8, 90-2, 94-6, 98-9, 101, 103-06, 108-11, 113, 116, 118, 121-22, 125
"The Smile" (Ballard) 1:79; 53:20, 55
"Smile" (Lawrence) 4:219
"The Smile" (Sansom) 21:125
"A Smile of Fortune" (Conrad) 9:142-43
"The Smile of Winter" (Carter) 13:2, 4
"The Smilers" (Fitzgerald) 6:56-7
The Smiles Gone (Keller)
    See *Das Verlorene Lachen*
"Smith and Jones" (Aiken) 9:4, 12-13
"Smith vs. Jones" (Twain) 34:297
Smog (Calvino)
    See *La nuvola di smog*
"Smoke" (Barnes) 3:18
"Smoke" (Chabon) 59:71, 76
"Smoke" (Faulkner) 1:178-80
Smoke (Appelfeld)
    See 'Ashan
Smoke, and Other Early Stories (Barnes) 3:17, 19
Smoke Bellew Tales (London) 4:289
"The Smoke Trees of San Pietro" (Trevor) 21:263
"Smokers" (Wolff) 63:266, 271-72, 282, 285-87, 290, 294-96, 299-301, 303, 305, 308, 310, 320, 322
The Smoking Mountain: Stories of Postwar Germany (Boyle) 5:56
"Smorgasbord" (Wolff) 63:340
"Smrt barona Gandary" (Čapek) 36:97, 102, 104
"Smrt u sinanovoj tekiji" (Andrić) 36:38, 43, 55, 79
"The Smuggler" (Singer) 3:389; 53:272, 274
"The Smuggling of Tie Co" (Far) 62:11, 39-41, 50, 77, 82, 86, 88-89, 99-100
"Snacker" (Caldwell) 19:14
"The Snag" (Pritchett) 14:285

"The Snail and the Rose-Tree" (Andersen) 6:7
"The Snake" (Andrić)
    See "Zmija"
"The Snake" (Steinbeck) 11:207-08, 225, 233, 237-38
"Snake and Hawk" (Benét) 10:145-46
The Snake Lady, and Other Stories (Lee) 33:302
"Snake Teeth" (Stuart) 31:226, 231, 245
"The Snake-Song" (Narayan) 25:141, 154
"Snapdragons" (Frame) 29:108, 112
"Snapshots of a Wedding" (Head) 52:201, 216-18, 227
"Sne talmide hakamim sehayu be'irenu" (Agnon) 30:53, 55
"Sneakers" (King) 17:295
"Sneedronningen" (Andersen) 6:4, 6-8, 13, 18-20, 24-8, 30, 36-7, 40; 56:12-16, 33-34, 37
"Sneewittchen" (Grimm and Grimm) 36:196, 204-05, 207-08, 223
"Snega" (Pilnyak) 48:285
"The Sniff" (Pritchett) 14:297
"The Sniper" (O'Flaherty) 6:261, 280
"A Snobbish Story" (Fitzgerald) 6:50
"Snopići" (Andrić) 36:38
"Snow" (Adams) 24:11
"Snow" (Beattie) 11:25-6, 29
"Snow" (Phillips) 16:330
"Snow Bound at the Eagle's" (Harte) 8:254
"The Snow Child" (Carter) 13:9-10, 28
"The Snow Guest" (Warner) 23:373
"The Snow Image: A Childish Miracle" (Hawthorne) 3:159, 177, 183
The Snow Image, and Other Twice-Told Tales (Hawthorne) 3:184
"The Snow Queen" (Andersen)
    See "Sneedronningen"
"The Snow Queen, a Folk Tale in Seven Parts" (Andersen)
    See "Sneedronningen"
The Snow Storm (Tolstoy)
    See *The Snowstorm*
"Snow Wind" (Pilnyak) 48:284
Snowbound: The Record of a Theatrical Touring Party (Stoker) 62:252
"Snowdrops" (Walser) 20:364
"Snowing in Greenwich Village" (Updike) 13:352
"Snowman, Snowman" (Frame) 29:97, 101, 112-15
Snowman, Snowman: Fables and Fantasies (Frame) 29:95-7, 113, 115
"Snowmen" (Millhauser) 57:154-55, 167, 177
"The Snowmen" (Pohl) 25:224, 229
"The Snows" (Pilnyak)
    See "Snega"
"The Snows of Kilimanjaro" (Hemingway) 1:214-15, 217-18, 229, 234; 25:79-81, 84-97, 99, 102-3, 105-7, 120-21, 125-28; 36:251, 273, 281, 289; 40:156, 208-09, 214-15, 250
The Snows of Kilimanjaro and Other Stories (Hemingway) 40:173
"Snowstorm" (Bulgakov) 18:86, 88
"The Snowstorm" (Pilnyak)
    See "Metel"
"The Snowstorm" (Pushkin)
    See "Metel"
"The SnowStorm" (Tolstoy)
    See "Metel"
The Snowstorm (Tolstoy) 9:382, 389
"Snow-White" (Grimm and Grimm)
    See "Sneewittchen"
"Snow-White and Rose-Red" (Grimm and Grimm)
    See "Schneeweisschen und Rosenrot"
"A Snowy Day" (Shiga) 23:346
"So Help Me" (Algren) 33:88, 101-02, 104, 111-14
"So Many Worlds" (Grau) 15:155
"So Much Water So Close to Home" (Carver) 8:5, 14-15, 19, 21, 29, 42, 53, 57-60; 51:5

"So On He Fares" (Moore) 19:308, 319-21, 324, 327-38
So zärtlich war Suleyken (Lenz) 33:315, 318
"Soames and the Flag" (Galsworthy) 22:71
"Soap" (Farrell) 28:92
"Soap" (Lu Hsun)
    See "Feizao"
Sobach'e serdtse (Bulgakov) 18:69-71, 73, 75, 82, 86, 93, 96-7, 103-08, 113-22
"Sobaka" (Turgenev) 7:316, 321, 323-24, 326, 335-36, 338; 57:311-12, 380
"The Sobbin' Women" (Benét) 10:144, 146, 148
"Sobremesa" (Pardo Bazán) 30:262, 295
Sochinenya (Gogol) 52:148
"The Sociable at Dudley's" (Garland) 18:154-55, 160
"Social Cares" (Zoshchenko) 15:388
"The Social Triangle" (Henry) 5:198
"A Society" (Woolf) 7:368, 371, 374, 377, 392-93, 396, 400-02, 404
"Society Chit-Chat" (Leacock) 39:266
"Socks" (Hood) 42:187
"Sodom in the Suburbs" (Perelman) 32:220
"Les soeurs Rondoli" (Maupassant) 1:256, 259, 270, 274, 283, 288
"Soffio" (Pirandello) 22:260
"The Soft Moon" (Calvino)
    See "La molle luna"
"The Soft Touch of Grass" (Pirandello) 22:240, 243
"The Soft Voice of the Serpent" (Gordimer) 17:166-67
The Soft Voice of the Serpent (Gordimer) 17:151-52, 157, 166, 186
"Soft-Boiled Eggs" (Pardo Bazán) 30:291
"Der Sohn" (Schnitzler) 15:351, 371
Die Söhne des Senators (Storm) 27:286
"Un soir" (Maupassant) 1:274, 280
"The Sojourner" (McCullers) 9:323, 332, 341, 345-46, 358; 24:232
Sokrovennyi chelovek (Platonov) 42:256-57
"A Soldier of Humour" (Lewis) 34:151, 158-60, 169, 176, 178
"A Soldier of the Empire" (Page) 23:2902
"Soldier, Red Soldier" (Kiely) 58:145
"A Soldier's Embrace" (Gordimer) 17:163-64
A Soldier's Embrace (Gordimer) 17:162, 164-65, 181, 191
"Soldier's Home" (Hemingway) 1:244; 40:155, 224, 251; 63:79, 90
"Soldier's Joy" (Wolff) 63:264, 301, 310, 316, 320-21
"A Soldier's Legacy" (Boell) 23:34
"Soldiers of the Republic" (Parker) 2:276, 281-82
"Soldiers Three" (Kipling) 5:269
Soldiers Three (Kipling) 5:259
"Solemn Advice to a Young Man about to Accept Undertaking as a Profession" (Saroyan) 21:137, 156
"A Solid House" (Rhys) 21:50-1, 53, 64-5, 69
"Solid Objects" (Woolf) 7:373, 377, 387, 397
"Solitaire" (Updike) 13:385
"The Solitary" (Cable) 4:50, 72-4
"A Solitary" (Freeman) 1:197; 47:106
"Solitary" (Wideman) 62:262-63, 288
"A Solitary Ewe" (Hood) 42:186
"The Solitary Snipe" (Akutagawa Ryūnosuke) 44:64
"La solitude" (Baudelaire) 18:39
"Solitude" (Maupassant) 1:262
"Solnechnyy udar" (Bunin) 5:91, 93, 104-06, 114, 119
"Un solo cabello" (Pardo Bazán) 30:261
"Solo Dance" (Phillips) 16:330
"Solus Rex" (Nabokov) 11:117
"Solution" (Dreiser) 30:153-55, 159
"Solution of a Forsyte" (Galsworthy) 22:75
"Solution Unsatisfactory" (Heinlein) 55:220
"Sombre récit, conteur plus sombre" (Villiers de l'Isle Adam) 14:381

"Sombre Tale, Sombre Teller" (Villiers de l'Isle Adam)
    See "Sombre récit, conteur plus sombre"
El sombrero de tres picos (Alarcon) 64:9, 17, 24, 31, 37, 39-44
"Some Account of the Latter Days of the Hon. Richard Marston of Dunoran" (Le Fanu) 14:247
"Some Approaches to the Problem of the Shortage of Time" (Le Guin) 12:235
"Some Are Born to Sweet Delight" (Gordimer) 17:178-79, 186, 188, 190-91
"Some Blue Hills at Sundown" (Gilchrist) 14:161
Some Champions (Lardner) 32:156
"Some Day" (Lawson) 18:239, 248, 250-51, 261
"Some Effects of a Hat" (Warner) 23:381
"Some Effects of the Mimer" (Levi) 12:278
Some Experiences of an Irish R.M. (Somerville & Ross) 56:290-5, 297-8, 303, 306-8, 312-16, 324, 329, 334-5
"Some Facts for Understanding the Perkians" (Cortázar)
    See "Datos para entender a los perqueos"
"Some Get Wasted" (Marshall) 3:303
"Some Hangover" (Bukowski) 45:62, 65, 68
"Some Innkeepers and Bestre" (Lewis) 34:166-67
Some Irish Yesterdays (Somerville & Ross) 56:294, 299-300, 308, 317
"Some Like Them Cold" (Lardner) 32:114, 117, 124, 131-32, 135, 141, 146, 150-52, 154-56, 160
"Some Monday for Sure" (Gordimer) 17:155, 160, 183
"Some Mother" (Bukowski) 45:51
"Some Notes on River Country" (Welty) 27:340
"Some of Us Have Been Threatening Our Friend Colby" (Barthelme) 55:119-21
Some Others and Myself (Suckow) 18:393-95, 413, 422-26
"Some Parishioners" (Moore) 19:330, 332, 334
"Some Passages in the Life of a Lion" (Poe) 35:339
Some People, Places, and Things That Will Not Appear in My Next Novel (Cheever) 1:92, 100; 38:61-2; 57:9
"Some Strange Disturbances in an Old House on Augier Street" (Le Fanu) 14:223-24, 238, 251
"Some Village Cronies" (Garland) 18:161
"Some Words with a Mummy" (Poe) 1:402; 54:228-29, 231
"Someone Has Disturbed the Roses" (García Márquez)
    See "Alguien desordena estas rosas"
"Someone to Trust" (O'Hara) 15:255, 264
"Someone Walking Around" (Cortázar)
    See "Alguien que anda por ahí"
"Something" (Andersen)
    See "Noget"
"Something" (Williams) 31:329, 332
"Something about a Viet Cong Flag" (Bukowski) 45:55
Something Childish, and Other Stories (Mansfield)
    See The Little Girl, and Other Stories
"Something Entirely Different" (Warner) 23:377
"Something for the Time Being" (Gordimer) 17:173
Something in Common, and Other Stories (Hughes) 6:122-23, 127, 133
"Something in His Nature" (Berriault) 30:96
"Something in It" (Stevenson) 51:239
Something I've Been Meaning to Tell You (Munro) 3:328, 331, 335, 339, 346
"Something Out There" (Gordimer) 17:169, 172, 174-76, 185-86, 192
Something Out There (Gordimer) 17:170, 173, 191

"Something Spurious From the Mindanao Deep" (Stegner) 27:220, 223-26
"Something Squishy" (Wodehouse) 2:355-56
"Something Terrible, Something Lovely" (Sansom) 21:84, 91, 124
Something Terrible, Something Lovely (Sansom) 21:112, 124
"Something That Happened" (Phillips) 16:335
Something to Remember Me By (Bellow) 14:60-1
"Something to Say" (Thurber) 47:383-84
"Something to Write About" (Andersen) 6:36
"Sometimes It's OK to Eat Inkwells" (Zoshchenko) 15:407
"Sometimes They Come Back" (King) 17:262; 55:249
"Somewhere a Roscoe ..." (Perelman) 32:204
"Somewhere Else" (Paley) 8:420
"Somewhere New" (Wilding) 50:346-48
Somewhere New: New and Selected Stories (Wilding) 50:373-74
"Sommerfuglen" (Andersen) 56:29
Die Sommernacht (Tieck) 31:282
Eine Sommerreise (Tieck) 31:290
"The Son" (Bunin) 5:81, 103-04, 106, 108-10
"The Son" (Schnitzler)
    See "Der Sohn"
"Son" (Turgenev) 7:321, 325-28, 338, 361; 57:311, 380
"Son" (Updike) 13:387
"The Son From America" (Singer) 3:374
"The Son of Andrés Aparicio" (Fuentes)
    See "El hijo de Andrés Aparicio"
"Son of Celluloid" (Barker) 53:136-39, 141, 143, 154, 158, 162, 168, 171-72
"The Son of God and His Sorrow" (Oates) 6:237
"The Son of Icarus" (Bradbury) 29:53
"A Son of the Celestial" (Cather) 2:100, 102; 50:76, 91, 183-84, 186, 210-11
"A Son of the Gods" (Bierce) 9:55-6, 60, 63-4
"The Son of the Sheik" (Norris) 28:204, 212, 214
A Son of the Sun (London) 4:266
"The Son of the Wolf" (London) 4:267
The Son of the Wolf: Tales of the Far North (London) 4:250-52, 258, 264, 278-79, 281-82, 284-87, 290
"Son of the Wolfman" (Chabon) 59:82-87
"El soñado" (Arreola) 38:9, 23
Sonatinas (Ferré) 36:146, 151
"The Song" (Babel) 16:27, 31, 52, 54-8
"The Song and the Sergeant" (Henry) 49:203
"The Song in the Garden" (Nin) 10:306
"A Song of Innocence" (Ellison) 26:11
"A Song of Love Triumphant" (Turgenev)
    See "Pesn' torzhestvuyushchey lyubvi"
"The Song of Peronelle" (Arreola) 38:12
"The Song of Songs" (Gilchrist) 14:162-63
"The Song of Songs" (Warner) 23:368
Song of the Blind (Fuentes)
    See Cantar de ciegos
"The Song of the Falcon" (Gorky)
    See "Pesnia o sokole"
"The Song of the Flying Fish" (Chesterton) 1:129, 138; 46:106, 113, 135
"Song of the Shirt, 1941" (Parker) 2:277, 280-81, 285-86
"Song of the Silencer" (Aldiss) 36:13-14
Song of the Silent Snow (Selby) 20:275, 280, 282
"The Song of the Siren" (Forster) 27:68
"The Song of the Stormy Petrel" (Gorky)
    See "Pesnia o burevestnike"
"The Song of the Triumphant Love" (Turgenev)
    See "Pesn' torzhestvuyushchey lyubvi"
"The Song of the Wren" (Bates) 10:139
"Song without Words" (O'Connor) 5:365, 371, 383, 398
"Songs My Father Sang Me" (Bowen) 3:41; 28:4, 7, 9

"Songs My Mother Taught Me" (Calisher) 15:8
Songs of a Dead Dreamer (Ligotti) 16:261, 269-70, 279, 282-85, 287, 293, 296
"The Songs of Distant Earth" (Clarke) 3:135-36
"Songs of Love and Seeking" (Davie) 52:11
"The Songs of Reba Love Jackson" (Wideman) 62:262, 315
Sonny Liston Was a Friend of Mine (Jones) 56:284-85
"Sonny's Blues" (Baldwin) 10:2-3, 5-7, 9, 12, 14-7, 21-5; 33:115-57
"Sono zenjitsu" (Endō) 48:198-99, 201
"The Son's Veto" (Hardy) 2:215-16, 223; 60:180, 194
"Sophistication" (Anderson) 1:30, 42, 44-5
"Soquots" (Caldwell) 19:23
"Sor Aparición" (Pardo Bazán) 30:264-66
"The Sorcerer's Apprentice" (O'Connor) 5:371-72
"The Sorceress's Head" (Calvino)
    See "La testa della maga"
"Sorcières espagnoles" (Mérimée) 7:283
"A Sordid Tale, or, Traceleen Continues Talking" (Gilchrist) 63:8, 21
"Sorel" (Farrell) 28:94
"Sorghum" (Mason) 4:25
"Soročinskaja jamarka" (Gogol) 4:85, 118, 121; 29:149, 171; 52:123, 164
Sorok Sorokov (Bulgakov) 18:106-07
"Sorrow" (Chekhov)
    See "Gore"
"The Sorrow of the Mermaid" (Tanizaki)
    See "Ningyo no nageki"
"The Sorrow of the Pagan Outcast" (Tanizaki)
    See "Itansha no kanashimi"
"Sorrow-Acre" (Dinesen) 7:164, 167, 170-71, 174, 177, 185-86, 188-90, 196, 205-08
"Sorrowful Mysteries" (Dubus) 15:83
"The Sorrows of a Summer Guest" (Leacock) 39:265
"The Sorrows of Gin" (Cheever) 1:100; 38:55, 87
"Sorry Fugu" (Boyle) 16:146, 148-49, 155
"Sorry, Right Number" (King) 17:295
"Sosedi" (Chekhov) 51:189
"Sosny" (Bunin) 5:98-9
Sotto il sole giaguro (Calvino) 3:119; 48:127-30, 174
"Sotto il sole glaguaro" (Calvino) 3:118-19; 48:128, 162-64, 168-70, 173-75
"Soul and Money" (Berriault) 30:103
Soul Clap Hands and Sing (Marshall) 3:299-304, 307-08, 316-17
"The Soul of Laploshka" (Saki) 12:316
"A Soulless Corporation" (Chesnutt) 7:14
"Souls Belated" (Wharton) 6:423-25
"The Sound" (Selby) 20:275, 280
"The Sound of the Hammer" (Dazai Osamu) 41:263, 276
"The Sound of the River" (Rhys) 21:50, 59, 64
"The Sound of the Singing" (Laurence) 7:254, 259-60, 268
"A Sound of Thunder" (Bradbury) 29:51; 53:193
"The Sound of Waiting" (Calisher) 15:7, 15, 19
"Sound Sweep" (Ballard) 1:68; 53:43, 49
"Sound Track" (Calisher) 15:9
"Soup on a Sausage Peg" (Andersen) 6:13-4
"The Source" (Porter) 4:339, 352, 363; 43:257, 303, 305
A Source of Embarrassment (McCarthy)
    See The Oasis
"Source of the World" (Bates) 10:121
"Sous la table, dialogue bachique sur plusieurs questions de haute morale" (Gautier) 20:5, 10-11, 22
"The South" (Borges)
    See "Le Sud"
South: Aspects and Images from Corsica, Italy, and Southern France (Sansom) 21:84, 93, 124-25

"The South Lingers On" (Fisher) **25**:9-10, 17-21, 25

South of No North (Bukowski) **45**:54-6, 58, 60

"South of the Slot" (London) **4**:254

South Sea Tales (London) **4**:266, 283

"A Southern Landscape" (Spencer) **57**:212, 215-16, 218-19, 239, 243

A Southern Landscape (Spencer) **57**:241

"The Southern Thruway" (Cortázar)
    See "La autopista del sur"

Southways (Caldwell) **19**:14, 25, 38, 54, 57

"The Southwest Chamber" (Freeman) **47**:109, 111

"The Southwest Experimental Fast Oxide Reactor" (Gilchrist) **63**:9, 29

"A Souvenir" (Freeman) **47**:149

"Souvenir" (Phillips) **16**:326-30

"A Souvenir of Japan" (Carter) **13**:4

"Souvenirs d'un gentilhomme italien" (Stendhal) **27**:247, 249

"Souvenirs occulte" (Villiers de l'Isle Adam) **14**:381-82, 389, 393

"Soy, tengo y quiero" (Alarcon) **64**:2-3, 8, 30

"Space for Reflection" (Aldiss) **36**:13

"Space Jockey" (Heinlein) **55**:164-65

Space, Time, and Nathaniel (Aldiss) **36**:5, 18

"The Spanish Bed" (Pritchett) **14**:263

"Spanish Blood" (Chandler) **23**:59, 80, 86, 97, 105-07, 109

"Spanish Blood" (Hughes) **6**:118, 132

"A Spanish Household" (Lewis) **34**:177

"The Spanish Lady" (Munro) **3**:339

"A Spanish Priest" (Maugham) **8**:380

The Spanish Virgin, and Other Stories (Pritchett) **14**:268-69, 271

Spanking the Maid (Coover) **15**:47, 52-3

"The Spark and Other Stories" (Davie) **52**:2, 7-11

"A Spark Neglected Burns the House" (Tolstoy) **9**:388

The Spark (The 'Sixties) (Wharton) **6**:439-40

"Sparkling Life" (Bulgakov) **18**:91

"Spat' xoetsja" (Chekhov) **6**:118-32; **51**:42, 105, 107, 153

"Der Spaziergang" (Walser) **20**:333, 335

"Lo specchio a tre luci" (Moravia) **26**:149

"Special Delivery" (Collier) **19**:104, 115

"The Special Sone" (Head) **52**:192, 201, 217, 227, 236

"The Specific of Doctor Menghi" (Svevo)
    See "Lo specifico del dottor Menghi"

"Lo specifico del dottor Menghi" (Svevo) **25**:350, 357, 359

"Speck's Idea" (Gallant) **5**:147

"The Spectacles" (Poe) **1**:407-08

"The Spectacles in the Drawer" (Ligotti) **16**:278-79, 284, 294

"The Spectral Estate" (Ligotti) **16**:297

"Spectral Horror" (Ligotti) **16**:287

"The Spectre Bridegroom" (Irving) **2**:240-41, 246, 251, 255-56; **37**:266

"The Spectre of Doom" (Stoker) **62**:246

"The Speculation of the Building Constructors" (Calvino)
    See "La speculazione edilizia"

"La speculazione edilizia" (Calvino) **3**:91, 111-12, 117-18; **48**:39, 147

La speculazione edilizia (Calvino) **48**:39, 84, 148, 153, 178, 180-81

"The Speech" (Pritchett) **14**:296-98

"Speed Trap" (Pohl) **25**:220, 225

"Spell Bereavement" (Lish) **18**:278, 283

"Spelling" (Munro) **3**:339

"Spending a Day at the Lottery Fair" (Pohl) **25**:236

"Speranza" (Pilnyak) **48**:291-92

"The Sphinx" (Poe) **22**:330

"The Sphinx without a Secret: An Etching" (Wilde) **11**:386, 399, 407

"The Sphynx Apple" (Henry) **5**:162

"The Spider Gardens of Madagascar" (Betts) **45**:3, 9, 30

"Spider, Spider" (Aiken) **9**:5, 12, 14, 32-3, 42

"Spider Town" (Moorhouse) **40**:293

Spiegel das Kätzchen (Keller) **26**:107, 125-27

Der Spiegel des Cyprianus (Storm) **27**:278

Spiel im Morgengrauen (Schnitzler) **15**:345, 367; **61**:290-91

"Spielerglück" (Hoffmann) **13**:188

Spielmann (Grillparzer)
    See *Der Arme Spielmann*

"Der Spielverderber" (Lenz) **33**:327

Der Spielverderber (Lenz) **33**:316

"The Spies in the Herb House" (Betts) **45**:10-12, 28-9

"Spike" (Ross) **24**:311, 323

"Spikes" (Chabon) **59**:82, 86

Spilled Time (Pilnyak) **48**:239

"Spillway" (Barnes) **3**:8-10, 24

Spillway (Barnes) **3**:4-5, 12-14, 16, 22

"Spindleberries" (Galsworthy) **22**:63-4, 75-6, 101

"The Spinoza of Market Street" (Singer) **3**:361, 368, 375, 384; **53**:301, 323, 329, 338

The Spinoza of Market Street, and Other Stories (Singer) **3**:370; **53**:324

"The Spinster and the Cat" (Suckow) **18**:393

"A Spinster's Tale" (Taylor) **10**:374-75, 386, 390, 397-98, 406, 409, 412-15, 417

"The Spiral" (Calvino)
    See "La spirale"

"La spirale" (Calvino) **3**:92, 103-04, 108-09; **48**:47, 67-9, 73, 78, 137, 139, 155-56, 160

"Spirit" (Frame) **29**:109, 118

"The Spirit of the Karroo" (Galsworthy) **22**:90

A Spirit Rises (Warner) **23**:372, 380

Spirite (Gautier) **20**:7-8, 20-1, 25, 30

"Spiritual Séance" (Bulgakov) **18**:92

"Spiritus" (Beattie) **11**:25, 29

Le spleen de Paris (Baudelaire)
    See *Petits poèmes en prose: Le spleen de Paris*

"The Split Second" (du Maurier) **18**:126, 138

"The Split-Tongue Sparrow" (Dazai Osamu) **41**:235-36

"Spoils" (Gordimer) **17**:177, 183-84, 187

"The Spooks of Long Gully" (Lawson) **18**:232, 234-36

"Sport" (Galsworthy) **22**:98

"The Sport of Kings" (Farrell) **28**:94

"Sport: The Kill" (O'Flaherty) **6**:261

"The Sportive Centre of Saint Vincent de Paul" (Hood) **42**:182, 214, 216-17, 240

A Sportsman's Sketches (Turgenev)
    See *Zapiski okhotnika*

"Sportsmanship" (O'Hara) **15**:248, 264-65

"A Spot of Konfrontation" (Aldiss) **36**:14

"The Spotted Dog" (Trollope) **28**:316-17, 321-22, 335, 339-40, 342-43, 349, 353-54, 357

"Spotted Horses" (Faulkner) **1**:167, 177

"The Spree" (Pritchett) **14**:260, 273, 285

"Spring" (Schulz)
    See "Wiosna"

"Spring Bandit" (Dazai Osamu) **41**:240, 244

"A Spring Evening" (Bunin) **5**:90, 92, 102

"Spring Fever" (Collier) **19**:110, 114

"Spring Floods" (Pilnyak) **48**:285-86

Spring Freshets (Turgenev)
    See *Veshnie vody*

"The Spring Hat" (Bates) **10**:123

"Spring in Fialta" (Nabokov)
    See "Vesna v Fial'te"

"A Spring Morning" (Pritchett) **14**:270, 298

"Spring Rain" (Malamud) **15**:235

"A Spring Romance" (Garland) **18**:163

"The Spring Running" (Kipling) **5**:287; **54**:90, 110, 112-13, 123

"Spring Song of the Frogs" (Atwood) **2**:22; **46**:38, 45, 49-51, 95

"Spring Sowing" (O'Flaherty) **6**:260-62, 264, 269, 271, 273, 281, 283

Spring Sowing (O'Flaherty) **6**:261-65, 278, 281, 283

"A Spring Sunday" (Jewett) **6**:156-57

"A Spring Time Case" (Tanizaki) **21**:192

"Springtime à la Carte" (Henry) **49**:197

Spring-Torrents (Turgenev)
    See *Veshnie vody*

"A Sprinkle of Comedy" (Barnes) **3**:18

"Spunk" (Hurston) **4**:135-37, 150, 152

Spunk: The Selected Stories of Zora Neale Hurston (Hurston) **4**:155

"SQ" (Le Guin) **12**:230-31, 241

"Squadron Commander Trunov" (Babel) **16**:24, 26, 28-30, 52, 57-8

The Square Egg, and Other Sketches, with Three Plays (Saki) **12**:322

"The Squaw" (Stoker) **62**:233, 243-44, 248, 253-54

"Squibs for the Guy" (Lewis) **40**:281

"Squire Napper" (Morrison) **40**:337, 367

"Squire Petrick's Lady" (Hardy) **60**:180, 205, 207

"Squire Toby's Will" (Le Fanu) **14**:223-24

"The Squire's Daughter" (Pushkin) **27**:163

"The Squire's Story" (Gaskell) **25**:55, 60

"The Squirrels" (Freeman) **47**:164

"Squirrles Have Bright Eyes" (Collier) **19**:98

"Sredni Vashtar" (Saki) **12**:287, 293-94, 297, 316-17, 320, 331, 333

"La srta. Cora" (Cortázar) **7**:62

"The S.S. Cow Wheat" (Babel) **16**:22

"Ssu-hsün" (P'u Sung-ling) **31**:205

"Ssu-wen lang" (P'u Sung-ling) **31**:199

"St. Anthony's Child" (Pardo Bazán)
    See "El niño de San Antonio"

St. Cecilia, or the Power of Music (Kleist)
    See *Die heilige Cäcilie; oder, die Gewalt der Musik*

"St. Christopher's Life" (Akutagawa Ryūnosuke) **44**:53, 62

"The St Louis Rotary Convention 1923, Recalled" (Moorhouse) **40**:289, 322

"The Stable of the Inn" (Page) **23**:308

"The Staech Affair" (Boell)
    See "Veränderungen in Staech"

"The Stage Coach" (Irving) **2**:245

"The Stage Tavern" (Jewett) **6**:159

"Stages" (Campbell) **19**:76

Stained Glass Elegies (Endō) **48**:191-92, 212

"The Stairs" (Bradbury) **29**:88

"Stalking the Nightmare" (Ellison) **14**:126-27

Stalky and Co. (Kipling) **5**:277-78, 282; **54**:80, 95-100, 103-4, 106-8

"The Stalled Ox" (Saki) **12**:296

"The Stalls of Barchester Cathedral" (James) **16**:228-30, 232, 237, 245, 253, 256-57

"The Stammerer" (Moravia) **26**:160

"The Stamp" (Davie) **52**:6

"Stamp Collection" (Čapek)
    See "Sbírka známek"

"The Stampeding of Lady Bastable" (Saki) **12**:313, 324

"The Standard of Living" (Parker) **2**:278, 281, 283

"Den standhaftige Tinsoldat" (Andersen) **6**:7, 16, 18-19, 36, 40-1; **56**:31, 36-7, 46

"The Standstill of Time" (Čapek) **36**:82

"Stanley" (Grau) **15**:148, 152, 160-61

"The Stanton Coachman" (Dunbar) **8**:122

"Stantsionnyi smotritel" (Pushkin) **27**:129, 141-45, 149, 163, 166, 168-71, 175, 182, 186-87; **55**:308

"Stantsye Baranovitsh" (Aleichem) **33**:25-6, 29, 61-5, 82-3

"The Star" (Clarke) **3**:125-27, 130, 136-38, 141-42

"The Star" (Wells) **6**:360-61, 365, 367, 382, 385-89, 393, 403, 406

"The Star in the Valley" (Murfree) **22**:188, 203, 206-08, 218

"The Star That Bids the Shepherd Fold" (O'Connor) **5**:383

"A Star Trap" (Stoker) **62**:242, 252-53

"The Star-Child" (Wilde) **11**:364, 374, 376, 384, 386, 394-95, 408

"The Stare" (Updike) **13**:375

"Stariki" (Kazakov) **43**:551, 53, 58, 67

"Starley" (Beattie) **11**:15, 17

"The Starlight Express" (Gilchrist) **14**:161-62

"Staroe vedro" (Solzhenitsyn) **32**:352

"Starosvetskie Pomeščiki" (Gogol) **4**:86, 119-20; **29**:124, 126, 132, 149, 152; **52**:107, 110, 135-36, 138-39, 151

"Starry Rash" (Bulgakov) **18**:86, 89

"The Stars Below" (Le Guin) **12**:223

"The Star's Great Night" (Verga)
    See "La Serata della Diva"

Starswarm (Aldiss) **36**:6, 18

"A Start in Life" (Dreiser) **30**:156-57, 159

"A Start in Life" (Suckow) **18**:389-91, 396, 398, 410, 418-19, 421

"Starting Again on Sherbrooke Street" (Hood) **42**:221

"Starting the Day" (Solzhenitsyn)
    See "Pristupaia ko dniu"

"Starukha Izergil" (Gorky) **28**:136, 144, 148, 152-54, 178, 183, 186-88

"The Starveling" (Colette) **10**:281

"Starye portrety" (Turgenev) **7**:327, 362-63

"Staryj genij" (Leskov) **34**:108

"State Champions" (Mason) **4**:26

"The State of Grace" (Aymé) **41**:3

The State of Ireland: A Novella and Seventeen Stories (Kiely) **58**:156-59, 163, 167-69

"State of Mind" (Aiken) **9**:5, 13-14, 19

"The Statement of Randolph Carter" (Lovecraft) **3**:258-60, 262, 282; **52**:264, 276, 286-87, 341

"The Station" (Bates) **10**:132

"The Station at Baranovitch" (Aleichem)
    See "Stantsye Baranovitsh"

"The Stationmaster" (Pushkin)
    See "Stantsionnyi smotritel"

"The Station-Master's Cradle" (Bulgakov) **18**:89-90

The Stations of the Body (Lispector)
    See *A via crucis do corpo*

"A Statue of Aphrodite" (Gilchrist) **63**:5-6, 16, 18

"The Statue of Liberty" (Wideman) **62**:258, 269

"Staze" (Andrić) **36**:50

"The Steadfast Tin Soldier" (Andersen)
    See "Den standhaftige Tinsoldat"

"Steady Hands at Seattle General" (Johnson) **56**:234, 237, 264

"Stealthily" (Svevo)
    See "Proditoriamente"

"The Steam Excursion" (Dickens) **17**:116-17

"Steam Tugs and Gray Tape" (Sansom) **21**:81, 99

"The Steel Cat" (Collier) **19**:110, 114

"Steel Throat" (Bulgakov) **18**:86, 88

"Steelman's Pupil" (Lawson) **18**:249

"The Steep Road" (Hesse) **49**:256

"Stefano Giogli, One and Two" (Pirandello) **22**:254

"Das Steinerne Herz" (Hoffmann) **13**:187

"Stella" (Nin) **10**:317, 320

"Stellavista" (Ballard)
    See "The Thousand Dreams of Stellavista"

"Step" (Chekhov) **2**:129-30, 143, 146, 151, 156; **28**:58; **51**:30, 39, 83, 85, 112, 124, 135, 150, 154, 177, 179-80, 196, 198

"Stepnoj korol' Lir" (Turgenev)
    See "Son"

"Stepnoy Korol 'Lir" (Turgenev) **7**:318-23, 336, 338, 358, 360-61

"The Steppe" (Chekhov)
    See "Step"

"Sterben" (Schnitzler) **15**:371

"The Sterile Millennia" (Aldiss) **36**:19

"Sterling Silver" (O'Hara) **15**:280

"The Steward" (Turgenev) **7**:313, 342

"Stickman's Laughter" (Algren) **33**:88, 106

"Sticks and Stones" (Michaels) **16**:302-03, 311-12, 321

"Stigmata" (Oates) **6**:224, 226

"Still" (Beckett) **16**:123, 126-27

"Still Life" (Malamud) **15**:171, 174-75, 182-84, 192-94, 222

"Still Life" (Updike) **13**:392

"Still Life with Watermelon" (Mason) **4**:27

"A Still Moment" (Welty) **1**:467-69, 482; **27**:340; **51**:256, 263-64, 277

"Still of Some Use" (Updike) **13**:403, 409

"The Still Small Voices" (Fante) **65**:94

Ein Stiller Musikant (Storm) **27**:283

"Stillness" (Gardner) **7**:223, 226, 235, 237, 240

"Stimmungen der See" (Lenz) **33**:316-19, 331

"Stinkpot" (Verga) **21**:298-99

"Stirling's Folly" (Auchincloss) **22**:49

"Stoat" (McGahern) **17**:299, 309

"The Stocking" (Campbell) **19**:74, 83, 91

"A Stoic" (Galsworthy) **22**:61, 69, 74, 76, 82, 94, 96, 99-100, 102

"The Stoker" (Kafka)
    See "Der Heizer"

"The Stolen Bacillus" (Wells) **6**:360, 374-75, 381-83, 395-99, 403

The Stolen Bacillus and Other Incidents (Wells) **6**:364-66, 380, 388, 403

"The Stolen Body" (Wells) **6**:381, 404

"The Stolen Bride" (Onetti)
    See "La novia robada"

"The Stolen Cactus" (Čapek)
    See "Ukradený kaktus"

"The Stolen Murder" (Čapek)
    See "UkradenaÁ vražda"

"The Stolen Papers 139/VII Dep. C." (Čapek)
    See "Ukradený spis 139/VII odd. C."

"Stolen Pleasures" (Berriault) **30**:104

"Stolen Pleasures" (Jewett) **6**:156-58

"The Stone" (O'Flaherty) **6**:281

"The Stone Boy" (Berriault) **30**:95-8

"Stone from Heaven" (P'u Sung-ling)
    See "Shih Ch'ing-hsü"

"The Stone on the Island" (Campbell) **19**:62, 72

"Stones in My Passway, Hellhound on My Trail" (Boyle) **16**:144

Stones of Many Colors (Stifter)
    See *Bunte Steine*

"Stoney Batter" (O'Flaherty) **6**:280-81

The Stony World (Borowski) **48**:3

"Stop" (Dixon) **16**:207

"Stop Staring at My Tits, Mister" (Bukowski) **45**:53

"Stopal'scik" (Leskov) **34**:108

"A Stop-Over at Tyre" (Garland) **18**:148, 154-55, 161, 163, 166

"Stoppenaalen" (Andersen) **56**:30

Storie naturali (Levi) **12**:274-76, 278-79

"Stories" (Peretz) **26**:193, 213

Stories (Andersen)
    See *Eventyr, fortalte for børn*

Stories (Bowen) **3**:39; **28**:10

Stories (Bulgakov) **18**:89, 91

Stories (Jolley) **19**:233, 243, 245-46

Stories (Pavese) **19**:386, 388

Stories about Lenin (Zoshchenko)
    See *Tales of Lenin*

Stories and Poems (Harte) **59**:291

Stories and Prose Poems: by Aleksandr Solzhenitsyn (Solzhenitsyn) **32**:394, 398

Stories and Sketches (Gissing) **37**:79-80

Stories and Tales (Turgenev) **57**:287

Stories by Erskine Caldwell (Caldwell) **19**:35

Stories for a Year (Pirandello)
    See *Novelle per un anno*

Stories for Every Day in the Year (Pirandello)
    See *Novelle per un anno*

Stories for Jewish Children (Aleichem)
    See *Mayses far yidishe kinder*

Stories from One Pocket (Čapek)
    See *Tales from Two Pockets*

Stories from the Other Pocket (Čapek)
    See *Tales from Two Pockets*

"Stories I Tell Myself" (Cortázar) **7**:69

The Stories of Bernard Malamud (Malamud) **15**:216, 218

The Stories of Breece D'J Pancake (Pancake) **61**:246-49, 251, 255, 273, 276, 280, 282-84

"Stories of Death and Society" (Auchincloss) **22**:51

The Stories of Elizabeth Spencer (Spencer) **57**:198, 208-12, 215, 219-20, 223, 238, 240-42

The Stories of Eva Luna (Allende)
    See *Cuentos de Eva Luna*

The Stories of F. Scott Fitzgerald (Fitzgerald) **6**:60

Stories of Five Decades (Hesse) **9**:232-33, 235-36

The Stories of Frank O'Connor (O'Connor) **5**:365

The Stories of Heinrich Böll (Boell) **23**:33, 35

The Stories of Henry Lawson (Lawson) **18**:206

The Stories of John Cheever (Cheever) **1**:105-06, 108-09; **38**:49, 52, 63, 83

The Stories of John Edgar Wideman (Wideman) **62**:273-75, 277, 282, 285

The Stories of Liam O'Flaherty (O'Flaherty) **6**:260, 265

"Stories of Lough Guir" (Le Fanu) **14**:223

The Stories of Muriel Spark (Spark) **10**:365-66, 368, 370-71

The Stories of Ray Bradbury (Bradbury) **29**:62-5

The Stories of Seán O'Faoláin (O'Faolain)
    See *Finest Short Stories of Seán O'Faoláin*

Stories of Sinebriukhov (Zoshchenko)
    See *The Tales by Nazar Ilyich Sinebriukhov*

Stories of Three Decades (Mann) **5**:308-09, 311

The Stories of Tobias Wolff (Wolff) **63**:321, 338, 341-42

The Stories of William Sansom (Sansom) **21**:92, 96, 112, 114, 118

Stories Told for Children (Andersen)
    See *Eventyr, fortalte for børn*

"The Storm" (Bowen) **3**:38-9

"The Storm" (Chopin) **8**:80, 84, 86, 91, 95

"Storm" (O'Brien) **10**:345-46

"The Storm" (Stuart) **31**:233, 263

"Storm Bird, Storm Dreamer" (Ballard) **53**:11, 61

"Storm Child" (Garland) **18**:147

"Storm in a Teacup" (Lu Hsun)
    See "Feng-po"

"A Storm in the Mountains" (Solzhenitsyn)
    See "Groza v gorakh"

"The Storm King" (Vinge) **24**:337, 344

"The Storm Ship" (Irving) **2**:254

"A Story" (Andrić)
    See "Priča"

"The Story" (Andrić)
    See "Priča"

The Story (Pasternak)
    See *Povest*

"A Story about Money" (Farrell) **28**:125

"The Story about the Anteater" (Benét) **10**:149

"A Story about the Little Rabbits" (Harris) **19**:170, 186, 195

Story Book (Hesse) **9**:230-31

"A Story by Angela Poe" (Benét) **10**:142, 144

Story Collection (Tagore)
    See *Galpa Guccha*

"The Story fo the Beetle Hunter" (Doyle) **12**:64

"Story from Bear Country" (Silko) **37**:310, 314

"A Story from the Dunes" (Andersen) **6**:18-9, 34

"The Story Hearer" (Paley) **8**:420

"Story in Harlem Slang" (Hurston) **4**:139

"The Story Not Shown" (Moorhouse) **40**:325

"The Story of a Blind Man" (Tanizaki)
    See "Mōmoku monogatari"

"The Story of a Conscience" (Bierce) **9**:64, 67

"The Story of a Disappearance and an Appearance" (James) **16**:230, 232, 237, 245

"The Story of a Horse" (Babel) **16**:25, 28, 50-3

"The Story of a Horse, Continued" (Babel) **16**:27

"The Story of a Lie" (Stevenson) **11**:269, 281; **51**:248

"The Story of a Little Chinese Seabird" (Far) **62**:50, 54-55

"The Story of a Mine" (Harte) **8**:216

"The Story of a Mother" (Andersen)
See "Hisbrien om en Moder"

"The Story of a Mouse" (Babel)
See "Istoriia moei golubiatni"

"The Story of a Non-Marrying Man" (Lessing) **6**:188, 211

"The Story of a Panic" (Forster) **27**:72-5, 81, 85-7, 97-8, 102-03, 111-13, 115, 119, 121-23

"Story of a Patron" (Warner) **23**:369-70

"The Story of an Hour" (Chopin) **8**:72-3, 79-80, 84, 87, 99, 102, 108

"A Story of Beer" (Bulgakov) **18**:90

"The Story of Bras-Coupé" (Cable) **4**:61

"The Story of Counter-Octave" (Pasternak) **31**:108-10, 115

"The Story of Father Alexis" (Turgenev)
See "Rasskaz ottsa Aleksaya"

"A Story of Historical Interest" (Wilson) **21**:329, 331, 333, 336, 342, 351

"The Story of Howling Wolf" (Garland) **18**:147, 167, 179-80, 188

"The Story of Iso" (Far) **62**:11

"The Story of Jees Uck" (London) **4**:271; **49**:316

"The Story of Keesh" (London) **4**:253

"The Story of Lahcen and Idir" (Bowles) **3**:80

"The Story of Lieutenant Ergunov" (Turgenev)
See "Istoriya leytenanta Ergunova"

"The Story of Mahlon" (Caldwell) **19**:41

"The Story of María Griselda" (Bombal)
See "La historia de María Griseld"

"The Story of Mr. Rabbit and Mr. Fox" (Harris) **19**:185

"The Story of Mrs. N.N." (Chekhov) **51**:84

"The Story of Muhammad Din" (Kipling) **5**:296; **54**:73

"The Story of My Dovecot" (Babel)
See "Istoriia moei golubiatni"

"The Story of Nature" (Moorhouse) **40**:302, 322

"The Story of One White Woman Who Married a Chinese" (Far) **62**:4, 50, 61-62, 75, 77, 100-101, 109, 111

"Story of Saint Joseph's Ass" (Verga) **21**:293, 298-99

"The Story of St. Vespaluus" (Saki) **12**:306

"A Story of Stories" (Dreiser) **30**:107, 122, 155, 157

"The Story of Teenchy-Tiny Duck" (Harris) **19**:196

"The Story of the Brazilian Cat" (Doyle) **12**:64

"A Story of the Days to Come" (Wells) **6**:389, 390, 403-04, 406-08

"The Story of the Deluge, and How It Came About" (Harris) **19**:195

"The Story of the Gadsbys" (Kipling) **54**:87-88
The Story of the Gadsbys (Kipling) **5**:260, 264-65, 274; **54**:87

"A Story of the Head Gardener" (Chekhov) **28**:60

"The Story of the Japanned Box" (Doyle) **12**:64

"The Story of the Knife" (Moorhouse) **40**:309

"The Story of the Late Mr. Elvesham" (Wells) **6**:361, 363, 366, 383, 388, 405

"The Story of the Nice Old Man" (Svevo)
See "La novella del buon vecchio e della bella fanciulla"

"The Story of the Oracle" (Lawson) **18**:250

"The Story of the Siren" (Forster) **27**:67, 69-71, 73-5, 83-5, 87, 99-100, 102-03, 112, 114
The Story of the Siren (Forster) **27**:75, 83-85, 87, 99-100, 102-03, 112, 114

"A Story of the Stone Age" (Wells) **6**:389-90, 403-04

"Story of the Vizier's Elephant" (Andrić)
See "Priča o vezirovom slonu"

"A Story of the War" (Harris) **19**:121, 179

"Story of the Warrior and the Captive" (Borges)
See "Historia del guerrero y de la cautiva"

"The Story of the Year" (Andersen) **6**:30

"The Story of the Young Italian" (Irving) **2**:260-61, 268

"Story of the Young Man with the Cream Tarts" (Stevenson) **11**:265

"The Story of the Young Robber" (Irving) **2**:255, 257, 262

"The Story of Tin-A" (Far) **62**:39-41, 55

"A Story of Tomoda and Matsunaga" (Tanizaki)
See "Tomoda to Matsunaga no hanashi"

"The Story of Two Dogs" (Lessing) **6**:198, 200, 203-04, 206, 208; **61**:131

"A Story of Yesterday" (Tolstoy) **9**:374

"A Story with a Pattern" (Lavin) **4**:163, 167-69, 184-85

"Story with Spiders" (Cortázar) **7**:69

"A Story without a Title" (Chekhov)
See "An Anonymous Story"

"Story without Words" (Čapek) **36**:121-22, 125

"The Story-Teller" (Saki) **12**:289, 291, 293, 295, 302

"Storyteller" (Silko) **37**:289, 295, 307, 315
Storyteller (Silko) **37**:287-90, 292-96, 298-99, 301, 303-12, 314-15

"Storyteller's Escape" (Silko) **37**:296

A Story-Teller's Holiday (Moore) **19**:293-96, 298-300, 305-09, 311-12, 345-46

"Storytellers, Liars, and Bores" (Michaels) **16**:306, 309, 311

"Storytelling" (Silko) **37**:289, 308

"The Stout Gentleman" (Irving) **2**:250-51, 254, 259; **37**:274

La strada che va in città (Ginzburg) **65**:116, 124, 132, 136, 138

"La strada di San Giovanni" (Calvino) **3**:97; **48**:37

"Straight Pool" (O'Hara) **15**:248, 264

"Strandhill, the Sea" (McGahern) **17**:302, 308, 318, 320

"The Strange Aberration of Mr. Ken Smythe" (Metcalf) **43**:74, 85-6, 91, 111, 162, 164

The Strange Case of Dr. Jekyll and Mr. Hyde (Stevenson) **11**:262, 264, 276, 279, 290-92, 301-02; **51**:230, 232, 236, 239, 242, 245-46, 248

"The Strange Case of John Boulnois" (Chesterton) **46**:152

"The Strange Child" (Kuhatschek)
See "Das Fremde Kind"

"Strange Comfort Afforded by the Profession" (Lowry) **31**:44-5, 47-8, 51-2, 54, 59-61, 64-5, 71, 73-4, 82, 84, 86

"The Strange Crime of John Boulais" (Chesterton) **1**:138; **46**:113

"A Strange Death" (Moore) **19**:342

"The Strange Design of Master Rignolo" (Ligotti) **16**:271, 277, 292, 296

"The Strange Disease" (O'Flaherty) **6**:262

"Strange Disturbances on Aungier Street" (Le Fanu)
See "Some Strange Disturbances in an Old House on Augier Street"

"A Strange Event in the Life of Schalken the Painter" (Le Fanu) **14**:220-21, 224-25, 232-36, 238-39, 252

"The Strange Experiences of Mr. Janík" (Čapek)
See "Případy pana Janíka"

"The Strange Girls" (Walser) **20**:355-56

"The Strange High House in the Mist" (Lovecraft) **3**:262, 277; **52**:270, 360

"Strange Island" (Akutagawa Ryūnosuke) **44**:52, 64

"A Strange Island" (Alcott) **27**:42

"Strange Meeting" (Sansom) **21**:127

"Strange Moonlight" (Aiken) **9**:4, 7-8, 13-14, 32-3, 35, 38, 40

"Strange News from Another Star" (Hesse) **9**:235

Strange News from Another Star, and Other Tales (Hesse) **9**:234-35, 244

"The Strange Ride of Morrowbie Jukes" (Kipling) **5**:262, 265, 273, 278, 299

"Strange Stories by a Nervous Gentleman" (Irving) **2**:251, 261

Strange Stories from a Chinese Studio (P'u Sung-ling)
See *Liao-chai chih-i*

Strange stories from the Refuge of My Study (P'u Sung-ling)
See *Liao-chai chih-i*

"A Strange Story" (Turgenev)
See "Strannaya istoriya"

"The Strange Story of the Three Golden Fishes: A Comedy of a Man Who Always Was Lucky—Especially in Marriage" (Moore) **19**:346

The Strange Tales of Liao-chai (P'u Sung-ling)
See *Liao-chai chih-i*

"A Strange Thing" (Galsworthy) **22**:63, 74, 79, 101

"A Strange Thing" (Machado de Assis)
See "Singular ocorrência"

Strange Things Happen Here (Valenzuela) **14**:366-67, 369-70

Strange True Stories of Louisiana (Cable) **4**:49, 51, 53, 58-62, 75

"The Stranger" (Baudelaire)
See "L'etranger"

"A Stranger" (de la Mare) **14**:80

"The Stranger" (Mansfield) **9**:280, 282-83

"The Stranger" (Schnitzler) **15**:342

"Stranger at the Table" (Apple) **50**:23, 38, 45

"Stranger, Bear Words to the Spartans We..." (Boell)
See "Wanderer, kommst du nach Spa..."

"A Stranger with a Bag" (Warner) **23**:374

A Stranger with a Bag, and Other Stories (Warner) **23**:380

"Strangers and Pilgrims" (de la Mare) **14**:80, 83, 86, 92

"Strangers in the Night" (Phillips) **16**:325

"The Stranger's Pew" (Page) **23**:308, 312

"The Strangest Thing" (Norris) **28**:213

"Strannaya istoriya" (Turgenev) **7**:315, 321, 324, 337, 358-59; **57**:306, 311, 313, 380

"Strašnaja mest'" (Gogol) **4**:103-04, 118-19; **29**:132, 149; **52**:144

"Die Strasse" (Walser) **20**:341

"The Strategy of the Were-Wolf Dog" (Cather) **2**:100; **50**:78, 93-4, 184

"Stratford-on-Avon" (Irving) **2**:245

"Strath" (Chekhov) **51**:189

"The Strawberry Season" (Caldwell) **19**:37

"Strawberry Spring" (King) **17**:265

"Strays" (Dybek) **55**:130, 132

"The Stream" (O'Flaherty) **6**:265, 277-78

"The Street" (Lovecraft) **3**:292

"The Street" (Morrison) **40**:348

"A Street" (Morrison) **40**:330, 335, 352, 354-55, 365-67, 370

"The Street" (Walser)
See "Die Strasse"

"Streetcorner Man" (Borges)
See "El Hombre de la esquina rosada"

"Streets" (Dixon) **16**:205

"The Streets—Morning" (Dickens) **17**:116, 134

"The Strength of Gideon" (Dunbar) **8**:128, 136, 141, 144

The Strength of Gideon and Other Stories (Dunbar) **8**:120-21, 124-25, 127, 131, 144-45

"The Strength of God" (Anderson) **1**:18

"The Strength of the Strong" (London) **4**:255

The Strength of the Strong (London) **4**:254-55, 283

Strictly Business (Henry) **5**:171

"Strictly from Hunger" (Perelman) **32**:211, 237
Strictly from Hunger (Perelman) **32**:205, 219
Strider (Tolstoy) **9**:393
"Strike" (Selby) **20**:253, 255, 258, 260, 262, 264-65, 267-69, 271-73, 279, 281
"The String Quartet" (Woolf) **7**:368-69, 374-75, 390, 392, 399
"Strir Patra" (Tagore) **48**:317, 320-21
"The Stroke" (Davie) **52**:8, 10-11
"The Stroke of Apelles" (Pasternak)
    See "Il tratto di Apelle"
"A Stroke of Good Fortune" (O'Connor) **23**:237
"Stroke of Lightning" (Galsworthy) **22**:75, 101
"The Stroll" (Andrić)
    See "Šetnja"
"Strong as Death is Love" (Singer) **3**:386
Strong Hearts (Cable) **4**:50, 62, 75
"Strong Horse Tea" (Walker) **5**:401, 403
"The Struggle" (O'Flaherty) **6**:264, 269
"A Struggle" (Svevo)
    See "Una lotta"
Struggling Spirit (Lagerkvist)
    See *Kämpande ande*
"The Stub Book" (Alarcon)
    See "El libro talonario"
"Stubborn in Poverty" (Dazai Osamu) **41**:226-28, 232
"The Stucco House" (Gilchrist) **63**:6
"Stučit!" (Turgenev)
    See "Stuk...stuk...stuk"
"Stud City" (King) **17**:272, 278-79, 285, 289-90
"The Student" (Chekhov) **2**:158; **51**:58, 60, 70, 150-51, 198-99
"The Student of Salamanca" (Irving) **2**:251, 254, 259
"The Student's Wife" (Carver) **8**:11, 46, 50-1, 53; **51**:13
Studien (Stifter) **28**:272, 286, 290-92, 298, 300-01
Studies (Stifter)
    See *Studien*
"Studies in Extravagance" (Galsworthy) **22**:60
"Studies in Horror" (Ligotti) **16**:287
"Studio 5, The Stars" (Ballard) **53**:7, 49, 72-3, 80, 127, 131
"Studs" (Farrell) **28**:90, 97, 122
"The Study of History" (O'Connor) **5**:376
"Stuk...stuk...stuk" (Turgenev) **7**:319, 321, 324-25, 338, 358-59; **57**:311, 313-14, 363-64, 367, 369-71
Eine Stunde hinter Mitternacht (Hesse) **9**:229-31
"The Stylish Child" (Dazai Osamu) **41**:255
"The Sub" (Dixon) **16**:207
"Subcommittee" (Henderson) **29**:321, 323-25
"A Subject of Childhood" (Paley) **8**:396, 398, 407
"Sublimating" (Updike) **13**:387
"The Subliminal Man" (Ballard) **1**:68-9, 77-8; **53**:9, 29, 50, 109-10
"Subpoena" (Barthelme) **2**:37, 39; **55**:32, 84, 111
"The Substitute" (Pardo Bazán) **30**:290
"A Suburban Fairy Tale" (Mansfield) **9**:311
Suburban Sketches (Howells) **36**:399-400
Success Stories (Banks) **42**:58-9
"Success Story" (Farrell) **28**:110
"The Successor" (Bowles) **3**:64-5, 80, 83
"Such Darling Dodos" (Wilson) **21**:324, 337, 345, 355, 357
Such Darling Dodos (Wilson) **21**:320, 328-29, 331, 336, 338, 345-46, 348-49, 354-55, 357-58, 364-65
"Such Is Life" (Pirandello) **22**:242-43
"Such Perfection" (Narayan) **25**:135, 138, 140, 156
"Sucker" (McCullers) **9**:332, 341-42, 344-45, 354-55
"Le Sud" (Borges) **4**:31; **41**:43-44, 46-47, 55, 58, 160
"The Sudden Afternoon" (Ballard) **53**:9

"A Sudden Trip Home in the Spring" (Walker) **5**:414
"Sudha Mahamaya" (Tagore) **48**:327, 338
"Le Sue giornate" (Moravia) **26**:174, 178
"Un sueño realizado" (Onetti) **23**:246, 249, 252, 279-80
Un sueño realizado y otros cuentos (Onetti) **23**:245-46, 251, 258
"La suerte de Teodoro Méndez Acubal" (Castellanos) **39**:48, 57
"Suffer the Little Children" (King) **17**:295
The Sugar Crock (Gass) **12**:148
"Sugar for the Horse" (Bates) **10**:117, 131
Sugar for the Horse (Bates) **10**:131
"The Sugawn Chair" (O'Faolain) **13**:314, 320
"Suicide Club" (Doyle) **12**:58
"The Suicide Club" (Stevenson) **51**:219, 246
The Suicide Club (Stevenson) **11**:280; **51**:248
"Suicides" (Gilchrist) **14**:150-51; **63**:20
"Suicides" (Pavese) **19**:374-75, 377-78, 387
"Suisen" (Dazai Osamu) **41**:254
"Suishō Gensō" (Kawabata) **17**:242
"The Suitcase" (Ozick) **15**:298-300, 311, 314-15, 319, 328-35; **60**:308, 313
"Suites and Single Rooms, with Bath" (Hood) **42**:237
Sukhodol (Bunin) **5**:81-3, 87, 90, 100-01
"Sul far del giorno" (Calvino) **48**:60
"Sulfur" (Levi) **12**:264, 268
"Sullivan's Trousers" (O'Faolain) **13**:309, 316
"Summer" (Boyle) **5**:54
"Summer" (Cortázar)
    See "Verano"
"Summer" (Frame) **29**:106
"Summer, an Elegy" (Gilchrist) **63**:2, 10, 24
"The Summer Before" (Steinbeck) **11**:253-54
"A Summer Day" (Stafford) **26**:275-76, 281, 289, 308
"Summer Dust" (Gordon) **15**:116, 119, 123, 126, 137, 139
"The Summer Farmer" (Cheever) **1**:99, 106; **38**:53, 66
"A Summer Holiday in the South" (Andrić) **36**:46
"A Summer in Maine" (Gilchrist) **14**:163-64
Summer in Maine (Gilchrist) **63**:21
"A Summer in Rouen" (Endō) **48**:204, 207-8
"A Summer in the South" (Andrić)
    See "A Summer Holiday in the South"
"Summer Morning in Dublin" (Farrell) **28**:126
"Summer Night" (Bowen) **3**:39, 41, 46, 51
"The Summer Night" (Bradbury) **29**:60; **53**:202-3, 205, 249-50, 253
"The Summer of the Beautiful White Horse" (Saroyan) **21**:169-71
"Summer People" (Beattie) **11**:25-6, 29
"The Summer People" (Jackson) **9**:258
"Summer Remembered" (Cheever) **38**:43
"Summer Shore" (Grau) **15**:161, 163-64
"Summer Storm" (Pavese) **19**:364, 373
Summer Storm, and Other Stories (Pavese) **19**:363
"Summer Swimmingpool" (Pavese) **19**:375
"Summer Theatre" (Cheever) **1**:99; **38**:63-6
"Summer Thunder" (Ross) **24**:302
"Summer Tryout" (Farrell) **28**:99, 122
"The Summer-House" (Trevor) **58**:210
"Summer's Day" (O'Hara) **15**:248-49, 252-53, 258, 270
"A Summer's Reading" (Malamud) **15**:168, 221
Summertime and Other Stories (Donoso)
    See *Veraneo y otros cuentos*
"Summertime on Icarus" (Clarke) **3**:130, 138, 147
"Summertime Was Nearly Over" (Aldiss) **36**:28
"The Summing Up" (Woolf) **7**:376, 381, 390, 392, 411
"The Sun" (Andrić)
    See "Sunce"
"Sun" (Lawrence) **4**:238, 240-42
"Sun and Moon" (Mansfield) **9**:282
"Sun and Shadow" (Tagore) **48**:331-33

"The Sun between Their Feet" (Lessing) **6**:198-99, 203, 212
"Sun Cured" (Lardner) **32**:117, 136-38, 140, 149
The Sun Dog (King) **17**:282, 284; **55**:259
"The Sun Rises Twice" (Bates) **10**:113
"Sunce" (Andrić) **36**:50
"Sunday" (Shiga) **23**:348
"Sunday Afternoon" (Bowen) **3**:41, 53
"Sunday Afternoon" (Gallant) **5**:141
"Sunday Afternoon" (Munro) **3**:343
"Sunday Afternoon Hanging" (Stuart) **31**:236, 262-63
"Sunday at Home" (Hawthorne) **3**:189; **39**:120, 122
"Sunday Brings Sunday" (Lavin) **4**:176
"Sunday Evening" (Bowen) **3**:53
"Sunday Evening" (Farrell) **28**:112
"Sunday Morning" (O'Hara) **15**:282, 289
"Sunday Morning, June 4, 1989" (Thomas) **20**:324-25, 328
"A Sunday Out of Town" (Dickens) **17**:120-21
"Sunday Teasing" (Updike) **13**:355
"Sunday under Three Heads" (Dickens) **17**:124
"The Sun-Dodgers" (O'Hara) **15**:282
"The Sun-Dog Trail" (London) **4**:253, 290
"Sunjammer" (Clarke) **3**:132
"Sunlight/Twilight" (Oates) **6**:236-37
"A Sunny Place" (Kawabata) **17**:252
"The Sunrise" (Atwood) **2**:17-18, 21-2; **46**:38, 43, 45-6, 49-50
"A Sunrise on the Veld" (Lessing) **6**:186
"Sunset" (Faulkner) **1**:177
Sunset (Babel)
    See *Zakat*
"Sunset Limited" (Harrison) **19**:211-14
"Sunshine and Shadow" (Beattie) **11**:10
"The Sunshine Club" (Campbell) **19**:82
Sunshine Sketches of a Little Town (Leacock) **39**:241, 242, 243, 245, 246, 247, 249, 250, 251, 252, 253, 254, 255, 256, 257, 258, 259, 260, 261, 269, 273, 274, 275
"Sunstroke" (Bunin)
    See "Solnechnyy udar"
A Sunstroke (Bunin) **5**:90
"Suora Scolastica" (Stendhal) **27**:249, 251, 263
"The Superintendent" (Cheever) **1**:99, 107; **38**:53
"Superiority" (Clarke) **3**:126, 150
The Supermale (Jarry)
    See *Le surmâle, roman moderne*
"Superman, My Son" (Jones) **56**:286-87
Supernatural Tales: Excursions into Fantasy (Lee) **33**:310
"The Supersonic Coward" (Wilding) **50**:346
"The Superstitious Man's Story" (Hardy) **2**:217
"Super-Toys Last All Summer Long" (Aldiss) **36**:20
"The Supper at Elsinore" (Dinesen) **7**:168, 177, 186, 190, 203-04
"A Supper by Proxy" (Dunbar) **8**:122, 135, 139
"Suppose a Wedding" (Malamud) **15**:173-75
"The Supreme Night" (Tagore) **48**:303
"Supruga" (Chekhov) **51**:172-74, 194
"El Sur" (Borges) **41**:41, 152
"Sur Catherine de Médicis" (Balzac) **59**:11-14
"Sur l'eau" (Maupassant) **64**:316
Sur l'eau (Maupassant) **1**:261-62, 265, 278
"Surfiction" (Wideman) **62**:268, 274, 278, 296-302
"The Surgeon's Daughter" (Scott) **32**:287, 299, 319
"Surgery" (Chekhov) **2**:130
Le surmâle, roman moderne (Jarry) **20**:44, 50-2, 54, 59, 62, 67, 70-2, 76
"A Surplus Woman" (Gilman) **13**:143
"'Surprise, Surprise!' from Matron" (Jolley) **19**:234, 245
"The Surveyor and Julka" (Andrić)
    See "Geometar i Julka"
"The Survival of Childhood" (Oates) **6**:224

"The Survival of the Fittest" (Thomas) **20**:324-25, 327

Survival Techniques (Calisher) **15**:21, 23

"The Survivor" (Bambara) **35**:17

"Survivor Type" (King) **17**:274-75; **55**:250

"Susan and the Doctor" (Suckow) **18**:393-94, 409, 416-17

"Susano-ono-mikoto" (Akutagawa Ryūnosuke) **44**:62

"Susedi" (Andrić) **36**:47

"Susy" (Harte) **8**:222, 251-52; **59**:307

"Suterareru made" (Tanizaki) **21**:195

"Suttee" (Auchincloss) **22**:14

"Suzette" (Chopin) **8**:100

"Svajatye gory" (Bunin) **5**:98

"Svidanie" (Turgenev) **57**:352-54, 356

"Svinedrengen" (Andersen) **6**:7, 18, 24, 26, 30-1, 34; **56**:31-3

"Svirel'" (Chekhov) **28**:58, 60-1

"Swaddling Clothes" (Mishima) **4**:313, 317, 322-23

"Swallows" (McGahern) **17**:299, 304, 308

"Swamp Boy" (Bass) **60**:16, 19, 38

"Swans" (Bass) **60**:41-42

"Swans" (Frame) **29**:100, 106, 108-09

"The Swan's Nest" (Andersen) **6**:4

"Swans on an Autumn River" (Warner) **23**:374

"The Swastika on Our Door" (Adams) **24**:2-3, 6

"The Sway-Backed House" (Chesnutt) **7**:33; **54**:48

"Sweat" (Hurston) **4**:136-38, 151, 155

"Sweet and Hot" (Perelman) **32**:204

"A Sweet Colleen" (O'Faolain) **13**:305

Sweet Diamond Dust and Other Stories (Ferré) **36**:146-47, 149-50

"Sweet Ermendarde" (Lovecraft) **52**:293

"Sweet Ladies, Good Night, Good Night" (Bradfield) **65**:62, 68

"The Sweet Sad Queen of the Grazing Isles" (Pohl) **25**:236

"The Sweet Singer of Omsk" (Saroyan) **21**:160

"Sweet Town" (Bambara) **35**:4, 6, 22, 32

"The Sweethearts" (Andersen) **6**:28, 30, 36

"Sweethearts" (Ford) **56**:144, 149, 152, 159, 170, 174, 194-95

"Sweethearts" (Phillips) **16**:326, 328

Sweethearts (Phillips) **16**:332

"The Sweetness of Twisted Apples" (Stegner) **27**:195, 197, 201, 204, 220

"Sweets for Angels" (Narayan) **25**:135, 141, 156

"A Swell-Looking Girl" (Caldwell) **19**:25, 46

"Swept and Garnished" (Kipling) **5**:275, 282

"The Swiftest Runners" (Andersen) **6**:10

"The Swimmer" (Cheever) **1**:94, 100, 102, 106, 108; **38**:44, 47-8, 51, 54, 57-61, 63-6, 72, 74, 76; **57**:3-34

"The Swineherd" (Andersen)
See "Svinedrengen"

"The Swing" (Bunin)
See "Kacheli"

"Swing Out, Sweet Chariot" (Perelman) **32**:201

"Swinging the Maelstrom" (Lowry) **31**:67

The Swiss Family Perelman (Perelman) **32**:219, 224, 233

"The Switchman" (Arreola)
See "El guardagujas"

"The Sword" (Betts) **45**:2, 28

"A s'y méprendre" (Villiers de l'Isle Adam) **14**:381, 388, 391

"The Sybarites" (Wilding) **50**:347

"Sylvania is Dead" (Stuart) **31**:227, 236-38, 255

"Sylvesternacht" (Hoffmann) **13**:189

"Sylvia" (Michaels) **16**:314, 317, 320

Sylvia: A Fictional Memoir (Michaels) **16**:317-18

Sylvie: Recollections of Valois (Nerval) **18**:328, 332-35, 337, 343-46, 355, 357, 359-62, 365, 367, 369-70, 376-77, 380, 383

"The Sympathetic Visitor" (Betts) **45**:2, 4, 22, 27-8

"Sympathy" (Woolf) **7**:409

La Symphonie pastorale (Gide) **13**:43, 48-52, 62, 72, 77, 98-9

Symphonies (Gide)
See *Two Symphonies*

"A Symphony in Lavender" (Freeman) **1**:199; **47**:84, 104, 195

"A Symposium" (Kundera) **24**:88-94, 97, 99-100, 103-04, 107, 114-16, 118, 122

"Syracuse; or, The Panther Man" (Morand) **22**:169

"The System" (Čapek) **36**:88, 109

"The System of Doctor Tarr and Professor Fether" (Poe) **1**:407; **22**:307-08, 330-31, 333; **35**:350; **54**:192, 196-202

"T" (Aldiss) **36**:19

T Zero (Calvino)
See *Ti con zero*

"Taarnv[dj]gteren" (Andersen) **56**:37

"The Tabernacle" (Pirandello) **22**:254

"The Table" (Trevor) **58**:200, 202, 206, 230

"The Table, the Ass and the Stick" (Grimm and Grimm)
See "The Magic Table, the Gold Donkey, and the Club in the Sack"

"Tabloid Tragedy" (Dreiser) **30**:155-56, 159

"Tactical Exercise" (Waugh) **41**:311

Tactical Exercise (Waugh) **41**:328

"Tadeo Limardo's Victim" (Bioy Casares)
See "La victima de Tadeo Limardo"

"The Tadpole and the Frog" (Stevenson) **51**:239

"Das Tagebuch der Redegonda" (Schnitzler) **15**:346

"The Tailor in Heaven" (Grimm and Grimm) **36**:229-30

"Tailors' Dummies" (Schulz)
See "Traktat o manekinach"

"Tails" (Dixon) **16**:211

"Taily-po" (Harris) **19**:196

"Tain't So" (Hughes) **6**:121, 131

"Take a Deep Breath" (Pohl) **25**:213

"Take Pity" (Malamud) **15**:169, 175, 212, 216-17, 219, 221, 223, 243

"Takes" (Dixon) **16**:218

"The Taking of Lungtungpen" (Kipling) **5**:260, 265

"The Taking of the Redoubt" (Mérimée)
See "L'enlèvement de la rédoute"

"Taking The Blue Ribbon at the County Fair" (Murfree) **22**:184, 203, 211

"Taking the Veil" (Mansfield) **9**:282, 310; **38**:230

"Taking the Wen" (Dazai Osamu)
See "Taking the Wen Away"

"Taking the Wen Away" (Dazai Osamu) **41**:233, 235-36, 276

"Takyr" (Platonov) **42**:250, 256, 259

Un tal Lucas (Cortázar) **7**:91-4

A Tale (Pasternak)
See *Povest*

"A Tale about the Safe-Breaker and the Fire-Raiser" (Čapek)
See "Příběh o kasaři a žháři"

"Tale for the Mirror" (Calisher) **15**:3

Tale for the Mirror: A Novella and Other Stories (Calisher) **15**:3-5, 7

"The Tale of a Dwarf" (Lewis) **40**:279

"Tale of a Vampire" (Hoffmann)
See "Der Vampyrismus"

"The Tale of Astolpho on the Moon" (Calvino) **3**:101

"The Tale of Captain Kopeykin" (Gogol) **52**:106

"The Tale of How Ivan Ivanovich Quarrelled with Ivan Nikiforovich" (Gogol) **4**:82, 84, 86, 105; **29**:124-26; **52**:83, 103, 106-7, 116, 121, 136, 138, 140, 144

"A Tale of Jerusalem" (Poe) **1**:407

"A Tale of Love and Politics" (Howells) **36**:398

"Tale of Moons" (Carpentier)
See "Histoire de lunes"

"The Tale of Rabbi Gadiel, the Infant" (Agnon) **30**:66

"The Tale of the Good Old Man and the Beautiful Girl" (Svevo)
See "La novella del buon vecchio e della bella fanciulla"

"The Tale of the Ingrate and His Punishment" (Calvino) **3**:101-02

"A Tale of the Ragged Mountains" (Poe) **1**:400, 402; **54**:218-23

"The Tale of the Scribe" (Agnon)
See "The Legend of the Scribe"

"The Tale of the Squint-Eyed Left-Handed Smith from Tula and the Steel Flea" (Leskov)
See "Levša"

"The Tale of the Unextinguished Moon" (Pilnyak)
See "Povest nepogašhennoy luny"

The Tale of the Unextinguished Moon, and Other Stories (Pilnyak)
See *Povest' nepogašennoj luny*

"The Tale of the Vizier's Elephant" (Andrić)
See "Priča o vezirovom slonu"

"A Tale of the White Pyramid" (Cather) **2**:100; **50**:91, 183, 184, 186

"Tale of the Wicker Chair" (Hesse) **9**:242, 244

"The Tale of Tod Lapraik" (Stevenson) **11**:303-06

"The Tale of Two Ivans" (Gogol)
See "The Tale of How Ivan Ivanovich Quarrelled with Ivan Nikiforovich"

"A Tale of Two Liars" (Singer) **3**:375

"A Tale of Two Sisters" (Singer) **3**:377

"A Tale of Unrequited Love" (Gorky) **28**:162

"The Tale of Urashima" (Dazai Osamu) **41**:234

"A Tale Without an End" (Aleichem) **33**:68-71

"The Talent Thou Gavest" (Evans) **43**:28-9, 41

Tales and Fantasies (Stevenson) **51**:236

Tales before Midnight (Benét) **10**:154, 158-59

Tales by Belkin (Pushkin)
See *Povesti Belkina*

Tales by Edgar A. Poe (Poe) **1**:388

The Tales by Nazar Ilyich Sinebriukhov (Zoshchenko) **15**:395

"Tales for Children" (Akutagawa Ryūnosuke)
See "Dowa"

Tales for Children (Tolstoy) **9**:382; **45**:135

Tales from Bective Bridge (Lavin) **4**:170-72, 185

Tales from Olden Times (Leskov) **34**:119

Tales from One Pocket (Čapek)
See *Povídky z druhé kapsy*

Tales from the Other Pocket (Čapek)
See *Povídky z jedné kapsy*

Tales from the Plum Grove Hills (Stuart) **31**:232-34, 260, 266

Tales from the White Hart (Clarke) **3**:131, 133

Tales from Two Pockets (Čapek) **36**:84, 93, 109, 120-21, 125-26, 128, 130

Tales of a Traveller (Irving) **2**:241, 244, 246, 250-51, 254-55, 258-62, 268

Tales of All Countries (Trollope) **28**:328, 332, 340, 342, 347

Tales of All Countries: First Series (Trollope) **28**:317, 323, 326, 332, 339

Tales of All Countries: Second Series (Trollope) **28**:318, 323, 326-27, 330-32

Tales of Ghosts and Men (Wharton)
See *Tales of Men and Ghosts*

Tales of Horror and the Supernatural (Machen) **20**:163, 186, 201

Tales of H.P. Lovecraft (Lovecraft) **52**:354

The Tales of Ivan Belkin (Pushkin)
See *Povesti Belkina*

Tales of Lenin (Zoshchenko) **15**:404, 407, 409

Tales of Manhattan (Auchincloss) **22**:9-10, 12, 17, 19, 20, 29, 34, 37, 39, 46, 49-51

Tales of Mean Streets (Morrison) **40**:328-332, 334-41, 343-45, 347-48, 350-51, 354-56, 364-68, 370-71, 375-75

Tales of Men and Ghosts (Wharton) **6**:421, 435

Tales of Mystery and Romance (Moorhouse) **40**:292-93, 297, 305-07, 309, 323-24
Tales of Odessa (Babel)
  See *The Odessa Tales*
Tales of Our Country (Platonov) **42**:250
Tales of Poland (Agnon) **30**:81-2
Tales of Sevastopol (Tolstoy) **9**:380
Tales of Soldiers and Civilians (Bierce) **9**:49-50, 55, 59, 65, 75
Tales of Space and Time (Wells) **6**:366-67, 380, 389
Tales of Tenderness and Power (Head) **52**:204, 209
Tales of Terror and Mystery (Doyle) **12**:60, 64
Tales of the Cthulhu Mythos (Lovecraft) **52**:269
Tales of the Grotesque and Arabesque (Poe) **1**:389-90; **22**:329, 333-34, 349; **35**:335-36; **54**:154
Tales of the Home Folks in Peace and War (Harris) **19**:182-83
Tales of the Jazz Age (Fitzgerald) **6**:45-6, 56, 58-9, 74, 101
Tales of the Long Bow (Chesterton) **1**:133; **46**:122
"Tales of the Moon" (Peretz) **26**:205
Tales of the Wilderness (Pilnyak) **48**:215
Tales of Twilight and the Unseen (Doyle) **12**:60
"Tales of Two Old Gentlemen" (Dinesen) **7**:173
Tales of Unrest (Conrad) **9**:151-52
Tales Told for Children (Andersen)
  See *Eventyr, fortalte for bøorn*
"The Talisman" (de la Mare) **14**:83
"A Talk among Leisured People" (Tolstoy) **9**:396
"Talk by the River" (Pavese) **19**:376
"The Talkative Man" (Narayan) **25**:136
"Talkin 'Bout Sonny" (Bambara) **35**:24
"Talking Horse" (Malamud) **15**:189, 190, 198, 220, 222
"Talking Skull" (Crace) **61**:33
The Talking Trees (O'Faolain) **13**:291, 313-14
"The Tall Men" (Faulkner) **1**:151, 162
"The Tall Woman" (Alarcon)
  See "La mujer alta"
"Tally Ho Budmâsh" (Galsworthy) **22**:90
"Talpa" (Rulfo) **25**:245, 249-53, 257-58, 262, 265, 274-75
"Tamango" (Mérimée) **7**:280-1, 283, 287-9, 300
"The Tambourine Lady" (Wideman) **62**:269
"Taming a Tartar" (Alcott) **27**:29, 57-8, 61
"The Taming of the Nightmare" (Chesterton) **1**:140
"Tamurlane" (Mukherjee) **38**:252, 254, 265
Tan triste como ella (Onetti) **23**:248, 260, 264-71, 275, 280
Tanagokoro no Shōsetsu (Kawabata) **17**:242, 251-58
"Tangerine" (Bradbury) **53**:267
"The Tangerines" (Akutagawa Ryūnosuke)
  See "Mikan"
"Tanhum" (Singer) **3**:380
"Tania" (Bunin) **5**:113
"Tanil" (Coppard) **21**:3
"Tante Cat'rinette" (Chopin) **8**:94
"Ho tante cose da dirvi . . ." (Pirandello) **22**:285
"Tante Tandpine" (Andersen)
  See "Auntie Toothache"
"Tanya" (Bunin)
  See "Tania"
Das Tanzlegendchen (Keller) **26**:101, 108
"Tao-hu" (P'u Sung-ling) **31**:191, 204
"An tAonach" (O'Flaherty) **6**:287-88
"Tapashwini" (Tagore) **48**:301, 303, 312-13
"The Tapestried Chamber" (Scott) **32**:319
"Tapiama" (Bowles) **3**:64-5, 80, 83
Taps at Reveille (Fitzgerald) **6**:46-7, 56, 60; **31**:15, 18-19, 21, 25-6, 29
"The Tar Baby" (Harris)
  See "The Wonderful Tar-Baby Story"
"Tarantula" (Jones) **56**:285
"Taras Bulba" (Gogol) **4**:83, 85-6, 117-19; **29**:128, 130, 132, 135, 149; **52**:104, 138

Taratuta (Donoso) **34**:42-3, 45-8
"Target One" (Pohl) **25**:227, 229-32, 234-35
"Tarquin of Cheapside" (Fitzgerald) **6**:58, 60
"Tarr and Fether" (Poe)
  See "The System of Doctor Tarr and Professor Fether"
"La tartaruga" (Pirandello) **22**:269
"A Taste of Honey" (Freeman) **1**:196; **47**:161
"Tatar Earrings" (Pilnyak) **48**:287
"Tatlin!" (Davenport) **16**:161-62, 165, 167-69, 171, 197
Tatlin! (Davenport) **16**:160-61, 163-68, 170-71, 173-77, 183, 185, 187, 195, 197
Tatterdemalion (Galsworthy) **22**:63, 97, 100-01
"Tattooer" (Tanizaki)
  See "Shisei"
Le taureau blanc (Voltaire) **12**:342
Tavern of Crossed Destinies (Calvino)
  See *La taverna dei destini incrociati*
La taverna dei destini incrociati (Calvino) **48**:48-50, 150
"The Taxidermist" (Cable) **4**:50
"The Taxpayer" (Bradbury) **53**:202-3, 205, 249, 252, 259
"Tea" (Gallant)
  See "Thank You for the Lovely Tea"
"Tea" (Saki) **12**:313
"Tea on the Mountain" (Bowles) **3**:61, 72, 79
"The Tea Time of Stouthearted Ladies" (Stafford) **26**:286
"Tea with an Artist" (Rhys) **21**:58, 62
"Tea with Mrs. Bittell" (Pritchett) **14**:272
"Teach Us to Outgrow Our Madness" (Oe)
  See "Warera no Kyoki o ikinobiru michi o oshieyo"
"The Teacher" (Anderson) **1**:18, 45, 52
"The Teacher of Literature" (Chekhov)
  See "Uitel' Slovesnosti"
"Teacher's Pet" (Thurber) **1**:422-23; **47**:380
"Teaching and Story Telling" (Maclean) **13**:278-79
"The Teachings of Don B.: A Yankee Way of Knowledge" (Barthelme) **2**:40
"A Teamster's Payday" (Farrell) **28**:118
"Teangabháil" (O'Flaherty) **6**:286-89
"Tears, Idle Tears" (Bowen) **3**:33, 41, 47
"The Tears of Ah Kim" (London) **4**:257, 270
"Tears—Idle Tears" (O'Connor) **5**:371, 395
"Technical Error" (Clarke) **3**:124-25, 129
"A Technical Error" (Henry) **5**:165
"Tèddi" (Kazakov) **43**:58, 62, 64, 66-7
"Teddy" (Kazakov)
  See "Tèddi"
"Teddy" (Salinger) **2**:293, 295, 300-01, 307, 309, 311-12, 316; **28**:262, 265; **65**:294, 304-5, 310, 316-18, 321
"The Teddy-Bears' Picnic" (Trevor) **21**:262, 265; **58**:231
"Ted's Wife" (Thomas) **20**:297, 305, 311
"The Teeth of My Father" (Metcalf) **43**:85, 95, 101, 112, 116, 160
The Teeth of My Father (Metcalf) **43**:75, 85, 102, 111-14, 116, 120
"Teibele and Her Demon" (Singer) **3**:375, 384; **53**:293, 301
"The Telegram" (Čapek) **36**:98, 127
"The Telegraph Girl" (Trollope) **28**:311, 322, 327, 333-34, 348, 355-56
"Telemachus, Friend" (Henry) **5**:179
"A Telephone Call" (Parker) **2**:274, 278, 280, 285
"A Telephone Call on Yom Kippur" (Singer) **3**:385-86
"The Telephone Game" (Trevor) **58**:300
"Television" (Beattie) **11**:31
"Tell Churchill that T. George McDowell is on His Feet" (Moorhouse) **40**:291
"Tell It Like It Is" (Ellison) **26**:11
"Tell Me a Riddle" (Olsen) **11**:164-68, 171, 174, 176, 178-79, 181, 185, 187, 195, 197
Tell Me a Riddle (Olsen) **11**:163, 169, 171, 174, 187-88, 193, 197-98

"Tell Me Who to Kill" (Naipaul) **38**:301, 303-04, 309, 312-13, 353-54
"Tell Me Yes or No" (Munro) **3**:335
"Tell the Women We're Going" (Carver) **8**:14, 30; **51**:5-6, 14
"Tell Them Not to Kill Me" (Rulfo)
  See "Díles que no me maten!"
"Telling" (Bowen) **3**:30, 33, 40
"Telling Mrs. Baker" (Lawson) **18**:213, 243, 252, 262
"The Tell-Tale Heart" (Poe) **1**:384, 393-94, 408; **34**:239-87; **35**:307-11, 314, 343, 345-46; **54**:198, 218
"El Tema del traidor y del héroe" (Borges) **4**:10, 23, 30, 39; **41**:40, 58, 147-48
"The Temperate Zone" (Wharton) **6**:428
"Tempesta solare" (Calvino) **48**:47, 155, 158
"Tempests" (Dinesen) **7**:171, 197
"The Temple" (Lovecraft) **3**:282, 289; **52**:265-66, 307-8, 343, 351
"The Temple at Thatch" (Waugh) **41**:350
"A Temple of the Holy Ghost" (O'Connor) **1**:343
"Temporary Shelter" (Gordon) **59**:237-38, 260-61, 263, 266, 268
Temporary Shelter (Gordon) **59**:229-32, 236-38, 249, 260-63, 266, 268, 278
"Le Temps mort" (Aymé) **41**:19-20
"Temps Perdi" (Rhys) **21**:35, 37-8, 53, 55, 67, 75-7
"Temptation" (Čapek) **36**:125
"The Temptation of Jack Orkney" (Lessing) **6**:188; **61**:97
The Temptation of Jack Orkney, and Other Stories (Lessing) **6**:188; **61**:93
The Temptation of Pescara (Meyer)
  See *Die Versuchung des Pescara*
The Temptation of Quiet Veronica (Musil)
  See *Die Versuchung der Stillen Veronika*
"The Temptation of St. Anthony" (Barthelme) **2**:37, 54; **55**:74, 83
"The Temptation of St. Ivo" (Gardner) **7**:214, 222, 229-30, 232
The Temptation of the Silent Veronika (Musil)
  See *Die Versuchung der Stillen Veronika*
"The Tempter" (Oates) **6**:227
"Ten Centavos" (Čapek) **36**:130
Ten Green Bottles (Thomas) **20**:285, 287-90, 292, 317, 320
"Ten Indians" (Hemingway) **63**:103, 107-8, 111, 113, 115
"Ten Minutes to Twelve" (Wilson) **21**:324, 363
"The Ten O'Clock People" (King) **17**:294-95
"Ten Pretty Girls" (Kiely) **58**:146
"The Ten Righteous" (Čapek) **36**:117, 129
"Ten Years Dead" (Garland) **18**:165
"The Tenant" (Mukherjee) **38**:235, 237-41, 245, 252-55, 261, 267, 271, 273, 275-76, 279-80, 282-84, 286
"Tenants of the Last Tree-House" (Gordimer) **17**:155-56
"The Tender Age" (Collier) **19**:113
"A Tender Man" (Bambara) **35**:11, 13, 27-9
"The Tender Shoot" (Colette)
  See "Le tendron"
Tendres stocks (Morand) **22**:156-59, 161, 164-65, 167-71, 178, 181
"The Tendrils of the Vine" (Colette) **10**:291
"Le tendron" (Colette) **10**:293-94
"Tenkibo" (Akutagawa Ryūnosuke) **44**:73, 82-3
"Tennessee's Partner" (Harte) **8**:210, 219, 221, 226, 230, 232-33, 236, 244, 255-56, 258-59; **59**:285-86, 289-90, 292, 311-12, 319, 322-23, 325, 338
"The Tennis Court" (Trevor) **21**:233; **58**:210
"The Tent" (O'Flaherty) **6**:262, 282
The Tent (O'Flaherty) **6**:262-65, 278-79, 283
"Les Tentations" (Baudelaire) **18**:15, 17, 19, 36, 38, 41
"The Tenth Clew" (Hammett) **17**:218, 220, 226
"The Tenth Man" (Aleichem) **33**:25
"The Tents of Kedar" (Kipling) **5**:261

"Teodoro Méndez's Luck" (Castellanos)
See "La suerte de Teodoro Méndez Acubal"
"Los teólogos" (Borges) **4**:5-6, 25, 28, 30; **41**:40, 148
"Teoría de Dulcinea" (Arreola) **38**:7, 9
"Teoria do medalhão" (Machado de Assis) **24**:128-29, 132
"Teotihuacan" (Porter) **43**:227, 232
"Tepeyac" (Cisneros) **32**:51
"Teraloyna" (Gordimer) **17**:177, 183, 185, 189-90
"La tercera resignación" (García Márquez) **8**:154-55, 169, 182
Tercets (Pirandello)
See *Terzetti*
"Teresa" (O'Faolain) **13**:286, 288, 293, 297, 312, 314
"Teresa's Wedding" (Trevor) **21**:247, 270, 277; **58**:229, 231
"Terminal" (Gordimer) **17**:171
"The Terminal Beach" (Ballard) **1**:69, 76, 80; **53**:4, 11-12, 14-15, 21-2, 32, 36, 46-7, 50, 105, 122-23
The Terminal Beach, and Other Stories (Ballard) **1**:68-70, 73
"Terminus" (Barthelme) **55**:95, 115
"The Termitary" (Gordimer) **17**:181
"Terra d'esilio" (Pavese) **19**:375, 377, 380, 387
"Terra incognita" (Nabokov) **11**:117, 154
"The Terrible Conflagration up at the Place" (Bradbury) **29**:65
"A Terrible Mistake" (Gissing) **37**:74
"The Terrible Old Man" (Lovecraft) **3**:292; **52**:265, 287, 294-95, 311, 335
"A Terrible Vengeance" (Gogol)
See "Strašnaja mest"
"Terror" (Anderson) **1**:30
"Terror" (Chekhov) **51**:125
"Terror" (Nabokov) **11**:124-25
"Terror" (Tanizaki) **21**:181
The Terror (Machen) **20**:155, 157, 163, 166, 182-83, 196, 200-01
"The Terror of Blue John Gap" (Doyle) **12**:61, 80
"The Terrorist" (O'Flaherty) **6**:262, 284
"The Terrorists" (Barnes) **3**:19
Terza pagina: Racconti e Saggi (Levi) **12**:273-78, 280-82
Terzetti (Pirandello) **22**:231, 275
"El tesoro" (Pardo Bazán) **30**:270
"El tesoro de la juventud" (Cortázar) **7**:95
Tessiner Herbsttag (Hesse) **49**:211
"The Test" (Garrett) **30**:172
"The Test of Courage" (O'Flaherty) **6**:281
"The Test of Elder Pill" (Garland)
See "Elder Pill, Preacher"
"La testa contro il muro" (Moravia) **26**:182
"La testa della maga" (Calvino) **48**:97
"Testament of Flood" (Warren) **4**:389, 394; **58**:310, 317, 354, 356
"Los testigos" (Cortázar) **7**:95
"Testimony of Trees" (Stuart) **31**:261, 264
"HaTe'udah" (Agnon) **30**:34, 38
"Tevye and Seri" (Peretz) **26**:201
"Tevye Goes to Palestine" (Aleichem) **33**:29
Tevye the Dairyman (Aleichem) **33**:7-8, 57
"Texarcana Was a Crazy Town" (Garrett) **30**:166, 180
The Texas Stories of Nelson Algren (Algren) **33**:111-14
"Text in a Notebook" (Cortázar) **7**:69
Textes pour rien (Beckett) **16**:71, 75-7, 110-14, 117-23, 130
Texts for Nothing (Beckett)
See *Textes pour rien*
"Texturologías" (Cortázar) **7**:93
"Texturologies" (Cortázar)
See "Texturologías"
"Thanasphere" (Vonnegut) **8**:428
"Thank You" (Kawabata) **17**:252-53
"Thank You for the Lovely Tea" (Gallant) **5**:138, 142

"Thanks for the Ride" (Munro) **3**:322, 329, 331, 336, 343
"Thanksgiving: Between Junetown and Caintown" (Hood) **42**:141, 168, 170-71, 187, 215, 220
"Thanksgiving Hunter" (Stuart) **31**:266
"Thanksgiving Spirit" (Farrell) **28**:89
The Thanksgiving Visitor (Capote) **47**:41-2, 45, 55-7
"That Accursed North" (Kazakov) **43**:69
"That Brute Simmons" (Morrison) **40**:329-30, 337, 366-67
"That Evening Sun" (Faulkner) **1**:147, 162, 181, 183
"That Fellow Tolstoy" (Coppard) **21**:8
"That Good May Come" (Wharton) **6**:424
"That I Had the Wings" (Ellison) **26**:8-9, 12, 21, 29.
"That in Aleppo Once..." (Nabokov) **11**:108-09, 111, 113, 129
That Old Gang O' Mine: The Early and Essential S. J. Perelman (Perelman) **32**:239-42
"That Pretty Girl in the Army" (Lawson) **18**:217, 220, 241, 243-44
"That Sophistication" (Anderson) **1**:50
"That There Dog o' Mine" (Lawson) **18**:244
"That Tree" (Porter) **4**:327-28, 330, 339-40, 349; **43**:170, 181, 223, 292
"That Was Me" (Chabon) **59**:84, 86
"That's the Way It's Always Been" (Algren) **33**:108
"Thawing Out" (Boyle) **16**:146-48, 154
"Theater" (Toomer) **1**:441, 443-45, 450, 452, 458, 460-61; **45**:228-30, 232, 237-38, 240-43, 260, 266, 268, 286-87, 327-28, 331, 336, 380-81
"Theatre of War" (Ballard) **1**:79, 82; **53**:57
"The Theatrical Young Gentleman" (Dickens) **17**:122
"Theft" (Porter) **4**:327, 329, 337-40, 342, 349, 360; **31**:154; **43**:170, 183, 223, 236-38, 292-93
A Theft (Bellow) **14**:48-50, 56, 59-61
"Theft in a Pastry Shop" (Calvino)
See "Furto in una pasticceria"
"Their Losses" (Taylor) **10**:391
"Their Pretty Ways" (Gissing) **37**:81
"Their Quiet Lives" (Warner) **23**:374
"Them Old Moth-Eaten Lovyers" (Murfree) **22**:213
"Theme of the Traitor and the Hero" (Borges)
See "El Tema del traidor y del héroe"
"The Theme of the Traitor and the Hero" (Borges)
See "El Tema del traidor y del héroe"
"Then It All Came Down" (Capote) **2**:81
"The Theologians" (Borges)
See "Los teólogos"
"The Theological Student" (Saroyan) **21**:155
"There" (Taylor) **10**:397
There and Now (Cortázar)
See *Ahí y ahora*
"There Are Meadows in Lanark" (Kiely) **58**:167
"There Are More Things" (Borges) **41**:120
There Are No Elders (Clarke) **45**:98, 109
"There Are No Thieves in This Town" (García Márquez) **8**:185
"There Are Smiles" (Lardner) **32**:135, 138, 140-41, 147
"There Goes a Dog" (Kazakov) **43**:67
"There Is a Tavern in the Town" (Stephens) **50**:313-14
"There Is No Hope for That" (Cortázar)
See "Ya no quedan esperanzas de"
"There She Is—She Is Taking Her Bath" (Anderson) **1**:50
"There Was a Man Dwelt by a Churchyard" (James) **16**:249, 251
"There Was an Old Woman" (Bradbury) **29**:65, 68, 86
"There Was Once" (Atwood) **46**:74-5

"There Was Something Shady about the Man" (Čapek)
See "Muž, který se nelíbil"
"There Will Come Soft Rains" (Bradbury) **29**:51; **53**:210-11, 246, 248-49, 251-52, 259-60
"There's a Garden of Eden" (Gilchrist) **14**:152; **63**:10, 22
"There's an Owl in My Room" (Thurber) **47**:367
"There's No Future in It" (Bates) **10**:139
"There's Someone Who Is Laughing" (Pirandello)
See "C'è qualcuno che ride"
There's Something in the Air (Bates) **10**:113-15
"Thérése á the Hotel" (Mauriac) **24**:184-85, 196, 202-03, 208
"Thérése and the Doctor" (Mauriac)
See "Thérése chez le docteur"
"Thérése chez le docteur" (Mauriac) **24**:184-85, 196, 202-03, 206-08
Thérèse Desqueyrous (Mauriac) **24**:167-69, 173, 180-82, 184, 188-95, 199, 201-03, 206-07
"Thermos Bottles" (Mishima) **4**:313-14, 316-18, 322
"Thermos Flasks" (Mishima)
See "Thermos Bottles"
"Thersites" (Čapek) **36**:116, 129
These Thirteen (Faulkner) **1**:180-81, 184
"These Walls Are Cold" (Capote) **2**:65; **47**:10, 44-7
"These Were Palaces" (Fuentes) **24**:61-4
Thésée (Gide) **13**:43, 48, 52, 54-7, 62, 71-2, 105-10, 112
Theseus (Gide)
See *Thésée*
"!!!The!!!Teddy!Crazy!!Show!!!" (Ellison) **14**:128
"They" (Heinlein) **55**:162-63, 214, 216
"They" (Kipling) **5**:266, 271-72, 275, 279-82, 284
"They Ain't the Men They Used to Be" (Farrell) **28**:105
"They All Had Grandfathers" (Bradbury) **53**:250, 253
"They Called for More Structure..." (Barthelme) **2**:50
"They Called Him 'Ally' for Short" (Lawson) **18**:218
"They Came" (Lewis) **40**:271-72, 277
"They Heard a Ringing of Bells" (Clarke) **45**:92, 94, 109
"They Landed on Mars" (Bradbury)
See "April 2000: The Third Expedition"
They of the High Trails (Garland) **18**:164
"They say there's a Boat on the River" (Lewis) **40**:279
"They That Walk in Darkness" (Zangwill) **44**:375, 387
They That Walk in Darkness (Zangwill) **44**:366, 387
"They Wait on the Wharf in Black" (Lawson) **18**:210, 215, 234
"They Way of a Man" (Grau) **15**:158, 165
"They Weren't Going to Die" (Boyle) **5**:63
"They're Hiding the Ham on the Pinball King, or, Some Came Stumbling" (Algren) **33**:109
"They're Not Coming Back" (Clarke) **45**:98
"They're Not Your Husband" (Carver) **8**:9, 34
"They've Given Us the Land" (Rulfo)
See "Nos han dado la tierra"
"The Thief" (O'Connor) **5**:371
"The Thief" (Tanizaki) **21**:181
"The Thief and His Master" (Grimm and Grimm) **36**:199
"The Thieves" (Chekhov)
See "Vory"
"The Thieves" (Grau) **15**:147
"Thieves" (O'Faolain) **13**:292, 316

"Thieves' Ears" (Bunin)
See "Petlistye ushi"
"The Thimble" (Lawrence) 4:235, 237
"Thimble, Thimble" (Henry) 5:159, 171
A Thin Ghost and Others (James) 16:238, 251, 255
"Thin Lips and False Teeth" (Lawson) 18:249
"The Thing" (Moravia) 26:171-73
"A Thing for Nothing" (O'Connor) 5:365
"A Thing is a Thing" (Moravia) 26:159, 165
"A Thing of the Past" (Gordimer) 17:154
"The Thing on the Doorstep" (Lovecraft) 3:259, 263, 272, 274-75, 283; 52:252, 256, 258, 276, 290-91, 322, 338
"A Thing They Wear" (Metcalf) 43:73
"Things" (Le Guin) 12:232
"Things" (Lawrence) 4:219
"Things as They Are" (Pritchett) 14:255, 285
Things As They Are (Stein) 42:283, 285-86, 292-94, 305-06, 311-17, 324, 339-40, 343-44, 346-48, 352, 355-57, 361
The Things That I Know (Hemingway)
See Across the River and into the Trees
"The Things They Carried" (Jones) 56:281
"The Things You Keep" (Grau) 15:156
"The Thinker" (Anderson) 1:43-5
"Thinking Makes It So" (Glasgow) 34:65, 67, 70-2, 77, 80, 100-02
Third Book of Laughable Loves (Kundera) 24:103
"The Third Capital" (Pilnyak) 48:239, 241-43, 245-46, 277-81
The Third Capital (Pilnyak)
See Tretya stolitsa
"The Third Circle" (Norris) 28:197, 199-200, 207, 213
The Third Circle (Norris) 28:199-200, 202, 208
"The Third Cock-Crow" (Bunin) 5:82-3
"The Third Day after Christmas" (Saroyan) 21:155
"The Third Expedition" (Bradbury)
See "April 2000: The Third Expedition"
"The Third Ingredient" (Henry) 5:181-82
The Third Metropolis (Pilnyak)
See Tretya stolitsa
"The Third Murder" (Lawson) 18:217
"The Third Party" (Trevor) 21:246, 248, 262; 58:255-56
"The Third Person" (James) 8:325
"A Third Presence" (Gordimer) 17:158
"The Third Prize" (Coppard) 21:29
"The Third Resignation" (García Márquez)
See "La tercera resignación"
"The Third Son" (Platonov) 42:250, 253
"The Third Thing that Killed My Father Off" (Carver) 8:14; 51:6
"Third Time Unlucky" (Hood) 42:235
"Thirst" (Andrić)
See "Zedj"
The Thirteen (Balzac)
See Histoire des treize
Thirteen Ghost-stories by Mr. James (James) 16:223
"Thirteen, New Parade" (Hardy) 60:188
Thirteen O'Clock: Stories of Several Worlds (Benét) 10:142, 154, 158
"Thirteen to Centaurus" (Ballard) 53:8, 44
Thirty Stories (Boyle) 5:56, 63
"The $30,000 Bequest" (Twain) 6:303, 328-30, 343-45
"Thirty-two Votes before Breakfast" (Stuart) 31:265
"This Indolence of Mine" (Svevo)
See "Il mio ozio"
"This International Stuff" (Leacock) 39:267
"This is Home" (Naipaul) 38:331, 334
"This Is Not a Film, This Is a Precise Act of Disbelief" (Abish) 44:4, 11, 18, 26-28, 30
"This Is the Place" (Stuart) 31:246, 263
"This Is Tibet!" (Boell)
See "Hier ist Tibten"

"This Is What Killed Dylan Thomas" (Bukowski) 45:55
"This Madness" (Dreiser)
See "This Madness—An Honest Novel About Love"
"This Madness—An Honest Novel About Love" (Dreiser) 30:147-49
"This Morning, This Evening, So Soon" (Baldwin) 10:5-7, 9
"This Mortal Coil" (O'Connor) 5:386, 389
"This Son of Mine" (Vonnegut) 8:432, 438
"This Time" (Campbell) 19:75
"This Wait" (Price) 22:384
This Was the Old Chief's Country (Lessing) 6:186, 196; 61:94, 99, 130-31, 135
"This Way for the Gas, Ladies and Gentlemen" (Borowski) 48:5, 7-8, 16
This Way for the Gas, Ladies and Gentlemen, and Other Short Stories (Borowski)
See Kamienny świat
"Thistledown" (Aiken) 9:12, 14, 30, 42
"Thistles" (Pilnyak)
See "Chertopolokh"
"Thix" (Thurber) 47:388
"The Thorn" (Gordon) 59:265, 267-68
"The Thorn in the Flesh" (Lawrence) 4:197, 202
"Thorns and Gifts" (Davie) 52:5, 10
"The Thorny Path of Honor" (Andersen) 6:4, 34
"Thoroughbred" (Norris) 28:205, 207
"Those Cousins from Sapucaia" (Machado de Assis) 24:152
"Those Days" (Akutagawa Ryūnosuke) 44:64
Those Days (Carver) 8:51
"Those Who Don't" (Cisneros) 32:5
"Thou Art the Man" (Poe) 1:406; 35:309; 54:156, 17 , 191, 235
"Thou Shall Not Covet" (Peretz)
See "Lo Sakhmod"
"Though One Rose from the Dead" (Howells) 36:389, 397
"Thought and the Violin" (Peretz) 26:205
"Thoughts about People" (Dickens) 17:116, 132, 136
The Thousand and One Nights (Andrić) 36:74
"A Thousand Deaths" (London) 4:277
"The Thousand Dreams of Stellavista" (Ballard) 53:7, 47, 73, 80, 115, 127-28, 131
"A Thousand Years" (Pilnyak) 48:289
"Thrawn Janet" (Stevenson) 11:268-69, 279, 281-82, 304-06; 51:218-19, 236, 240-44
"The Thread of a Spider's Web" (Akutagawa Ryūnosuke)
See "Kumonoito"
"Three" (Čapek) 36:92-3, 124
"Three" (Grau) 15:149, 160
Three (Sansom) 21:81, 83-4, 124
"Three Angry People" (Stephens) 50:313, 315-16, 338
"Three Bears Cottage" (Collier) 19:104, 109, 112
"The Three Brothers" (Pilnyak) 48:237
Three by Flannery O'Connor (O'Connor) 61:241-42
"Three Calls" (Peretz) 26:205
"Three Chapters from a Tale" (Pasternak) 31:108
"Three Courses and a Dessert: Being a New and Gastronomic Version of the Game of Consequences" (Forster) 27:90
"Three Deaths" (Pilnyak)
See "Tri Smerti"
Three Deaths (Tolstoy)
See Tri smerti
"Three Degrees Over" (Aldiss) 36:28
"Three Dogs of Siena" (Sansom) 21:86, 90, 95, 97
"Three Encounters" (Turgenev)
See "Three Meetings"

"The Three Eras of Libbie Marsh" (Gaskell)
See "Libbie Marsh's Three Eras"
Three Exemplary Novels and a Prologue (Unamuno)
See Tres novelas ejemplares y un prólogo
"Three Fantasies in Minor Key" (Bioy Casares) 17:95
"Three Fat Women of Antibes" (Maugham) 8:379
"The Three Feathers" (Grimm and Grimm) 36:188
"The Three Friends" (de la Mare) 14:68, 83, 90
"Three Gifts" (Peretz)
See "Drei Matones"
"The Three Girls" (Pavese) 19:377, 387
"The Three Golden Apples" (Lee) 33:307, 310
"Three Halves of a House" (Hood) 42:138, 181, 201, 225-26, 230-31, 235
"Three Happy Places" (Stephens) 50:305, 314, 316, 338
"Three Heavy Husbands" (Stephens) 50:305, 314, 327-28, 338
"The Three Hermits" (Tolstoy) 9:373-74, 388
"Three Heroines" (Taylor) 10:408
"The Three Holy Men" (Barthelme) 55:5
"The Three Horsemen of the Apocalypse" (Chesterton) 46:125
"Three Hundred Acres of Elbow Room" (Stuart) 31:244, 251
The Three Impostors (Machen) 20:156-57, 159, 162-63, 165, 173-74, 176, 186, 190, 196-97, 199, 201, 205-07
"Three Knots in the Net" (Castellanos)
See "Tres nudos en la red"
"Three Kopeks" (Bulgakov) 18:89
"Three Lambs" (O'Flaherty) 6:264, 274
"Three Letters" (Williams) 31:329
"Three Lindens" (Hesse) 9:242-43
"The Three Little Men in the Wood" (Grimm and Grimm) 36:205
Three Lives (Stein) 42:274-78, 280, 282-83, 286-87, 292-94, 310-24, 326, 328, 332-36, 338, 343, 345-52, 354
"Three Lovers Who Lost" (Stephens) 50:314-16, 327-28, 338
"Three Meetings" (Turgenev) 7:314-15, 324-25, 328, 335; 57:293-94
"The Three Million Yen" (Mishima) 4:313-14, 316-18, 322
"Three Miraculous Soldiers" (Crane) 7:103, 106; 56:110
"The Three Notorious Fools" (Arnim)
See "Die drei Erznarren"
"Three Partners" (Harte) 8:216, 222, 248; 59:307
"Three People" (Trevor) 58:300-301
"Three Pictures" (Woolf) 7:408, 410-12
"Three Portraits" (Turgenev)
See "Tri portreta"
"Three Portraits and a Prayer" (Pohl) 25:220
Three Professional Studies (Williams) 31:329
"Three Questions" (Tolstoy) 9:388
"Three Raps" (Turgenev)
See "Stuk...stuk...stuk"
The Three Righteous Combmakers (Keller)
See Die drei gerechten Kammacher
"Three Rounds" (Morrison) 40:328, 361
"Three Shots" (Hemingway) 40:250; 63:53
"Three Sisters" (Agnon) 30:65-7, 71
"The Three Sisters" (Cisneros) 32:6, 28-29, 32, 43
The Three Sisters (Chekhov)
See Tri Sestry
Three Sisters: A Drama in Four Acts (Chekhov)
See Tri Sestry
"The Three Sisters and the Old Beau" (Freeman) 47:84
"The Three Snake Leaves" (Grimm and Grimm) 36:228-29
"The Three Souls of Ah So Nan" (Far) 62:50
"Three Stories" (Saroyan) 21:132

Three Stories (Gogol) **29**:142

Three Stories and Ten Poems (Hemingway) **1**:206

"The Three Strangers" (Hardy) **2**:202-03, 205, 208, 212-15, 218, 220, 223, 226-27

"Three Tales" (Singer) **53**:294

Three Tales (Flaubert)
    See *Trois contes: Un coeur simple; La légende de Saint-Julien l'hospitalier; Hérodias*

Three Tales (Mauriac)
    See *Trois Récits*

"Three Thousand Years among the Microbes" (Twain) **6**:333, 336, 338, 350-53; **26**:325, 330, 333, 358-64

Three Times Three (Saroyan) **21**:141, 143, 146, 153, 158-60, 163, 168

"Three Tools" (Chesterton) **1**:136

"The Three Tools of Death" (Chesterton) **46**:132

"The Three Treasures" (Akutagawa Ryūnosuke) **44**:53

Three Uneasy Pieces (White) **39**:347-48

"Three Vagabonds of Trinidad" (Harte) **8**:245, 251; **59**:294

"Three Without, Doubled" (Lardner) **32**:145, 148

"Three Women" (Cather)
    See "Old Mrs. Harris"

Three Women (Musil)
    See *Drei Frauen*

"Three Women and Two Men" (Thomas) **20**:317

"Three Women Who Wept" (Stephens) **50**:305, 314-15, 328, 338

"Three Years" (Chekhov)
    See "Tri goda"

"Three Young Wives" (Stephens) **50**:315, 338-39

The Three-Cornered Hat (Alarcon)
    See *El sombrero de tres picos*

"The Three-Day Blow" (Hemingway) **1**:208, 219, 244; **36**:291, 310; **40**:185, 209, 219-22, 229-30, 233; **63**:72, 75

"The Threefold Destiny" (Hawthorne) **3**:160, 177-78, 182-83, 189

"The Threepenny Piece" (Stephens) **50**:314, 327

"Throat of a Black Cat" (Cortázar)
    See "Cuello de gatito negro"

"Through the Gates of the Silver Key" (Lovecraft) **3**:262, 267, 272-73, 286, 294; **52**:262, 275, 277, 286

"Through the Looking Glass" (Oates) **6**:228

"Through the Midnight Sky" (Platonov) **42**:254

"Through the Panama" (Lowry) **31**:40-1, 43-5, 47-50, 52-5, 59-63, 71-5, 82, 84, 86-7

"Through the Quinquina Glass" (Sansom) **21**:87, 92

"Through the Streets of My Own Labyrinth" (Nin) **10**:303

"Through the Veil" (Doyle) **12**:80

"Through the Walls" (Levi) **12**:277

"The Thrower-Away" (Boell)
    See "Der Wegwerfer"

"Thrown Away" (Kipling) **5**:261; **54**:79

"Thumbelina" (Andersen)
    See "Tommelise"

"Thumbling" (Andersen)
    See "Poor Thumbling"

"Thumbling's Travels" (Grimm and Grimm) **36**:199, 223, 229-30

"Thundermug" (Algren) **33**:111, 113

The Thurber Album (Thurber) **47**:369, 382

The Thurber Carnival (Thurber) **1**:416, 426

"Thus I Refute Beelzy" (Collier) **19**:98, 101, 103, 105, 107

"Le Thyrse" (Baudelaire) **18**:59, 63

"The Thyrsus" (Baudelaire)
    See "Le Thyrse"

"Ti con zero" (Calvino) **3**:93; **48**:48, 59, 86-8, 134

Ti con zero (Calvino) **3**:92, 94-6, 98-9, 107, 117; **48**:33-5, 48, 57-9, 61, 63, 65, 74, 76-8, 103, 105-6, 109, 113-15, 127, 131-32, 136, 142-43, 150, 167

"Ti Démon" (Chopin) **8**:100

"Ti Frére" (Chopin) **8**:72

La tía Tula (Unamuno) **11**:313-14, 317, 324-25, 327, 330, 335, 344-45, 347-48

"Tian Shan's Kindred Spirit" (Far) **62**:18-19, 50, 57, 74, 77

"Tic ... tac" (Alarcon) **64**:3, 5, 7

"The Tick of the Clock" (Greene) **29**:218

"A Ticket on Skoronski" (Algren) **33**:96, 108

"Tickets" (Barthelme) **55**:117-18

"Tickets, Please" (Lawrence) **4**:222-23, 226, 228, 231, 233-35, 242-46

"The Tide" (O'Flaherty) **6**:262, 279, 285

"The Tide Line" (Metcalf) **43**:108-9

"Tide Pools" (Adams) **24**:17-18

"A Tidewater Morning" (Styron) **25**:312-13, 317-18

"The Tie" (Kipling) **5**:278

"La tierra que nos han dado" (Rulfo)
    See "Nos han dado la tierra"

"The Tiger" (Saroyan) **21**:143-44, 163

"Tiger, Tiger" (Frame) **29**:105, 106

"Tiger! Tiger!" (Kipling) **54**:83, 110, 122, 134-35

"Tigers Are Better-Looking" (Rhys) **21**:57, 69

Tigers Are Better-Looking (Rhys) **21**:33, 39, 41, 48, 57, 60-1, 63-7, 69-71

"The Tiger's Bride" (Carter) **13**:6, 9, 23, 25, 27, 30-32

"The Tiger's Claw" (Narayan) **25**:139

The Tiger's Daughter (Mukherjee) **38**:243

"A Tight Boat" (Chesnutt) **7**:13

"Till September Petronella" (Rhys) **21**:39, 41-3, 48-9, 54, 60, 65, 67, 70

"The Tillotson Banquet" (Huxley) **39**:155, 168, 171, 174-75, 177

"Tim" (Stuart) **31**:239-40

"Timber" (Galsworthy) **22**:67, 101

"Timbuktu" (Thomas) **20**:290, 294-95, 298, 318

"Time" (Čapek)
    See "Čas"

"Time" (Pavese) **19**:375

"Time and Again" (Pancake) **61**:249, 284

"Time and Ebb" (Nabokov) **11**:108, 127, 130

"Time and Place" (Sansom) **21**:89, 91, 95

Time and the Hunter (Calvino)
    See *Ti con zero*

"The Time Capsule" (Gilchrist) **14**:161-62; **63**:4

"Time Checkmated" (Levi) **12**:280

"Time Did" (Gordimer) **17**:164, 193

"The Time Element" (O'Hara) **15**:289, 291

The Time Element, and Other Stories (O'Hara) **15**:286

"Time Expired" (Bates) **10**:117

"Time, Gentlemen!" (Calisher) **15**:8, 15-17, 19

"Time Gents, Please" (Sansom) **21**:108, 110-11, 126

"The Time Handsome Brown Ran Away" (Caldwell) **19**:48, 51-2

"The Time Ma Spent the Day at Aunt Bessie's" (Caldwell) **19**:51

"Time of Bitter Children" (Garrett) **30**:173

"The Time of Death" (Munro) **3**:329-30

"The Time of Friendship" (Bowles) **3**:63-7, 81-2

The Time of Friendship (Bowles) **3**:63-5, 70, 79-81, 84

"Time of Passage" (Ballard) **53**:10, 42

"The Time of Their Lives" (O'Faolain) **13**:320

"The Time of Year" (Trevor) **21**:247

"Time Stands Still" (Čapek) **36**:92

"Time the Tiger" (Lewis) **34**:157

"The Time the Wolves Ate the Vice-Principal" (Steinbeck) **11**:248

"Time to Go" (Dixon) **16**:207-08, 212

Time to Go (Dixon) **16**:206-08, 212-15

"The Time Tombs" (Ballard) **53**:8, 46

"Times" (Beattie) **11**:29

The Times Are Never So Bad: A Novella and Eight Short Stories (Dubus) **15**:76, 81, 83, 88, 97

"Time's Arrow" (Clarke) **3**:133-34, 142

"Timothy's Birthday" (Trevor) **58**:253-54, 263-64, 273, 275

"Timothy's Narrow Squeak" (Galsworthy) **22**:71

"A Tin Can" (O'Flaherty) **6**:276

"The Tin Soldier" (Andersen)
    See "Den standhaftige Tinsoldat"

"Tin Soldier" (Vinge) **24**:340-41, 351

"Tin Tan Tann" (Cisneros) **32**:35, 38

"The Tinder-Box" (Andersen)
    See "Fyrtøjet"

"The Tinkerer" (Coover) **15**:47

"The Tins" (Cowan) **28**:77; 80

The Tins and Other Stories (Cowan) **28**:77-78

"Le tir et le cimetière" (Baudelaire) **18**:3, 18, 35

"Tired Courtesan" (Moravia)
    See "Cortigiana stanca"

"A Tiresomesome Story" (Chekhov)
    See "A Dreary Story"

"Tišina" (Bunin) **5**:98

"The Titanic Bar" (Andrić)
    See "Bife titanik"

"Titanium" (Levi) **12**:264, 268

"Titbull's Alms-houses" (Dickens) **17**:123

"Tite Poulette" (Cable) **4**:52, 62, 67-8, 76-7

"The Tithe of the Lord" (Dreiser) **30**:157-59

"Title" (Barth) **10**:42-3, 46-8, 54-5, 61, 63-4, 73-4, 76, 79-81, 85-8, 91, 97-100

"HaTizmoret" (Agnon) **30**:38

"Tlactocatzine en el jardin de Flandes" (Fuentes) **24**:30, 37-8, 41, 43-8, 53-5, 61-2, 69-70, 82

"Tlactocatzine in the Garden of Flanders" (Fuentes)
    See "Tlactocatzine del jardin de Flandes"

"Tlön, Uqbar, Orbis Tertius" (Borges) **4**:6-7, 10-12, 15, 18, 25, 29, 33, 35, 43; **41**:55, 62-64, 79, 83-86, 138, 144-47, 158

"To a Person Sitting in Darkness" (Twain) **26**:354

"To Be Filed for Reference" (Kipling) **54**:79

"To Be Read at Dusk" (Dickens) **17**:124

"To Bell the Cat" (Vinge) **24**:341

"To Bow Bridge" (Morrison) **40**:338, 368

"To Build a Fire" (London) **49**:325-68

"To Build a Fire (1902)" (London) **4**:272-74

"To Build a Fire (1908)" (London) **4**:265, 267, 272-76, 278, 280-82, 289-93

"To Come So Far" (Warner) **23**:369

"To Cool the Air" (Warner) **23**:369

"To Da-duh, In Memoriam" (Marshall) **3**:301, 303, 307, 313-15, 317

"To Die in Jerusalem" (Zangwill) **44**:367, 370, 373, 375, 388

"To Father's House" (Agnon) **30**:4

"To Hell with Dying" (Walker) **5**:403, 406, 419, 422

"To London and Rome" (Barthelme) **55**:16, 24

"To Market, to Market" (Stuart) **31**:265

"To Nature and Back Again" (Leacock) **39**:264

"To Room Nineteen" (Lessing) **6**:198, 201-02, 208, 214, 218, 220; **61**:88-89, 91, 93-96, 104, 140

To Room Nineteen (Lessing) **61**:93

"To See You Again" (Adams) **24**:19, 23, 25

To See You Again (Adams) **24**:9-11, 15

"To Set Our House in Order" (Laurence) **7**:252, 262, 264-65, 269

"To Sleep, Perchance to Steam" (Perelman) **32**:204, 222, 231

"To Sleep, Sleep...!" (Chekhov) **51**:78

"To the Chicago Abyss" (Bradbury) **29**:46; **53**:214

"To the Doctor" (Agnon)
    See "El haRofe"

"To the Man on Trail" (London) **4**:250, 267, 277, 279

"To the Rescue!" (Sansom) **21**:92

"To the Sea Serpent" (Fuentes)
   See "A la Víbora de la mar"
"To the Snake of the Sea" (Fuentes)
   See "A la Víbora de la mar"
"To the Unknown God" (Moravia) **26**:173
"To Thy Chamber Window, Sweet" (Gordon)
   15:106, 120, 129
"To Whom It May Concern" (Farrell) **28**:96
"To Yearn Is Subhuman, to Forestall Divine"
   (Perelman) **32**:235-36
"Toad's Mouth" (Allende) **65**:13-14, 17, 35, 47,
   51
"Tobacco and the Devil" (Akutagawa
   Ryūnosuke)
   See *Tobaku tu akuma*
Tobaku tu akuma (Akutagawa Ryūnosuke)
   44:42, 57-9
"Tobermory" (Saki) **12**:287, 302, 304, 312, 333
"Tobe's Tribulations" (Chesnutt) **54**:44-5, 51
"Tobias Mindernickel" (Mann) **5**:322, 334, 336
"Tobin's Palm" (Henry) **49**:196
"Tobold" (Walser) **20**:353
"Tocayos" (Donoso) **34**:21, 25, 29-30, 35-36,
   41-42, 49
"Toc...toc...toc" (Turgenev)
   See "Stuk...stuk...stuk"
Der Tod des Dichters (Tieck) **31**:289-90
Der Tod in Venedig (Mann) **5**:307, 309-11, 313-
   14, 319, 322-27, 331, 338-40, 342-45, 348,
   355-56
"Today Is Friday" (Hemingway) **1**:228-29
"Todos los fuegos el fuego" (Cortázar) **7**:61, 69
Todos los fuegos el fuego (Cortázar) **7**:52-4, 60,
   62, 64
"Together and Apart" (Woolf) **7**:376, 381, 388
"Tóir Mhic Uí Dhíomasuigh" (Moore) **19**:307,
   319-26, 328-32, 334, 341
"La toison d'or" (Gautier) **20**:8, 14-15
Tokyo hakkei (Dazai Osamu) **41**:247-50, 256-59
"Told by the Schoolmaster" (Galsworthy) **22**:73
*Told by Uncle Remus: New Stories of the Old
   Plantation* (Harris) **19**:149, 164, 187, 191,
   197
"Told in the Drooling Ward" (London) **4**:255-
   56, 266
"Told in the Tavern" (Jewett) **6**:159
"Der Tolle Invalide auf dem Fort Ratonneau"
   (Arnim) **29**:2-6, 30-5
"The Toll-Gatherer's Day" (Hawthorne) **3**:158
"The Tolstoy Pitch" (Hood) **42**:186
"The Tolstoy Touch" (Hood) **42**:139
"Tom Carroll" (Farrell) **28**:114, 125-6
"Tom Outland's Story" (Cather) **50**:141
"Tom Rivers" (Gordon) **15**:106-07
"The Tomb" (Lovecraft) **52**:252, 263, 267, 287-
   88, 290, 340-45, 351, 354, 356
"The Tomb of His Ancestors" (Kipling) **5**:266;
   54:70, 72
"The Tomb of Pletone" (Forster) **27**:115, 117
"Les tombales" (Maupassant) **1**:263; **64**:333,
   351-53
"The Tomb-Herd" (Campbell) **19**:66, 89
The Tomb-Herd and Others (Campbell) **19**:87
"The Tomb-Legions" (Lovecraft) **52**:311
"The Tombling Day" (Bradbury) **29**:65
"Tomelen'je duxa" (Leskov) **34**:108, 111
"Tommelise" (Andersen) **6**:27-8, 36; **56**:31, 36
"Tommy" (Wideman) **62**:264-65, 276, 288-89
"The Tommy Crans" (Bowen) **3**:33, 41
Tommy Gallagher's Crusade (Farrell) **28**:93-4,
   96-7, 120, 126
"Tommy, the Unsentimental" (Cather) **2**:100,
   105; **50**:59, 78, 92, 152, 157, 168-69, 184,
   226-27
"Tomoda to Matsunaga no hanashi" (Tanizaki)
   21:194
"Tomorrow" (Conrad) **9**:143
"Tomorrow" (Faulkner) **1**:165, 179, 181
"Tomorrow" (Lu Hsun)
   See "Mingtian"
"Tomorrow and Tomorrow" (Farrell) **28**:114,
   116

"Tomorrow and Tomorrow and So Forth"
   (Updike) **13**:352
"Tomorrow and Tomorrow and Tomorrow"
   (Vonnegut) **8**:425, 429-31
"Tomorrow is a Million Years" (Ballard) **53**:9-
   10, 54
Tomorrow Times Seven (Pohl) **25**:232
"Tomorrow's Child" (Bradbury) **29**:49, 65
"The Tomorrow-Tamer" (Laurence) **7**:249, 261
The Tomorrow-Tamer (Laurence) **7**:245-50,
   260-61, 272
"Tom's Warm Welcome" (Chesnutt) **7**:14
"Tonelli's Marriage" (Howells) **36**:396-97
"The Tongue-Cut Sparrow" (Dazai Osamu)
   41:238
Tonio Kröger (Mann) **5**:307, 310-11, 316, 318,
   324, 331, 342-44, 355
Tonka (Musil) **18**:292-97, 305, 313-17, 322-25
"Tony" (Čapek) **36**:130
"Tony and the Beetles" (Dick) **57**:107
"Tony Kytes, the Arch Deceiver" (Hardy)
   2:206-07
"Tony's Story" (Silko) **37**:295, 308-9
"Too Bad" (Parker) **2**:274, 280, 285
"Too Dearly Bought" (Gissing) **37**:70
"Too Early Spring" (Benét) **10**:144
Too Far to Go: The Maples Stories (Updike)
   13:373, 383, 387-88
"Too Much Tolerance" (Waugh) **41**:339
"Too Rich" (Moravia) **26**:142, 155
"Too Young" (O'Hara) **15**:248, 265, 270
"The Tooth" (Jackson) **9**:249, 258-60, 266;
   39:210, 211, 212, 224, 227, 229, 231
"A Tooth for Paul Revere" (Benét) **10**:143, 154,
   159
"The Top" (Kafka)
   See "Der Kreisel"
"The Top and the Ball" (Andersen) **6**:18, 32
"The Topaz Cufflinks Mystery" (Thurber)
   47:375-76
"Topham's Chance" (Gissing) **37**:51-2, 80
"Topos" (Arreola) **38**:4, 7, 11
"Toppan" (Norris) **28**:207
Tor Hapela'ot (Appelfeld) **42**:3, 8, 15, 29-34,
   36-37
"Torch Song" (Cheever) **1**:89, 99, 106, 109-10;
   38:53, 84
"Torito" (Cortázar) **7**:54, 88-9
"The Torn Lace" (Pardo Bazán) **30**:290
"Torokko" (Akutagawa Ryūnosuke) **44**:71, 79
"Torpid Smoke" (Nabokov) **11**:117, 154-6
"The Torque" (Forster) **27**:90, 96, 105, 107,
   117
"A Torrent Dammed" (O'Connor) **5**:387
The Torrents of Spring (Turgenev)
   See *Veshnie vody*
"Torridge" (Trevor) **21**:262; **58**:201
"The Torture" (Andrić)
   See "Zlostavljanje"
"La torture par l'espérance" (Villiers de l'Isle
   Adam) **14**:378, 398
"Tosca" (Allende) **65**:11, 39, 47, 49, 53
"Toshishun" (Akutagawa Ryūnosuke) **44**:69-72
"Toska" (Chekhov) **2**:128, 130, 155; **51**:52, 89,
   108, 155-56, 159, 168
"Total Environment" (Aldiss) **36**:20
"Total Loss" (Warner) **23**:373
"Der toten schweigern" (Schnitzler) **15**:345,
   376; **61**:306, 308
"Totentanz" (Wilson) **21**:319, 322, 332-33, 337-
   39, 346-47, 355-57
"The Touch" (O'Flaherty) **6**:265, 285
"A Touch of Autumn in the Air" (O'Faolain)
   13:289, 293-95, 314, 320
The Touch of Nutmeg (Collier) **19**:103, 105,
   115
"The Touch of Nutmeg Makes It" (Collier)
   19:103, 109, 113
"A Touch of Realism" (Saki) **12**:294, 306
A Touch of the Sun (Sansom) **21**:84
"Touched with Fire" (Bradbury) **29**:67, 88

"A Touching Story of George Washington's
   Boyhood" (Twain) **34**:343
The Touchstone (Wharton) **6**:413
"A Tough Tussle" (Bierce) **9**:49, 67
"A Tour of the Forest" (Turgenev) **7**:320,
   337-38
A Tour on the Prairies (Irving) **2**:244
"The Tourist City in the South" (Hesse) **9**:244
"Tourmaline" (Stifter) **28**:284, 286-88, 290
"The Tout of Yarmouth Bridge" (Gissing) **37**:55
Le toutounier (Colette) **10**:263
"Toward Evening" (Updike) **13**:355
Toward the Setting Sun (Platonov) **42**:250
"Towel with a Rooster" (Bulgakov) **18**:86
"Tower from Yuggoth" (Campbell) **19**:72, 89
"Town and Country Lovers" (Gordimer)
   17:164-65, 193-94
"Town Crier Exclusive, Confessions of a
   Princess Manque: How Royals Found Me
   Unsuitable to Marry Their Larry" (Elkin)
   12:119-20
"The Town of Gradov" (Platonov) **42**:248
"The Town of the Little People" (Aleichem)
   See "Di shtot fun di kleyne mentshelek"
"The Town Philosopher's Banquet"
   (Moorhouse) **40**:298, 311
"The Town Poor" (Jewett) **6**:151
"Townies" (Dubus) **15**:77, 79-81, 88, 96
"Townsend" (Dreiser) **30**:149
"The Toys of Peace" (Saki) **12**:285
The Toys of Peace, and Other Papers (Saki)
   12:285, 289, 322, 328-29
"Traceleen, She's Still Talking" (Gilchrist)
   See "A Sordid Tale, or, Traceleen Continues
   Talking"
"Traceleen Turns East" (Gilchrist) **14**:162-63
"Track 12" (Ballard) **1**:68; **53**:7, 49
"A Tractate Middoth" (James) **16**:232, 234, 240,
   245, 252, 255, 257
"The Tractor" (Cowan) **28**:75; 79-80; 82
"The Tradesman's Return" (Hemingway)
   25:113
"A Tradition of 1804" (Hardy) **2**:215, 220-21
Traffics and Discoveries (Kipling) **5**:266, 272,
   283; **54**:75
"A Tragedy" (Lavin) **4**:165, 176, 183
"The Tragedy at Three Corners" (Dunbar)
   See "The Tragedy at Three Forks"
"The Tragedy at Three Forks" (Dunbar) **8**:121-
   22, 125, 136
"Tragedy in a Greek Theatre" (Pritchett)
   14:268-69, 273
"A Tragedy of Error" (James) **8**:302
"A Tragedy of Two Ambitions" (Hardy) **2**:205-
   06, 214-17, 223; **60**:180
"Tragic" (Hesse) **9**:232, 236
"The Trail of the Green Blazer" (Narayan)
   25:135, 140, 153
Trailerpark (Banks) **42**:54-5
"The Train" (Carver) **8**:25-6, 34
"The Train" (O'Connor) **61**:243
"The Train and the City" (Wolfe) **33**:346, 348,
   366, 375, 380, 401
"Train from Rhodesia" (Gordimer) **17**:167, 173,
   186
"The Train Station" (Coover) **15**:48
"The Train Was on Time" (Boell)
   See "Der Zug war pünktlich"
"The Train Whistled" (Pirandello)
   See "Il treno ha fischiato"
"Training" (Atwood) **2**:3-4, 7-8, 10, 12-13, 16;
   46:26-7, 33, 35-6, 42
"The Trains" (Saroyan) **21**:161
"Le traitement du docteur Tristan" (Villiers de
   l'Isle Adam) **14**:381-82
"The Traitor" (Maugham) **8**:368, 377
"Traitorously" (Svevo)
   See "Proditoriamente"
"Traitors" (Lessing) **6**:217
"Traktat o manekinach" (Schulz) **13**:328-30,
   333, 335, 338

"Tralala" (Selby) **20**:253-54, 256, 259, 261-63, 265-69, 272, 277, 279
La trama celeste (Bioy Casares) **17**:54, 59, 61, 75, 85, 87
"The Tramp" (O'Flaherty) **6**:275, 285
"La trampa" (Arreola) **38**:25
"The Tramp's Tale" (Čapek) **36**:108
"La transaction" (Balzac) **5**:24
"Transaction" (O'Hara) **15**:257-58
"Transcendent Horror" (Ligotti) **16**:287
"The Transformation" (Appelfeld)
　　See "Hahishtanut"
"The Transformation of Martin Burney" (Henry) **5**:197
"The Transformation of Vincent Scoville" (Oates) **6**:230
"Transience" (Clarke) **3**:127, 135, 142
"Transients in Arcadia" (Henry) **5**:158, 189
"Transit Bed" (Calvino)
　　See "Un letto di passaggio"
"Transit of Earth" (Clarke) **3**:147
"A Transit of Venus" (Leacock) **39**:265
"The Transition of Juan Romero" (Lovecraft) **52**:264
"Transitional" (Zangwill) **44**:367, 375-76, 387
"Transmigrations of a Melody" (Peretz) **26**:202
A Transparent Tree: Fictions (Kelly) **50**:286-88, 292-93, 295-96, 299
The Transposed Heads (Mann)
　　See *Die vertauschten Köpfe*
"The Trap" (Pirandello)
　　See "La trappola"
"The Trap" (Singer) **53**:272
Trapné providky (Čapek) **36**:81-3, 92-3, 96-7, 124-26
"Trapped" (O'Flaherty) **6**:273, 276, 279, 283
"La trappola" (Pirandello) **22**:275
"Trash" (Thomas) **20**:324, 326
"Trastevere" (Lavin) **4**:183, 185
"Il tratto di Apelle" (Pasternak) **31**:98, 104-06, 108, 110, 116-18
Traumnovelle (Schnitzler) **15**:344, 353-54, 366, 372, 374; **61**:287-310
"Travel Notes" (Bulgakov) **18**:90
"A Travel Piece" (Atwood) **2**:3-4, 6-7, 10, 12, 15-16; **46**:26, 33, 35, 41-2, 57-8, 62, 93
"Traveler" (Gilchrist)
　　See "Traveller"
"The Traveler" (Stegner) **27**:205, 219-20, 223, 225
"Traveling Salesman" (Dybek) **55**:126
"Traveling Together" (Adams) **24**:16
"Traveller" (Davie) **52**:10
"Traveller" (Gilchrist) **14**:150-51; **63**:10, 13, 23-24
"Traveller, If You Come to the Spa" (Boell)
　　See "Wanderer, kommst du nach Spa..."
"Traveller, If You Go to Spa" (Boell)
　　See "Wanderer, kommst du nach Spa..."
A Traveller's Room (Davie) **52**:3-8, 10-12
Traveller's Samples (O'Connor) **5**:371
"Travelling Abroad" (Dickens) **17**:123
"Travelling along the Oka" (Solzhenitsyn)
　　See "Puteshestvuia vdol' Oki"
"The Travelling Companion" (Andersen)
　　See "Reisekammeraten"
"The Travelling Companion" (Stevenson) **51**:230, 239-40
"Travelling Companions" (James) **32**:106
"The Travelling Entertainer" (Jolley) **19**:220, 230, 243
The Travelling Entertainer (Jolley) **19**:220-21, 233
"Travelling Northward" (Metcalf) **43**:154, 156-57, 166
"The Travelling Sister" (Freeman) **47**:84, 105
"Travelogue" (Lardner) **32**:135, 140, 146, 149, 167
"La Traversée de Paris" (Aymé) **41**:30-35
"Travis Hallett's Half-Back" (Norris) **28**:205
"Treacherously" (Svevo)
　　See "Proditoriamente"

"Treason" (Babel) **16**:27-8, 51
"Treasure" (Frame) **29**:104
"The Treasure" (Maugham) **8**:380
"Treasure of Abbot Thomas" (James) **16**:225, 228-29, 232-34, 236, 244, 251-53, 255-57
"The Treasure of Far Island" (Cather) **50**:59, 72, 75, 104-05, 146-47, 150, 126-87, 191-94, 201, 204, 208, 226-27, 234
"The Treasure of Franchard" (Stevenson) **11**:268-69, 281, 284; **51**:248
"The Treasure of Youth" (Cortázar)
　　See "El tesoro de la juventud"
"The Treasure Ship" (Saki) **12**:295, 308, 312
Treat 'Em Rough: Letters from Jack the Kaiser Killer (Lardner) **32**:144
"A Treatise on Housing" (Bulgakov) **18**:92
"Treatise on Tailors' Dummies" (Schulz)
　　See "Traktat o manekinach"
"The Tree" (Bombal)
　　See "El árbol"
"The Tree" (de la Mare) **14**:66, 85-6
"The Tree" (Lovecraft) **52**:265, 267, 283, 285-86, 307
"The Tree" (Thomas) **3**:399, 402, 408-09; **44**:322, 327, 331, 333-34, 337-38, 341, 346, 348-49, 354-55, 359
"A Tree. A Rock. A Cloud." (McCullers) **9**:322-23, 327, 329-30, 332, 341, 345-46, 353-54; **24**:232
"The Tree Fort" (Gilchrist) **14**:161-62
"Tree Frogs" (Shiga) **23**:346
"The Tree of Justice" (Kipling) **5**:292
"The Tree of Knowledge" (Evans) **43**:18
"The Tree of Knowledge" (Freeman) **47**:101
"The Tree of Knowledge" (James) **8**:301
"The Tree of Life" (Kawabata)
　　See "Inochi no Ki"
"The Tree of Life" (Machen) **20**:178
"A Tree of Night" (Capote) **2**:61-3, 66, 69, 72-5; **47**:12-13, 28-31, 35, 44-5, 50-2, 54-5
A Tree of Night, and Other Stories (Capote) **2**:61-4, 72, 74, 83; **47**:17, 28, 59
"A Tree to Be Desired" (Gilchrist) **63**:8
"The Trees of Pride" (Chesterton) **1**:122
"La tregua" (Castellanos) **39**:48, 57, 66, 67, 70
The Trembling of a Leaf (Maugham) **8**:370-72
"Il treno ha fischiato" (Pirandello) **22**:255, 270
Trent's Trust and Other Stories (Harte) **59**:310
"Trenzas" (Bombal) **37**:38
Tres novelas ejemplares y un prólogo (Unamuno) **11**:313, 317, 323, 331, 345, 348
Tres novelitas burguesas (Donoso) **34**:8, 12-13, 17, 32, 34
"Tres nudos en la red" (Castellanos) **39**:74
"Três tesouros perdidos" (Machado de Assis) **24**:128, 151
"Tretii syn" (Platonov) **42**:256
Tretya stolitsa (Pilnyak) **48**:239, 241-43, 245-46, 277-81
"Tri goda" (Chekhov) **2**:131, 155-57, **28**:59; **51**:28, 83, 129, 136, 191, 193-94, 197-98, 207
"Tri portreta" (Turgenev) **7**:313, 318, 320, 323; **57**:289, 291
Tri Sestry (Chekhov) **51**:29
"Tri Smerti" (Pilnyak) **48**:254
Tri smerti (Tolstoy) **9**:382-83, 389-90; **45**:136-37, 159-62
"Trial by Combat" (Jackson) **9**:250; **39**:211, 215, 219, 224, 227
"The Trial of Pan" (Greene) **29**:221
"The Trial of the Old Watchdog" (Thurber) **1**:426
"The Trial Sermon on Bull-Skin" (Dunbar) **8**:118, 121, 127, 136
"The Triangle" (Stephens) **50**:315, 327-28
"The Tribe" (Svevo)
　　See "La tribù"
"La tribù" (Svevo) **25**:357-58
Tribulat Bonhomet (Villiers de l'Isle Adam) **14**:378-79

"The Tribunal" (Čapek) **36**:82, 93, 124-25
"Tribuneaux rustiques" (Maupassant) **1**:259, 286
"The Trick" (Campbell) **19**:76, 78
"Trick of Nature" (Bulgakov) **18**:90
"The Tricksters" (Chekhov)
　　See "Fokusniki"
"Trigo errante" (Fuentes) **24**:31, 37-8, 43
"A Trillion Feet of Gas" (Updike) **13**:355
"Trilobites" (Pancake) **61**:246, 248-51, 253, 255-57, 259-61, 263, 265, 271, 275, 277-78, 281-82, 284-85
"The Trimmed Lamp" (Henry) **5**:171, 185, 198
The Trimmed Lamp (Henry) **5**:155, 192; **49**:205
"A Trinity" (Trevor) **58**:229
"The Trinket Box" (Lessing) **6**:196-97, 212-20
"Trinket's Colt" (Somerville & Ross) **56**:333, 340
"Trio" (Rhys) **21**:61, 70
"Trio em lá menor" (Machado de Assis) **24**:128
"The Trip" (O'Hara) **15**:252, 261, 280-81
"A Trip in a Horse Car" (Far) **62**:11
"A Trip to Chancellorsville" (Fitzgerald) **6**:47
"A Trip to the Head" (Le Guin) **12**:232-33
Trip to the Orient (Nerval)
　　See *Voyage en Orient*
"The Triplets" (Auchincloss) **22**:45
Tristan (Mann) **5**:307-11, 321, 323-24
"The Triumph of Night" (Wharton) **6**:418, 428, 431-32
"The Triumph of Reason" (Gilchrist) **63**:8
The Triumph of the Egg: A Book of Impressions from American Life in Tales and Poems (Anderson) **1**:20, 23, 27, 30, 34, 37-8, 40, 47, 52, 54-55; **46**:16-20
"The Triumphs of a Taxidermist" (Wells) **6**:380, 384, 388
Trois contes: Un coeur simple; La légende de Saint-Julien l'hospitalier; Hérodias (Flaubert) **11**:37, 52-3, 56-7, 62-6, 70-1, 76-84, 87, 96-9, 101; **60**:110-12, 116, 119, 124, 126, 142, 154, 161
"Les trois filles de Milton" (Villiers de l'Isle Adam)
　　See "Les filles de Milton"
Trois Récits (Mauriac) **24**:183, 196, 203-05
The Troll Garden (Cather) **2**:90, 93, 96, 103, 113; **50**:52, 56, 58-9, 81, 83, 100, 104, 106-07, 110, 112-15, 119-24, 133, 135-39, 146, 152-53, 187, 193-95, 199-200, 236, 238, 241-3, 249, 763-65, 279
Trolley Ride (Calisher)
　　See *The Last Trolley Ride*
"Trop de faveur tue" (Stendhal) **27**:249, 263
"Tropic of Eden" (Ballard) **53**:131
"Trotsky's Garden" (Michaels) **16**:307, 309
"The Trouble" (Powers) **4**:368-69, 372
"The Trouble about Sophiny" (Dunbar) **8**:122
"Trouble in Wilton Road Victoria" (Sansom) **21**:105, 108
"Trouble Is My Business" (Chandler) **23**:65-6, 72, 89, 110
"The Trouble of Marcie Flint" (Cheever) **1**:90; **38**:53, 55, 85, 87-8
"Trouble on Lost Mountain" (Harris) **19**:124, 131, 179, 181
"The Trouble with Stamps" (Bulgakov) **18**:89
"Trouble with the Angels" (Hughes) **6**:112, 118-19, 122, 131
"Trouble with the Natives" (Clarke) **3**:124, 149
The Trouble with Tigers (Saroyan) **21**:142-46, 153, 158, 163
"Troubled Sleep" (Price) **22**:387-88
"The Troublemaker" (Tagore)
　　See "Apada"
"The Troubles of Dr. Thoss" (Ligotti) **16**:261, 263, 271, 274, 278, 283, 289
"The Troublesome Grandfathers" (Zoshchenko) **15**:388
"Troubling of the Water" (Henderson) **29**:326, 328
"The Trousers" (Dunbar) **8**:122

"The Trousseau" (Chekhov) **51**:34
"The Trout" (O'Faolain) **13**:297
"The Truant" (Irving) **2**:265
"The Truck" (Akutagawa Ryūnosuke)
　　See "Torokko"
"Trucks" (King) **17**:261-62
"A True Story" (Borowski) **48**:15
"A True Story" (Thomas)
　　See "The True Story"
"The True Story" (Thomas) **44**:331, 343-44,
　　346
The True Story of Ah Q (Lu Hsun)
　　See "Ah Q zheng zhuan"
"The True Story of Lavinia Todd"
　　(Auchincloss) **22**:5, 38
"True Thomas" (Benét) **10**:148
"True Trash" (Atwood) **46**:98
"The Trumpet" (de la Mare) **14**:88-90, 93
"The Trumpet Shall Sound" (Warner) **23**:369
"Trumpeter" (Gardner) **7**:225-26, 233, 235
"Trup" (Andrić) **36**:33
Trust Me (Updike) **13**:401-02, 409
"The Trust Property" (Tagore) **48**:335
"The Trustfulness of Polly" (Dunbar) **8**:122,
　　128, 147
"Trut" (Andrić) **36**:38
"The Truth" (Pirandello) **22**:252-53
"The Truth About Pyecraft" (Wells) **6**:360, 392,
　　404
"The Truth about the Ill-dressed" (Alarcon)
　　See "Verdades de paño pardo"
"The Truth About Toads" (Thurber) **47**:363
"Truth and Lies" (Price) **22**:370, 386
"Truth or Consequences" (Adams) **24**:11
"Try the Girl" (Chandler) **23**:59, 65, 67-8, 72,
　　80, 82, 87, 96, 98-9, 107-10
"The Tryst" (Chekhov) **51**:153
"The Tryst" (Oates) **6**:251-52
"The Tryst" (Turgenev) **7**:342-43; **57**:266
"A Tryst at an Ancient Earthwork" (Hardy)
　　2:210, 214-15
"The Tsalal" (Ligotti) **16**:292, 295, 297
"Le tsar noir" (Morand) **22**:169, 174
"Tselaya zhizn" (Pilnyak) **48**:253-55, 257-58,
　　272
"Tseytl un Rikl" (Singer) **53**:315
"Ts'u-chih" (P'u Sung-ling) **31**:191, 198
"Tu más profunda piel" (Cortázar) **7**:95
"Tu tzuch'un" (Akutagawa Ryūnosuke) **44**:52
"Tubal-Cain Forges A Star" (García Márquez)
　　See "Tubal-Caín forja una estrella"
"Tubal-Caín forja una estrella" (García
　　Márquez) **8**:154, 156
"Tudor Witch" (Lewis) **40**:280
"The Tuesday Afternoon Siesta" (García
　　Márquez)
　　See "Tuesday Siesta"
"Tuesday Night" (Beattie) **11**:14, 16
"Tuesday Siesta" (García Márquez) **8**:183, 185
"Le tueur de cygnes" (Villiers de l'Isle Adam)
　　14:397
"The Tug of Love" (Zangwill) **44**:378
"The Tugging" (Campbell) **19**:66, 73, 90
"The Tuggses at Ramsgate" (Dickens) **17**:117,
　　138
"Tulip" (Hammett) **17**:201, 203, 206, 227, 229
"Tuman" (Bunin) **5**:98
Una tumba sin nombre (Onetti)
　　See *Para una tumba sin nombre*
"Tung shêng" (P'u Sung-ling) **31**:204
"The Tunnel Under the World" (Ballard) **53**:110
"The Tunnel Under the World" (Pohl) **25**:213,
　　220, 222, 224-27, 229-32, 234, 237
"Tupejnyi xudožnik" (Leskov) **34**:110-11
A Tupolev Too Far (Aldiss) **36**:27
"A Turbulent Year" (Andrić)
　　See "Nemirna godina"
An T-úr-Ghort (Moore) **19**:300, 303-10, 312,
　　314, 316-25, 328-39, 341, 344-47, 352
"A Turkey Hunt" (Chopin) **8**:88
"The Turkey Season" (Munro) **3**:346

"Turkeyneck Morning" (Bukowski) **45**:52
"The Turkish Bath" (Trollope) **28**:321, 335,
　　340, 348
"The Turkish Night" (Morand)
　　See "La nuit Turque"
"Turmalin" (Stifter)
　　See "Tourmaline"
The Turn Inward (Hesse)
　　See *Der Weg nach Innen*
Turn Left at Thursday (Pohl) **25**:232
"The Turn of the Screw" (Oates) **6**:225
The Turn of the Screw (James) **8**:271-76, 283,
　　291-96, 298, 316, 318, 320, 325-26; **47**:200-
　　359
"Turn the Page" (Henderson) **29**:316
"Turned" (Gilman) **13**:126, 141
"The Turning Wheel" (Dick) **57**:104
"The Turtle Who Conquered Time" (Thurber)
　　47:264
"The Turtles of Tasman" (London) **4**:255-56,
　　266
Tuscan Fairy Tales (Lee) **33**:307, 310
"The Tutor's Tale" (Waugh) **41**:327
"Tutti Frutti" (Sansom) **21**:87, 105
"Tutto in un punto" (Calvino) **3**:92; **48**:47, 72-3,
　　166
"The Twelve Brothers" (Grimm and Grimm)
　　36:225-26
"Twelve Flying Monkeys Who Won't Copulate
　　Properly" (Bukowski) **45**:54
Twelve Men (Dreiser) **30**:110-11, 122, 133-34,
　　147-51
"The Twelve Months" (Grimm and Grimm)
　　36:237
"The Twelve Mortal Men" (McCullers) **9**:322,
　　338
"Twelve O'Clock" (Crane) **7**:108; **56**:79-80
"Twelve O'Clock" (Kluge) **61**:74
Twelve Stories and a Dream (Wells) **6**:366-67,
　　380, 391, 400
"Twenty Minutes" (Salter) **58**:172, 174-76, 179,
　　194-96
"Twenty-Five Bucks" (Farrell) **28**:87
*Twenty-Five Short Stories by Stephen Vincent
　　Benét* (Benét) **10**:143, 156
"Twenty-Four Hours in a Strange Diocese"
　　(Powers) **4**:380
"Twenty-Nine Inventions" (Oates) **6**:225
Twenty-one Stories (Agnon) **30**:3-4, 21
Twenty-One Stories (Greene) **29**:186, 213-14
"Twenty-Six and One" (Gorky)
　　See "Dvadtsat' shest' i odna"
"Twenty-Six Men and a Girl" (Gorky)
　　See "Dvadtsat' shest' i odna"
Twice-Told Tales (Hawthorne) **3**:154-55, 157-
　　61, 180, 184-85, 190; **39**:126
"Twilight at the Towers" (Barker) **53**:154, 156,
　　158, 162
"Twin Beds in Rome" (Updike) **13**:386
"The Twinkle in His Eye" (O'Hara) **15**:287,
　　291
"The Twins" (Spark) **10**:350, 352, 354, 356,
　　366
The Twins of Table Mountain (Harte) **59**:311
"The Twitching Colonel" (White) **39**:284, 293,
　　333-35
Twixt Land and Sea: Tales (Conrad) **9**:141, 148
"Two" (Singer) **3**:381; **53**:305
Two Adolescents (Moravia) **26**:132-34, 136,
　　140-41, 156
"Two Augurs" (Villiers de l'Isle Adam)
　　See "Deux augures"
"Two Blue Birds" (Lawrence) **4**:220
"Two Boys and a Girl" (Wolff) **63**:275
"Two Boys at Grinder Brothers" (Lawson)
　　18:202
"Two Bridgeport Tales" (Hood) **42**:235
"The Two Brothers" (Hesse) **9**:241-43
"The Two Brothers" (Pritchett) **14**:280, 285-86,
　　298, 305
"The Two Captains" (Lewis) **34**:163, 165
"Two Colonials" (Calisher) **15**:4, 14

"Two Corpses Go Dancing" (Singer) **3**:370;
　　53:323
"The Two Damsels" (Cervantes)
　　See "Las dos doncellas"
"Two Days Wasted in Kansas City" (Saroyan)
　　21:134
"Two Doctors" (James) **16**:245, 256
"Two Dogs and a Fence" (Lawson) **18**:233, 244
"The Two Drovers" (Scott) **32**:287, 292-93,
　　297-305, 310-12, 314-22, 324, 326
"The Two Elenas" (Fuentes)
　　See "Las dos Elenas"
"Two Fallen Angels" (Alarcon)
　　See "Dos ángeles caídos"
Two Fallen Angels and Other Forgotten Works
　　(Alarcon)
　　See *Dos ángeles caidos y otros escritos
　　olvidados*
"Two Families" (Lish) **18**:268
"The Two Flags" (Levi) **12**:276
Two Forsyte Interludes (Galsworthy) **22**:97
"Two Friends" (Cather) **2**:100, 109, 115, 117-
　　18; **50**:64, 105, 126, 130-31, 141, 143-44,
　　103, 208, 210-12, 252-53, 257
"Two Friends" (Freeman) **47**:123-25, 175
Two Friends (Turgenev) **7**:327; **57**:295-97
"Two Gallants" (Joyce) **3**:200-01, 205-06, 209,
　　214, 220-21, 225, 231-34, 237, 246; **26**:39,
　　46-7, 50; **44**:265-66; **64**:231, 257
"The Two Generals" (Trollope) **28**:319, 323,
　　326, 341, 346, 348
"Two Gentle People" (Greene) **29**:202, 212
"The Two Heroines of Plumplington"
　　(Trollope) **28**:314-15, 321, 325, 327, 339,
　　342-43, 348, 355-57
"The Two Hunchbacks" (Calvino)
　　See "I due gobbi"
Two Hussars (Tolstoy) **9**:376, 389
"Two in December" (Kazakov)
　　See "Dvoe v dekabre"
"Two in the Bush" (Thomas) **20**:290, 292, 294,
　　319
"Two in the Bush, and Other Stories"
　　(Thomas) **20**:289, 290
"Two Ivans" (Babel) **16**:50, 56, 58
"The Two Ivans" (Gogol)
　　See "The Tale of How Ivan Ivanovich Quar-
　　relled with Ivan Nikiforovich"
"The Two Kings and Their Two Labyrinths"
　　(Borges)
　　See "Los dos reyes y los dos laberintos"
"Two Ladies in Retirement" (Taylor) **10**:379-
　　80, 382, 384, 392, 418
"Two Little Confederates" (Page) **23**:295
Two Little Confederates (Page) **23**:285, 291-92,
　　308, 319
*Two Lives: Reading Turgenev; My House in
　　Umbria* (Trevor) **21**:258-59, 261, 263,
　　265; **58**:216-17, 219-22, 239-42, 264,
　　270-71
"Two Looks" (Galsworthy) **22**:63, 101
"Two Lovely Beasts" (O'Flaherty) **6**:269-70,
　　274, 281-82, 285
Two Lovely Beasts, and Other Stories
　　(O'Flaherty) **6**:262-63, 265, 276, 278,
　　281-83, 285
The Two Magics (James) **8**:296
"The Two Maidens" (Cervantes)
　　See "Las dos doncellas"
"Two Markets" (Singer) **3**:377
"The Two Masks" (Pirandello)
　　See "Le due maschere"
"Two Meditations" (Barth) **10**:42, 54-5, 75, 89-
　　90, 98, 100
Two Memorable Fantasies (Bioy Casares) **17**:48
"Two Men" (Johnson) **56**:234-35, 238, 259, 264
"Two Men, A Railway Story" (Moore)
　　See "Le Sinistre de Tonbridge"
"Two Men Running" (Jolley) **19**:223, 236-37,
　　244
"Two More Gallants" (Trevor) **21**:246-47;
　　58:231, 243-47, 270, 279

Two Mothers (Unamuno)
See *Dos madres*
"The Two Numantias" (Fuentes) 24:79
"Two of a Trade" (Morrison) 40:365
"Two Old Lovers" (Freeman) 1:197, 200-01;
47:83, 192
"Two Old Men" (Tolstoy) 9:377, 387
"Two Old-Timers" (Fitzgerald) 6:71
"Two or Three Graces" (Huxley) 39:158,
173-74
Two or Three Graces (Huxley) 39:157, 171
"Two Portraits" (Chopin) 8:72, 87, 98, 110
"Two Potters" (Lessing) 6:200
"Two Rivers" (Stegner) 27:196-97, 199
"Two Scholars Who Lived in Our Town"
(Agnon)
See "Sne talmide hakamim sehayu be'ir-
enu"
"Two Sheep" (Frame) 29:97-8, 115
"Two Ships" (Boyle) 16:145-46
"Two Sisters" (Farrell) 28:101
"Two Sisters" (Stifter)
See "Zwei Schwestern"
"Two Soldiers" (Faulkner) 1:151
Two Stories of the Seen and Unseen (Oliphant)
25:182, 184, 203
"Two Summers and Two Souls" (Chopin) 8:99
Two Symphonies (Gide) 13:42-3
"The Two Temples" (Melville) 1:303, 323
"Two Thanksgiving Day Gentlemen" (Henry)
5:187
"Two Thousand and Some Odd Dollars"
(Saroyan) 21:134
"The Two Travelers" (Grimm and Grimm)
36:229-30
"Two Useful Visits" (Price) 22:385, 388
"Two Views of a Cheap Theatre" (Dickens)
17:123
"Two White Beans" (Benét) 10:149
"Two Worlds" (Maclean) 13:278
"Two Wrongs" (Fitzgerald) 6:51, 60, 61
Two-faced Herma (Pirandello)
See *Erma bifronte*
"Typhoon" (Dreiser) 30:122, 153
"Typhoon" (Shiga) 23:348
Typhoon (Conrad) 9:141, 143-45, 147, 151-52,
157, 160, 163, 166, 186-88
"Tyrannosaurs Rex" (Bradbury) 29:47; 53:215
"The Tyranny of Realism" (Greene) 29:219-20
"The Tyrant" (O'Flaherty) 6:264
"Tyrants Destroyed" (Nabokov) 11:126
Tyrants Destroyed, and Other Stories
(Nabokov) 11:122-24
"Tyrant's Territory" (Aldiss) 36:20
"Le tzar et les grands-ducs" (Villiers de l'Isle
Adam) 14:396
"Tzvishen Zwee Berg" (Peretz) 26:196, 202,
220
"U istoka dnej" (Bunin) 5:98-9
"U musafirhani" (Andrić) 36:33
"U Stadionu" (Andrić) 36:51
"U vodenici" (Andrić) 36:33
"U zindanu" (Andrić) 36:33, 38
"U znakomykh" (Chekhov) 51:211-12
"Den uartige Dreng" (Andersen) 56:36
"Ubiistvo" (Chekhov) 51:200-2
"Uitel' Slovesnosti" (Chekhov) 2:128, 131-32,
155; 28:59; 51:58, 60, 84, 130, 146, 192,
194
"L'ufficiale inglese" (Moravia) 26:138, 151,
163
"The Ugliest Pilgrim" (Betts) 45:5, 7-8, 18-20,
31-32, 35
Ugly Anna (Coppard) 21:16
"The Ugly Duckling" (Andersen)
See "Den grimme [dJ]lling"
"Uglypuss" (Atwood) 2:18, 22; 46:45-6, 49,
52, 96
"Uisce faoi Dhraíocht" (O'Flaherty) 6:287-88
"UkradenaÁ vražda" (Čapek) 36:97
"Ukradený kaktus" (Čapek) 36:99, 102, 127

"Ukradený spis 139/VII odd. C." (Čapek) 36:96,
102, 105, 126
"Ukridge Sees Her Through" (Wodehouse)
2:354
"The Ulcerated Milkman" (Sansom) 21:115
The Ulcerated Milkman (Sansom) 21:101, 115,
127
Ulick and Soracha (Moore) 19:299
"Ulrike" (Borges) 41:131-34
"La última calaverada" (Alarcon) 64:3, 5-6, 9,
30
"Ultima ilusión" (Pardo Bazán)
See "La última ilusión de don Juan"
"La última ilusión de don Juan" (Pardo Bazán)
30:265, 267-69
La última niebla (Bombal) 37:2-3, 9, 12-17,
19-21, 23-30, 32-33, 36, 38, 40-41, 46-47
"Ultima Thule" (Galsworthy) 22:60, 74, 79, 99
"Ultima Thule" (Nabokov) 11:117
"The Ultimate City" (Ballard) 1:72, 74, 83-4
The Ultimate City (Ballard) 53:22, 62
"The Ultimate Melody" (Clarke) 3:133-34
"The Ultimate Millennia" (Aldiss) 36:19
"The Ultimate Safari" (Gordimer) 17:178, 180,
184-85, 188, 191
"Último capítulo" (Machado de Assis)
24:128-29
Ultimo round (Cortázar) 7:53, 70-1, 80, 91,
94-5
"El último viaje del buque fantasma" (García
Márquez) 8:154, 160, 167-68, 170-72, 186
Ultimo viene il corvo (Calvino) 3:106, 116;
48:53, 56
"Ultor de Lacy" (Le Fanu) 14:252
"Umbertino" (Svevo) 25:334, 351, 361
"The Umbrella" (Pirandello) 22:241
"Umney's Last Case" (King) 17:295
"The Unacknowledged Champion of
Everything" (Algren) 33:108
Un'altra vita (Moravia) 26:180
"Unapproved Route" (O'Connor) 5:371
"Unattractive" (Kazakov) 43:67
"An Unbiased Criticism" (Twain) 34:324
"Unbreakable Doll" (Narayan) 25:142
"Unc' Edinburg's Drowndin'" (Page) 23:284-
85, 291, 293, 297, 301-02, 316-17, 325-26
"Uncertain Flowering" (Laurence) 7:271-72
"Unchain My Heart" (Jones) 56:273-74
"Uncle" (Narayan) 25:139, 155, 167
"Uncle Anne" (Boyle) 5:54
"Uncle Casper" (Stuart) 31:261
"Uncle Fonse Laughed" (Stuart) 31:263
"Uncle Gabe's White Folks" (Page) 23:290
"Uncle Grant" (Price) 22:361, 388
"Uncle Henry's Love Nest" (Caldwell) 19:14
"Uncle Jeff" (Stuart) 31:231, 239-41
"Uncle Jim and Uncle Billy" (Harte) 8:227,
244; 59:317
"Uncle John, The Baptist" (Stuart) 31:249
"Uncle Ned's Short Stay" (Caldwell) 19:41, 51
"Uncle Otto's Truck" (King) 17:274; 55:250-51
"Uncle Peter's House" (Chesnutt) 7:12, 27;
54:52
"Uncle Remus" (Harris) 19:131
Uncle Remus and Brer Rabbit (Harris) 19:196
*Uncle Remus and His Friends: Old Plantation
Stories, Songs and Ballads* (Harris)
19:130, 133, 163-64, 187
*Uncle Remus and His Legends of the Old
Plantation* (Harris) 19:121
Uncle Remus and the Little Boy (Harris) 19:196
*Uncle Remus, His Songs and His Sayings:
Folklore of the Old Plantation* (Harris)
19:133, 136, 139, 144, 148, 160-62, 166-67,
169, 185, 187, 189, 193, 195-96
"Uncle Remus Initiates the Little Boy" (Harris)
19:185, 189, 197
"Uncle Simon's Sunday Out" (Dunbar) 8:122,
127, 144
"Uncle Spencer" (Huxley) 39:156, 173, 176

Uncle Tom's Children (Wright) 2:360-61, 363,
365-68, 370-71, 373-75, 379, 381-84,
386-88
"Uncle Valentine" (Cather) 2:98, 113-15; 50:76,
105-06, 141, 153, 208, 232, 247-48, 280-82
"Uncle Wellington's Wives" (Chesnutt) 7:3, 16,
23, 28-9, 33, 37; 54:44, 51, 58
"Uncle Wiggily in Connecticut" (Salinger)
2:290, 292, 295, 299, 305-06, 313-14
"Uncle Wiggly in Connecticut" (Salinger)
65:294-95, 304, 306, 308, 317
"Uncle Willy" (Faulkner) 1:151
"Unclean" (O'Flaherty) 6:259
"Uncles" (Atwood) 46:98
"Uncles" (Taylor) 10:379
"Uncle's Dream" (Dostoevsky) 2:164, 172, 184
"Uncle's Letters" (Narayan) 25:139, 155
*The Uncollected Short Stories of Sarah Orne
Jewett* (Jewett) 6:156, 166; 44:219
The Uncollected Wodehouse (Wodehouse) 2:343
"The Uncomfortable Pause Between Life and
Art" (Aldiss) 36:20, 25-6
The Uncommercial Traveller (Dickens) 17:123
"The Uncommon Prayer-Book" (James) 16:229-
32, 239, 241, 244-45
"The Unconquered" (Maugham) 8:380
"Uncovenanted Mercies" (Kipling) 5:271, 283;
54:77
"The Undefeated" (Hemingway) 1:209, 216,
218-19, 224, 230, 234; 36:252, 270, 325;
40:191, 209, 212, 215, 219
"Under a Glass Bell" (Nin) 10:299, 303-04
Under a Glass Bell (Nin) 10:299-300, 302-06
"Under a Glass Sky" (Bulgakov) 18:90
"Under Glass" (Atwood) 2:3, 6, 10, 13, 16;
46:33, 36, 38-9, 49-50, 76-7
"Under New Management" (Warner) 23:370-71
"Under the Banyan Tree" (Narayan) 25:135,
138
"Under the Boardwalk" (Phillips) 16:328-29
Under the Crust (Page) 23:287, 307
"Under the Deck Awnings" (London) 4:291
Under the Deodars (Kipling) 5:265
"Under the Fan" (Moore) 19:339-40, 342
"Under the Garden" (Greene) 29:187-88, 190,
195-200, 212-13, 215, 217, 226, 229-30
"Under the Greenwood Tree" (Williams)
31:325, 333
"Under the Jaguar Sun" (Calvino) 3:118-19
Under the Jaguar Sun (Calvino)
See *Sotto il sole giaguro*
"Under the Knife" (Singer) 3:362
"Under the Knife" (Wells) 6:360, 389, 393-94,
405
"Under the Lion's Paw" (Garland) 18:142, 148,
150, 154-55, 159, 163, 167-69, 172, 176,
182-83
"Under the Microscope" (Updike) 13:360, 387
"Under the Pyramids" (Lovecraft) 52:292
"Under the Radar" (Ford) 56:184, 196
"Under the Rose" (Pynchon) 14:308, 331, 334-
38, 341-42, 344, 347-48
"Under the Shrinking Royalty the Village
Smithy Stands" (Perelman) 32:235
"Under the Sky" (Bowles) 3:59, 61-2, 67, 79
"Under the Spreading Atrophy" (Perelman)
32:231
"Under the Sunset" (Stoker) 62:251
Under the Sunset (Stoker) 62:231, 235-36,
251-52
"Under the Volcano" (Lowry) 31:42
"Under the Willow-Tree" (Andersen) 6:4
"The Underground" (Dostoevsky) 2:187
"Underground Lady" (Yamamoto) 34:359
"Understanding Alvarado" (Apple) 50:9, 20-1,
27, 30-1, 42, 44
Understudies (Freeman) 47:87, 103, 105, 132,
160, 162, 164
"The Undertaker" (Pushkin)
See "Grobovshchik"
"Undertakers" (Kipling) 5:293; 54:136
"Underwater" (Bioy Casares) 17:94, 96

"Undine" (Dazai Osamu) 41:276
Undiscovered Country: The New Zealand Stories of Katherine Mansfield (Mansfield) 9:281
"The Undismayed Operator" (Bulgakov) 18:89
"Unearthing Suite" (Atwood) 2:17, 22; 46:38, 46, 50-1, 78-9, 96-7
"Unequally Yoked" (Norris) 28:205
"The Unexpected" (Chopin) 8:72, 100
"The Unexpected" (London) 4:253, 260-62
"Unexpected Guests" (Boell) 23:7
"An Unfinished Collection" (Wodehouse) 2:343
"An Unfinished Love Story" (Lawson) 18:201, 248, 250-51
"Unfinished Short Story" (Forster) 27:117
"An Unfinished Story" (Henry) 5:163, 171, 178-79, 182, 185; 49:197
"The Unfortunate" (Turgenev)
    See "Neschastnaya"
"The Unfortunate Lover" (Moravia)
    See *L'amante infelice*
The Unfortunate Lover (Moravia)
    See *L'amante infelice*
The Unfortunate Ones (White) 39:292
"An Unhappy Girl" (Turgenev)
    See "Neschastnaya"
"Unholy Living and Half Dying" (O'Faolain) 13:301, 305
"The Unholy Three" (Auchincloss) 22:29
"Unicorn" (Tanizaki)
    See "Kirin"
"The Unicorn in the Garden" (Thurber) 1:427-28, 431; 47:374-75, 387
"The Uniformed Stray" (Moorhouse) 40:293
"Uninhabitedness" (Pasternak) 31:108
"The Uninsured" (Gilchrist) 63:6
"The Union Buries Its Dead" (Lawson) 18:201-02, 206, 211, 213, 218, 220-21, 233-35, 237-38, 241, 243, 259, 261
"Union Reunion" (Wilson) 21:318, 321, 332, 344, 351, 357
Unions (Musil)
    See *Vereinigungen*
"The Unit" (Čapek) 36:92
"The United Idolaters" (Kipling) 54:96, 99
A Universal History of Infamy (Borges)
    See *Historia universal de la infamia*
A Universal History of Iniquity (Borges) 41:157
Universe (Heinlein) 55:171-73, 176, 182, 214, 232
"The University of Death" (Ballard) 53:16, 98
"The Unkindest Blow" (Saki) 12:295-96
"The Unknowable God" (Abe) 61:20
"The Unknown" (Bombal) 37:45
"An Unknown Man's Story" (Chekhov) 51:79, 129-30
"The Unknown Masterpiece" (Balzac)
    See "Le Chef d'oeuvre inconnu"
"The Unknown Quantity" (Henry) 5:197
"The Unknown Woman" (Villiers de l'Isle Adam)
    See "L'inconnue"
"The Unknown Woman of the Seine" (Nin) 10:304
"Unlighted Lamps" (Anderson) 1:27, 30, 39, 46-7, 53, 55
Unlucky for Pringle (Lewis) 34:163-64, 170, 178
"An Unmarried Man's Summer" (Gallant) 5:122, 130-31
"Unmistakably the Finest" (Bradfield) 65:60-61, 63, 65
"The Unnameable" (Lovecraft) 3:262, 276, 293-94; 52:284, 286, 314, 341
"The Unnatural Mother" (Gilman) 13:126; 62:190-91
"Uno de dos" (Arreola) 38:25
"Uno dei tre è ancora vivo" (Calvino) 48:41-2, 80-1
"Unpaid Consultant" (Vonnegut) 8:436
"The Unparalleled Adventure of One Hans Pfaall" (Poe) 1:400, 402, 406; 54:191

"The Unparalleled Invasion" (London) 4:255
"An Unpleasant Predicament" (Dostoevsky) 2:166, 184
"The Unpleasant Profession of Jonathan Hoag" (Heinlein) 55:186-87, 189-90, 215
"An Unpleasantness" (Chekhov) 28:58
The Unploughed Land (Cowan) 28:76
"Unpopular Gals" (Atwood) 46:75
"Unprofessional" (Kipling) 5:285
"An Unprotected Female at the Pyramids" (Trollope) 28:318, 323, 328-29, 332, 347
"Unready to Wear" (Vonnegut) 8:434
"The Unrest Cure" (Saki) 12:287, 300, 324, 326
"An Unsavoury Interlude" (Kipling) 54:96-97
"The Unseen" (Singer) 3:358, 362, 383-84
"Unser Karl" (Harte) 8:220
"Unshorn Locks and Bogus Bagels" (Perelman) 32:230
Unspeakable Practices, Unnatural Acts (Barthelme) 2:29-31, 35, 37-8, 51
"Unspoiled Monsters" (Capote) 47:64-7
"The Unspoiled Reaction" (McCarthy) 24:221-24
"Unstuck" (Updike) 13:404, 409
Unterhaltungen deutscher Ausgewanderten (Goethe) 38:161-62, 166, 187
"Until Forsaken" (Tanizaki)
    See "Suterareru made"
"Until One Is Deserted" (Tanizaki) 21:208
The Untilled Field (Moore)
    See *An T-úr-Ghort*
"Untitled Piece" (McCullers) 9:343, 345, 356-57
"The Untold Lie" (Anderson) 1:21, 34, 39, 41-2, 44, 52; 46:18
"'Unused'" (Anderson) 1:23, 27, 30, 39-40, 46-7, 53, 55; 55:3-4, 6, 8, 12, 28, 32-3, 35-6, 38, 44, 49, 52-3, 66, 74, 111
The Unvanquished (Faulkner) 1:151, 170, 177, 180; 35:176; 42:114
Unveröffentlichte Prosadichtungen (Walser) 20:333, 335
"The Unvexed Isles" (Warren) 4:387, 389-90, 395, 400; 58:310, 354
"Unwanted Heroine" (Wilson) 21:358, 361
"Unwelcome Words" (Bowles) 3:85-6
Unwelcome Words: Seven Stories (Bowles) 3:85
"An Unwilling Guest" (Freeman) 47:193
"The Unworthy Friend" (Borges) 4:18
"The Unwriteable Words" (Abe) 61:20
"An Unwritten Novel" (Woolf) 7:368, 371-72, 375-76, 378, 382, 388, 392, 397-99, 405, 408-09
"Unzen" (Endō) 48:192
"L'uomo che guarda" (Moravia) 26:142, 149
"L'uomo e la teoria darwiniana" (Svevo) 25:360
"Uomo nei gerbidi" (Calvino) 3:96; 48:36
"Up, Aloft in the Air" (Barthelme) 2:38; 55:23
"Up Among the Eagles" (Valenzuela) 14:359, 361, 366
Up Among the Eagles (Valenzuela)
    See *Donde viven las águilas*
"Up in Michigan" (Hemingway) 1:207, 219; 40:221; 63:40, 55, 79, 124-25
"Up North" (Cowan) 28:78
"Up the Bare Stairs" (O'Faolain) 13:300, 302, 304, 306-07
"Up the Coulée" (Garland) 18:142, 144, 148, 150, 154-56, 158-59, 161, 163, 168-70, 172, 175-76, 182, 193
"Upon the Dull Earth" (Campbell) 19:81
"Upon the Dull Earth" (Dick) 57:114-18, 137
"Upon the Sweeping Flood" (Oates) 6:224-25
Upon the Sweeping Flood, and Other Stories (Oates) 6:224-25
The Uprising in the Cévennes (Tieck)
    See *Der Aufruhr in den Cevennen*
"Uprooted" (Chekhov) 2:130
"Uprooted" (O'Connor) 5:369, 371, 375-77, 383, 397

"Uprooted" (Suckow) 18:394, 399-400, 405, 407-08, 415
"Upstairs in the Wineshop" (Lu Hsun)
    See "Zai jiulou shang"
"The Upturned Face" (Crane) 7:109, 143-45; 56:88, 105-10
"Uriah's Son" (Benét) 10:146
Urien's Voyage (Gide)
    See *Le voyage d'Urien*
Ursula (Keller) 26:91, 107-08, 111, 113
"Das Urteil" (Kafka) 5:225-26, 228-29, 232, 240, 243-45, 252-55; 35:227-28, 243, 262-63, 290; 60:225-27, 229-33, 235, 245, 247-51, 254, 257, 297-98
"The Use of Force" (Williams) 31:304-05, 312, 315, 317-23, 325, 333, 335-36, 338-39, 344-46, 351, 363-64
"The Used-Boy Raisers" (Paley) 8:399, 406-07
USFS 1919: The Ranger, The Cook and a Hole in the Sky (Maclean) 13:260, 270-71
"Usher II" (Bradbury) 29:50-1; 53:193-94, 198-99, 207-8, 222, 247-48, 250, 254, 257-58, 262
"Usomnivshiisia Makar" (Platonov) 42:248, 256
"Ustricy" (Chekhov) 51:102, 104
"Usurpation (Other People's Stories)" (Ozick) 15:302, 305, 311, 315-17, 326
"Utenok" (Solzhenitsyn) 32:352, 395
"Uvod" (Andrić) 36:63-4, 68
"V gorod" (Kazakov) 43:63,66
"V ovrage" (Chekhov) 2:128, 131-32, 145, 156-57; 28:59, 61; 51:26-7, 31, 124, 136, 150, 194, 199-203, 205-7, 209, 211
"V rodnom uglu" (Chekhov) 2:139, 142, 155, 157-58; 51:83, 130, 132, 204
"V ssylke" (Chekhov) 2:157; 51:70, 111, 113, 189
"V Stepi" (Gorky) 28:150, 190
"V zvezdnoj pustyne" (Platonov) 42:266
"Va bene" (Pirandello) 22:228
"Va' così che vai bene" (Calvino) 48:80
"The Vacant Lot" (Freeman) 47:111-12
"Vacation Time" (Boyle) 5:54
"Vacations in the South" (Andrić)
    See "Letovanje na jugu"
"Le Vaches" (Aymé) 41:14
The Vagabond (Colette)
    See *La vagabonde*
Vagabondaggio (Verga) 21:291, 297
La vagabonde (Colette) 10:257, 272-73, 291
"Valaida" (Wideman) 62:258-59, 268
"The Valentine" (Howells) 36:399
Valentino (Ginzburg) 65:116, 118-20, 123, 145
"The Valet" (Barnes) 3:22-4
"The Valiant Woman" (Powers) 4:380-81, 383
"The Valley" (Bass) 60:16-17, 20
"The Valley Between" (Marshall) 3:303, 308-09, 312, 315, 317
"The Valley of Childish Things" (Wharton) 6:427
The Valley of the Moon (London) 4:254
"The Valley of the Shadow" (Kipling) 5:261
"The Valley of the Spiders" (Wells) 6:361
"Vals capricho" (Castellanos) 39:36, 42
"The Vampire of the Village" (Chesterton) 46:130
"Vampirism" (Hoffmann)
    See "Der Vampyrismus"
"Eine Vampyrgeschichte" (Hoffmann)
    See "Der Vampyrismus"
"Der Vampyrismus" (Hoffmann) 13:186, 215, 228, 230
"Van Gogh's Room at Arles" (Elkin) 12:119-20
"Vanadium" (Levi) 12:256, 258, 265-67
"Vanddraaben" (Andersen) 56:35
"The Vane Sisters" (Nabokov) 11:116, 122-23, 125, 144
"Vanguard Reaches Menton" (Calvino)
    See "Gli avanguardisti a Mentone"
"Vanina Vanini" (Stendhal) 27:231, 248-49, 260

"The Vanishing of Vaudrey" (Chesterton) **1**:131; **46**:110-11, 135

"The Vanishing Prince" (Chesterton) **1**:122

"Vanishings" (Hood) **42**:226

"Vanity and Some Sables" (Henry) **5**:187

"Vánka" (Chekhov) **2**:130; **51**:48-9, 78, 105, 157-59

"Vanka Mazin" (Gorky) **28**:161

"Vanvild Kava" (Singer) **3**:383

"Varangian Times" (Pilnyak) **48**:288, 290

"Varenka Olesova" (Gorky) **28**:151

Varia Invención (Arreola) **38**:3, 8-12, 30

"The Variable Man" (Dick) **57**:104

Várias histórias (Machado de Assis) **24**:153

"Variation on a Theme" (Collier) **19**:98, 110, 114

"Varieties of Exile" (Gallant) **5**:134-35, 143

Various Inventions (Arreola)
　　See *Varia Invención*

"Various Temptations" (Sansom) **21**:90, 92-5, 112-13, 124

"Le vase étrusque" (Mérimée) **7**:278, 280-1, 283, 286-91, 300, 304

"Vashti in the Dark" (Crane) **56**:95

"Vastarien" (Ligotti) **16**:263-64, 267, 269, 274, 276-80, 283, 285-89, 294

"Vaster than Empires and More Slow" (Le Guin) **12**:208-10, 216, 231-33

"The Vats" (de la Mare) **14**:66, 82, 90

"Vayber" (Singer) **53**:322

"A vayse kapore" (Aleichem) **33**:38-9

"Večer nakanune Ivana Kupala" (Gogol) **4**:88, 119-21; **29**:132, 135

Vechera ná khutore bliz Dikanki (Gogol) **4**:85-7, 98, 117; **52**:82, 104, 144, 146, 165

Vechny muzh (Dostoevsky) **2**:166-67, 175-77, 184-85; **44**:160

"Vegetable Love" (Apple) **50**:5-6, 9-13, 20, 26, 30-2, 34-5, 38

"Vehaya he'akov lemishor" (Agnon) **30**:7-8

"The Veldt" (Bradbury) **29**:42, 51; **53**:252

"Velga" (Bunin) **5**:98

"Vendée" (Faulkner) **1**:171

"Une vendetta" (Maupassant) **1**:277

"La vendetta revenge" (Balzac) **5**:4, 22, 29, 31

"The Venerable" (Coppard)
　　See "The Old Venerable"

"The Venerated Bones" (Lagerkvist) **12**:195

"La vengeance d'une femme" (Barbey d'Aurevilly) **17**:11, 15, 18-21, 33-4, 36-7, 44

"The Vengeance of 3902090" (Thurber) **1**:419

"The Vengeance of the Damned" (Bukowski) **45**:63

"Venice" (Sansom) **21**:86

"The Venomous Viper of the Volga" (Lardner) **32**:132

"Il ventaglino" (Pirandello) **22**:233, 284-86

"The Venturers" (Henry) **5**:159, 190-91

"The Venus" (Williams) **30**:301, 343, 345, 360

"Venus, Cupid, Folly, and Time" (Taylor) **10**:391, 407, 409, 419

"La Vénus d'Ille" (Mérimée) **7**:276, 279-80, 283-6, 288, 290, 293-5, 297, 301, 306

"The Venus of Ille" (Mérimée)
　　See "La Vénus d'Ille"

"Venus Smiles" (Ballard) **53**:72, 78-9, 81, 91, 128, 131

"Véra" (Villiers de l'Isle Adam) **14**:377, 379, 381-82, 384, 387, 390, 396, 398, 403, 408

"Veränderungen in Staech" (Boell) **23**:35

"Veraneo" (Donoso) **34**:5-6, 21-23, 29-31, 35, 49

Veraneo y otros cuentos (Donoso) **34**:3, 24, 29,49

"Verano" (Cortázar) **7**:61-3

"Verba testamentária" (Machado de Assis) **24**:128-29, 132

"Verbal Transcription—6 AM" (Williams) **31**:322, 334

"Verboten" (Gordon) **59**:274

"Verdades de paño pardo" (Alarcon) **64**:10

"The Verdict" (Wharton) **6**:435

El verdugo (Balzac) **5**:21, 31

Vereinigungen (Musil) **18**:288, 290-93, 317

"Verlie I Say unto You" (Adams) **24**:5

Die Verlobung (Tieck) **31**:270-71, 286

Die Verlobung in St. Domingo (Kleist) **22**:122-24, 146, 151-52

Die verlorene Ehre der Katharina Blum: oder, Wie Gewalt entstehen und wohin sie führen kann (Boell) **23**:13-15, 19, 25-6, 28-30, 33, 36, 39

Das Verlorene Lachen (Keller) **26**:91, 107, 121

"Das Verlorene Spiegelbild" (Hoffmann) **13**:183, 200

Vermilion Sands (Ballard) **1**:78; **53**:6-7, 11, 32, 67, 69, 71, 73, 75, 77-80, 115, 120, 127-31

"Verochka" (Chekhov) **51**:41-2, 83, 109, 159, 211

Veronika (Storm) **27**:281

"Versamina" (Levi) **12**:278-79

Die Versuchung der Stillen Veronika (Musil) **18**:288-89, 291-93, 302, 317, 320-22

Die Versuchung des Pescara (Meyer) **30**:187-88, 204-05, 236-38, 240-42

Die vertauschten Köpfe (Mann) **5**:312-13, 315, 323, 326

"The Vertical Ladder" (Sansom) **21**:90-92

"Vertigo" (Čapek) **36**:128

Die verwandlung (Kafka) **5**:210-13, 215, 217-20, 224-25, 231, 234, 239-40, 245, 252; **29**:340-42, 346, 349, 355, 365, 369-70; **35**:215-96; **60**:226-27, 232, 235, 245, 247-57, 297-98

Very Far Away from Anywhere Else (Le Guin) **12**:231, 241

"A Very Fine Fiddle" (Chopin) **8**:88, 103

Very Good, Jeeves (Wodehouse) **2**:346

"The Very Good Mother" (Svevo)
　　See "La buonissima madre"

"The Very Image" (Villiers de l'Isle Adam)
　　See "A s'y méprendre"

"A Very Late Spring" (Caldwell) **19**:34

A Very Long Way from Anywhere Else (Le Guin)
　　See *Very Far Away from Anywhere Else*

"The Very Old Are Beautiful" (Betts) **45**:9, 17, 27

"A Very Old Man with Enormous Wings" (García Márquez)
　　See "Un Señor muy viejo con unas alas enormes"

"The Very Proper Gander" (Thurber) **1**:431

"A Very Short Story" (Hemingway) **63**:79-80

Das verzauberte Haus (Musil)
　　See *Die Versuchung der Stillen Veronika*

"Der Verzicht" (Lenz) **33**:318, 320

"Veselyi dvor" (Bunin) **5**:87

Veshnie vody (Turgenev) **7**:316-17, 320-21, 324-25, 327-29, 334, 336-38, 357-58, 361-62; **57**:305, 385

"Vesna v Fial'te" (Nabokov) **11**:112, 114, 128-29

Vešnie vody (Turgenev)
　　See *Veshnie vody*

"The Vessel of Wrath" (Maugham) **8**:375, 378

"The Vest" (Thomas) **44**:334, 337, 344

"La veste lunga" (Pirandello) **22**:250, 283-85

"Vesti iz rodiny" (Bunin) **5**:98

"Vestiges: Harlem Sketches" (Fisher)
　　See "The South Lingers On"

"Věštkyně" (Čapek) **36**:96, 98-9, 127

"A Veteran Falls" (Hughes) **6**:122

"Veteran of the Private Evacuations" (Ballard) **1**:70

"Les veuves" (Baudelaire) **18**:4, 9, 17, 32, 39, 60

"Via Crucis" (Lispector) **34**:207, 213

A via crucis do corpo (Lispector) **34**:203-05, 209-15

The Via Crucis of the Body (Lispector)
　　See *A via crucis do corpo*

"Via negativa" (Salter) **58**:186, 190, 192

"Il viaggio" (Pirandello) **22**:255, 275, 277, 283-84, 286

"Un viaggio con le mucche" (Calvino) **48**:83

"Viaje a la semilla" (Carpentier) **35**:91, 95, 106, 110, 113, 126

"Viaje de novios" (Pardo Bazán) **30**:272

"El viajero" (Pardo Bazán) **30**:264

"The Vice-Consul" (Pritchett) **14**:273

"A Victim of Circumstances" (Gissing) **37**:64

A Victim of Circumstances (Gissing) **37**:80

"A Victim of Heredity" (Chesnutt) **54**:43

"Victim of Justice" (Dreiser)
　　See "Nigger Jeff"

"Victim or Hero?" (Farrell) **28**:125

"La vìctima de Tadeo Limardo" (Bioy Casares) **17**:70, 73

"The Victor" (Dreiser) **30**:122

"Victor Blue" (Beattie) **11**:15, 18, 21

"Victoria Kazimirovna" (Zoshchenko) **15**:400-01

"Victory" (Faulkner) **1**:148

"The Victory" (Tagore) **48**:301

"The Victory Burlesk" (Atwood) **2**:19

"Victory over Japan" (Gilchrist) **63**:11, 28

Victory over Japan (Gilchrist) **14**:152-55, 157-59, 162-63; **63**:5, 8, 12, 17-19, 21, 27-28, 30

"Vida Interminable" (Allende) **65**:33, 39, 47-48, 54

"La vida no es muy seria en sus cosas" (Rulfo) **25**:244

"Vida nueva" (Pardo Bazán) **30**:262

"La vida privada" (Arreola) **38**:9, 12-13

"El vidrio roto" (Pardo Bazán) **30**:272

"La vie boheme" (Gordimer) **17**:167

"Vieja moralidad" (Fuentes) **24**:29, 32, 45, 56, 58, 62, 71, 73

"Vienne" (Rhys) **21**:53, 61-2, 67, 74-5

Viennese Idylls (Schnitzler) **61**:290

"The Viennese Opera Ball" (Barthelme) **2**:28; **55**:16, 20

"Le vieux saltimbanque" (Baudelaire) **18**:4-5, 15, 17-18, 27-32

"View from a Height" (Vinge) **24**:336, 342-43

"A View from a Hill" (James) **16**:231, 233, 237, 240, 244

"The View from the Balcony" (Stegner) **27**:195, 197, 202, 224

"A View from the Treetop" (Kiely) **58**:148

A View of Dawn in the Tropics (Cabrera Infante)
　　See *Vista del amanecer en el trópico*

"The View of Rome" (Warner) **23**:373-74

"A View of the Woods" (O'Connor) **1**:342-45, 356; **61**:202,204

"A View of the Yasukuni Festival" (Kawabata)
　　See "Shōkonsai Ikkei"

"Viewfinder" (Carver) **51**:5, 7, 12, 20

"Views of My Father Weeping" (Barthelme) **2**:31, 42, 46, 48, 55; **55**:5, 11, 34-6

"Vigilante" (Steinbeck) **11**:208, 225, 232-33, 241-42, 244

"La vigna" (Pavese) **19**:369, 376, 385

"A Vignette" (James) **16**:251, 254

The Viking Portable Library Dorothy Parker (Parker) **2**:276, 278

"De vilde Svaner" (Andersen) **6**:13, 19, 30, 35, 40; **56**:37

"The Villa" (Spencer) **57**:198

"Villa on the Hill" (Pavese) **19**:387

"Villa Violetta" (Lavin) **4**:183, 185

"The Village" (Dixon) **16**:217

"The Village Angler" (Irving) **37**:266

"The Village Inside" (Hood) **42**:214, 219-20, 222, 239-42

"A Village Lear" (Freeman) **47**:85

"A Village Lear" (Turgenev)
　　See "Stepnoy Korol 'Lir"

"Village of Goryukhino" (Pushkin)
　　See *Istoriia sela Goriukhino*

The Village of Stepanchikovo (Dostoevsky)
　　See *The Friend of the Family*

"The Village Olujaci" (Andrić)
See "Olujaci"
A Village Romeo and Juliet (Keller)
See Romeo und Julia auf dem Dorfe
"The Village Saint" (Head) 52:188, 195-96, 199, 201, 227
"A Village Singer" (Freeman) 1:197, 200, 47:105, 108, 134, 145-46, 148-49, 180, 194
"The Village That Voted the Earth Was Flat" (Kipling) 5:277, 280, 282
"The Villager" (Jackson) 39:210, 215, 216, 217, 223, 225
"Villon's Wife" (Dazai Osamu)
See "Buiyon no tsuma"
"Le Vin de Paris" (Aymé) 41:3, 11, 17, 32-33
"Vinden fort[dj]ller om Valdemar Daae og hans Døttre" (Andersen) 56:37
"The Vindication of Jared Hargot" (Dunbar) 8:138
Vinegar Puss (Perelman) 32:229, 236
"The Vineyard" (Pavese)
See "La vigna"
"Viney's Free Papers" (Dunbar) 8:122, 127, 131, 133, 144
"Vino" (Andrić) 36:50
"Vino generoso" (Svevo) 25:329, 331, 335-36, 351, 354, 357, 359-60
"A Vintage Thunderbird" (Beattie) 11:4-5, 17, 29
Vinter-Eventyr (Dinesen)
See Winter's Tales
Viola tricolor (Storm) 27:282
"Violation" (Gordon) 59:231, 267
"The Violent Noon" (Ballard) 53:39, 41
"Violet" (Mansfield) 38:203, 231
"The Virgin and the Gipsy" (Lawrence) 4:205-06
The Virgin and the Nun (Keller)
See Die Jungfrau und die Nonne
The Virgin as Knight (Keller)
See Die Jungfrau als Ritter
"The Virgin of Seven Daggers" (Lee) 33:302, 308, 310-11
"Virgin Violeta" (Porter) 4:341, 350; 31:163, 178; 43:223, 230, 237, 253, 292
"Virginia and Paul" (Villiers de l'Isle Adam)
See "Virginie et Paul"
"The Virginians Are Coming" (Farrell) 28:127
"Virginie et Paul" (Villiers de l'Isle Adam) 14:379, 381, 384, 386-87, 390, 394, 396
"Virgínius: narrativa de um advogado" (Machado de Assis) 24:155
"Virgins" (Trevor) 21:246, 248
"The Virgin's Gift" (Trevor) 58:299-301
"Virility" (Ozick) 15:298, 300, 313
"Virtue" (Galsworthy) 22:101
"Virtue" (Maugham) 8:378
"A Virtuoso's Collection" (Hawthorne) 3:171
"Virus X" (Gallant) 5:139
Il visconte dimezzato (Calvino) 3:90-1, 94, 99, 106, 117; 48:44-5, 90, 150, 164, 178
"Vision" (Gordon) 59:261
"Vision" (Tagore) 48:301
La vision de Babouc (Voltaire) 12:340-1
"La vision de Charles XI" (Mérimée) 7:287, 289
"A Vision of Judgment" (Wells) 6:360, 391
"The Vision of the Fountain" (Hawthorne) 3:178, 182
"A Vision of the World" (Cheever) 1:93-6, 105; 38:54-5, 61, 66; 57:9
"The Vision of Tom Chuff" (Le Fanu) 14:220, 223
"Visions" (Turgenev) 7:315
"Visions: A Fantasy" (Turgenev)
See "Prizraki. Fantaziya"
"Visions of Budhardin" (Dybek) 55:125, 127, 134, 141-42
"A Visit" (Millhauser) 57:189
"The Visit" (Spencer) 57:197, 240
"A Visit in Bad Taste" (Wilson) 21:322, 327, 332, 339, 344, 352-53

"A Visit Next Door" (Jewett) 6:158
"A Visit of Charity" (Welty) 1:470; 51:306, 340
"A Visit of Condolence" (Lawson) 18:201
"A Visit to America" (Thomas) 3:393
"A Visit to Anselm Oakes" (Isherwood) 56:205
"A Visit to Avoyelles" (Chopin) 8:72, 84
"A Visit to Grandpa's" (Thomas) 3:397, 402, 405, 410, 412; 44:324, 350, 359
"A Visit to Mingus County" (Caldwell) 19:41
"A Visit to Morin" (Greene) 29:187, 189, 198, 211
"A Visit to Newgate" (Dickens) 17:110, 116-17, 121
"A Visit to the Cemetery" (Lavin) 4:164-66, 168-69
"A Visit to the Dentist" (Sansom) 21:99, 116, 126
"Visit to the Fair" (Williams) 31:331, 350, 359, 361
"The Visit to the Museum" (Nabokov) 11:117, 145, 147, 152
"A Visit to the Zoo" (Davie) 52:7
"La visita" (Pirandello) 22:261, 269
"Una visita al viejo poeta" (Unamuno) 11:312
"The Visitants from Yesterday" (Murfree) 22:220-22
"Visitation" (Schulz) 13:333, 339
"Le Visiteur" (Trevor) 58:300
"Le visiteur nocturne" (Mauriac) 24:197, 203-05
"The Visiting of Mother Danbury" (Dunbar) 8:127
"Visiting with King Ahasuerus" (Aleichem) 33:20
"The Visitor" (Bowen) 3:40
"A Visitor" (Dazai Osamu) 41:238, 240, 242
"The Visitor" (Thomas) 3:400, 407, 409; 44:322, 330, 333-34, 336-38, 348, 355-58
"A Visitor and His Opinions" (Oliphant) 25:204
"Visitors" (Barthelme) 2:56; 55:93, 109, 111, 113
"Visitors" (Mukherjee) 38:238-41, 252, 255, 265, 271
"The Visitors April '34" (Thomas) 44:333
Visňevyi sad (Chekhov) 51:30, 35
"Uma vista de Alcebíades" (Machado de Assis) 24:129
Vista del amanecer en el trópico (Cabrera Infante) 39:2-19, 21
"Visti alla mensa" (Calvino) 48:41
Vita dei campi (Verga) 21:280-81, 285-86, 291, 294, 298-99, 301-02, 305, 308, 313
"La vita difficile" (Calvino) 48:80, 84
"La vita nuda" (Pirandello) 22:231
La vita nuda (Pirandello) 22:231, 275
"Vitamins" (Carver) 8:26, 32
"Vittoria Accoramboni, duchesse de Bracciano" (Stendhal) 27:231, 249, 260-61
"Vittoria delle formiche" (Pirandello) 22:270
"La viuda de Montiel" (García Márquez) 8:187-90
"El viudo Román" (Castellanos) 39:30, 34, 37, 38, 73
"Viva la introyección!" (Unamuno) 11:312
"Vive la France" (Boell) 23:38
"Viver!" (Machado de Assis) 24:127-29
"Vivian Thanks God" (Farrell) 28:112
"Viy" (Gogol) 4:82, 86, 102-03; 29:149; 52:103-4, 107, 113, 122, 139, 169, 171
"Vizitnye kartochki" (Bunin) 5:114
"Vladýcnyj sud" (Leskov) 34:111
"Vlemk the Box-Painter" (Gardner) 7:223-26, 238-41
"A Vocation and a Voice" (Chopin) 8:72, 78, 93, 97, 99, 100, 102
"Les vocations" (Baudelaire) 18:5
"La Vocazione de Suora Agnese" (Verga) 21:294
Le voci della sera (Ginzburg) 65:116-19, 125-26, 130, 132, 139-40, 146
Die Vogelscheuche (Tieck) 31:275, 286-87

"The Voice" (Cowan) 28:75
"The Voice" (Nin) 10:300-01, 307-11, 314-15, 317, 322-23
"The Voice" (Pritchett) 14:271, 286
"A Voice Foretold" (Wideman) 62:278
"The Voice in the Bones" (Ligotti) 16:271, 274, 280, 288, 296, 297
"The Voice of . . ." (Galsworthy) 22:99
"The Voice of the Beach" (Campbell) 19:66, 70-1, 73, 80, 84, 88, 90
"The Voice of the City" (Henry) 5:171, 191, 194
The Voice of the City (Henry) 5:155, 192; 49:205
"The Voice of the Mountain" (Moore) 19:345
The Voice of the People (Peretz) 26:204-05
"The Voice of the Turtle" (Maugham) 8:379
Voices (Cowan) 28:81-83
Voices at Play (Spark) 10:353, 355, 359
"Voices from the Dust" (Vinge) 24:337, 343
"Voices from the Moon" (Dubus) 15:94, 96, 100-01
Voices From the Moon (Dubus) 15:81-3, 85-6, 89-96, 98
Voices in the Evening (Ginzburg)
See Le voci della sera
"Voices Lost in the Snow" (Gallant) 5:135, 139
"The Voices of Adamo" (Laurence) 7:245, 249-50
"The Voices of Time" (Ballard) 1:71, 80; 53:10-14, 22, 31-2, 45, 47, 50, 83, 85-90
"Voitel' nica" (Leskov) 34:111-12, 117, 125
"The Volcano" (Stegner) 27:195, 220, 224
"The Volcano Dances" (Ballard) 53:11
"Vollendung der Liebe" (Musil) 18:288-93, 317-20
"Volodja boloj i Volodja malen'kij" (Chekhov) 51:175, 191, 193
"The Volunteer" (Stegner) 27:198
Von Jenseit des Meeres (Storm) 27:278, 283-84
"Von Kempelen and His Discovery" (Poe) 1:402
"Vor dem gesetz" (Kafka) 5:254; 29:339, 351; 60:240-42
"Vorgeschichte" (Lenz) 33:321-23, 325-27
"Voron" (Bunin) 5:113
"Vory" (Chekhov) 51:111, 180
"Vos heyst 'neshome'" (Peretz) 26:218
"Vox populi" (Villiers de l'Isle Adam) 14:381-82, 386, 394-96
"The Voyage" (Mansfield) 9:278, 282, 303-04; 38:203
Le voyage d'Urien (Gide) 13:57-61, 63, 72
Voyage en Orient (Nerval) 18:328, 334, 336, 346-47, 366
"The Voyage to Rosewood" (Oates) 6:231
"Vozdushnye puti" (Pasternak) 31:96-8, 113-14, 117, 120
"Vprok" (Platonov) 42:255-56, 259
Les vrilles de la vigne (Colette) 10:261, 263
La vuelta al día en ochenta mundos (Cortázar) 7:53, 61, 91, 94
"V.V.: or Plots and Counterplots" (Alcott) 27:3-5, 32
"Vystrel" (Pushkin) 27:129, 134-44, 163, 166-68, 182-83, 186-87
"Die Waage der Baleks" (Boell) 23:6-8, 22
"Wa-ch'u" (P'u Sung-ling) 31:192
"Waga namida o nuguitamo, hi" (Oe)
See "Mizu kara waga namida o nuguitamo hi"
"The Wages of Sin" (Dreiser) 30:155
"The Waging of the Peace" (Pohl) 25:223, 237
"A Wagner Concert" (Cather) 2:90-1, 96, 103, 105, 108;
"A Wagner Matinée" (Cather) 2:90-1, 96, 103, 105, 108; 50:57-9, 62, 82, 106-07, 112, 123, 133-35, 137, 139, 197-98, 239-41, 245, 264, 275, 279
"The Wagnerians" (Auchincloss) 22:29
"Wahiah—A Spartan Mother" (Garland) 18:147, 178
"A Waif of the Plains" (Harte) 8:222, 251

"The Waif Woman" (Stevenson) **51**:240
"Wailing Well" (James) **16**:242, 244, 251
"The Wait" (Borges)
See "La espera"
"Waiting" (Beattie) **11**:13, 22
"The Waiting" (Borges)
See "La espera"
"Waiting" (Chang) **28**:26; 31; 34
"Waiting" (Dubus) **15**:89
"Waiting" (Oates) **6**:232
"Waiting at Dachau" (Price) **22**:366, 369, 376, 378-79, 384, 388
"Waiting for Santy" (Perelman) **32**:211
"Waiting for Stella" (Adams) **24**:12
"Waiting for the Moving of the Water" (Leskov) **34**:128
"Waiting for the Postman to Knock" (Clarke) **45**:87, 92, 94, 109
"Waiting for the Universe to Begin" (Aldiss) **36**:19
Waiting for Winter (O'Hara) **15**:276-79, 283-86
"The Waiting Grounds" (Ballard) **1**:68, 76; **53**:8, 31-2, 45
"The Waiting Room" (Boell) **23**:38
"The Waiting Room" (Čapek)
See "Čekárna"
"The Waiting Supper" (Hardy) **2**:211, 215-16, 219, 223; **60**:182
"Waiting Up" (Updike) **13**:387
Wakai (Shiga) **23**:339, 344, 346, 350-58, 363
"The Wake" (Dybek) **55**:127, 134, 136, 139-41
"Wake for the Living" (Bradbury) **29**:51
"The Wake of Patsy McLaughlin" (Farrell) **28**:100
"Wakefield" (Hawthorne) **3**:154, 159, 161-62, 178, 189, 191
Waking Nightmares (Campbell) **19**:76-8, 87
Waldeinsamkeit (Tieck) **31**:286
"Waldemar Daa and His Daughters" (Andersen)
See "The Wind Tells of Valdemar Daae and His Daughters"
"Der Waldgänger" (Stifter) **28**:273, 297
Waldo and Magic, Inc. (Heinlein) **55**:217
"Der Waldsteig" (Stifter) **28**:287, 290, 299
Waldwinkel (Storm) **27**:286, 314
"Walimai" (Allende) **65**:16, 54
"The Walk" (Donoso)
See "Paseo"
"The Walk" (Walser) **20**:336-37, 349, 360-61
The Walk, and Other Stories (Walser) **20**:337
"A Walk in the Dark" (Clarke) **3**:124, 147-49
"Walk in the Moon Shadows" (Stuart) **31**:226-27, 236
"A Walk in the Wheat" (Kiely) **58**:148
"A Walk in the Woods" (Bowen) **3**:54
"Walker Brothers Cowboy" (Munro) **3**:321, 329, 343, 347
"A Walking Delegate" (Kipling) **5**:279
"Walking Lessons" (Price) **22**:365-66, 368, 372-73, 385, 387
"Walking on Water" (Atwood) **46**:65-6, 68-9
"Walking on Water" (Munro) **3**:331, 346
"Walking Out" (Beckett) **16**:100
"Walking Round the City" (Metcalf) **43**:107
"Die Walkuere" (Mann) **5**:310
"The Wall" (Sansom) **21**:81-2, 90-2, 95, 122-24
"The Wall" (Sartre)
See "Le Mur"
The Wall, and Other Stories (Sartre)
See *Le mur*
"The Wall of Darkness" (Clarke) **3**:125, 129, 147
The Wall: The Crime of Mr. S. Karuma (Abe)
See *Kabe-S. Karuma shi no hansai*
"Walled City" (Oates) **6**:251-52
"A Walled Garden" (Taylor) **10**:382, 410
"The Wallet" (Updike) **13**:402
"The Walls of Jericho" (Dunbar) **8**:122, 136, 149
"Wally" (Auchincloss) **22**:48
"Wally Whistles Dixie" (Beattie) **11**:16, 23, 28

"The Walnut Hunt" (Caldwell) **19**:9
Wälsungenblut (Mann) **5**:310-11, 321, 323, 344
"Walt" (Gordon) **59**:262
"Walt and Will" (Apple) **50**:23, 32, 34, 41, 45
"Walter Briggs" (Updike) **13**:390, 400
"Walter Kömpff" (Hesse) **9**:235
"Walter T. Carriman" (O'Hara) **15**:264, 269
"The Waltz" (Parker) **2**:274, 281, 283, 285-86
"Waltz Caprice" (Castellanos)
See "Vals capricho"
"Wan Lee, the Pagan" (Harte) **8**:249; **59**:294
"Wanda's" (Beattie) **11**:16
"The Wanderer" (Kazakov) **43**:58
"Wanderer, kommst du nach Spa..." (Boell) **23**:37
"The Wanderers" (Lewis) **40**:272, 276-77, 280-82
"Wanderers" (Suckow) **18**:389, 415
"The Wanderers" (Welty) **1**:479, 493; **51**:275, 278, 283, 290, 292, 297, 305, 310, 322-23, 329, 338
Wandering (Lu Hsun)
See *P'anghuang*
"The Wandering Jew" (Akutagawa Ryūnosuke) **44**:62
"Wandering Willie's Tale" (Scott) **32**:288-89, 291, 299-300, 303, 306, 308-10, 314, 320
"A Wand'ring Minstrel, I" (Gordimer) **17**:153
"Wang Ch'eng" (P'u Sung-ling) **31**:191, 206
"Wang Tzu-an" (P'u Sung-ling) **31**:199
"Wang-che" (P'u Sung-ling) **31**:192
"A Waning Moon" (Sansom) **21**:89-92, 95, 114
"Wants" (Paley) **8**:397, 399, 416
"Wapping Workhouse" (Dickens) **17**:123
"The War" (Saroyan) **21**:133, 136
"War and Peace" (Saroyan) **21**:161
"The War Baby" (Lewis) **34**:153, 165, 172, 175
"War Between Saints" (Verga) **21**:300
"War Fever" (Ballard) **53**:56, 67
War Fever (Ballard) **53**:35-6, 67, 113, 117
"The War Generation" (Endō) **48**:192-93
"The War in Spain" (Saroyan) **21**:163
"The War in the Bathroom" (Atwood) **2**:4, 6-8, 10; **46**:26, 33, 38, 40-1, 76, 92, 94
"War Memories" (Crane) **56**:87-8
"The War Millennia" (Aldiss) **36**:19
"The War of the Wall" (Bambara) **35**:42
The War of Time (Carpentier)
See *Guerra del tiempo*
"Ward No. Six" (Chekhov)
See "Palata No. 6"
"Ward O 3 b" (Lewis) **40**:272-73, 277, 279, 283
"A Ward of Colonel Starbottle's" (Harte) **8**:249
"The Warden" (Gardner) **7**:213-14, 218, 222, 231
"The Wardrobe" (Mann) **5**:330
"The Warehouse" (Singer) **3**:358, 360
"Warera no Kyoki o ikinobiru michi o oshieyo" (Oe) **20**:223-28
"The Wares in Rio" (Ellison) **14**:146
"The Warlock" (Stafford) **26**:300
"The Warm, Quiet Valley of Home" (Saroyan) **21**:144, 150
"Warm River" (Caldwell) **19**:4, 6
"A Warning to the Curious" (James) **16**:232-33, 236-37, 252, 256
A Warning to the Curious (James) **16**:238, 251, 255
"The Warrior Princess Ozimbu" (Price) **22**:361, 384-85
"Der Wärter" (Hauptmann) **37**:258
"Was" (Faulkner) **1**:148, 173-74, 182; **35**:146-47, 157, 186, 195
"Wash" (Faulkner) **1**:166, 180
Waste of Timelessness, and Other Early Stories (Nin) **10**:305-06
"Watakushi no mono" (Endō) **48**:192, 197-99
"The Watch" (Bass) **60**:4-5, 30-32, 40
"The Watch" (Dixon) **16**:200, 211
"The Watch" (Turgenev)
See "Časy"

The Watch (Bass) **60**:3-4, 6, 8-10, 16, 18, 20, 24, 27-28, 30, 39
"Watch and Ward" (Pirandello) **22**:244
"Watch Out for Daddy" (Algren) **33**:96, 98
"Watch the Birdie" (Campbell) **19**:77
"Watch This Space" (Clarke) **3**:133
"The Watch Towers" (Ballard) **53**:8, 44, 110
"Watch Town" (Moorhouse) **40**:291
"The Watcher" (Le Fanu)
See "The Familiar"
The Watcher (Calvino)
See *La giornata d'uno scrutatore*
The Watcher, and Other Stories (Calvino)
See *La giornata d'uno scrutatore*
"A Watcher by the Dead" (Bierce) **9**:49
"A Watcher of the Dead" (Gordimer) **17**:151-52
"The Watchers" (Bradbury) **53**:201, 205, 253, 259
"The Watchers" (Calisher) **15**:5, 17-18
"The Watchful Poker Chip of Henri Matisse" (Bradbury) **29**:88
"Watching the Tango" (Gordon) **59**:260-61
"The Watchman" (Narayan) **25**:133, 139, 141, 156
"Water" (Galsworthy) **22**:73
"The Water Baby" (London) **4**:270
"The Water Hen" (O'Flaherty) **6**:268
The Water Is Wide (Le Guin) **12**:231
"The Water of Izli" (Bowles) **3**:68
"Water Them Geraniums" (Lawson) **18**:202, 204, 220-23, 226-27, 229-30, 232, 234, 262
"The Watercress Girl" (Bates) **10**:120, 131-33
"The Watercress Girl" (Coppard) **21**:4, 10, 20, 26
The Watercress Girl, And Other Stories (Bates) **10**:120-21
"The Waterfall" (Gordon) **15**:142
"Watermelon Story" (Wideman) **62**:263-64, 301
"Water-Message" (Barth) **10**:41-3, 46-8, 54, 56, 60, 63, 67, 79, 84, 87, 89, 91, 95, 97-101
"The Waters of Strife" (Somerville & Ross) **56**:306, 316-17, 332, 337
"The Watertight VW" (Wilding) **50**:347
"Benson #Watts is Dead in Virginia" (Betts) **45**:3, 31
"The Wave" (O'Flaherty) **6**:261, 264, 268, 285
"The Wave of Osiris" (Lagerkvist) **12**:181
"The Waves of Lake Balaton" (Lenz) **33**:337
"The Wax Madonna" (Pirandello) **22**:228
"The Way Back" (Grau) **15**:148
"The Way Back" (Moore) **19**:312-17, 319-22, 330-31, 333, 336
"Way Down Deep in the Jungle" (Jones) **56**:283
"Way Down on Lonesome Cove" (Murfree) **22**:196-97, 209
"Way in the Middle of the Air" (Bradbury) **29**:42; **53**:193, 198-99, 207-8, 210, 247-48, 250, 253
"The Way It Has to Be" (Pancake) **61**:259-60, 263
"The Way It Was" (Pohl) **25**:235
"The Way of a Woman" (Dunbar) **8**:122, 128, 136
"The Way of the Cross" (du Maurier) **18**:129, 137
"The Way of the Earth" (Evans) **43**:13, 15, 27-8, 39
"The Way of the World" (Cather) **2**:102-03; **50**:85, 95-6, 105, 167-68, 184-85, 187, 192, 226
"The Way of the World" (Norris) **28**:204
"The Way Some People Live" (Cheever) **38**:43
The Way Some People Live (Cheever) **1**:87-8, 92, 98-100; **38**:61, 63; **57**:9
"The Way to Majorca" (O'Hara) **15**:277, 284
"The Way to the Churchyard" (Mann) **5**:322, 328-29, 334-37
"The Way to the Dairy" (Saki) **12**:314
The Way Within (Hesse)
See *Der Weg nach Innen*
"A Way You'll Never Be" (Hemingway) **1**:218, 245, 247; **40**:155, 209, 212, 214; **63**:66, 91

"A Wayfaring Couple" (Freeman) 47:164
The Ways of White Folks (Hughes) 6:109-10, 121-23, 126-29, 131-34, 136-38, 140-42
Wayside Courtships (Garland) 18:160
Wayside Crosses (Čapek)
    See *Boži muka*
"A Wayside Episode" (Davis) 38:95, 110
"The Wayside Inn" (Turgenev)
    See "The Inn"
The Wayward and the Seeking: A Collection of Writing by Jean Toomer (Toomer) 45:245, 340, 347
The Wayward Wife, and Other Stories (Moravia)
    See *I racconti*
"We Also Walk Dogs" (Heinlein) 55:164, 212, 236
"We Are Looking at You, Agnes" (Caldwell) 19:27
"We Are Norsemen" (Boyle) 16:142-43, 151
We Are the Living (Caldwell) 19:4-6, 9, 11-12, 25, 34-5, 54, 57
"We Are Very Poor" (Rulfo)
    See "Es que somos muy pobres"
"We Can Remember It for You Wholesale" (Dick) 57:103, 140-41, 143-44, 149, 151
"We Crown Three King" (Tagore)
    See "Rajtika"
"We Didn't" (Dybek) 55:157
"We Don't Live Here Anymore" (Dubus) 15:69-71, 73, 76, 82, 87, 91, 98
We Don't Live Here Anymore (Dubus) 15:81, 91-3
"We Drink the Wine in France" (Walker) 5:401
"We Love Glenda So Much" (Cortázar) 7:69
We Love Glenda So Much, and Other Tales (Cortázar)
    See *Queremos tanto a Glenda*
"We Often Think of Lenin in The Clothespin Factory" (Davenport) 16:198
"We Purchased People" (Pohl) 25:226
"We Shall Never Die" (Solzhenitsyn)
    See "My-to ne umrem"
"We Want a Touchdown" (Saroyan) 21:143
"We Were Spending an Evening at Princess D.'s Dacha" (Pushkin) 27:164
"A Weak Heart" (Dostoevsky)
    See "A Faint Heart"
"Weak Heart" (Mansfield) 9:282
"The Weaker Sex" (Kawabata)
    See "Yowaki Utsuwa"
The Weaker Vessel (Kawabata)
    See "Yowaki Utsuwa"
The Weakling (Mauriac) 24:160-62
The Weakling and the Enemy (Mauriac) 24:160
"A Weary Hour" (Mann) 5:330
"The Weaver and the Worm" (Thurber) 1:428; 47:362
"The Weavers at the Mill" (Kiely) 58:148
"The Web of Circumstance" (Chesnutt) 7:3, 16, 19, 22-3, 29-33, 37; 54:15-16, 51, 58
The Web of Earth (Wolfe) 33:346-49, 351, 354, 369, 372, 374-76, 380
"The Wedding" (Bates) 10:113
"The Wedding" (Gogol) 29:120-21
"The Wedding" (O'Flaherty) 6:260, 265, 277-78, 285
"The Wedding" (Pritchett) 14:281, 299
"A Wedding Chest" (Lee) 33:302, 307
"Wedding Day" (Boyle) 5:54-5, 65, 70-2
Wedding Day, and Other Stories (Boyle) 5:54
"The Wedding Dress" (Moore)
    See "An Gúnna-Phósta"
"The Wedding Feast" (Moore) 19:310, 335
"The Wedding Gig" (King) 55:250-51
"The Wedding Gown" (Moore)
    See "An Gúnna-Phósta"
"The Wedding Guest" (Auchincloss) 22:43
"A Wedding in Brownsville" (Singer) 3:360, 363, 376
"A Wedding in Jackson" (Gilchrist) 63:5, 19-20

"The Wedding in the Garden" (Trevor) 21:246-47, 260, 262, 270, 274
"A Wedding in Toronto" (Clarke) 45:95
"The Wedding Knell" (Hawthorne) 3:154
"The Wedding March" (Wescott) 35:364, 369-72, 374-75, 379
"The Wedding of the Painted Doll" (Jolley) 19:233
"Wedding Pictures" (Phillips) 16:325, 328
"Wedding Preparations in the Country" (Kafka)
    See "Hochzeitsvorbereitungen auf dem Lande"
"Wedding Trip" (Pavese) 19:374-75, 387
"Wednesdays and Fridays" (Jolley) 19:245
"Wednesday's Child" (Oates) 6:225
"Wee Willie Winkie" (Kipling) 5:269
"Wee Winkie's Wanderings" (Cather) 50:94
"The Weeds" (McCarthy) 24:215-16, 225
"A Week in the Country" (Le Guin) 12:210, 213, 215-16, 245, 249
"Weekend" (Beattie) 11:6-7, 14, 17, 29
"Weekly Serial" (Coover) 15:39
"Weep No More, My Lady" (Stuart) 31:233-34, 244, 250, 252-53
"Weep Not My Wanton" (Coppard) 21:11
"The Weeping Man" (Lewis) 34:163-64
Weg nach Innen (Hesse)
    See *Der Weg nach Innen*
Der Weg nach Innen (Hesse) 9:211; 49:214, 230, 264
"Der Wegwerfer" (Boell) 23:6-8, 10
"Weight" (Atwood) 46:80-1, 98-9
"Weir of Hermiston" (Stevenson) 11:296, 299-300
Weir of Hermiston (Stevenson) 11:268-69, 282, 286
Weird Women (Barbey d'Aurevilly)
    See *Les diaboliques*
"Welcome, Bob" (Onetti)
    See "Bienvenido, Bob"
"The Welcome Table" (Walker) 5:401, 403, 406, 410-11
Welcome to the Monkey House: A Collection of Short Works (Vonnegut) 8:424-30, 435-36
The Well (Onetti)
    See *El pozo*
"We'll Have Fun" (O'Hara) 15:286
"The Well of Days" (Bunin) 5:100
"The Well of Miriam" (Agnon) 30:34
"The Well of Pen-Morfa" (Gaskell) 25:58, 65, 71
"Well, That's That" (Farrell) 28:87
"Well We All Had Our Willie and Wade Records..." (Barthelme) 55:115
"Welt" (Walser)
    See "Das Ende der Welt"
We're Friends Again (O'Hara) 15:250-51, 272
"We're Very Poor" (Rulfo)
    See "Es que somos muy pobres"
"The Werewolf" (Carter) 13:5, 7, 27
"The Werewolf" (Pavese) 19:368
Werewolves in Their Youth (Chabon) 59:82-84, 86-87
Wessex Tales (Hardy) 2:202-03, 205, 212, 214-15, 220, 223, 225-26, 229; 60:177-78, 183, 185, 189-92, 198
"West End" (Aiken) 9:9, 12, 14
"A West Indian Slave Insurrection" (Cable) 4:59, 75
"The West Midland Underground" (Wilding) 50:352
The West Midland Underground (Wilding) 50:349
West of Rome (Fante) 65:75, 106, 108
"The Westbound Train" (Cather) 2:102; 50:77, 96, 104
The Western Stories of Stephen Crane (Crane) 7:153
"Westminster Abbey" (Irving) 2:244-45, 250-51
"Westward" (Levi) 12:278-79

Westward Ha!; or, Around the World in Eighty Clichés (Perelman) 32:211, 219, 230, 233
"A Wet Night" (Beckett) 16:65, 92-3
"The Wet Nurse" (Pirandello) 22:229
"Wet Saturday" (Collier) 19:103, 109, 111
"Whacky" (Clarke) 3:134
"The Whale Tooth" (London) 4:266
"The Whale's Story" (Alcott) 27:42
"Whales Weep" (Boyle) 16:146
"The Wharf" (de la Mare) 14:80, 82, 88, 90
"What a Misfortune" (Beckett) 16:69, 92
"What a Thing, to Keep a Wolf in a Cage!" (Calisher) 15:3
"What about the Cat?" (Far) 62:50, 56
"What Becomes of the Pins" (Alcott) 27:43
What Christmas Is as We Grow Older (Dickens) 49:165
"What Daddy Does Is Always Right" (Andersen)
    See "What Father Does is Always Right"
"What Death with Love Should Have to Do" (Oates) 6:224, 226
"What Destiny Wanted" (Fuentes)
    See "Fortuna lo que ha querido"
"What Do Hippos Eat?" (Wilson) 21:322-23, 332-33, 345, 354
"What Do You Do in San Francisco?" (Carver) 8:32, 34
"What Do You Mean It Was Brillig?" (Thurber) 1:428
"What Do You See, Madam?" (Barnes) 3:18
"What Does It Matter? A Morality" (Forster) 27:91, 104, 107-08
"What Dreams May Come" (de la Mare) 14:80, 83, 84
"What Else" (Abish) 44:12, 37
"What Fanny Heard" (Alcott) 27:43
"What Father Does" (Andersen)
    See "What Father Does is Always Right"
"What Father Does is Always Right" (Andersen) 6:18, 26, 30
"What Goes Up" (Clarke) 3:134
"What Happened" (Clarke) 45:94
"What Happened To Charles" (Thurber) 47:363
"What He Saw" (Wideman) 62:274, 277, 331-32, 341-43
What I Know So Far (Lish) 18:266-68, 270, 274, 278, 280, 284
"What I Saw of Shiloh" (Bierce) 9:98-9
"What Is It?" (Carver) 8:4, 10, 32
"What Is Left to Link Us" (Lish) 18:284
"What Is Soul?" (Peretz)
    See "Vos heyst 'neshome'"
"What it was like, sometimes" (Wilding) 50:359-63, 367
"What Kind of Day Did You Have?" (Bellow) 14:41-2, 50-1, 53-6, 58
"What Men Live By" (Tolstoy) 9:387
"What old Johanne told" (Andersen)
    See "Hvad gamle Johanne fotalte"
"What the Nightingale Sang" (Zoshchenko) 15:387, 395
"What the Old Man Does is Always Right" (Andersen)
    See "What Father Does is Always Right"
"What the Red Glare Meant" (Lovecraft) 52:314
"What the Shepherd Saw" (Hardy) 2:210; 60:182
"What the Swallows Did" (Alcott) 27:41
"What to Do Next" (Barthelme) 55:14, 87
"What to Do Till the Analyst Comes" (Pohl) 25:224, 228-29, 230-31, 235
"What to Wear" (Adams) 24:16-17
"What Was Mine" (Beattie) 11:30-1
What Was Mine, and Other Stories (Beattie) 11:30-2
"What We Talk about When We Talk about Love" (Carver) 8:15, 17-23, 26, 30, 32, 34, 37-44, 46-8, 51, 56-9; 51:1-21
What We Talk about When We Talk about Love (Carver) 8:13, 15, 17-23, 26, 30, 32, 37-40, 43-4, 46, 48, 56-9; 51:4-8, 11, 15, 17-19

"What Were You Dreaming?" (Gordimer) 17:183, 188-89
"What You Hear from 'Em?" (Taylor) 10:379, 396, 399, 401, 407, 411, 415
"What You Want" (Henry) 5:187
"What's in Alaska?" (Carver) 8:7, 10-11, 32, 34, 53
"What's the Purpose of the Bayonet?" (Garrett) 30:164-65, 179-80
"The Wheel" (Bradbury) 53:248, 253
The Wheel of Love, and Other Stories (Oates) 6:247
"The Wheelbarrow" (Pritchett) 14:268, 280, 287
"Wheels" (Dixon) 16:208
"Wheels" (McGahern) 17:301-02, 307-09, 318, 323-24
"When a Man Falls, a Crowd Gathers" (Crane) 56:88
"When Alice Told Her Soul" (London) 4:257, 270
"When Boyhood Dreams Come True" (Farrell) 28:96, 127-8
When Boyhood Dreams Come True (Farrell) 28:126
"When Everyone Was Pregnant" (Updike) 13:358, 387
"When God Laughs" (London) 4:253
When God Laughs, and Other Stories (London) 4:253-54
"When Greek Meets Greek" (Greene) 29:183-84, 217
"When He Was Free and Young and He Used to Wear Silks" (Clarke) 45:72, 91, 96
When He Was Free and Young and He Used to Wear Silks (Clarke) 45:72, 87, 93-5, 109
"When I First Met Dr. Hickey" (Somerville & Ross) 56:320
"When I Was a Witch" (Gilman) 13:125; 62:190-91
When I Was Mad (Pirandello)
    See *Quand'ero matto*
"When It Happens" (Atwood) 2:4, 6-7, 10, 13, 16; 46:26, 33, 36, 39-40, 94
"When It's Time to Go" (Wideman) 62:269
"When My Girl Comes Home" (Pritchett) 14:261, 266-67, 301
When My Girl Comes Home (Pritchett) 14:267, 286
"When Old Baldy Spoke" (Murfree) 22:201
"When the Dead Rise from Their Graves" (Bulgakov) 18:90
"When the Light Gets Green" (Warren) 4:389-90, 394, 396, 399, 401; 58:310, 336, 354
"When the Old Century Was New" (Dreiser) 30:122, 127, 129, 132
"When the Sun Went Down" (Lawson) 18:198, 239
When the War Began (Boell)
    See "Als der Krieg ausbrach"
When the War Started (Boell)
    See "Als der Krieg ausbrach"
"When the Waters Were Up at Jules" (Harte) 8:214
When the World Screamed (Doyle) 12:81
When Things of the Spirit Come First: Five Early Tales (Beauvoir)
    See *Quand prime le spirituel*
"When We Were Nearly Young" (Gallant) 5:148
"When Women Love Men" (Ferré)
    See "Cuando las mujeres quieren a los hombres"
When Women Rule (Clarke) 45:72-9, 81-5, 88, 96-7
"When You Think of Me" (Caldwell) 19:42
When You Think of Me (Caldwell) 19:41
"Where All Is Emptiness There Is Room to Move" (Bradbury) 53:267
"Where Are You Going, Where Have You Been?" (Oates) 6:238, 244-46
"Where I Lived, and What I Lived For" (Oates) 6:225, 234-35

"Where I'm Calling From" (Carver) 8:17, 26-8, 32, 51
Where I'm Calling From: New and Selected Stories (Carver) 8:41, 45-6, 48-50, 55, 57, 59-61; 51:18-19
"Where Is Everyone?" (Carver) 8:18, 32, 59-60
"Where is the Har of the Beautiful Dancing Birds in the Sun-wind?" (Head) 52:220
"Where is the Voice Coming From" (Welty) 27:353-54; 51:318
"Where It Was, There I Must Begin to Be" (Davenport)
    See "Wo es war, soll ich werden"
"Where Love Is, God Is" (Tolstoy) 9:387
"Where Mountain Lion Lay Down with Deer" (Silko) 37:309
"Where Tawe Flows" (Thomas) 3:397, 406, 411-12; 44:350-51
"Where the Cloud Breaks" (Bates) 10:139
"Where the Eagles Dwell" (Valenzuela)
    See "Up Among the Eagles"
"Where the Girls Were Different" (Caldwell) 19:25-6
"Where the Harrycans Comes From" (Harris) 19:196
"Where the Heart Is" (Campbell) 19:77-8
"Where the Myth Touches Us" (Hood) 42:137-39, 146, 189, 205, 233
"Where the Sea Used to Be" (Bass) 60:23-25
"Where the Trail Forks" (London) 4:258, 286
Where You'll Find Me, and Other Stories (Beattie) 11:25, 28-9, 32
"Where's Duncan?" (Harris) 19:147, 173, 181
"Which Is the True One?" (Baudelaire)
    See "Laquelle est la vraie?"
"Which New Era Would That Be?" (Gordimer) 17:153, 161
"Which Was It?" (Twain) 6:331-34, 337, 350
"Which Was the Dream?" (Twain) 6:331-34, 337, 340, 350
"While the Auto Waits" (Henry) 5:158, 189
While the Billy Boils (Lawson) 18:198, 200, 208, 215, 248-50, 254, 257, 259, 261-62
Whilomville Stories (Crane) 7:104; 56:111
"The Whimper of Whipped Dogs" (Ellison) 14:105, 118
"The Whining" (Campbell) 19:74, 86
"The Whip-Poor-Will" (Thurber) 1:422; 47:381-82
The Whir of Gold (Ross) 24:323
Whirligigs (Henry) 5:182
"The Whirlpool Rapids" (Atwood) 46:65-8
"Whirlwind" (Tanizaki)
    See "Hyōfū"
"A Whisper in the Dark" (Alcott) 27:22-8, 45-50, 59
"The Whisperer in Darkness" (Lovecraft) 3:258-60, 263, 269-71, 274-75, 278-80, 284, 291, 294; 52:255, 258, 272-73, 283-84, 289, 320-21, 338, 349, 356
"Whispering Leaves" (Glasgow) 34:56, 61-3, 74-6, 80, 89-90, 95-6, 102
"The Whistle" (Welty) 1:468; 51:281, 321
"Whistling Dick's Christmas Stocking" (Henry) 5:161, 170
Whistling in the Dark (Garrett) 30:184
"The Whistling Swan" (Wescott) 35:363-64, 366-67, 371-73, 379
"Whit Monday" (Lewis) 40:281
White and Black (Pirandello)
    See *Bianche e nere*
"The White Ape" (Lovecraft)
    See "Facts concerning the Late Arthur Jermyn and His Family"
"The White Azalea" (Spencer) 57:198, 207, 239-40
"The White Birch" (Freeman) 47:165
"The White Cat of Drumgunniol" (Le Fanu) 14:223
"The White Counterpane" (Dunbar) 8:127, 134
"White Dump" (Munro) 3:347-49
"The White Eagle" (Chopin) 8:99

"The White Flower" (Kawabata) 17:251
"The White Flower" (Narayan) 25:138-40, 156, 160
"White Girl, Fine Girl" (Grau) 15:149, 156
"White Glow" (Lu Hsun)
    See "Bai guang"
"The White Goddess and the Mealie Question" (Gordimer) 17:153
"The White Hair" (Pardo Bazán) 30:290
"The White Heron" (Jewett)
    See "A White Heron"
"A White Heron" (Jewett) 6:157, 160, 170-73; 44:179-232
A White Heron, and Other Stories (Jewett) 6:171
"The White Horse" (Jones) 56:274, 281
"The White Horse" (Pardo Bazán)
    See "El caballo blanco"
"The White Horses of Vienna" (Boyle) 5:63-4
"The White Knight" (Moorhouse) 40:325
"A White Lie" (Sansom) 21:87
"The White Man's Way" (London) 4:253
"The White Mulberry Tree" (Cather) 50:232
"White Nights" (Dostoevsky) 2:171-72
"The White Old Maid" (Hawthorne) 3:154, 159, 180-81
The White People (Machen) 20:161, 165, 175-77, 183, 186, 194, 196-201
"The White Pony" (Bates) 10:132
"The White Pyramid" (Cather) 50:184
"The White Quail" (Steinbeck) 11:207-08, 221, 225, 227-28, 230, 233-36; 37:334, 339, 351, 354-55, 357, 359, 361
"The White Rabbit" (Pritchett) 14:269
"The White Rabbit Caper" (Thurber) 1:431
"The White Scapegoat" (Aleichem)
    See "A vayse kapore"
"The White Sea" (Kipling) 5:293
"The White Ship" (Lovecraft) 52:285, 297, 331, 342, 355, 357-59
"The White Silence" (London) 4:250-51, 258, 267, 277, 281-84, 287-88; 49:340-42
"The White Snake" (Grimm and Grimm) 36:189
"White Spot" (Anderson) 1:52
"The White Stocking" (Lawrence) 4:198, 202, 230
"White Weeds" (Chesnutt) 54:50, 60
"The White Wild Bronco" (Kiely) 58:144, 148, 154-55, 157
"A White Woman Who Married a Chinese" (Far)
    See "The Story of One White Woman Who Married a Chinese"
"The Whiteboys" (Somerville & Ross) 56:318, 332
"Whitechapel" (Morrison) 40:334, 365
"White-Eyes, Bulbuls, and a Bat" (Shiga) 23:346
"Who Am I This Time?" (Vonnegut)
    See "My Name is Everyone"
Who Can Replace a Man? (Aldiss) 36:6
"Who Crosses Storm Mountain?" (Murfree) 22:210
"Who Dealt?" (Lardner) 32:117, 127, 139-41, 145
"Who Do You Think You Are?" (Munro) 3:343
Who Do You Think You Are? (Munro) 3:333, 335-40, 342-43, 345-47
"Who Do You Wish Was with Us" (Thomas) 3:395, 398, 403, 406, 411-12; 44:351, 360
"Who for Such Dainties?" (Wilson) 21:360
"Who Has Seen the Wind" (McCullers) 9:332, 342-44, 347, 354, 360
"Who Is It Can Tell Me Who I Am?" (Berriault) 30:103-04
"Who Is This Tom Scarlett?" (Barnes) 3:18
"Who Knows What's Up in the Attic?" (Rhys) 21:56
"Who Made Yellow Roses Yellow?" (Updike) 13:355
"Who Pays the Piper . . ." (Pirandello) 22:244
"Who Stand for the Gods" (Dunbar) 8:122

"Whoever Was Using This Bed" (Carver) **8**:43
"Whole Days in the Trees" (Duras)
    See "Des Journées entières dans les arbres"
Whole Days in the Trees (Duras)
    See *Des journées entières dans les arbres*
"A Whole Life" (Pilnyak)
    See "Tselaya zhizn"
"A Whole Loaf" (Agnon)
    See "Pat Shlema"
"The Whole Town's Sleeping" (Bradbury)
    53:266
"The Whole World Knows" (Welty) **1**:474, 479-
    80, 483; **51**:260, 271, 319, 321-26, 328-29,
    334, 339
"A Whole Year Drunk and Purim Sober"
    (Peretz) **26**:216
Whom Do We Write For? (Calvino)
    See "Senza colori"
"Whoopee for the New Deal!" (Farrell) **28**:94-5
"Whores on the Half-Doors" (Kiely) **58**:168
"Who's Passing for Who?" (Hughes) **6**:132,
    141
"Who's Paying for This Call?" (Hood) **42**:184,
    187, 204
"Who's There" (Clarke) **3**:134
"The Whosis Kid" (Hammett) **17**:219, 221
"Why Brer Possum Loves Peace" (Harris)
    19:130, 171
"Why Brother Bear Has No Tail" (Harris)
    19:196
"Why Brother Fox's Legs Are Black" (Harris)
    19:196
"Why Brother Wolf Didn't Eat the Little
    Rabbits" (Harris) **19**:195
"Why Don't You Dance" (Carver) **8**:32, 37,
    42-3, 47-8, 51; **51**:2, 5, 7, 12, 20
"Why Frau Frohmann Raised Her Prices"
    (Trollope) **28**:311, 322-23, 355
*Why Frau Frohmann Raised Her Prices and
    Other Stories* (Trollope) **28**:311, 322-23,
    332-33, 339, 350, 354
"Why Heisherik Was Born" (Singer) **3**:385, 387
"Why Honey?" (Carver) **8**:32
"Why I Live at the P. O." (Welty) **51**:281, 314,
    318, 329, 340
"Why I Want to Fuck Ronald Reagan"
    (Ballard) **1**:70, 75, 82; **53**:17, 26, 95
"Why Mr. Cricket Has Elbows on His Tail"
    (Harris) **19**:196
"Why Mr. Possum Has No Hair on His Tail"
    (Harris) **19**:157
"Why Mr. Possum Loves Peace" (Harris)
    See "Why Brer Possum Loves Peace"
"Why the Alligator's Back Is Rough" (Harris)
    19:196
"Why the Confederacy Failed" (Harris) **19**:125
"Why the Darkey Loves Chicken" (Chesnutt)
    54:43
"Why the Guinea-Fowls Are Speckled"
    (Harris) **19**:196
"Why the Little Frenchman Wears His Arm in
    a Sling" (Poe) **1**:407; **35**:316
"Why the Negro Is Black" (Harris) **19**:140, 195
"Why the Waves Have Whitecaps" (Hurston)
    4:140
"Why was she blond?" (Alarcon)
    See "¿Por qué era rubia?"
"Why, Who Said So?" (Moravia) **26**:161
"Why, You Reckon?" (Hughes) **6**:118, 132
"Wicked Girl" (Fante) **65**:35
"A Wicked Voice" (Lee) **33**:302, 305, 309,
    311-12
"The Widder Tree Shadder Murder" (Jolley)
    19:248
"Wide Missouri" (Wideman)
    See "Across the Wide Missouri"
"The Wide Net" (Welty) **1**:467, 469, 471, 494;
    51:260, 262
The Wide Net, and Other Stories (Welty) **1**:466-
    68, 471, 482, 496; **51**:280, 319
"The Widow" (Babel) **16**:26, 50, 53-4, 58

"The Widow and Her Son" (Irving) **2**:240-41,
    251
"A Widow Woman" (Evans) **43**:3, 20
"The Widower" (Schnitzler)
    See "Der wittwer"
"The Widower Roman" (Castellanos)
    See "El viudo Román"
"Widows" (Baudelaire)
    See "Les veuves"
"Widows" (Trevor) **58**:252, 259-60, 263, 276
"A Widow's Dilemma" (Pirandello) **22**:236
"The Widow's Might" (Gilman) **13**:126;
    62:190-91
"The Widow's Mite" (Trollope) **28**:317, 320,
    326, 341, 348
The Widows of Thornton (Taylor) **10**:388-89,
    411, 415
"The Widow's Ordeal" (Irving) **2**:241
"The Widow's Son" (Irving)
    See "The Widow and Her Son"
"Widow's Walk" (Grau) **15**:163
"Das Wiedergefundene Paradies" (Arnim)
    29:9-10
Der wiederkehrende griechische Kaiser (Tieck)
    31:276
"Wiedersehen in der Allee" (Boell) **23**:4
"Wiedersehen mit Drüng" (Boell) **23**:4
"The Wife" (Chekhov)
    See "ena"
"The Wife" (Irving) **2**:240-41, 243, 245, 251
Wife (Mukherjee) **38**:243
"A Wife for Dino Rossi" (Fante) **65**:74, 89, 103
"The Wife of a King" (London) **4**:258, 282,
    284, 286
"The Wife of Another and the Husband under
    the Bed" (Dostoevsky) **2**:171, 193
"The Wife of his Youth" (Chesnutt) **7**:2, 15-16,
    23, 33-7; **54**:8-10, 13-14, 19-20, 27, 47-9,
    41, 58-9, 61, 63-4
*The Wife of his Youth, and Other Stories of the
    Color Line* (Chesnutt) **7**:2-3, 15, 19, 21-3,
    26, 30, 33, 37-8; **54**:8-9, 11, 14-16, 19, 25,
    27-8, 46-52, 57-8, 64
"A Wife of Nashville" (Taylor) **10**:415-16
"The Wife of the Autumn Wind" (Kawabata)
    17:252
"The Wife of Usher's Well" (James) **16**:234
"The Wife-Killer" (Singer) **3**:358; **53**:323
"Wife's Holiday" (Narayan) **25**:139-40, 155
"A Wife's Letter" (Tagore)
    See "Strir Patra"
"The Wife's Story" (Davis) **38**:110, 114, 119-20
"The Wife's Story" (Le Guin) **12**:235
"A Wife's Story" (Mukherjee) **38**:235, 237-38,
    240-41, 244, 250, 252-54, 257-59, 261, 266,
    279-80, 282-84, 286
"Wife-Wooing" (Updike) **13**:348-50, 373, 384,
    395
The Wild Ass' Skin (Balzac)
    See *La peau de chagrin*
"The Wild Blue Yonder" (Thomas) **20**:323, 327
The Wild Blue Yonder (Thomas) **20**:323-28
The Wild Body (Lewis) **34**:146-47, 149-54, 156,
    158-60, 162-67, 169-75, 179
"The Wild Boy" (Kiely) **58**:149
"Wild Flowers" (Caldwell) **19**:13-14, 38
"The Wild Goat's Kid" (O'Flaherty) **6**:260, 262,
    264, 268-69
"The Wild Goose" (Moore) **19**:303, 305, 308,
    312, 330, 333
"Wild Horses" (Bass) **60**:6, 8, 31
"A Wild Irishman" (Lawson) **18**:206
"The Wild Man and the Gentle Boy" (Far) **62**:50
The Wild Palms (Faulkner) **1**:159-61, 167-68;
    35:157
"Wild Rover No More" (Kiely) **58**:145, 147
"The Wild Swan" (O'Flaherty) **6**:268
The Wild Swan, and Other Stories (O'Flaherty)
    6:259, 271
"The Wild Swans" (Andersen)
    See "De vilde Svaner"
Die wilde Engländerin (Tieck) **31**:287

"The Wilderness" (Bradbury) **29**:78; **53**:198,
    254-55
"Wilderness" (Henderson) **29**:327
"Wilderness Tips" (Atwood) **46**:81, 98-9
Wilderness Tips (Atwood) **46**:75-6, 78-81, 92
"The Wildgoose Chase" (Coppard) **21**:19-21
"Wilfrid Holmes" (Moore) **19**:296, 298, 300,
    310
"The Will" (Lavin) **4**:165-66
"Will as a Boy" (Dixon) **16**:215
"Will o' the Mill" (Stevenson) **11**:268-69, 281;
    51:218-19, 236-37, 239, 248
"A Will of Iron" (Leskov) **34**:127
"The Will of Stanley Brooke" (Campbell)
    19:61-2, 72, 81
"The Will to Happiness" (Mann) **5**:322-23
"Will You Please Be Quiet, Please?" (Carver)
    8:3-4, 7, 10-11, 18-19, 22, 32
Will You Please Be Quiet, Please? (Carver)
    8:3-6, 17-18, 26, 29, 32, 34, 45, 50, 54;
    51:6, 12-13, 20
"Will You Tell Me" (Barthelme) **2**:27; **55**:16,
    18, 23
"Will You Walk into My Parlor?" (Dreiser)
    30:107
*Willa Cather's Collected Short Fiction,
    1892-1912* (Cather) **2**:103, 105; **50**:59, 65,
    167, 182, 226-28, 233-34, 245-46, 257, 279
"The Willful Child" (Grimm and Grimm)
    36:199
"Willi" (Gallant) **5**:138
"William Bacon's Man" (Garland) **18**:148
"William Reilly and the Fates" (Benét) **10**:160
"William the Conqueror" (Kipling) **5**:283;
    54:70, 72
"William Wilson" (Poe) **1**:378, 385-86, 394-97,
    407; **22**:293, 351; **34**:251, 274; **35**:309, 331,
    333-36; **54**:142-44, 146-51
"William's Wedding" (Jewett) **6**:180
Willie Masters' Lonesome Wife (Gass) **12**:125,
    128, 141-46, 148-50, 152-53
"Willie Waugh" (Coppard) **21**:11
"Willie Winkie" (Andersen) **6**:24
"The Willing Muse" (Cather) **2**:98, 103; **50**:200-
    01, 203
"A Willing Slave" (Narayan) **25**:135, 154, 156,
    158
"Willows" (de la Mare) **14**:71
"The Willow-Ware" (Freeman) **47**:84, 86
"Willy-Wagtails by Moonlight" (White) **39**:279-
    80, 285-86, 290, 292-93, 298, 312-16, 325,
    328-29, 335, 345
"The Wilshire Bus" (Yamamoto) **34**:349, 359
"Wilt Thou Leave Me Thus" (Coppard) **21**:10
"Wind" (Ballard) **53**:80
"The Wind" (Bradbury) **29**:67; **53**:245
"The Wind and the Boy" (Head) **52**:188, 200,
    206, 228, 244
"The Wind at Beni Midar" (Bowles) **3**:64, 85
"The Wind Blows" (Mansfield) **9**:282, 284, 302,
    305; **23**:139, 153; **38**:230
The Wind Blows Over (de la Mare) **14**:89, 92
"The Wind Box" (Bradfield) **65**:61, 65-68
"The Wind in the Rosebush" (Freeman) **47**:109,
    132, 136-37
*The Wind in the Rosebush, and Other Stories
    of the Supernatural* (Freeman) **47**:86, 107,
    109-13, 136-37
"The Wind Shifting West" (Grau) **15**:148, 152,
    150, 164
The Wind Shifting West (Grau) **15**:147-48, 152,
    154, 160-61
"The Wind Tells of Valdemar Daae and His
    Daughters" (Andersen) **6**:12, 15, 18, 24
"The Wind Tells the Story of Valdemar Daa
    and his Daughters" (Andersen)
    See "The Wind Tells of Valdemar Daae and
    His Daughters"
"The Windfall" (Caldwell) **19**:19, 41
"The Window" (Andrić) **36**:43
"The Window" (Moore) **19**:308, 345
A Window in Mrs. X's Place (Cowan) **28**:79

"The Windowpane Check" (O'Hara) **15**:283
"The Windows" (Sansom) **21**:86
"The Winds" (Welty) **1**:472; **51**:303
"The Wind's Tale" (Andersen)
    See "The Wind Tells of Valdemar Daae and
      His Daughters"
The Wind's Twelve Quarters (Le Guin) **12**:209,
    212, 219, 224, 231, 234, 245
"Windy Day at the Reservoir" (Beattie) **11**:30-1,
    34
"Wine" (Andrić)
    See "Vino"
"The Wine Breath" (McGahern) **17**:304, 309,
    319, 322
"The Wine of Paris" (Aymé)
    See "Le Vin de Paris"
"Wine of Surany" (Caldwell) **19**:41
"Wine of Wyoming" (Hemingway) **40**:251
The Wine of Youth (Fante) **65**:75-76, 78-79, 83,
    95-101, 104, 111
"The Wine Worm" (Akutagawa Ryūnosuke)
    44:42, 57-8
Winesburg, Ohio (Anderson) **1**:17-9, 22, 24-35,
    38-46, 48, 51-2, 55, 57-8; **46**:16-21
"Winged Creatures" (Warner) **23**:383, 385
"Wingfield" (Wolff) **63**:282, 294-96, 298, 300,
    310-12, 318, 320-21
"The Winner" (Hood) **42**:238
Winner Take Nothing (Hemingway) **1**:211, 216-
    17; **25**:113; **40**:172, 210, 237, 245, 247,
    249-50, 256-60, 263
"Winner Takes All" (Waugh) **41**:323, 331
Winsome Winnie (Leacock) **39**:265
"Winter" (Dubus) **15**:96
"Winter" (Gilchrist) **14**:163-64
"Winter: 1978" (Beattie) **11**:9, 23-4
"Winter Cruise" (Maugham) **8**:380
"Winter Dreams" (Fitzgerald) **6**:46, 59, 66, 69,
    76, 88, 90-1, 100, 102, 104
"The Winter Father" (Dubus) **15**:75, 82
"Winter in July" (Lessing) **6**:186, 191, 213-14,
    217-18; **61**:100, 103-4
Winter in the Air, and Other Stories (Warner)
    23:370-71, 380
"The Winter Market" (Gibson) **52**:16-17, 21-2,
    27-30, 34, 36, 53-5, 59
"Winter Nelis" (Jolley) **19**:234, 246
"Winter Night" (Boyle) **5**:55
"The Winter of Artifice" (Nin) **10**:309-12, 314-
    17, 319-20, 323
The Winter of Artifice (Nin) **10**:300-02, 305-06,
    317, 319, 322, 324
"Winter of the Lion" (Salter) **58**:180
"Winter Rain" (Adams) **24**:4, 7
"Winter Sun" (Appelfeld)
    See "Shemesh shel horef"
"Winter Wind" (Munro) **3**:331
Der Wintergärten (Arnim) **29**:5, 9-10, 17, 25-30
"Winterkill" (Ford) **56**:144-45, 152, 156, 160,
    175, 194
"The Winters and the Palmeys" (Hardy) **2**:207,
    209; **60**:192
"A Winter's Day" (Leskov)
    See "Zimnij den'"
"Winter's King" (Le Guin) **12**:231-32
"A Winter's Tale" (Kelly) **50**:286, 288, 302
"A Winter's Tale" (Stafford) **26**:276, 278-80,
    307
"A Winter's Tale" (Thomas) **20**:317-18
"A Winter's Tale" (Thomas) **44**:334
Winter's Tales (Dinesen) **7**:164, 166, 170-71,
    175, 180, 193, 195-96, 199-200, 205, 208
"Winterton" (Dreiser) **30**:149-50
The Winthrop Covenant (Auchincloss) **22**:27,
    29, 33, 35, 39, 43-4, 47, 50-1
"Winthrop's Adventure" (Lee) **33**:312
"Wintry Peacock" (Lawrence) **4**:231, 234-35
"Wiosna" (Schulz) **13**:327
"Wipeout" (Jones) **56**:273-74
"Wir Besenbinder" (Boell) **23**:5
"Wireless" (Kipling) **5**:266, 275, 280; **54**:76

The Wisdom of Father Brown (Chesterton)
    1:120-21, 124; **46**:116, 130, 133, 151
"The Wisdom of Silence" (Dunbar) **8**:122, 126,
    132, 135, 146
"The Wisdom of the New" (Far) **62**:13, 19, 50-
    52, 57-60, 64, 75, 95, 97, 99
"The Wisdom of the Trail" (London) **4**:282-85,
    288
"Wise Guy" (O'Hara) **15**:264
"The Wise Men" (Crane) **7**:101, 126
"The Wise She-Frog" (Ferré) **36**:149
"Wiser than a God" (Chopin) **8**:69-70, 73, 84,
    99
"The Wish House" (Kipling) **5**:275, 280-81
"Wisteria" (Spencer) **57**:198
"The Witch" (Chekhov) **51**:89, 153
"The Witch" (Jackson) **9**:255-56; **39**:211, 217,
    218, 219, 220, 227
"The Witch" (Singer) **3**:377
"The Witch à La Mode" (Lawrence) **4**:220
"Witchbird" (Bambara) **35**:15, 27, 29-30
"Witchcraft" (Head) **52**:199-200, 210, 217, 227-
    28, 236
"Witchcraft" (Machen) **20**:160
"Witcherley Ways: A Christmas Tale"
    (Oliphant) **25**:204
"The Witches" (Pavese) **19**:369
"Witches Loaves" (Henry) **5**:184
"Witch's Money" (Collier) **19**:98-9, 104, 110,
    113-14
"With Bill in the Desert" (Abish) **44**:11
"With Che at Kitty Hawk" (Banks) **42**:57
"With Che at the Plaza" (Banks) **42**:57, 67-8
"With Che in New Hampshire" (Banks) **42**:57,
    66-7
"With Justifiable Pride" (Cortázar)
    See "Con legítimo orgullo"
"With Old Man Makhno" (Babel) **16**:22
"With Smiles as Wide as Summer" (Bradbury)
    53:267
"With the Death of the Saint" (Agnon) **30**:68
"With the Nameless Dead" (Dreiser) **30**:118
"With the Nationalists" (Warner) **23**:386-87
"With the Night Mail" (Kipling) **5**:268
"The Withered Arm" (Hardy) **2**:202-03, 205,
    208, 213-14, 217-20, 227-28, 231-34;
    60:177, 183, 190-93
"Withered Fields" (Akutagawa Ryūnosuke)
    See "Karenoshō"
"The Withered Flowers" (Chang) **28**:34
"Withered Skin of Berries" (Toomer) **45**:245-
    46, 249-50, 265, 274, 277-78, 317, 340
"Within a Grove" (Akutagawa Ryūnosuke)
    See "Yabu no naka"
Within the Wall (Agnon) **30**:71
"Without a Hero" (Boyle) **16**:156-57
Without a Hero, and Other Stories (Boyle)
    16:156-57
"Without Benefit of Clergy" (Kipling) **5**:262,
    291, 295-97, 299; **54**:120
"Without Benefit of Galsworthy" (Collier)
    19:108-09
"Without Colors" (Calvino) **3**:104, 108-09
"Without Title" (Chekhov) **51**:77-8
"Without Visible Means" (Morrison) **40**:328,
    367
"The Witness" (Porter) **4**:339-40, 358; **43**:258,
    260, 264, 281, 306
"Witness to the Crucifixion" (Gilchrist) **63**:8
"The Witnesses" (Cortázar)
    See "Los testigos"
"The Witnesses" (Sansom) **21**:86-7
"The Witnesses" (Updike) **13**:358
"Der wittwer" (Schnitzler) **15**:345, 376-77;
    61:306-8
"The Wives of the Dead" (Hawthorne) **3**:159,
    164, 186
"The Wizards of Pung's Corners" (Pohl)
    25:213, 222-23, 237
"Wo es war, soll ich werden" (Davenport)
    16:199-200
Wo warst du, Adam? (Boell) **23**:36

Wodehouse on Crime (Wodehouse) **2**:352
"The Wolf" (Hesse) **9**:230, 235
"The Wolf" (Stephens) **50**:315
"Wolf Alice" (Carter) **13**:7, 9, 27-8
"Wolf Dreams" (Beattie) **11**:11, 19-20
"Wolf Lonigan's Death" (O'Flaherty) **6**:261,
    276, 280
"The Wolf Who Went Places" (Thurber) **47**:363
"Wolfert Webber" (Irving) **2**:241, 247, 249,
    251-52, 262, 266, 268
"Wolfert's Roost" (Irving) **2**:246
"Wolf's Head" (Murfree) **22**:212
"The Wolves of Cernogratz" (Saki) **12**:306, 317,
    329
"A Woman" (Galsworthy) **22**:74, 93
"The Woman at the Store" (Mansfield) **9**:281,
    284, 302, 305
"A Woman Called Shizu" (Endō) **48**:212
The Woman Destroyed (Beauvoir)
    See *La femme rompue*
"Woman Hollering Creek" (Cisneros) **32**:15-7,
    21, 24-5, 37
Woman Hollering Creek and Other Stories
    (Cisneros) **32**:7-8, 11, 15, 17, 25, 34, 36,
    38, 51-52
Woman in a Lampshade (Jolley) **19**:221-23,
    233-34, 240, 242, 244-45, 248
"The Woman in Black" (Moravia) **26**:173
"A Woman in the House" (Caldwell) **19**:5, 23
"The Woman Lit by Fireflies" (Harrison)
    19:212-14, 218
The Woman Lit by Fireflies (Harrison) **19**:207,
    210-15
"The Woman Nobody Called On" (Cather)
    50:104
"A Woman of Fifty" (Maugham) **8**:380
A Woman of Means (Taylor) **10**:379, 388
Woman of the River (Alegria)
    See "A Temple of the Holy Ghost"
"A Woman of Tomorrow" (Glasgow) **34**:77
"A Woman on a Roof" (Lessing) **6**:199, 206
"The Woman on the Rock" (Andrić)
    See "Žena na kamenu"
"A Woman Seldom Found" (Sansom) **21**:89,
    126
"The Woman Who Came at Six O'Clock"
    (García Márquez) **8**:172, 183, 185
*The Woman Who Could Not Read, and Other
    Tales* (Zoshchenko) **15**:388, 390
"The Woman Who Fainted" (Dybek) **55**:130,
    141-42
"The Woman Who Had Five A's in Her
    Name" (Kelly) **50**:789
"The Woman Who Had Imagination" (Bates)
    10:130
*The Woman Who Had Imagination, and Other
    Stories* (Bates) **10**:112
"The Woman Who Married Clark Gable"
    (O'Faolain) **13**:293, 322
"The Woman Who Rode Away" (Lawrence)
    4:219, 226, 239
*The Woman Who Rode Away, and Other
    Stories* (Lawrence) **4**:230
"The Woman Who Sowed Iniquity" (Evans)
    43:37
"The Woman Who Was Everybody" (Calisher)
    15:2, 5
"The Woman Who Was Not Allowed to Keep
    Cats" (White) **39**:280, 282, 284, 286, 289,
    291-95, 312, 316-18, 325, 327, 343
"A Woman with a Past" (Fitzgerald) **6**:50
"The Woman with Blue Eyes" (Gorky)
    See "Zhenshchina s golubymi glazami"
"A Woman without a Country" (Cheever) **1**:95,
    100
"A Woman, Young and Old" (Paley) **8**:388, 390,
    396, 398
"The Woman-Hater" (Aiken) **9**:5, 14
"The Womanizer" (Ford) **56**:150-51, 160-61,
    163-64, 166, 168, 185, 187
The Womanizer (Ford) **56**:141

"A Woman's Arms" (Machado de Assis) **24**:138, 153

"A Woman's Hand" (White) **39**:301, 303-04, 306, 308-09, 311, 319, 324-25, 329, 337, 345

"A Woman's Kingdom" (Chekhov)
See "Bab'e carstuo"

"A Woman's Revenge" (Barbey d'Aurevilly)
See "La vengeance d'une femme"

"Womb Ward" (Lessing) **61**:123

"Women" (Lardner) **32**:132, 135, 140, 145

"Women" (Singer) **3**:358

The Women from Sarajevo (Andrić)
See "Gospodjicd"

Women in Their Beds: New and Selected Stories (Berriault) **30**:103, 105

"The Women of Madison Avenue" (O'Hara) **15**:282

"The Women on the Wall" (Stegner) **27**:191, 195, 197, 203-05, 220, 227

The Women on the Wall (Stegner) **27**:194, 196-97, 199, 219

"Women, Politics and Murder" (Hammett) **17**:200

Women with Men (Ford) **56**:150, 160-61, 167, 169, 177, 185, 192-94

"A Women's Restaurant" (Boyle) **16**:140-42

Wonder Stories Told for Children (Andersen)
See *Eventyr, fortalte for bøorn*

"The Wonderful Death of Dudley Stone" (Bradbury) **29**:89

"The Wonderful Old Gentleman" (Parker) **2**:274, 281, 283

Wonderful Tales (Andersen)
See *Eventyr, fortalte for bøorn*

Wonderful Tales for Children (Andersen)
See *Eventyr, fortalte for bøorn*

"The Wonderful Tar-Baby Story" (Harris) **19**:140, 173, 195

"A Wonderful Woman" (Adams) **24**:9, 19

Wondering Where to Turn (Lu Hsun)
See *P'anghuang*

"The Wonder-Worker" (Peretz)
See "Der Kuntsenmakher"

"The Wondrous Child" (Stoker) **62**:236-37, 251-52

"The Wood Duck" (Thurber) **1**:414, 422; **47**:380

"The Woodcutter's Third Son" (Hood) **42**:193, 205

"The Wooden Cross" (Alarcon)
See "La cruz de palos"

"The Wooden Dove of Archytas" (Davenport) **16**:178, 192

"The Woodfelling" (Tolstoy) **9**:375

"Woof Woof" (Saroyan) **21**:144

"The Wooing of Becfola" (Stephens) **50**:318

"Word and the Flesh" (Stuart) **31**:263

The Word for World Is Forest (Le Guin) **12**:207-10, 216, 219, 223, 234, 242-43

"The Word of Unbinding" (Le Guin) **12**:231-32

"The Word Processor of the Gods" (King) **17**:276; **55**:251

"Words" (Andrić)
See "Reci"

"The Words of a Dwarf" (Akutagawa Ryūnosuke)
See "Shuju no kotoba"

The Words that Count (Campbell) **19**:70, 86

"Work" (Johnson) **56**:234-35, 260-61

"Work, Death, and Sickness" (Tolstoy) **9**:388

"Work Not in Progress" (Greene) **29**:223, 226

"The Work on Red Mountain" (Harte) **8**:231, 254

"Work Suspended" (Waugh) **41**:311

Work Suspended (Waugh) **41**:330

"The Workers" (Galsworthy) **22**:82

"The Working Girl" (Beattie) **11**:33

"Working on the Spaceship Yards" (Aldiss) **36**:11

"The Working Party" (Bowen) **3**:30, 40, 49

Works (Alarcon)
See *Obras completas*

"Work'us" (Stoker) **62**:252

"The World according to Hsü" (Mukherjee) **38**:252, 254-55, 264, 272, 277-78

"The World and the Bubble" (Dreiser) **30**:129

"The World and the Door" (Henry) **5**:182

"The World & the Theatre" (Saroyan) **21**:139, 142, 159

The World Is Too Much With Us (Bates) **10**:124

"The World of Apples" (Cheever) **1**:112; **38**:45, 47, 49, 56, 63, 66

The World of Apples (Cheever) **1**:97-8, 101; **38**:45, 65

"A World of Glass" (Sansom) **21**:95

"World of Stone" (Borowski) **48**:10

The World of Stone (Borowski) **48**:16

"A World of Talent" (Dick) **57**:107

"The World (This One), the Flesh (Mrs. Oedipa Maas), and the Testament of Pierce Inverarity" (Pynchon) **14**:308

"The World to Come" (Peretz)
See "Oylem ha-be"

"The World with One Eye Shut" (Crace) **61**:32

"Worldly Goods" (Wolff) **63**:282, 292-96, 300, 303, 305, 308

"World's End" (Williams) **31**:305, 323-24, 332, 339-40, 344

The Worlds of Robert A. Heinlein (Heinlein) **55**:229

"The Worm in The Apple" (Cheever) **38**:56, 85-6

"A Worn Path" (Welty) **1**:466, 470, 491-92, 494; **27**:332-66; **51**:259-60, 318

"The Worn-Out Dancing Shoes" (Grimm and Grimm) **36**:228

"The Worn-Out Man" (Walser) **20**:355-56

"Worship" (Atwood) **2**:20

"The Worst Crime in the World" (Chesterton) **1**:129, 138; **46**:107, 113, 125, 135

"The Worst Thing of All" (Gordimer) **17**:155

Worstward Ho (Beckett) **16**:109, 129-34

"Would You Do It for a Penny?" (Ellison) **14**:126

"Would You Suggest Writing as a Career?" (Bukowski) **45**:53-4

"The Wounded Cormorant" (O'Flaherty) **6**:260, 262, 268, 282-83

"The Wounded Soldier" (Garrett) **30**:166, 173, 180

Wounds in the Rain: A Collection of Stories Relating to the Spanish-American War of 1898 (Crane) **7**:104, 108

"Wrack" (Barthelme) **55**:115

"Das Wrack" (Lenz) **33**:317, 329, 331-32

"The Wrath of God" (Fante) **65**:74, 95, 99-100

"Wratislaw" (Saki) **12**:317

"The Wreath" (O'Connor) **5**:372, 389

"The Wreath" (Pirandello) **22**:242

A Wreath for Garibaldi (Garrett) **30**:174

"Wrens and Starlings" (Powers) **4**:380

"The Wren's Nest" (O'Flaherty) **6**:274, 279

"Wressley of the Foreign Office" (Kipling) **5**:279

"Write on Me" (Davie) **52**:6

"The Writer" (Galsworthy) **22**:60, 99

Writes of Passage (Cabrera Infante) **39**:21

"A Writing Lesson" (Gordon) **59**:260, 266

"The Writing of God" (Borges)
See "La escritura del Dios"

"Writing Short Stories" (O'Connor) **61**:222

"Writing Yourself a Proper Narrative" (Moorhouse) **40**:308

"The Wrong House" (Mansfield) **9**:279

"Wrong Pigeon" (Chandler) **23**:110

"The Wrong Set" (Wilson) **21**:321, 323, 325, 327, 330-32, 336, 338-39, 342-44, 350, 352, 354

The Wrong Set, and Other Stories (Wilson) **21**:318-22, 326, 331, 335-36, 338, 341, 344, 348-49, 351, 353-54, 357-58, 364-65

"The Wrong Shape" (Chesterton) **1**:121, 129-30, 136; **46**:107, 109, 125, 132, 141, 149

"The Wrong Trousers" (Bulgakov) **18**:90

"A Wronged Husband" (Pirandello) **22**:236

"Wu hsiao-lien" (P'u Sung-ling) **31**:206, 208-09

"The Wub" (Dick)
See "Beyond Lies the Wub"

"Wunderkind" (McCullers) **9**:322, 332, 342-43, 345, 347-48, 350, 354-55; **24**:232

Das Wunderkind (Mann) **5**:324, 330-31

Die Wundersüchtigen (Tieck) **31**:275, 286

"Xanadu" (Thomas) **20**:290-93, 317

"Xingu" (Wharton) **6**:418, 422, 428-29, 437

Xingu, and Other Stories (Wharton) **6**:417-19, 421, 435

Xozjain i rabotnik (Tolstoy)
See *Khozyáin i rabotnik*

"Ya no quedan esperanzas de" (Cortázar) **7**:95

"Yabu no naka" (Akutagawa Ryūnosuke) **44**:45, 51-2, 60, 63, 78-9

"The Yachting Cap" (Lewis) **34**:163-65

"Yah! Yah! Yah!" (London) **4**:266

"Yajima Ryūdō" (Shiga) **23**:346

Yakov Pasynkov (Turgenev) **7**:314, 320, 324; **57**:299

"Yam Gruel" (Akutagawa Ryūnosuke)
See "Imogayu"

"The Yankee Fox" (Benét) **10**:150

"The Yanks Are Coming, in Five Breathless Colors" (Perelman) **32**:222

"Yao" (Lu Hsun) **20**:128, 140-41

"A Yard of String" (Stuart) **31**:249

"Yasukichi no techōkara" (Akutagawa Ryūnosuke) **44**:79, 89

"Ya-t'ou" (P'u Sung-ling) **31**:196-97, 207, 209

"The Yattering and Jack" (Barker) **53**:139-40, 156, 158, 161, 163

"Ye Olde Cheshire Cheese" (Pilnyak) **48**:292-93

"Year by Year the Evil Gains" (Aldiss) **36**:17

"The Year of Heaven" (Saroyan) **21**:144

"The Year of the Jackpot" (Heinlein) **55**:166, 184-85, 204

"A Year of Their Life" (Pilnyak)
See "God ikh zhizni"

"Yearning for My Mother" (Tanizaki)
See "Haha no kouru ki"

"The Years in Exile" (Metcalf) **43**:74, 85-6, 93-4, 112-14, 160, 164

"Yegipetskiye nochi" (Pushkin) **55**:317

"Yeh-ch'a kuo" (P'u Sung-ling) **31**:200

"Yeh-kou" (P'u Sung-ling) **31**:200

"The Yelagin Affair" (Bunin)
See "The Elaghin Affair"

"Yellow" (Beckett) **16**:70

"The Yellow Beret" (Lavin) **4**:167

"The Yellow Bird" (Chesterton) **1**:124-25, 133; **46**:145

"A Yellow Flower" (Cortázar)
See "Una flor amarilla"

"Yellow Girl" (Caldwell) **19**:19

"The Yellow Gown" (Anderson) **1**:52

"Yellow Streak" (Farrell) **28**:99

"The Yellow Streak" (Maugham) **8**:367, 372

"The Yellow Wallpaper" (Gilman) **13**:118-19, 121-25, 128-41, 145, 147-62, 166, 168, 170-71, 175; **62**:122-229

The Yellow Wallpaper (Gilman) **62**:124, 174

"Yellow Woman" (Silko) **37**:295, 302-3, 308

"Yemelyan Pilyai" (Gorky)
See "Emelyan Pilyai"

"Yen Shih" (P'u Sung-ling) **31**:196

"Yentl the Yeshiva Boy" (Singer) **3**:359, 384; **53**:275-76, 295, 301, 305, 337-38, 340, 344-50, 352

Yepifan Locks (Platonov) **42**:251

"Yermolai and the Miller's Wife" (Turgenev) **7**:342; 266, 268

"Yermolay and the Miller's Wife" (Turgenev)
See "Yermolai and the Miller's Wife"

"Yesterday Was the Last Time" (Betts)
See "The Gentle Insurrection"

"Les yeux des pauvres" (Baudelaire) **18**:4, 6, 33, 47-51, 53

"Yi yüan kuan" (P'u Sung-ling) **31**:204-05

"Yid Somersault" (Leskov)
See "Židovskaja kuvyrkalegija"

"A Yiddish 'Hamlet'" (Zangwill) **44**:378

"Yiddish in America" (Ozick)
   See "Envy: or, Yiddish in America"
"Yijian xiaoshi" (Lu Hsun) **20**:146-47
"Ying-ning" (P'u Sung-ling) **31**:192, 196-97
"Ylla" (Bradbury) **29**:50; **53**:191, 202-4, 209, 246-50, 252-53
"The Yogurt of Vasirin Kefirosky" (Apple) **50**:5, 29
"A Yom Kippur Scandal" (Aleichem) **33**:82
"Yonder Peasant, Who Is He?" (McCarthy) **24**:215-16
"Yoneko's Earthquake" (Yamamoto) **34**:348, 350, 352, 354-55, 358, 360-62, 364-65, 367, 369, 379, 387-90
"Der yontefdiker tsimes" (Aleichem) **33**:38
"York Beach" (Toomer) **45**:214, 233, 235
Yoshinokuzu (Tanizaki) **21**:219-22, 224, 226
"Yostie" (O'Hara) **15**:278, 283
"You and Me and the Continuum" (Ballard) **53**:32, 96
"You Are as Brave as Vincent Van Gogh" (Barthelme) **55**:87
"You Are Not I" (Bowles) **3**:59-61, 66, 68-9, 72, 76-7
You Are Now Entering the Human Heart (Frame) **29**:112-13
"You Broke My Dream" (Lewis) **34**:178-79
"You Can Always Tell Newark" (O'Hara) **15**:251
You Can't Keep a Good Woman Down (Walker) **5**:412-14
"You Can't Step into the Same Street Twice" (Dybek) **55**:139
"You Can't Tell a Man by the Song He Sings" (Roth) **26**:257, 265, 268
"You Could Look It Up" (Thurber) **47**:365, 377-78, 382
"You Have Left Your Lotus Pods on the Bus" (Bowles) **3**:69
You Know Me Al: A Busher's Letters (Lardner) **32**:113-14, 117, 121-22, 127, 131, 141-45, 148-50, 152, 155-56, 159, 165, 170-71, 180
"You Know Me, Carlo" (Moravia) **26**:160
"You Know They Got a Hell of a Band" (King) **17**:294-95
"You Know What" (Beattie) **11**:30, 33-4
"You Make Your Own Life" (Pritchett) **14**:269, 271, 297
You Make Your Own Life (Pritchett) **14**:269, 293
"You Must Know Everything" (Babel) **16**:34
You Must Know Everything: Stories, 1915-1937 (Babel) **16**:34
"You Must Remember This" (Coover) **15**:61-2
"You Name It" (Gordimer) **17**:194
"You Should Have Seen the Mess" (Spark) **10**:350, 355, 359, 363, 369
"You Were Perfectly Fine" (Parker) **2**:272, 278, 281
"You Were Too Trusting, Captain" (Babel) **16**:22
"You'll Catch Your Death" (Hood) **42**:236
You'll Catch Your Death (Hood) **42**:235
"You'll Never Know, Dear, How Much I Love You" (Updike) **27**:327-28
"Young Archimedes" (Huxley) **39**:162, 168-70
"The Young Aunt with the White Hair" (Cable) **4**:49
"The Young Girl" (Mansfield) **9**:279, 310
"The Young Girl and the American Sailor" (Moorhouse) **40**:293
"The Young Glory of Him" (Hughes) **6**:127
"Young Goodman Brown" (Hawthorne) **3**:164-68, 171-74, 177-78, 180, 182-83, 185-87, 189, 191-93; **29**:233-313; **39**:91, 105, 115, 128
"The Young Italian" (Irving)
   See "The Story of the Young Italian"
"The Young King" (Wilde) **11**:364, 373, 375-76, 381-82, 384-86, 394-97, 407-09
"The Young Lady-Peasant Girl" (Pushkin)
   See "Baryshnia-krest'ianka"

"Young Lochinvar" (Benét) **10**:150
Young Lucretia (Freeman) **47**:83
"The Young Man from Kalgoorlie" (Bates) **10**:113, 139
Young Man in Chains (Mauriac)
   See *L'enfant chargé de chaînes*
A Young Man in Search of Love (Singer) **53**:326
"The Young Man with the Carnation" (Dinesen) **7**:164, 191-92, 194, 198
"The Young Man with the Cream Tarts" (Stevenson) **51**:218
The Young Master Carpenter (Tieck)
   See *Der junge Tischlermeister*
Young Men in Spats (Wodehouse) **2**:325, 328
"The Young Robber" (Irving)
   See "The Story of the Young Robber"
"Young Robin Gray" (Harte) **8**:223
"A Young Woman in Green Lace" (Parker) **2**:273, 283
"The Youngest Doll" (Ferré)
   See "La muñeca menor"
The Youngest Doll (Ferré)
   See *Papeles de Pandora*
"Your Doctor Loves You" (Adams) **24**:16
"Your Lover Just Called" (Updike) **13**:387
Your Lover Just Called: Stories of Joan and Richard Maple (Updike)
   See *Too Far to Go: The Maples Stories*
"Your Most Profound Skin" (Cortázar)
   See "Tu más profunda piel"
"Your Obituary, Well Written" (Aiken) **9**:4-5, 7, 12, 14, 30, 34
"Youth" (Conrad) **9**:140, 143-44, 146-47, 152, 157, 160-66, 171, 175-78
Youth (Tolstoy)
   See *Yunost*
Youth: A Narrative, and Two Other Stories (Conrad) **9**:151
Youth and the Bright Medusa (Cather) **2**:91-2, 94, 98, 103, 111-13; **50**:56-7, 119, 139, 182, 194-95, 198, 208, 236, 241, 243
"Youth and the Lady" (Warner) **23**:372
"Youth from Vienna" (Collier) **19**:110, 112
"The Youth of Daidōji Shinsuke" (Akutagawa Ryūnosuke)
   See "Daidoji Shinsuke no Hansei"
"The Youthful Years" (Chang) **28**:28; 35
"Youths and Death" (Akutagawa Ryūnosuke) **44**:56
"Yowaki Utsuwa" (Kawabata) **17**:247
"Yoysef" (Aleichem) **33**:39
"Yü Ch'ü-wo" (P'u Sung-ling) **31**:199
"Yucca Knolls" (O'Hara) **15**:259
"Yü-ch'ien" (P'u Sung-ling) **31**:199
"Yugashima no Omoide" (Kawabata) **17**:249-50
"Yume no ukihashi" (Tanizaki) **21**:180-81, 183, 198, 203-04, 210-11, 217, 225-27
Yunost (Tolstoy) **9**:375
"Yveline Samoris" (Maupassant) **1**:283
"Yvette" (Maupassant) **1**:263, 275, 283; **64**:346-47
"Z. Marcas" (Balzac) **5**:27, 31, 33
"Za logorovanja" (Andrić) **36**:66-7
"Zagrowsky Tells" (Paley) **8**:412
"The Zahir" (Borges)
   See "El Zahir"
"El Zahir" (Borges) **4**:10, 25; **41**:51
"Zai jiulou shang" (Lu Hsun) **20**:140-42, 149-50
"Zajačij remiz" (Leskov) **34**:108-10, 117
Zakat (Babel) **16**:35
"Zakhar-Kalita" (Solzhenitsyn) **32**:341, 361-62, 364-65, 392, 394
"Zakhar-the-Pouch" (Solzhenitsyn)
   See "Zakhar-Kalita"
"Zakoldovannoe mesto" (Gogol) **4**:117, 121; **29**:135; **52**:165
"Zametki neizvestnogo" (Leskov) **34**:108
"Zamostye" (Babel) **16**:27, 54, 57-8
"Zanos i stradanja Tome Galusa" (Andrić) **36**:47, 52
"Zapax xleba" (Kazakov) **43**:62, 65-6

"Zapečatlennyj angel" (Leskov) **34**:109-10, 113-15, 127-30
Zapiski iunogo vracha (Bulgakov) **18**:75, 86, 88-9
Zapiski iz podpol'ya (Dostoevsky) **2**:164-65, 168, 172-73, 178-83, 186, 188-89; **33**:158-30; **44**:112-13, 155, 158, 160
Zapiski okhotnika (Turgenev) **57**:259, 263-67, 270, 276, 278, 281-84, 287, 317, 352, 354
"Zapiski sumasshedshego" (Gogol) **52**:174-76
Zapiski sumasshedshego (Tolstoy) **9**:366-68, 377, 388
Zářivé hlubiny (Čapek) **36**:81-2, 87, 96, 109
"Zatvorena vrata" (Andrić) **36**:48
Das Zauberschloss (Tieck) **31**:275, 285-87
"Zaveshchanie" (Gogol) **52**:170
"Zaydlus der ershter" (Singer) **53**:294, 323
"Zazubrina" (Gorky) **28**:137, 192
"Zeal" (Powers) **4**:370
"Zedj" (Andrić) **36**:46, 70-1
"Zeidlus the Pope" (Singer)
   See "Zaydlus der ershter"
"Zeitl and Rickel" (Singer) **3**:359
"Zeke Hammertight" (Stuart) **31**:226, 238-39
"Zeko" (Andrić) **36**:36, 46-9
"Železnaja volja" (Leskov) **34**:108, 110, 112, 114
"ena" (Chekhov) **51**:35, 84, 111-12, 128, 177, 182, 189
"Zena iz slonove kosti" (Andrić) **36**:50-1
"Žena na kamenu" (Andrić) **36**:46-7, 49
"Zero Hour" (Bradbury) **29**:57-8
"Zetland: By a Character Witness" (Bellow) **14**:41-2
"Zhenia's Childhood" (Pasternak)
   See "Detstvo Luvers"
"Zhenikh vo polunochi" (Pilnyak) **48**:216, 237, 254, 268-70, 273
"Zhenshchina s golubymi glazami" (Gorky) **28**:190
"Zhitié odnói báby" (Leskov) **34**:131
"Zhufu" (Lu Hsun) **20**:140-42
"Zibn Gite Yor" (Peretz) **26**:197, 217
"Židovskaja kuvyrkalegija" (Leskov) **34**:112
Zig-Zags at the Zoo (Morrison) **40**:349
"Zigzags of Treachery" (Hammett) **17**:200
"Zimnij den'" (Leskov) **34**:108, 127, 130
Zimzum (Lish) **18**:285-86
"Zinc" (Levi) **12**:256-57, 259, 262
"Lo zio acquativo" (Calvino) **3**:92-3, 109; **48**:47, 66, 71, 73, 104, 133-35, 154-56, 160
"Životi" (Andrić) **36**:66, 68
"Živý plamen" (Čapek) **36**:96
"Zločin na poště" (Čapek) **36**:98-9, 105-06, 127
"Zločin v chalupě" (Čapek) **36**:102, 128
"Zloj mal' ik" (Chekhov) **51**:104
"Zlostavljanje" (Andrić) **36**:47-8, 50
"Zmija" (Andrić) **36**:35-6, 46-7
"Znakovi pored puta" (Andrić) **36**:35, 38, 50
"Zodiac 2000" (Ballard) **1**:79; **53**:20, 63, 65
"A Zokn" (Singer) **3**:355-56
"Zoku Akuma" (Tanizaki) **21**:195
"The Zombies" (Barthelme) **55**:96
"Zone of Quiet" (Lardner) **32**:131, 133, 135, 138, 140-41, 146, 149, 152-55, 159, 166-67, 174-75, 193-95
"Zone of Terror" (Ballard) **1**:68; **53**:10-12, 50, 113
"Zooey" (Salinger) **2**:291, 293-94, 296-97, 302-05, 308; **28**:221-29, 231-34, 236-40, 244-45, 248-50, 253-55, 259, 262, 266, 268-69; **65**:299, 301, 332
"Der Zug war pünktlich" (Boell) **23**:34, 36
"Zuja" (Andrić) **36**:65, 67
Die Zürcher Novellen (Keller) **26**:106, 108-09, 111, 113, 115
"Zwei Herzen in die Drygoods Schlock" (Perelman) **32**:235
"Zwei Schwestern" (Stifter) **28**:291, 298-99
Der Zweikampf (Kleist) **22**:105-10, 113, 116-17, 123-24, 128, 131